ALLIED AIRCRAFT OF WORLD WAR II

1939–1945

THE WORLD'S GREAT WEAPONS

ALLIED AIRCRAFT OF WORLD WAR II

1939–1945

THE WORLD'S GREAT WEAPONS

Chris Chant

amber
BOOKS

The material in this volume has previously appeared in:
The Essential Aircraft Identification Guide: Allied Fighters 1939–45 and *The Essential Aircraft Identification Guide: Allied Bombers 1939–45*.

Published by
Amber Books Ltd
74–77 White Lion Street
London
N1 9PF
United Kingdom
www.amberbooks.co.uk
Appstore: itunes.com/apps/amberbooksltd
Facebook: www.facebook.com/amberbooks
Twitter: @amberbooks

ISBN: 978-1-78274-207-4

Project Editor: Michael Spilling
Design: Colin Hawes and Andrew Easton
Picture Research: Terry Forshaw

Printed in China

Picture Credits
All photographs courtesy of Art-Tech/Aerospace
except for 12, 174 and 192 courtesy of Cody Images

All artworks are courtesy of Alcaniz Fresno's S.A. and Art-Tech/Aerospace

Contents

Volume One:
Allied Fighters

Introduction

The fighter is essentially a defensive weapon
whose capabilities can also be used offensively.
In the Battle of Britain, for example, the Royal Air Force's
fighters were used purely defensively to protect the United
Kingdom, either by destroying the German bombers or
tackling the German escort fighters to allow other RAF
fighters an easier approach to the German bombers.
Modified by time and occasion, the same basic tenet held
true throughout the war. As in World War I, therefore, the
fighter of World War II was an arbiter of the air war as it
either aided or prevented other warplanes from going
about the tasks that could affect the course of the war
in direct terms – such as bombing industrial targets and
supporting ground offensives.

◀ **Hurricanes in 'vic' formation**

This photograph of some uncoded, newly-delivered Hawker Hurricane Mk Is shows two sets of three aircraft
in the classic 'vic' formation used by the RAF up until 1941, before the British adopted the more effective
'finger four' based on the German Schwarm.

▲ Polikarpov I-16s in flight

Although obsolete in 1941 when the Germans invaded the Soviet Union, the Polikarpov I-16 proved to be a tough and manoeuvrable aircraft that gave a good account of itself against the superior German Bf 109.

THE BASICS OF FIGHTER tactics were unaltered in concept from those developed in World War I, and were therefore derived from speed, climb rate, overall agility with emphasis on turn rate, armament and the pilot's reaction time and exploitation of sun and cloud. Surprise remained the trump card. The major advance between the wars was the advent of voice communication by radio, which allowed pilots to pass on and receive information and orders, and from a time very late in the 1930s to receive instruction from ground controllers watching the development of the air battle on radar.

In September 1939, Royal Air Force (RAF) Fighter Command's tactics were derived from the concept that the air threat to the UK would comprise German bombers, flying in close formation and unescorted by fighters as the latter were unable to reach Britain's shores from airfields in Germany. It was believed that the era of the dogfight had passed, and thus rigid air fighting tactics were introduced. By means of complex and lengthy manoeuvres, these were designed to bring the maximum number of guns to bear on the bomber formation. The fighting unit was thus the tight 'vic' (V formation) of three fighters.

As events very rapidly proved, such formulaic attacks were of no use. The *Luftwaffe*'s fighter arm was decidedly superior as its pilots had gained invaluable tactical experience under real combat conditions during the Spanish Civil War (1936–39), and had devised and proved the ideal fighter formation, the *Rotte*. This comprised two fighters, spaced some 180m (600ft) apart, and the primary task of wingman was to guard his leader from an attack from the beam or the rear as the leader made the tactical decisions and also covered his wingman.

The four-fighter *Schwarm* was the logical expansion of the *Rotte*, with two pairs of aircraft rather than just two aircraft. When, in 1941, the RAF eventually copied the *Luftwaffe* and adopted this pattern, it was called the 'finger-four', as the relative positions of the fighters was similar to the tips of the finger.

Battle of Britain

Despite the lessons of the brief air fighting during Germany's attack on the Low Countries and France, in June 1940 the British entered the Battle of Britain with the unwieldy 'vic'. The *Luftwaffe* failed to exploit opportunities, such as the RAF's radar gap at low level, however, and as the battle continued and grew more intense, more able tactical leaders adopted the looser type of formation which improved manoeuvrability without sacrificing cover. This meant that the British fighters were steadily better placed to engage the German fighters as the latter were switched, quite wrongly, from free-roaming hunts for British fighters to close escort of the bombers, so losing the advantage of the fighters' agility and surprise.

The British also evolved different tactics against the bombers. In one popular approach, the fighters, flying line abreast, flew head-on at the bombers to minimize the time in which the fighter escort could intervene, and also often to break up the bomber formation for piecemeal engagement by the fighters. In another, based on the so-called 'big wing' concept, a large formation was grouped to make a simultaneous attack more effective than the same number of aircraft arriving separately. The Duxford Wing, of three and later five squadrons, was created but not notably successful as its formation in the air almost always took too long.

After the battle of Britain, Fighter Command tried to retain the initiative by luring the *Luftwaffe* to battle over France with 'Circus' operations, but this failed to gain the sought-for advantage as the Germans generally refused to rise to the bait.

Soviet air tactics

The Soviet air arm still used the three-aircraft 'vic' at the start of the German invasion of the Soviet Union in June 1941, but the pilots who survived the mass destruction of the Soviet air units in the first weeks of the campaign then started to copy the German fighter tactics in the form of eight fighters in two loose sections of four. This improved matters, but the efforts of the Soviet fighter arm were still severely hampered by the lack of ground-control

▼ **P-51D 'Finger Four'**
In this photograph from 1944, four USAAF P-51D Mustangs from the 308th Fighter Squadron fly in the classic 'finger four' formation used by most Allied air forces from 1942 onwards.

radar, the general absence of radio (forcing pilots to communicate visually) and the lack of adequate air gunnery training, which meant that fire was all too often inaccurate and opened at too great a range. The training of pilots had always emphasised adherence to group attacks rather than the exercise of small unit or individual initiative, and the inevitable fragmentation of units in combat had a decidedly adverse effect on Soviet pilots' ability to function effectively.

Generally, the pilots were reluctant to engage the German bombers closely, and often ended their attacks too quickly before inflicting decisive damage. When engaged by German fighters, the Soviet pilots adopted the defensive circle manoeuvre learned in the Spanish Civil War, in which each fighter covered that ahead of it, before seeking to break away at low level.

However, by late 1943, the quality of Soviet fighter pilots and their equipment had improved radically, and, in combination with their huge numerical superiority, they gradually gained total command of the air over the Eastern Front.

US fighter tactics

Although the United States Army Air Force's (USAAF) fighter tactics from the involvement of the United States in World War II from December 1941 were still too rigid, moves toward the 'finger four' had already begun, and spread rapidly through the USAAF and US Navy. The major innovation of the concept was the 'Thach weave' developed by Lieutenant Commander John Thach of the US Navy in a largely successful effort to give the Grumman F4F Wildcat a better chance against the technically superior Mitsubishi A6M 'Zero'. The new tactic was based on two pairs of fighters abreast of each other with the pairs about 365m (1200ft) apart. When an attack was made on one pair, the other broke towards it to engage, and the pair being attacked broke towards the pair protecting it. This created a scissors effect as the two pairs crossed, and meant that the pursuing Japanese fighter(s) were faced with a beam attack if they held their course, a head-on attack if they turned towards the attackers, or a rear attack if they turned away.

Ultimately the US advantage in training, experience and aircraft capability meant that American pilots were able to meet the Axis pilots on more than equal terms and decimate their opponents, who were, from 1944, decidedly inferior in experience and numbers.

Chapter 1

France

By 1939, the French Air Force was beginning
to emerge from the political and technical doldrums in
which it had languished since World War I. New thinking
and new aircraft were evident, but the problem the *Armée
de l'Air* now had to face was whether it was too little or too
late, or worst of all, both too little and too late.
The fighter arm had at last disposed of nearly all of its
obsolete first-generation monoplane fighters, but was still
reliant on the indifferent Morane-Saulnier MS.406,
pending the arrival of more advanced fighters such
as the Dewoitine D.520.

◀ **First-generation monoplane fighter**
The Morane-Saulnier MS.406C.1 was created on the basis of several modern features, but was at best an
indifferent fighter with performance decidedly inferior to that of the German fighters it would have to face.

The *Armée de l'Air*
1939–40

The *Armée de l'Air* was numerically large and appeared formidable, but was in fact dependent largely on obsolescent aircraft, and was still suffering from the effects of political antipathies and the nationalization of the French aero industry in the mid-1930s.

B Y 1937, IT WAS CLEAR that the French air force needed more modern aircraft to replace inferior fighters such as the Dewoitine D.500 and D.501, which were still in service with fighter squadrons including the famous *Cigognes* (storks). This squadron, which was part of *Groupe de Chasse* (GC) I, was initially stationed at Chartres-Champbol. However, only a matter of days before Germany triggered World War II by invading Poland on 1 September 1939, it moved to Beauvais-Tillé after replacing its D.500 and D.501 fighters with Morane-Saulnier MS.406 machines (each armed with one 20mm/0.79in cannon). These were among the most modern fighters on the strength of the *Armée de l'Air* at the start of World War II. France's programme to manufacture more than 2500 modern

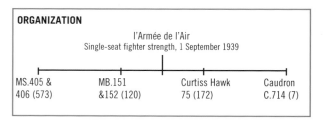

aircraft, including Bloch MB.170 bombers as well as Dewoitine D.520 fighters, was a direct response to the difficulties in which the government had found itself through a comment apparently made by the commander-in-chief of the air force. He said that less than half of France's total of about 1400 first-line aircraft would be ready for action at a moment's notice, and that most of these machines were also

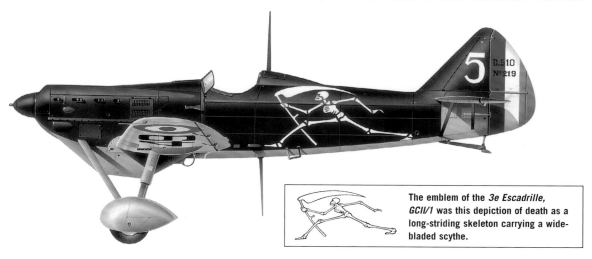

The emblem of the *3e Escadrille, GCII/1* was this depiction of death as a long-striding skeleton carrying a wide-bladed scythe.

Specifications

Crew: 1

Powerplant: 641kW (860hp) Hispano-Suiza
  liquid-cooled V-12

Maximum speed: 402km/h (250mph)

Range: 700km (435 miles)

Service ceiling: 11,000m (36,090ft)

Dimensions: span 12.09m (39ft 8.25in);
  length 7.94m (26ft 0.5in);
  height 2.42m (7ft 11.25in)

Weight: 1929kg (4244lb) loaded

Armament: 1 x 20mm (0.79in) HS9 cannon and
  2 x 7.5mm (0.295in) MAC1934 MGs

▲ **Dewoitine D.510C.1**

3e Escadrille / Groupe de Chasse II/1 (GC IV/1), Etampes, 1938

The D.510 was an interim monoplane fighter with fixed landing gear and open accommodation, but moderately good armament in the form of one 20mm (0.79in) fixed forward-firing cannon (between the cylinder banks to fire through the hollow propeller shaft) and two 7.5mm (0.295in) machine guns.

FIGHTER AIRCRAFT: DEWOITINE D.520C.1			
Unit	Operational	Victories	Losses
GC I/3	17/04/40	50 +18 prob	32
GC II/3	10/05/40	31 +15 prob	20
GC II/7	20/05/40	12 + 4 prob	14
GC III/3	28/05/40	8 + 2 prob	17
GC III/6	10/06/40	7 + 0 prob	2

obsolescent. There was a large element of truth in this, but it also reflected the political pressure to which service commanders customarily resorted to secure resources in the face of demands by the other two service commanders.

And while resources were one matter, another was the air force's lack of clear thought about how it should best be used. Even within the service there were several schools of operational and tactical

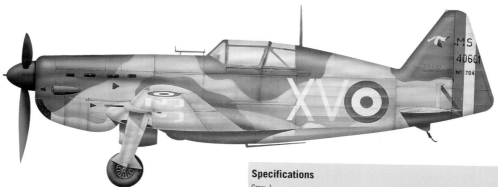

▲ **Morane Saulnier MS.406C.1**

1e Escadrille / GC I/2 / Nimes, July 1940

The MS.406 was France's first 'modern' monoplane fighter, but was in all major respects, except firepower, an indifferent warplane with little to commend it except ease of manufacture and availability.

Specifications

Crew: 1
Powerplant: 641kW (860hp) Hispano-Suiza liquid-cooled V-12
Maximum speed: 490km/h (304mph)
Range: 750km (466 miles)
Service ceiling: 9400m (30,840ft)

Dimensions: span 10.62m (34ft 9.5in);
length 8.17m (26ft 9.33in);
height 3.25m (10ft 8in)
Weight: 2471kg (5448lb) loaded
Armament: 1 x 20mm (0.79in) HS9 or HS404 cannon and 2 x 7.5mm (0.295in) MAC1934 MGs

▲ **Dewoitine D.520C.1**

GC II/7 / France, July 1940

The D.520 was without doubt the best single-seat fighter available to the French in the first part of World War II, but was at that time delivered in only small numbers, and its pilots could therefore exercise no real impact on events.

Specifications

Crew: 1
Powerplant: 686kW (920hp) Hispano-Suiza 12Y-45 liquid-cooled V-12
Maximum speed: 535km/h (332mph)
Range: 900km (553 miles)
Service ceiling: 11,000m (36,090ft)

Dimensions: span 10.20m (33ft 5.5in);
length 8.76m (28ft 8.75in);
height 2.57m (8ft 5.25in)
Weight: 2783kg (6134lb) loaded
Armament: 1 x 20mm (0.79in) Hispano-Suiza HS-404 cannon and 4 x 7.5mm (0.295in) MAC1934 MGs

▼ The Armée de l'Air Groupe de Chasse

The French core fighter unit in 1939/40 was the groupe de chasse (wing), which comprised a number of escadrilles (squadrons) sometimes on different bases and, in time of war, themselves allocated to various groupements (groups) with other types of aircraft. Thus on 10 May 1940 Groupement de Chasse 21 in the Zone d'Operations Aeriennes Nord, comprised GC I/1 at Chantilly-les-Aigles, GC II/1 at Buc, GC III/3 at Beauvais-Tille, GC II/10 at Rouen-Boos and GC III/10 at Le Havre-Octeville.

1e Escadrille

2e Escadrille

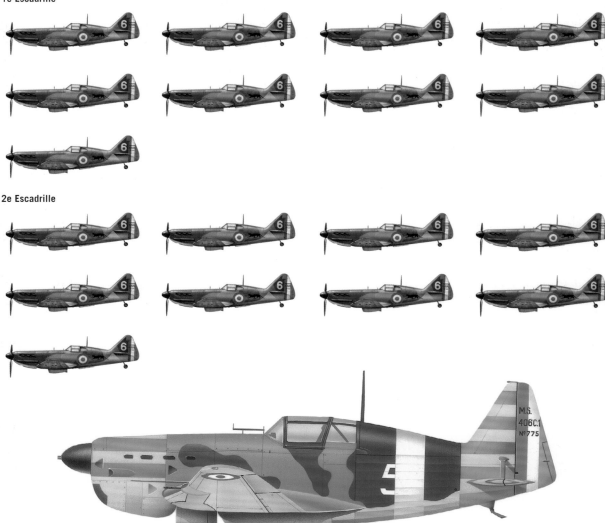

Specifications

Crew: 1

Powerplant: 641kW (860hp) Hispano-Suiza
12Y-31 liquid-cooled V-12

Maximum speed: 490km/h (304mph)

Range: 750km (466 miles)

Service ceiling: 9400m (30,840ft)

Dimensions: span 10.62m (34ft 9.5in);
length 8.17m (26ft 9.33in);
height 3.25m (10ft 8in)

Weight: 2471kg (5448lb) loaded

Armament: 1 x 20mm (0.79in) HS-9 or
HS-404 cannon and 2 x 7.5mm (0.295-in)
MAC1934 MGs

▲ Morane-Saulnier MS.406C.1

Escadron de Entrainment / Toulouse, 1941

The MS.406C.1 was numerically the most important French fighter in the campaign that led to France's defeat in May–June 1940. Production amounted to 1077 aircraft, and the survivors were used mostly for training from 1941.

thought, and this led to interminable argument and delay. All this wrangling continued even as Germany, France's eastern neighbour on the other side of the great Rhine river, was steadily building up her forces on the basis of a fairly concentrated industrial effort, and within the context of clear military imperatives and only limited inter-service rivalry.

Operational deficiencies

The combined effect of France's inadequate aeronautical programmes and the indecision evident at all levels, from the government right down to the middle echelons of the armed forces, inevitably meant that the French Air Force was materially and operationally deficient relative to the air force it would have to face in combat after September 1939. The problem was exacerbated by the fact that while the French air force had no experience of air warfare under modern conditions, the German air force certainly did. The commitment of the Legion Condor to the Spanish Civil War (1936–39) had brought it that considerable advantage. Fighting on the side of the victorious Nationalists, German fighters and their pilots had been tried against modern Soviet fighters flying on behalf of the Republican side.

Germany's fighters were therefore combat-proven and in the process of steady development, while their pilots had worked out a system of tactics that were admirably suited to the demands of high-speed air

▲ **First flight**
This photograph shows pilot Marcel Doret taking a Dewoitine D.520 on its first flight in October 1938.

combat. The Germans had also developed a high level of skill in the cooperation of the various elements of their air force, and in the flying of independent bombing campaigns and the means whereby the air force could best provide tactical air support for the ground forces.

When it became evident in the mid-1930s that another major European war was probably if not actually certain, France sought to respond through an intense programme of re-equiping and modernization in 1938–39. However, this was an effort that was taken much too late to be meaningful, and much too inadequately to be effective.

Specifications

Crew: 1

Powerplant: 768kW (1030hp) Rolls-Royce
Merlin III liquid-cooled V-12

Maximum speed: 582km/h (362mph)

Range: 636km (395 miles)

Service ceiling: 9725m (31,900ft)

Dimensions: span 11.22m (36ft 10in);
length 9.11m (29ft 11in);
height 2.69m (8ft 10in)

Weight: 2624kg (5784lb) loaded

Armament: 8 x 7.7mm (0.303in)
Browning MGs

▲ **Supermarine Spitfire Mk I**
Experimental and development service, France 1940
The French Air Force did not use the British-designed Spitfire as an operational fighter, but received one aeroplane in 1938 for experimental and development purposes. It is believed that this aeroplane was captured by the Germans late in the Battle of France, during June 1940.

The defeat of France
MAY–JUNE 1940

Woefully ill-prepared, and with only small British forces available to aid her, France lacked the strength and organization to halt, let alone defeat, the German ground and air onslaught that fell on her on 10 May 1940. Less than seven weeks later, she was compelled to surrender.

WHEN THE WAR STARTED, the *Armée de l'Air* was in a very poor state, and could muster only 826 combat-ready fighters. More aircraft had been built, but these lacked essential equipment or final preparation: some lacked gun sights or propellers, and others had guns that had not been harmonized.

Thus when the German offensive started in May 1940, the Germans could deploy not only more aircraft but also more experienced pilots, many of them veterans of the Spanish Civil War. The Germans advanced swiftly through France and both out-thought and out-fought all Allied opposition. The French and their British allies struggled hard over France, but could achieve nothing significant to stem the German tide. In the air, the French fighter arm was at times able to achieve local successes, but these were of little use when the air support squadrons and their covering fighters were often out of contact

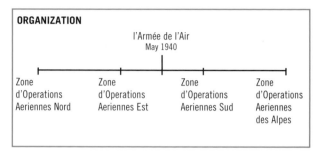

ORGANIZATION

l'Armée de l'Air
May 1940

| Zone d'Operations Aeriennes Nord | Zone d'Operations Aeriennes Est | Zone d'Operations Aeriennes Sud | Zone d'Operations Aeriennes des Alpes |

FIGHTER AIRCRAFT: ZOAN (GROUPEMENT DE CHASSE 21)

Unit	Type	Base	Serviceable
GC I/1	MB.152	Chantilly	n/a
GC II/1	MB.152	Buc	n/a
GC II/10	MB.151/152	Rouen	n/a
GG III/10	MB.151/152	Le Havre	n/a

Specifications

Crew: 1

Powerplant: 746kW (1000hp) Gnome-Rhone 14N-25 air-cooled 14-cylinder radial

Maximum speed: 509km/h (316mph)

Range: 540km (335 miles)

Service ceiling: not available

Dimensions: span 10.54m (34ft 7in); length 9.10m (29ft 10.25in); height 3.03m (9ft 11.33in)

Weight: 2800kg (6160lb) loaded

Armament: 2 x 20mm (0.79in) Hispano-Suiza HS-404 cannon and four 7.5mm (0.295in) MAC1934 MGs

▲ **Bloch MB.152C.1**

3e Escadrille / GC II/1 / Buc, May 1940

This unit was part of the Groupement de Chasse 21 facing the main German offensive. Of some 300 such aircraft delivered by January 1940, about two-thirds were non-operational for lack of the required propeller.

with the French Army units they were tasked to support, in part due to the poor coordination of communications between the army and the air force, and in part to the army's obsolescent and unreliable radio equipment.

As it became clear that the campaign was lost, the French high command ordered what remained of the *Armée de l'Air* to French colonies in North Africa – in order, it believed at the time, that the fight could be continued. Yet the Vichy government, which became the official German-approved power in occupied France after the armistice, now ordered the dissolution of many of the air force squadrons. During the Battle of France, the French lost more than 750 aircraft, and the Germans more than 850 – the French fighters did inflict significant casualties.

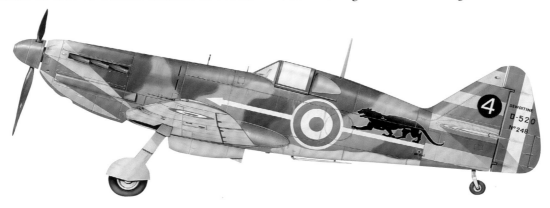

Specifications

Crew: 1

Powerplant: 686kW (920hp) Hispano-Suiza
  12Y-45 liquid-cooled V-12

Maximum speed: 535km/h (332mph)

Range: 900km (553 miles)

Service ceiling: 11,000m (36,090ft)

Dimensions: span 10.20m (33ft 5.5in);
  length 8.76m (28ft 8.75in);
  height 2.57m (8ft 5.25in)

Weight: 2783kg (6134lb) loaded

Armament: 1 x 20mm (0.79in) Hispano-Suiza
  HS-404 cannon and 4 x 7.5mm (0.295in)
  MAC1934 MGs

▲ Dewoitine D.520C.1

4e Escadrille / Groupe de Chasse II/7 / Tunisia, 1942

(Vichy French air force)

The D.520 was one of the modern warplanes that Vichy France was allowed to keep and, indeed, to manufacture. In the Battle of France, the D.520 was credited with shooting down 114 German aircraft for the loss of 83 of its own number.

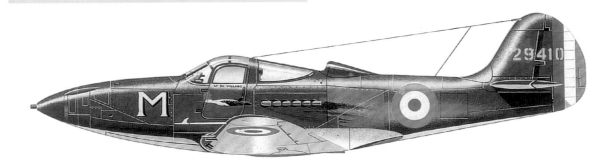

▲ Bell P-39N Airacobra

GC II/6 'Travail' / Free French Air Force, 1943

The American-made Airacobra was one of several types of Allied warplane used by the French Air Force later in World War II. With its sturdy construction, good protection and heavy armament, the P-39 was an effective ground-attack fighter.

Specifications

Crew: 1

Powerplant: 895kW (1200hp) Allison V-1710-
  85 liquid-cooled V-12

Maximum speed: 605km/h (376mph)

Range: 483km (300 miles)

Service ceiling: 11,665m (38,270ft)

Dimensions: span 10.36m (34ft 0in); length
  9.19m (30ft 2in); height 3.79m (12ft 5in)

Weight: 3992kg (8800lb) loaded

Armament: 1 x 37mm (1.46in) M4 cannon,
  2 x 12.7mm (0.5in) Browning MGs, 4 x
  7.62mm (0.3in) Browning MGs, and 227kg
  (500lb) of bombs

Chapter 2

United Kingdom and Commonwealth

The UK started World War II with a fighter arm
that was comparatively small and inexperienced, but had
good aircraft in its Hawker Hurricane and Supermarine
Spitfire fighters. Over the next six-and-a-half years, this
fighter arm grew greatly in size and capability through
its successes in the Battle of Britain and the
campaigns that followed in Burma, North Africa, Italy and,
finally, northwest Europe. The Spitfire remained in steady
development and was supplemented by last-generation
piston-engined fighters as well as the Gloster Meteor,
the only jet-powered Allied fighter to see service
in World War II.

◀ **Supermarine Spitfire Mk XII**
The first production variant of the Spitfire with a Griffon engine, the clipped-wing Spitfire Mk XII entered
service in 1943 and was built to the extent of 100 aircraft. The engine drove a four-blade propeller.

RAF Fighter Command
1939–41

Fighter Command was dedicated to the air defence of the UK. It was growing rapidly in the years before the war, and provided fighters for the French campaign. It was Fighter Command that prevented the *Luftwaffe* from winning the Battle of Britain, and then went on the offensive.

FIGHTER COMMAND was created in 1936 in recognition of the fact that as the RAF expanded during the rearmament phase before World War II, more specialized applications were needed for fighter, bomber and coastal aircraft. On 20 May 1926, Fighter Command had been established as a group within the Inland Area, and on 1 June 1926 this Fighting Area, as it was then called, was transferred to the Air Defence of Great Britain. The Fighting Area was raised to command status in 1932 and renamed on 1 May 1936.

In the following years, the command was expanded greatly and its obsolescent biplanes were replaced by two of the most celebrated warplanes ever to fly with the RAF, namely the Hawker Hurricane and Supermarine Spitfire monoplanes. Fighter Command's decisive moment arrived in the summer of 1940 as the *Luftwaffe* tried to gain air supremacy over the English and UK as a prerequisite to the launch of a seaborne invasion.

Fighter Command was divided into a number of groups, each allocated its own area of the UK. No. 11 Group covered the main weight of the German attack, as it operated over south-east England and London. It was reinforced by No. 10 Group, which covered south-west England, and No. 12 Group, which covered the Midlands and the north of England. In the end, the Germans failed to win air superiority, although the RAF had eaten very deep into its reserves of pilots by the middle of the battle. Aircraft shortages were never a major problem, but the numbers and physical/psychological state of their pilots was of great concern. Pilots were being killed or severely wounded at a rate greater than they could be replaced from training schools. It took Fighter Command some months to recover from its losses in the Battle of Britain and go over to the offensive.

As 1941 began, Fighter Command began the task of winning air superiority over north-western France.

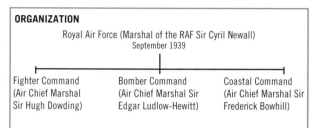

ORGANIZATION

Royal Air Force (Marshal of the RAF Sir Cyril Newall)
September 1939

| Fighter Command (Air Chief Marshal Sir Hugh Dowding) | Bomber Command (Air Chief Marshal Sir Edgar Ludlow-Hewitt) | Coastal Command (Air Chief Marshal Sir Frederick Bowhill) |

RAF COMBAT SQUADRONS (SEPTEMBER 1939)

Type	UK	NW Europe	Mediterranean
Fighter	41	4	6
Heavy/medium bomber	40	2	0
Light bomber	12	6	8
Torpedo bomber	1	0	1
Flying boat	4	0	1

▲ **Scramble**

These Hurricanes from No. 87 Squadron were committed to the Air Component of the BEF during the Battle of France. This photograph was taken somewhere in France, March 1940.

By May, the British squadrons began to operate as wings under the control of a experienced wing leader. Several types of short-penetration operations were tried in an effort to draw the *Luftwaffe* into an attritional campaign and keep large numbers of fighters pinned in France, particularly after the German invasion of the Soviet Union in June 1941. Large numbers of Spitfires were despatched with small numbers of medium bombers in often vain attempts to lure the German fighters into

combat. The results of these efforts were decidedly mixed, and the Germans were able to leave a mere two experienced *Jagdgeschwadern* (180 aircraft at most) in Western Europe.

Most of the tactical factors that had allowed Fighter Command to win the Battle of Britain were now reversed, and 1941 saw Fighter Command claim some 731 *Luftwaffe* fighters (although in reality only 236 were lost from all causes) for the loss of about 530 of its own fighters.

▲ **Supermarine Spitfire Mk IA**

No. 603 'City of Edinburgh' Squadron

Within two weeks of the outbreak of war in September 1939, the squadron began to receive Spitfires. It was operational with Spitfires in time to intercept the first German air raid on the British Isles on 16 October, when it destroyed the first enemy aircraft to be shot down over Britain in World War II.

Specifications

Crew: 1

Powerplant: 768kW (1030hp) Rolls-Royce
    Merlin III liquid-cooled V-12

Maximum speed: 582km/h (362mph)

Range: 636km (395 miles)

Service ceiling: 9725m (31,900ft)

Dimensions: span 11.22m (36ft 10in);
    length 9.11m (29ft 11in);
    height 2.69m (8ft 10in)

Weight: 2624kg (5784lb) loaded

Armament: 8 x 7.7mm (0.303in)
    Browning MGs

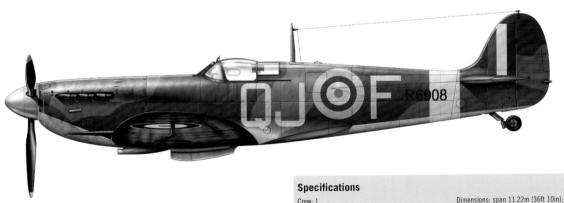

▲ **Supermarine Spitfire Mk IB**

No. 92 Squadron / RAF Fighter Command, 1940

The Spitfire Mk IB marked an important evolutionary step in the firepower of the Spitfire family, four of the the eight 7.7mm (0.303in) machine guns of the Spitfire Mk IA being replaced by two 20mm (0.79in) cannon.

Specifications

Crew: 1

Powerplant: 768kW (1030hp) Rolls-Royce
    Merlin III liquid-cooled V-12

Maximum speed: 582km/h (362mph)

Range: 636km (395 miles)

Service ceiling: 9725m (31,900ft)

Dimensions: span 11.22m (36ft 10in);
    length 9.11m (29ft 11in);
    height 2.69m (8ft 10in)

Weight: about 2624kg (5784lb) loaded

Armament: 2 x 20mm (0.79in) Hispano cannon
    and 4 x 7.7mm (0.303in) Browning MGs

RAF Component of the BEF
1939–40

Controlled by the so-called British Air Forces in France (BAFF), which also commanded the bomber squadrons of the Advanced Air Striking Force (AASF), the RAF Component of the British Expeditionary Force (BEF) provided reconnaissance and fighter capabilities.

THE RAF COMPONENT of the British Air Forces in France began life as Air Vice Marshal P. H. L. Playfair's Advanced Air Striking Force (AASF), which was formed on 24 August 1939 out of 10 light and medium bomber squadrons (Nos 12, 15, 40, 88, 103, 105, 142, 150, 218 and 226) of the Royal Air Force's No. 1 Group. This was transferred to France so that its warplanes would be able to operate against targets in western Germany.

The AASF was initially a command independent of the BEF, and as such reported directly to the Air Ministry in London. This arrangement soon proved to impractical, however, so on 15 January 1940 the AASF was made immediately subordinate to the headquarters of Air Marshal Sir Arthur S. 'Ugly' Barratt's BAFF. The BAFF also took under command Air Vice Marshal C. H. B. Blount's RAF Component of the BEF, whose Nos 1, 2, 4, 13, 16, 26, 53, 59, 73, 85, 87, 613 and 614 Squadrons comprised five Westland Lysander tactical reconnaissance, four

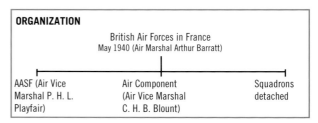

ORGANIZATION

British Air Forces in France
May 1940 (Air Marshal Arthur Barratt)

AASF (Air Vice Marshal P. H. L. Playfair)	Air Component (Air Vice Marshal C. H. B. Blount)	Squadrons detached

Bristol Blenheim long-range reconnaissance and four (later six) Hawker Hurricane single-seat fighter units, the last later increased to six to protect installations and escort reconnaissances.

The BAFF's elements entered full-scale action, after limited skirmishing in the 'phoney war', on 10 May 1940 as the Germans launched their strategic offensive to the west through the Netherlands, Belgium and France. Like those of the French, the British air units suffered a stream of reverses and even disasters, for the aircraft types and numbers were wholly inadequate against a technically and

▲ **Hawker Hurricane Mk IA**

No. 1 Squadron / RAF Fighter Command, 1940

With its sturdy airframe and wide-track main landing gear units, the Hurricane was well suited for operations from the grass strips typical of Fighter Command's satellite airfields.

Specifications

Crew: 1	Service ceiling: 10,180m (33,400ft)
Powerplant: 768kW (1030hp) Rolls-Royce	Dimensions: span 12.19m (40ft 0in); length
Merlin II liquid-cooled V-12	9.55m (31ft 4in); height 4.07m (13ft 4.5in)
Maximum speed: 496km/h (308mph)	Weight: 2820kg (6218lb) loaded
Range: 845km (525 miles)	Armament: 8 x 7.7mm (0.303in) Browning MGs

tactically superior air adversary, and ground forces possessing excellent light anti-aircraft artillery. The Fairey Battle light bomber failed badly, most being shot down in the course of their first few missions, and the Blenheim light bomber did little better: during an attack on the bridges at Maastricht late in May, the AASF lost 40 out of 71 aircraft. As the Germans advanced, the BAFF retreated south, but by mid-June it was clear that defeat was imminent and the remnants of the BAFF began to withdraw to the UK, where the headquarters were eventually disbanded on 26 June 1940.

FIGHTER SQUADRONS OF THE RAF COMPONENT (SPRING 1940)			
Unit	Type	Strength	Base
No. 1 Squadron	Hurricane I	12	Vassincourt
No. 73 Squadron	Hurricane I	12	n/a
No. 85 Squadron	Hurricane I	12	Lille
No. 87 Squadron	Hurricane I	12	n/a
No. 607 Squadron	Hurricane I	12	Merville
No. 615 Squadron	Hurricane I	12	Poix

▼ 1940 RAF Squadron

In 1940, before it had come into full and extended contact with the more advanced fighter tactics used by the Luftwaffe, the Royal Air Force had its 12-aircraft fighter squadrons organized in four flights each of three aircraft, and the flights and squadrons were trained to make formation attacks. Thereafter, the RAF quickly changed to a squadron organization and tactics most akin to those of the Germans, with the emphasis on pairs of fighters (leader and wingman) operating together.

'A' Flight   'B' Flight   'C' Flight   'D' Flight

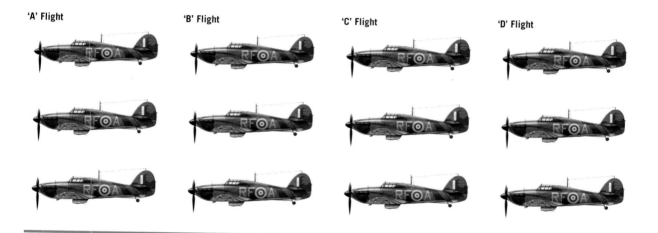

Battle of France
MAY 1940

From the first stages of the German offensive, the British air forces based in France had a torrid time of it. The reconnaissance and bomber units were savaged by technically more advanced adversaries, but the Hurricane fighter units were more effective and inflicted heavy losses.

THE BAFF's airfields in northern France escaped essentially unscathed in the concentrated *Luftwaffe* attacks that accompanied the start of the invasion of the Low Countries and France on 10 May 1940. However, it was not long before the aircraft of the squadrons based on these airfields began to suffer a spate of losses as they came up against skilled German pilots. The enemy pilots had honed their capabilities in Spain and Poland, and were flying advanced warplanes, including (as the standard fighter) the first-class Messerschmitt Bf 109E single-engined warplane.

Although the Hawker Hurricane was a worthy, sturdy and easily maintained fighter, it was not in the same league as the Bf 109. The BAFF's other primary fighter, although in the last stages of being phased out of service, was the Gloster Gladiator biplane with only four rather than eight machine guns, and fixed landing gear.

As always, the fighters were tasked with the protection of key installations in France against German bomber attack, and the escort of Bristol Blenheim twin-engined light bombers and long-range reconnaissance aircraft, plus Fairey Battle single-engined light bombers and Westland Lysander battlefield reconnaissance aircraft.

▲ Hawker Hurricane Mk I

No. 303 Squadron / RAF Fighter Command, Northolt, August 1940

The Hawker Hurricane was an excellent blend of old (steel tube in the structure and largely fabric covering) and new (low-set cantilever wing, enclosed cockpit, retractable main landing gear units and eight-gun main armament). In the Battle of Britain, the Hurricane was Fighter Command's highest-scoring fighter.

Specifications

Crew: 1
Powerplant: 768kW (1030hp) Rolls-Royce
Merlin II liquid-cooled V-12
Maximum speed: 496km/h (308mph)
Range: 845km (525 miles)

Service ceiling: 10,180m (33,400ft)
Dimensions: span 12.19m (40ft 0in); length
9.55m (31ft 4in); height 4.07m (13ft 4.5in)
Weight: 2820kg (6218lb) loaded
Armament: 8 x 7.7mm (0.303in) Browning MGs

Specifications

Crew: 1
Powerplant: 768kW (1030hp) Rolls-Royce
Merlin II liquid-cooled V-12
Maximum speed: 496km/h (308mph)
Range: 845km (525 miles)

Service ceiling: 10,180m (33,400ft)
Dimensions: span 12.19m (40ft 0in); length
9.55m (31ft 4in); height 4.07m (13ft 4.5in)
Weight: 2820kg (6218lb) loaded
Armament: 8 x 7.7mm (0.303in) Browning MGs

▲ Hawker Hurricane Mk IA

No. 87 Squadron / No. 60 Wing

With the introduction of Hurricane Mk II variants armed with cannon, aircraft with machine-gun armament received the letter 'A' as a suffix to their designation. The Hurricane was very sturdy, and later became an excellent fighter-bomber.

With escort, the Blenheim could achieve limited successes, but the Battle and Lysander were very quickly revealed as fatally vulnerable not only to fighter attack but also to the capabilities of the anti-aircraft guns that the Germans deployed very strongly in calibres between 20mm (0.79in) and 88mm (3.465in).

Air support role

While fighters despatched by the UK-based Fighter Command attempted to provide air support for the Dutch and Belgians, the BAFF's 416 aircraft, including 96 Hurricanes in six squadrons, were facing a losing battle slightly further to the west, even though they were reinforced by another three Hurricane units, Nos 3, 79 and 501 Squadrons.

The nature of the British air element's task is indicated by the fact that on the day of its arrival, on 10 May, No. 501 Squadron refuelled and immediately rose into combat, two of the Hurricanes becoming embroiled with 40 or more Heinkel He 111 bombers. During the day, the BAFF flew 161 fighter sorties, 81 leading to combat and resulting in claims for 36 German aircraft downed at the cost of two Hurricanes lost.

As the campaign progressed, the kill/loss ratio veered steadily in favour of the Germans as the Allies' loss of territory compounded servicing and maintenance problems, and as pilots became

▲ **BAFF Gladiators**

Pilots from No. 615 Squadron sit besides their Gladiator Mk II fighters as part of the Air Component of the British Expeditionary Force, early in 1940. The Gladiator proved no match for the more modern warplanes of the Luftwaffe.

increasingly exhausted. Rightly believing that France would be defeated, Air Chief Marshal Sir Hugh Dowding, commanding Fighter Command, refused to allow Supermarine Spitfire squadrons to be transferred to France, and the BAFF was pulled out late in June so that the RAF could prepare for the Battle of Britain. The Battle of France had cost the RAF 959 aircraft, including 477 invaluable fighters.

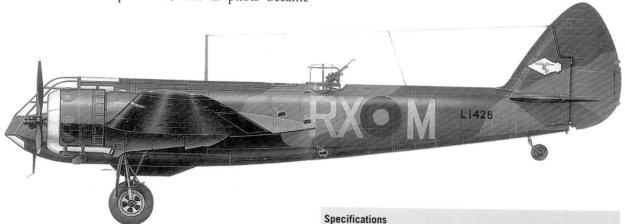

▲ **Bristol Blenheim Mk IF**

No. 25 Squadron / RAF Fighter Command, Hawkinge, Kent, summer 1940

The Blenheim Mk IF was an interim fighter created out of the Blenheim Mk I light bomber by the addition of a ventral pack carrying four 7.7mm (0.303in) Browning fixed forward-firing machine guns.

Specifications

Crew: 2

Powerplant: 2 x 626kW (840hp) Bristol Mercury VIII air-cooled 9-cylinder radial

Maximum speed: 447km/h (278mph)

Range: 1690km (1050 miles)

Service ceiling: 8315m (27,280ft)

Dimensions: span 17.17m (56ft 4in); length 12.12m (39ft 9in); height 3.00m (9ft 10)

Weight: 5534kg (12,200lb) loaded

Armament: 5 x 7.7mm (0.303in) Browning MGs and 1 x 7.7mm (0.303in) Vickers 'K' MG

Battle of Britain

JULY–OCTOBER 1940

The Battle of Britain was a major turning point in World War II, for it was the first occasion on which the Germans suffered a strategic defeat. To launch a seaborne invasion of the UK, the Germans needed air supremacy, but failed to win this in the Battle of Britain.

THE BATTLE OF BRITAIN was the first major battle to be fought entirely by air forces. The Germans thought that a successful amphibious assault on the UK could not be made until the RAF had been neutralized, and this led to the battle dated by British historians to the period between 10 July and 31 October 1940, in which the Germans' major daylight effort was made. German historians usually record the battle as starting in mid-August 1940 and ending in May 1941, when the German bomber arm was withdrawn for the invasion of the USSR.

In an effort to finish the war in the west, on 16 July Hitler ordered the rapid preparation of the *Seelöwe* (Sea Lion) invasion for launch in mid-August. The *Luftwaffe* was now facing an opponent more capable than the French Air Force, for the RAF was well-trained, well coordinated, high in morale and equipped with fighters fully the equal of the Messerschmitt Bf 109E single-engined and Bf 110 twin-engined fighters.

The primary weight of the RAF's fighting fell on the Hurricane Mk I, but the Germans now came to appreciate that the newer Spitfire Mk I was a superb

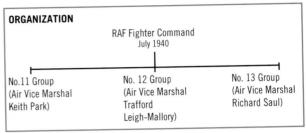

ORGANIZATION

RAF Fighter Command
July 1940

No.11 Group	No. 12 Group	No. 13 Group
(Air Vice Marshal Keith Park)	(Air Vice Marshal Trafford Leigh-Mallory)	(Air Vice Marshal Richard Saul)

NO.12 GROUP: SINGLE-ENGINED FIGHTER SQUADRONS (JULY 1940)			
Unit	Type	Strength	Serviceable
No.19 Squadron	Spitfire	8	5
No. 264 Squadron	Defiant	11	7
No. 66 Squadron	Spitfire	12	4
No. 242 Squadron	Hurricane	10	4
No. 222 Squadron	Spitfire	12	4
No. 46 Squadron	Hurricane	15	3
No. 611 Squadron	Spitfire	3	11

▼ **Hurricane fighters**
A pair of Mk I Hurricanes from No. 111 Squadron prepare to do battle with the Luftwaffe over southeast England, summer 1940.

fighter. The British had fewer experienced pilots at the start of the battle, and it was this shortage of trained pilots which became the greatest concern for Air Chief Marshal Sir Hugh Dowding. Drawing from regular RAF forces as well as the Auxiliary Air Force and the Volunteer Reserve, the British could muster some 1103 fighter pilots on 1 July. The Germans could muster 1450 fighter pilots, and these were generally more experienced.

In the early phases of the battle, the RAF was hindered by its reliance on dated formations. These restricted squadrons to tight 12 aircraft formations composed of three-aircraft 'sections' in tight 'vics'. With four sections flying together in tight

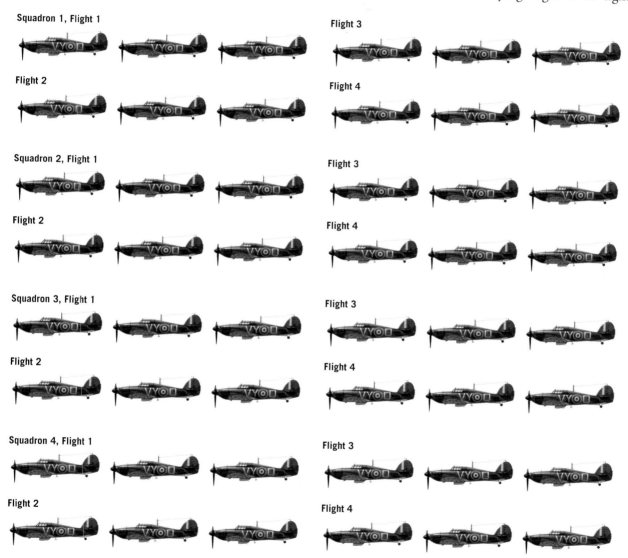

Squadron 1, Flight 1

Flight 2

Flight 3

Flight 4

Squadron 2, Flight 1

Flight 2

Flight 3

Flight 4

Squadron 3, Flight 1

Flight 2

Flight 3

Flight 4

Squadron 4, Flight 1

Flight 2

Flight 3

Flight 4

▲ **1940 RAF 'Big Wing'**

The brainchild of Squadron Leader D. R. S. Bader and Air Vice Marshal Leigh-Mallory of No. 12 Group, the 'big wing' was based on the idea that four squadrons operating together would inflict more damage than four squadrons operating independently. However, it took so long to assemble the 'big wing' in the air that it could not intercept the Germans bombers before they had attacked London, and Air Vice Marshal Park of No. 11 Group, supported by Dowding, argued that any type of pre-attack interception was better in degrading the bombers' effectiveness.

▲ Supermarine Spitfire Mk IA

No. 66 Squadron / RAF Fighter Command, 1940

With 12 serviceable and four unserviceable aircraft on 1 July 1940, No. 66
Squadron was part of No. 12 Group and based at Coltishall in East Anglia.

Specifications

Crew: 1

Powerplant: 768kW (1030hp) Rolls-Royce
  Merlin III liquid-cooled V-12

Maximum speed: 582km/h (362mph)

Range: 636km (395 miles)

Service ceiling: 9725m (31,900ft)

Dimensions: span 11.22m (36ft 10in);
  length 9.11m (29ft 11in);
  height 2.69m (8ft 10in)

Weight: 2624kg (5784lb) loaded

Armament: 8 x 7.7mm (0.303in)
  Browning MGs

▲ Supermarine Spitfire Mk IA

No. 602 Squadron / RAF Fighter Command, 1940

With 12 serviceable and four unserviceable aircraft on 1 July 1940, No. 602
Squadron was part of No. 13 Group and based at Drem in Scotland.

Specifications

Crew: 1

Powerplant: 768kW (1030hp) Rolls-Royce
  Merlin III liquid-cooled V-12

Maximum speed: 582km/h (362mph)

Range: 636km (395 miles)

Service ceiling: 9725m (31,900ft)

Dimensions: span 11.22m (36ft 10in);
  length 9.11m (29ft 11in);
  height 2.69m (8ft 10in)

Weight: 2624kg (5784lb) loaded

Armament: 8 x 7.7mm (0.303in)
  Browning MGs

formation, only the squadron leader at the front was
free to search for the enemy. British training also
emphasized formulaic attacks by sections breaking
away in sequence. Fighter Command recognized
the weaknesses of this rigid structure early in the
battle, but it was felt too risky to change tactics as the
fighting continued.

A compromise allowed the squadron formations
to fly looser formations with one or two 'weavers'
flying above and behind for greater observation and
rear protection. After the battle, RAF pilots adopted
a variant on the German *Schwarm* (two pairs, each
consisting of a leader and a wingman). Each *Schwarm*
in a *Staffel* (squadron) flew staggered and with

plenty of room between them, making the formation
difficult to spot at longer ranges and allowing for
greater flexibility.

The *Luftwaffe* regrouped after the Battle of
France into three *Luftflotten* (air fleets) on the
UK's southern and northern flanks. *Luftflotte
2*, commanded by *Generalfeldmarschall* Albert
Kesselring, was responsible for the bombing of
south-east England and the London area. *Luftflotte
3*, under *Generalfeldmarschall* Hugo Sperrle, targeted
the West Country, Midlands and north-west
England. *Luftflotte 5*, under *Generaloberst* Hans-
Jürgen Stumpff from his headquarters in Norway,
targeted the north of England and Scotland.

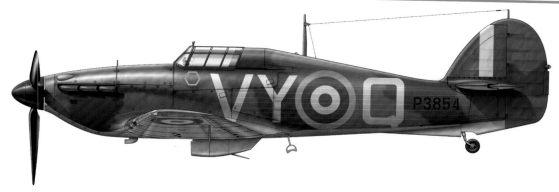

▲ **Hawker Hurricane Mk IA**

No. 85 Squadron / RAF Fighter Command, August 1940

With 15 serviceable and three unserviceable aircraft on 1 July 1940, No. 85 Squadron was part of No. 12 Group and based at Martlesham in East Anglia.

Specifications

Crew: 1

Powerplant: 768kW (1030hp) Rolls-Royce Merlin II liquid-cooled V-12

Maximum speed: 496km/h (308mph)

Range: 845km (525 miles)

Service ceiling: 10,180m (33,400ft)

Dimensions: span 12.19m (40ft 0in); length 9.55m (31ft 4in); height 4.07m (13ft 4.5in)

Weight: 2820kg (6218lb) loaded

Armament: 8 x 7.7mm (0.303in) Browning MGs

No. 10 Group

JUNE–DECEMBER 1940

A late arrival in the establishment of RAF Fighter Command, No. 10 Group helped to lift the operational burden from the all-important No. 11 to its east, and also provided this latter group with replacement pilots and aircraft to keep up the fighter strength in south-east England.

THE FIRST No. 10 Group of the Royal Air Force was formed on 1 April 1918 in No. 2 Area. On 8 May of the following year, it was transferred to the South-Western Area, and in 1918 it was further transferred to the Coastal Area, with which the group remained until it was disbanded on 18 January 1932.

New group

No. 10 Group was re-established on 1 June 1940 within Air Chief Marshal Sir Hugh Dowding's Fighter Command. The rationale for this expansion of Fighter Command's subordinate formations was to allow what was now the neighbouring No. 11 Group, previously responsible for the protection of the whole of southern England, to concentrate its efforts on just south-east England, which would clearly be the area most centrally threatened by German air attack from bases in occupied northern France, Belgium and the Netherlands. Thus the new No. 10 Group

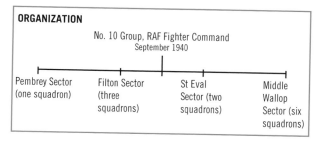

ORGANIZATION

No. 10 Group, RAF Fighter Command
September 1940

| Pembrey Sector (one squadron) | Filton Sector (three squadrons) | St Eval Sector (two squadrons) | Middle Wallop Sector (six squadrons) |

was allocated south-west England and the portions of England and Wales flanking the Bristol Channel as its area of responsibility.

Under the command of Air Vice Marshal Sir Christopher Brand, No. 10 Group supported No. 11 Group in the Battle of Britain by rotating squadrons, transferring extra fighter support when this was required, and making more pilots available when necessary. It is notable that Air Vice Marshal Keith Park, commanding the decisive No. 11 Group,

▲ Supermarine Spitfire Mk IA

No. 609 Squadron / 10 Group

No. 609 Squadron was formed at RAF Yeadon, now Leeds Bradford International Airport, on 10 February 1936, as one of the 20 flying Squadrons of the Royal Auxiliary Air Force. During the Battle of Britain, the squadron moved to RAF Middle Wallop, west of London, as part of Fighter Command's efforts to defend the south coast of England.

enjoyed a far better relationship with Brand than with Air Vice Marshal Trafford Leigh-Mallory of No. 12 Group.

As well as providing support for No. 11 Group, No. 10 Group had a number of squadrons equipped with aircraft whose obsolescence rendered them unsuitable for active use in the combat arena of the

▼ Bristol Beaufighter

The Beaufighter Mk IF was the first effective night-fighter in British service, a role for which it was cleared in July 1940. Large and powerful, the Beaufighter possessed adequate performance, but carried AI. Mk IV radar and the fixed forward-firing armament of four 20mm (0.79in) cannon. This was a machine of No. 604 Squadron.

Specifications

Crew: 1

Powerplant: 768kW (1030hp) Rolls-Royce Merlin III liquid-cooled V-12

Maximum speed: 582km/h (362mph)

Range: 636km (395 miles)

Service ceiling: 9725m (31,900ft)

Dimensions: span 11.22m (36ft 10in); length 9.11m (29ft 11in); height 2.69m (8ft 10in)

Weight: 2624kg (5784lb) loaded

Armament: 8 x 7.7mm (0.303in) Browning MGs

NO. 10 GROUP SQUADRONS, 1 SEPTEMBER 1940			
Unit	Type	Strength	Serviceable
No. 87 Squadron	Hurricane	15	9
No. 92 Squadron	Spitfire	16	12
No. 152 Squadron	Spitfire	16	12
No. 213 Squadron	Hurricane	15	8
No. 234 Squadron	Spitfire	17	12
No. 236 Squadron	Blenheim	17	12
No. 238 Squadron	Hurricane	15	11
No. 249 Squadron	Hurricane	16	15
No. 604 Squadron	Blenheim	14	11
No. 609 Squadron	Spitfire	14	11

Battle of Britain. These types included the Gloster Gladiator biplane and the Boulton Paul Defiant turret fighter.

No. 10 Group layout

No. 10 Group had its headquarters at Box in Wiltshire, and its primary sectors in September were Pembrey, Filton (with other airfields at Exeter, Bibury and Colerne), St Eval (with another airfield at Roborough), and Middle Wallop (with other airfields at Warmwell and Boscombe Down). There were also operational training units at Aston Down, Sutton Bridge and Hawarden airfields. After the end of the Battle of Britain, No. 10 Group was responsible for offensive missions into north-west France by the Westland Whirlwind twin-engined attack fighter,

and also provided fighter cover for the all-important convoys of merchant ships approaching and leaving the British Isles via the South-Western Approaches. Any pilots posted to a squadron of No. 10 Group from either No. 12 Group or No. 13 Group knew that they would soon be transferred to No. 11 Group, where the weight of the growing British air offensive against German fighters and their bases in northern France was concentrated from early in 1941. These pilots, therefore, took every advantage of No. 10 Group's comparatively safe area of operation to hone their skills in preparation for a more active level of service.

It is worth noting that No. 10 Group was finally reabsorbed into No. 11 Group on 2 May 1945, only days before the end of World War II in Europe.

No. 11 Group

JULY–SEPTEMBER 1940

The story of No. 11 Group is in large measure the story of Fighter Command in the Battle of Britain. Based in the south-east of England, the group bore the brunt of the German air offensive during the fighter and bomber phases of the battle, and emerged scarred but unbeaten.

A No. 11 GROUP was first formed on 1 April 1918 in No. 2 Area, and was transferred to the South-Western Area the next month on 8 May.

The group was disbanded on 17 May of the same year, only to be re-formed in the North-Western Area on 22 August. In May 1920, No. 11 Group was reduced to No. 11 Wing. Then on 14 July 1936, No. 11 Group became the first group to be established within Fighter Command, and had responsibility for the defence of southern England, including London.

Group organization

The group was organized using the Dowding system

of fighter control. The group's HQ was at RAF Uxbridge, from where commands were passed to the various sector airfields, each of which coordinated several airfields and fighter squadrons. No. 11 Group's sectors (A, B, C, D, E, F, Y and Z) airfields were Tangmere, Kenley, Biggin Hill, Hornchurch, North Weald, Debden, Middle Wallop and Northolt.

New commander

Air Vice Marshal Keith Park assumed command of No. 11 Group on 20 April 1940 and led it throughout its period of enduring fame in the Battle of Britain. Pilots posted to No. 11 Group's squadrons

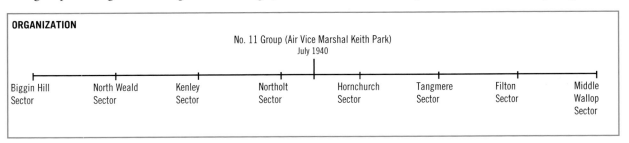

ORGANIZATION

No. 11 Group (Air Vice Marshal Keith Park)
July 1940

| Biggin Hill Sector | North Weald Sector | Kenley Sector | Northolt Sector | Hornchurch Sector | Tangmere Sector | Filton Sector | Middle Wallop Sector |

knew they would see extensive action, while the pilots leaving the group knew that they were going to comparatively safer duty.

Enjoying the full support of the commanders of Nos 10 and 13 Groups, Park received only modest support from No. 12 Group's Air Vice Marshal Trafford Leigh-Mallory, who did not agree with Park's tactics.

Restructured command

Park orchestrated his command very carefully in the five phases of the battle. In the first (10 July–7 August), the British and Germans lost 169 and 192 aircraft during fighting over the English Channel and the British ports along it.

In the second phase (8–23 August), the losses were 303 and 403 respectively as the Germans attacked radar stations and forward fighter bases.

In the third (24 August–6 September) the losses were 262 and 378 as the Germans attacked inland fighter bases and fighter factories to force the RAF into the air.

In the fourth (7–30 September), the losses were 380 and 435 in German daylight attacks on London, before the Germans switched to fighter-bomber raids in the fifth phase (1–31 October), when they lost 325 aircraft to the British 265, and thereafter

NO. 11 GROUP FIGHTER SQUADRONS (1 AUGUST 1940)			
Unit	Type	Strength	Serviceable
No. 1 Squadron	Hurricane	16	13
No. 17 Squadron	Hurricane	19	14
No. 25 Squadron	Blenheim	14	7
No. 32 Squadron	Hurricane	15	11
No. 41 Squadron	Spitfire	16	10
No. 43 Squadron	Hurricane	19	18
No. 56 Squadron	Hurricane	17	5
No. 64 Squadron	Spitfire	16	12
No. 65 Squadron	Spitfire	16	11
No. 74 Squadron	Spitfire	15	12
No. 85 Squadron	Hurricane	18	12
No. 111 Squadron	Hurricane	12	10
No. 145 Squadron	Hurricane	17	10
No. 151 Squadron	Hurricane	18	13
No. 257 Squadron	Hurricane	15	10
No. 266 Squadron	Spitfire	18	13
No. 501 Squadron	Hurricane	16	11
No. 600 Squadron	Blenheim	15	9
No. 601 Squadron	Hurricane	18	14
No. 610 Squadron	Spitfire	15	12
No. 615 Squadron	Hurricane	16	14

Specifications

Crew: 1

Powerplant: 768kW (1030hp) Rolls-Royce Merlin III liquid-cooled V-12

Maximum speed: 582km/h (362mph)

Range: 636km (395 miles)

Service ceiling: 9725m (31,900ft)

Dimensions: span 11.22m (36ft 10in); length 9.11m (29ft 11in); height 2.69m (8ft 10in)

Weight: 2624kg (5784lb) loaded

Armament: 8 x 7.7mm (0.303in) Browning MGs

▲ **Supermarine Spitfire Mk IA**

No. 74 Squadron / RAF Fighter Command, 1940

In July 1940, No. 74 Squadron was based at Hornchurch in No. 11 Group.

switched to night bombing. With the battle over, Leigh-Mallory and Air Marshal Sholto Douglas managed to have Park and Air Chief Marshal Sir Hugh Dowding removed, moving into their positions at the head of No. 11 Group and Fighter Command respectively.

Specifications

Crew: 2

Powerplant: 2 x 1119kW (1500hp) Bristol Hercules XI air-cooled engine

Maximum speed: 492km/h (306mph)

Range: 2414km (1500 miles)

Service ceiling: 8810m (28,900ft)

Dimensions: span 17.63m (57ft 10in); length 12.60m (41ft 4in); height 4.82m (15 ft 10in)

Weight: 9435kg (21,100lb) loaded

Armament: 4 x 20mm (0.79in) cannon and 6 x 7.7mm (0.303in) MGs

▲ Bristol Beaufighter Mk IF

No. 25 Squadron / RAF Fighter Command

The Beaufighter multi-role warplane saw its first service as a heavy fighter, and most especially as a night-fighter. As such, it was the RAF's first effective means of tackling German night-bombers.

▲ Hawker Hurricane Mk I

No. 249 Squadron / No. 11 Group

Based at RAF North Weald, this Hurricane was flown by Squadron Leader John Grandy. The squadron was formed as a fighter unit on 16 May 1940 at Church Fenton. It was equipped with Spitfires for the first month, but these were changed to Hurricanes in June.

Specifications

Crew: 1

Powerplant: 768kW (1030hp) Rolls-Royce Merlin II liquid-cooled V-12

Maximum speed: 496km/h (308mph)

Range: 845km (525 miles)

Service ceiling: 10,180m (33,400ft)

Dimensions: span 12.19m (40ft 0in); length 9.55m (31ft 4in); height 4.07m (13ft 4.5in)

Weight: 2820kg (6218lb) loaded

Armament: 8 x 7.7mm (0.303in) Browning MGs

▲ Supermarine Spitfire Mk IA

No. 74 Squadron / Fighter Command, 1940

Led by Squadron Leader F. L. White, No. 74 Squadron was based at Hornchurch as one of the three Spitfire units operating in No. 11 Group's Hornchurch sector. The squadron had 15 aircraft at this time, 12 of them serviceable.

Specifications

Crew: 1
Powerplant: 768kW (1030hp) Rolls-Royce
  Merlin III liquid-cooled V-12
Maximum speed: 582km/h (362mph)
Range: 636km (395 miles)
Service ceiling: 9725m (31,900ft)

Dimensions: span 11.22m (36ft 10in);
  length 9.11m (29ft 11in);
  height 2.69m (8ft 10in)
Weight: 2624kg (5784lb) loaded
Armament: 8 x 7.7mm (0.303in)
  Browning MGs

▲ Hawker Hurricane Mk IA

No. 501 Squadron / 11 Group / RAF Fighter Command, 1940

Based at Gravesend in the Biggin Hill Sector of No. 11 Group on 1 September 1940, No. 501 Squadron was led by Squadron Leader H. A. V. Hogan and on this day had a strength of 17 Hurricane fighters, only 11 of them serviceable.

Specifications

Crew: 1
Powerplant: 768kW (1030hp) Rolls-Royce
  Merlin II liquid-cooled V-12
Maximum speed: 496km/h (308mph)
Range: 845km (525 miles)
Service ceiling: 10,180m (33,400ft)

Dimensions: span 12.19m (40ft 0in); length
  9.55m (31ft 4in); height 4.07m (13ft 4.5in)
Weight: 2820kg (6218lb) loaded
Armament: 8 x 7.7mm (0.303in)
  Browning MGs

▼ 1940 RAF Spitfire 'Big Wing'

The rationale of the 'big wing', according to its protagonists, was that while its assembly time might deny it the opportunity to effect an interception before the bombers attacked, it would deliver so heavy a blow as the bombers streamed home that the Germans' ability to sustain the bomber offensive would soon be degraded. This factor would, in turn, ease the task of the defending fighters and lead to a steadily escalating German loss rate.

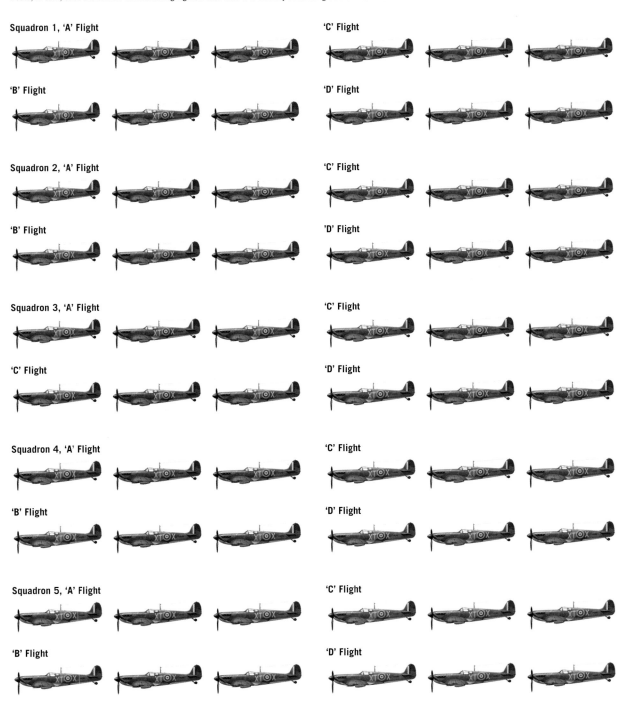

Squadron 1, 'A' Flight

'B' Flight

'C' Flight

'D' Flight

Squadron 2, 'A' Flight

'B' Flight

'C' Flight

'D' Flight

Squadron 3, 'A' Flight

'C' Flight

'C' Flight

'D' Flight

Squadron 4, 'A' Flight

'B' Flight

'C' Flight

'D' Flight

Squadron 5, 'A' Flight

'B' Flight

'C' Flight

'D' Flight

▲ Supermarine Spitfire Mk IA

No. 603 Squadron / RAF Fighter Command, 1940

In 1 July 1940, No. 603 Squadron was part of No. 13 Group, and based at Turnhouse in Scotland with flights detached to Dyce and Montrose.

Specifications

Crew: 1

Powerplant: 768kW (1030hp) Rolls-Royce Merlin III liquid-cooled V-12

Maximum speed: 582km/h (362mph)

Range: 636km (395 miles)

Service ceiling: 9725m (31,900ft)

Dimensions: span 11.22m (36ft 10in); length 9.11m (29ft 11in); height 2.69m (8ft 10in)

Weight: 2624kg (5784lb) loaded

Armament: 8 x 7.7mm (0.303in) Browning MGs

▲ Supermarine Spitfire Mk I

No. 66 Squadron / 11 Group

Based at RAF Biggin Hill, the Spitfires of 66 Squadron were commandered by Squadron Leader Rupert Leigh. The squadron received its first Spitfires in late 1938, and flew operational patrols over Dunkirk in the withdrawal from France in May 1940. The squadron joined 11 Group in September 1940.

Specifications

Crew: 1

Powerplant: 768kW (1030hp) Rolls-Royce Merlin III liquid-cooled V-12

Maximum speed: 582km/h (362mph)

Range: 636km (395 miles)

Service ceiling: 9725m (31,900ft)

Dimensions: span 11.22m (36ft 10in); length 9.11m (29ft 11in); height 2.69m (8ft 10in)

Weight: 2624kg (5784lb) loaded

Armament: 8 x 7.7mm (0.303in) Browning MGs

▲ **On patrol**
Spitfire Mk IA fighters of No. 11 Group's No. 610 Squadron, based at RAF Biggin Hill, in June 1940. The aircraft are flying in flights of three aircraft.

No. 12 Group

JULY–SEPTEMBER 1940

Covering the Midlands of England, No. 12 Group was not as hard pressed as No. 11 Group, and was thus well placed to come to the aid of its southern neighbour, which had more squadrons but always, despite the advantages offered by radar, lacked time to assemble in numbers.

N O. 12 GROUP of the Royal Air Force first came into existence during April 1918 at Cranwell, Lincolnshire, as part of the No. 3 Area. On 8 May 1918, the group transferred to the Midland Area, and then on 18 October of the same year to the Northern Area. On 1 November 1918, the group became the RAF (Cadet) College.

Reconstituted group

No. 11 Group was reconstituted on 1 April 1937 as part of Fighter Command. In World War II, No. 12 Group was entrusted with the task of providing air defence for the Midlands of England, and as such was of importance second only to that of No. 11 Group. As No. 12 Group's area of responsibility included many industrial areas, it received a large number of German bombing attacks.

The commander of No. 12 group during the summer and autumn of 1940 was Air Vice Marshal Trafford Leigh-Mallory, an ambitious officer who had assumed command of the group in December 1937. Despite his length of service in the RAF, Leigh-Mallory had been passed over for command of the more important No. 11 Group in favour of Air Vice Marshal Keith Park. Feeling that he had been slighted, Leigh-Mallory thereafter had a distinctly cool relationship with Park, hardly the ideal situation for the commanders of the UK's two most important air defence groups.

'Big wing' tactics

In September 1940, No. 12 Group's sectors were Duxford, Coltishall, Wittering, Digby, Kirton-in-Lindsey (three airfields) and Church Fenton (three airfields) with elements of 17 squadrons. In addition to providing regional air defence over the Midlands,

NO. 12 GROUP FIGHTER SQUADRONS (1 SEPTEMBER 1940)			
Unit	Type	Strength	Serviceable
No. 19 Squadron	Spitfire	15	11
No. 23 Squadron	Blenheim	17	11
No. 29 Squadron	Blenheim	14	10
No. 46 Squadron	Hurricane	17	15
No. 74 Squadron	Spitfire	16	11
No. 222 Squadron	Spitfire	16	10
No. 229 Squadron	Hurricane	16	12
No. 242 Squadron	Hurricane	15	11
No. 264 Squadron	Defiant	15	8
No. 266 Squadron	Spitfire	12	8
No. 310 Squadron	Hurricane	14	10
No. 611 Squadron	Spitfire	18	12

No. 12 Group was also allocated the task of providing cover for No. 11 Group's airfields during the Battle of Britain, but on several occasions these

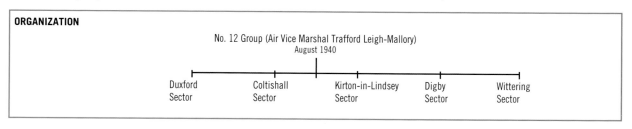

ORGANIZATION

No. 12 Group (Air Vice Marshal Trafford Leigh-Mallory)
August 1940

| Duxford Sector | Coltishall Sector | Kirton-in-Lindsey Sector | Digby Sector | Wittering Sector |

Specifications

Crew: 2

Powerplant: 768kW (1030hp) Rolls-Royce
Merlin III liquid-cooled V-12

Maximum speed: 489km/h (304mph)

Range: 748km (465 miles)

Service ceiling: 9250m (30,350ft)

Dimensions: span 11.99m (39ft 4in);
length 10.77m (35ft 4in);
height 3.71m (12ft 2in)

Weight: 3773kg (8318lb) loaded

Armament: 4 x 7.7mm (0.303in) Browning MGs
in the power-operated dorsal turret

▲ **Boulton Paul Defiant Mk I**

No. 264 Squadron / RAF Fighter Command, mid-1940

This Defiant Mk I was flown by Squadron Leader P. A. Hunter. The Defiant scored some initial success when the nature of its turreted armament was not comprehended, but once the Germans knew that the aircraft lacked both fixed forward-firing guns and agility, they were able to shoot the type down with ease.

vital installations were left undefended. When Park complained about it, Leigh-Mallory responded that greater results would accrue from the implementation of the 'big wing' tactic, but that the assembly of a concentrated force in the air took time.

The 'big wing' was certainly an effective air fighting force whenever it was actually assembled and managed to effect an interception with the massed enemy air units, but this happened on only a limited number of occasions. Even so, opponents of Park and Air Chief Marshal Sir Hugh Dowding were able to exploit the low incidence of these successes after the end of the battle and so engineer the removal of Park and Dowding, who were replaced by Leigh-Mallory and Air Marshal Sir William Sholto Douglas respectively.

Crew: 1	Dimensions: span 11.22m (36ft 10in);
Powerplant: 768kW (1030hp) Rolls-Royce	length 9.11m (29ft 11in);
Merlin III liquid-cooled V-12	height 2.69m (8ft 10in)
Maximum speed: 582km/h (362mph)	Weight: 2624kg (5784lb) loaded
Range: 636km (395 miles)	Armament: 8 x 7.7mm (0.303in) Browning MGs
Service ceiling: 9725m (31,900ft)	

▲ **Supermarine Spitfire Mk IA**
No. 66 Squadron / RAF Fighter Command, 1940

Led by Squadron Leader R. H. A. Leigh, No. 66 Squadron had 16 aircraft, 12 of them serviceable, on 1 August 1940. The squadron was part of No. 12 Group's strength, and was based at Coltishall as one of the two squadrons in the Coltishall sector. The other unit was No. 242 Squadron with Hurricanes.

Specifications

Crew: 1	Dimensions: span 11.22m (36ft 10in);
Powerplant: 768kW (1030hp) Rolls-Royce	length 9.11m (29ft 11in);
Merlin III liquid-cooled V-12	height 2.69m (8ft 10in)
Maximum speed: 582km/h (362mph)	Weight: about 2624kg (5784lb) loaded
Range: 636km (395 miles)	Armament: 2 x 20mm (0.79in) Hispano cannon
Service ceiling: 9725m (31,900ft)	and 4 x 7.7mm (0.303in) Browning MGs

▲ **Supermarine Spitfire Mk IB**
No. 19 Squadron / RAF Fighter Command, 1940

No. 19 Squadron was the first unit to receive Spitfire fighters, in August 1938. At the beginning of September 1940, the unit was based at Fowlmere in the Duxford sector as part of No. 12 Group. Led by Squadron Leader P. C. Pinkham, No. 19 Squadron had 15 aircraft on this date, 11 of them serviceable.

RAF Fighter Command
1941–43

With the Battle of Britain won but the Germans still bombing British cities in the 'Blitz', the early weeks of 1941 saw Fighter Command go over to the offensive, trying several types of tactic to pin German air forces in Western Europe and draw them into the air for a battle of attrition.

FROM THE START of 1941, Fighter Command began an attempt to wrest control of the air from the Germans over north-west Europe. By May 1941, the squadrons on the main air bases had been grouped into fighter wings under a single experienced leader.

Several short-penetration fighter tactics were tested in an effort to draw the Luftwaffe into a war of attrition, and to pin German fighter forces in north-west Europe, especially after the June 1941 German invasion of the USSR.

The fighter best suited to the task was the Supermarine Spitfire, which was used in large numbers with medium bomber forces whose task was to attack the targets that the Germans fighters would seek to protect. In general, though, the Germans responded only when the situation favoured them, and the general inaccuracy of the bombing meant that the British attacks were seldom effective.

Thus the results of such operations in 1941 were very mixed. One major problem was the short range of the Spitfire, which had been designed as a limited-endurance interceptor and therefore could

SELECTED FIGHTER COMMAND HURRICANE SQUADRONS (1941)		
Unit	Type	Base
No. 71 Squadron	Hurricane	Church Fenton
No. 91 Squadron	Hurricane	Hawkinge
No. 92 Squadron	Hurricane	Biggin Hill
No. 116 Squadron	Hurricane	Hatfield
No. 121 Squadron	Hurricane	Kirton-in-Lindsey
No. 128 Squadron	Hurricane	Hastings
No. 133 Squadron	Hurricane	Coltishall
No. 136 Squadron	Hurricane	Kirton-in-Lindsey
No. 181 Squadron	Hurricane	Duxford
No. 182 Squadron	Hurricane	Martlesham Heath
No. 239 Squadron	Hurricane	Hatfield
No. 247 Squadron	Hurricane	Roborough
No. 255 Squadron	Hurricane	Kirton-in-Lindsey
No. 306 Squadron	Hurricane	Church Fenton
No. 308 Squadron	Hurricane	Speke
No. 315 Squadron	Hurricane	Acklington
No. 316 Squadron	Hurricane	Pembrey
No. 317 Squadron	Hurricane	Acklington
No. 331 Squadron	Hurricane	Catterick
No. 401 Squadron	Hurricane	Digby
No. 402 Squadron	Hurricane	Digby

◄ **Ground attack Hurricane**

Soon hard-pressed in the interceptor role, the Hurricane was converted into a ground attack aircraft, armed with Vickers 40mm (1.5in) cannons. The first of this type to enter service flew in the Western Desert in mid-1942.

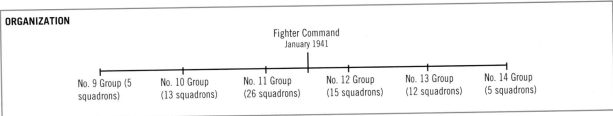

ORGANIZATION

Fighter Command
January 1941

No. 9 Group (5 squadrons) — No. 10 Group (13 squadrons) — No. 11 Group (26 squadrons) — No. 12 Group (15 squadrons) — No. 13 Group (12 squadrons) — No. 14 Group (5 squadrons)

not remain long over France. In these circumstances, the *Luftwaffe* was able to reduce its strength in France to just two *Jadgdeschwadern* of some 180 fighters, although these units were the very capable JG 2 and JG 26. The situation in which British fighters were operating at short range over home territory, with all its recovery and repair facilities, was now entirely reversed in the favour of the Germans. In 1941, therefore, Fighter Command lost some 530 aircraft

and the Germans only 236, although British pilots claimed 731. As 1941 ended, the Focke-Wulf Fw 190 appeared as a fighter superior to the Spitfire Mk V, and 1942 and 1943 were therefore harder years in which the offensive was pressed, regardless of losses, to show support for the USSR. Over the UK, meanwhile, improved British night-fighters made the Blitz very costly, and in May it was called off to allow German concentration of effort against the USSR.

Offensive sweeps
1941–43

Fighter Command initially attempted to draw the *Luftwaffe* into the air with massed fighter sweeps, known as 'Rhubarb' operations, but the Germans generally refused to respond. Little more success attended the 'Circus' operations, which were fighter-escorted bomber raids.

THE FIRST TYPE of offensive developed in 1941 by No. 11 Group was the 'Rhubarb', a sweep by the aircraft of one or sometimes two fighter wings. As the sweeps offered little real threat, the Germans largely ignored them. No. 11 Group, therefore, devised the 'Circus', which involved large numbers of fighters escorting a few bombers whose attentions were designed to inflict real damage, and so spur a German reaction. Between January and June 1941,

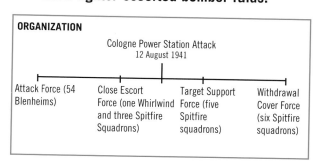

ORGANIZATION

	Cologne Power Station Attack 12 August 1941		
Attack Force (54 Blenheims)	Close Escort Force (one Whirlwind and three Spitfire Squadrons)	Target Support Force (five Spitfire squadrons)	Withdrawal Cover Force (six Spitfire squadrons)

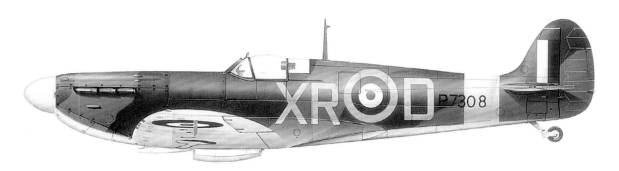

Specifications

Crew: 1

Powerplant: 768kW (1030hp) Rolls-Royce
Merlin III liquid-cooled V-12

Maximum speed: 582km/h (362mph)

Range: 636km (395 miles)

Service ceiling: 9725m (31,900ft)

Dimensions: span 11.22m (36ft 10in);
length 9.11m (29ft 11in);
height 2.69m (8ft 10in)

Weight: 2624kg (5784lb) loaded

Armament: 8 x 7.7mm (0.303in) Browning
MGs in wings

▲ **Supermarine Spitfire Mk IA**

No. 71 'Eagle' Squadron / Fighter Command, 1941

The pilots of this squadron were primarily American volunteers, and this aeroplane was flown by Pilot Officer W. Dunn.

▼ 1941 'Circus' sweep

A typical 'Circus' operation of 1941 might involve 120 aircraft in the form of 12 Bristol Blenheim light bombers (one squadron) escorted and covered by 108 Supermarine Spitfire fighters (nine squadrons each comprising four flights of three aircraft). While part of the Spitfire force provided escort for the vulnerable Blenheim bombers, the rest of the force operated semi-independently at higher altitude, ready to pounce on any German fighters that rose to the challenge.

Blenheim squadron

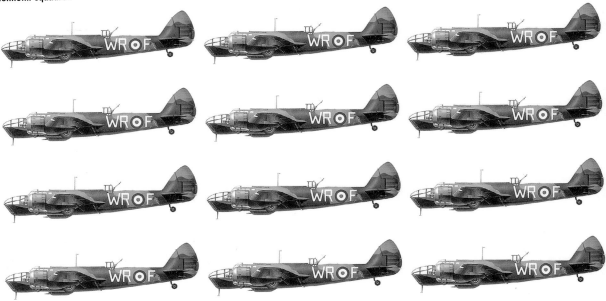

Escort squadron (1 of 9)

Flight 1   **Flight 2**   **Flight 3**   **Flight 4**

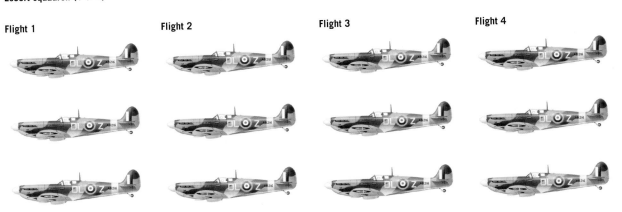

the Circuses involved 190 bomber sorties, while the Rhubarbs and Circuses combined involved 2700 fighter sorties.

During these, Fighter Command lost 51 pilots, and claimed the destruction of 44 German aircraft, though the total was in fact somewhat lower. The number of Circuses was increased in the second half of 1941 and into 1942–43. Even though the British had introduced the improved Spitfire Mk V, the Germans had responded initially with the fine Messerschmitt Bf 109F and then in September 1941 with the excellent Focke-Wulf Fw 190A, the latter decidedly better than the Spitfire Mk V. Moreover, the German radar system was now better than the British system had been in 1940, and this made it almost impossible for the Circuses to achieve surprise. Even so, Leigh-Mallory claimed that between 14 June and 3 September 1941, No. 11 Group had destroyed 437 German fighters, with another 182 claimed as probables.

The *Luftwaffe* had no more than about 260 (200 serviceable) single-engined fighters in France and the Low Countries, so the real figures were, in fact, 128 lost and 76 damaged. Fighter Command itself lost 194 pilots during this period. For the period between 14 June and 31 December, Fighter Command claimed 731 'kills' for the loss of 411 aircraft, while the actual German losses were just 154.

Better used in other theatres?

Fighter Command retained 75 day fighter squadrons in the UK in the later part of 1941. The same basic tactical situation prevailed during 1942 and 1943, and is perhaps typified by the amphibious 'reconnaissance in force' to Dieppe on 19 August 1942. The Canadian 2nd Division and supporting elements assaulted under cover of the guns of eight destroyers and Hurricanes firing 20mm (0.79in) cannon, and the operation was a disaster despite an air umbrella of 70 squadrons, including 61

of fighters. Leigh-Mallory claimed 43 German bombers and 49 fighters destroyed, 10 bombers and 29 fighters probably destroyed, and 56 bombers and 84 fighters damaged. In fact, the German losses were 25 bombers and 23 fighters destroyed, and 16 bombers and eight fighters damaged. The RAF lost 106 aircraft, of which 88 were fighters.

▲ **Fighter-bomber**

Loaded with a pair of 114kg (250lb) bombs under its wing, this Hawker Hurricane Mk IIB of No. 402 Squadron, RCAF, prepares for a cross-Channel sortie in 1941.

Specifications

Crew: 1

Powerplant: 876kW (1175hp) Rolls-Royce Merlin XII liquid-cooled V-12

Maximum speed: 570km/h (354mph)

Range: 636km (395 miles)

Service ceiling: 11,457m (37,600ft)

Dimensions: span 11.22m (36ft 10in); length 9.11m (29ft 11in); height 2.69m (8ft 10in)

Weight: 2803kg (6172lb) loaded

Armament: 8 x 7.7mm (0.303in) Browning MGs in wings

▲ **Supermarine Spitfire Mk II**

No. 312 Squadron / RAF Fighter Command, 1941

The aircraft of No. 312 Squadron were flown by Czechoslovakian pilots who had escaped from their homeland at the time of the German takeover in 1939, and this aeroplane was flown by Lieutenant Vybiral. Many of the Czech pilots had gained combat experience with the French Air Force in May and June 1940.

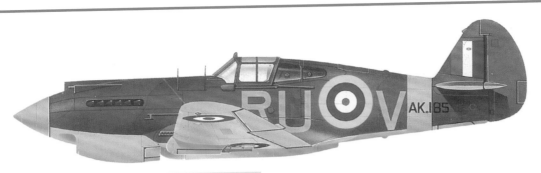

Specifications

Crew: 1

Powerplant: 860kW (1150hp) Allison piston
    engine

Maximum speed: 580km/h (360mph)

Range: 1100km (650 miles)

Service ceiling: 8800m (29,000ft)

Dimensions: span 11.38m (37ft 4in);
    length 9.66m (31ft 8in);
    height 3.76m (12ft 4in)

Weight: 3760kg (8280lb) loaded

Armament: 6 x 12.7mm (0.5in) M2 Browning
    MGs

▲ Curtiss Tomahawk Mk IIB

No. 414 Squadron / RAF, Croydon, early 1941

In theory, the Tomahawk offered adequate capabilities and was readily available from the USA, but experience soon revealed the type's complete unsuitability for use against a technically sophisticated opponent such as the Luftwaffe.

Specifications

Crew: 1

Powerplant: 860kW (1150hp)

Maximum speed: 580km/h (360mph)

Range: 1100km (650 miles)

Service ceiling: 8800m (29,000ft)

Dimensions: span 11.38m (37ft 4in); length
    9.66m (31ft 8in); height 3.76m (12ft 4in)

Weight: 3760kg (8280lb) loaded

Armament: 6 x 12.7mm (0.5in) M2 Browning
    MGs

▲ Curtiss Tomahawk Mk IB

No. 400 Squadron / Royal Canadian Air Force / Odiham, late 1941

After working up in the UK, most Tomahawk squadrons were diverted to secondary theatres, such as those in North Africa, and served in the ground-attack role, a role in which they faced mainly inferior Italian aircraft and AA fire.

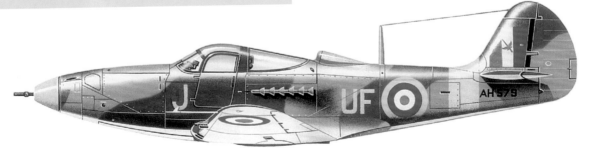

Specifications

Crew: 1

Powerplant: 895kW (1200hp) Allison V-1710-
    85 liquid-cooled V-12

Maximum speed: 605km/h (376mph)

Range: 483km (300 miles)

Service ceiling: 11,665m (38,270ft)

Dimensions: span 10.36m (34ft 0in); length
    9.195m (30ft 2in); height 3.785m (12ft 5in)

Weight: 3992kg (8800lb) loaded

Armament: 1 x 37mm (1.46in) M4 cannon,
    2 x 12.7mm (0.5in) Browning MGs, 4 x
    7.62mm (0.3in) Browning MGs

▲ Bell Airacobra Mk I

No. 601 (County of London) Squadron / Duxford, late 1941–early 1942

The British ordered 675 examples of the Airacobra, but deliveries were halted after the arrival of only 80 aircraft. Some of these went to No. 601 Squadron, which was the only British squadron to be equipped with the type. The Airacobra remained in first-line British service only between October and December 1941.

Fighter-bombers over the Channel
JANUARY–JULY 1942

The British learned much from their first year of sweeps across the English Channel, but also suffered heavy losses. The Germans maintained the technical ascendancy, and the British had to rethink their tactical concepts in the first stages of 1942.

DESPITE EARLIER losses and the need for reinforcements deploying to overseas theatres, the RAF relaunched its offensive operations into northern Europe during March 1942. On 13 March, Circuses were resumed and 'Ramrods' were authorized, the latter focusing on damaging worthwhile land targets, not seeking to draw up and defeat the German fighter arm. Also resumed were Rhubarbs and 'Roadsteads', the last directed at German coastal shipping. At this time, Fighter Command had just over 57 squadrons of Spitfire Mk V fighters (1130 aircraft), in addition to several squadrons equipped with Hurricane Mk IIs, Beaufighters, Whirlwinds and Havocs.

New offensive

The renewed offensive started on 8 March when No. 2 (Bomber) Group's new Boston medium bombers were involved in Circuses against Comines and Abbeville against light opposition. Other Circuses and Ramrods followed, No. 11 Group selecting targets within the combat radius of the Spitfire Mk V. Few were airfields, favoured targets being marshalling yards, chemical plants and small

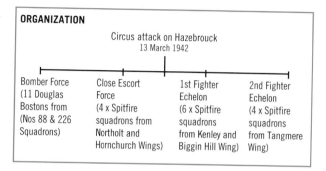

ORGANIZATION

Circus attack on Hazebrouck
13 March 1942

Bomber Force (11 Douglas Bostons from (Nos 88 & 226 Squadrons)	Close Escort Force (4 x Spitfire squadrons from Northolt and Hornchurch Wings)	1st Fighter Echelon (6 x Spitfire squadrons from Kenley and Biggin Hill Wing)	2nd Fighter Echelon (4 x Spitfire squadrons from Tangmere Wing)

factories. At the same time, No. 10 Group flew the occasional operation to north-western France, while No. 12 Group limited its efforts to Rhubarbs and 'Rodeos' over the southern Netherlands.

During the first month, Fighter Command claimed 53 aircraft downed, 27 probables and 36 damaged, and lost 32 of its own aircraft together with 28 pilots killed or missing. The actual German losses were 12 aircraft. However, April 1942 was a critical month for Fighter Command. In northern France, moves had already been made to strengthen the defence and, on a limited basis, go over to the

Specifications

Crew: 1

Powerplant: 860kW (1150hp)

Maximum speed: 580km/h (360mph)

Range: 1100km (650 miles)

Service ceiling: 8800m (29,000ft)

Dimensions: span 11.38m (37ft 4in); length 9.66m (31ft 8in); height 3.76m (12ft 4in)

Weight: 3760kg (8280lb) loaded

Armament: 6 x 12.7mm (0.5in) M2 Browning MGs

▲ **Curtiss Tomahawk Mk I**

No. 400 Squadron / RAF, late 1941

Another US warplane ordered in large numbers, the Tomahawk proved inadequate at all but low levels for lack of adequate supercharging, and was allocated to 16 home-based tactical reconnaissance squadrons, seeing only limited use before being replaced by North American Mustangs.

offensive with specially created *Jagdbomberstaffeln* (fighter-bomber squadrons) supplementing some initial units that had already undertaken successful tip-and-run attacks on British south coast towns, convoys and radar stations. During the 'Circus' operations of April 1942, claims of 40 destroyed, 32 probable and 63 damaged were made for the loss of 81 aircraft, but the losses of *Jagdgeschwader* 2 (JG 2) and JG 26 were in fact only 21 fighters.

July 1942 saw the introduction of the so-called 'Mass Rhubarb', a tactic in which 120 or more Spitfires roamed northern France at tree-top height

FIGHTER COMMAND WHIRLWIND SQUADRONS, 1941		
Unit	Type	Base
No. 137 Squadron	Whirlwind	Charmy Down
No. 263 Squadron	Whirlwind	Charmy Down

to attack targets of opportunity. The German anti-aircraft guns exacted a heavy toll. In the six months to the end of July 1942 on the Channel Front, Fighter Command lost 335 fighters, whereas the Germans lost only 84 fighters.

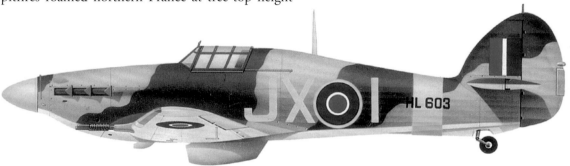

▲ Hawker Hurricane Mk IIC

No. 1 Squadron / RAF Fighter Command, 1942

By early in 1942, the Hurricane no longer possessed the performance to operate in the pure fighter role, but the Hurricane Mk IIC fighter-bomber remained in limited service from British bases. It was used in larger numbers and with greater success in the North Africa and Burma theatres.

Specifications

Crew: 1

Powerplant: 954kW (1280hp) Rolls-Royce Merlin XX liquid-cooled V-12

Maximum speed: 529km/h (329mph)

Range: 1480km (920 miles)

Service ceiling: 10,850m (35,600ft)

Dimensions: span 12.19m (40ft 0in); length 9.81m (32ft 2.25in); height 3.98m (13ft 1in)

Weight: 3629kg (8044lb) loaded

Armament: 4 x 20mm (0.79in) Hispano cannon and up to 544kg (1000lb) of bombs or rocket projectiles

Specifications

Crew: 1

Powerplant: 1685kW (2260hp)

Maximum speed: 650km/h (405mph)

Range: 980km (610 miles)

Service ceiling: 10,400m (34,000ft)

Dimensions: span 12.67m (41ft 7in); length 9.73m (31ft 11in); height 4.66m (15ft 4in)

Weight: 5170kg (11,400lb) loaded

Armament: 4 x 20mm (0.8in) Hispano-Suiza HS.404 cannons, 2 x 454 kg (1000lb) bombs

▲ Hawker Typhoon Mk IB

No. 3 Squadron / RAF Fighter Command, May 1943

Conceived as an interceptor and introduced in September 1941, the Typhoon failed in its intended role, but possessed excellent speed at low altitude. But the type was important in defeating the German 'tip-and-run' fighter-bomber raids on the south coast of the UK, and then became a superb ground-attack fighter.

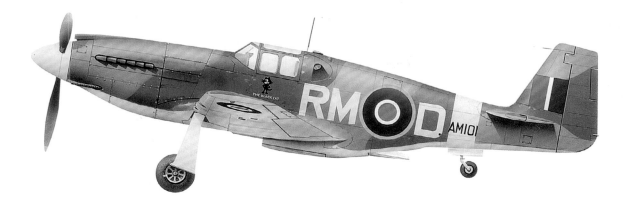

Specifications

Crew: 1

Powerplant: 858kW (1150hp) Allison V-1710-
  39 V12 engine

Maximum speed: 690km/h (430mph)

Range: 1215km (755 miles)

Service ceiling: 12,649m (41,500ft)

Dimensions: span 11.27m (37ft);
  length 9.84m (32ft 4in);
  height 4.15m (13ft 8in)

Weight: 4173kg (9200lb) loaded

Armament: 4 x 12.7mm (0.5in) and 4 x
  7.62mm (0.3in) Browning MGs

▲ **North American Mustang Mk I**

No. 26 Squadron / RAF Army Cooperation Command, Gatwick, mid–late 1942

Powered by an Allison V-1710 V-2 engine of the type also used in the Tomahawk, the Mustang Mk I also possessed inferior performance at altitude, and after entering service in April 1942 was used in the low-altitude reconnaissance fighter role.

Coastal defence
1941–43

While the bulk of the RAF's fighter strength was devoted to offensive operations over north-west Europe, the Germans still possessed the capability to make individually small but cumulatively significant attacks on British ports and coastal convoys. Fighter Command had to respond.

THROUGHOUT WORLD WAR II, the UK remained reliant on her ports. At the ports arrived convoys delivering vital food, raw supplies, men and weapons from her empire, the United States and other countries; and from them men, equipment and other exports went off to different theatres and, ultimately, northwest France for the Allied invasion of Normandy in June 1944. Thus the major and even minor ports around the country's long coastline were inevitable objectives for German attack, and both oceanic and coastal convoys also proved to be very important targets for the *Luftwaffe* and *Kreigsmarine*.

German raids

Much of the work against ports and coastal convoys was undertaken by submarines and coastal craft with torpedoes and mines, while submarines and

COASTAL COMMAND BEAUFIGHTER SQUADRONS (1941–45)	
Unit	Date
No. 143 Squadron	June 1941 – October 1944
No. 144 Squadron	May 1943 – May 1945
No. 235 Squadron	December 1941 – June 1944
No. 236 Squadron	October 1941 – May 1945
No. 248 Squadron	July 1941 – January 1944
No. 252 Squadron	December 1940 – December 1946
No. 254 Squadron	June 1942 – October 1946
No. 404 Squadron (RCAF)	September 1942 – April 1945
No. 406 Squadron (RCAF)	June 1941 – August 1944
No. 455 Squadron (RAAF)	December 1943 – May 1945
No. 498 Squadron (RNZAF)	November 1943 – August 1945

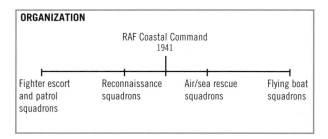

RAF Coastal Command
1941

Fighter escort and patrol squadrons

Reconnaissance squadrons

Air/sea rescue squadrons

Flying boat squadrons

long-range aircraft targeted oceanic convoys with torpedoes and bombs. Yet there was also a part to be

played by the *Luftwaffe*'s fighter-bombers and coastal aircraft, the former delivering pinpoint attacks that could secure limited useful physical results at times, but also served on a larger scale to tie down British forces and keep the British defences off balance. German coastal aircraft served by laying mines in the estuaries of British rivers and other natural chokepoints off British ports.

The German air activity was normally undertaken at low level to ensure that the fighter-bombers and minelayers suffered the minimum possibility

▲ Bristol Beaufighter Mk IF

RAF Fighter Command, UK, 1941

Carrying antennae on its nose and the leading edges of its outer wing panels, the Beaufighter Mk IF was the world's first effective radar-equipped night-fighter.

Specifications

Crew: 2

Powerplant: 2 x 1119kW (1500hp) Bristol Hercules XI air-cooled engine

Maximum speed: 492km/h (306mph)

Range: 2414km (1500 miles)

Service ceiling: 8810m (28,900ft)

Dimensions: span 17.63m (57ft 10in); length 12.60m (41ft 4in); height 4.82m (15 ft 10in)

Weight: 9435kg (21,100lb) loaded

Armament: 4 x 20mm (0.79in) cannon and 6 x 7.7mm (0.303in) MGs in the wings, and 1 x 7.7mm (0.303in) Vicker rearward-firing MG in dorsal turret

▲ Boulton Paul Defiant Mk II

No. 151 Squadron / RAF Fighter Command, 1941

Though never a truly effective fighter, the Defiant was better as a night-fighter than as a conventional day-fighter.

Specifications

Crew: 2

Powerplant: 954kW (1280hp) Rolls-Royce Merlin XX liquid-cooled V-12

Maximum speed: 504km/h (313mph)

Range: 748km (465 miles)

Service ceiling: 9250m (30,350ft)

Dimensions: span 11.99m (39ft 4in); length 10.77m (35ft 4in); height 3.71m (12ft 2in)

Weight: 3821kg (8424lb) loaded

Armament: 4 x 7.7mm (0.303in) Browning MGs in the power-operated dorsal turret

of radar-directed interception. This tactic in turn required the British to operate a system of standing patrols from the many air bases, large and small, located round the coast of the UK. With the aid of such radar direction as was possible, and visual sightings by shore-based observers and the personnel of coastal shipping, at least a modicum of a defence could be made, and sufficient losses inflicted on the Germans to deter their efforts.

Along the south coast of England, 'tip-and-run' raids made by high-performance German fighter aircraft, such as the manouevrable Focke-Wulf Fw 190A and fast-turning Messerschmitt Bf 109F, could only be countered by British fighters of equal performance, typically the latest variants of the redoubtable Supermarine Spitfire and then the Hawker Typhoon.

The Typhoon was known for its excellent turn of low-altitude speed and the devastating armament of four 20mm (0.79in) cannon, which could wreck almost any aircraft with only a half-second burst. These aircraft had effectively halted the main German

Specifications

Crew: 1	Dimensions: span 12.19m (40ft 0in);
Powerplant: 954kW (1280hp) Rolls-Royce	length 9.81m (32ft 2.25in);
Merlin XX liquid-cooled V-12	height 3.98m (13ft 1in)
Maximum speed: 529km/h (329mph)	Weight: about 3649kg (8044lb) loaded
Range: 1480km (920 miles)	Armament: 12 x 7.7mm (0.303in) Browning
Service ceiling: 10,850m (35,600ft)	MGs

▲ Hawker Hurricane Mk IIA
No. 253 Squadron / RAF Fighter Command, 1941

The all-black finish, alleviated only by national and unit markings, was designed to make the Hurricane 'invisible' in the night sky.

Specifications

Crew: 1	Dimensions: span 13.72m (45ft);
Powerplant: 2 x 659kW (885hp) Peregrine	length 9.83m (32ft 3in);
engines	height 3.53m (11ft 7in)
Maximum speed: 580km/h (360mph)	Weight: 4697kg (10,356lb) loaded
Range: 1300km (808 miles)	Armament: 4 x Hispano 20mm (0.8in) cannon
Service ceiling: 9240m (30,315ft)	in nose (60 rounds per gun, 240 rounds total)

▲ Westland Whirlwind
No. 263 Squadron / RAF Fighter Command, west of England, 1942

No. 263 Squadron was one of only two squadrons equipped with the Whirlwind twin-engined long-range fighter and fighter-bomber. With its good range and considerable firepower, the Whirlwind was well suited to the coastal role, in defence as well as offence.

effort by the end of 1942. Along the rest of the UK's coast, where the threat was posed by lower-performance aircraft such as the Heinkel He 115 twin-engined floatplane and Messerschmitt Bf 110 twin-engined multi-role warplane, older aircraft were used since these were adequate to the task and were no longer needed for cutting-edge operations.

So there was a steady flow of fighter patrols, supported by other aircraft, over the coasts and coastal waters of the UK during the mid years of the war. These patrols served a useful primary purpose, and also provided a facility for the locating and marking of men from downed aircraft or sunken ships, allowing air or sea rescue craft to be called in and directed to the right spot.

The patrols also provided useful flying and navigation training for inexperienced pilots and those recovering from wounds or being rested for tiredness.

Fleet Air Arm
1939–43

Returning to the full control of the Royal Navy after years in the technical doldrums under the control of the RAF, the Fleet Air Arm was poorly equipped at the technical level for the type of warfare it would have to wage between 1939 and 1945, but was full of ideas and spirit.

THE ROYAL NAVAL AIR SERVICE was merged with the Royal Flying Corps (RFC) on 1 April 1918 to create the Royal Air Force. The RAF kept control of the Naval Air Branch until 1937, when it was returned to Admiralty control.

At the start of World War II, it had become the Fleet Air Arm (FAA) and comprised 20 squadrons with only 232 aircraft, most of them obsolescent and none up to the standards of modern land-based warplanes.

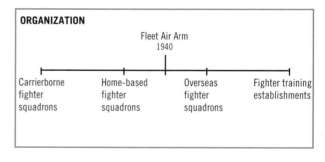

Naval fighters

The naval fighters of this time were the Blackburn Roc and then the Fairey Fulmar, and the FAA then progressed through the Sea Hurricane and Supermarine Seafire to US types such as the Grumman Hellcat and Vought Corsair. By the end of World War II, when the FAA had been deployed all over the world, the FAA was operating from 59 aircraft carriers (fleet, light and escort) and 56 air stations, and had some 3700 aircraft and 72,000 men.

FLEET AIR ARM ROC SQUADRONS		
Unit	Type	Base
No. 801 Squadron	Roc	Hatston
No. 803 Squadron	Roc	n/a
No. 806 Squadron	Roc	Eastleigh
No. 759 Squadron	Roc	n/a
No. 760 Squadron	Roc	n/a
No. 769 Squadron	Roc	n/a
No. 772 Squadron	Roc	n/a
No. 773 Squadron	Roc	n/a

SELECTED FLEET AIR ARM FULMAR SQUADRONS		
Unit	Type	Base
No. 800X Squadron	Fulmar	HMS Furious
No. 800Y Squadron	Fulmar	HMS Argus
No. 800Z Squadron	Fulmar	HMS Victorious
No. 803 Squadron	Fulmar	India & Ceylon
No. 804 Squadron	Fulmar	HMS Eagle
No. 805 Squadron	Fulmar	Egypt & Crete
No. 806 Squadron	Fulmar	HMS Illustrious

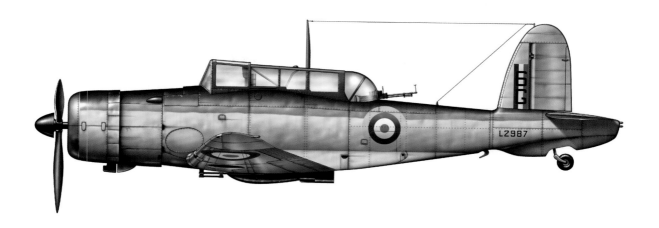

▲ Blackburn Skua Mk II

No. 5 Maintenance Unit, Kemble, 1939

The Skua Mk II was the production variant of the Skua Mk I prototype. Through designed as a carrierborne dive-bomber, the Skua doubled as a naval fighter, but was ineffective in each role and withdrawn from first-line service in 1941.

Specifications

Crew: 2

Powerplant: 664kW (890hp) Bristol Perseus XII radial engine

Maximum speed: 362km/h (225mph)

Range: 1223km (760 miles)

Service ceiling: 6160m (20,200ft)

Dimensions: span 14.07m (46ft 2in); length 10.85m (35ft 7in); height 3.81m (12ft 6in)

Weight: 3732kg (8228lb) loaded

Armament: 4 x 7.7mm (0.303in) MGs in wings; Lewis rear gun; 1 x 227kg (500lb) bomb beneath fusilage

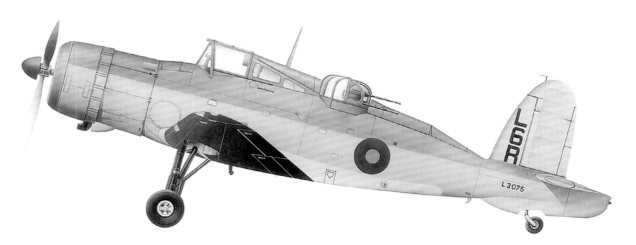

▲ Blackburn Roc

No. 2 AACU / Fleet Air Arm

Essentially the naval counterpart of the land-based Boulton Paul Defiant, the Roc was based on the turret fighter concept and suffered the same basic failings as the Defiant. These were the weight of the power-operated turret, a poor power/weight ratio, and the lack of agility and fixed forward-firing armament.

Specifications

Crew: 2

Powerplant: 675kW (905hp) Bristol Perseus XII radial engine

Maximum speed: 359km/h (223mph)

Range: 1304km (810 miles)

Service ceiling: 5485m (18,000ft)

Dimensions: span 14.02m (46ft); length 10.85m (35ft 7in); height 3.68m (12ft)

Weight: 3606kg (7950lb) loaded

Armament: 4 x 7.7mm (0.303in) MGs in dorsal turret

▲ **Gloster Sea Gladiator Mk I**

RAF service, June 1940

The Sea Gladiator Mk I was the full-standard carrierborne fighter derived closely from the Gladiator, which was the UK's last land-based biplane fighter.

Specifications

Crew: 1	Service ceiling: 9845m (32,300ft)
Powerplant: 619kW (830hp) Bristol Mercury VIIIAS air-cooled 9-cylinder radial	Dimensions: span 9.83m (32ft 3in); length 8.36m (27ft 5in); height 3.52m (11ft 7in)
Maximum speed: 407km/h (253mph)	Weight: 2272kg (5020lb) loaded
Range: 684km (425 miles)	Armament: 4 x 7.7mm (0.303in) Browning MGs

Early war
1939–40

On the outbreak of World War II, the Fleet Air Arm was small and possessed only indifferent aircraft. Even so, imbued with the offensive spirit of the Royal Navy, the FAA's squadrons were soon involved in active air operations in many parts of the world.

DESPITE THEIR SMALL numbers, the squadrons of the FAA were able to fulfil an important role early in World War II. On 1 September 1939, the FAA had 232 aircraft, and of these most were inferior to their RAF counterparts. The most modern type in the fighter, dive-bomber and fighter-reconnaissance role was the Blackburn Skua, operational with Nos 800, 801, 803 and 806 Squadrons, which had just

ORGANIZATION

FAA, Royal Navy
1 September 1939

Ark Royal & Furious (Home Fleet)	Courageous & Hermes (Channel Force)	Glorious (Mediterranean Fleet)	Eagle (China Station)

FAA CARRIERBORNE AIRCRAFT STRENGTHS (1939)

Ship	Aircraft type	Strength
Eagle	Swordfish	18
Hermes	Swordfish	9
Furious	Swordfish, Skua & Roc	18, 8 & 4
Courageous	Swordfish	24
Glorious	Swordfish & Sea Gladiator	36 &12
Ark Royal	Swordfish & Skua	42 & 18

36 aircraft. The primary attacker was the Fairey Swordfish Mk I torpedo and reconnaissance biplane, of which 140 were in service, with the 457mm (18in) torpedo as their primary weapon. The rest of the FAA comprised either shipborne or shore-based spotter and reconnaissance types such as the Supermarine Walrus and Fairey Seafox.

From the beginning of hostilities, the FAA undertook anti-submarine patrols with HMS *Ark Royal*, *Hermes* and *Courageous* in the North-West

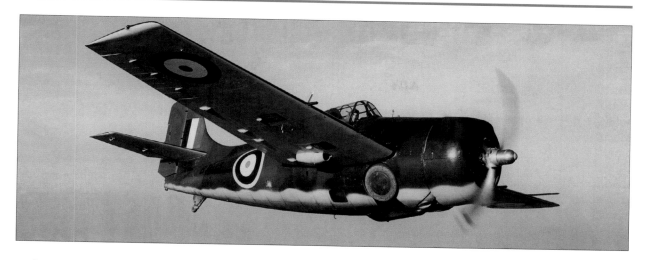

▲ Early Martlet

This Martlet Mk I was one of the French Cyclone-powered Martlets delivered in September 1940.

and South-West Approaches under the Home Fleet, and with Nos 800, 803, 810, 820, 821, 822 and 814 Squadrons embarked. HMS *Furious*, *Glorious* and *Eagle* were in the Atlantic, off Aden and in the East Indies respectively, and early operations included patrols off the Cape Verde Islands and Brazil, and unsuccessful searches for the *Graf Spee* in the South Atlantic.

The shore-based Nos 800 and 804 Squadrons, based at Hatston-Kirkwall, operated against the German Navy off Norway in April 1940. The *Furious* was involved in attacks in Narvikfjord on 10 April, and again towards the end of the month, until

relieved by the *Glorious* and *Ark Royal* with Skua, Roc and Sea Gladiator Mk I warplanes, which saw action off Namsos, Bodo and Narvik.

During September and October 1940, the *Furious* launched two strikes on Tromso and Trondheim. With the loss of the *Glorious* in June 1940, the *Ark Royal* was the only carrier left to Home Fleet, with the others either ferrying or in stations in the Mediterranean and Indian Ocean.

▲ Grumman Martlet Mk I

No. 804 Squadron / Fleet Air Arm, Hatston, 1940

The Martlet Mk I was the British version of the Grumman F4F-3, and entered service with the FAA in September 1940, initially with No. 804 Squadron based in the Orkney Islands for the defence of the Home Fleet's great anchorage and base in Scapa Flow.

Specifications

Crew: 1

Powerplant: 880kW (1180hp) Pratt & Whitney R-1830-86 engine

Maximum speed: 512km/h (318mph)

Range: 2173km (1350 miles)

Service ceiling: 10,900m (35,700ft)

Dimensions: span 11.58m 38ft); length 8.76m (28ft 8in); height 2.81m (9ft 3in)

Weight: 3607kg (7952lb) loaded

Armament: 4 x 12.7mm (0.5in) MGs in wings; 2 x 113kg (249lb) bombs

Convoy protection
JANUARY 1941 – MAY 1943

One of the most important tasks undertaken by the Fleet Air Arm was the protection of convoys crossing the Atlantic. Here the FAA's fighters were needed to drive off or shoot down German long-range reconnaissance and bombing aircraft, and keep a constant watch for U-boats.

B Y THE END OF 1940, the Allies and many neutral states trading across the Atlantic had lost 1281 ships, some 585 of them to U-boat attack and the others to attacks by aircraft, surface ships both large and small, and mines.

Over the same 16-month period, the Germans had lost only 32 U-boats, none of them to air attack alone. Yet the battle was now beginning to sway in the opposite direction as the British began to field longer-range maritime patrol aircraft, about one-sixth of them fitted with air-to-surface search radar. Larger numbers of better escort vessels were becoming available, and better coordination of air and naval assets was arriving after the creation of the RAF's No. 19 Group.

Convoy attacks

Yet the scale of the task was reflected in a pair of events in February 1941. On 8–12 February, a U-boat

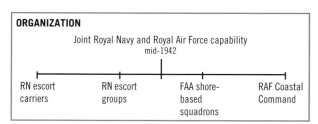

ORGANIZATION

Joint Royal Navy and Royal Air Force capability mid-1942

| RN escort carriers | RN escort groups | FAA shore-based squadrons | RAF Coastal Command |

vectored Focke Fw 200 long-range aircraft and the cruiser *Admiral Hipper* onto two convoys, which lost 16 out of 26 ships, and then, on 26 February, Fw 200 aircraft were called in by U-boat to sink seven ships of a single convoy and damage another four. In May, Swordfish attack aircraft of the *Ark Royal* were instrumental in damaging and slowing the battleship *Bismarck*, which was then caught and sunk by British surface forces.

So far as convoys were concerned, though, there remained a 'black hole' in the centre of the Atlantic,

Specifications

Crew: 1

Powerplant: 880kW (1180hp) Pratt & Whitney R-1830-86 engine

Maximum speed: 512km/h (318mph)

Range: 2173km (1350 miles)

Service ceiling: 10,900m (35,700ft)

Dimensions: span 11.58m 38ft);

length 8.76m (28ft 8in);

height 2.81m (9ft 3in)

Weight: 3607kg (7952lb) loaded

Armament: 4 x 12.7mm (0.5in) MGs in wings;

2 x 113kg (249lb) bombs

▲ **Grumman Martlet Mk I**

No. 804 Squadron / Fleet Air Arm, Hatston, Orkney Islands, early 1941

Used for the air defence of Scapa Flow, this aeroplane was based on the US Navy's F4F-3, and was one of 91 aircraft originally built to a French order. The type had a fixed wing, Wright Cyclone single-row radial engine, and a fixed forward-firing armament of four 12.7mm (0.5in) machine guns.

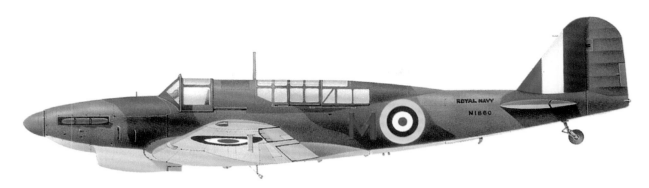

Specifications

Crew: 2

Powerplant: 805kW (1080hp) Rolls-Royce
Merlin VIII V-12 engine

Maximum speed: 398km/h (247mph)

Range: 1336km (830 miles)

Service ceiling: 21,500m (6555ft)

Dimensions: span 14.14m (46ft 4in);
length 12.24m (40ft 2in);
height 4.27m (14ft)

Weight: 4387kg (9672lb) loaded

Armament: 8 x 7.7mm (0.303in) MGs in wings

▲ **Fairey Fulmar Mk I**

No. 806 Squadron / Fleet Air Arm, 1942

While its layout, powerplant and fixed forward-firing armament were akin to those of contemporary land-based fighters, the Fulmar was rendered a wholly indifferent fighter by the Royal Navy's demand that it have two- rather than one-seat accommodation in a longer and weightier fuselage. The second occupant wielded no armament, so undertook just the observer, navigator and radio operator roles.

too far from the UK and North America to be reached even by long-range aircraft, and here the U-boat was almost impossible to defeat.

Fleet aircraft carriers were too few in number and too valuable to be risked in these circumstances, but an initial answer came with the CAM-ship. This was a merchant vessel fitted with a catapult to launch a Hawker Hurricane fighter, which had to ditch in the sea close to a ship at the end of its single mission, the pilot being recovered. These Hurricanes made life very difficult for the Fw 200 long-range reconnaissance aircraft that called in the U-boat packs, and also spotted for and attacked the U-boats.

The CAM-ship was recognized from the start as only a palliative, and the true solution was found in the escort carrier, which was a merchant vessel adapted for the carriage, launch and recovery of small numbers of fighters and anti-submarine aircraft, increasingly the Grumman Wildcat and Grumman Avenger respectively.

The first such vessel was HMS *Audacity*. The ship survived only to December 1941 before being lost to a torpedo, but the concept had been proved and the subsequent construction of escort carriers in US and British yards allowed the cheap yet effective little aircraft carriers to provide just the type of air escort the Atlantic convoys needed. The Germans responded with measures that included greater use of night cover, heavier anti-aircraft armament and

radar warning receivers, to which the Allies in turn responded with better radio direction-finders and improved anti-submarine weapons for ships. For aircraft came heavy fixed forward-firing armament, radar that the Germans found difficult to detect and, for a night-attack capability, the Leigh Light – an underwing searchlight turned on only in the final stages of a radar-guided approach, illuminating the target U-boat for accurate visual attack.

The turning point in the Battle of the Atlantic was May 1943. In this month, the Germans lost 41 U-boats, 38 of them in the Atlantic or in the Bay of Biscay, the latter as U-boats attempted to pass between French ports and their operating areas deep in the Atlantic. There were still successes and reverses for each side, but Germany could no longer sustain U-boat losses at the rate of May 1943.

ROYAL NAVY ESCORT CARRIERS (1941–43)			
Class	Displacement	Speed	Air strength
'Audacity' (1)	11,000 tons	15kt	6
'Activity' class (1)	14,250 tons	18kt	11
'Vindex' (2)	16,830 tons	18kt	18
'Campania' (1)	15,970 tons	16kt	18
'Archer' (1)	12,860 tons	16.5kt	16
'Avenger' (3)	15,300 tons	16.5kt	15
'Attacker' (11)	14,170 tons	18.5kt	18–24

RAF Desert Air Force
1940–42

One of the lessons of the unsuccessful British *Battleaxe* offensive of June 1941 was the need of the Allied ground forces for air support that was both better organized and larger in scope and capability. This led to the creation of the Desert Air Force to provide tactical air support.

T HE DESERT AIR FORCE (DAF; later 1st Tactical Air Force) was created in North Africa to provide close air support to the British Eighth Army, and comprised British, Australian, South African and finally US squadrons. Before the creation of the Desert Air Force, several RAF formations operated in North Africa.

By the time of Italy's declaration of war in June 1940, the British air commander in the Middle East, Air Vice Marshal Sir Arthur Longmore, had only 29 squadrons with fewer than 300 aircraft. In 1941,

ORGANIZATION

Air Headquarters Western Desert (Air Vice Marshal A. Coningham)
23 October 1941

| No. 201 Group (Air Commodore L. H. Slatter) | No. 202 Group (Air Commodore T. W. Elmhirst) | No. 205 Group (Air Commodore L. L. MacLean) | No. 206 Group (Air Commodore C. B. Cooke) |

WDAF FIGHTER & TACTICAL RECCE SQUADRONS (26 MAY 1942)		
Unit	Type	Base
No. 2 Sqn, SAAF	Kittyhawk	Gambut
No. 3 Sqn, RAAF	Kittyhawk	Gambut
No. 4 Sqn, SAAF	Tomahawk	Gambut
No. 5 Sqn, SAAF	Tomahawk	Gambut
No. 15 Sqn, SAAF	Blenheim IVF	Amiriya, Kufra
No. 33 Sqn, RAF	Hurricane	Gambut
No. 40 Sqn, SAAF	Hurricane, Tomahawk	El Adem
No. 73 Sqn, RAF	Hurricane	El Adem
No. 80 Sqn, RAF	Hurricane	Gambut
No. 112 Sqn, RAF	Kittyhawk	Gambut
No. 145 Sqn, RAF	Hurricane	Gambut
No. 208 Sqn, RAF	Hurricane, Tomahawk	El Adem
No. 250 Sqn, RAF	Kittyhawk	Gambut
No. 260 Sqn, RAF	Kittyhawk	Gambut
No. 274 Sqn, RAF	Hurricane	Gambut
No. 450 Sqn, RAAF	Kittyhawk	Gambut

▲ **Curtiss Tomahawk Mk IIB**

No. 112 Squadron / Western Desert Air Force, Sidi Haneich, October 1941
Tomahawk Mk IIB was the designation that the Royal Air Force applied to the British-ordered version of the Hawk 81A-2 ordered by France but delivered to the UK after the fall of France for service with the designation Tomahawk Mk IIA.

Specifications

Crew: 1
Powerplant: 860kW (1150hp)
Maximum speed: 580km/h (360mph)
Range: 1100km (650 miles)
Service ceiling: 8800m (29,000ft)

Dimensions: span 11.38m (37ft 4in);
length 9.66m (31ft 8in);
height 3.76m (12ft 4in)
Weight: 3760kg (8280lb) loaded
Armament: 6 x 12.7mm (0.5in) M2 Browning
MGs in wings

command passed to Air Marshal Arthur Tedder, who reorganized his strength into wings, of which the first was No. 253 Wing for close support. The first

command-level formation, formed on 21 October 1941, was the Air Headquarters Western Desert (AHWD), created by revision of No. 204 Group.

Specifications

Crew: 1

Powerplant: 477kW (640hp) Rolls-Royce Kestrel
VI engine

Maximum speed: 359km/h (223mph)

Range: 435km (270 miles)

Service ceiling: 8990m (29,500ft)

Dimensions: span 9.14m (30ft);
length 8.15m (26ft 9in);
height 3.10m (10ft 2in)

Weight: 1637kg (3609lb) loaded

Armament: 2 x 7.7mm (.303in) Vickers forward
firing MGs

▲ **Hawker Fury Mk II**

No. 43 Squadron / South African Air Force

The South African Air Force bought seven of these aircraft in 1936, and at the start of World War II received 24 ex-RAF aircraft. A number of Furys were used against Italian forces in East Africa in 1941.

North Africa
1942–43

After a promising tactical start blunted by the German air units' technical edge, the Desert Air Force matured steadily into an exceptional tactical air arm whose later aircraft and fully fledged tactics set the pattern for the tactical air support in the mainland European campaigns.

THE AHWD INITIALLY OPERATED in three wings as Nos 258 and 269 Wings over the front and No. 262 Wing over the Nile delta. On 20 January 1942, the AHWD became Air Headquarters Libya, but on 3 February reverted to AHWD.

On 31 January 1943 command was assumed by Air Vice Marshal H. Broadhurst, and on 10 July 1943 the force was renamed as the DAF, which was subordinated to the North-West African (later Mediterranean and 1st) Tactical Air Force.

Given Fighter Command's priority, the North African force was generally equipped with obsolescent aircraft types such as the Gloster

Gladiator, but nonetheless performed well against the Italian air force. As the direct threat to the UK declined, North Africa started to receive more modern aircraft, including the Hawker Hurricane, and the US-built Curtiss Tomahawk/Kittyhawk

FIGHTER WINGS OF NO. 211 GROUP, DAF (MID-APRIL 1943)		
Unit & Squadrons	Type	Strength
No. 7 Wing, SAAF Nos 2, 4, 5	Kittyhawk	63
US 57th Fighter Group 64th, 65th, 66th & 314th	Kittyhawk	80
US 79th Fighter Group 85th, 86th, 87th & 316th	Kittyhawk	80
No. 239 Wing, RAF Nos 3 & 450 RAAF, & Nos 112, 250, 260 & 450 RAF	Kittyhawk	105
No. 244 Wing, RAF No. 1 SAAF, No. 417 RCAF, & Nos 6, 92, 145 & 601 RAF	Hurricane & Spitfire	126
No. 285 Wing, RAF No. 40 SAAF, & No. 73 RAF	Hurricane & Spitfire	39

series, which was not suitable for operations in northern Europe.

Numbers advantage

The DAF always outnumbered its Axis opponents, and devoted its primary effort to tactical support and long-range interdiction. These pitted the DAF's warplanes against the technically superior Messerschmitt Bf 109F fighters of the *Luftwaffe's*

Jagdgeschwader 27, whose pilots in general had the advantage of altitude and surprise over the comparatively slow and low-altitude DAF fighters, which suffered heavy losses.

During 1942, the DAF revised its tactics and received more modern aircraft, the latter including the Supermarine Spitfire from August 1942 for use in the air superiority role, and this helped to tun the tide in the DAF's favour. The DAF adapted the German concept of fighter-bombers controlled by forward air controllers using radio and attached to frontline ground units. The DAF improved the concept by introducing 'cab ranks' of fighter-bombers waiting to be directed at a specific tactical targets.

In this way, the DAF provided vital and decisive air support to the Eighth Army until the end of the war, fighting through Egypt, Libya, Tunisia, Sicily and mainland Italy. The tactics that had proved successful in the latter part of the North African campaign were also adopted with even greater success during the invasion of Europe in 1944.

Commonweath flyers

The major Commonwealth contributor to the DAF was South Africa, which provided more than 12 squadrons. North Africa was the South Africans' primary theatre of service, as their government had decided that no South African formations should fight outside Africa. The Australian element included No. 3 Squadron, which reached North Africa late

▲ **Curtiss Kittyhawk Mk I**

No. 112 Squadron / Western Desert Air Force, 1942

Like the closely related Tomahawk, the Kittyhawk was a member of the tactical fighter family known to the US Army Air Forces as the P-40. The type operated almost exclusively in the low-level fighter-bomber role with weapons such as a 227kg (500lb) bomb under the fuselage.

Specifications

Crew: 1

Powerplant: 895kW (1200hp) Allison piston
engine

Maximum speed: 563km/h (350mph)

Range: 1738km (1080 miles)

Service ceiling: 9450m (31,000ft)

Dimensions: span 11.36m (37ft 4in);
length 10.16m (33ft 4in);
height 3.76m (12ft 4in)

Weight: 3511kg (7740lb) loaded

Armament: 4 x 12.7mm (0.5in) Browning MGs
in wings

in 1940 and served with the DAF until the closing stages of the war in Europe. Many foreign personnel also flew in RAF squadrons, some of the most numerous being Polish pilots and other aircrew.

The US Army Air Forces (USAAF) provided more strength: the 57th and 79th Fighter Groups, which flew the P-40, and one medium bomber group, which flew the North American B-25, served with the DAF from mid-1942 until they were absorbed into the new US Ninth Air Force.

The Western Desert Air Force had about 1000 warplanes by late 1941. By the time of the second battle of El Alamein late in 1942, the DAF had more than 1500, more than double the number of Axis aircraft.

BRITISH SQUADRONS IN THE MEDITERRANEAN THEATRE		
Date	Fighter	Light bomber
September 1939	6	8
July 1940	8	9
December 1941	29	10
December 1942	47	17
December 1943	49	13
September 1944	41	7
March 1945	33	6

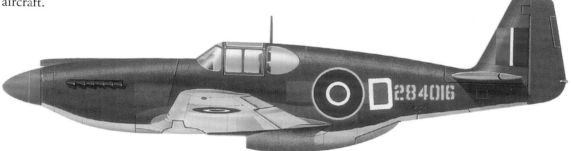

Specifications

Crew: 1

Powerplant: 988kW (1325hp) Allison V-1710-87 liquid-cooled piston V12 engine

Maximum speed: 590km/h (365mph)

Range: 885km (550 miles)

Service ceiling: 7650m (25,100ft)

Dimensions: span 11.28m (37ft 1in); length 9.83m (32ft 3in); height 3.71m (12ft 2in)

Weight: 4535kg (10,000lb) loaded

Armament: 6 x 12.7mm (0.50in) M2 Browning MGs in wings

▲ North American A-36A

No. 1437 Strategic Reconnaissance Flight

Fast at low level and possessing good range, the A-36 was well suited to the reconnaissance role. This aircraft was used in Tunisia early in 1943.

Specifications

Crew: 1

Powerplant: 860kW (1150hp)

Maximum speed: 580km/h (360mph)

Range: 1100km (650 miles)

Service ceiling: 8800m (29,000ft)

Dimensions: span 11.38m (37ft 4in); length 9.66m (31ft 8in); height 3.76m (12ft 4in)

Weight: 3760kg (8280lb) loaded

Armament: 6 x 12.7mm (0.5in) M2 Browning MGs in wings

▲ Curtis Tomahawk Mk IIB

No. 112 Squadron / North Africa, 1942

With a sturdy airframe and its Allison V-1710 engine optimized for low-altitude performance, the Tomahawk was better suited to the close support and tactical reconnaissance roles than the pure fighter task at higher altitudes.

Specifications

Crew: 1

Powerplant: 895kW (1200hp)

Maximum speed: 512km/h (318mph)

Range: 2012km (1250 miles)

Service ceiling: 10,365m (34,000ft)

Dimensions: span 11.58m (38ft);

length 8.76m (28ft 9in);

height 2.81m (9ft 5in)

Weight: 7952kg (3607lb) loaded

Armament: 6 x 12.7mm (0.5in) MGs in leading

edge of wings

▲ Grumman Wildcat Mk III

No. 805 Squadron / Fleet Air Arm, Western Desert, 1941

This aeroplane was flown over the Western Desert by Sub-Lieutenant Walsh.

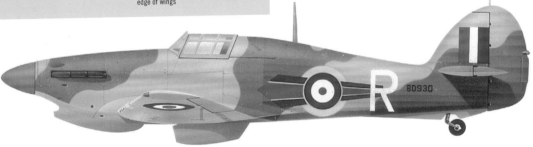

▲ Hawker Hurricane Mk IIB

No. 73 Squadron / Western Desert, 1942

Wearing a stylized version of the squadron's peacetime flash insignia, this Hurricane is in desert camouflage and has a Vokes filter under its nose.

Specifications

Crew: 1

Powerplant: 954kW (1280hp) Rolls-Royce

Merlin XX liquid-cooled V-12

Maximum speed: 529km/h (329mph)

Range: 1480km (920 miles)

Service ceiling: 10,850m (35,600ft)

Dimensions: span 12.19m (40ft 0in);

length 9.81m (32ft 2.25in);

height 3.98m (13ft 1in)

Weight: about 3649kg (8044lb) loaded

Armament: 12 x 7.7mm (0.303in) Browning

MGs and up to 454kg (1000lb) of bombs

▲ Hawker Hurricane Mk IIB

No. 73 Squadron / Western Desert, 1942

Wearing desert camouflage and a stylized version of the squadron's prewar marking on the side of the fuselage, this Hurricane Mk IIB has visible desert equipment in the form of the duct under the nose for the Vokes air filter.

Specifications

Crew: 1

Powerplant: 954kW (1280hp) Rolls-Royce

Merlin XX liquid-cooled V-12

Maximum speed: 529km/h (329mph)

Range: 1480km (920 miles)

Service ceiling: 10,850m (35,600ft)

Dimensions: span 12.19m (40ft 0in);

length 9.81m (32ft 2.25in);

height 3.98m (13ft 1in)

Weight: about 3649kg (8044lb) loaded

Armament: 12 x 7.7mm (0.303in) Browning

MGs and up to 454kg (1000lb) of bombs

▲ Hawker Hurricane Mk IIC

Royal Air Force / Western Desert, 1942

With its fixed forward-firing armament of four 20mm(0.79in) Hispano cannon, the Hurricane Mk IIC made an excellent close support and ground-attack fighter even though it was outmatched in the pure fighter role by German fighters such as the Messerschmitt Bf 109F.

Specifications

Crew: 1

Powerplant: 954kW (1280hp) Rolls-Royce
    Merlin XX liquid-cooled V-12

Maximum speed: 529km/h (329mph)

Range: 1480km (920 miles)

Service ceiling: 10,850m (35,600ft)

Dimensions: span 12.19m (40ft 0in);
    length 9.81m (32ft 2.25in);
    height 3.98m (13ft 1in)

Weight: about 3649kg (8044lb) loaded

Armament: 4 x 20mm (0.8in) Hispano cannon
    and up to 454kg (1000lb) of bombs

Specifications

Crew: 2

Powerplant: 2 x 1119kW (1500hp) Bristol
    Hercules XI air-cooled engine

Maximum speed: 492km/h (306mph)

Range: 2414km (1500 miles)

Service ceiling: 8810m (28,900ft)

Dimensions: span 17.63m (57ft 10in);
    length 12.60m (41ft 4in);
    height 4.82m (15 ft 10in)

Weight: 9435kg (21,100lb) loaded

Armament: 4 x 20mm (0.79in) cannon and
    6 x 7.7mm (0.303in) MGs

▲ Bristol Beaufighter Mk IC

No. 252 Squadron / RAF Coastal Command, Ecdu, Egypt, mid-1942

The aeroplane is a standard Coastal Command Beaufighter in the Middle East camouflage scheme of dark earth and mid-stone.

▲ **Hurricanes over the Western Desert**
These are Hurricane Mk IIC tropicalized aircraft of No. 239 Squadron, with an undernose Vokes filter.

Battle for Malta
1940–43

The story of air warfare over the Mediterranean is, in effect, the story of the battle for Malta, which controls the east–west lines of communication that the British needed, and the north–south lines that the Italians and Germans needed.

THE AXIS SIEGE OF MALTA was of great import, and Malta become one of the most intensively bombed areas of World War II: some 3000 raids took place during the two years of the siege, and the civilian losses came to a total of some 1493 dead and 3674 wounded. Between June 1940 and December 1942, British and Commonwealth fighters claimed the destruction of some 863 Axis aircraft (the actual losses were about 570 aircraft in action) for the loss of 289 Spitfires and Hurricanes in action, and some 844 aircraft lost to all causes in the air and on the ground. The *Luftwaffe* alone claimed some 446 Allied aircraft (of all types) shot down.

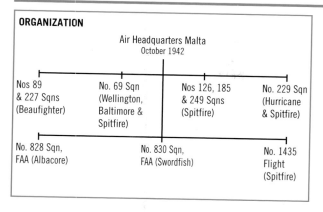

ORGANIZATION

Air Headquarters Malta
October 1942

| Nos 89 & 227 Sqns (Beaufighter) | No. 69 Sqn (Wellington, Baltimore & Spitfire) | Nos 126, 185 & 249 Sqns (Spitfire) | No. 229 Sqn (Hurricane & Spitfire) |
| No. 828 Sqn, FAA (Albacore) | | No. 830 Sqn, FAA (Swordfish) | No. 1435 Flight (Spitfire) |

Faith, Hope and Charity

When Italy entered the war in June 1940, Malta was essentially undefended, as the British felt that the island could not be defended effectively. Thus there were only 4000 soldiers and a few obsolete biplanes on the island. The first Italian air attack came on 11 June, one day after Italy's declaration of war, and the failure of the initial attacks persuaded the British government that the island could indeed be held. It therefore sent reinforcements – a policy that was maintained for the rest of the war.

By the start of July, the Gladiators had been reinforced by Hawker Hurricanes to create No. 261 Squadron. More aircraft were delivered by aircraft carrier in August in the first of many such efforts. During the first five months of the siege, Malta's aircraft claimed some 37 Italian aircraft destroyed or damaged. In January 1941, the German X *Fliegerkorps* arrived in Sicily, and there was immediately a major increase in the bombing of Malta. The appearance in February of a *Staffel* of Bf 109E fighters of *Jagdgeschwader* 26 led to a rapid escalation in Hurricane losses: during the following four months, 7./JG 26 claimed 42 air victories without loss. In mid-1941, the British formed Nos 126 and 185 Squadrons, and the defence was bolstered by cannon-armed Hurricane Mk II fighters.

Beaufighter reinforcement

In April and May, the first Bristol Blenheim and Bristol Beaufighter attack warplanes arrived. The weight of the Axis attack declined later in the year as German units were diverted to the Eastern Front. But in December 1941 German forces turned their attention back to Malta.

All the necessities had to be brought in by sea, and resupply became very difficult and the island was almost cut off: 31 Allied ships were lost to bombing, and while the defence claimed some 191 aircraft shot down from June 1940 to December 1941, its own losses were 94 fighters.

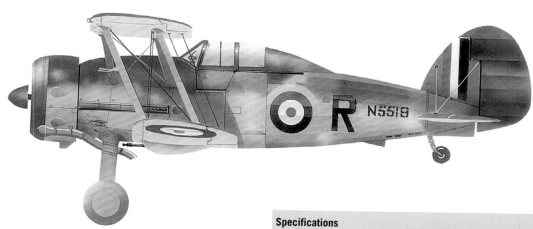

▲ **Gloster Sea Gladiator Mk II**

RAF Air Defence of Malta, 1940

Flown by Sergeant Pilot Robertson, this Sea Gladiator Mk II was one of several assembled on Malta from spares left for the use of the Sea Gladiators embarked on the carrier HMS Glorious but found unused.

Specifications

Crew: 1	Dimensions: span 8.94m (29ft 4in);
Powerplant: 298kW (400hp)	length 6.17m (20ft 3in);
Maximum speed: 243km/h (151mph)	height 2.82m (9ft 3in)
Endurance: 2 hours 45 minutes	Weight: 1189kg (2622lb) loaded
Service ceiling: 7010m (23,000ft)	Armament: 2 x 7.7mm (.303in) Vickers MGs in
	upper part of forward fuselage

With the Hurricane now decidedly outclassed by the new Messerschmitt Bf 109Fs of JG 53 and Italian Macchi C.202s, the first Supermarine Spitfire Mk Vs flew into Malta in March 1942 , and the number of carrier deliveries increased through 1942 for the use of Nos 601 and 603 Squadrons.

By mid-1942, the Axis air strength against the island had reached its peak at about 520 German and 300 Italian aircraft. Throughout this period, Royal Navy submarines, RAF bombers and FAA torpedo aircraft operating from Malta continued to wreak havoc on Axis shipping, severely curtailing vital supplies and reinforcements to the German and Italian forces in North Africa. Even so, by this time the Axis powers thought that Malta had been effectively neutralized, and therefore that some of their strength could be diverted to other theatres.

George Cross

On 15 April 1942, King George VI awarded the island of Malta the George Cross, the highest civilian award for gallantry in the Commonwealth. In the first six months of 1942, there was only one 24-hour period without air raids. *Luftwaffe* records indicate that between 20 March and 28 April 1942, Malta was subjected to 11,819 sorties and 6557 tonnes (6452 tons) of bombs.

The British took advantage of the lull to fly in more fighters, but all other supplies remained in critically short supply. There was a new wave of attacks in October, but the Allied efforts in the Middle East were beginning to have their effect, and supplies were reaching Malta. As the Axis forces were progressively defeated in North Africa, the siege of Malta was lifted.

Tunisia
JANUARY–MAY 1943

Caught between Allied forces advancing from the west and east, and finding it almost impossible to get supplies of weapons and all other essentials, the Axis forces in North Africa were compressed into a lodgement in northern Tunisia and forced to surrender in May 1943.

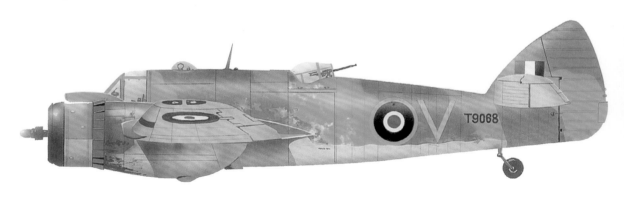

▲ **Bristol Beaufighter Mk IC**

No. 272 Squadron / RAF, North African and Mediterranean theatre, 1942

The Beaufighter Mk IC was the variant of the Beaufighter Mk I heavy fighter optimized for the coastal role with improved radio and navigation equipment as well as more fuel. The type's cannon armament proved very effective against light coastal vessels and installations.

Specifications

Crew: 2

Powerplant: 2 x 1119kW (1500hp) Bristol Hercules XI air-cooled engine

Maximum speed: 492km/h (306mph)

Range: 2414km (1500 miles)

Service ceiling: 8810m (28,900ft)

Dimensions: span 17.63m (57ft 10in); length 12.60m (41ft 4in); height 4.82m (15 ft 10in)

Weight: 9435kg (21,100lb) loaded

Armament: 4 x 20mm (0.79in) cannon and 6 x 7.7mm (0.303in) MGs in the wings, and 1 x 7.7mm (0.303in) Vicker rearward-firing MG in dorsal turret

B Y THE START OF 1943, the advance of the British Eighth Army and Allied First Army, from east and west respectively, was placing the Axis forces in an increasingly difficult position. Without any significant Axis maritime lift capability to Tunisia, the Axis lodgement had been strengthened by air in November 1942, but Allied air power was now so rampant that any continuation of this process was impossible, as was air support for the Axis ground forces. However, although the Axis forces were trapped, the capable *Generalfeldmarschall* Erwin

Rommel was nonetheless able to stall the Allies with a series of defensive operations, most notably with the battle of the Kasserine Pass, but the Axis forces were now outflanked, outgunned and outnumbered.

Under cover of increasingly powerful air forces, the Allies slowly squeezed the shattered Axis forces into northern Tunisia, where they capitulated on 13 May 1943, surrendering more than 275,000 men to become prisoners of war. It was a shattering defeat hastened by the skilful exercise of Allied air power.

Specifications

Crew: 1

Powerplant: 895kW (1200hp) Pratt & Whitney R-1830-86 14-cylinder engine

Maximum speed: 507km/h (315mph)

Range: 1851km (1150 miles)

Service ceiling: 10,900m (35,700ft)

Dimensions: span 11.58m 38ft);
length 8.76m (28ft 8in);
height 2.81m (9ft 3in)

Weight: 3607kg (7952lb) loaded

Armament: 6 x 12.5mm (0.5in) MGs in wings;
2 x 113kg (249lb) bombs

▲ Grumman Martlet Mk II

No. 888 Squadron / Fleet Air Arm / HMS Formidable, *November 1942*

The aeroplane is wearing US and British markings for use in Torch, the Allied amphibious landings in French northwest Africa in November 1942. Soon known as the Wildcat Mk II, this was a variant of the Martlet Mk I with folding rather than fixed wing panels and two more guns, and as such was effectively similar to the US Navy's F4F-4.

▲ Grumman Wildcat Mk IV

No. 888 Squadron / Fleet Air Arm / HMS Formidable, *November 1942*

This is the aeroplane flown by Squadron Leader Fleet for the Allied Torch landings in French northwest Africa, and wears a mix of British and US markings, the latter in an effort to persuade the Vichy French forces not to fire on any such aircraft.

Specifications

Crew: 1

Powerplant: 895kW (1200hp)

Maximum speed: 512km/h (318mph)

Range: 2012km (1250 miles)

Service ceiling: 10,365m (34,000ft)

Dimensions: span 11.58m (38ft);
length 8.76m (28ft 9in);
height 2.81m (9ft 5in)

Weight: 7952kg (3607lb) loaded

Armament: 6 x 12.7mm (0.5in) MGs in leading edge of wings

Specifications

Crew: 1

Powerplant: 1096kW (1470hp) Merlin 50
  engine

Maximum speed: 594km/h (369mph)

Range: 1827km (1135 miles)

Service ceiling: 11,125m (36,500ft)

Dimensions: span 11.23m (36ft 10in);
  length 9.12m (29ft 11in);
  height 3.02m (9ft 11in)

Weight: 2911kg (6417lb) loaded

Armament: 4 x 7.7mm (0.303in) MGs and 2 x
  20mm (0.8in) cannons in wings

▲ **Supermarine Spitfire Mk VB**

No. 224 Wing / Goubrine South, Tunisia, April 1943

This was the aeroplane in which Wing Commander Ian Gleed was shot down while trying to intercept and destroy German transport aircraft on 16 April 1943. Over the course of the war, 3923 Spitfire Mk VBs were built.

The Invasion of Sicily

JULY 1943

With their Axis foes driven from North Africa or captured, the Allies now turned their attention to a weakened Italy. The first step was clearly the short stride to the large island of Sicily, which would become a springboard for an Allied descent on the mainland.

T HE ALLIED LANDINGS round the southern tip of Sicily began on 9 July 1943 and ended on 17 August with an Allied victory following a major Allied amphibious and airborne operation and subsequent advance. The assault formations were the US Seventh Army on the left and British Eighth Army on the right, while the Axis defence was made up of some 365,000 Italian and about 40,000 German troops.

Landings

The landings took place in a strong wind, which made them difficult, and two British and two US airborne drops were carried out just after midnight during the night of 9/10 July. The American paratroopers were mainly from the 505th Parachute Infantry Regiment of the 82nd Airborne Division, making their first combat drop. The strong winds caused aircraft to go off course and scattered them widely;

the result was that around half the US paratroopers failed to reach their rallying points. British glider-landed troops fared little better, only one of 12 gliders landing on target, and many ditching at sea. Nevertheless, the scattered airborne troops maximized their opportunities, attacking patrols and creating confusion wherever possible.

Because of the adverse weather, many men were landed in the wrong place, wrong order and well behind time, but the British nonetheless took the port of Syracuse virtually unopposed. Only in the American centre was a substantial counterattack made, at exactly the point where the airborne force should have been. On 11 July, the US commander, Lieutenant-General George C. Patton, ordered his reserve parachute regiments to drop and reinforce the centre. Not every unit had been informed of the drop, and the 144 Douglas C-47 transports, which arrived shortly after an Axis air raid, were

▲ **Curtiss Kittyhawk Mk III**

No. 250 Squadron / RAF, southern Italy, autumn 1943

The Kittyhawk remained in useful service during the North African and Italian campaigns.

Specifications

Crew: 1	Dimensions: span 11.36m (37ft 4in);
Powerplant: 895kW (1200hp) Allison piston	length 10.16m (33ft 4in);
engine	height 3.76m (12ft 4in)
Maximum speed: 563km/h (350mph)	Weight: 3511kg (7740lb) loaded
Range: 1738km (1080 miles)	Armament: 4 x 12.7mm (0.5in) Browning MGs
Service ceiling: 9450m (31,000ft)	in wings

engaged by Allied warships: 33 were shot down and 37 damaged, resulting in 318 casualties to friendly fire. Even so, during the first two days progress was excellent; Vizzini in the west and Augusta in the east were taken. Then resistance in the British sector stiffened, and General Sir Bernard Montgomery persuaded the Allied army group commander to shift the inter-army boundaries so that the British could bypass resistance and retain the key role of capturing Messina.

After a week's fighting, Patton looked for a greater role for his army and opted to take Palermo, the capital. This spurred a coup against the Italian leader, Benito Mussolini, who was deposed. After the capture of Palermo, with the British still bogged down south

of Messina, a two-pronged advance was ordered on this key port city. On 24 July, Montgomery suggested to Patton that his Seventh Army should take Messina, as it was better placed. The Seventh Army started its attack on what was now a German defence line at Troina, which held, and the Germans managed to keep the bulk of their forces beyond reach of capture and maintain their evacuation plans: men of the US 3rd Infantry Division entered Messina just after the last Axis troops left Sicily.

The Axis losses totalled 29,000, with 140,000 captured. The US Army lost 2237 killed and 6544 wounded and captured, while the British suffered 2721 dead and 10,122 wounded and captured. Allied air power was again dominant.

Italian Campaign

SEPTEMBER 1943 – MAY 1945

The Allies landed on the mainland of Italy on 9 September 1943, and any hopes of swift victory were soon dashed. The Italians secured an armistice, but the Germans were masters of defensive warfare, and held out grimly in the face of overwhelming Allied air power.

ON 9 SEPTEMBER 1943, the US and British forces of the US Fifth Army landed against strong German opposition at Salerno on the 'shin' of the Italian 'leg' and elements of the British Eighth Army

landed virtually unopposed at Taranto on the 'instep'. Italy had surrendered, but any Allied hopes that the Germans would pull out of Italy were unrealistic. The Eighth Army was able to make good progress for a time along the east coast, taking the port of Bari and the important airfields around Foggia. Despite the fact that it was not reinforced, the Germans came very close to defeating the landing at Salerno, which had been selected as it was within striking distance of the great port of Naples, the most northerly port that could be covered by Allied fighters operating from Sicilian bases.

Natural defences

As the Allies advanced north, increasingly difficult mountain and river terrain checked all possibility of rapid advance and offered the German forces ideal opportunities for extended defence. Early in October 1943, Adolf Hitler was persuaded by his army group commander in southern Italy that the defence of Italy should be undertaken as far away from Germany as possible, and making optimum use of the natural defensive geography while at the same time denying the Allies the easy capture of a succession of airfields steadily closer to Germany.

*Generalfeldmarsch*all Albert Kesselring was now given command of the whole of Italy, and he ordered the construction of a series of defence lines across Italy to the south of Rome.

Two lines, the Volturno Line and the Barbara Line, were used to delay the Allies and so yield the opportunity to prepare the most formidable

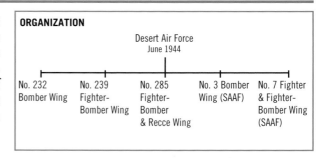

defensive positions that formed the Winter Line. The Winter Line was the overall designation of the Gustav Line and two auxiliary defence lines, the Bernhardt and Adolf Hitler Lines, to the west of the Apennine mountains. The Winter Line proved a major obstacle to the Allies at the end of 1943, halting the advance of the Fifth Army on the western side of Italy. Although the Eighth Army broke through the Gustav Line in the east and took Ortona, truly dreadful weather at the very end of 1943 brought Allied efforts to a halt.

The Allies then focused on the western front where an attack through the Liri valley would open the way to Rome. Landings at Anzio behind the line were intended to destabilize the Germans' Gustav Line defence, but the anticipated early thrust inland to cut off the German defence did not happen and the Anzio force was held.

ORGANIZATION

Desert Air Force
June 1944

| No. 232 Bomber Wing | No. 239 Fighter-Bomber Wing | No. 285 Fighter-Bomber & Recce Wing | No. 3 Bomber Wing (SAAF) | No. 7 Fighter & Fighter-Bomber Wing (SAAF) |

▲ **Curtis Kittyhawk Mk IV**

No. 112 Squadron / No. 239 Wing, Cutella, Italy, 1944

112 Squadron operated the Tomahawk IIB from July to December 1941 and at this time adopted the Sharkmouth markings for which it is now famous. The underfuselage hardpoint of the 'Kittybomber' could carry one 113kg (250lb) bomb, or a 227kg (500lb) bomb as shown here, or a 454kg (1000 kg) bomb.

Specifications

Crew: 1
Powerplant: 895kW (1200hp) Allison piston
engine
Maximum speed: 563km/h (350mph)
Range: 1738km (1080 miles)
Service ceiling: 9450m (31,000ft)

Dimensions: span 11.36m (37ft 4in);
length 10.16m (33ft 4in);
height 3.76m (12ft 4in)
Weight: 3511kg (7740lb) loaded
Armament: 4 x 12.7mm (0.5in) Browning MGs
in wings

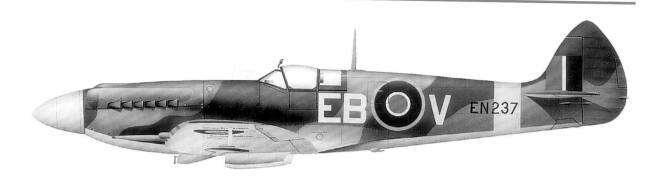

Specifications

Crew: 1

Powerplant: 1170kW (1565hp) 12-cylinder
Rolls-Royce Griffon 2 engine

Maximum speed: 642km/h (410mph)

Range: 698km (435 miles) on internal fuel tanks

Service ceiling: 12,650m (41,500ft)

Dimensions: span 11.23m (36ft 10in);
length 9.47m (31ft 1in);
height 3.86m (12ft 8in)

Weight: 3343kg (7370lb) loaded

Armament: 4 x 7.7mm (0.303in) MGs and 2 x
20mm (0.8in) cannons

▲ Supermarine Spitfire Mk XII

No. 41 Squadron / Italy, 1944

Later-mark Supermarine Spitfire fighters were characterized by enlargement of
the vertical tail surface, including a broader-cord rudder to maintain directional
authority despite the larger nose with its Rolls-Royce Griffon engine.

▲ North American Mustang Mk III

No. 112 Squadron / RAF, Italy, 1945

This was the aeroplane of Flight Lieutenant Raymond V. Hearn, commander of the
Squadron's 'B' Flight. Hearn was killed by German anti-aircraft fire on 18 February
1945 during his last scheduled sortie. The nose is painted with 112 Squadron's
famous 'sharkmouth' markings.

Specifications

Crew: 1

Powerplant: 1081kW (1450hp) V-1650-3
engine

Maximum speed: 690km/h (430mph)

Range: 1215km (755 miles)

Service ceiling: 12,649m (41,500ft)

Dimensions: span 11.27m (37ft);
length 9.84m (32ft 4in);
height 4.15m (13ft 8in)

Weight: 4173kg (9200lb) loaded

Armament: 4 x 12.7mm (0.5in) MGs

It took four major offensives between January
and May 1944 before the line was eventually broken
by a combined assault of the Fifth and Eighth
Armies concentrated along a 32km (20-mile) front
between Monte Cassino and the west coast.

At the same time, the forces at Anzio broke out
of their beachhead, but Fifth Army preferred to
take Rome, on 4 June, rather than cut off sizeable
German forces. From June to September, the

Allies advanced beyond Rome, taking Florence
and approaching the Gothic Line. This last major
defensive line, just south of Bologna, was penetrated
during the autumn campaign, but there was no
decisive breakthrough until April 1945.

Then the German armies, shattered and virtually
without fuel as a result of the domination of the
Allied air forces, which also decimated all ground
movement, finally collapsed.

RAF Fighter Command
1942–45

The years 1942 and 1943 were marked by battles of attrition with the *Luftwaffe*, but as German strength declined and Fighter Command started to introduce new fighters as well as advanced versions of its current fighters, the British gained a clear ascendancy over the *Luftwaffe*.

THE PROCESS OF WEARING down the *Luftwaffe* over France, which Fighter Command had started in 1941, continued in various forms during 1942–43. However, the expansion of the war effort in other theatres resulted in the outward transfer of many experienced pilots and squadrons. Thus the units left to No. 11 Group found it increasingly difficult to gain superiority over the small but very capable

▲ North American Mustang Mk I
No. 414 (Canadian) Squadron / RAF Army Cooperation Command, Middle Wallop, 1942

The RAF received 620 examples of the Mustang Mk I, which replaced the Curtiss Tomahawk in service with Army Cooperation squadrons for the reconnaissance-fighter role. There were also 150 cannon-armed Mustang Mk IAs and 50 long-range Mustang Mk II aircraft.

Specifications
Crew: 1
Powerplant: 858kW (1150hp) Allison V-1710-
  39 V12 engine
Maximum speed: 690km/h (430mph)
Range: 1215km (755 miles)
Service ceiling: 12,649m (41,500ft)

Dimensions: span 11.27m (37ft);
  length 9.84m (32ft 4in);
  height 4.15m (13ft 8in)
Weight: 4173kg (9200lb) loaded
Armament: 4 x 12.7mm (0.5in) and 4 x
  7.62mm (0.3in) Browning MGs

▲ Supermarine Spitfire Mk VC
No. 91 Squadron / RAF Fighter Command, Hawkinge, 1942

The Spitfire Mk VC was the development of the Spitfire Mk V with the 'universal' wing able to carry machine-gun or cannon/machine-gun armament. The wing could also have its tips removed for a greater roll rate at low altitude, or extended for greater ceiling. This has the 'B' type cannon/machine-gun armament.

Specifications
Crew: 1
Powerplant: 1102kW (1478hp) Rolls-Royce
  Merlin 45 engine
Maximum speed: 594km/h (369mph)
Range: 1827km (1135 miles)
Service ceiling: 11,125m (36,500ft)

Dimensions: span 11.23m (36ft 10in);
  length 9.12m (29ft 11in);
  height 3.02m (9ft 11in)
Weight: 2911kg (6417lb) loaded
Armament: 4 x 7.7mm (0.303in) MGs and 2 x
  20mm (0.8in) cannons

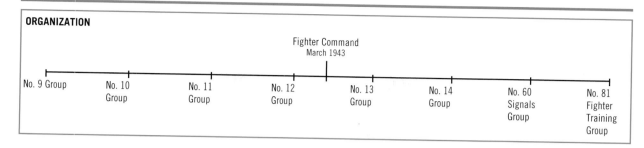

ORGANIZATION

Fighter Command
March 1943

No. 9 Group — No. 10 Group — No. 11 Group — No. 12 Group — No. 13 Group — No. 14 Group — No. 60 Signals Group — No. 81 Fighter Training Group

fighter units that the Germans left in France. The squadrons were additionally committed to exhausting defensive patrols against small units of Focke-Wulf Fw 190 fighter-bombers flying low-level 'hit and run' raids against ports and towns along the south coast of England. Yet the new Hawker Typhoon fighter proved itself able to catch these raiders.

Dieppe raid

The most notable offensive battle took place over the 'reconnaissance in force' against Dieppe in August 1942. The *Luftwaffe* and RAF fought it out over the failed assault, and though Fighter Command managed to prevent the *Luftwaffe* from attacking the assault shipping (its primary objective) the British success proved illusory. Despite the claims of the day that more German than British aircraft had been shot down, later analysis revealed exactly the opposite.

In 1943, the most notable event was the division of Fighter Command into the Air Defence of Great Britain (ADGB) and the 2nd Tactical Air Force (TAF). As its designation indicates, the ADGB was entrusted with the task of defending the UK from air attack, while the 2nd TAF was tasked with the support of ground forces after the eventual invasion of Europe.

The year 1944 saw the ADGB's greatest effort. *Overlord*, the Allied invasion of northern France, was launched on 6 June 1944. British fighters wove over the battle area and, together with their US brothers in arms, completely suppressed the efforts of the miniscule German opposition.

They also directly supported ground forces by strafing enemy positions and transport. Later in the year, the final major trial of what had become Fighter Command once again in October 1944, occurred with the defeat of the V-1 flying bomb campaign. In World War II, Fighter Command lost 3690 men killed, 1215 wounded and 601 taken prisoner, as well as 4790 aircraft lost.

Specifications

Crew: 1

Powerplant: 1170kW (1565hp) 12-cylinder Rolls-Royce Merlin 61 engine

Maximum speed: 642km/h (410mph)

Range: 698km (435 miles) on internal fuel tanks

Service ceiling: 12,650m (41,500ft)

Dimensions: span 11.23m (36ft 10in); length 9.47m (31ft 1in); height 3.86m (12ft 8in)

Weight: 3343kg (7370lb) loaded

Armament: 4 x 7.7mm (0.303in) MGs and 2 x 20mm (0.8in) cannons

▲ **Supermarine Spitfire Mk IX**

Special Service Flight, Northolt, 1942

Although developed as an interim type with the airframe of the Spitfire Mk V and the Rolls-Royce Merlin 60 series engine, the Spitfire Mk IX was produced in larger numbers than any other Spitfire variant.

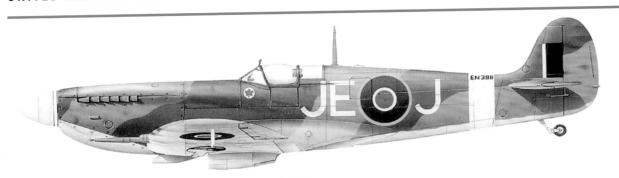

Specifications

Crew: 1

Powerplant: 1170kW (1565hp) 12-cylinder
  Rolls-Royce Merlin 61 engine

Maximum speed: 642km/h (410mph)

Range: 698km (435 miles) on internal tanks

Service ceiling: 12,650m (41,500ft)

Dimensions: span 11.23m (36ft 10in);
  length 9.47m (31ft 1in);
  height 3.86m (12ft 8in)

Weight: 3343kg (7370lb) loaded

Armament: 4 x 7.7mm (0.303in) MGs and 2 x
  20mm (0.8in) cannons

▲ **Supermarine Spitfire Mk IXE**

Kenley Wing / RAF Fighter Command, Kenley, 1943–44

This was the personal aeroplane of Wing Commander J. E. 'Johnnie' Johnson,
commanding the Kenley Wing and later No. 127 (Canadian) Wing at Kenley, and
as such sporting his initials rather than a squadron coding.

Night-fighters
1942–45

The Air Defence of Great Britain was one part of Fighter Command after this had been divided to allow the creation of the 2nd Tactical Air Force. Although only short-lived, the ADGB has its place in history as the air formation that helped to defeat the V-1 flying bomb campaign.

THE FIRST INCARNATION of the Air Defence of
Great Britain (ADGB) happened in 1925, as
the command of this name was created for the
supervision of home defences, which at the time

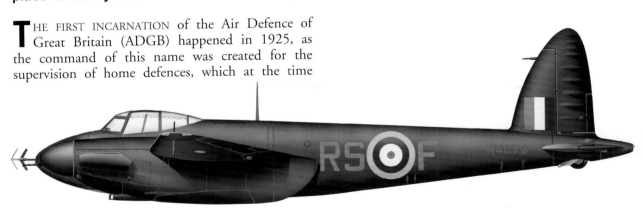

Specifications

Crew: 2

Powerplant: 2 x 918kW (1230hp) Rolls-Royce
  Merlin XX engines

Maximum speed: 612km/h (380mph)

Range: 1963km (1220 miles)

Service ceiling: 9449m (31,000ft)

Dimensions: span 16.51m (54ft 2in);
  length 12.43m (40ft 10in);
  height 4.65m (15ft 3in)

Weight: 5942kg (13,100lb) loaded

Radar: AI.Mk IV interceptor radar

Armament: 4 x 20mm (0.8in) Hispano cannon
  and 4 x 7.7mm (0.303in) Browning MGs

▲ **de Havilland Mosquito NF.Mk II**

No. 157 Squadron / RAF Fighter Command, Castle Camps, mid-1942

The first fighter Mosquito introduced into service was the NF. Mk II in mid-1942.
The Mosquito NF. Mk II brought an altogether better capability to the RAF's
night-fighter arm, for it offered a much higher level of performance than the
Beaufighter.

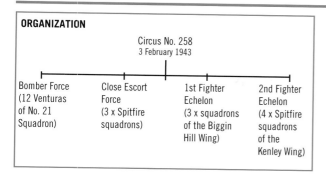

ORGANIZATION

Circus No. 258
3 February 1943

Bomber Force
(12 Venturas
of No. 21
Squadron)

Close Escort
Force
(3 x Spitfire
squadrons)

1st Fighter
Echelon
(3 x squadrons
of the Biggin
Hill Wing)

2nd Fighter
Echelon
(4 x Spitfire
squadrons
of the
Kenley Wing)

and the Fighting Area. In 1936, the ADGB was disestablished, whereupon the erstwhile Bombing Area became Bomber Command, and the Fighting Area became Fighter Command.

The second incarnation of the Air Defence of Great Britain designation came when it was adopted for what was left of Fighter Command after the 2nd Tactical Air Force (TAF) had been hived off Fighter Command in 1943. The new ADGB was tasked with the air defence of Britain.

It was nonetheless nothing more than a small Fighter Command, and this fact was recognized in 1944 when the command reverted to the Fighter Command designation.

included bombers as well as fighters. This first ADGB was split into two areas controlling regular squadrons. These were the Wessex Bombing Area

Specifications

Crew: 2

Powerplant: 2 x 954kW (1280hp) Rolls-Royce
    Merlin XX engines

Maximum speed: 492km/h (306mph)

Range: 2414km (1500 miles)

Service ceiling: 8810m (28,900ft)

Dimensions: span 17.63m (57ft 10in);
    length 12.60m (41ft 4in);
    height 4.82m (15 ft 10in)

Weight: 9435kg (21,100lb) loaded

Armament: 4 x 20mm (0.79in) cannon and
    6 x 7.7mm (0.303in) MGs in the wings

▲ **Bristol Beaufighter Mk II**

No. 307 (Polish) Squadron / Exeter, April 1943

The red-and-white checkerboard marking, derived from the Polish flag, was a standard adornment of the aircraft flown by Polish-manned squadrons.

Specifications

Crew: 3

Powerplant: 1193kW (1600hp) Wright R-2600-
    23 radial piston engine

Maximum speed: 510km/h (317mph)

Range: 1521km (945 miles)

Service ceiling: 7225m (23,700ft)

Dimensions: span 18.69m (61ft 4in);

length 14.63m (47ft 11in);
    height 5.36m (17ft 7in)

Weight: 10,964kg (24,127lb) loaded

Armament: 6 x 12.7mm (0.5in) forward-firing
    Browning M2 MGs; 2 x 2.7mm (0.5in) MGs
    in power-operated dorsal turret; 2 x 2.7mm
    (0.5in) rearward firing MGs in ventral tunnel

▲ **Douglas Havoc Mk I**

No. 23 Squadron / RAF Fighter Command, Ford, 1943

The Havoc fighter development of the DB-7 bomber made a moderately useful interim night-fighter, but was too large an aeroplane for the role.

Flying bomb interceptors
1944

The first of Germany's 'vengeance' weapons was the V-1 flying bomb, a primitive cruise missile guided by an autopilot and powered by a pulsejet. The V-1 was comparatively fast at low level and inaccurate, but it carried a large warhead and was a real menace to civilian morale.

THE CAMPAIGN AGAINST the V-1 involved balloon barrages, belts of anti-aircraft guns and fighters. The latter recorded its first interception on 14/ 15 June 1944. When the V-1 campaign began in mid-June of 1944, there were fewer than 30 examples of the Hawker Tempest, the only fighter with the low-altitude speed needed to catch a V-1, and these were allocated to No. 150 Wing.

Tempest wing

The Tempest wing was increased to more than 100 aircraft by September. P-51s and Griffon-engined Spitfire Mk XIVs were also specially tuned to give them the speed needed, and at night de Havilland Mosquitoes were used. There was no need for radar since the V-1's exhaust plume was visible from far away. Daylight V-1 chases were chaotic and often unsuccessful until a special defence zone was declared between London and the coast, in which only the fastest fighters were permitted to operate.

Between June and 5 September 1944, the handful of No. 150 Wing Tempests shot down 638 flying bombs, No. 3 Squadron claiming 305. Next most successful were the Mosquito (428), Spitfire Mk XIV (303) and Mustang (232).

Meteor speed

Even though it was not fully operational, the jet-powered Gloster Meteor was rushed into service with No. 616 Squadron RAF to fight the V-1s. It had ample speed, but its cannon were prone to jamming. By September 1944, the V-1 threat to England was removed when all its launch sites were overrun by the advancing Allied armies. Some 4261 V-1s had been destroyed by fighters, anti-aircraft fire and barrage balloons.

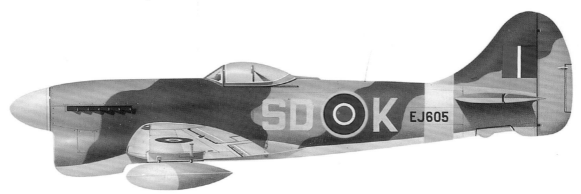

▲ Hawker Tempest Mk V (Series 2)

No. 501 Squadron / RAF, 1944–45

A conceptual development of the Typhoon with a thinner wing, among other changes, the Tempest was an altogether superior fighter. Delivered in August 1944, the Tempests of 501 Squadron specialized in defensive operations against the V-1 flying bombs.

Specifications

Crew: 2	length 10.26m (33ft 8in);
Powerplant: 1626kW (2180hp) Napier Sabre IIA	height 4.90m (16ft 1in)
H-type piston engine	Weight: 6142kg (13,540lb) loaded
Maximum speed: 686km/h (426mph)	Armament: 4 x 20mm (0.8in) Hispano
Range: 2092km (1300 miles)	cannon in wings, plus up to 907kg (2000lb)
Service ceiling: 10,975m (36,000ft)	disposable stores consisting of either 2 x
Dimensions: span 12.50m (41ft);	bombs or 8 rockets for ground attack role

Specifications

Crew: 1

Powerplant: 1081kW (1450hp) V-1650-3 engine

Maximum speed: 690km/h (430mph)

Range: 1215km (755 miles)

Service ceiling: 12,649m (41,500ft)

Dimensions: span 11.27m (37ft); length 9.84m (32ft 4in); height 4.15m (13ft 8in)

Weight: 4173kg (9200lb) loaded

Armament: 4 x 12.7mm (0.5in) MGs

▲ North American Mustang Mk IIIB

No. 316 (Polish) Squadron / Coltishall, June 1944

The Mustang Mk III was the British counterpart of the USAAF's P-51B and was employed for a time as flying bomb interceptor.

Specifications

Crew: 1

Powerplant: 1081kW (1450hp) V-1650-3 engine

Maximum speed: 690km/h (430mph)

Range: 1215km (755 miles)

Service ceiling: 12,649m (41,500ft)

Dimensions: span 11.27m (37ft); length 9.84m (32ft 4in); height 4.15m (13ft 8in)

Weight: 4173kg (9200lb) loaded

Armament: 4 x 12.7mm (0.5in) MGs

▲ North American Mustang Mk III

No. 306 'Torunski' (Polish) Squadron / UK, 1944

This aeroplane has the British 'Malcolm hood' in place of the original framed canopy, much improving the pilot's fields of vision.

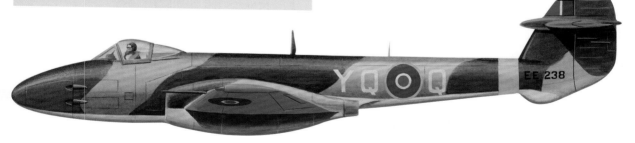

Specifications

Crew: 1

Powerplant: 2 x 7.56kN (1700lb st) Rolls-Royce W.2B/23C Welland turbojet engines

Maximum speed: 668km/h (415mph)

Service ceiling: 12,190m (40,000ft)

Dimensions: span 13.11m (43ft); length 12.57m (41ft 3in); height 3.96m (13ft)

Weight: 6257kg (13,795lb) maximum take-off

Armament: 4 x 20mm (0.8in) Hispano cannon fixed forward-firing in nose

▲ Gloster Meteor Mk I

No. 616 Squadron / RAF, 1945

Although it offered better performance than the piston-engined fighters of the day, the Meteor was little more than a turbojet-powered development of an airframe that was otherwise typical of piston-engined thinking.

RAF 2nd Tactical Air Force

1943–45

The 2nd Tactical Air Force was created using the tactics developed in North Africa by the Desert Air Force and then translated to the Italian campaign of 1943. It was designed to provide the British and Canadian forces with superb air support in the northwest Europe campaign.

THE 2ND TACTICAL AIR FORCE (TAF) was one of the three tactical air forces that were established within the Royal Air Force during and after World War II.

The 2nd TAF comprised squadrons and personnel from the air forces of the British Commonwealth and the air units of various governments in exile, as well as from the RAF itself.

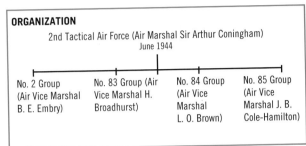

ORGANIZATION

2nd Tactical Air Force (Air Marshal Sir Arthur Coningham)
June 1944

| No. 2 Group (Air Vice Marshal B. E. Embry) | No. 83 Group (Air Vice Marshal H. Broadhurst) | No. 84 Group (Air Vice Marshal L. O. Brown) | No. 85 Group (Air Vice Marshal J. B. Cole-Hamilton) |

2nd TAF established

The 2nd TAF was established during June 1943, even before the DAF (1st TAF) had moved from North Africa to Italy to perfect its tactics under European mainland conditions. It was part of the Allied preparations already advanced for the invasion of northwest Europe, an operation planned for the summer of 1944.

The 2nd TAF drew units from many elements of the RAF commands in the UK in order to build up a force able to provide a high level of support for the British Army in the field.

Bomber Command provided its No. 2 Group, which was equipped with light bombers and fighter-bombers, and Fighter Command was divided into two portions, namely the Air Defence of Great Britain, which retained fighter units for the air defence of the UK, and Nos 83 and 84 Groups for allocation to the 2nd TAF.

▲ **Supermarine Spitfire Mk IXE**

No. 144 (Canadian) Wing / Kenley, March 1943

This was the personal aeroplane of Wing Commander J. E. 'Johnnie' Johnson.

Specifications

Crew: 1

Powerplant: 1170kW (1565hp) 12-cylinder Rolls-Royce Merlin 61 engine

Maximum speed: 642km/h (410mph)

Range: 698km (435 miles) on internal fuel tanks

Service ceiling: 12,650m (41,500ft)

Dimensions: span 11.23m (36ft 10in); length 9.47m (31ft 1in); height 3.86m (12ft 8in)

Weight: 3343kg (7370lb) loaded

Armament: 4 x 7.7mm (0.303in) MGs and 2 x 20mm (0.8in) cannons

The new force's first commander was Air Marshal Sir John d'Albiac. But on 21 January 1944, d'Albiac was followed by the commander most usually associated with the 2nd TAF, namely Air Marshal Sir Arthur Coningham.

This officer possessed vast experience of the type of air operations needed for the effective support of fast-moving land warfare, for he had commanded the DAF in North Africa and Italy, and now perfected the 2nd TAF to meet any and all the demands that would be placed on it. One of the primary tactics was the 'cab rank' system of on-call close support developed in North Africa and Italy.

By mid-1944, the *Luftwaffe* was nothing like the force it once had been, so air opposition to the 2nd TAF was limited. The force could therefore concentrate on the support of the British and Canadian forces on the left flank of the Allied invasion of France and subsequent advance east toward Germany.

Bodenplatte

One exception to this general situation came with *Bodenplatte*, the *Luftwaffe's* last major effort launched on 1 January 1945, when the 2nd TAF

suffered serious losses on the ground. But the *Luftwaffe's* standards of training were now so low that many aircraft were shot down by ground fire or Allied fighters, and others ran out of fuel and crashed because of their pilots' navigational errors.

WINGS OF NO. 83 GROUP, 2ND TAF (JUNE 1944)		
Wing	Squadrons	Aircraft
No. 39, RCAF	168 & 414 430	Mustang Spitfire
No. 121	174, 175 & 245	Typhoon
No. 122	19, 65 & 122	Typhoon
No. 122	19, 65 & 122	Mustang
No. 124	181, 182 & 247	Typhoon
No. 125	132, 453 & 602	Spitfire
No. 126, RCAF	401, 411 & 412	Spitfire
No. 127, RCAF	403, 416 & 421	Spitfire
No. 129, RCAF	184	Typhoon
No. 143, RCAF	438, 439 & 440	Typhoon
No. 144, RCAF	441, 442 & 443	Spitfire
Air observation post	652, 653, 658, 659 & 662	Auster

▲ Hawker Typhoon Mk IB

No. 247 Squadron / No. 124 Wing / No. 83 Group / 2nd TAF, 1944

Although the Typhoon is best known in the attack role, with an underwing load of eight 76mm (3in) unguided rockets, it also operated in the close support role with two bombs of up to 454kg (1000lb) size under the wing.

Specifications

Crew: 1

Powerplant: 1685kW (2260hp) Napier Sabre II liquid cooled H-24 in-line piston engine

Maximum speed: 650km/h (405mph)

Range: 980km (610 miles)

Service ceiling: 10,400m (34,000ft)

Dimensions: span 12.67m (41ft 7in); length 9.73m (31ft 11in); height 4.66m (15ft 4in)

Weight: 5170kg (11,400lb) loaded

Armament: 4 x 20mm (0.8in) Hispano-Suiza HS.404 cannons, 2 x 454 kg (1000lb) bombs

▲ **Hawker Typhoon Mk IB**

No. 198 Squadron / No. 123 Wing / No. 84 Group / 2nd TAF

Depicted in the time before the Overlord invasion of Normandy, which it supported, this Typhoon Mk IB lacks 'invasion stripe' markings.

Specifications	
Crew: 1	Dimensions: span 12.67m (41ft 7in);
Powerplant: 1685kW (2260hp) Napier Sabre II	length 9.73m (31ft 11in);
liquid cooled H-24 in-line piston engine	height 4.66m (15ft 4in)
Maximum speed: 650km/h (405mph)	Weight: 5170kg (11,400lb) loaded
Range: 980km (610 miles)	Armament: 4 x 20mm (0.8in) Hispano-Suiza
Service ceiling: 10,400m (34,000ft)	HS.404 cannons, 2 x 454 kg (1000lb) bombs

Normandy landings
JUNE–AUGUST 1944

The period between the landing in Normandy (6 June) and the German escape from the Falaise pocket (20 August) saw the use of great Allied airpower, but the development of this capability was hindered by operations from the UK until airfields had been captured or created in France.

THE ALLIED INVASION and reconquest of northwest Europe started on 6 June 1944 with the launch of *Overlord*, the Allied 21st Army Group's amphibious landings in Normandy under cover of Air Chief Marshal Sir Trafford Leigh-Mallory's Allied Expeditionary Air Force (AEAF). The primary British and Commonwealth component of the AEAF was Air Marshal Sir Arthur Coningham's 2nd TAF operating from bases in southern England.

The Germans were taken completely by surprise, and in any case had only small air forces in France. The Allies, therefore, had matters completely their own way on 6 June as the light bombers of the 2nd TAF aided the heavy bombers of Bomber Command in attacking beach defences and installations, and then moved their attentions inland to destroy the Germans' last surviving lines of communication as the assault forces progressed south.

Here the light bombers collaborated with the 2nd TAF's attack aircraft under a cover of late-generation

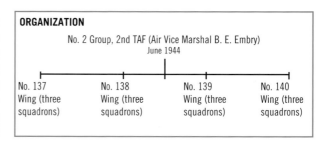

ORGANIZATION

No. 2 Group, 2nd TAF (Air Vice Marshal B. E. Embry)
June 1944

| No. 137 Wing (three squadrons) | No. 138 Wing (three squadrons) | No. 139 Wing (three squadrons) | No. 140 Wing (three squadrons) |

fighters, while low-level tactical reconnaissance planes swept ahead of the advancing ground forces in search of German defensive strongpoints and the possible arrival of German reinforcements, especially of armour. During that day, Allied air forces flew 14,674 sorties and lost only 113 aircraft, some of the losses being unfortunate victims of 'friendly fire'. The *Luftwaffe* was able to respond with a mere 319 sorties, which achieved only negligible results.

The nature of the campaign that was now under way was reflected on the following day, when the warplanes of Nos 83 and 84 Groups attacked a German Panzer division moving toward the front, destroying 90 trucks, 40 fuel tankers, five tanks and 84 other armoured vehicles, including assault guns and self-propelled artillery. The Allies gained the use of their first airstrip in Normandy on 10 June, and in the British and Commonwealth portion of the lodgement 31 more such strips were later developed, allowing the transfer of squadrons from the UK and thus longer endurance over the battlefield.

Luftwaffe response

The *Luftwaffe* responded as and when it could in the face of the essentially total air superiority of the Allies, who could thus use their tactical air power as and when they weather permitted. Even so, the Germans performed wonders in getting men, tanks, artillery and essential supplies to the front, and so seriously delayed the 21st Army Group. The German front finally began to unravel on 24 July as the Americans broke out in the west and then swung round to the east. The Germans were now threatened with a major encirclement in a pocket near Falaise, but managed to extricate many of their men before the neck of the pocket could be closed.

Even so, it was a major disaster for the Germans at Falaise, who lost most of their armour, artillery and motor transport. The pocket held 19 German

▲ **Fighter bomber**
Armed with eight rocket projectiles, this Typhoon Mk IB carries a typical Typhoon warload for low-level missions.

divisions, including nine Panzer divisions. Before they could escape, the Allied tactical squadrons, spearheaded by Hawker Typhoon fighter-bomber units, effectively destroyed the 5. and 7. *Panzerarmees* over a three-day period (17–19 July), destroying or forcing the abandonment of all but about 120 of 2300 German armoured vehicles.

The Germans tried to respond in the air, but the *Luftwaffe* was only a shadow of its former self and by mid-August *Luftflotte 3* had been reduced to just 75 aircraft.

▲ **Hawker Typhoon IB**

No. 486 Squadron / Air Defence of Great Britain, spring 1944
Not all Hawker Typhoon fighter-bomber units were allocated to the 2nd TAF, this squadron remaining on the strength of Fighter Command (later the ADGB) at Tangmere on the coast of Sussex in southern England.

Specifications

Crew: 1	length 9.73m (31ft 11in);
Powerplant: 1685kW (2260hp)	height 4.66m (15ft 4in)
Maximum speed: 650km/h (405mph)	Weight: 5170kg (11,400lb) loaded
Range: 980km (610 miles)	Armament: 4 x 20mm (0.8in) Hispano-Suiza
Service ceiling: 10,400m (34,000ft)	HS.404 cannons, 8 x 27kg (60lb) rockets for
Dimensions: span 12.67m (41ft 7in);	ground attack purposes

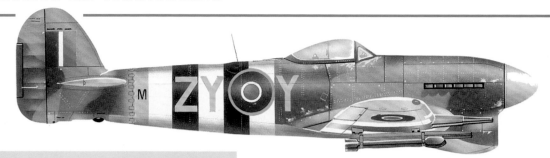

Specifications

Crew: 1

Powerplant: 1685kW (2260hp) Napier Sabre II
 piston engine

Maximum speed: 650km/h (405mph)

Range: 980km (610 miles)

Service ceiling: 10,400m (34,000ft)

Dimensions: span 12.67m (41ft 7in); length
 9.73m (31ft 11in); height 4.66m (15ft 4in)

Weight: 5170kg (11,400lb) loaded

Armament: 4 x 20mm (0.8in) Hispano-Suiza
 HS.404 cannons, 8 x 27kg (60lb) rockets for
 ground attack purposes

▲ Hawker Typhoon Mk IB
No. 193 Squadron / No. 146 Wing / No. 84 Group / 2nd TAF

Seen here wearing northern European day-fighter camouflage and black-and-white recognition strips for the invasion of Europe, the Typhoon Mk IB proved itself a decisive weapon in the northwestern Europe campaign as an attack fighter well able to deal with German armoured vehicles and artillery.

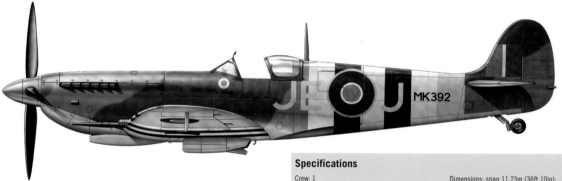

▲ Supermarine Spitfire Mk IX
No. 127 (Canadian) Wing / northwest Europe, autumn 1944

This was another of Wing Commander J. E. 'Johnnie' Johnson's personal aircraft, from the time he commanded another Canadian wing in the northwest European campaign from bases in France.

Specifications

Crew: 1

Powerplant: 1170kW (1565hp) 12-cylinder
 Rolls-Royce Merlin 61 engine

Maximum speed: 642km/h (410mph)

Range: 698km (435 miles) on internal fuel tanks

Service ceiling: 12,650m (41,500ft)

Dimensions: span 11.23m (36ft 10in);
 length 9.47m (31ft 1in);
 height 3.86m (12ft 8in)

Weight: 3343kg (7370lb) loaded

Armament: 4 x 7.7mm (0.303in) MGs and 2 x
 20mm (0.8in) cannons

▲ Supermarine Spitfire Mk XIV
Northwest Europe, autumn 1944

The Mk XIV was used by the 2nd Tactical Air Force as their main high-altitude air superiority fighter in northern Europe. In total, 957 Mk XIVs were built, over 400 of which were FR Mk XIVs. This fighter also bears the personal markings of Wing Commander J. E. 'Johnnie' Johnson.

Specifications

Crew: 1

Powerplant: 1528kW (2050hp) Griffon 65 series
 engine

Maximum speed: 720km/h (448mph)

Range: 965km (600 miles) using additional
 rear fuel tank

Service ceiling: 13,560m (44,500ft)

Dimensions: span 11.23m (36ft 10in); length
 9.96m (32ft 8in); height 3.86m (12ft 8in)

Weight: 3343kg (7370lb) loaded

Armament: 4 x 7.7mm (0.303in) MGs and 2 x
 20mm (0.8in) cannons

Specifications

Crew: 1

Powerplant: 1170kW (1565hp) 12-cylinder
Rolls-Royce Merlin 61 engine

Maximum speed: 642km/h (410mph)

Range: 698km (435 miles) on internal fuel tanks

Service ceiling: 12,650m (41,500ft)

Dimensions: span 11.23m (36ft 10in);
length 9.47m (31ft 1in);
height 3.86m (12ft 8in)

Weight: 3343kg (7370lb) loaded

Armament: N/A

▲ Supermarine Spitfire PR.Mk IX

Photographic reconnaissance squadron / RAF, 1944

Though carrying no armament, the Spitfire PR.Mk IX was very important to the
Allied war effort – its ability to fly fast and high over long ranges made it
an excellent photo-reconnaissance aeroplane.

▼ Supermarine Spitfire Mk VII

RAF Fighter Command, summer 1944

The Spitfire Mk VII was optimized for the high-altitude role with the Merlin 61
engine, a longer-span wing with more pointed tips and a retractable tailwheel.
Production amounted to 471 aircraft, which served with 11 Squadrons based
mostly in the UK.

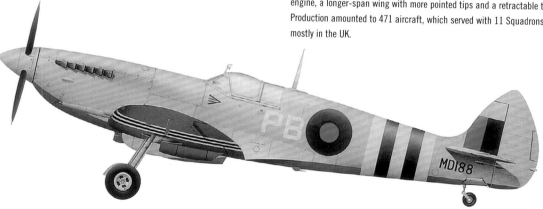

Specifications

Crew: 1

Powerplant: 1170kW (1565hp) 12-cylinder
Rolls-Royce Merlin 61 engine

Maximum speed: 642km/h (410mph)

Range: 698km (435 miles) on internal fuel tanks

Service ceiling: 12,650m (41,500ft)

Dimensions: span 11.23m (36ft 10in);
length 9.47m (31ft 1in);
height 3.86m (12ft 8in)

Weight: 3343kg (7370lb) loaded

Armament: 4 x 7.7mm (0.303in) MGs and 2 x
20mm (0.8in) cannons

▶ Spitfire Mk IXC

This is part of No. 306 Torunski Squadron, a Polish-manned unit based at Northolt
in 1943–44 and engaged in daylight sweeps over Europe.

▲ Hawker Tempest Mk V Series 2

No. 274 Squadron, RAF / summer 1944

No. 274 Squadron converted from the Supermarine Spitfire Mk IX to the Tempest
Mk V at Hornchurch during August 1944, and moved to Belgium in the following
month. For the rest of World War II, the squadron flew armed reconnaissance
missions, which led to many combats deep behind the frontline.

Specifications

Crew: 2

Powerplant: 1626kW (2180hp) Napier Sabre IIA
  H-type piston engine

Maximum speed: 686km/h (426mph)

Range: 2092km (1300 miles)

Service ceiling: 10,975m (36,000ft)

Dimensions: span 12.50m (41ft);

length 10.26m (33ft 8in);

height 4.90m (16ft 1in)

Weight: 6142kg (13,540lb) loaded

Armament: 4 x 20mm (0.8in) Hispano
  cannon in wings, plus up to 907kg (2000lb)
  disposable stores consisting of either 2 x
  bombs or 8 rockets for ground attack role

No. 2 Group
1944–45

**No. 2 Group was formed on 20 March 1936, with five wings of ten squadrons. Four of the wings
were allocated to the Advanced Air Striking Force (AASF), and a Bristol Blenheim of No. 2 Group
made the first British operational sortie to cross the German frontier in World War II.**

THE 2ND TAF's primary mission was to support the
fighting troops on the ground. The fighters and
fighter-bombers of the 83rd and 84th Groups were
more suitable for what is now known as close-support
– ground attack with rockets, cannon and bombs – in
pinpoint and diving attacks against single targets such
as tanks, trains, bridges and field fortifications. The
agility of these light aircraft enabled them to make
precision attacks in a way that the larger bombers,
committed to horizontal bombing runs, could not.

In May 1943, No. 2 Group was detached from
Bomber Command, now increasingly concerned with
heavy night bombing, and allocated to the 2nd TAF.
The group was very active in the northwest Europe
campaign for tactical bombing, and in the closing
months of the war was based on the continent.
No. 2 Group started the war with 79 Blenheims
and finished with more than 260 Mosquitoes and
Mitchells. It flew more than 57,000 operational
sorties at a cost of 2671 men killed or missing and
396 wounded.

ORGANIZATION

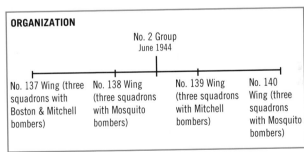

No. 2 Group
June 1944

No. 137 Wing (three
squadrons with
Boston & Mitchell
bombers)

No. 138 Wing
(three squadrons
with Mosquito
bombers)

No. 139 Wing (three
squadrons with Mitchell
bombers)

No. 140
Wing (three
squadrons
with Mosquito
bombers)

WINGS OF NO. 2 GROUP (1944)

Wing	Squadrons	Aircraft	Role
No. 137	Nos 88, 226 & 342	Boston & Mitchell	Light bomber
No. 138	Nos 107, 305 & 613	Mosquito	Light bomber
No. 139	Nos 98, 180 & 320	Mitchell	Light bomber
No. 140	Nos 21, 464 & 487	Mosquito	Light bomber

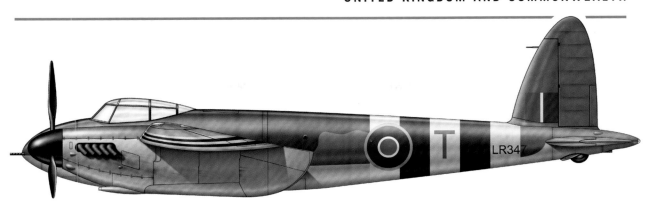

Specifications

Crew: 2

Powerplant: 2 x 1103kW (1480hp) Rolls-Royce
Merlin 23 engines

Maximum speed: 595km/h (370mph)

Range: 2744km (1705 miles)

Service ceiling: 10,515m (34,500ft)

Dimensions: span 16.51m (54ft 2in);
length 13.08m (42ft 11in);
height 5.31m (17ft 5in)

Weight: 9072kg (20,000lb) loaded

Armament: 4 x 20mm (0.8in) cannons in
wings, plus 4 x 7.7mm (0.303in) MGs in nose

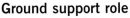 **de Havilland Mosquito FB.Mk VI**

No. 138 Wing / RAF, 1944

With two Merlin engines and a low-drag airframe built largely of a plywood/balsa/plywood sandwich material for low weight and considerable strength, the Mosquito was very adaptable and fast, and in fighter-bomber form carried four cannon, four MGs, up to 907kg (2000lb) of bombs (half this figure internally) and, in some cases, eight unguided rocket projectiles.

No. 83 Group
1944–45

No. 83 Group was notably important to the British and Commonwealth forces, for it had four reconnaissance and five air observation post squadrons as well as 25 squadrons of fighters and fighter-bombers in nine wings. Five of these wings, with 12 squadrons, were Canadian.

No. 83 GROUP was formed in the UK on 1 April 1943, and came under the command of Air Vice Marshal W. F. Dickson on 21 March 1943. The group had been planned and created as a primary element of the 2nd TAF. In this formation, No. 83 Group served alongside No. 84 Group, both being supported in the field by the efforts of Air Vice Marshal J. B. Cole-Hamilton's – and from 10 October 1944, Air Vice Marshal C. R. Steele's – No. 85 (Base) Group of 12 squadrons in six wings, as well as essential support elements, including three airfield construction squadrons.

Ground support role

Nos 83 and 84 Groups were both entrusted with the task of providing provide direct support to British and Canadian forces in the field during the Allied liberation of Europe from 6 June 1944. The two groups played an important part in establishing

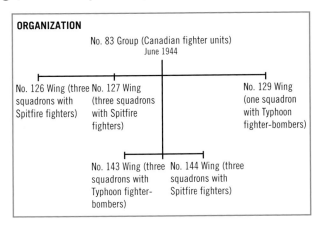

ORGANIZATION

No. 83 Group (Canadian fighter units)
June 1944

No. 126 Wing (three squadrons with Spitfire fighters)

No. 127 Wing (three squadrons with Spitfire fighters)

No. 129 Wing (one squadron with Typhoon fighter-bombers)

No. 143 Wing (three squadrons with Typhoon fighter-bombers)

No. 144 Wing (three squadrons with Spitfire fighters)

air superiority and attacking German installations and communications before the commitment of the Allied invasion of Europe in *Overlord*. Air Vice Marshal H. Broadhurst assumed command on 24 March 1944, and by the eve of the landings

No. 83 Group had a strength of 29 squadrons, with fighter and ground-attack units predominating, but including four tactical reconnaissance and five artillery observation post squadrons.

Invasion commitment

The group was committed right from the start of the invasion, and squadrons were moved from the southern part of England to the Normandy lodgement as soon as there were airstrips available for their use. Throughout the northwest Europe campaign, No. 83 Group provided a very high quantity and quality of air support for the formations of the 21st Army Group, including the failed *Market Garden* operations to take and hold bridges over the Rhine river as far north as Arnhem, and the

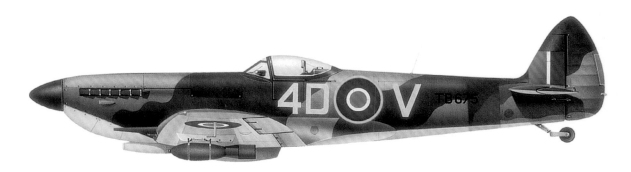

Specifications

Crew: 1

Powerplant: 1180kW (1580hp) 12-cylinder
   Merlin Packard 266 engine

Maximum speed: 642km/h (410mph)

Range: 698km (435 miles)

Service ceiling: 12,650m (41,500ft)

Dimensions: span 11.23m (36ft 10in);
   length 9.47m (31ft 1in);
   height 3.86m (12ft 8in)

Weight: 3343kg (7370lb) loaded

Armament: 2 x 12.7mm (0.5in) MGs and 2 x
   20mm (0.8in) cannons; plus 2 x 114kg (250lb)
   bombs under each wing

▲ Supermarine Spitfire Mk XVI
No. 74 Squadron / RAF, early 1945

The low-flying Spitfire Mk XVI was the last major production variant of the Merlin-engined Spitfire family, and was powered by a US-made Merlin. Other features were the clear-view canopy and a more pointed vertical tail surface. Some 1054 such aircraft were delivered from October 1944.

▲ de Havilland Mosquito FB.Mk VI
RAF, 1945

The Mosquito FB. Mk VI was the classic fighter-bomber variant of the Mosquito multi-role warplane family, and production totalled 2718 aircraft. The variant entered service in October 1943, and was operated in the day/night intruder and tactical support roles.

Specifications

Crew: 2

Powerplant: 2 x 1103kW (1480hp) Rolls-Royce
   Merlin 23 engines

Maximum speed: 595km/h (370mph)

Range: 2744km (1705 miles)

Service ceiling: 10,515m (34,500ft)

Dimensions: span 16.51m (54ft 2in);
   length 13.08m (42ft 11in);
   height 5.31m (17ft 5in)

Weight: 9072kg (20,000lb) loaded

Armament: 4 x 20mm (0.8in) cannons in
   wings, plus 4 x 7.7mm (0.303in) MGs in nose

squadrons 'leapfrogged' between airfields close to the frontline in order to keep pace with the Allied advance and exert pressure wherever there was a requirement.

The most important aircraft types flown by No. 83 Group at this time were the Hawker Typhoon Mk I fighter-bomber, Supermarine Spitfire Mk IX fighter and fighter-bomber, and North American Mustang Mk I reconnaissance fighter.

By the time of the German surrender in May 1945, the forward squadrons of No. 83 Group were operating from former *Luftwaffe* airfields in Germany itself, and the group then became part of the British occupation forces before being disbanded, with its squadrons subsequently absorbed into No. 84 Group on 21 April 1946.

WINGS OF NO. 83 GROUP (LATE 1944)			
Wing	Squadrons	Aircraft	Role
No. 39	Nos 168, 400 & 414	Mustang	Recce
No. 39	No. 420	Spitfire	Recce
No. 121	Nos 174, 175 & 245	Typhoon	Attack
No. 122	Nos 19, 65 & 122	Mustang	Fighter
No. 124	Nos 181, 182 & 247	Typhoon	Attack
No. 125	Nos 132, 453 & 602	Spitfire	Fighter
No. 126	Nos 401, 411 & 412	Spitfire	Fighter
No. 127	Nos 403, 416 & 421	Spitfire	Fighter
No. 129	No. 184	Typhoon	Attack
No. 143	Nos 438,439 & 440	Typhoon	Attack
No. 144	Nos 441, 442 & 443	Spitfire	Fighter

▲ 'County of Chester' Squadron

No. 610 Squadron of the Royal Auxiliary Air Force flew the Spitfire throughout the war, converting to the superlative Spitfire Mk XIV (pictured here) in January 1944.

No. 84 Group
1944–45

The partner of No. 83 Group within the 2nd TAF, No. 84 Group had AOP and reconnaissance units but was strongest in fighter and fighter-bomber units, with 26 squadrons in eight wings. No. 84 Group also included many units with personnel from occupied countries.

COMMANDED BY Air Vice Marshal L. O. Brown, No. 84 Group partnered No. 83 Group in the 2nd TAF, and had essentially the same role and therefore a comparable composition. The group had three rather than four reconnaissance squadrons with North American Mustang and Supermarine Spitfire aircraft, and two rather than five AOP squadrons with Auster aircraft. The main strength of No. 84 Group lay in its nine wings of Hawker Typhoon ground-attack

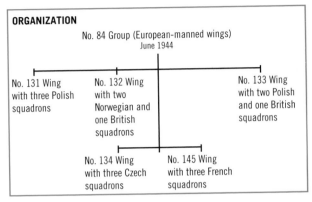

ORGANIZATION

No. 84 Group (European-manned wings)
June 1944

No. 131 Wing with three Polish squadrons

No. 132 Wing with two Norwegian and one British squadrons

No. 133 Wing with two Polish and one British squadrons

No. 134 Wing with three Czech squadrons

No. 145 Wing with three French squadrons

FIGHTER-BOMBER WINGS OF NO. 84 GROUP (JUNE 1944)			
Wing	**Squadrons**	**Aircraft**	**Role**
No. 123	Nos 98 & 609	Typhoon	Attack
No. 131	Nos 302, 308 & 317	Spitfire	Fighter
No. 132	Nos 66, 331 & 332	Spitfire	Fighter
No. 133	Nos 129, 306 & 315	Mustang	Fighter
No. 134	Nos 310, 312 & 313	Spitfire	Fighter
No. 135	Nos 222, 349 & 485	Spitfire	Fighter
No. 136	Nos 164 & 183	Typhoon	Attack
No. 145	Nos 329, 340 & 341	Spitfire	Fighter
No. 146	Nos 193, 197, 257 & 266	Typhoon	Attack

aircraft (three wings with eight squadrons), Mustang fighter-bombers (one wing with three squadrons) and Spitfire fighters and fighter-bombers (five wings with 15 squadrons). No. 84 Group also included large numbers of 'expatriate' pilots, for its overall order of battle included many foreign squadrons: five Polish, three Czechoslovak, two French, two Norwegian, one Belgian and one New Zealand.

▲ **North American Mustang Mk III**

No. 133 (Polish) Wing / 2nd TAF / northwest Europe, summer–autumn 1944

This was the personal aeroplane of No. 133 Wing's leader, Wing Commander Stanislaw Skalski, the highest-scoring Polish ace of World War II with at least 19 victories. The wing comprised the British No. 129 Squadron, and the Polish Nos 306 and 315 Squadrons.

Specifications

Crew: 1

Powerplant: 1081kW (1450hp) V-1650-3 engine

Maximum speed: 690km/h (430mph)

Range: 1215km (755 miles)

Service ceiling: 12,649m (41,500ft)

Dimensions: span 11.27m (37ft);

length 9.84m (32ft 4in);

height 4.15m (13ft 8in)

Weight: 4173kg (9200lb) loaded

Armament: 4 x 12.7mm (0.5in) MGs

▲ **Supermarine Spitfire Mk IXC**

No. 306 Squadron / No. 133 (Polish) Wing / No. 84 Group, summer 1944

No. 306 Squadron was one of the two Polish-manned squadrons in this wing.

Specifications

Crew: 1

Powerplant: 1175kW (1580hp) 12-cylinder
 Rolls-Royce Merlin 66 engine

Maximum speed: 642km/h (410mph)

Range: 698km (435 miles) on internal fuel tanks

Service ceiling: 12,650m (41,500ft)

Dimensions: span 11.23m (36ft 10in);
 length 9.47m (31ft 1in);
 height 3.86m (12ft 8in)

Weight: 3343kg (7370lb) loaded

Armament: 4 x 7.7mm (0.303in) MGs and 2 x
 20mm (0.8in) cannons

No. 85 Group
1944–45

No. 85 Group provided a number of support facilities for Nos 83 and 84 Groups. It aided the ground forces directly, but also covered the airfields from which the two more forward groups operated, providing nocturnal coverage against German bombers and fighter-bombers.

COMMANDED BY AIR Vice Marshal J. B. Cole-Hamilton and then, from 10 July, by Air Vice Marshal C. R. Steele, No. 85 Group provided backing for Nos 83 and 84 Groups with airfield construction, beach and balloon squadrons as well as frontline units. It had two wings of day-fighters and four wings of de Havilland Mosquito night-fighters, the latter tasked with protecting the 21st Army Group and all its installations from night attack by the *Luftwaffe*. The night-fighter wings totalled six squadrons, of which three were British, two Canadian and one New Zealand. The squadrons were very effective and, in the period between June 1944 and the end of World War II in Europe in May 1945, were credited with the destruction of some 200 German aircraft.

No. 85 Group's other two combat elements were Nos 141 and 150 Wings, each equipped with day-fighters. No. 141 Wing had three squadrons equipped with Supermarine Spitfire fighters, while No. 150 wing also possessed three squadrons. Of

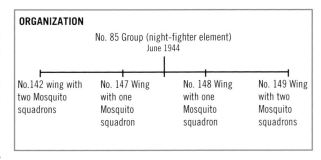

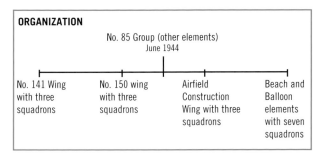

these three units, No. 56 Squadron was initially equipped with the Spitfire but converted to the superlative Hawker Tempest fighter on 6 July 1944 and thus flew the same type of warplane as its two sister units, namely Nos 3 and 486 Squadrons.

Initially based on airfields in the southeast of England, No. 85 Wing moved to France as soon as the situation permitted, and then followed in the wake of Nos 83 and 84 Groups as it had longer-range aircraft.

WINGS OF NO. 85 GROUP (1944)			
Wing	Squadrons	Aircraft	Role
No. 141	Nos 91, 124 & 322	Spitfire	Fighter
No. 142	Nos 264 & 602	Mosquito	Night-fighter
No. 147	No. 29	Mosquito	Night-fighter
No. 148	No. 409	Mosquito	Night-fighter
No. 149	Nos 410 & 488	Mosquito	Night-fighter
No. 150	No. 56	Spitfire	Fighter
No. 150	Nos 3 & 486	Tempest	Fighter

Push through Northwest Europe
SEPTEMBER 1944 – MAY 1945

By September 1944, the British and Canadian forces of the 21st Army Group had entered Belgium. After the setback of the Arnhem airborne operation and delay as the port of Antwerp was opened, they drove forward into north Germany to reach Hamburg by the end of the war.

THE SHAPE OF AIR fighting's future was foreshadowed in October 1944, even as the Allied armies were driving toward Germany's western frontier, by the arrival in service of the Messerschmitt Me 262 turbojet-powered fighter. Available only in small numbers and powered by very unreliable engines, the Me 262 was conceived specifically for this type of powerplant, unlike the slightly earlier straight-winged Arado Ar 234 bomber and the Gloster Meteor that was little more than a conventional fighter recast with two jet engines. The nature of the tactical air war remained

▲ **Hawker Typhoon Mk IB**

No. 175 Squadron / 2nd TAF, late 1944

No. 175 Squadron received Typhoons in mid 1943, when they became a part of the newly-formed 2nd TAF. The squadron supported the Normandy landings in June 1944, helping to wreck enemy communications networks. The squadron supported Twenty-First Army Group in the ground-attack role through the Low Countries and Germany until the end of the war.

Specifications

Crew: 1

Powerplant: 1685kW (2260hp) Napier Sabre II liquid cooled H-24 in-line piston engine

Maximum speed: 650km/h (405mph)

Range: 980km (610 miles)

Service ceiling: 10,400m (34,000ft)

Dimensions: span 12.67m (41ft 7in); length 9.73m (31ft 11in); height 4.66m (15ft 4in)

Weight: 5170kg (11,400lb) loaded

Armament: 4 x 20mm (0.8in) Hispano-Suiza HS.404 cannons, plus 8 x 27kg (60lb) rockets for ground attack purposes essentially unaltered, however, as the Germans lacked the numbers of aircraft and trained aircrew to make a dent in the Allied support for their ground forces, and they were also further constrained by increasingly scarce fuel reserves. The Allies could therefore operate essentially at will, watchful for only small numbers of German aircraft, with only the Me 262 and a dwindling number of aces flying late-model Focke-Wulf Fw 190s and Messerschmitt Bf 109s posing any real threat.

Two classic fighter-bomber raids of this period were undertaken by de Havilland Mosquito aircraft. On 31 October 1944, 25 Mosquitoes of Nos 21, 464 and 487 Squadrons made a very low-level attack on the Gestapo HQ at Aarhus in Denmark, destroying the building, killing 200 Germans and burning all the files on the Danish resistance. Then, on 31 December, Mosquitoes of No. 627 Squadron made a less successful attack of the same type on the Gestapo HQ in the Norwegian capital, Oslo.

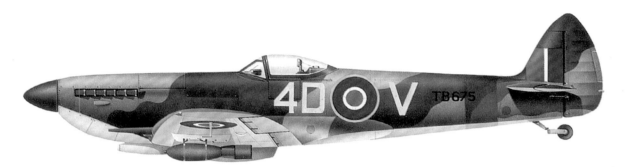

▲ Supermarine Spitfire Mk XVIE
No. 74 Squadron / 2nd TAF, Belgium, late 1944
Optimized for the lower-level role with bombs or rocket projectiles carried externally, the Spitfire Mk XVIE was a definitive member of the Spitfire family, and its 'E' type wing had two 20mm (0.79in) cannon and two 12.7mm (0.5in) MGs.

Specifications

Crew: 1
Powerplant: 1529kW (2050hp) 12-cylinder
  Griffon 65 engine
Maximum speed: 707km/h (439mph)
Range: 636km (395 miles)
Service ceiling: 12,650m (41,500ft)

Dimensions: span 11.23m (36ft 10in);
  length 9.47m (31ft 1in)
  height 3.86m (12ft 8in)
Weight: 3844kg (8475lb) loaded
Armament: 2 x 12.7mm (0.5in) MGs and 2 x
  20mm (0.8in) cannons; plus 2 x 114kg (250lb)
  bombs under each wing

▲ Supermarine Spitfire F.Mk XIVE
No. II Squadron, 1944
The Spitfire XIVE had shortened wings to improve the aircraft's rate of roll at low altitudes. This improved performance in the gound attack role, but gave the wings a 'clipped' appearance.

Specifications

Crew: 1
Powerplant: 1529kW (2050hp) 12-cylinder
  Griffon 65 engine
Maximum speed: 707km/h (439mph)
Range: 636km (395 miles)
Service ceiling: 12,650m (41,500ft)

Dimensions: span 11.23m (36ft 10in);
  length 9.47m (31ft 1in);
  height 3.86m (12ft 8in)
Weight: 3844kg (8475lb) loaded
Armament: 2 x 12.7mm (0.5in) MGs and 2 x
  20mm (0.8in) cannons

The *Luftwaffe*'s final raid

The *Luftwaffe* made its final major offensive one day later, sending some 800 aircraft against Allied air bases. The attack gained complete surprise and caused the loss of some 300 Allied aircraft, which could easily be replaced, while the Germans lost a comparable number, including some 200 by their own anti-aircraft guns. The Germans could not replace the few experienced men who were lost, and the tide of the air war flowed even more strongly in favour of the Allies, who were thus untroubled in the air for the rest of the war.

▼ 1944 Fighter Wing

By 1944, the Allies had fully absorbed the implications of the Germans' more loosely organized fighter practice, based on the key team of the leader and his wingman. The fighter wing of 1944, therefore, had three or four 16-aircraft squadrons, each operating in four flights, each comprising four aircraft in leader and wingman teams. Combined with superior equipment, such as the Hawker Tempest and late-model Supermarine Spitfire, this arrangement gave the British the tactical advantage.

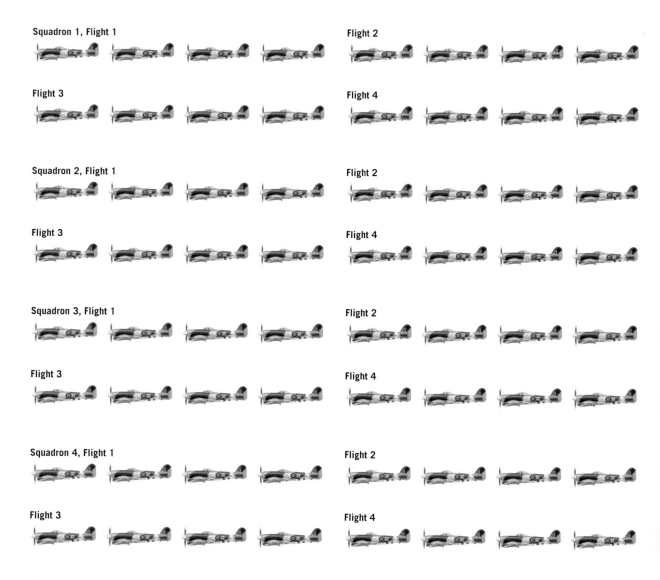

Squadron 1, Flight 1   Flight 2

Flight 3   Flight 4

Squadron 2, Flight 1   Flight 2

Flight 3   Flight 4

Squadron 3, Flight 1   Flight 2

Flight 3   Flight 4

Squadron 4, Flight 1   Flight 2

Flight 3   Flight 4

RAF Coastal Command
1943–45

Established in July 1936 to succeed the RAF's Coastal Area, Coastal Command protected the UK from naval attack, sought to destroy German surface raiders and U-boats while covering convoys and took the air war to Germany's coastal shipping. By 1943, it was winning its war.

COASTAL COMMAND was controlled operationally by the Admiralty for much of the war to maximize the UK's sea and air response to German surface and submarine threats. Within this context it also collaborated with the shore-based elements of the Fleet Air Arm in the UK, and with the Royal Navy's carrier forces in home waters and the North Atlantic.

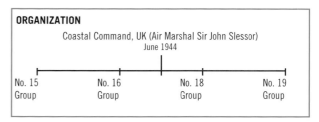

ORGANIZATION

Coastal Command, UK (Air Marshal Sir John Slessor)
June 1944

| No. 15 Group | No. 16 Group | No. 18 Group | No. 19 Group |

Coastal Command structure
In September 1939, the command had four groups, three of them operational round the coast of the UK: No. 16 Group in the eastern half of the English Channel and the southern half of the North Sea, No. 18 Group in the rest of the North Sea and areas to the north and west of Scotland, and No. 15 Group in the rest. In February 1941, No. 19 Group became active between Nos 18 and 15 Groups. In November 1940, No. 200 Group at Gibraltar was transferred to the control of Coastal Command from RAF Mediterranean, and in December 1941 No. 200 Group became RAF Gibraltar. Coastal Command also had in Iceland No. 30 Wing, which in July 1941 became RAF Iceland, and from mid-1943 No. 247 Group in the Azores.

Command aircraft
The command's equipment was initially inferior, especially where land-based aircraft were concerned.

Specifications
Crew: 3
Powerplant: 2 x 742kW (995hp) Bristol Mercury XV nine cylinder engine
Maximum speed: 266km/h (428mph)
Range: 2350km (1460 miles)
Service ceiling: 6705m (22,000ft)
Dimensions: span 17.17m (56ft 4in);
length 12.98m (42ft 7in);
height 3.90m (12ft 9in)
Weight: 6804kg (15,000lb) loaded
Armament: 1 x 7.7mm (.303in) MG in lead edge of port wing, 2 x 7.7mm (.303in) trainable MGs in dorsal turret, 2 x 7.7mm (.303in) forward-firing MGs in undernose blister position

▲ Bristol Blenheim Mk IVF
No. 248 Squadron / Coastal Command

No. 248 Squadron was one of 11 Coastal Command squadrons that flew the Blenheim Mk IVF in the medium-range fighter role, roaming out into the waters off the British Isles to watch for Germans surface raiders and U-boats, and to destroy German bomber and reconnaissance aircraft. They also attacked light craft in coastal waters.

▲ **Rocket attack**
The Beaufighter was a lethal maritime strike aircraft. Here, a Mk. X from No. 455 Squadron releases all eight rocket at once against a seaborne target.

MAJOR COASTAL COMMAND AIRCRAFT TYPES		
Aircraft	Role	No. of sqds
Avro Anson	Short-range recce	21
Bristol Beaufort	Torpedo	6
Bristol Beaufighter	Attack	13
Consolidated Catalina	Long-range recce	9
Consolidated Liberator	Long-range recce	12
de Havilland Mosquito	Attack	7
Handley Page Hampden	Torpedo & weather	7
Lockheed Hudson	Medium-range recce	17
Short Sunderland	Long-range recce	14
Vickers Warwick	Rescue & recce	10
Vickers Wellington	Medium-range recce	14

However, as the war progressed and the threat to convoys increased, Coastal Command received a higher priority, and by 1943 was well equipped in terms of its flying boats and land-based reconnaissance bombers.

Flying boats included the Short Sunderland and Consolidated Catalina, while the land-based types included the Vickers Wellington, Boeing B-17 Fortress and Consolidated Liberator. The first and the last two offered the ability to roam deep into the Arctic and Atlantic Oceans.

The arrival of the de Havilland Mosquito freed the Bristol Beaufighter for Coastal Command use in the shorter-range role. The Beaufighter became a very useful short-range aeroplane, operating with rockets and depth charges against U-boats in the Bay of Biscay. The type was also used in attacks on German shipping, even attacking German flak vessels. The Beaufighter was later supplemented in this role by the Mosquito fighter-bomber.

By the start of 1943, improvements in tactics and the introduction of electronic aids vastly improved the command's capability, and as shipping losses declined the U-boat kill rate rose. It was not so much the number sunk as the constant harassment they could inflict which made the aircraft effective: if the U-boats approached to make contact in daylight, they risked interception, and even night-time attacks were perilous.

During the war, Coastal Command flew more than 240,000 sorties, sank 212 U-boats and destroyed 478,000 tons of shipping, in the process losing 1777 aircraft and as many as 10,875 men.

Coastal Command strike wings
1944–45

The units that took the anti-ship war to the Germans were Coastal Command's strike wings, mostly located on the east coast of Scotland. They crossed the North Sea in search of coastal shipping in the Leads of occupied Norway's long western shore.

THE TWO AIRCRAFT types generally associated with the strike wings were the Bristol Beaufighter and de Havilland Mosquito twin-engined heavy fighter-bombers, the former armed with a torpedo and rockets, and the latter with bombs, rockets and occasionally a 57mm (2.24in) gun.

On 1 September 1944, No. 18 Group assumed control of RAF Banff, and the No. 144 Squadron's

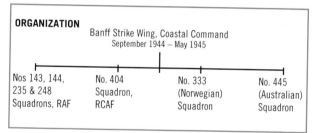

ORGANIZATION

Banff Strike Wing, Coastal Command
September 1944 – May 1945

Nos 143, 144, 235 & 248 Squadrons, RAF	No. 404 Squadron, RCAF	No. 333 (Norwegian) Squadron	No. 445 (Australian) Squadron

▲ **Banff Strike Wing**
No. 404 Squadron, RCAF, flew the Bristol Beaufighter from September 1942, receiving these Beaufighter TF.Mk X machines in September 1943.

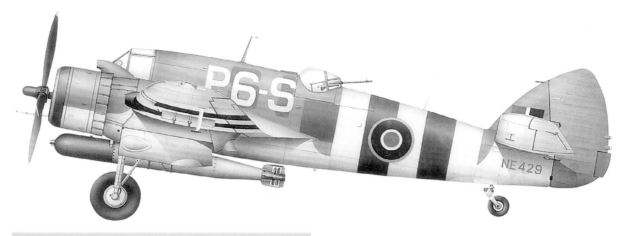

Specifications

Crew: 2

Powerplant: 2 x 1320kW (1770hp) Bristol

  Hercules XVII radial piston engines

Maximum speed: 488km/h (303mph)

Range: 2366km (1470 miles)

Service ceiling: 4570m (15,000ft)

Dimensions: span 17.63m (57ft 10in);

length 12.70m (41ft 8in);

height 4.83m (15ft 10in)

Weight: 11,431kg (25,200lb) loaded

Armament: 4 x 20mm (0.8in) cannon and 6

  x 7.7mm (.303in) MGs in wings; 1 x 7.7mm

  (.303in) Vickers MG in dorsal turret; 1 x

  torpedo

▲ Bristol Beaufighter TF.Mk X

No 489 (New Zealand) Squadron / RAF Coastal Command, UK, 1944–45

Sturdy and fast at low altitude, the Beaufighter TF.Mk X carried an air-launched torpedo under its fuselage, or rocket projectiles under its outer wing panels.

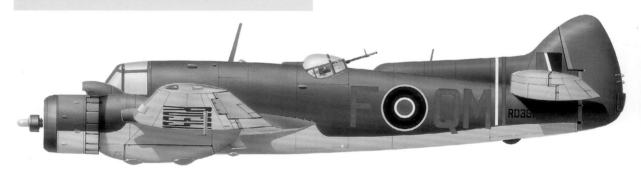

Specifications

Crew: 2

Powerplant: 2 x 1320kW (1770hp) Bristol

  Hercules XVII radial piston engines

Maximum speed: 488km/h (303mph)

Range: 2366km (1470 miles)

Service ceiling: 4570m (15,000ft)

Dimensions: span 17.63m (57ft 10in);

length 12.70m (41ft 8in);

height 4.83m (15ft 10in)

Weight: 11,431kg (25,200lb) loaded

Armament: 4 x 20mm (0.8in) cannon and 6

  x 7.7mm (.303in) MGs in wings; 1 x 7.7mm

  (.303in) Vickers MG in dorsal turret

▲ Bristol Beaufighter TF.Mk X

No. 254 Squadron / North Coates Strike Wing / RAF Coastal Command, UK, 1944

Late-service examples of the Beaufighter TF.Mk X were operated in a two-tone grey camouflage scheme optimized for use in the sky and sea conditions and colours prevalent in the North Sea and Norwegian Sea.

Beaufighters and Nos 235 and 248 Squadrons' Mosquitoes arrived, together with 'P' flight of No. 333 (Norwegian) Squadron (with Mosquitoes to act as outriders on the basis of its knowledge of the Norwegian coast), and finally No. 404 (Canadian) Squadron's Beaufighters. The commanding officer was Wing Commander F. W. Pierce.

First raid

The wing's first major effort was made on 14 September, when 25 Mosquitoes of Nos 235 and 248 squadrons, along with four of No. 248 Squadron's Mosquito Mk XVIIIs with the 57mm (2.24in) gun, flew a 'Rover' armed patrol with 19 Beaufighters of Nos 144 and 404 Squadrons. The

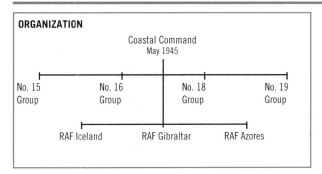

Coastal Command
May 1945

No. 15 Group   No. 16 Group   No. 18 Group   No. 19 Group

RAF Iceland   RAF Gibraltar   RAF Azores

COASTAL COMMAND SQUADRON TOTALS (MAY 1945)		
Group	Anti-submarine squadrons/strength	Anti-ship squadrons/strength
No. 15	7/100	0
No. 16	2.5/28	5/94
No. 18	8/105	9.5/180
No. 19	13/183	0
Iceland	2/30	0
Gibraltar	2/35	0
Azores	2/30	0

mission found four motor vessels with two escorts off Kristiansund and attacked, hits being scored on all vessels and fires started. The 268-tonne (264-ton) flagship *Sulldorf* was sunk and the 3376-tonne (3323-ton) merchant vessel *Iris* was damaged. The flak was intense, which forced one Beaufighter to ditch offshore.

On 19 September, another Rover with 21 Beaufighters and 11 Mosquitoes attacked a convoy of three ships near Askevold, sinking two of the merchantmen, one of 1389 tonnes (1367 tons) and the other of 3129 tonnes (3080 tons), for the loss of one No. 144 Squadron Beaufighter. On 21 September, 21 Beaufighters escorted by 17 Mosquitoes attacked and sank two merchant vessels, and five days later 16 Mosquitoes sank the *Biber* and damaged the *Storfsund* off the Hjeltefjord. Late in the month, the Mosquitoes were modified

to carry eight rockets. On 21 October, Mosquitoes of Nos 235 and 248 Squadrons and Beaufighters of No. 404 Squadron attacked shipping in Haugesend harbour, sinking the 1954-tonne (1923-ton) *Eckenheim* and 1455-tonne (1432-ton) *Vestpa* for the loss of one aeroplane.

North Sea raids

On 5 December, Mosquitoes of Nos 143, 235 and 248 Squadrons flew a major attack on shipping in the Nordgulenfjord, which resulted in four German vessels being damaged. These were the *Ostland*, *Tucuman*, *Magdalena* and *Helene Russ*. During this action, two Mosquitoes were badly hit, one of No. 143 Squadron reaching Sumburgh in the Shetlands on one engine and crash-landing, and the

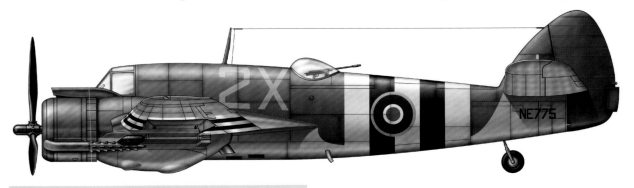

▲ **Beaufighter Mk VI**

RAF Coastal Command, 1944

Features of all but the first Beaufighters were the dihedralled rather than flat tailplane and, as development continued, enlargement of the vertical tail area with a long dorsal fillet.

Specifications

Crew: 2

Powerplant: 2 x 1230kW (1650hp) Bristol Hercules VI radial piston engines

Maximum speed: 488km/h (303mph)

Range: 2366km (1470 miles)

Service ceiling: 4570m (15,000ft)

Dimensions: span 17.63m (57ft 10in);

length 12.70m (41ft 8in);

height 4.83m (15ft 10in)

Weight: 11,431kg (25,200lb) loaded

Armament: 4 x 20mm (0.8in) cannon and 6 x 7.7mm (.303in) MGs in wings; 1 x 7.7mm (.303in) Vickers MG in dorsal turret; 8 x 41kg (90lb) rockets

ARMAMENT OF SELECTED COASTAL COMMAND AIRCRAFT			
Type	Guns	Bombs	Torpedo/rocket
Avro Anson I	2 x 7.7mm (0.3in)	163kg (360lb)	0
Bristol Beaufighter VI	4 x 20mm (0.8in) & 4x 7.7mm (0.3in)	2 x 113kg (250lb)	1/8
de Havilland Mosquito VI	4 x 20mm (0.8in) & 4x 7.7mm (0.3in)	4 x 227kg (500lb)	0/8
Consolidated Catalina I	4 x 7.7mm (0.3in)	907kg (2000lb)	0/0
Short Sunderland V	2 x 12.7mm (0.5in) & 12 x 7.7mm (0.3in)	907kg (2000lb)	0/0
Vickers Wellington III	8 x 7.7mm (0.3in)	2040kg (4500lb)	0/0

other of No. 248 Squadron being shot down. The latter aeroplane was seen to make an attack on a large, heavily armed ocean-going tug, and was on fire before making the attack. It later crashed into the sea. During the attack in the Nordgulenfjord, all aircraft encountered intense light flak from the whole of the eastern end of the anchorage, especially from the northern shore, some of the guns being positioned several hundred feet up the mountain side. Five other aircraft also had to land away from base, three of them on one engine; another four suffered damage.

On 7 December, a mixed sortie by 25 Mosquitoes from Banff and 40 Beaufighters from Dallachy, escorted by 12 Mustangs of No. 315 (Polish) Squadron, attacked the fighter airfield at Gossen in Norway. The formation was attacked by 12 Messerschmitt Bf 109 and Focke-Wulf Fw 190 fighters, and in the air battle that followed No. 315 Squadron claimed four Bf 109s downed. One Mustang, one Beaufighter and two Mosquitoes were lost.

On 10 December, an attack by Nos 143, 235 and 248 Squadrons' Mosquitoes attacked shipping in the Flekkefjord, and sank the 1508-tonne (1485-ton) *Gijdrun*. No aircraft were lost during the attack.

On 16 December, an attack force of Nos 143, 235 and 248 Squadrons attacked shipping at Malloy and Kraakbellesund. At the former the 5775-tonne (5684-ton) *Ferndale* was sunk, while at the latter the tug *Parat* was also sunk. During these actions, two Mosquitoes were lost. One was an aeroplane of No. 248 Squadron, which was hit by flak. This machine managed a controlled ditching. Both members of the crew were seen to leave the aeroplane and climb into their dinghy. A Vickers Warwick air-sea rescue aeroplane dropped a Lindholme dinghy. Up to the time when escorting aircraft had to return to base as they ran short of fuel, the two men were seen to be sitting up in the dinghy, but despite an intensive search of the area they were never found.

Thus the effort continued right into May 1945.

▼ **Coastal Command Squadron (1943–45)**

By the middle period of World War II, the organization of Coastal Command had settled into the workable pattern suggested by experience in the more fraught early stages of the war. The attack squadrons of Coastal Command, flying aircraft such as the Bristol Beaufighter and de Havilland Mosquito (below) in the second half of the war, thus had 12 aircraft subdivided into four three-aircraft flights.

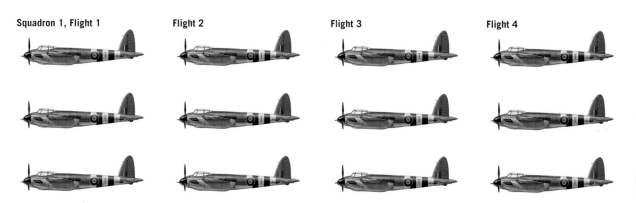

Squadron 1, Flight 1   Flight 2   Flight 3   Flight 4

Maritime fighters
1943–45

The fighters serving with Coastal Command and the Fleet Air Arm fell into two basic forms as large twin-engined strike fighters used only by Coastal Command, and smaller single-engined fighters used only by the FAA for both the carrierborne and land-based roles.

THE PRIMARY STRIKE fighters of RAF Coastal Command were a pair of substantial twin-engined aircraft, namely the Bristol Beaufighter and de Havilland Mosquito. The Beaufighter had been designed as a heavy fighter possessing a high degree of conceptual similarity with the Blenheim light bomber and Beaufort torpedo-bomber, and was powered by two Bristol Hercules radial engines.

Anti-shipping role

Entering service in September 1940, the Beaufighter was developed in four main variants for Coastal Command: 1) the initial Beaufighter Mk IC; 2) the Beaufighter Mk VIC with provision for an underfuselage torpedo; 3) the Beaufighter TF.Mk X development of the Mk VIC with greater power, radar and provision for underwing rockets; 4) the Beaufighter TF.Mk XI with no torpedo capability. Beaufighter-equipped strike wings became the

ORGANIZATION

Coastal Command Strike Wings
November 1942–May 1945

North Coates Strike Wing (Nos 143, 236 & 254 Squadrons)	Langham and Dallachy Strike Wing (Nos 455, 489 Squadrons)	Strubby and Dallachy Strike Wing (Nos 144 & 404 Squadrons)	Banff Strike Wing (Nos 143, 235, 248 & 333 Squadrons)

scourge of German shipping in the North Sea and English Channel; in two days during April 1945, Beaufighters sank five U-boats.

New fighter

Entering service in May 1943 in its fighter form, the de Havilland Mosquito was powered by two Rolls-Royce Merlin V-12 engines, and was used by Coastal Command in two primary variants. These entered

Specifications

Crew: 2

Powerplant: 2 x 1320kW (1770hp) Bristol Hercules XVII radial piston engines

Maximum speed: 488km/h (303mph)

Range: 2366km (1470 miles)

Service ceiling: 4570m (15,000ft)

Dimensions: span 17.63m (57ft 10in);

length 12.70m (41ft 8in);

height 4.83m (15ft 10in)

Weight: 11,431kg (25,200lb) loaded

Armament: 4 x 20mm (0.8in) cannon and 6 x 7.7mm (.303in) MGs in wings; 1 x 7.7mm (.303in) Vickers MG in dorsal turret; 2 x 113kg (250lb) bombs

▲ **Bristol Beaufighter TF.Mk X**

No. 455 (Australian) Squadron / Langham & Dallachy Strike Wing, mid-1944

One of the favourite weapons of Beaufighter strike squadrons was the 76mm (3in) rocket fitted with either an 11kg (25lb) solid armour-piercing or 27kg (60lb) explosive-filled semi-armour-piercing warhead. The projectile's accuracy was limited, but the full salvo of 16 such weapons was truly devastating.

service in May 1944, and were the Mosquito FB.Mk VI fighter-bomber (essentially similar to that used by Fighter Command with machine-gun and cannon armament as well as bombs or rocket projectiles), and the Mosquito FB.Mk XVIII, known as the 'Tsetse' for its sting in the offensive role, as the standard four 20mm (0.79in) cannon were replaced by a single 57mm (2.24in) adapted anti-tank gun.

Fleet Air Arm – North Atlantic
1943–45

Using increasing numbers of aircraft delivered by the United States as the primary equipment for its growing force of escort carriers, the Fleet Air Arm became a vital weapon in the battle of the North Atlantic against German U-boats.

D URING 1943, the Royal Navy's escort carrier strength increased rapidly, and this allowed most major convoys to be escorted by at least one such vessel. Built to mercantile rather than naval standards, and smaller than the fleet's large and light carriers, the escort carrier could be produced fairly quickly, and it was less of a loss, although still a blow, when such a vessel was sunk.

Several types of warplane saw service on the escort carriers, but the three most important were all products of the Grumman company. These

MAJOR DELIVERIES OF GRUMMAN AIRCRAFT TO THE ROYAL NAVY			
Aircraft	Role	Number	US Navy
Wildcat I, II & III	Fighter	100, 90 &10	F4F-3A
Wildcat IV	Fighter	200	F4F-4
Wildcat V & VI	Fighter	312 & 370	FM-1 & -2
Hellcat I	Fighter-bomber	252	F6F-3
Hellcat II	Fighter-bomber	930	F6F-5
Avenger I	Torpedo bomber	402	TBF-1
Avenger II & III	Torpedo bomber	334 & 222	TBM-1C & -3

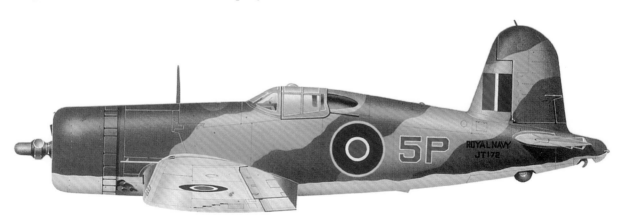

▲ **Vought Corsair Mk I**

No. 1835 Squadron / Fleet Air Arm / Brunswick, Nova Scotia, late 1943

The Royal Navy was an early operator of the Corsair, a highly effective land-based and carrierborne fighter well able to tackle surface as well as air targets.

Specifications

Crew: 1

Powerplant: 1678kW (2250hp) Pratt & Whitney R-2800-18W 18-cylinder radial engine

Maximum speed: 718km/h (446mph)

Range: 2511km (1560 miles)

Service ceiling: 12,650m (41,5000ft)

Dimensions: span 12.49m (41ft); length 10.27m (33ft 8in); height 4.50m (14ft 9in)

Weight: 6149kg (13,555lb) loaded

Armament: 6 x 12.7mm (0.5in) forward-firing MGs in wings

were the Wildcat (originally Martlet) fighter, the Hellcat fighter-bomber, and the Avenger torpedo and level bomber. All were powered by very reliable air-cooled radial engines, and while the Wildcat was useful primarily for patrol round the convoy and attacks on U-boats with its machine-gun armament, the Hellcat offered greater performance as well as the ability to carry two 454kg (1000lb) bombs or eight rocket projectiles, both effective anti-submarine weapons.

The Avenger offered a different level of capability with much longer endurance and the ability to carry one torpedo, or 907kg (1000lb) of bombs or rockets.

Specifications

Crew: 1

Powerplant: 1491kW (2000hp) Pratt & Whitley R-2800-10W radial piston engine

Maximum speed: 597km/h (371mph)

Range: 1674km (1040 miles)

Service ceiling: 11,186m (36,700ft)

Dimensions: span 13.06m (42ft 10in); length 10.24m (33ft 7in); height 4.39m (33ft 7in)

Weight: 4178kg (9212lb) loaded

Armament: 6 x 12.7mm (0.5in) wing-mounted MGs plus 6 x 27kg (60lb) rockets or 2 x 454kg (1000lb) bombs

▲ Grumman Hellcat Mk I

No. 800 Squadron / Fleet Air Arm / embarked on HMS Emperor, 1944

The potent carrierborne fighter known to the British as the Hellcat Mk I was the Lend-Lease counterpart of the US Navy's F6F-3 Hellcat, the first production variant of this successor to the Wildcat. Deliveries to the UK amounted to 252 aircraft.

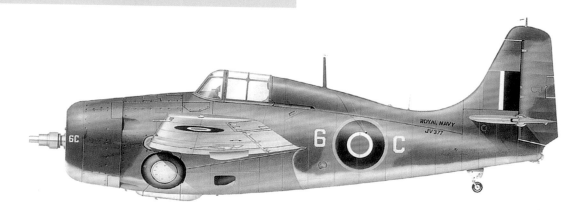

▲ Grumman Wildcat Mk VI

No. 882 Squadron / Fleet Air Arm

Wildcat Mk VI was the British designation for the FM-2, the last variant of the F4F Wildcat family and built by General Motors rather than Grumman. Some 370 FM-2s were transferred to the UK under the terms of the Lend-Lease Act.

Specifications

Crew: 1

Powerplant: 1007kW (1350hp) Pratt & Whitney R-1830-86 14-cylinder engine

Maximum speed: 507km/h (315mph)

Range: 1851km (1150 miles)

Service ceiling: 10,900m (35,700ft)

Dimensions: span 11.58m 38ft); length 8.76m (28ft 8in); height 2.81m (9ft 3in)

Weight: 3607kg (7952lb) loaded

Armament: 6 x 12.5mm (0.5in) MGs in wings; 2 x 113kg (249lb) bombs

Chapter 3

United States

In December 1941, when the United States was drawn
into World War II by the Japanese attack on Pearl Harbor,
the US Army Air Forces (USAAF) had 4002 combat aircraft.
By August 1945, at the time of Japan's surrender, this
strength had increased to 39,192, while over the same
period non-combat strength had grown from 12,297
to 63,475. Within the combat totals, the USAAF's fighter
strength rose from 2170 to 16,799 aircraft. This huge
growth in less than five years, was made possible only by
the USA's timely prewar decision to start a programme
of massive rearmament, and also to boost industrial
production to meet not only its own requirements
but those of the European nations fighting
the Germans.

◀ Cadillacs of the sky
P-51D Mustang fighters of the 357th Fighter Squadron, 361st Fighter Group, fly above England on their way to Germany, 1944.

Early organization
1942–43

The strategic air formation that the United States based in the UK was the Eighth Air Force. This formation grew from 1942 totals of four fighter, one medium bomber and 10 heavy bomber groups to March 1945 figures of nine fighter and 43 heavy bomber groups.

THE AMERICAN CONCEPT of how a major enemy should be defeated was already well established before the USA was drawn into World War II by the Japanese attack of 7 December 1941 on Pearl Harbor in the Hawaiian Islands. This event enlarged World War II by a huge extent, and what was now truly a

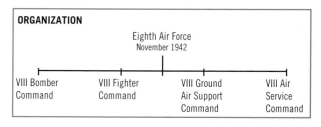

ORGANIZATION

Eighth Air Force
November 1942

| VIII Bomber Command | VIII Fighter Command | VIII Ground Air Support Command | VIII Air Service Command |

global conflict was further widened by Germany's declaration of war on the USA.

US military doctrine had long emphasized the paramount importance of a direct attack on a major enemy in massive strength and by the most direct route. This was primarily the task of the US Army, which would enjoy the benefits of powerful tactical air support from the USAAF, but a further role was planned for air power. This was the destruction, or at least the severe degradation, of the enemy's ability to wage or sustain a modern war by the systematic application of strategic air power.

The target of this strategic air power was the destruction of the German war industries by precision daylight bombing. The main targets for this effort

▲ **Mustang ace**

Fighter leader Captain Don Gentile scored 15.5 kills in the North American P-51 Mustang, flying with the 336th Fighter Squadron of the Eighth Air Force's 4th Fighter Group.

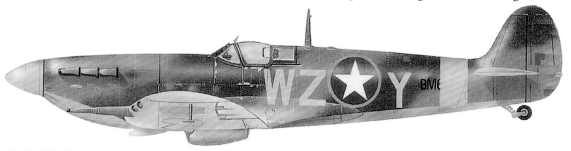

Specifications

Crew: 1

Powerplant: 1096kW (1470hp) Rolls-Royce
  Merlin 50 engine

Maximum speed: 594km/h (369mph)

Range: 1827km (1135 miles)

Service ceiling: 11,125m (36,500ft)

Dimensions: span 11.23m (36ft 10in);
  length 9.12m (29ft 11in);
  height 3.02m (9ft 11in)

Weight: 2911kg (6417lb) loaded

Armament: 4 x 7.7mm (0.303in) MGs and 2 x
  20mm (0.8in) cannons in wings

▲ **Supermarine Spitfire Mk VB**

309th Fighter Squadron / 31st Fighter Group, late 1942

To boost the number of capable combat aircraft available to it, the USAAF used small numbers of British aircraft, including this Spitfire Mk VB, which came with ex-'Eagle' squadron personnel, and later passed to the 67th Observation Group.

were most obviously key industrial targets, such as the factories in which aircraft and tanks were made, and – most importantly of all – any chokepoints in the industrial process, such as the few ball-bearing manufacturing facilities, whose destruction would reduce Germany's capacity for the manufacture of engines for aircraft, tanks and submarines, and even the machine tools on which all modern industrial processes were dependent. Another major target area was the communications needed to move raw material to the factories and deliver completed weapons to the armed forces.

PRODUCTION TOTALS FOR US FIGHTERS OPERATED OVER EUROPE			
Aircraft	Type	Entered service	Number built
Bell P-39 Airacobra	Fighter-bomber	1941	9590
Bell P-63 Kingcobra	Fighter-bomber	1943	3505
Lockheed P-38 Lightning	Fighter	1941	9393
North American P-51 Mustang	Fighter	1942	15,469
Republic P-47 Thunderbolt	Fighter	1943	15,634

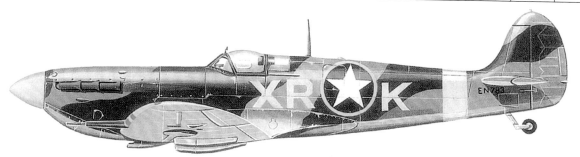

▲ **Supermarine Spitfire Mk VB**

334th Fighter Squadron / 4th Fighter Group, early 1943

The 4th Fighter Group was activated on 12 September 1942, as the RAF's Nos 71, 121 and 133 'Eagle' Squadrons (personnel and aircraft) were transferred to become the 334th, 335th and 336th Fighter Squadrons. The 4th Fighter Group claimed the highest total of German aircraft destroyed in the air and on the ground, and on 28 July 1943 was the first Eighth Air Force fighter group to fly over Germany itself.

Specifications

Crew: 1

Powerplant: 1096kW (1470hp) Rolls-Royce
   Merlin 50 engine

Maximum speed: 594km/h (369mph)

Range: 1827km (1135 miles)

Service ceiling: 11,125m (36,500ft)

Dimensions: span 11.23m (36ft 10in);
   length 9.12m (29ft 11in);
   height 3.02m (9ft 11in)

Weight: 2911kg (6417lb) loaded

Armament: 4 x 7.7mm (0.303in) MGs and 2 x
   20mm (0.8in) cannons in wings

Specifications

Crew: 1

Powerplant: 1891kW (2535hp) Pratt & Whitney
   R-2800-59W Double Wasp

Maximum speed: 697km/h (433mph)

Range: 3060km (1900 miles) with drop tanks

Service ceiling: 12,495m (41,000ft)

Dimensions: span 12.42m (40ft 9in);
   length 11.02m (36ft 2in);
   height 4.47m (14ft 8in)

Weight: 7938kg (17,500lb) maximum take-off

Armament: 8 x 12.7mm (0.5in) MGs in wings

▲ **Republic P-47C Thunderbolt**

334th Fighter Squadron / 4th Fighter Group, Debden, March 1943

After flying the Spitfire Mk V fighters it brought from service in the RAF's No. 71 'Eagle' Squadron, the 334th Fighter Squadron converted to P-47C heavy fighters.

Strategic bomber escort
1943–45

The Americans initially believed that the Boeing B-17 heavy bomber's high performance and defensive armament would permit daylight precision bombing without the need for fighter escort. Events proved them wrong, and the search was launched for a long-range escort.

THE USA BELIEVED that the way to win the war in Europe was by direct attack on Germany's primary strength by the ground forces, whose task would be aided by the air-delivered destruction of Germany's industrial and military production capabilities. This was the task of the strategic bomber forces which, the USAAF thought, had the right weapon in the form of the Boeing B-17 four-engined heavy bomber with the advanced Norden bomb sight. This was intended to allow bombing by day from high altitude with the accuracy to destroy key German industrial facilities.

'Box' formation

The bombers would fly at more than 7620m (25,000ft) in three-dimensional 'box' formations, these designed so that each bomber was covered by the guns of surrounding bombers. The 'boxes' were supposed to be relatively immune from interception except by small numbers of fighters, which would be defeated by the bombers' massed 12.7mm (0.5in) trainable machine guns.

It was a vain hope, as the Eighth Air Force's first forays into German air space soon revealed. Radar allowed the Germans to scramble fighters early enough to reach high altitude in some numbers. The German fighter pilots quickly established that the bombers were most vulnerable to head-on attacks,

ESCORT FIGHTERS OF THE EIGHTH AIR FORCE			
Type	Armament	Standard range	Range with drop tanks
Lockheed P-38L	1 x 20mm (0.79in) 4 x 12.7mm (0.5in)	1890km (1175 miles)	4185km (2600 miles)
North American P-51D	6 x 20mm (0.79in)	1530km (950 miles)	3700km (2300 miles)
Republic P-47D	8 x 12.7mm (0.5in)	1270km (790 miles)	2775km (1725 miles)

▲ 'Ferocious Frankie'
This bomb-loaded P-51D Mustang was the regular mount of Major Wallace Hopkins, commanding officer of the 374th Fighter Squadron, 361st Fighter Group.

and that it was possible to break into these 'boxes'. What the bombers needed was escort by fighters with the agility and firepower, and with the range to accompany the bombers to and from their targets.

The Republic P-47 and Lockheed P-38 provided a partial solution, but lacked the agility to cope with the superior German fighters (such as the Fw 190) and the range to remain with the bombers right through the mission. The solution appeared in the form of the P-51 Mustang, which was in itself a superb fighter, had considerable internal fuel capacity, and was finally fitted with drop tanks for prodigious range. The tanks were dropped before combat took place, the fighters then returning home after the sortie on internal fuel.

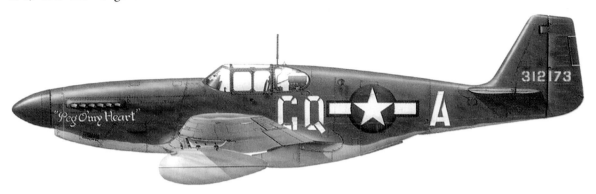

▲ North American P-51B Mustang

354th Fighter Squadron / 355th Fighter Group, spring 1944

The 355th Fighter Group reached Staple Morden, its home for the rest of the war, in July 1943, and its 354th, 357th and 358th Fighter Squadrons were equipped with the P-47D until February 1944. The group claimed more strafing victories than any other group of the Eighth Air Force.

Specifications

Crew: 1

Powerplant: 1044kW (1400hp) Rolls-Royce Merlin V-1650-3 12-cylinder engine

Maximum speed: 690km/h (430mph)

Range: 3540km (2200 miles)

Service ceiling: 12,649m (41,500ft)

Dimensions: span 11.27m (37ft); length 9.84m (32ft 4in); height 4.15m (13ft 8in)

Weight: 4173kg (9200lb) loaded

Armament: 6 x 12.7mm (0.5in) MGs

▲ Lockheed P-38L-5-LO Lightning

55th Fighter Squadron / 20th Fighter Group / King's Cliffe, mid-1944

The 57th, 77th and 79th Fighter Squadrons of the 20th Fighter Group took up station at King's Cliffe in August 1943 with the P-38H and P-38J variants of the Lightning, but converted to the P-51C in December 1944.

Specifications

Crew: 2

Powerplant: 2 x 1194kW (1600hp) Allison V-1710-111/113

Maximum speed: 666km/h (414mph)

Range: 4184km (2600 miles)

Service ceiling: 13,410m (20,000ft)

Dimensions: span 15.85m (52ft); length 11.53m (37ft 10in); height 2.99m (9ft 10in)

Weight: 9798kg (21,600lb) maximum takeoff

Armament: 1 x 20mm (0.8in) cannon and 4 x 12.7mm (0.5in) MGs in nose, plus 2 x 907kg (2000lb) bombs

Specifications

Crew: 1

Powerplant: 1081kW (1450hp) Rolls-Royce
  Merlin V-1650-3 12-cylinder engine

Maximum speed: 690km/h (430mph)

Range: 1215km (755 miles)

Service ceiling: 12,649m (41,500ft)

Dimensions: span 11.27m (37ft);
  length 9.84m (32ft 4in);
  height 4.15m (13ft 8in)

Weight: 4173kg (9200lb) loaded

Armament: 4 x 12.7mm (0.5in) MGs

▲ North American P-51B Mustang

374th Fighter Squadron / 361st Fighter Group, Bottisham, mid-1944

The 361st Fighter Group arrived at Bottisham with its 374th, 375th and 376th Fighter Squadrons in November 1943. The group first flew the P-47D, but converted to the P-51 in May 1944. Later homes were Little Walden, St Dizier, Chievres and, finally, Little Walden once more.

Specifications

Crew: 1

Powerplant: 1264kW (1695hp) Packard Merlin
  V-1650-7 V-12 piston engine

Maximum speed: 703km/h (437mph)

Range: 3347km (2080 miles)

Service ceiling: 12,770m (41,900ft)

Dimensions: span 11.28m (37ft);
  length 9.83m (32ft 3in);
  height 4.17m (13ft 8in)

Weight: 5488kg (12,100lb) loaded

Armament: 6 x 12.7mm (0.5in) MGs in wings,
  plus up to 2 x 454kg (1000lb) bombs

▲ North American P-51D Mustang

362nd Fighter Squadron / 357th Fighter Group, Leiston, mid-1944

Always equipped with Mustang variants, the 357th Fighter Group began its life in the Eighth Air Force at Raydon during November 1943, but two months later moved to Leiston with its 362nd, 363rd and 364th Fighter Squadrons.

Specifications

Crew: 2

Powerplant: 2 x 1276kW (1710hp) Rolls-Royce
  Merlin 12 cylinder piston engines

Maximum speed: 657km/h (408mph)

Range: 1963km (1220 miles)

Service ceiling: 9449m (31,000ft)

Dimensions: span 16.50m (54ft 2in);
  length 12.65m (41ft 6in);
  height 4.65m (15ft 3in)

Weight: 11,756kg (25,917lb) maximum takeoff

Armament: 4 x 20mm (0.8in) Hispano cannon
  and 4 x 7.7mm (0.303in) Browning MGs

▲ de Havilland Mosquito PR.Mk XVI (F-8)

653rd Bombardment Squadron / 25th Bombardment Group, Watton, mid-1944

Comprising the 652nd Bombardment Squadron (Heavy), 653rd Bombardment Squadron (Light) and 654th Bombardment Squadron (Special Purpose), the 25th Bombardment Group settled at Watton in April 1944. The heavy squadron flew the B-24, then B-17 four-engined bombers for weather reconnaissance over the Atlantic, while the light squadron flew the Mosquito in the same task over Europe.

▲ **Republic P-47D Thunderbolt**

USAAF, European theatre, late 1944

Operating in a basic plain metal finish with only small areas of olive drab on the upper fuselage, the P-47D was used late in World War II primarily for the heavy fighter-bomber role, carrying considerable ordnance and exploiting its speed and sturdy airframe.

Specifications

Crew: 1

Powerplant: 1891kW (2535hp) Pratt & Whitney R-2800-59W Double Wasp

Maximum speed: 697km/h (433mph)

Range: 3060km (1900 miles) with drop tanks

Service ceiling: 12,495m (41,000ft)

Dimensions: span 12.42m (40ft 9in); length 11.02m (36ft 2in); height 4.47m (14ft 8in)

Weight: 7938kg (17,500lb) maximum take-off

Armament: 8 x 12.7mm (0.5in) MGs in wings, plus provision for 1134kg (2500lb) external bombs or rockets

US Eighth Air Force
1942–45

The Eighth Air Force was schemed as a major formation of the USAAF to be based in England. It would fly Boeing B-17 and Consolidated B-24 four-engined heavy bombers in precision attacks to destroy Germany's industrial capacity and its ability to make and sustain modern warfare.

THE EIGHTH AIR FORCE had the specific task of strategic heavy bombing, attacking pinpoint targets in German industrial, communications and resources facilities. This, the Americans believed, would materially damage the ability of the Germans to make and sustain a modern type of warfare.

Accuracy was the keynote of the concept, and was to be provided by the use of the advanced Norden bomb sight by heavy bombers flying by day, and at high altitude to reduce the chances of the German fighter arm being able to effect any significant interceptions. This bombing campaign lasted from the summer of 1942 to the end of the war in Europe in May 1945.

USAAF COMBAT GROUPS IN THE EUROPEAN THEATRE			
Date	Light bomber	Medium bomber	Fighter
December 1942	1	6	14
December 1943	1	10	30
December 1944	4	13	29
March 1945	4	13	31

On 2 January 1942, the order creating the Eighth Air Force was signed, and the initial HQ was formed at Savannah, Georgia, on 28 January. On 8 January, it was announced that the organization of US Forces in the British Isles had been created, and the VIII

Bomber Command was established in England on 22 February 1942, with its initial HQ at RAF Bomber Command headquarters at High Wycombe. Additional commands of the Eighth Air Force were the VIII Air Support Command and VIII Fighter Command. During most of its existence in the UK, the Eighth Air Force had its headquarters at the Wycombe Abbey School for Girls in Buckinghamshire, and during World War II the Eighth Air Force was commanded successively by Major-General Carl A. Spaatz, Major General Ira C. Eaker, and Lieutenant-General 'Jimmy' Doolittle,

the last best known as the leader of the April 1942 carrier-launched B-25 'Doolittle' raid on Tokyo and a few other Japanese targets. The Eighth Air Force later became the US Air Forces in Europe.

First blood

On 4 July 1942, six US crews from the 15th Bombardment Group (Light), together with six RAF crews, took off from RAF Swanton Morley, in Norfolk, on a daylight attack against four airfields in the German-occupied Netherlands. This was the first occasion on which US airmen had flown in

▲ North American P-51B Mustang

353rd Fighter Squadron / 354th Fighter Group, mid 1944

The P-51B was the first Mustang variant with the Packard V-1650 (Rolls-Royce Merlin) engine instead of the Allison V-1710 unit. This turned the Mustang into a superb fighter. Other features of this machine are the bulged 'Malcolm' hood for improved fields of vision, and a dorsal fin for enhanced directional authority.

Specifications

Crew: 1	Dimensions: span 11.27m (37ft);
Powerplant: 1044kW (1400hp) Packard V-1650	length 9.84m (32ft 4in);
Rolls-Royce Merlin engine	height 4.15m (13ft 8in)
Maximum speed: 690km/h (430mph)	Weight: 4173kg (9200lb) loaded
Range: 3540km (2200 miles)	Armament: 6 x 12.7mm (0.5in) MGs
Service ceiling: 12,649m (41,500ft)	

▲ Supermarine Spitfire PR.Mk IX

14th Photographic Squadron / 7th Photographic Group, Mount Farm, 1944

Reaching its English base in July 1943, the 7th Photographic Group's components were the 13th, 14th, 22nd and 27th Photographic Squadrons. The group's standard aircraft early in its career were the F-4 and F-5 variants of the P-38 Lightning, but there were also some Spitfires and, later, the P-51D and P-51K.

Specifications

Crew: 1	Dimensions: span 11.23m (36ft 10in);
Powerplant: 1170kW (1565hp) 12-cylinder	length 9.47m (31ft 1in);
Rolls-Royce Merlin 61 engine	height 3.86m (12ft 8in)
Maximum speed: 642km/h (410mph)	Weight: 3343kg (7370lb) loaded
Range: 698km (435 miles) on internal fuel tanks	Armament: 4 x 7.7mm (0.303in) MGs and 2 x
Service ceiling: 12,650m (41,500ft)	20mm (0.8in) cannons

American-built bombers against a German target. The event was of considerable historical importance, but in itself the raid was not in any way a significant success. Two of the US-crewed aircraft succumbed to German anti-aircraft fire. A start had been made, and before it ended its campaign the Eighth Air Force flew 332,904 sorties and dropped 633,260 tonnes (623,288 tons) of bombs on German targets on the European mainland. The campaign cost the Eighth Air Force large numbers of men and aircraft, losses peaking at 420 machines in April 1944.

USAAF TACTICAL WARPLANE STRENGTHS		
Date	Light/medium bomber	Fighter
December 1941	1544	2170
December 1942	3757	5303
December 1943	6741	11,875
December 1944	9169	17,198
August 1945	8463	16,799

Specifications

Crew: 1

Powerplant: 1044kW (1400hp) Packard V-1650
 Rolls-Royce Merlin engine

Maximum speed: 690km/h (430mph)

Range: 3540km (2200 miles)

Service ceiling: 12,649m (41,500ft)

Dimensions: span 11.27m (37ft);
 length 9.84m (32ft 4in);
 height 4.15m (13ft 8in)

Weight: 4173kg (9200lb) loaded

Armament: 6 x 12.7mm (0.5in) MGs

▲ North American P-51B Mustang

364th Fighter Squadron / 357th Fighter Group, Leiston, early 1944

Among the distinctions of the 357th Fighter Group were the facts that it was the first Mustang group in the Eighth Air Force, had a faster rate of aerial victories than any other Eighth Air Force group in the last 12 months of the war, and had the highest claims for one mission, on 14 January 1945, at 45 shot down and 56 probably downed.

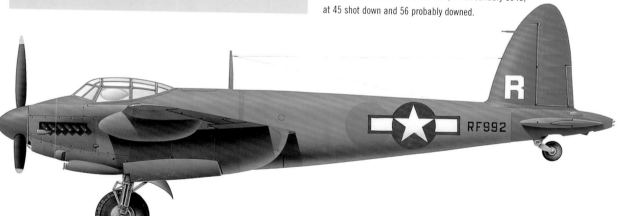

▲ de Havilland Mosquito PR.Mk XVI

25th Bombardment Group (Reconnaissance) / 325th Photographic Wing, Watton, summer 1944

Able to fly high and fast over German-held territory with only minimum chance of interception, the Mosquito PR.Mk XVI was used for weather reconnaissance.

Specifications

Crew: 2

Powerplant: 2 x 1276kW (1710hp) Rolls-Royce
 Merlin 12-cylinder piston engines

Maximum speed: 657km/h (408mph)

Range: 1963km (1220 miles)

Service ceiling: 9449m (31,000ft)

Dimensions: span 16.50m (54ft 2in);
 length 12.65m (41ft 6in);
 height 4.65m (15ft 3in)

Weight: 11,756kg (25,917lb) maximum takeoff

Armament: 4 x 20mm (0.8in) Hispano cannon
 and 4 x 7.7mm (0.303in) Browning MGs

▼ 1944 US Eighth Air Force Fighter Group

The standard fighter group of the Eighth Air Force in 1944 was three squadrons each of four flights, each flight being composed of two elements, each comprising a leader and his wing man. This organization gave the squadron 16 aircraft, and the group 48 aircraft. By this time, US production and training were running at rates so high that squadrons seldom lacked either aircraft or the pilots to man them.

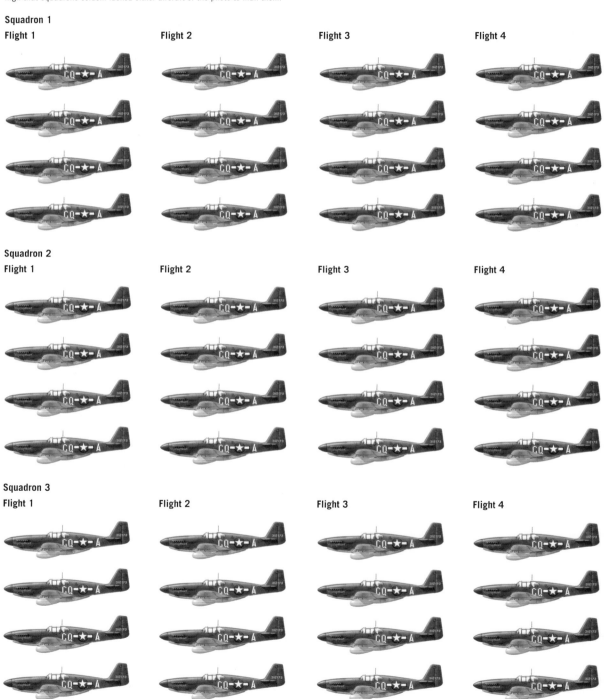

Squadron 1

Flight 1   Flight 2   Flight 3   Flight 4

Squadron 2

Flight 1   Flight 2   Flight 3   Flight 4

Squadron 3

Flight 1   Flight 2   Flight 3   Flight 4

VIII Fighter Command
1942–45

VIII Fighter Command was created largely to provide escort for the bombers of VIII Bomber Command. Early tactics laying down the advisability of close escort gradually gave way to the practice of searching out the opposition and destroying it in the air and on the ground.

THE VIII FIGHTER Command was the fighter arm of the Eighth Air Force, and eventually consisted of 15 three-squadron groups in three wings. It was led for most of its existence by Major-General Willliam E. Kepner, who assumed command in August 1943. In June 1944, the command had six Thunderbolt, five Mustang and four Lightning groups, the last soon disappearing and only one unit still flying the Thunderbolt at the end of the war. Providing escort for VIII Bomber Command was the command's primary role.

Limited range

The P-47 lacked the range to take bombers far beyond the German border, and the P-38 had high-altitude engine problems. But with the arrival of large

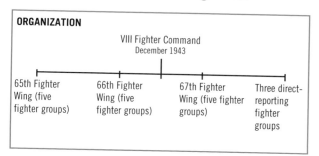

ORGANIZATION

VIII Fighter Command
December 1943

65th Fighter Wing (five fighter groups)	66th Fighter Wing (five fighter groups)	67th Fighter Wing (five fighter groups)	Three direct-reporting fighter groups

numbers of P-51s early in 1944, the tide stared to turn. From January 1944, the fighters were no longer tied closely to the bombers but were freed to take the air war to the Germans at all altitudes, including their airfields. *Luftwaffe* losses rose to unsustainable levels, but bomber losses fell.

Specifications

Crew: 1

Powerplant: 1264kW (1695hp) Packard Merlin V-1650-7 V-12 piston engine

Maximum speed: 703km/h (437mph)

Range: 3347km (2080 miles)

Service ceiling: 12,770m (41,900ft)

Dimensions: span 11.28m (37ft); length 9.83m (32ft 3in); height 4.17m (13ft 8in)

Weight: 5488kg (12,100lb) loaded

Armament: 6 x 12.7mm (0.5in) MGs in wings, plus up to 2 x 454kg (1000lb) bombs

▲ **North American P-51D Mustang**

487th Fighter Squadron / 352nd Fighter Group, Chievres and Bodney, April 1945

This was the aeroplane of Major William Halton, commander of the squadron. By this late stage of the war, most US warplanes were flown in plain metal finish leavened by national, unit and personal markings.

▲ North American P-51D-5-NA Mustang
343rd Fighter Squadron / 55th Fighter Group, early 1945
This aircraft was flown by American ace Lt. E. Robert Welch. He notched up six kills and 12 aircraft destroyed on the ground. The red 'prancing horse' logo on the tailplane was used by the squadron from late 1944 onwards.

Specifications
Crew: 1

Powerplant: 1264kW (1695hp) Packard Merlin
V-1650-7 V-12 piston engine

Maximum speed: 703km/h (437mph)

Range: 3347km (2080 miles)

Service ceiling: 12,770m (41,900ft)

Dimensions: span 11.28m (37ft);
length 9.83m (32ft 3in);
height 4.17m (13ft 8in)

Weight: 5488kg (12,100lb) loaded

Armament: 6 x 12.7mm (0.5in) MGs in wings,
plus up to 2 x 454kg (1000lb) bombs

▲ North American P-51D Mustang
352nd Fighter Squadron / 353rd Fighter Group, late 1944–early 1945
Like most US fighter groups, the 353rd Fighter Group removed most of the camouflage from its P-51D and P-51K aircraft as being unnecessary in the face of the Luftwaffe's decline, adding weight and increasing drag.

Specifications
Crew: 1

Powerplant: 1264kW (1695hp) Packard Merlin
V-1650-7 V-12 piston engine

Maximum speed: 703km/h (437mph)

Range: 3347km (2080 miles)

Service ceiling: 12,770m (41,900ft)

Dimensions: span 11.28m (37ft);
length 9.83m (32ft 3in);
height 4.17m (13ft 8in)

Weight: 5488kg (12,100lb) loaded

Armament: 6 x 12.7mm (0.5in) MGs in wings,
plus up to 2 x 454kg (1000lb) bombs

ALLIED FIGHTER PRODUCTION		
Year	UK	USA
1939	1324	n/a
1940	4283	1162
1941	7064	4416
1942	9849	10,769
1943	10,727	23,988
1944	10,730	38,873
1945	5445	20,742

BOMB TONNAGES DROPPED IN EUROPE		
Year	Bomber Command	US Eighth Air Force
1942	18,703	1411
1943	157,367	44,185
1944	525,518	389,119
1945	181,740	188,573
Totals	883,328	623,288

65th Fighter Wing
1942–45

While the fighter group, with its three squadrons, was the cornerstone of the Eighth Air Force's ability to provide tactical support for its bombers, it was administratively sensible to concentrate the groups into three high-level command bodies, namely the fighter wings.

THE EIGHTH AIR FORCE'S fighter groups were assigned for administrative purposes to three fighter wings, each of them under the direct control of VIII Fighter Command until September 1945, when each of the three wings was assigned to one of the three bomb (later air) divisions. This restructing simplified the chain of command and also facilitated the planning of fighter support for the bombers of each division. It should be noted, however, that while each fighter wing was intended to support the bombers of its own division, in practice the fighter wings often provided support for the bombers of other divisions.

In the short term, VIII Fighter Command retained responsibility for three training organizations, namely the 495th and 496th Fighter Groups and the 1st Combat Crew Gunnery School, but late in November 1944 these too passed to the direct control

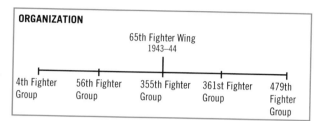

ORGANIZATION

65th Fighter Wing
1943–44

| 4th Fighter Group | 56th Fighter Group | 355th Fighter Group | 361st Fighter Group | 479th Fighter Group |

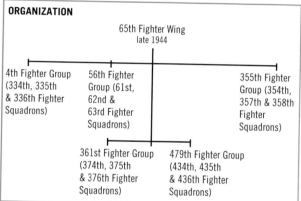

ORGANIZATION

65th Fighter Wing
late 1944

4th Fighter Group (334th, 335th & 336th Fighter Squadrons)

56th Fighter Group (61st, 62nd & 63rd Fighter Squadrons)

355th Fighter Group (354th, 357th & 358th Fighter Squadrons)

361st Fighter Group (374th, 375th & 376th Fighter Squadrons)

479th Fighter Group (434th, 435th & 436th Fighter Squadrons)

▲ **North American P-51D Mustang**

375th Fighter Squadron / 361st Fighter Group, early 1945

The P-51 was a superb example of the fighter designer's art, with excellently harmonized controls. The ventral radiator installation lowered drag and actually produced some thrust as the heated cooling air was discharged, and the contents of the cheap impregnated paper drop tanks added considerable range.

Specifications

Crew: 1

Powerplant: 1264kW (1695hp) Packard Merlin V-1650-7 V-12 piston engine

Maximum speed: 703km/h (437mph)

Range: 3347km (2080 miles)

Service ceiling: 12,770m (41,900ft)

Dimensions: span 11.28m (37ft); length 9.83m (32ft 3in); height 4.17m (13ft 8in)

Weight: 5488kg (12,100lb) loaded

Armament: 6 x 12.7mm (0.5in) MGs in wings, plus up to 2 x 454kg (1000lb) bombs

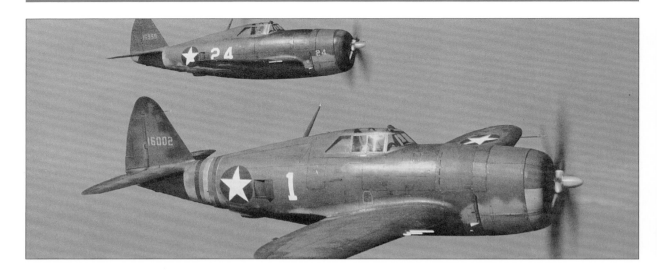

▲ **'Razorback' design**

These early P-47Bs have the classic 'razorback' design. The lead aircraft is flown by P-47 ace Hubert Zemke.

of the air divisions. The VIII Fighter Command order of battle was based on three fighter wings, as noted above, and the lowest numbered of these was the 65th Fighter Wing, which had its headquarters at the Dane Bradbury School at Saffron Walden, and in September 1944 was reassigned from the VIII Fighter Command to the 2nd Bomb Division (from January 1945, the 2nd Air Division).

The 65th Fighter Wing's components consisted of the following: the 4th Fighter Group 'The Eagles' (the 334th, 335th and 336th Fighters Squadrons with the Spitfire, Thunderbolt and Mustang respectively) based at Debden from September 1942 to April 1943, and then at Steeple Morden to the end of the war; the 56th Fighter Group (61st, 62nd and 63rd Fighter Squadrons with the Thunderbolt) based at King's Cliffe, Horsham St Faith, Halesworth, Boxted and Little Walden between January 1943 and the end of the war; the 355th Fighter Group (354th, 357th and

Specifications

Crew: 1	Dimensions: span 11.28m (37ft);
Powerplant: 1264kW (1695hp) Packard Merlin	length 9.83m (32ft 3in);
V-1650-7 V-12 piston engine	height 4.17m (13ft 8in)
Maximum speed: 703km/h (437mph)	Weight: 5488kg (12,100lb) loaded
Range: 3347km (2080 miles)	Armament: 6 x 12.7mm (0.5in) MGs in wings,
Service ceiling: 12,770m (41,900ft)	plus up to 2 x 454kg (1000lb) bombs

▲ **North American P-51D Mustang**

355th Fighter Group, Steeple Morden, 1945

This was the aeroplane of the group's commander, Lieutenant-Colonel Claiborne H. Kinnard, Jr., who led the group between 21 February and 7 June 1945.

358th Fighter Squadrons with Thunderbolt and Mustang) based at Steeple Morden from July 1943 to the end of the war; the 361st Fighter Group (374th, 375th and 376th Fighter Squadrons with Thunderbolt and Mustang) based at Bottisham, Little Walden, St Dizier, Chievres and, finally, Little Walden once again; and lastly the 479th Fighter Group, known as 'Riddle's Raiders' (434th, 435th and 436th Fighter Squadrons with the Lightning and Mustang), based at Wattisham from May 1944.

THUNDERBOLT ACES OF THE 56TH FIGHTER GROUP		
Name	Unit	Victories
Francis Gebreski	56th FG	28
Robert S. Johnson	56th FG	27
David Schilling	56th FG	22.5
Fred Christenson	56th FG	21.5
Walter Mahurin	56th FG	19
Hubert Zemke	56th FG	18
Gerald Johnson	56th FG	16.5

66th Fighter Wing
1942–45

Like the other fighter wings of the VIII Fighter Command, the 66th Fighter Wing was based on the standard five-group organization, and from its inception in December 1942 became one of the finest fighting elements of the Eighth Air Force.

THE 66TH FIGHTER Wing had its headquarters at Sawston Hall, near Cambridge, and was later transferred from the control of the VIII Fighter Command to the 3rd Bomb Division (later 3rd Air Wing). The 66th Fighter Wing was of standard fighter wing strength inasmuch as it controlled five fighter groups.

ORGANIZATION

66th Fighter Wing
1943–45

| 55th Fighter Group | 78th Fighter Group | 339th Fighter Group | 353rd Fighter Group | 357th Fighter Group |

Specifications

Crew: 1

Powerplant: 1264kW (1695hp) Packard Merlin V-1650-7 V-12 piston engine

Maximum speed: 703km/h (437mph)

Range: 3347km (2080 miles)

Service ceiling: 12,770m (41,900ft)

Dimensions: span 11.28m (37ft); length 9.83m (32ft 3in); height 4.17m (13ft 8in)

Weight: 5488kg (12,100lb) loaded

Armament: 6 x 12.7mm (0.5in) MGs in wings, plus up to 2 x 454kg (1000lb) bombs

▲ **North American P-51K Mustang**

362nd Fighter Squadron / 357th Fighter Group, Leiston, early 1945

From December 1944 many of the 357th Fighter Group's P-51D and P-51K fighters were stripped of camouflage, but for anti-glare purposes retained green paint on the upper fuselage forward of the cockpit.

The 55th Fighter Group was based at Nuthampstead from September 1943 and then Wormingford from April 1944 to the end of the war. It had the 38th, 338th and 343rd Fighter Squadrons flying Lightnings and then Mustangs. The 78th Fighter Group was based at Goxhill from December 1942 and then Duxford from April 1943 to the end of the war, and had the 82nd, 83rd and 84th Fighter Squadrons with the Lightning, Thunderbolt and Mustang. The 339th Fighter Group based at Fowlmere from April 1944 to the end of the war had the 503rd, 504th and 505th Fighter Squadrons with the Mustang. The 353rd Fighter Group was based at Goxhill between June and August 1943, Metfield between August 1943 and April 1944, and finally Raydon for the rest of the war. It had the 350th, 351st and 352nd Fighter Squadrons with the Thunderbolt and then the Mustang. Finally the 357th Fighter Group, based at Raydon between November 1943 and January 1944, and then Leiston for the rest of the war, had the 362nd, 363rd and 364th Fighter Squadrons with the Mustang, which it introduced in the Eighth Air Force.

▲ **North American P-51K Mustang**

362nd Fighter Squadron / 357th Fighter Group, Leiston, late 1944

This was the aeroplane of Captain Leonard Kit Carson, who on 27 November 1944 shot down five German fighters in a single engagement.

Specifications

Crew: 1

Powerplant: 1264kW (1695hp) Packard Merlin V-1650-7 V-12 piston engine

Maximum speed: 703km/h (437mph)

Range: 3347km (2080 miles)

Service ceiling: 12,770m (41,900ft)

Dimensions: span 11.28m (37ft); length 9.83m (32ft 3in); height 4.17m (13ft 8in)

Weight: 5488kg (12,100lb) loaded

Armament: 6 x 12.7mm (0.5in) MGs in wings, plus up to 2 x 454kg (1000lb) bombs

Specifications

Crew: 1

Powerplant: 1264kW (1695hp) Packard Merlin V-1650-7 V-12 piston engine

Maximum speed: 703km/h (437mph)

Range: 3347km (2080 miles)

Service ceiling: 12,770m (41,900ft)

Dimensions: span 11.28m (37ft); length 9.83m (32ft 3in); height 4.17m (13ft 8in)

Weight: 5488kg (12,100lb) loaded

Armament: 6 x 12.7mm (0.5in) MGs in wings, plus up to 2 x 454kg (1000lb) bombs

▲ **North American P-51D Mustang**

362nd Fighter Squadron / 357th Fighter Group, late 1944

The omission of most camouflage paint, which was not needed in the absence of effective German fighter opposition, saved maintenance time and cost, and added slightly to the aeroplane's maximum speed.

67th Fighter Wing
1943–45

Another five-group formation, the 67th Fighter Wing provided escort for the bombers of the Eighth Air Force, and was then let off the leash to a modest degree to serve the bombers better by taking the war to the German fighter arm on the ground as well as in the air.

THE 67TH FIGHTER Wing was headquartered at Walcot Hall, near Stamford, and in September 1944 was reallocated from the VIII Fighter Command to the 1st Bomb Division (from January 1945 the 1st Air Division, an integrated formation with its own bomber and fighter elements). The 67th Fighter Wing had the standard five fighter groups.

The 20th Fighter Group was based at King's Cliffe from August 1943, and its three component units were the 55th, 77th and 79th Fighter Squadrons, which flew the P-38 Lightning to July 1944, when they transitioned to the P-51 Mustang for the rest of the war. The 352nd Fighter Group was based at Bodney from July 1943, with detachments at Asche and Chievres on the European mainland between December 1944 and April 1945. Its components were the 328th, 486th and 487th Fighter Squadrons with the Thunderbolt in its P-47D variant between July 1943 and April 1944, and then the Mustang in its P-51B, P-51C, P-51D and P-51K variants thereafter for the rest of the war. The 356th Fighter

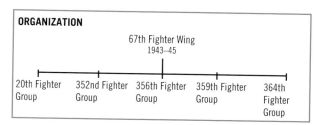

ORGANIZATION

67th Fighter Wing
1943–45

| 20th Fighter Group | 352nd Fighter Group | 356th Fighter Group | 359th Fighter Group | 364th Fighter Group |

Group was based at Goxhill between August and October 1943 before settling at Martlesham Heath for the rest of the war, and its components were the 359th, 360th and 361st Fighter Squadrons, which flew the Thunderbolt in its P-47D form to November 1944 before transitioning to the Mustang in its P-51D and P-51K forms for the rest of the war.

The 359th Fighter Group was based at East Wretham from October 1943 to the end of the war, and its components were the 368th, 369th and 370th Fighter Squadrons, which flew the Thunderbolt in its P-47D form to May 1944, when they transitioned to the Mustang, in its P-51B, P-51C, P-51D and P-51K forms, for the rest of the war.

The 364th Fighter Group was based at Honington from February 1944 to the end of the war, and its components were the 382rd, 384th and 385th Fighter Squadrons, which flew the Lightning in its P-38J form to July 1944 before converting to the Mustang, in its P-51D form, for the rest of the war.

▲ **P-51 power**

This P-51D Mustang carries the auxiliary fuel tanks introduced in late 1943 for long-range bomber escort duties.

MUSTANG ACES OF THE EIGHTH AIR FORCE		
Name	Unit	Victories
George Preddy	352nd FG	25.83
John Meyer	352nd FG	24
Ray Wetmore	359th FG	21.25
Don Gentile	4th FG	19.83
Duncan Glenn	353rd FG	19
Walter Beckham	353rd FG	18
Duane Beeson	4th FG	17.33

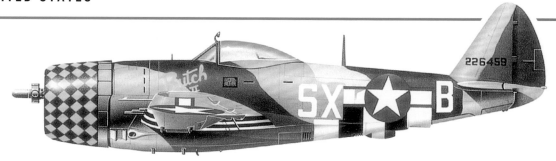

Specifications

Crew: 1

Powerplant: 1891kW (2535hp) Pratt & Whitney
R-2800-59W Double Wasp

Maximum speed: 697km/h (433mph)

Range: 3060km (1900 miles) with drop tanks

Service ceiling: 12,495m (41,000ft)

Dimensions: span 12.42m (40ft 9in); length
11.02m (36ft 2in); height 4.47m (14ft 8in)

Weight: 7938kg (17,500lb) maximum take-off

Armament: 8 x 12.7mm (0.5in) MGs in wings,
plus provision for 1134kg (2500lb) external
bombs or rockets

▲ Republic P-47D Thunderbolt

352nd Fighter Squadron / 353rd Fighter Group, Raydon, July 1944

The Thunderbolt was much improved as a fighter in its later forms with the
original pattern of framed canopy, forward of the 'razorback' upper rear fuselage,
replaced by a clear-view canopy and cut-down rear decking.

Specifications

Crew: 1

Powerplant: 1264kW (1695hp) Packard Merlin
V-1650-7 V-12 piston engine

Maximum speed: 703km/h (437mph)

Range: 3347km (2080 miles)

Service ceiling: 12,770m (41,900ft)

Dimensions: span 11.28m (37ft);
length 9.83m (32ft 3in);
height 4.17m (13ft 8in)

Weight: 5488kg (12,100lb) loaded

Armament: 6 x 12.7mm (0.5in) MGs in wings,
plus up to 2 x 454kg (1000lb) bombs

▲ North American P-51D Mustang

*369th Fighter Squadron / 359th Fighter Group, East Wretham,
November 1944*

This was the aeroplane of 1st Lieutenant Claude Crenshaw, who ended the war
with seven air and three ground 'kills'. His best day was 21 November 1944,
when Crenshaw downed four Focke-Wulf Fw 190 fighters.

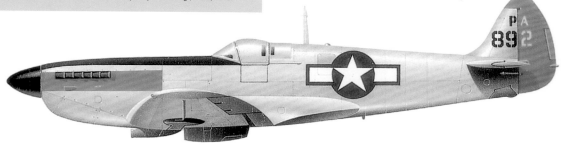

Specifications

Crew: 1

Powerplant: 1170kW (1565hp) 12-cylinder Rolls-
Royce Merlin 61 engine

Maximum speed: 642km/h (410mph)

Range: 698km (435 miles) on internal fuel tanks

Service ceiling: 12,650m (41,500ft)

Dimensions: span 11.23m (36ft 10in); length
9.47m (31ft 1in); height 3.86m (12ft 8in)

Weight: 3343kg (7370lb) loaded

Armament: 4 x 7.7mm (0.303in) MGs and 2 x
20mm (0.8in) cannons

▲ Supermarine Spitfire PR.Mk IX

7th Photographic Group

The group flew a combination of F-5 (P-38), P-51 and Spitfire IX photo/recon
aircraft to obtain information about bombardment targets and damage inflicted
by bombardment operations. The group also provided mapping service for air and
ground units; observed and reported on enemy transportation, installations, and
positions; and obtained data on weather conditions.

Specifications

Crew: 1

Powerplant: 1044kW (1400hp) Packard
V-1650-3 Rolls-Royce Merlin engine

Maximum speed: 690km/h (430mph)

Range: 3540km (2200 miles)

Service ceiling: 12,649m (41,500ft)

Dimensions: span 11.27m (37ft);
length 9.84m (32ft 4in);
height 4.15m (13ft 8in)

Weight: 4173kg (9200lb) loaded

Armament: 6 x 12.7mm (0.5in) MGs

▲ North American P-51B Mustang

354th Fighter Squadron / 355th Fighter Group, Steeple Morden, April 1944

This was the aeroplane, in standard olive drab and neutral grey colour, of 2nd
Lieutenant Henry Brown, who ended the war with 17.2 kills in air-to-air combat.

Specifications

Crew: 1

Powerplant: 1044kW (1400hp) Packard
V-1650-3 Rolls-Royce Merlin engine

Maximum speed: 690km/h (430mph)

Range: 3540km (2200 miles)

Service ceiling: 12,649m (41,500ft)

Dimensions: span 11.27m (37ft);
length 9.84m (32ft 4in);
height 4.15m (13ft 8in)

Weight: 4173kg (9200lb) loaded

Armament: 6 x 12.7mm (0.5in) MGs

▲ North American P-51B Mustang

487th Fighter Squadron / 352nd Fighter Group, Bodney, May 1944

1st Lieutenant William Wisner achieved 16 victories in this fighter and one
other aeroplane.

▲ North American P-51B Mustang

336th Fighter Squadron / 4th Fighter Group, Debden, May 1944

The fighter of Captain Willard 'Millie' Milikan, who achieved 13 victories despite
earlier rejection by the US Army Air Corps and receiving a poor rating for flying
skill when he joined the Royal Canadian Air Force. Milikan commanded a unit
equipped with Republic F-84 jet-powered warplanes in the Korean War.

Specifications

Crew: 1

Powerplant: 1081kW (1450hp) Packard
V-1650-3 Rolls-Royce Merlin engine

Maximum speed: 690km/h (430mph)

Range: 1215km (755 miles)

Service ceiling: 12,649m (41,500ft)

Dimensions: span 11.27m (37ft);
length 9.84m (32ft 4in);
height 4.15m (13ft 8in)

Weight: 4173kg (9200lb) loaded

Armament: 4 x 12.7mm (0.5in) MGs

▲ North American P-51B Mustang

328th Fighter Squadron / 352nd Fighter Group, Bodney, July 1944

Fitted with a 'Malcolm hood', this P-51B was the aeroplane of 1st Lieutenant John F. Thornell, Jr., one of the 352nd Fighter Group's leading aces with 17.25 victories.

Specifications

Crew: 1

Powerplant: 1044kW (1400hp) Packard
V-1650-3 Rolls-Royce Merlin engine

Maximum speed: 690km/h (430mph)

Range: 3540km (2200 miles)

Service ceiling: 12,649m (41,500ft)

Dimensions: span 11.27m (37ft);
length 9.84m (32ft 4in);
height 4.15m (13ft 8in)

Weight: 4173kg (9200lb) loaded

Armament: 6 x 12.7mm (0.5in) MGs

▲ North American P-51D Mustang

354th Fighter Squadron / 355th Fighter Group, Steeple Morden, late summer 1944

This was the second aircraft of Captain Henry Brown, leading ace of the 355th Fighter Group (14.2 air-to-air and 14.5 air-to-surface victories) before being taken prisoner on 3 October 1944.

Specifications

Crew: 1

Powerplant: 1264kW (1695hp) Packard Merlin
V-1650-7 V-12 piston engine

Maximum speed: 703km/h (437mph)

Range: 3347km (2080 miles)

Service ceiling: 12,770m (41,900ft)

Dimensions: span 11.28m (37ft);
length 9.83m (32ft 3in);
height 4.17m (13ft 8in)

Weight: 5488kg (12,100lb) loaded

Armament: 6 x 12.7mm (0.5in) MGs in wings,
plus up to 2 x 454kg (1000lb) bombs

▲ North American P-51D Mustang

343rd Fighter Squadron / 55th Fighter Group, Worningford, September 1944

The fighter of Lieutenant E. Robert Welch, who achieved 12 victories.

Specifications

Crew: 1

Powerplant: 1264kW (1695hp) Packard Merlin
V-1650-7 V-12 piston engine

Maximum speed: 703km/h (437mph)

Range: 3347km (2080 miles)

Service ceiling: 12,770m (41,900ft)

Dimensions: span 11.28m (37ft);
length 9.83m (32ft 3in);
height 4.17m (13ft 8in)

Weight: 5488kg (12,100lb) loaded

Armament: 6 x 12.7mm (0.5in) MGs in wings,
plus up to 2 x 454kg (1000lb) bombs

▼ 56th Fighter Group – 1944

Based at Boxted from 18 April 1944, and commanded in this period by Colonel Hubert A. Zemke until 12 August, then by Colonel David C. Schilling until 27 January 1945, and finally (in World War II) by Lieutenant-Colonel Lucian A. Dade, Jr., the 56th Fighter Group was of the standard triangular pattern of the USAAF. Its three squadrons, each comprising four flights of four aircraft (two leader and wingman pairs) for 48 aircraft in all, were the 61st, 62nd and 63rd Fighter Squadrons.

61st Fighter Squadron

Flight 1   Flight 2   Flight 3   Flight 4

62nd Fighter Squadron

Flight 1   Flight 2   Flight 3   Flight 4

63rd Fighter Squadron

Flight 1   Flight 2   Flight 3   Flight 4

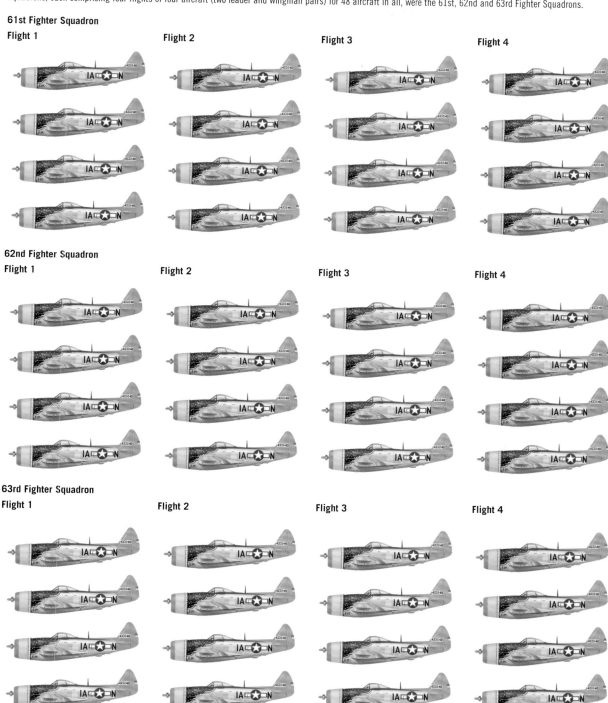

US Ninth Air Force
1942–45

Created for service in North Africa as a multi-role air force, the Ninth Air Force came into its own when translated into a highly capable tactical air force to support the US armies in the northwest Europe campaign of 1944–45.

THE US NINTH AIR FORCE was the tactical counterpart of the Eighth Air Force, initially intended for service in North Africa, and was created on 12 November 1942 to win air superiority, prevent Axis forces from supplying or rebuilding their forces, and provide the ground forces with close support.

By the end of 1942, a total of 370 aircraft had been ferried to the Ninth Air Force, the majority of them fighter-bombers, medium bombers and heavy bombers. In February 1943, the Germans took the

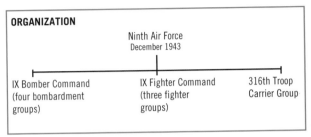

ORGANIZATION

	Ninth Air Force December 1943	
IX Bomber Command (four bombardment groups)	IX Fighter Command (three fighter groups)	316th Troop Carrier Group

US NINTH ARMY AIR FORCE (1942–43)	
Unit	Aircraft type
IX Fighter Command	
57th FG	P-40F
79th FG	P-40F
324th FG	P-40F
IX Bomber Command	B-24D/B-25C
316th Troop Carrier Group	C-47

offensive and drove through the Kasserine Pass in southern Tunisia. The US II Corps took a beating, but the Germans were checked with the aid of Ninth and Twelfth Air Force elements.

Sicilian campaign

The Axis forces in North Africa surrendered in May 1943, and the Allies prepared to invade Sicily. After the Allied victory in Tunisia, Ninth Air Force groups attacked airfields and rail facilities in Sicily and Italy, and then in July supported the Allied forces in the Sicilian campaign.

Specifications

Crew: 2

Powerplant: 2 x 1194kW (1600hp) Allison V-1710-111/113

Maximum speed: 666km/h (414mph)

Range: 4184km (2600 miles)

Service ceiling: 13,410m (20,000ft)

Dimensions: span 15.85m (52ft); length 11.53m (37ft 10in); height 2.99m (9ft 10in)

Weight: 9798kg (21,600lb) maximum takeoff

Armament: 1 x 20mm (0.8in) cannon and 4 x 12.7mm (0.5in) MGs in nose, plus 2 x 907kg (2000lb) bombs

▲ **Lockheed P-38J Lightning**

401st Fighter Squadron / 370th Fighter Group, Florennes, Belgium, November 1944

By this late stage of World War II, the Lightning was used mostly in the long-range fighter-bomber role, a low-altitude task in which the altitude limitations of its Allison V-1710 liquid-cooled V-12 engines were not a problem.

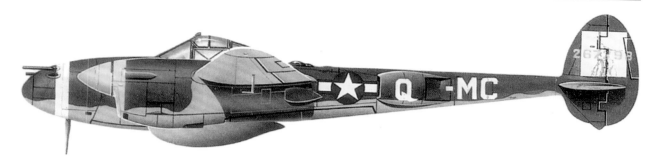

Specifications

Crew: 2

Powerplant: 2 x 1194kW (1600hp) Allison
V-1710-111/113

Maximum speed: 666km/h (414mph)

Range: 4184km (2600 miles)

Service ceiling: 13,410m (20,000ft)

Dimensions: span 15.85m (52ft); length 11.53m
(37ft 10in); height 2.99m (9ft 10in)

Weight: 9798kg (21,600lb) maximum takeoff

Armament: 1 x 20mm (0.8in) cannon and
4 x 12.7mm (0.5in) MGs in nose, plus 2 x 907kg
(2000lb) bombs

▲ **Lockheed P-38J Lightning**

79th Fighter Squadron / 20th Fighter Group, early 1944

Its size and weight militated against use of the twin-engined Lighting as an air combat fighter, but its high performance, especially in speed and range, suggested that the type might find gainful employment in the bomber escort role until it found its métier in the long-range fighter-bomber and attack roles.

Specifications

Crew: 2

Powerplant: 2 x 1194kW (1600hp) Allison
V-1710-111/113

Maximum speed: 666km/h (414mph)

Range: 4184km (2600 miles)

Service ceiling: 13,410m (20,000ft)

Dimensions: span 15.85m (52ft); length 11.53m
(37ft 10in); height 2.99m (9ft 10in)

Weight: 9798kg (21,600lb) maximum takeoff

Armament: 1 x 20mm (0.8in) cannon and
4 x 12.7mm (0.5in) MGs in nose, plus 2 x 907kg
(2000lb) bombs

▲ **Lockheed P-38 Lightning**

365th Fighter Squadron / 358th Fighter Group, England, mid-1944

On 1 February 1944, the Eighth Air Force's 358th Fighter Group was passed to the Ninth Air Force, which in turn reallocated its Mustang-equipped 357th Fighter Group to the Eighth Air Force.

IX FIGHTER COMMAND (NOVEMBER 1943)		
Unit	Base	Aircraft type
67th Recon Group	RAF Membury	F-5/P-38
354th FG	RAF Boxted	P-51
357th FG (to 1 Feb 44)	RAF Leiston	P-51
358th FG (from 1 Feb 44)	RAF Leiston	P-47

In August and September 1943, the Ninth Air Force was tasked to move to the UK, and transferred its units in North Africa to the Twelfth Air Force. The Ninth Air Force was deactivated in Egypt on 16 October 1943, the day on which its new HQ was reactivated at Burtonwood in England, and then became a decisive tactical air force led by Lieutenant-General Hoyt S. Vandenberg.

The nucleus of the Ninth Air Force was formed in November 1943 by the transfer of some Eighth Air Force tactical bomber, fighter and troop carrier groups, and during the following winter the Ninth Air Force expanded very rapidly so that by the end of May 1944, when the last combat group became operational, its complement ran to 45 flying groups operating some 5000 aircraft.

Together with the Eighth Air Force, the Ninth Air Force was tasked with destroying the *Luftwaffe* in the air and on the ground and thus gaining air supremacy before the launch of the Allied invasion of France in June 1944. By early August, most Ninth Air Force groups had been transferred to bases in France, and were then assigned to tactical air commands

(TACs) supporting the ground forces: the XXIX TAC supported the Ninth Army in the north, the IX TAC the First Army in the centre, and the XIX TAC the Third Army in the south; air cover was provided by the IX Air Defense Command.

In December 1944 and January 1945, the Ninth Air Force's fighters and bombers were critical in defeating the Germans in the so-called Battle of the Bulge, and for the rest of the war the Ninth Air Force provided excellent support for the US forces. With victory won, the Ninth Air Force was deactivated on 2 December 1945.

▲ North American P-51B Mustang
355th Fighter Squadron / 354th Fighter Group, England, late 1943
This is an example of the first Mustang variant with the Packard V-1650 (Rolls-Royce Merlin) liquid-cooled V-12 engine, and is carrying 284l (75 US gal) drop tanks for extended range.

Specifications

Crew: 1
Powerplant: 1044kW (1400hp) Packard V-1650-3 Rolls-Royce Merlin engine
Maximum speed: 690km/h (430mph)
Range: 3540km (2200 miles)
Service ceiling: 12,649m (41,500ft)
Dimensions: span 11.27m (37ft); length 9.84m (32ft 4in); height 4.15m (13ft 8in)
Weight: 4173kg (9200lb) loaded
Armament: 6 x 12.7mm (0.5in) MGs

▲ North American F-6B Mustang
107th Tactical Reconnaissance Squadron, Europe, 1944
The F-6B was the tactical reconnaissance derivative of the P-51A fighter, with the basic armament retained but a pair of K-24 cameras installed.

Specifications

Crew: 1
Powerplant: 1044kW (1400hp) Packard V-1650-3 Rolls-Royce Merlin engine
Maximum speed: 690km/h (430mph)
Range: 3540km (2200 miles)
Service ceiling: 12,649m (41,500ft)
Dimensions: span 11.27m (37ft); length 9.84m (32ft 4in); height 4.15m (13ft 8in)
Weight: 4173kg (9200lb) loaded
Armament: 6 x 12.7mm (0.5in) MGs

Normandy and Northwest Europe
JUNE 1944 – MAY 1945

The Ninth Air Force offered the armies of the US 12th Army Group the type of tactical air support that the British 2nd Tactical Air Force gave to the Anglo-Canadian 21st Army Group in the northwest Europe campaign, greatly speeding the Allied advance and reducing losses.

THE NINTH AIR FORCE was a key element in the planning for the debouchment of the US forces in *Overlord*, the Allied amphibious invasion of France over the beaches of Normandy in June 1944. The Ninth Air Force had already played a major role in destroying the German lines of communication in France and the Low Countries behind all the possible invasion areas, and thus isolating the German forces and depriving them of a realistic chance of reinforcement or major resupply.

Like the British 2nd TAF, the US Ninth Air Force had also been instrumental with the Allied heavy bomber forces in destroying much of the coastal defence system that the Germans had built so expensively and laboriously over the previous years, with particular emphasis placed on the destruction of the artillery emplacements that could otherwise have crippled the seaborne approach of the Allied invasion forces.

ORGANIZATION

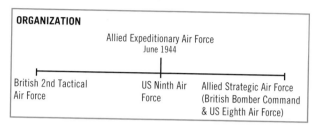

Allied Expeditionary Air Force
June 1944

British 2nd Tactical Air Force | US Ninth Air Force | Allied Strategic Air Force (British Bomber Command & US Eighth Air Force)

US FIGHTER-BOMBER ARMAMENT

Type	Guns	Disposable
Bell P-39Q	1 x 20mm (0.79in) 4 x 12.7mm (0.5in)	227kg (500 lb)
Curtiss P-40N	6 x 12.7mm (0.5in)	680kg (1500lb)
Lockheed P-38L	1 x 20mm (0.79in) 4 x 12.7mm (0.5in)	1814kg (4000lb)
North American P-51D	6 x 12.7mm (0.5in)	907kg (2000lb)
Republic P-47D	8 x 12.7mm (0.5in)	1134kg (2500lb)

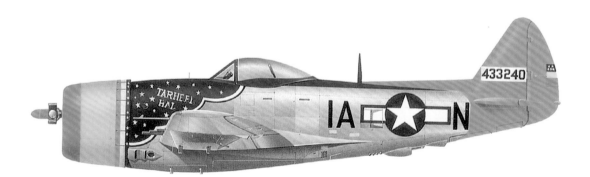

Specifications

Crew: 1

Powerplant: 1891kW (2535hp) Pratt & Whitney R-2800-59W Double Wasp

Maximum speed: 697km/h (433mph)

Range: 3060km (1900 miles) with drop tanks

Service ceiling: 12,495m (41,000ft)

Dimensions: span 12.42m (40ft 9in); length 11.02m (36ft 2in); height 4.47m (14ft 8in)

Weight: 7938kg (17,500lb) maximum takeoff

Armament: 8 x 12.7mm (0.5in) MGs in wings, plus provision for 1134kg (2500lb) external bombs or rockets

▲ Republic P-47D Thunderbolt

336th Fighter Squadron / 358th Fighter Group, Toul, France, late 1944

Later production examples of the P-47D introduced a small dorsal fillet to reduce a tail flutter problem. This aeroplane carries the orange tail markings of the 1st Tactical Air Force.

With the ground forces ashore and the lodgement area enlarged steadily if slowly, the fighter and then the medium bomber groups of the Ninth Air Force could be transferred from England to France, either extending their tactical radii deeper into German-held territory or increasing their loiter times in the areas over or immediately beyond the frontline.

Hard fighting

Thereafter, the Ninth Air Force moved east through France and Belgium toward the western part of Germany. There was occasion for hard fighting in the air, but as often as not it was the weather rather than the Germans that was the greater hindrance. Air support was provided for the ground forces with concentration and accuracy, and in the later stages of the campaign this proved of immense value in speeding the US advance and reducing losses. During the invasion of southern France in August 1944, two fighter groups of the Ninth Air Force were reallocated to the provisional US/French 1st TAF supporting the invasion force's drive north, and for the Arnhem operation of September the Ninth Air Force transferred its IX Troop Carrier Command (14 C-47 groups) to the 1st Allied Airborne Army.

In December 1944 and January 1945, the Ninth Air Force committed its warplanes, as and when the weather permitted, to stem and then defeat the German offensive in the 'Battle of the Bulge'. The Ninth Air Force's troop carrier groups delivered paratrooper and glider units during the Allied airborne crossing of the Rhine on 24 March 1945, which was the largest single airborne drop in history.

▲ Photo reconnaissance

An F-4 Lightning of the 3rd Photographic Reconnaissance Group banks towards the photographer. The 3rd Group arrived in Algeria in late 1942 and flew countless missions in support of the Allied armies in Europe.

IX Fighter Command
JUNE 1944 – MAY 1945

The IX Fighter Command was one of the three formations in the US Ninth Air Force and, despite its designation, it was optimized for the fighter-bomber role in support of the ground forces. The command did have a number of Mustang units, however, offering some genuine fighter ability.

IN THE SUMMER OF 1944, command of the US Ninth Air Force was in the hands of Lieutenant-General Lewis H. Brereton, an officer with widespread command experience in the Far East and Middle East before he arrivd in the UK. On 24 August, Brereton was reassigned to become the commander of the Allied First Airborne Army, and his place at the head of the US Ninth Air Force was subsequently assumed by Lieutenant-General

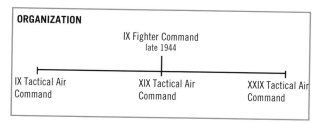

ORGANIZATION

IX Fighter Command
late 1944

IX Tactical Air Command	XIX Tactical Air Command	XXIX Tactical Air Command

FIGHTER ACES OF THE NINTH AIR FORCE	
Name	Victories
Glenn T. Eagleston	18.5
Don M. Beerbower	15.5
Jack T. Bradley	15
Bruce W. Carr	14
Wallace N. Emmer	14
Kenneth H. Dahlberg	14
Robert W. Stephens	13
Lowell K. Brueland	12.5
James H. Howard	12.3
Clyde B. East	12

Hoyt S. Vandenberg. IX Fighter Command was headquartered at Middle Wallop in the south of England until it moved to Les Obeaux in France during August and then five other towns in France, Belgium and Germany as the US forces moved east. It was commanded by Major-General R. Etheral, and from the summer of 1944 was largely an administrative organization that ensured the smooth operation of the eventual total of the three tactical air commands for which it had responsibility. These were the IX, XIX and XXIX TACs, allocated to support the initial trio of US armies that took the ground war to the Germans from 6 June 1944.

Specifications
Crew: 1

Powerplant: 1264kW (1695hp) Packard Merlin
V-1650-7 V-12 piston engine

Maximum speed: 703km/h (437mph)

Range: 3347km (2080 miles)

Service ceiling: 12,770m (41,900ft)

Dimensions: span 11.28m (37ft);
length 9.83m (32ft 3in);
height 4.17m (13ft 8in)

Weight: 5488kg (12,100lb) loaded

Armament: 6 x 12.7mm (0.5in) MGs in wings,
plus up to 2 x 454kg (1000lb) bombs

▲ **North American P-51D Mustang**
354th Fighter Group, European theatre, 1944–45
As suggested by the motif pained on the cowling of the Packard V-1650 liquid-cooled V-12 engine, this is the aeroplane of Lieutenant-Colonel Glenn T. Eagleston, commander of the 354th Fighter Group and an ace with 24 confirmed victories.

IX Tactical Air Command
JUNE 1944 – MAY 1945

The IX Tactical Air Command was the subordinate formation within the IX Fighter Command, tasked with the support of the US First Army. In this task, it operated from quickly prepared advanced landing grounds close behind the front for minimum response times.

ESTABLISHED LATE in 1943, the IX Tactical Air Command was led by Major-General Elwood Quesada, and comprised three fighter-bomber wings and one reconnaissance group.

In June 1944, on the eve of the Allied invasion of France, the IX TAC had three fighter-bomber wings. The 70th Fighter Wing comprised Colonel George Wertenbaker's Ibsley-based 48th Fighter Group (492nd, 493rd and 494th Fighter Squadrons) flying the P-47 Thunderbolt, Colonel Charles Young's Stoney Cross-based 367th Fighter Group (392nd, 393rd and 394th Fighter Squadrons) flying the P-38 Lightning, Colonel Bingham Kleine's Bisterne-based 371st Fighter Group (404th, 405th and 406th Fighter Squadrons) flying the P-47 Thunderbolt, and Colonel Clinton Wasem's Warmwell-based 474th Fighter Group (428th, 429th and 430th Fighter Squadrons) flying the P-38 Lightning.

The 71st Fighter Wing comprised Lieutenant-Colonel Norman Holt's Thruxton-based 366th Fighter Group (389th, 390th and 391st Fighter

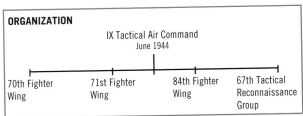

ORGANIZATION

	IX Tactical Air Command June 1944		
70th Fighter Wing	71st Fighter Wing	84th Fighter Wing	67th Tactical Reconnaissance Group

Squadrons) flying the P-47 Thunderbolt, Colonel Gil Meyers' Chilboton-based 368th Fighter Group (395th, 396th and 397th Fighter Squadrons) flying the P-47 Thunderbolt, and Colonel Seth McKee's Andover-based 370th Fighter Group (401st, 402nd and 385th Fighter Squadrons) flying the P-38 Lightning.

The 84th Fighter Wing comprised Colonel William Greenfield's Lymington-based 50th Fighter Group (10th, 81st and 313rd Fighter Squadrons) flying the P-47 Thunderbolt, Colonel Ray Steckers's Beaulieu-based 365th Fighter Group (386th, 387th and 388th Fighter Squadrons) flying

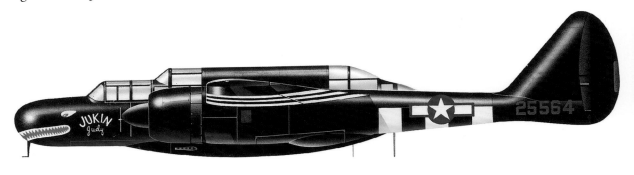

Specifications

Crew: 2/3

Powerplant: 2 x 1678kW (2250hp) Pratt & Whitney R-2800-65 18 cylinder radial engines

Maximum speed: 594km/h (369mph)

Range: 3058km (1900 miles)

Service ceiling: 10.090m (33,100ft)

Dimensions: span 20.12m (66ft); length 14.91m (48ft 11in); height 4.46m (14ft 8in)

Weight: 15,513kg (34,200lb) maximum takeoff

Armament: 4 x 20mm (0.8in) cannon in underside of forward fuselage

▲ **Northrop P-61A Black Widow**

422nd Night-Fighter Squadron / IX Fighter Command, Scorton, 1944

One of two night-fighter squadrons, the other being the 425th Night-Fighter Squadron, which reported directly to the headquarters of the IX Fighter Command, the 422nd Night-Fighter Squadron worked up at Scorton in Yorkshire before moving south to its operational base at Charmy Down.

367TH & 474TH FIGHTER GROUPS, 70TH FIGHTER WING			
Unit	Type	Strength	Serviceable
392nd FS	P-38	16	n/a
393rd FS	P-38	16	n/a
394th FS	P-38	16	n/a
428th FS	P-38	16	n/a
429th FS	P-38	16	n/a
430th FS	P-38	16	n/a

48TH & 371ST FIGHTER GROUPS, 70TH FIGHTER WING			
Unit	Type	Strength	Serviceable
492nd FS	P-47	16	n/a
493rd FS	P-47	16	n/a
494th FS	P-47	16	n/a
404th FS	P-47	16	n/a
405th FS	P-47	16	n/a
406th FS	P-47	16	n/a

the P-47 Thunderbolt, Colonel Carol McColpin's Winkton-based 404th Fighter Group (506th, 507th and 508th Fighter Squadrons) flying the P-47 Thunderbolt, and Colonel Robert Delashew's Christchurch-based 405th Fighter Group (509th, 510th and 511th Fighter Squadrons) flying the P-47 Thunderbolt.

Reconnaissance elements

The IX TAC was completed by its own organic tactical and photo-reconnaissance element in the form of Colonel George Peck's 67th Tactical Reconnaissance Group, which was based largely at Chalgrove and Middle Wallop, and comprised the 107th and 109th Tactical Reconnaissance Squadrons flying the P-51 Mustang, and the 30th and 33rd Photo-Reconnaissance Squadrons flying the F-5 reconnaissance version of the P-38 Lightning.

After providing support for the initial stages of the Allied invasion from across the Channel, these

wings moved to France as and when there were facilities available, and moved forward according to the general Allied advance.

▲ **Ground attack**

Here, a Ninth Air Force Lightning strafes a train in German-occupied Europe in late 1944. Note the' invasion stripes' on the wings.

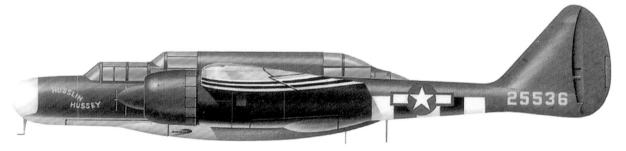

Specifications

Crew: 2/3

Powerplant: 2 x 1678kW (2250hp) Pratt & Whitney R-2800-65 18 cylinder radial engines

Maximum speed: 594km/h (369mph)

Range: 3058km (1900 miles)

Service ceiling: 10.090m (33,100ft)

Dimensions: span 20.12m (66ft); length 14.91m (48ft 11in); height 4.46m (14ft 8in);

Weight: 15,513kg (34,200lb) maximum takeoff

Armament: 4 x 20mm (0.8in) cannon in underside of forward fuselage

▲ **Northrop P-61A Black Widow**

422nd Night-Fighter Squadron / IX Fighter Command, Scorton, summer 1944

The 422nd Night-Fighter Squadron was the first unit equipped with the P-61 to reach the UK, and flew its first operational sortie in July 1944 from Hurn, near Bournemouth.

Specifications

Crew: 1

Powerplant: 1044kW (1400hp) Packard
V-1650-3 Rolls-Royce Merlin engine

Maximum speed: 690km/h (430mph)

Range: 3540km (2200 miles)

Service ceiling: 12,649m (41,500ft)

Dimensions: span 11.27m (37ft);
length 9.84m (32ft 4in);
height 4.15m (13ft 8in)

Weight: 4173kg (9200lb) loaded

Armament: 6 x 12.7mm (0.5in) MGs

▲ **North American P-51B Mustang**

356th Fighter Squadron / 354th Fighter Group, UK, 1944

This was the second aeroplane with this name flown by Major James Howard, the commander of the 356th Fighter Squadron. This officer had previously flown with the American Volunteer Group in China, hence the six 'meatball' markings above the six swastika kill markings below the cockpit.

XIX Tactical Air Command
June 1944 – May 1945

The XIX Tactical Air Command was the formation entrusted with the provision of tactical air support for the US Third Army. This was the fastest-moving of the US armies, and the XIX TAC therefore became very adept in the art of fast relocation farther forward.

E STABLISHED IN 1944, the XIX Tactical Air Command was led by Major-General Otto Weyland, and initially comprised two fighter-bomber wings and one reconnaissance group.

Thus as General George S. Patton's newly activated Third Army began to move south-east through France in an advance that would eventually take its spearhads into western Czechoslovakia by May 1945, the XIX TAC had two fighter-bomber wings.

The 100th Fighter Wing comprised Colonel George Bickell's 48th Fighter Group (353rd, 355th and 366th Fighter Squadrons) originally based at Lashenden and flying the P-51 Mustang, Colonel Cecil Wells' 358th Fighter Group (365th, 366th and 367th Fighter Squadrons) originally based at High Halden and flying the P-47 Thunderbolt, Colonel Morton Magaffin's 362nd Fighter Group (377th, 378th and 379th Fighter Squadrons) originally based at Headcorn and flying the P-47 Thunderbolt, and Colonel Jim Tipton's 363rd Fighter Group (380th,

ORGANIZATION

XIX Tactical Air Command
September 1944

100th Fighter Wing	303rd Fighter Wing	10th Photo Group

381st and 382nd Fighter Squadrons) originally based at Staplehurst and flying the P-51 Mustang.

303rd Fighter Wing

The 303rd Fighter Wing comprised Colonel Lewis Curry's 36th Fighter Group (22nd, 23rd and 53rd Fighter Squadrons), originally based at Kingsnorth and flying the P-47 Thunderbolt, Colonel William Schwarz's 373rd Fighter Group (410th, 411th and 412th Fighter Squadrons), first based at Woodchurch and flying the P-47 Thunderbolt, and Colonel Anthony Grossetta's 40th Fighter Group (412th, 513th and 514th Fighter Squadrons) originally based at Ashford and flying the P-47 Thunderbolt. On 15 September, the 303rd Fighter Wing was transferred to the XXIX TAC.

The XIX TAC was completed by its own organic tactical and photo reconnaissance element in the form of Colonel William Reid's 10th Photo Group, which comprised the 12th and 15th Tactical Reconnaissance Squadrons flying the P-51 Mustang, and the 31st and 34th Photo-Reconnaissance Squadrons flying the P-38 Lightning. All these units soon moved from southern England to France and then points farther east and south.

NINTH AAF LOSSES IN EUROPE (NOVEMBER 1943 – MAY 1945)	
Aircraft type	Number
Douglas A-20/F-3 Havoc	57
Douglas A-26 Invader	35
Martin B-26 Marauder	179
Douglas C-47	92
Lockheed P-38/F-5 Lightning	213
Republic P-47 Thunderbolt	616
North American P-51/F-6 Mustang	233
Northrop P-61 Black Widow	4

▲ **North American P-51B Mustang**

353rd Fighter Squadron / 354th Fighter Group, Lashenden, summer 1944

This was the second aeroplane flown by Captain Donald M. 'Buzz' Beerbower to carry the name 'Bonnie B'.

Specifications

Crew: 1

Powerplant: 1044kW (1400hp) Packard V-1650-3 Rolls-Royce Merlin engine

Maximum speed: 690km/h (430mph)

Range: 3540km (2200 miles)

Service ceiling: 12,649m (41,500ft)

Dimensions: span 11.27m (37ft); length 9.84m (32ft 4in); height 4.15m (13ft 8in)

Weight: 4173kg (9200lb) loaded

Armament: 6 x 12.7mm (0.5in) MGs

Specifications

Crew: 1

Powerplant: 1264kW (1695hp) Packard Merlin V-1650-7 V-12 piston engine

Maximum speed: 703km/h (437mph)

Range: 3347km (2080 miles)

Service ceiling: 12,770m (41,900ft)

Dimensions: span 11.28m (37ft); length 9.83m (32ft 3in); height 4.17m (13ft 8in)

Weight: 5488kg (12,100lb) loaded

Armament: 6 x 12.7mm (0.5in) MGs in wings

▲ **North American F-6D Mustang**

15th Tactical Reconnaissance Squadron / 10th Photographic Group / XIX Tactical Air Command, northern France, late summer 1944

This was the reconnaissance development of the P-51D, with cameras in the rear fuselage to the rear of the radiator installation.

Specifications

Crew: 1

Powerplant: 1044kW (1400hp) Packard
V-1650-3 Rolls-Royce Merlin engine

Maximum speed: 690km/h (430mph)

Range: 3540km (2200 miles)

Service ceiling: 12,649m (41,500ft)

Dimensions: span 11.27m (37ft);

length 9.84m (32ft 4in);

height 4.15m (13ft 8in)

Weight: 4173kg (9200lb) loaded

Armament: 6 x 12.7mm (0.5in) MGs

▲ **North American P-51B Mustang**

382nd Fighter Squadron / 363rd Fighter Group / XIX Tactical Air Command, northern France, summer 1944

This was the fighter flown by Robert McGee after the move of the 363rd Fighter Group to France, as indicated by the yellow spinner adopted at this time.

Specifications

Crew: 1

Powerplant: 1264kW (1695hp) Packard Merlin
V-1650-7 V-12 piston engine

Maximum speed: 703km/h (437mph)

Range: 3347km (2080 miles)

Service ceiling: 12,770m (41,900ft)

Dimensions: span 11.28m (37ft);

length 9.83m (32ft 3in);

height 4.17m (13ft 8in)

Weight: 5488kg (12,100lb) loaded

Armament: 6 x 12.7mm (0.5in) MGs in wings,

plus up to 2 x 454kg (1000lb) bombs

▲ **North American P-51D Mustang**

402nd Fighter Squadron / 370th Fighter Group / IX Tactical Air Command, France, late 1944

This was the aeroplane used almost exclusively in the fighter-bomber role by the pilot Robert Bohna.

Specifications

Crew: 1

Powerplant: 1044kW (1400hp) Packard
V-1650-3 Rolls-Royce Merlin engine

Maximum speed: 690km/h (430mph)

Range: 3540km (2200 miles)

Service ceiling: 12,649m (41,500ft)

Dimensions: span 11.27m (37ft);

length 9.84m (32ft 4in);

height 4.15m (13ft 8in)

Weight: 4173kg (9200lb) loaded

Armament: 6 x 12.7mm (0.5in) MGs

▲ **North American F-6C Mustang**

15th Tactical Reconnaissance Squadron / 10th Photographic Group, France, autumn 1944

The aeroplane of John Hoefker, who ended World War II with 10.5 victories. He was shot down on the German side of the frontline in December 1944 but escaped capture to return to his squadron.

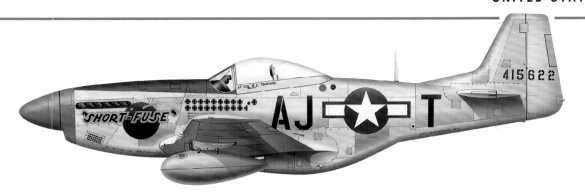

Specifications

Crew: 1

Powerplant: 1264kW (1695hp) Packard Merlin

  V-1650-7 V-12 piston engine

Maximum speed: 703km/h (437mph)

Range: 3347km (2080 miles)

Service ceiling: 12,770m (41,900ft)

Dimensions: span 11.28m (37ft);

  length 9.83m (32ft 3in);

  height 4.17m (13ft 8in)

Weight: 5488kg (12,100lb) loaded

Armament: 6 x 12.7mm (0.5in) MGs in wings,

  plus up to 2 x 454kg (1000lb) bombs

▲ **North American P-51D Mustang**

356th Fighter Squadron / 354th Fighter Group / XIX Tactical Air Command, 1944–45

This was the aeroplane of Lieutenant-Colonel Richard Turner, commander of the 356th Fighter Squadron.

XXIX Tactical Air Command
SEPTEMBER 1944 – MAY 1945

Activated only in September 1944 as the Allied armies swept east through northern France into Belgium and toward western Germany, the XXIX Tactical Air Command was allocated the task of providing the US Ninth Amy with tactical air support.

IT WAS DURING SEPTEMBER 1944 that the XXIX TAC was officially activated under the command of Brigadier-General Richard E. Nugent for the tactical air support of the US Ninth Army. At this stage, the command's assets were only the 303rd Fighter Wing transferred from the XIX TAC, and the 363rd Reconnaissance Group.

303rd Fighter Wing

Operating from a number of bases in parts of France liberated from German occupation, the 303rd Fighter Wing comprised Colonel Lewis Curry's Athis-based 36th Fighter Group (22nd, 23rd and 53rd Fighter Squadrons) flying the P-47 Thunderbolt, Colonel William Schwarz's Reims-based 373rd Fighter Group (410th, 411th and 412th Fighter Squadrons) flying the P-47 Thunderbolt, and Colonel Anthony Grossetta's Mourmelon le Grand-based 40th Fighter Group (512th, 513th and 514th Fighter Squadrons) also flying the P-47 Thunderbolt.

ORGANIZATION

XXIX Tactical Air Command
September 1944

303rd Fighter Wing   363rd Reconnaissance Group

In the following month, having received units from the IX and XIX TACs, the XXIX TAC became operational in support of the US Ninth Army, and one of the new formation's most important assets was Major Richard Leghorn's 33rd Photo Reconnaissance Squadron, equipped with the F-5 photo-reconnaissance derivative of the P-38 Lightning. which had been received from the IX TAC's 67th Reconnaissance Group and remained with the 363rd Tactical Reconnaissance Group for the rest of World War II.

The capabilities of the XXIX TAC, which remained smaller than the other two tactical air commands of the IX Fighter Command, were revealed on the first day of *Grenade*, the Ninth Army's crossing of the Roer river on 23 February 1945. For this undertaking, the XXIX TAC could call on its reconnaissance group and, more immediately significant, the armed power of its five groups of fighter-bombers, totalling some 375 aircraft. The Americans crossed the river without undue difficulty, but had then to face German counterattacks.

The Ninth Army's artillery was very effective, and was ably supported in this task by the Thunderbolt squadrons of the XXIX TAC, which operated at very low level to drop their bombs with commendable accuracy before strafing the hapless Germans soldiers with their devastating batteries of eight 12.7mm (0.5in) Browning machine guns.

'Plunder'

Much the same level of capability was revealed in the days before the launch of the *Plunder* offensive to take the Allied 21st Army Group, including the US Ninth Army, across the great Rhine river into Germany proper on 23 March 1945. As part of the interdiction effort designed to isolate the German

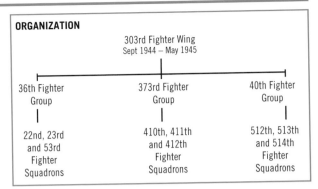

ORGANIZATION

303rd Fighter Wing Sept 1944 – May 1945		
36th Fighter Group	373rd Fighter Group	40th Fighter Group
22nd, 23rd and 53rd Fighter Squadrons	410th, 411th and 412th Fighter Squadrons	512th, 513th and 514th Fighter Squadrons

▶ **Ground attack master**

Fitted with eight 12.7mm (0.5in) machine guns and capable of carrying bombs and rockets, the P-47 was the ideal ground attack platform.

Specifications

Crew: 1

Powerplant: 1891kW (2535hp) Pratt & Whitney R-2800-59W Double Wasp

Maximum speed: 697km/h (433mph)

Range: 3060km (1900 miles) with drop tanks

Service ceiling: 12,495m (41,000ft)

Dimensions: span 12.42m (40ft 9in); length 11.02m (36ft 2in); height 4.47m (14ft 8in)

Weight: 7938kg (17,500lb) maximum takeoff

Armament: 8 x 12.7mm (0.5in) MGs in wings, plus provision for 1134kg (2500lb) external bombs or rockets

▲ **Republic P-47D Thunderbolt**

512th Fighter Squadron / 406th Fighter Group, Nordholz, Germany, summer 1945

The red/yellow/red band round the rear fuselage indicates that this unit had been allocated to the air element of the occupation forces.

P-51B Mustang
To many pilots, the P-51B was the finest variant of the P-51 Mustang. When fitted with the British 'Malcolm hood', it was lighter and faster, and handled more crisply, than the bubble-canopied P-51D. This P-51B flew with the 354th Fighter Squadron.

side of the river, the Allied air forces had since the middle of February been running a major bombing effort. This was designed to seal the Ruhr from the rest of Germany by destroying rail bridges and viaducts, and by attacking canal traffic along a broad arc running from Bremen near the North Sea south and south-west around the eastern edge of the Ruhr to the Rhine south of the industrial region.

Attacks were aimed at critical German communications centres, railway marshalling yards, supply dumps, industrial plants and any other comparable targets. From mid-February to 21 March, much of the Allied air strength had been focused on this task whenever other operations permitted. Heavy and medium bombers made some 1792 sorties against 17 rail bridges and viaducts

along the arc round the Ruhr. By 21 March, 10 of the bridges had been destroyed and five others rendered unusable. The destruction of these bridges significantly impaired German movement.

Final push
The fighters and fighter-bombers of the British 2nd TAF and XXIX TAC now joined the Ruhr campaign. Most of the 7311 sorties flown by these pilots between 11 and 21 March were directed against the rail and road systems of the Ruhr. In the last three days before the operation's start, some 2000 medium bombers of the US 9th Bombardment Division struck at communications centres, rail yards and flak positions, and thus the area was effectively isolated.

US Twelfth Air Force
1942–45

The US Twelfth Air Force came into being as a direct result of the decision by US planners that proposed operations in north-west Africa required more air support than was currently available. The formation then went on to vital service in the Italian campaign.

THE ORIGINS OF THE US Twelfth Air Force date to the meetings held between British and US planning staffs in mid-1942. The aim was to develop the strategy that would see the introduction of US forces into combat against the Germans for the first time, namely the *Torch* amphibious landings in French north-west Africa and the subsequent eastward advance to Tunisia. This was

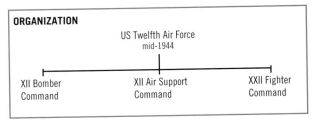

ORGANIZATION

US Twelfth Air Force
mid-1944

| XII Bomber Command | XII Air Support Command | XXII Fighter Command |

an operation and subsequent campaign of such size and complexity that it would require considerable air support. Indeed, recognizing that a new command organization would have to be established to control the personnel and equipment involved, the planners decided to create a new US Twelfth Air Force.

The new Twelfth Air Force was activated on 20 August 1942 at Bolling Field, Maryland, and on 23 September Brigadier-General 'Jimmy' Doolittle assumed command with Colonel Hoyt S. Vandenberg as chief of staff. Time for the preparation of the new air force was short. In fact, it was only four months

USAAF GROUP STANDARD ORGANIZATION AND STRENGTH

Unit	No. of aircraft	No. of crews
Medium bomber	96	96
Light bomber	96	96
Single-engine fighter	110–125	108–125
Twin-engine fighter	110–125	108–125
Night-fighter	18	16
Tactical recce	27	23
Photo recce	24	21

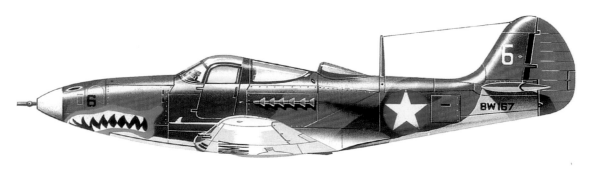

▲ **Bell P-39L Airacobra**

93rd Fighter Squadron / 81st Fighter Group

The wheel turned full circle as the US forces flew Airacobra aircraft initially delivered to the UK as Airacobra Mk I warplanes. The Airacobra's strength and heavy armament made it a good attack fighter.

Specifications

Crew: 1

Powerplant: 895kW (1200hp) Allison V-1710-85 liquid-cooled V-12

Maximum speed: 605km/h (376mph)

Range: 483km (300 miles)

Service ceiling: 11,665m (38,270ft)

Dimensions: span 10.36m (34ft 0in); length

9.195m (30ft 2in); height 3.785m (12ft 5in)

Weight: 3992kg (8800lb) loaded

Armament: 1 x 37mm (1.46in) M4 cannon, 2 x 12.7mm (0.5in) Browning MGs, 4 x 7.62mm (0.3in) Browning MGs, and 227kg (500lb) of bombs before the Twelfth Air Force was committed to active service with the descent of Allied forces on north-west Africa on 8 November 1942. The Twelfth Air Force was very active in the period leading to the final defeat of the Axis forces in North Africa during May 1943, and after this it was reduced for further service in the Mediterranean theatre. The US military leadership was basically opposed to the continuance of operations in this theatre (believing it to be a diversion from the primary aim of defeating the Germans by the most direct assault from northern France into Germany), but was persuaded to agree to operations that saw the Twelfth Air Force in action over Sicily, Italy and southern France.

By May 1945, the Twelfth had flown some 430,681 sorties, dropped 220,630 tonnes (217,156 tons) of bombs, claimed destruction of 2857 aircraft and lost 2667 of its own. The Twelfth Air Force was eventually deactivated at Florence, Italy, on 31 August 1945.

▲ **Supermarine Spitfire Mk VC**

308th Fighter Squadron / 31st Fighter Group

Fitted under the nose with a Vokes filter to prevent North African dust and grit being drawn into the engine, this Spitfire Mk VC was one of a modest number of British aircraft operated in North Africa by the US air forces.

Specifications

Crew: 1	Dimensions: span 11.23m (36ft 10in);
Powerplant: 1096kW (1470hp) Rolls-Royce	length 9.12m (29ft 11in);
Merlin 50 engine	height 3.02m (9ft 11in)
Maximum speed: 594km/h (369mph)	Weight: 2911kg (6417lb) loaded
Range: 1827km (1135 miles)	Armament: 4 x 7.7mm (0.303in) MGs and 2 x
Service ceiling: 11,125m (36,500ft)	20mm (0.8in) cannons in wings

North Africa and the Mediterranean
1942–45

The Mediterranean theatre was never anything more than a sideshow to the US armed forces. As a result of British pressure, however, the Americans agreed to an extension of the success in North Africa to begin operations against Italy, first on Sicily and then the mainland.

AFTER THE DEFEAT of the Axis forces in North Africa, the Allies decided, despite US reluctance, to pursue them into Italy. The first step was the *Husky* invasion of Sicily by the US Seventh and British Eighth Armies in July 1943. The Allies then prepared to assault the mainland, starting with the *Avalanche* descent on Salerno in September 1943 by the US Fifth and British Eighth Armies. Italy secured an armistice just as this operation was launched, but the Germans decided to fight.

Very ably led and including a number of high-grade formations, the German armies were able to make the best of Italy's formidable campaigning terrain to fight a series of hard-fought delaying actions as they were slowly and very bloodily driven north along the Italian peninsula.

Defensive barrier

The British were largely on the east and the Americans on the west. The Apennine mountains made the basis of superb defensive lines, which the Germans held strongly before falling back in good order, and the Allies were never able to outflank these defences in any significant manner.

Nevertheless, the Fifth Army captured Rome in June 1944, and with potent and overwheming air support, fought north to eventual victory in April 1945.

▲ **Grumman F4F-4 Wildcat**

VGR-28 / USS Suwannee, *northwest Africa, November 1942*

Used in the reconnaissance fighter role, this US Navy warplane reflects the removal of red from the US national insignia and the adoption of a large yellow surround to lessen the chances of confusion with Axis markings.

Specifications

Crew: 1	Dimensions: span 11.58m 38ft);
Powerplant: 895kW (1200hp) Pratt & Whitney	length 8.76m (28ft 8in);
R-1830-86 14-cylinder engine	height 2.81m (9ft 3in)
Maximum speed: 507km/h (315mph)	Weight: 3607kg (7952lb) loaded
Range: 1851km (1150 miles)	Armament: 6 x 12.5mm (0.5in) MGs in wings;
Service ceiling: 12,010m (39,400ft)	2 x 45kg (100lb) bombs

Specifications

Crew: 1	Dimensions: span 11.36m (37ft 4in);
Powerplant: 895kW (1200hp) Allison piston	length 10.16m (33ft 4in);
engine	height 3.76m (12ft 4in)
Maximum speed: 563km/h (350mph)	Weight: 3511kg (7740lb) loaded
Range: 1738km (1080 miles)	Armament: 4 x 12.7mm (0.5in) Browning MGs
Service ceiling: 9450m (31,000ft)	in wings

▲ **Curtiss P-40L Warhawk**

325th Fighter Group, Tunisia, 1943

This was the aeroplane of the group's commander, Lieutenant-Colonel Gordon H. Austin. The aeroplane was completed in the standard 'sand and spinach' camouflage of the theatre below national, unit and personal markings.

Bomber escort – Italian campaign
1942–45

The US Twelfth Air Force was brought into being as a balanced air formation able to satisfy all the requirements of the US Army's senior commanders in North Africa. The formation therefore included all of the elements for modern air warfare over and beyond the land battlefield.

THE TWELFTH AIR FORCE was planned from the outset as a balanced air formation able to provide all levels of bombing, air support and fighter capabilities complemented by a small but adequate reconnaissance capability. The main weight of its offensive capability was, of course, its bomber arm, and the XII Bomber Command was constituted on 26 February 1942 and activated on 13 March at the MacDill base in Florida. It was assigned to the Twelfth Air Force in August and transferred, without personnel and equipment, to High Wycombe in England, where the command was re-established before being moved to Tafaraoui in Algeria on 22 November 1942 to support the US and British ground forces after the *Torch* landings.

The XII Bomber Command was operational in the Mediterranean theatre until 1 November 1943, when most of its personnel were withdrawn. The command

received more men in January 1944 and served in combat until 1 March 1944, but was disbanded in Corsica on 10 June 1944.

Bomber escort

Known elements of the XII Bomber Command were the 5th Bombardment Wing comprising five bombardment groups with the B-17, two bombardment groups with the B-24, one bombardment group with the A-20 and A-26, two

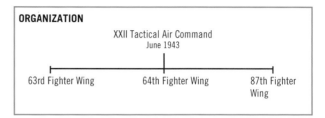

ORGANIZATION

XXII Tactical Air Command
June 1943

63rd Fighter Wing   64th Fighter Wing   87th Fighter Wing

▼ **US Fighter Squadron, 1942–43**

The standard organization of the USAAF fighter and fighter-bomber squadron in the Mediterranean campaign was based on a strength of 16 aircraft tactically disposed as four flights each with four aircraft, the aircraft of each flight operating in two pairs in leader and wingman combinations. The arrangement worked well, and remained essentially unaltered for the rest of World War II.

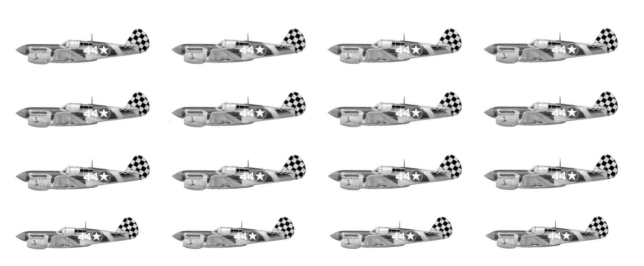

fighter groups with the P-38, one fighter group with the P-40, and one reconnaissance group with the P-38, P-39, P-40, P-51, A-20, A-36, B-17 and B-24. The 42nd Bombardment Wing comprised three bombardment groups with the B-26, one fighter group with the P-38 and one fighter group with the P-40; the 47th Bombardment Wing comprised two bombardment groups with the B-24, two bombardment groups with the B-25 and three bombardment groups with the B-26, one fighter group with the P-38, and three fighter groups with the P-40. The 57th Bombardment Wing comprised

five bombardment groups with the B-25, one bombardment with the A-20 and A-26, and two fighter groups with the P-40.

USAAF COMBAT GROUPS IN THE MEDITERRANEAN THEATRE			
Date	Fighter	Light/medium bomber	Heavy bomber
December 1942	10	6	3
December 1943	13	8	9
December 1944	12	8	19
March 1945	10	8	19

▲ **North American P-51A Mustang**

522nd Fighter-Bomber Squadron

Optimized for the long-range role, the P-51A was a fighter with good speed but was limited in the air-combat role by the poor performance of its Allison V-1710 liquid-cooled V-12 engine. As Merlin-engined Mustangs with better altitude capability were introduced, the P-51A became a useful fighter-bomber.

Specifications

Crew: 1

Powerplant: 895kW (1200hp) Allison V-1710-81 engine

Maximum speed: 690km/h (430mph)

Range: 3540km (2200 miles)

Service ceiling: 12,649m (41,500ft)

Dimensions: span 11.27m (37ft); length 9.84m (32ft 4in); height 4.15m (13ft 8in)

Weight: 4173kg (9200lb) loaded

Armament: 4 x 12.7mm (0.5in) MGs

▲ **Apaches in the Desert**

The A36A Apache was first used by the USAAF in the North African campaign in early 1943. This aircraft was rejected for widespread production in favour of the Mustang, but it was instrumental in the development of later Mustang variants.

Specifications

Crew: 1

Powerplant: 988kW (1325hp) Allison V-1710-
 87 liquid-cooled piston V12 engine

Maximum speed: 590km/h (365mph)

Range: 885km (550 miles)

Service ceiling: 7650m (25,100ft)

Dimensions: span 11.28m (37ft 1in);
 length 9.83m (32ft 3in);
 height 3.71m (12ft 2in)

Weight: 4535kg (1000lb) loaded

Armament: 6 x 12.7mm (0.50in) M2 Browning
 MGs in wings

▲ **North American A-36A Apache**

524th Fighter-Bomber Squadron, Italy, 1943

The A-36A was the attack fighter brother of the P-51 Mustang fighter, as suggested by the indifferent altitude performance of its Allison V-1710 liquid-cooled V-12 engine. The type was flown in Italy by the 27th and 86th Fighter-Bomber Groups. Only 500 such aircraft were built.

XII Tactical Air Command
1942–45

The formation that finally became the XII Tactical Air Command was initially created as the XII Ground Air Support Command. It was intended to provide the US forces of the Allied First Army in North Africa with a powerful yet flexible air support.

THE XII TACTICAL Air Command (TAC) was constituted on 10 September 1942 with the initial designation XII Ground Air Support Command, and was activated on 17 September. It was allocated to the new Twelfth Air Force, receiving the revised designation XII Air Support Command before finally becoming the XII TAC in the course of April 1944.

The XII Air Support Command arrived in French Morocco from 9 November 1942 as the major part of the US air component that supported the Allied *Torch* landings.

Mediterranean base
The XII TAC was operational in the Mediterranean and European theatres until May 1945, and then remained in Europe as part of the occupation force of the United States Air Forces in Europe (USAFE). It was deactivated at Bad Kissingen in the US occupation zone of Germany on 10 November 1947.

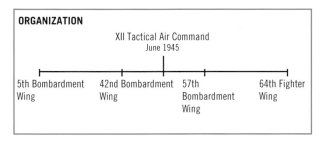

ORGANIZATION

XII Tactical Air Command
June 1945

5th Bombardment Wing — 42nd Bombardment Wing — 57th Bombardment Wing — 64th Fighter Wing

Known XII TAC components included three bombardment wings transferred from the XII Bomber Command when this was deactivated in the course of June 1944. These three units were the 5th Bombardment Wing for the heavy bomber role with the 2nd Bombardment Group (1944–45), the 97th Bombardment Group (1944–45), the 99th Bombardment Group (1944–45), the 301st Bombardment Group (1944–45), the 463rd Bombardment Group (1944–45) and the 483rd

Bombardment Group (1944–45), all flying the B-17 Flying Fortress four-engine bomber. For the medium bomber role, the 42nd Bombardment Wing with the 17th Bombardment Group (1944–45) and 320th Bombardment Group (1944–45) both flying the B-26 Marauder twin-engine bomber; and the 57th Bombardment Wing also for the medium bomber role with the 310th Bombardment Group (1944–45), 319th Bombardment Group (1944–45), 321st Bombardment Group (1944–45) and 340th Bombardment Group (1944–45), all flying the B-25 Mitchell twin-engine bomber.

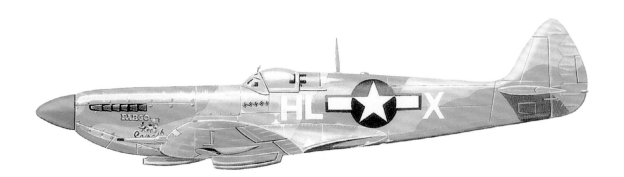

▲ **Supermarine Spitfire Mk VIII**

308th Fighter Squadron / 31st Fighter Group, Italy, 1944

This was the aeroplane of 1st Lieutenant L. P. Molland, commanding officer of the 308th Fighter Squadron.

Specifications

Crew: 1

Powerplant: 1170kW (1565hp) 12-cylinder Rolls-Royce Merlin 61 engine

Maximum speed: 642km/h (410mph)

Range: 698km (435 miles) on internal fuel tanks

Service ceiling: 12,650m (41,500ft)

Dimensions: span 11.23m (36ft 10in); length 9.47m (31ft 1in); height 3.86m (12ft 8in)

Weight: 3343kg (7370lb) loaded

Armament: 4 x 7.7mm (0.303in) MGs and 2 x 20mm (0.8in) cannons

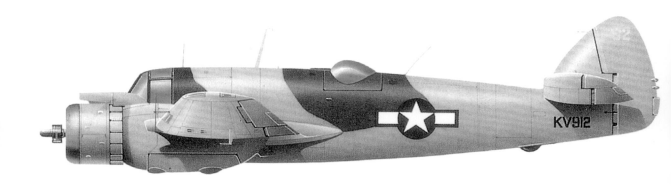

Specifications

Crew: 2

Powerplant: 2 x 1230kW (1650hp) Bristol Hercules VI radial piston engines

Maximum speed: 488km/h (303mph)

Range: 2366km (1470 miles)

Service ceiling: 4570m (15,000ft)

Dimensions: span 17.63m (57ft 10in);

length 12.70m (41ft 8in);

height 4.83m (15ft 10in)

Weight: 11,431kg (25,200lb) loaded

Armament: 4 x 20mm (0.8in) cannon and 6 x 7.7mm (.303in) MGs in wings; 1 x 7.7mm (.303in) Vickers MG in dorsal turret

▲ **Bristol Beaufighter Mk VIF**

416th Night-Fighter Squadron, Corsica, 1943–44

Another British type that saw limited service with the USAAF was the Beaufighter, seen here in its Mk VIF form as a radar-equipped night-fighter.

Post-war service

The last of the XII TAC's components was the 64th Fighter Wing, which was added for service on post-war USAFE occupation duties. This wing comprised the 27th Fighter Group (1946–47), 36th Fighter Group (1945–46), 86th Fighter Group (1945–46), 324th Fighter Group (1945) and 406th Fighter Group (1945–46) all flying the P-47 Thunderbolt single-engine heavy fighter; and the 52nd Fighter Group (1946–47), 354th Fighter Group (1945–46) and 355th Fighter Group (1945), all flying the P-51 Mustang single-engined multi-role fighter.

Specifications

Crew: 1

Powerplant: 1891kW (2535hp) Pratt & Whitney
R-2800-59W Double Wasp

Maximum speed: 697km/h (433mph)

Range: 3060km (1900 miles) with drop tanks

Service ceiling: 12,495m (41,000ft)

Dimensions: span 12.42m (40ft 9in); length
11.02m (36ft 2in); height 4.47m (14ft 8in)

Weight: 7938kg (17,500lb) maximum takeoff

Armament: 8 x 12.7mm (0.5in) MGs in wings,
plus provision for 1134kg (2500lb) external
bombs or rockets

▲ **Republic P-47D Thunderbolt**

86th Fighter Squadron / 79th Fighter Group, Fano, Italy, February 1945

While serving in Italy, the 79th Fighter Group used a non-standard group designation system (x plus a number), which it had first adopted in the USA before transfer overseas.

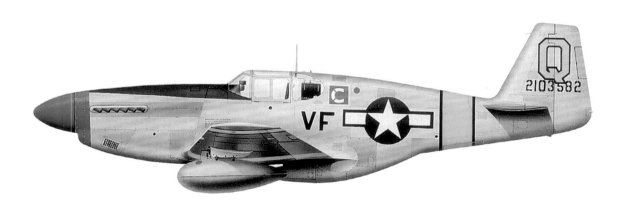

Specifications

Crew: 1

Powerplant: 1044kW (1400hp) Packard
V-1650-3 Rolls-Royce Merlin engine

Maximum speed: 690km/h (430mph)

Range: 3540km (2200 miles)

Service ceiling: 12,649m (41,500ft)

Dimensions: span 11.27m (37ft);
length 9.84m (32ft 4in);
height 4.15m (13ft 8in)

Weight: 4173kg (9200lb) loaded

Armament: 6 x 12.7mm (0.5in) MGs

▲ **North American P-51C Mustang**

5th Fighter Squadron / 52nd Fighter Group, Italy, 1944

This was the aeroplane of Lieutenant Calvin D. Allen, Jr.

▲ **Republic P-47D Thunderbolt**

USAAF, European Theatre, 1944

This is the original pattern of P-47D with a framed canopy sliding to the rear over the 'razorback' turtledeck upper decking of the rear fuselage. Even with drop tanks, the P-47D possessed range that was adequate rather than exceptional.

Specifications

Crew: 1	Dimensions: span 12.42m (40ft 9in); length
Powerplant: 1891kW (2535hp) Pratt & Whitney	11.02m (36ft 2in); height 4.47m (14ft 8in)
R-2800-59W Double Wasp	Weight: 7938kg (17,500lb) maximum takeoff
Maximum speed: 697km/h (433mph)	Armament: 8 x 12.7mm (0.5in) MGs in wings,
Range: 3060km (1900 miles) with drop tanks	plus provision for 1134kg (2500lb) external
Service ceiling: 12,495m (41,000ft)	bombs or rockets

XXII Tactical Air Command
1942–45

Despite its several names, the XXII TAC provided the US Twelfth Air Force with very useful ground-attack and close support capabilities, and also the wherewithal to provide fighter escort for its bomber forces.

T HE LAST MAJOR component of the US Twelfth Air Force, and optimized for the tactical role, was the XXII TAC. This was constituted on the same day as the XII Bomber Command, on 26 February 1942, and was activated on 5 March, thus predating the XII Ground Air Support Command, which later became the XII TAC. The XXII TAC was redesignated as the XII Fighter Command in May 1942, but reverted to its original designation as the XXII TAC during the course of November 1944.

North African posting

The XII Fighter Command was allocated to the Twelfth Air Force in August 1942. Establishedt at Wattisham in England during September 1942, it moved to its designated operational area in North Africa, reaching Tafaraoui in French Algeria on 8 November 1942 as part of the air component for

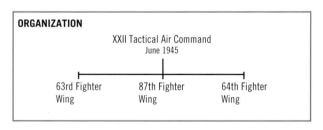

ORGANIZATION

XXII Tactical Air Command
June 1945

63rd Fighter Wing — 87th Fighter Wing — 64th Fighter Wing

the Allied forces involved in the *Torch* landings in French north-west Africa and the advance toward Tunisia, the last part of North Africa held by the Axis forces until they were thrown out in May 1943.

The XXII TAC served in the combat role within the Mediterranean theatre until the end of World War II, and was then deactivated at Pomigliano, Italy, on 4 October 1945.

Known components of the XXII TAC were a pair of wings flying the P-47 Thunderbolt single-engine heavy fighter. These units were the 63rd Fighter Wing comprising the 52nd Fighter Group (1943–44) and the 350th Fighter Group (1943–44), and the 87th Fighter Wing comprising the 57th Fighter Group (1944), 79th Fighter Group (1944) and 86th Fighter Group (1944).

Thunderbolt flyers

Between them, these five groups mustered a total of 15 squadrons with some 240 aircraft. In a theatre essentially bereft of German fighter opposition and bombers that could otherwise have been the targets of their heavy fixed forward-firing armament of six or eight 12.7mm (0.5in) machine guns, the Thunderbolts were operated almost exclusively in the fighter-bomber role. This role was especially important in the Italian theatre, as artillery was more limited in its applications than it would otherwise have been in less rugged terrain.

The Germans displayed skill and industry in creating excellent defensive complexes, which carefully exploited the advantages offered to the defence by the backbone-like Apennine mountains, together with the hills scoured into a myriad steep gorges by fast-flowing rivers extending west and east from them. The fighter-bomber was therefore amongst the major weapons of choice for the Allied

▲ **Heavy cruiser**

The P-47N was the fastest and heaviest of the Thunderbolts to fly in World War II, and included square-cut wing tips and extra fuel cells in the root of each wing.

air forces. With useful firepower and disposable loads, the single-engine fighter-bomber could operate in twisty valleys at low level, strafing convoys in the open and bombing defensive emplacements.

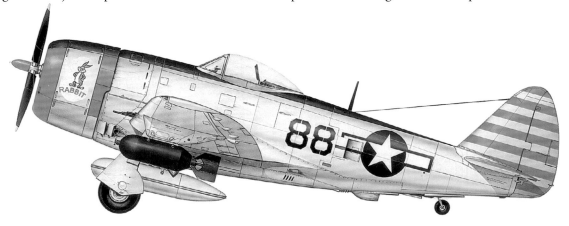

▲ **Republic P-47D-25-RE Thunderbolt**

527th Fighter Squadron / 86th Fighter Group, Pisa, Italy, 1944

Sturdy and well armed with heavy machine guns and disposable weapons under the wing, the P-47D was a classic heavy fighter-bomber, and extra range was provided by the drop tank.

Specifications

Crew: 1	Dimensions: span 12.42m (40ft 9in); length
Powerplant: 1891kW (2535hp) Pratt & Whitney	11.02m (36ft 2in); height 4.47m (14ft 8in)
R-2800-59W Double Wasp	Weight: 7938kg (17,500lb) maximum takeoff
Maximum speed: 697km/h (433mph)	Armament: 8 x 12.7mm (0.5in) MGs in wings,
Range: 3060km (1900 miles) with drop tanks	plus provision for 1134kg (2500lb) external
Service ceiling: 12,495m (41,000ft)	bombs or rockets

▼ 1945 Fighter Wing

By 1945, the USAAF's fighter strength had been integrated into powerful fighter wings. Each of these comprised three fighter groups, which in turn consisted of three fighter squadrons. Each fighter squadron had four flights each of four aircraft in the form of two tactical pairs, each based on a two-aeroplane team (leader and his wingman). In overall terms, therefore, this gave the fighter wing a total of 144 aircraft.

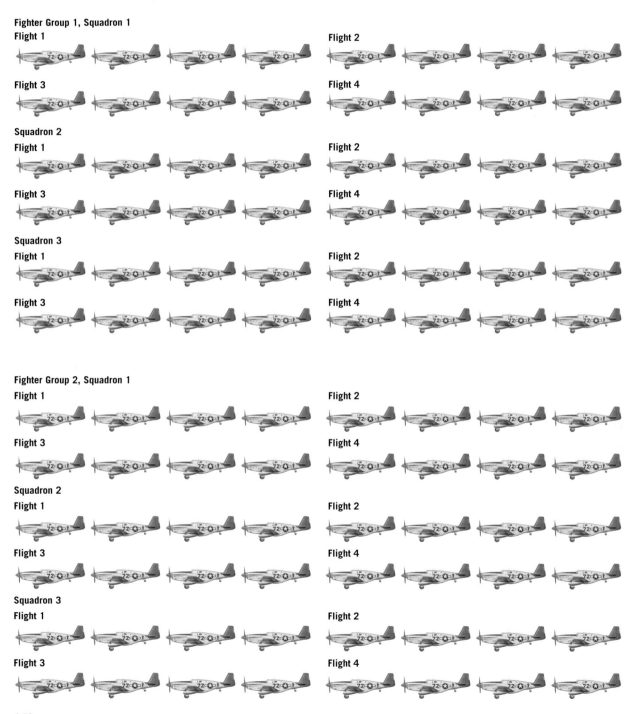

Fighter Group 1, Squadron 1
Flight 1

Flight 2

Flight 3

Flight 4

Squadron 2
Flight 1

Flight 2

Flight 3

Flight 4

Squadron 3
Flight 1

Flight 2

Flight 3

Flight 4

Fighter Group 2, Squadron 1
Flight 1

Flight 2

Flight 3

Flight 4

Squadron 2
Flight 1

Flight 2

Flight 3

Flight 4

Squadron 3
Flight 1

Flight 2

Flight 3

Flight 4

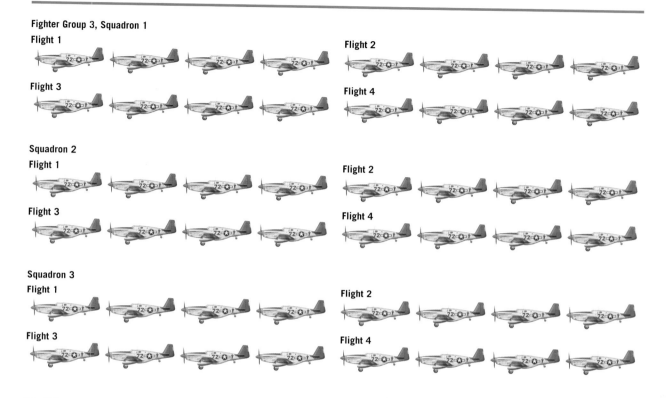

Fighter Group 3, Squadron 1

Flight 1

Flight 2

Flight 3

Flight 4

Squadron 2

Flight 1

Flight 2

Flight 3

Flight 4

Squadron 3

Flight 1

Flight 2

Flight 3

Flight 4

US Fifteenth Air Force
1943–45

The Fifteenth Air Force was the southern counterpart of the UK-based Eighth Air Force, and gave the United States the ability to undertake the strategic bomber role in Italy, the Balkans as far east as the Black Sea, and central European areas.

THE US FIFTEENTH AIR Force was one of the later additions to the overall command organization of the USAAF in World War II for service in the Mediterranean theatre. It was conceived as a strategic air force, with emphasis therefore placed on its heavy bomber capability, and it embarked on its programme of combat operations only one day after it had been established. This was made possible by the fact that the new air force inherited already well-established units, and the Fifteenth Air Force commander, Lieutenant-General 'Jimmy' Doolittle, was well-experienced in the organization and control of strategic bomber operations and was thus in the position to press ahead without delay.

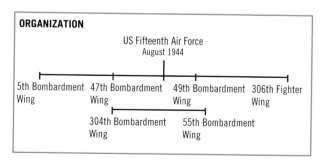

ORGANIZATION

US Fifteenth Air Force
August 1944

5th Bombardment Wing 47th Bombardment Wing 49th Bombardment Wing 306th Fighter Wing

304th Bombardment Wing 55th Bombardment Wing

The new air force force drew its operational elements from the heavy bomber units of the IX Bomber Command of the Ninth Air Force, which was being relocated to the UK to become the USAAF's primary exponent of tactical air power in the north-west Europe campaign, the XII Bomber Command of the Twelfth Air Force, and diversion of groups for the Eighth Air Force.

Strategic role

Operating mainly from bases in southern Italy, the Fifteenth Air Force, along with the Eighth Air Force and RAF Bomber Command, became the Allied instruments of the strategic air war waged against Germany. The Fifteenth Air Force lost 2110 bombers from its 15 B-24 and six B-17 bombardment groups, while its seven fighter groups claimed a total of 1836 German aircraft destroyed. The Fifteenth Air Force was deactivated on 15 September 1945.

▲ **North American P-51C Mustang**

302nd Fighter Squadron / 322nd Fighter Group, Italy

This was the aeroplane of the ace Lieutenant Lee 'Buddy' Archer.

Specifications

Crew: 1

Powerplant: 1044kW (1400hp) Packard
V-1650-3 Rolls-Royce Merlin engine

Maximum speed: 690km/h (430mph)

Range: 3540km (2200 miles)

Service ceiling: 12,649m (41,500ft)

Dimensions: span 11.27m (37ft);
length 9.84m (32ft 4in);
height 4.15m (13ft 8in)

Weight: 4173kg (9200lb) loaded

Armament: 6 x 12.7mm (0.5in) MGs

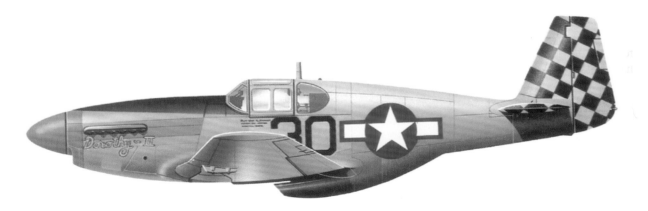

Specifications

Crew: 1

Powerplant: 1044kW (1400hp) Packard
V-1650-3 Rolls-Royce Merlin engine

Maximum speed: 690km/h (430mph)

Range: 3540km (2200 miles)

Service ceiling: 12,649m (41,500ft)

Dimensions: span 11.27m (37ft);
length 9.84m (32ft 4in);
height 4.15m (13ft 8in)

Weight: 4173kg (9200lb) loaded

Armament: 6 x 12.7mm (0.5in) MGs

▲ **North American P-51B Mustang**

318th Fighter Squadron / Fifteenth Air Force

The one major limitation of the otherwise excellent P-51B was its framed canopy, whose large areas of metal impaired the pilot's lateral fields of vision.

Italy and Southern Europe
1943–45

The aircraft of the US Fifteenth Air Force, operating primarily from bases in the flat areas near the 'heel' of Italy, played a major part in curtailing the flow of supplies to Germans forces seeking desperately to hold onto the northern half of Italy from the summer of 1944.

A S THE TWO ALLIED armies, the US Fifth Army in the west and the British Eighth Army in the east, advanced north from the line of Rome, which fell on 4 June 1944, they continued to encounter the standard pattern of skilled German defence.

Tactical air power was of vital importance in winkling the Germans from their defences through the use of light bombers and ground-attack aircraft, while medium bombers attacked farther to the north in an effort to cut the Germans' lines of communication and destroy rear-area facilities.

Targeting strategic facilities

There was also scope for heavy bombers to roam still deeper behind the front to attack strategic targets in the Balkans and the southern part of central Europe, including aircraft production facilities, tank manufacturing factories, and key industrial facilities and fuel production centres all across the region.

There was also the opportunity to disrupt, if not actually to sever, the limited number of routes that the Germans could use to nourish their ground forces in Italy. These rail and road routes included natural chokepoints such as the Brenner Pass, and also included major marshalling yards in cities such as Vienna and Ljubljana.

The same type of effort was also waged against the German communications to their forces in Greece, Albania and southern Yugoslavia. Little praised at the time or later, this strategic bombing effort played a major part in crippling the Germans.

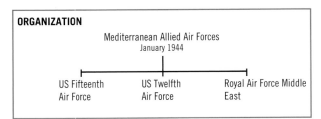

ORGANIZATION

Mediterranean Allied Air Forces
January 1944

US Fifteenth Air Force	US Twelfth Air Force	Royal Air Force Middle East

▲ **Fighter ace**
Captain Andrew Turner (left), commanding officer of the 302nd Fighter Squadron, 332nd Fighter Group, and Lieutenant Clarence 'Lucky' Lester (right) discuss a recent mission.

306th Fighter Wing
1943–45

Like all other strategic air forces of the USAAF, the Fifteenth Air Force in Italy had the heavy bomber at its core, but also needed escort fighters. This capability was provided by the 25 fighter groups controlled by the 306th Fighter Group.

THE 306TH FIGHTER Group was the escort fighter element of the US Fifteenth Air Force, and operated two types of fighter in the form of the Lockheed P-38 Lightning twin-engine warplane and the North American P-51 Mustang single-engine fighter. The three Lightning elements were the 1st, 14th and 82nd Fighter Groups, which were based at Salsola, Triolo and Vincenzo respectively.

The 1st Fighter Group, which moved to Aghione in Corsica for a time in August 1944 to support the *Dragoon* landings in southern France, comprised the 27th, 71st and 94th Fighter Squadrons; the 14th Fighter Group comprised the 37th, 37th and 48th Fighter Squadrons; and the 82nd Fighter Group comprised the 95th, 96th and 97th Fighter Squadrons.

Mustang flyers

The four Mustang elements were the 31st, 52nd, 325th and 332nd Fighter Groups, which were based at San Severo, Madna, Lesina and Ramitelli respectively. The 31st Fighter Group comprised the 307th, 308th and 309th Fighter Squadrons; the 52nd Fighter Group comprised the 2nd, 4th and 5th Fighter Squadrons; the 325th Fighter Group comprised the 317th, 318th and 319th Fighter Squadrons; and the 332nd Fighter Group comprised the 99th, 100th, 301st and 302nd Fighter Squadrons,

▲ **Mountain cruising**
'Bubbletop' Mustangs of the 325th (foreground), 332nd, 52nd and 31st Fighter Groups pose for the camera late in the war. Note the lack of colourful markings on the Mustang from the 332nd Fighter Group.

although it should be noted that the 99th Fighter Squadron was allocated to the 86th Fighter Group of the US Twelfth Air Force, and flew the Curtiss P-40 Warhawk and the Republic P-47 Thunderbolt as well as the Mustang.

Free roaming role

While the primary task of these fighters units was the escort of the Fifteenth Air Force's B-24 Liberator heavy bombers, the decline of the *Luftwaffe*'s fighter arm, whose remnants were increasingly concentrated for the defence of Germany, meant that the Allied fighters had what was, in effect, a roving commission to search out German air power at low as well and medium and high altitudes, and in the absence of aerial 'trade' to search for targets of opportunity such as convoys, trains, fuel storage facilities and anything resembling a military dump.

306TH FIGHTER WING		
Base	**Group**	**Squadrons**
Salsola	1st FG	27th, 71st & 94th FSs
Triolo	14th FG	37th, 47th & 48th FSs
San Severo	31st FG	307th, 308th & 309th FSs
Madna	52nd FG	2nd, 4th & 5th FSs
Vincenzo	82nd FG	95th, 96th & 97th FSs
Lesina	325th FG	317th, 318th & 319th FSs
Ramitelli	332nd FG	99th, 100th, 301st & 302nd FSs

ORGANIZATION

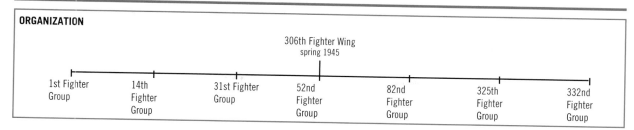

306th Fighter Wing
spring 1945

| 1st Fighter Group | 14th Fighter Group | 31st Fighter Group | 52nd Fighter Group | 82nd Fighter Group | 325th Fighter Group | 332nd Fighter Group |

▲ **North American P-51D Mustang**

307th Fighter Squadron / 31st Fighter Group, Italy, 1944–45

This was the aeroplane of Lieutenant James Brooks, a pilot of the
US Fifteenth Air Force.

Specifications

Crew: 1

Powerplant: 1264kW (1695hp) Packard Merlin
V-1650-7 V-12 piston engine

Maximum speed: 703km/h (437mph)

Range: 3347km (2080 miles)

Service ceiling: 12,770m (41,900ft)

Dimensions: span 11.28m (37ft);
length 9.83m (32ft 3in);
height 4.17m (13ft 8in)

Weight: 5488kg (12,100lb) loaded

Armament: 6 x 12.7mm (0.5in) MGs in wings,
plus up to 2 x 454kg (1000lb) bombs

Specifications

Crew: 1

Powerplant: 1264kW (1695hp) Packard Merlin
V-1650-7 V-12 piston engine

Maximum speed: 703km/h (437mph)

Range: 3347km (2080 miles)

Service ceiling: 12,770m (41,900ft)

Dimensions: span 11.28m (37ft);
length 9.83m (32ft 3in);
height 4.17m (13ft 8in)

Weight: 5488kg (12,100lb) loaded

Armament: 6 x 12.7mm (0.5in) MGs in wings,
plus up to 2 x 454kg (1000lb) bombs

▲ **North American P-51D Mustang**

317th Fighter Squadron / 325th Fighter Group, Italy 1944–45

This was the aeroplane of Lieutenant Walter R. Hinton, a pilot of the
US Fifteenth Air Force. Note the diagonal-chequered pattern on the tailplane,
used by all aircraft throughout the 325th Fighter Group.

Chapter 4

Soviet Union

Although the Soviet air forces were numerically strong in 1939, they were in a poor state of training and the vast majority of their aircraft were obsolete. The 'Winter War' of 1939–40 with Finland proved this point, and the Soviet Union accelerated the modernization programme it had already begun on the basis of some advanced warplanes under development. This process was wholly incomplete at the time of the German invasion of June 1941, but the destruction of vast numbers of Soviet aircraft was something of a blessing in disguise. A new Soviet air arm began to emerge on the basis of good warplanes optimized for Soviet production and operating conditions, and a training programme that emphasized skills rather than an adherence to set procedures. From 1943, the Soviets steadily swept the Germans from the skies.

◀ **On patrol**
Two Polikarpov I-16 fighters patrol over the vast forests of northern Russia before the outbreak of war with Nazi Germany.

Russo-Finnish War
1939–40

When he ordered the invasion of Finland in November 1939, Stalin believed that the Soviet forces would secure quick and total victory. Despite being totally outnumbered, in the air as on the ground, the Finns resisted with great determination and there followed a bloody campaign.

THE FINNS POSSESSED 145 frontline aircraft, of which only 114 were serviceable, while the Soviets could call on up to 3800 aircraft. After early reverses, the Soviets sent in larger numbers of more modern aircraft, but the Finns were for some time able to cope with this as a result of their superior tactics. Finland used the 'finger four' formation – four aircraft flying as two pairs, one low and the other high, each fighting independently but supporting its wingman in combat. This was better than the Soviet tactic of three fighters in a 'vic' formation. The Finnish tactics, combined with the Finnish belief in attack rather than defence, regardless of the odds, contributed to the failure of Soviet bombers to inflict substantial damage on Finnish positions, industries and population centres.

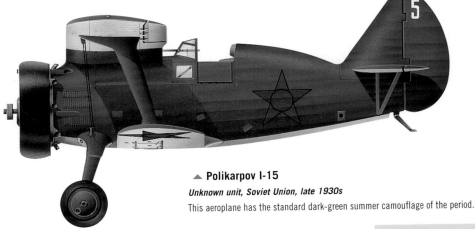

Specifications
Crew: 1
Powerplant: 358kW (480hp) M-22
  radial piston engine
Maximum speed: 278km/h (173mph)
Range: 560km (348 miles)
Service ceiling: 7500m (24,605ft)
Dimensions: span 10.24m (33ft 7in);
  length 6.78m (22ft 3in)
Weight: 934kg (2059lb) unloaded
Armament: 2 x 7.62mm (03in) PV-1
  MGs, plus 2 x 20kg (44lb) bombs

▲ **Polikarpov I-15**
Unknown unit, Soviet Union, late 1930s
This aeroplane has the standard dark-green summer camouflage of the period.

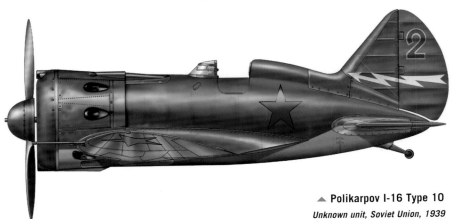

Specifications
Crew: 1
Powerplant: 746kW (1000hp) M-62
  radial piston engine
Maximum speed: 490km/h (304mph)
Range: 600km (373 miles)
Service ceiling: 9470m (31,070ft)
Dimensions: span 8.88m (29ft 2in);
  length 6.04m (19ft 10in)
Weight: 2060kg (4542lb) loaded
Armament: 4 x 7.62mm (03in) ShKAS
  MGs (sometimes 2 x 20mm/0.8in
  replacing 2 x ShKAS MGs in wings);
  up to 200kg (441lb) bomb load

▲ **Polikarpov I-16 Type 10**
Unknown unit, Soviet Union, 1939
This version is depicted in the standard green summer camouflage.

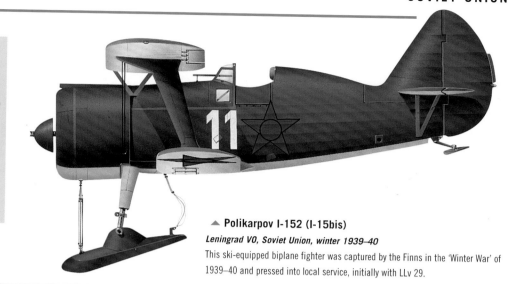

Specifications

Crew: 1

Powerplant: 578kW (775hp) M-25V
radial piston engine

Maximum speed: 370km/h (230mph)

Range: 560km (348 miles)

Service ceiling: 9500m (31,070ft)

Dimensions: span 10.20m (33ft 6in);
length 6.27m (20ft 7in)

Weight: 1900kg (4189lb) loaded

Armament: 4 x 7.62mm (03in)
ShKAS MGs; up to 150kg (331lb)
bomb load

▲ **Polikarpov I-152 (I-15bis)**

Leningrad VO, Soviet Union, winter 1939–40

This ski-equipped biplane fighter was captured by the Finns in the 'Winter War' of 1939–40 and pressed into local service, initially with LLv 29.

Soviet V-VS

1941–42

When the Germans unleashed Operation *Barbarossa*, the invasion of the Soviet Union in June 1941, the Soviet air forces were large but technically obsolete and in a dismal state of training that emphasized orthodoxy rather than initiative. Change was under way, but it was too late to prevent catastrophic losses during 1941.

THE SOVIET AIR FORCE, which is also known by the abbreviation V-VS (*Voenno-Vozdushnye Sily*), was the official designation of one of the air forces of the Soviet Union, the other being the Soviet Anti-Air Defence (PVO). The origins of the V-VS can be found in the the so-called Workers' and Peasants' Air Fleet established in 1918 as the Soviet successor to the Imperial Russian Air Force.

After the service was placed under control of the Red Army, which led to the change of designation to V-VS in 1930, the air force was much less influenced by the thinking and planning of the Communist party and more geared towards serving the needs of the professional Red Army.

After the creation of the Soviet Union, many efforts were made both to modernize the Soviet aero industry on a national basis and to enlarge aircraft production. As a result, the production of aircraft increased rapidly and dramatically in the USSR in the early years of the 1930s. In the middle and late years of that decade, the V-VS could therefore introduce Polikarpov I-15 biplane and Polikarpov

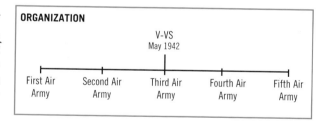

ORGANIZATION

V-VS
May 1942

First Air Army — Second Air Army — Third Air Army — Fourth Air Army — Fifth Air Army

I-16 monoplane fighters, the former including a variant with retractable main landing gear units, and also the Tupolev SB-2 and Ilyushin DB-3 monoplane bombers, the former generally acknowledged as the best high-speed bomber of its time.

Early test

One of the first real tests of the V-VS and the Soviet aero industry came in 1936 with the start of the Spanish Civil War. The Soviet Union decided to aid the Republican government side with equipment and some manpower, and here the best of the V-VS was put to the test against German and Italian detachments flying for the Nationalist rebel side

SOVIET FIGHTER TYPES JUNE 1941			
Type	Speed	Armament	Number built
Lavochkin LaGG-3	560km/h (348mph)	1 x 20mm cannon 2 x 12.7mm MGs	6527
Mikoyan MiG-3	640km/h (398mph)	1 x 12.7mm 2 x 7.62mm MGs	3322
Polikarpov I-15bis	370km/h (230mph)	4 x 7.62mm MGs	2408
Polikarpov I-153	365km/h (227mph)	4 x 7.62mm MGs	3437
Polikarpov I-16	525km/h (326mph)	2 x 20mm cannon 2 x 7.62mm MGs	c.6500
Yakovlev Yak-1	580 km/h (360mph)	1 x 20mm cannon 2 x 7.62mm MGs	8720

and testing their own latest types. Early success with the I-16 was wasted because of the limited use of this fighter, and the arrival of the Messerschmitt Bf 109 later in the war secured air superiority for the Nationalists. At the start of World War II, the Soviet military was not yet ready for developing modern technology suitable for winning a war.

In 1939, the V-VS used its bombers to attack Finland in the 'Winter War', but the losses inflicted on it by the relatively small Finnish air arm showed the air force's shortcomings, mostly due to loss of personnel in the purges of the late 1930s.

Specifications

Crew: 1

Powerplant: 820kW (1100hp) M-63 radial
  piston engine

Maximum speed: 2490km/h (304mph)

Range: 600km (373 miles)

Service ceiling: 9470m (31,070ft)

Dimensions: span 8.88m (29ft 2in);

length 6.04m (19ft 10in)

Weight: 2060kg (4542lb) loaded

Armament: 4 x 7.62mm (03in) ShKAS MGs
  (sometimes 2 x 20mm [0.8in] replacing 2 x
  ShKAS MGs in wings); up to 200kg (441lb)
  bomb load

▼ **Polikarpov I-16 Type 24**

Unknown squadron of the Leningrad Military District, Soviet Union,
summer 1939

The I-16 was very tricky to fly as a result of its short and tubby fuselage, and
nearly all pilots preferred an open cockpit.

Barbarossa: the first months

JUNE–AUGUST 1941

In the first three months of their campaign against the Soviet Union, the Germans swept all before them. The V-VS lost many thousands of aircraft and men, but already manufacture of more modern aircraft was being stepped up, and training was improved.

THE GERMAN INVASION of the Soviet Union started on 22 June 1941. Three-fifths of the *Luftwaffe's* strength was deployed along the frontier with the Soviet Union. Some 1400 of the 1945 operational aircraft, 1280 of them serviceable, were gathered

in four *Luftflotten*: 650 fighters, 831 bombers, 324 dive-bombers and 140 reconnaissance aircraft, as well as 200 transports plus coastal and reconnaissance machines. The Germans had allied support, including 299 Finnish aircraft just a short time later, but

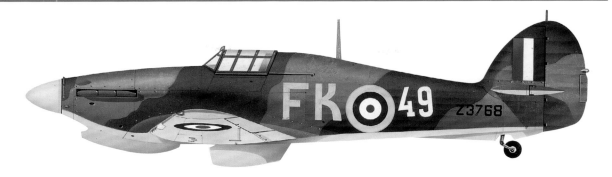

Specifications

Crew: 1

Powerplant: 954kW (1280hp) Rolls-Royce
Merlin XX liquid-cooled V-12

Maximum speed: 529km/h (329mph)

Range: 1480km (920 miles)

Service ceiling: 10,850m (35,600ft)

Dimensions: span 12.19m (40ft 0in); length
9.81m (32ft 2.25in); height 3.98m (13ft 1in)

Weight: 3629kg (8044lb) loaded

Armament: 8 x 7.7mm (0.303in)
Browning MGs

▲ **Hawker Hurricane Mk IIB**

No. 18 Squadron / No. 151 Wing / RAF, Vaenga, autumn 1941

In an effort to show solidarity with the Soviet people after the German invasion of the Soviet Union in June 1941, the British sent a wing of Hurricane fighters, complete with air and ground crews, in the late summer of 1941. The aircraft flew with Soviet markings superimposed on the British camouflage.

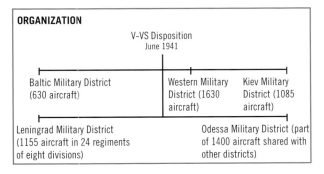

ORGANIZATION

V-VS Disposition
June 1941

Baltic Military District
(630 aircraft)

Western Military
District (1630
aircraft)

Kiev Military
District (1085
aircraft)

Leningrad Military District
(1155 aircraft in 24 regiments
of eight divisions)

Odessa Military District (part
of 1400 aircraft shared with
other districts)

the Axis air strength was wholly overshadowed in numerical terms by the V-VS' strength of some 12,000–15,000 operational aircraft, about 7000 of them in the west, in 23 air divisions.

The Soviets were currently working their way through a great programme of re-equipment and retraining. Not expecting a German attack, they were also based in undispersed form on airfields right up against the frontier. However, the *Luftwaffe* possessed a huge advantage in terms of experience, and also in terms of the superior quality of the aircraft available to them.

Surprise attack

The first attack was made just after 3 a.m. by 637 bombers and 331 fighters against 31 airfields. The Soviets were caught completely by surprise, and the Germans lost a mere two aircraft. There followed a stream of later raids, and by the end of the day

1489 Soviet aircraft had been claimed on the ground and 322 in the air as the German ground forces swept forward.

The Germans' standard tactic was the employment of dive-bombers and heavy fighters in direct support of the armoured spearheads, these aircraft acting as airborne artillery while medium bombers attacked supply and concentration areas, railway communications, convoys and targets deeper behind the front. In the first seven days, the Soviets lost 4990 aircraft and the Germans just 179.

The greatest battles of the war up to this time took place as the German spearheads approached Minsk on 30 June. Large formations of unescorted Soviet bombers were committed, and one German unit, *Jagdgeschwader* 51, claimed 114 of these shot down. Further north, while defending bridges captured over the Duna river, JG 54 claimed the destruction of 65 bombers shot down, and on 6 July some 65 of 73 bombers attacking a German bridgehead at Ostrov were destroyed.

The first air raid on Moscow was flown on 22 July: 127 bombers dropped 106 tonnes (104 tons) of bombs. On the following night, 115 bombers attacked, and 100 more went back on the day after this. Thereafter Moscow was bombed regularly by day as well as night. During the summer months, the superior German fighters were notably active, and the unfortunate Soviet aircraft were shot down in almost unbelievable numbers.

The defence of Moscow
NOVEMBER 1941 – FEBRUARY 1942

The Germans had gambled on winning a swift victory in the Soviet Union, but were then checked in front of Moscow by renewed Soviet strength and the onset of truly bitter winter conditions. Then the Soviets counterattacked, driving the Germans back.

DURING SEPTEMBER 1941, the Soviets had attempted several counterattacks on the German Army Group Centre directed towards Moscow but, now woefully short of armoured vehicles as well as aircraft, they could not attempt a strategic counteroffensive. On 2 October, the Germans committed Army Group Centre to a final push on the capital. In front of this formation was a complex of defence lines, but the Germans broke through the first of these without difficulty and took Orel some 120km (75 miles) behind it. The Germans then closed in and trapped huge numbers of Soviet

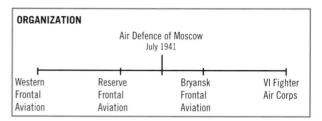

ORGANIZATION

Air Defence of Moscow
July 1941

Western Frontal Aviation	Reserve Frontal Aviation	Bryansk Frontal Aviation	VI Fighter Air Corps

personnel, leaving the Soviets with just 90,000 men and 150 tanks for the defence for Moscow. But the weather was worsening steadily, and the Germans paused to regroup, which allowed the Soviets to bring in fresh troops from Siberia. The Germans got under way once more on 15 November, by 2 December reaching a point only 24km (15 miles) west of central Moscow. But the first blizzards of the winter were now beginning, and the Germans forces lacked the equipment for winter survival, let alone combat. The Soviets now counterattacked and by February 1942 had pushed the Germans back.

GERMAN & SOVIET FRONTLINE AIR STRENGTHS		
Date	**German**	**Soviet**
June 1941	2130	8100
July 1941	1050	2500
December 1941	2500	2500
May 1942	3400	3160

▲ **Mikoyan-Gurevich MiG-3P**
6th IAP (Fighter Aviation Regiment) / 6th IAK (Fighter Aviation Corps) / PVO / Moscow Air Defence Zone, early 1942
This aeroplane was flown by A. V. Shlopov.

Specifications

Crew: 1

Powerplant: 1007kW (1350hp) Mikuli AM-35A
V12 piston engine

Maximum speed: 640km/h (398mph)

Range: 1195km (743 miles)

Service ceiling: 12,000m (39,370ft)

Dimensions: span 10.20m (33ft 6in);

length 8.26m (27ft 1in); height 3.50m
(11ft 6in)

Weight: 3350kg (7385lb) loaded

Armament: 1 x 12.7mm (0.5in) Beresin and
2 x 7.62mm (0.3in) ShKAS MGs; up to 200kg
(441lb) bomb load or 6 x RS-82 rockets on
underwing racks

Specifications

Crew: 1

Powerplant: 1007kW (1350hp) Mikuli AM-35A
V12 piston engine

Maximum speed: 640km/h (398mph)

Range: 1195km (743 miles)

Service ceiling: 12,000m (39,370ft)

Dimensions: span 10.20m (33ft 6in);

length 8.26m (27ft 1in); height 3.50m
(11ft 6in)

Weight: 3350kg (7385lb) loaded

Armament: 1 x 12.7mm (0.5in) Beresin and
2 x 7.62mm (0.3in) ShKAS MGs; up to 200kg
(441lb) bomb load or 6 x RS-82 rockets on
underwing racks

▲ **Mikoyan-Gurevich MiG-3**

34th IAP / 6th IAK, Moscow, winter 1941–42

'Za Stalina' (For Stalin) was a common legend on Soviet aircraft of the period.

Specifications

Crew: 1

Powerplant: 925kW (1240hp) Klimov M-105PF
V12 piston engine

Maximum speed: 560km/h (348mph)

Range: 650km (404 miles)

Service ceiling: 9600m (31,490ft)

Dimensions: span 9.80m (32ft 2in);
length 8.90m (29ft 3in)

Weight: 3280kg (7231lb) loaded

Armament: 2 x 20mm (0.8in) cannon (firing
through propeller hub), 2 x 12.7mm ((0.5in)
MGs in nose

▲ **Lavochkin LaGG-3**

6th IAK / Moscow Air Defence Zone, summer 1942

The unusual black and green camouflage was the result of the aeroplane being built in a factory that had previously manufactured tractors, which had always been completed in black or green.

The defence of Leningrad

AUGUST 1941 – FEBRUARY 1942

Named for the first leader of the Soviet Union, Leningrad had a huge symbolic attraction to Hitler. The Germans closed on the city in August 1941, but the Soviets were wholly determined to hold the city, no matter how heavy the cost.

ON 1 SEPTEMBER 1941, the forces of the German Army Group North were close enough to the great city of Leningrad to start their artillery bombardment. The Germans, who had decided against a direct assault on the city, now began the process of encircling it with the aid of the Finnish Army in the north, aiming to starve the city's garrison and civil population and so force them to surrender.

On 15 September, with the capture of Schlusselburg on the southern edge of Lake Ladoga, the city was completely cut off from overland communication with the rest of the Soviet Union. The food remaining in the city was sufficient, if carefully rationed, for about one month, and people began to succumb to starvation during October and November, some 11,000 deaths recorded in the latter month. A supply route from Tikhvin to Lednevo had been used to get some food across the lake in barges, but on 9 November the Germans took Tikhvin, and in the middle of the month the ice on the lake made navigation impossible while not yet being thick enough to support heavy motor vehicles such as laden trucks.

A new road from Zaboriye via Karpino to Lednevo was opened on 6 December, but the combination of the poor surface conditions and deteriorating weather meant that trucks could achieve little more than 30km (19 miles) per day on it. On 9 December, as part of the Red Army's winter counteroffensive, Tikhvin was recaptured and the Germans were pushed back to the Volkhov river. The railway was repaired and an ice road opened across the lake, facilitating a proper supply line to the city. But the supply situation remained precarious; on 25 December alone, 3700 people died. The situation became more desperate in the spring of 1942, when the thaw of the ice made the survival of Leningrad still more problematical.

▼ Fighter regiment, 1943

In 1943, the Soviet fighter arm was based on the fighter regiment, itself subordinated to the fighter division (three regiments) or the composite division (one fighter, one bomber and one ground-attack regiments). In basic terms the regiment comprised three fighter squadrons, each with about 12 aircraft, each squadron being subdivided into three sections of four aircraft. Each squadron tended to be equipped with the same type of aircraft, but a regiment might include a mixture of types, as shown here.

1st Squadron (12 x MiG-3s)

2nd Squadron (12 x Yak-1s)

3rd Squadron (12 x Yak 1-Ms)

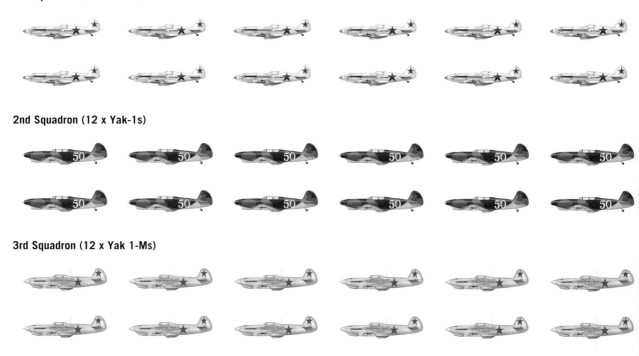

Soviet V-VS
1942–45

During 1942, the V-VS began to recover strongly from its decimation in 1941, with new aircraft and better training. Soviet production also grew in 1942, and by 1943 the fighter arm of the V-VS was in a position to start challenging and then getting the better of the *Luftwaffe*.

AS IT STARTED TO recover from the disasters of 1941, the V-VS was able to rebuild, largely from the efforts of factories that had been uprooted from European Russia and re-erected to the east of the Ural mountain barrier, an area in which other factories also sprang up. Initially the V-VS received the same types of aircraft it had been operating in 1941, for which the manufacturing skills already existed and which made large-scale use of materials readily available in the Soviet Union, most notably two forms of plywood created from local wood. The same materials also featured in the new types of aircraft that began to emerge from the production lines in 1942. So far as fighters were concerned, these were primarily the products of the Lavochkin, Mikoyan-Gurevich and Yakovlev design organizations. The two most important were the first and third, which created basic designs of advanced concept that could then be built in large numbers and steadily enhanced by incremental improvement.

Fighter power

The Soviets' main strength was always its fighters, for which emphasis was placed on simple manufacture and maintenance, strength to absorb battle damage and the rigours of operating on primitive airfields,

▲ **Mikoyan-Gurevich MiG-3 squadron**
Here, pilots of the 12th Soviet Fighter Regiment take the 'oath of the guard', following combat successes in the winter of 1942.

ORGANIZATION

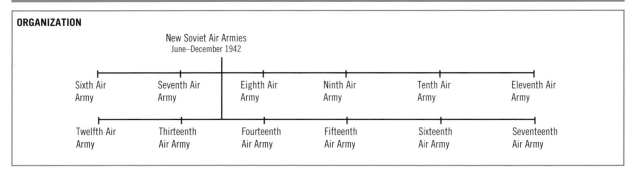

New Soviet Air Armies
June–December 1942

Sixth Air Army	Seventh Air Army	Eighth Air Army	Ninth Air Army	Tenth Air Army	Eleventh Air Army
Twelfth Air Army	Thirteenth Air Army	Fourteenth Air Army	Fifteenth Air Army	Sixteenth Air Army	Seventeenth Air Army

▲ Bell P-39Q Airacobra

16th Guards IAP, Eastern Front, 1944

This was one of the P-39 aircraft flown by Aleksandr Pokryshkin, the second highest-scoring Soviet ace, who shot down 48 of his eventual 59 'kills' while flying the Airacobra. Pokryshkin's memoirs and personal notebooks put his score at over 100. However, the Soviet air force did not officially confirm kills whose wreckage could not be found, and so many aircraft shot down over enemy territory were never confirmed.

Specifications

Crew: 1

Powerplant: 895kW (1200hp) Allison V-1710-85 liquid-cooled V-12

Maximum speed: 605km/h (376mph)

Range: 483km (300 miles)

Service ceiling: 11,665m (38,270ft)

Dimensions: span 10.36m (34ft 0in); length 9.195m (30ft 2in); height 3.785m (12ft 5in)

Weight: 3992kg (8,800lb) loaded

Armament: 1 x 37mm (1.46in) M4 cannon, 2 x 12.7mm (0.5in) Browning MGs, 4 x 7.62mm (0.3in) Browning MGs

▲ Lavochkin La-5FN

240th IAP, Eastern Front, April 1944

This aeroplane was flown by Ivan Kozhedub, a Hero of the Soviet Union and the highest-scoring Soviet ace of World War II. The legend below the cockpit translates as 'from collective farm worker Konev, Vasili Viktorovich'.

Specifications

Crew: 1

Powerplant: 1380kW (1850hp) Shvetsov M-82FN radial piston engine

Maximum speed: 665km/h (413mph)

Range: 635km (395 miles)

Service ceiling: 10.800m (35,435ft)

Dimensions: span 9.80m (32ft 2in); length 8.60m (28ft 3in)

Weight: 3280kg (7231lb) loaded

Armament: 2 x 20mm (0.8in) Beresin B-20 cannon in nose; plus up to 200kg (441lb) bomb load good performance and handling, powerful armament, and engines optimized for performance at up to 5000m (16,400ft). The qualities of these aircraft resulted from the decision made in the 1930s that the Soviet air forces would concentrate on tactical air warfare above the front in support of the ground forces, which were seen as the decisive arm. By 1943, therefore, the V-VS was considerably more of a match for the *Luftwaffe*, and in 1944 and 1945 achieved almost total air superiority.

GERMAN & SOVIET FRONTLINE AIR STRENGTHS		
Date	German	Soviet
November 1942	2450	3100
July 1943	2500	8300
January 1944	1800	8500
June 1944	1710	11,800
January 1945	1430	14,500
April 1945	1500 (all fronts)	17,000

Specifications

Crew: 1

Powerplant: 880kW (1180hp) Klimov M-105PF
V-12 liquid-cooled engine

Maximum speed: 592km/h (368mph)

Range: 700km (435 miles)

Service ceiling: 10,050m (33,000ft)

Dimensions: span 10 m (32ft 10in);
length 8.5m (27ft 11in)

Weight: 2883kg (6343lb) loaded

Armament: 1 x 20mm (0.8in) ShVAK cannon,
1 x 12.7mm (0.5in) Berezin UBS MG

▲ **Yakovlev Yak-1M**

1st 'Warszawa' IAP, Eastern Front, late 1944

This squadron was manned by Polish units in the Soviet army. A single one-second burst from the Yak-1s combined machine guns using high-explosive ammunition produced a highly destructive 2kg (4.4lb) weight of fire.

Specifications

Crew: 1

Powerplant: 925kW (1240hp) Klimov M-105PF
V12 piston engine

Maximum speed: 560km/h (348mph)

Range: 650km (404 miles)

Service ceiling: 9600m (31,490ft)

Dimensions: span 9.80m (32ft 2in);
length 8.90m (29ft 3in)

Weight: 3280kg (7231lb) loaded

Armament: 2 x 20mm (0.8in) cannon (firing
through propeller hub), 2 x 12.7mm (0.5in)
MGs in nose

▲ **Lavochkin LaGG-3**

9th IAP / V-VS ChF (Black Sea Air Force), southern Soviet Union, May 1944

Flown by Yuri Shchipov, this aeroplane carried the pilot's own 'lion's head' marking and eight victory symbols below the cockpit.

The Eastern Front
1942–43

The Soviets stunned the Germans with their counteroffensives late in 1941, and pressed their advantage into the spring thaw of 1942. Then the Germans replied with their own offensives, taking them towards the Caucasus and, fatally, the city of Stalingrad on the Volga river.

THE YEAR 1942 STARTED with the continuation of the Soviet counteroffensive that had checked the Germans in front of Moscow, this counteroffensive stretching along the full length of the Eastern Front. It ended in stalemate only after the advent of the spring thaw. Germany planned to regain the strategic initiative with a summer offensive towards the Caspian Sea and the important oilfields of the Caucasus, and preliminary offensives between early May and late June paved the way for this effort. A subsidiary undertaking took Sevastopol on the western side of the Crimea.

The German offensive, Operation Blue, began on 28 June and initially made good progress. Hitler then changed his mind about the objective, and added Stalingrad as one of the two major objectives. Divided aims meant divided forces, and Germany now lacked the strength to make fast progress on two diverging fronts. Even though the Soviet forces

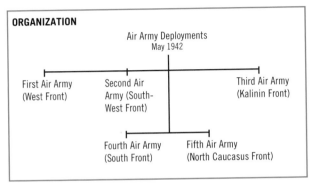

ORGANIZATION

Air Army Deployments
May 1942

First Air Army (West Front)

Second Air Army (South-West Front)

Third Air Army (Kalinin Front)

Fourth Air Army (South Front)

Fifth Air Army (North Caucasus Front)

were in disarray, the determination of the Soviet high command, combined with the huge distances that the Germans were trying to cover, meant that the offensive slowed and then stalled. Through the summer, the *Luftwaffe* kept local air superiority, but the V-VS introduced advanced bombers and fighters operated by competent aircrews.

▲ **Order of the Red Banner**
Overflying the Crimea, the lead aeroplane in this formation of Yakovlev Yak-9 fighters carries the Order of the Red Banner, indicating that all of these aircraft belong to a Guards unit.

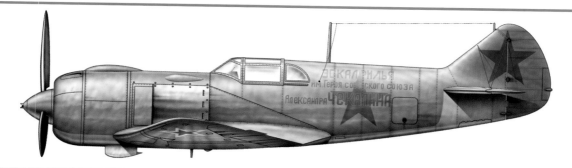

Specifications

Crew: 1

Powerplant: 1380kW (1850hp) Shvetsov
 M-82FN radial piston engine

Maximum speed: 665km/h (413mph)

Range: 635km (395 miles)

Service ceiling: 10.800m (35,435ft)

Dimensions: span 9.80m (32ft 2in);
 length 8.60m (28ft 3in)

Weight: 3280kg (7231lb) loaded

Armament: 2 x 20mm (0.8in) Beresin B-20
 cannon in nose; plus up to 200kg (441lb)
 bomb load

▲ Lavochkin La-5

Unknown unit, Eastern Front, 1943

This is an early example without the later variants' cut-down rear fuselage and
revised canopy, which offered much improved all-round fields of vision.

Specifications

Crew: 1

Powerplant: 962kW (1290hp) Klimov
 VK-105PF-2 V12 liquid-cooled piston engine

Maximum speed: 646km/h (401mph)

Range: 650km (405 miles)

Service ceiling: 10,700m (35,000ft)

Dimensions: span 9.2m (30 ft 2in);
 length 8.5m (27ft 11in); height 2.39m
 (7ft 11in)

Weight: 2692kg (5864lb) loaded

Armament: 1 x 20mm (0.8in) ShVAK cannon,
 2 x 12.7mm (0.5in) Berezin UBS MG

▲ Yakovlev Yak-3

Unknown unit, Eastern Front, 1943

In common with many Soviet warplanes, this Yak-3 bears an exhortatory slogan on
the side of the fuselage below the cockpit.

Specifications

Crew: 1

Powerplant: 880kW (1180hp) Klimov M-105PF
 V-12 liquid-cooled engine

Maximum speed: 592km/h (368mph)

Range: 700km (435 miles)

Service ceiling: 10,050m (33,000ft)

Dimensions: span 10 m (32ft 10in);
 length 8.5m (27ft 11in)

Weight: 2883kg (6343lb) loaded

Armament: 1 x 20mm (0.8in) ShVAK cannon,
 1 x 12.7mm (0.5in) Berezin UBS MG

▲ Yakovlev Yak-1M

37th Guards IAP / 6th Guards AD, Eastern Front, 1943

This aeroplane was flown by Major B. N. Yevemen, and the legend under the
cockpit translates as 'to the pilot of the Stalingrad Front Guards Major Comrade
Yeven from the collective farm workers of the collective farm "Stakhanov",
comrade F. P. Golovatov'.

Kursk
JULY 1943

The Battle of Kursk was the defining moment of the war on the Eastern Front. Here the Germans tried, for the last time, to regain the strategic initiative they had lost in the Battle of Stalingrad, and were decisively defeated by Soviet armoured, artillery and tactical air strength.

IN FEBRUARY 1943, the German Sixth Army, trapped and starving in the ruins of Stalingrad, was forced to surrender its last 93,000 men after the *Luftwaffe* failed to deliver the tonnages of supplies it had promised to keep the beleaguered army in fighting trim. The Soviet forces launched a major offensive across the Donets river to take Kharkov, which the Germans then retook in an example of extraordinary combat and generalship skills. Both sides spent the period between March and July rebuilding their strengths, and planning for the summer. The lull in the fighting from March had left the Soviets with a large salient, centred on Kursk, bulging into the German lines beyond Orel in the north and Kharkov in the south.

Here the Germans saw an opportunity for a pincer offensive to strike south-east and north-east to meet behind Kursk, pinch out the salient and trap huge Soviet forces for annihilation. They gathered major armoured formations, rushed new armoured fighting

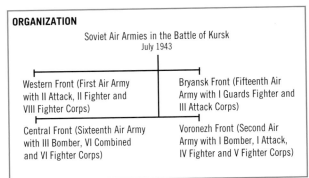

ORGANIZATION

Soviet Air Armies in the Battle of Kursk
July 1943

Western Front (First Air Army with II Attack, II Fighter and VIII Fighter Corps)

Bryansk Front (Fifteenth Air Army with I Guards Fighter and III Attack Corps)

Central Front (Sixteenth Air Army with III Bomber, VI Combined and VI Fighter Corps)

Voronezh Front (Second Air Army with I Bomber, I Attack, IV Fighter and V Fighter Corps)

vehicles into service and massed considerable air strength. But the Soviets were warned by their agents of the details of the German scheme, and prepared defences in great depth, with lines of earthworks, minefields, huge quantities of artillery and armour, and powerful air forces now able to meet the *Luftwaffe* in qualitative terms while exceeding it in quantitative terms.

▲ **Lavochkin La-5FN**

Unknown unit, Eastern Front, 1943–44

The La-5 series of very capable fighters remained in production into 1944, 9920 such aircraft being delivered.

Specifications

Crew: 1

Powerplant: 1380kW (1850hp) Shvetsov M-82FN radial piston engine

Maximum speed: 665km/h (413mph)

Range: 635km (395 miles)

Service ceiling: 10,800m (35,435ft)

Dimensions: span 9.80m (32ft 2in); length 8.60m (28ft 3in)

Weight: 3280kg (7231lb) loaded

Armament: 2 x 20mm (0.8in) Beresin B-20 cannon in nose; plus up to 200kg (441lb) bomb load

The Battle of Kursk lasted between 5 and 16 July, and was a huge Soviet success. The northern half of the undertaking achieved little for the Germans, while their southern offensive managed to batter its way deeper into the Soviet lines before being checked.

A major armoured battle, possibly the world's largest ever tank-versus-tank engagement, developed round Prokhorovka as the Germans tried to smash their way forward and the Soviets called in part of their huge reserve to defeat this effort.

Specifications

Crew: 1

Powerplant: 880kW (1180hp) Klimov M-105PF
 V-12 liquid-cooled engine

Maximum speed: 592km/h (368mph)

Range: 700km (435 miles)

Service ceiling: 10,050m (33,000ft)

Dimensions: span 10 m (32ft 10in);
 length 8.5m (27ft 11in)

Weight: 2883kg (6343lb) loaded

Armament: 1 x 20mm (0.8in) ShVAK cannon,
 1 x 12.7mm (0.5in) Berezin UBS MG

▲ Yakovlev Yak-1

18th Guards IAP, Khationki, Eastern Front, spring 1943

This was the aeroplane of Lieutenant-Colonel A. E. Golubov. Golubov finished the war with 39 kills.

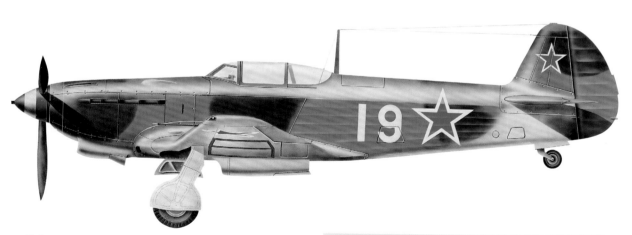

▲ Yakovlev Yak-9

Normandie-Niémen Squadron / French Air Force, Eastern Front, 1943–44

The Normandie-Niémen Squadron was formed from Free French fighter pilots at the suggestion of Charles de Gaulle, and served on the Eastern Front from March 1943 until the end of the war. During this time, the unit destroyed 273 enemy aircraft and received many orders, citations and decorations from both France and the Soviet Union.

Specifications

Crew: 1

Powerplant: 880kW (1180hp) Klimov M-105 PF
 V-12 liquid-cooled piston engine

Maximum speed: 591 km/h (367mph))

Range: 884km (549 miles)

Service ceiling: 9100m (30,000ft)

Dimensions: span 9.74m (31ft 11in);
 length 8.55m (28ft); height 3m (9ft 10in)

Weight: 3117kg (6,858lb) loaded

Armament: 1 x 20mm (0.8in) ShVAK cannon,
 1 x 12.7mm (0.5in) Berezin UBS MG

NEW-GENERATION SOVIET FIGHTERS USED AT KURSK			
Type	Speed	Armament	Number built
Lavochkin La-5FN	650km/h (404mph)	2 x 20 or 23mm cannon	10,000
Yakovlev Yak-3	655km/h (407mph)	1 x 20mm cannon 2 x 12.7mm MGs	4848
Yakovlev Yak-7B	615km/h (382mph)	1x 20mm cannon 1 x 12.7mm MG	6399
Yakovlev Yak-9D	600km/h (372mph)	1 x 20mm cannon 1 x 12.7mm MG	16,769

Overhead the fighters of the V-VS prevented the *Luftwaffe* from playing a decisive part, and then supported the Soviet attack bombers, ground-attack aircraft and anti-tank warplanes in wreaking havoc on the German forces.

It is believed that the Germans lost something in the order of 3000 armoured fighting vehicles and 1400 aircraft at Kursk, and while their losses were equally as great the Soviets had decisively beaten the Germans. Hence between 12 July and 26 November the Soviets could unleash a number of great offensives between Smolensk and the Black Sea from which the *Wehrmacht* never recovered.

The push west

DECEMBER 1943 – SEPTEMBER 1944

Soviet forces swept west after Kursk, and the Germans were able to inflict no more than local reverses that merely delayed rather than halted the Soviet forces. Only after huge advances did logistical exhaustion finally bring the Red Army to a halt in the late summer of 1944.

SUPPORTED BY ever larger numbers of tactical warplanes, such as the Ilyushin Il-2 ground-attack and Petlyakov Pe-2 light bomber types, and operating under an umbrella of ever more capable Lavochkin and Yakovlev fighters, the Soviet ground forces lifted the siege of Leningrad on 19 January 1944 even as the current winter offensive, launched late in the previous year, moved west.

▲ **Yakovlev Yak-9D**

Unknown unit, Eastern Front, 1944–45

The Yak-9D was the extended-range development of the basic Yak-9 fighter, with fuel capacity increased from 440l (115 US gal) to 650l (170 US gal), giving a maximum range of 1360km (845 miles).

Specifications

Crew: 1
Powerplant: 880kW (1180hp) Klimov M-105 PF
V-12 liquid-cooled piston engine
Maximum speed: 591 km/h (367mph))
Range: 1360km (845 miles)
Service ceiling: 9100m (30,000ft)

Dimensions: span 9.74m (31ft 11in);
length 8.55m (28ft); height 3m (9ft 10in)
Weight: 3117kg (6858lb) loaded
Armament: 1 x 20mm (0.8in) ShVAK cannon,
1 x 12.7mm (0.5in) Berezin UBS MG

◄ **Dive-bomber**

As well as being a superb interceptor, the Yak-9 was also used in the ground-attack role.

Between January and April, the Soviet forces in the south crossed the great Dniepr river and liberated Ukraine before advancing into Romania, leading to the defection of that country and Bulgaria to the Soviet side in September.

With the launch of the Red Army's greatest ever ground offensive, Operation Bagration, in June and July, the Soviets liberated Belorussia in the Eastern Front's central sector, and exerted major pressure

▲ **Lavochkin La-7**

Unknown unit, central part of the Eastern Front, 1944–45

The La-7 was the final development of the already excellent La-5.

Specifications

Crew: 1

Powerplant: 1380kW (1850hp) Shvetsov M-82FN radial piston engine

Maximum speed: 680km/h (425mph)

Range: 990km (618 miles)

Service ceiling: 9500m (31,160ft)

Dimensions: span 9.80m (32ft 2in); length 8.60m (28ft 3in)

Weight: 3280kg (7231lb) loaded

Armament: 2 x 20mm (0.8in) ShVAK cannon or 3 x 20mm (0.8in) Berezin B-20 cannon in nose; plus up to 200kg (441lb) bomb load

▲ **Lavochkin La-7**

163rd Guards IAP, Eastern Front, 1944–45

The La-7 was without doubt one of the finest fighters of World War II, and this example is believed to have been the personal aeroplane of the 163rd Guards IAP's commander.

Specifications

Crew: 1

Powerplant: 1380kW (1850hp) Shvetsov M-82FN radial piston engine

Maximum speed: 680km/h (425mph)

Range: 990km (618 miles)

Service ceiling: 9500m (31,160ft)

Dimensions: span 9.80m (32ft 2in); length 8.60m (28ft 3in)

Weight: 3280kg (7231lb) loaded

Armament: 2 x 20mm (0.8in) ShVAK cannon or 3 x 20mm (0.8in) Berezin B-20 cannon in nose; plus up to 200kg (441lb) bomb load on the Finns in the north, leading to Finland's armistice in September. The Soviet summer offensive did not end with the liberation of Byelorussia, but continued remorselessly onwards. Even though they were approaching the point of exhaustion and their lines of communication were stretched to the very limit, the Red Army advanced into eastern Poland before finally halting outside Warsaw on 1 August.

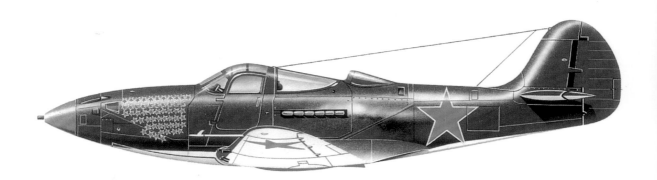

▲ Bell P-39Q Airacobra

Unknown unit, southern Soviet Union, 1944

This is another of the Bell P-39s flown by Major Aleksandr Pokryshkin, the second-highest scoring Soviet ace with a total of 59 victories. On 16 July 1944, Pokryshkin fought a group of Ju-87s and Hs-129s, shooting down three Ju-87s and one Hs-129.

Specifications

Crew: 1

Powerplant: 895kW (1200hp) Allison V-1710-85 liquid-cooled V-12

Maximum speed: 605km/h (376mph)

Range: 483km (300 miles)

Service ceiling: 11,665m (38,270ft)

Dimensions: span 10.36m (34ft 0in); length 9.195m (30ft 2in); height 3.785m (12ft 5in)

Weight: 3992kg (8800lb) loaded

Armament: 1 x 37mm (1.46in) M4 cannon, 2 x 12.7mm (0.5in) Browning MGs, 4 x 7.62mm (0.3in) Browning MGs

Assault on the Reich
OCTOBER 1944 – MAY 1945

The Soviets advanced into the Baltic states during September 1944, trapping a complete army group, and then through the Balkans right until the end of the year. By the start of 1945, they were poised for their advance through Germany, culminating in the capture of Berlin.

BY THE AUTUMN OF 1944, the V-VS was rampant over the Eastern Front. It prevented the rapidly declining German air strength from achieving anything of note and provided the Soviet ground forces with tactical support of unparalleled capability over the battlefield and against the German lines of communication.

Overwhelming odds

The German continued to fight hard on the ground, but were outnumbered and completely outgunned, and therefore could not halt the Soviet steamroller. The Soviets cleared the Baltic states, except for an isolated pocket in which a German army group survived to the end of the war to no good purpose, and at the same time moved through the Balkans to approach Yugoslavia and enter eastern Hungary.

On 12 January 1945, the Soviets launched a huge offensive between the Carpathian mountains in the south and the Baltic Sea in the north, while at the same time another thrust advanced through Hungary to reach Vienna on 15 April.

Push for Berlin

The prize most desired by the Soviets, however, was Berlin, and it was on 22 April that the Soviet advance guards reached the outskirts of the German capital, which had been surrounded by 25 April. The Battle of Berlin lasted until 2 May, three days after Hitler's suicide and just six days before Germany's unconditional surrender.

The Soviets estimated, probably correctly, that in the previous three months the Germans had lost about one million men killed, while Soviet captures amounted to 800,000 men, 6000 aircraft, 12,000 armoured fighting vehicles and 23,000 pieces of artillery. The Red Army and its air forces had delivered a final, terrible revenge upon Germany and its people.

Specifications

Crew: 1

Powerplant: 1380kW (1850hp) Shvetsov
 M-82FN radial piston engine

Maximum speed: 680km/h (425mph)

Range: 990km (618 miles)

Service ceiling: 9500m (31,160ft)

Dimensions: span 9.80m (32ft 2in);
 length 8.60m (28ft 3in)

Weight: 3280kg (7231lb) loaded

Armament: 2 x 20mm (0.8in) ShVAK cannon
 or 3 x 20mm (0.8in) Berezin B-20 cannon in
 nose; plus up to 200kg (441lb) bomb load

▲ **Lavochkin La-7**

Unknown unit, Eastern Front, 1944–45

With its powerful air-cooled radial engine and clean lines, the La-7 offered excellent performance.

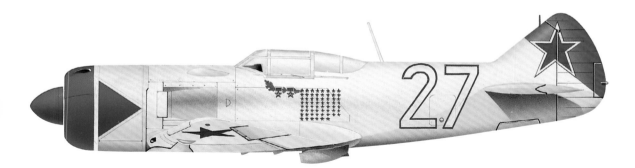

▲ **Lavochkin La-7**

176th Guards IAP / 302nd IAD (Fighter Division), Eastern Front, 1944–45

This was one of the aircraft flown by Colonel Ivan Kozhedub, the Soviet Union's highest-scoring ace. Three times decorated as Hero of the Soviet Union, Kozhedub is credited with downing 62 enemy aircraft.

Specifications

Crew: 1

Powerplant: 1380kW (1850hp) Shvetsov
 M-82FN radial piston engine

Maximum speed: 680km/h (425mph)

Range: 990km (618 miles)

Service ceiling: 9500m (31,160ft)

Dimensions: span 9.80m (32ft 2in);
 length 8.60m (28ft 3in)

Weight: 3280kg (7231lb) loaded

Armament: 2 x 20mm (0.8in) ShVAK cannon
 or 3 x 20mm (0.8in) Berezin B-20 cannon in
 nose; plus up to 200kg (441lb) bomb load

Chapter 5

Other Allied Air Forces

While the French, British, US and Soviet fighter
arms dominated the fighting in Europe during World War II,
there were also a number of smaller air arms involved. First
of these was the Polish Air Force, which fought gallantly and
with some success in the war's first campaign
against a German opponent tactically, technically and
operationally superior. But smaller European air arms
that should also be mentioned, not least because they
provided the Allies with aircrews after the defeat of their
countries, were Denmark, Norway, the Netherlands, Belgium,
Yugoslavia and Greece. Finally, there was Brazil, which
sent a small expeditionary force to support the Allied cause
during the Italian campaign, in which there was also
a small Italian Co-Belligerent Air Force.

◀ Gull-winged fighter
The fighters of the PZL organization were the mainstays of the Polish fighter arm in the 1930s. These are
P.11 aircraft, which by 1939 were of obsolescent design.

Polish Air Force

SEPTEMBER 1939

The Polish Air Force was only just moving into the era of the 'modern' monoplane design in 1939, and was outclassed by a *Luftwaffe* equipped with more advanced aircraft and, just as importantly, using tactics proved in the Spanish Civil War. Even so, the Poles fought hard.

MOST OF POLAND'S first-line warplanes at the time of the German invasion of 1 September were products of the PZL organization, and of these the most advanced were the P.23 Karas single-engine and P.37 Los twin-engine aircraft operated in the reconnaissance and bomber roles.

The squadrons flying these types were aggressive in their efforts, but lacked the training and fighter cover to survive long in the face of the Germans' very capable fighter arm. From the middle of September, moreover, the Germans concentrated a considerable effort against the Polish airfields and soon deprived the Poles of the bases from which the surviving aircraft could operate.

Aggressive tactics

The Polish fighter arm was still more determined and aggressive in its tactics, but was poorly served in its aircraft, which were gull-winged fighters with

ORGANIZATION

Polish Air Force
September 1939

Dispositional Air Force   Armies' Air Force

AIRCRAFT OF THE DISPOSITIONAL AIR FORCE'S PURSUIT BRIGADE		
Unit	Type	Strength
III/1 (111 & 112 Squadrons)	PZL P.11	20
IV/1 (113 & 114 Squadrons)	PZL P.11	20
III/2 (123 Squadron)	PZL P.7a	10

fixed landing gear. The oldest of these in service in September 1939 was the P.7, which had entered service in 1932. The P.11 was conceptually very similar but with a more powerful engine, and claimed 125 victories in the air before the defeat of Poland.

▲ **Breguet Bre.19**

Unknown unit, Polish Air Force, 1930s

An obsolete type, the Bre.19 remained in Polish service well into the 1930s, latterly in second-line roles.

Specifications

Crew: 2

Powerplant: 336kW (450hp) Lorraine 12Ed
  piston

Maximum speed: 214km/h (133mph)

Range: 800km (497 miles)

Service ceiling: 7200m (23,620ft)

Dimensions: span 14.83m (48ft 7in);

length 9.61m (31ft 6in); height 3.69m
  (12ft 1in)

Weight: 1387kg (3058lb)

Armament: 1 x fixed forward 7.62mm (0.3in)
  Vickers MG, and two flexibly mounted rear
  7.62mm (0.3in) Lewis MGs

Specifications

Crew: 1
Powerplant: 470kW (630hp) Bristol
    Mercury V S2 radial engine
Maximum speed: 375km/h (233mph)
Range: 550km (341 miles)
Service ceiling: 8000m (26,246ft)
Dimensions: span 10.72 m (35ft 2in);
    length 7.55m (24ft 9in); height
    2.85m (9ft 4in)
Weight: 1650kg (3638lb) loaded
Armament: 2–4 7.92mm (0.312in)
    MGs; plus 50kg (110lb) bomb load

▲ **PZL P.11c**

No. 113 Squadron / 1st Air Regiment, Warsaw, late 1930s

The P.11 was much liked by its pilots for its good handling in the air.

Specifications

Crew: 1
Powerplant: 470kW (630hp) Bristol
    Mercury V S2 radial engine
Maximum speed: 375km/h (233mph)
Range: 550km (341 miles)
Service ceiling: 8000m (26,246ft)
Dimensions: span 10.72 m (35ft 2in);
    length 7.55m (24ft 9in); height
    2.85m (9ft 4in)
Weight: 1650kg (3638lb) loaded
Armament: 2–4 7.92mm (0.312in)
    MGs; plus 50kg (110lb) bomb load

▲ **PZL P.11c**

Unknown Polish unit, late 1930s

Although it had moderately good performance by the standards of the mid-1930s, the P-11 was obsolete at the start of World War II and easily outclassed by the airplanes of the Luftwaffe.

Specifications

Crew: 1
Powerplant: 470kW (630hp) Bristol
    Mercury V S2 radial engine
Maximum speed: 375km/h (233mph)
Range: 550km (341 miles)
Service ceiling: 8000m (26,246ft)
Dimensions: span 10.72 m (35ft 2in);
    length 7.55m (24ft 9in); height
    2.85m (9ft 4in)
Weight: 1650kg (3638lb) loaded
Armament: 2–4 7.92mm (0.312in)
    MGs; plus 50kg (110lb) bomb load

▲ **PZL P.11c**

No. 122 Squadron / 2nd Air Regiment, Krakow, late 1930s

This was numerically the most important fighter in Polish service at the time of the German invasion of September 1939.

Low Countries
MAY 1940

When Germany invaded the Netherlands and Belgium in May 1940, both of these countries had small air forces, but they lacked operational experience and the size to do anything but inflict modest losses on the Germans as their ground forces were driven into defeat.

THE FOKKER company had designed and built large numbers of capable warplanes, mainly for export, during the 1920s, but had then started to fall behind as larger nations began to introduce the 'modern' type of monoplane warplane with a cantilever wing and retractable main landing gear units.

Thus the country's most modern aircraft was the Fokker G.I twin-engine heavy fighter with adequate performance and heavy armament. However, only 23 were operational at the time of the German invasion of 10 May 1940, and these could be of little real use in the five-day campaign culminating in the Netherlands' defeat, by which time only one of the aircraft was left.

The most important Dutch fighter was the Fokker D.XXI, which may be categorized as an interim type since it had a low-set cantilever wing and enclosed cockpit, but retained fixed main landing gear units and an obsolescent metal-framed structure covered with fabric. The type had first flown in 1936, and by May 1940, 36 of the aircraft had been delivered, of which 29 were used in the five-day campaign. The

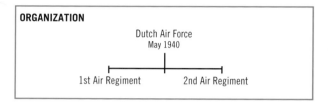

ORGANIZATION

Dutch Air Force
May 1940

1st Air Regiment   2nd Air Regiment

FIGHTER UNITS OF THE DUTCH AIR FORCE			
Unit	Type	Strength	Base
1st Fighter Sqn/1 Reg	Fokker D.XXI	11	de Kooy
2nd Fighter Sqn/1 Reg	Fokker D.XXI	9	Schiphol
3rd Fighter Sqn/1 Reg	Fokker G.IA	11	Waalhaven
4th Fighter Sqn/1 Reg	Fokker G.IA	12	Bergen-op-Zoom
1st Fighter Sqn/2 Reg	Fokker D.XXI	8	Ypenberg
3rd Fighter Sqn/2 Reg	Douglas DB-8A	11	Ypenberg

Dutch pilots flew their aircraft with considerable courage, but most of the aircraft were destroyed either in the air or on the ground.

▶ **Fokker D.XXI**

Dutch Air Force, 1939–40

The D.XXI was an interim monoplane with a cantilever wing and enclosed cockpit, but had an obsolete structure and fixed landing gear. When it entered service in 1938, it was a quantum leap forward for the Dutch Army Aviation Group. Until then, its fighter force had consisted of ageing biplanes with open cockpits. The new Fokker proved to be an extremely sturdy aircraft.

Specifications

Crew: 1

Powerplant: 619kW (830hp) Bristol Mercury VIII air-cooled, 9-cylinder, radial

Maximum speed: 418km/h (260mph)

Range: 930km (574 miles)

Service ceiling: 9350m (30,675ft)

Dimensions: span 11m (36ft 1in); length 8.20m (26ft 11in); height 2.95m (9ft 8in)

Weight: 1970kg (4399lb) maximum takeoff

Armament: 4 x 7.92mm (0.34in) FN Browning M36 MGs

▲ Hawker Hurricane Mk I

2e Escadrille / 2e Regiment de l'Aeronautique / Belgian Air Force, Diest Schaffen, 1940

Some 11 of the 18 Hurricane aircraft that Belgium received were in service at the time of the German invasion in May 1940.

Specifications

Crew: 1	Service ceiling: 10,180m (33,400ft)
Powerplant: 768kW (1030hp) Rolls-Royce Merlin II liquid-cooled V-12	Dimensions: span 12.19m (40ft 0in); length 9.55m (31ft 4in); height 4.07m (13ft 4.5in)
Maximum speed: 496km/h (308mph)	Weight: 2820kg (6218lb) loaded
Range: 845km (525 miles)	Armament: 8 x 7.7mm (0.303in) Browning MGs

▲ Hawker Hurricane Mk IA

2e Escadrille / 2e Regiment de l'Aeronautique / Belgian Air Force, Diest Schaffen, 1940

Belgium ordered 20 British-built Hurricane Mk IAs and 80 for local construction, but received 15 and built three respectively.

Specifications

Crew: 1	Dimensions: span 12.19m (40ft 0in);
Powerplant: 768kW (1030hp) Rolls-Royce Merlin II liquid-cooled V-12	length 9.55m (31ft 4in); height 4.07m (13ft 4.5in)
Maximum speed: 496km/h (308mph)	Weight: 2820kg (6218lb) loaded
Range: 845km (525 miles)	Armament: 8 x 7.7mm (0.303in)
Service ceiling: 10,180m (33,400ft)	Browning MGs

Belgian Air Force

With only a small indigenous aircraft manufacturing industry and limited financial resources, Belgium opted to concentrate on the local manufacture or assembly of British aircraft by the Belgian subsidiary of the Fairey company of the UK.

The air force also flew 23 examples of a late-generation Italian biplane fighter, the Fiat CR.42 Falco, derived from the CR.32 that had performed creditably in the Spanish Civil War. The CR.42 was

ORGANIZATION

Belgian Air Force
May 1940

1st Air Regiment (six army co-operation squadrons)	2nd Air Regiment (six fighter squadrons)	3rd Air Regiment (four reconnaissance bomber squadrons)

wholly outclassed by the Germans' Messerschmitt Bf 109 monoplane fighter. Much the same can be said of the Gloster Gladiator, the last British biplane fighter to enter service. At the time of the German invasion, the Belgians had 15 of these fighters in service contained in one squadron.

Without doubt the best fighter in Belgian service was another British type, the Hawker Hurricane, of which there were 11 in service with more on order. The Hurricane was a capable blend of obsolescent and modern, the former represented by its metal-framed and largely fabric-covered airframe, and the latter by its overall configuration, retractable main landing gear units, enclosed cockpit, and powerful fixed forward-firing armament of eight rifle-calibre machine guns in the leading edges of its wing.

This mix of fighters could avail the Belgian Air Force little in May 1940 before inevitable defeat.

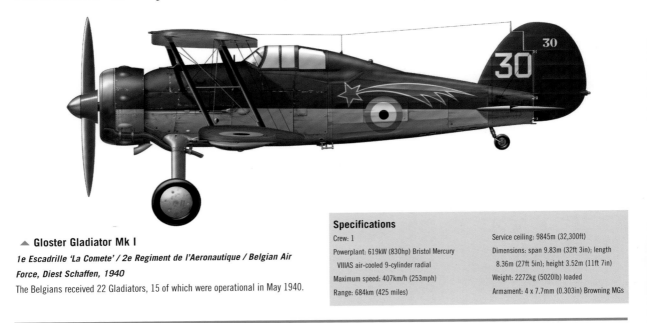

▲ **Gloster Gladiator Mk I**

1e Escadrille 'La Comete' / 2e Regiment de l'Aeronautique / Belgian Air Force, Diest Schaffen, 1940

The Belgians received 22 Gladiators, 15 of which were operational in May 1940.

Specifications

Crew: 1

Powerplant: 619kW (830hp) Bristol Mercury VIIIAS air-cooled 9-cylinder radial

Maximum speed: 407km/h (253mph)

Range: 684km (425 miles)

Service ceiling: 9845m (32,300ft)

Dimensions: span 9.83m (32ft 3in); length 8.36m (27ft 5in); height 3.52m (11ft 7in)

Weight: 2272kg (5020lb) loaded

Armament: 4 x 7.7mm (0.303in) Browning MGs

Scandinavia
APRIL–MAY 1940

Before turning its attention to the west, where the Netherlands and Belgium were defeated as part of the great German offensive against France from 10 May, Germany decided to secure its northern flank by the swift overrunning of Denmark and the defeat of Norway.

SMALL IN SIZE AND and with only the most limited of armed forces, Denmark could offer no realistic opposition to the German invasion of 9 April 1940, which was intended to provide support for the more important conquest of Norway. Denmark's air force was miniscule and wholly obsolete in its aircraft, the most modern type being the Gloster Gladiator that replaced the Bristol Bulldog in one squadron from 1935. Morevoer, it saw no combat since Denmark swiftly

capitulated in return for the German offer of limited independence in internal matters.

Norwegian Air Force

Reflecting the country's larger size and greater population, the defence establishment of Norway was larger than that of Denmark. The army and navy each had their own air arms, both of which had operated the indigenously designed Hover MF.9 fighter, which was out of service by 1940. By this time, the army and naval air arms had establishments that permitted 36 and 20 fighters respectively, and the fighters in service were the Curtiss Hawk 75A first-generation 'modern' monoplane from the United States and the Gloster Gladiator last-generation biplane from the United Kingdom.

In these circumstances, therefore, the Norwegian air arms could offer little effective resistance to the German invasion. The Norwegian pilots flew with courage and determination, but their lack of operational experience and the obsolescence of their equipment made the result a foregone conclusion. The Norwegian losses were comparatively heavy but, like the Poles before them, the Norwegians flew some of their aircraft to safety, in this instance to the UK. Numbers of Norwegian personnel escaped to carry on the fight from the United Kingdom and, in the case of naval personnel, Canada.

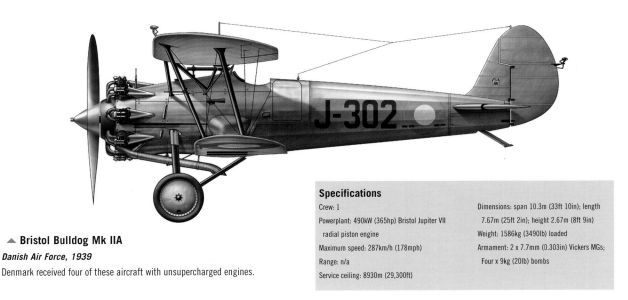

▲ Bristol Bulldog Mk IIA

Danish Air Force, 1939

Denmark received four of these aircraft with unsupercharged engines.

Specifications

Crew: 1

Powerplant: 490kW (365hp) Bristol Jupiter VII radial piston engine

Maximum speed: 287km/h (178mph)

Range: n/a

Service ceiling: 8930m (29,300ft)

Dimensions: span 10.3m (33ft 10in); length 7.67m (25ft 2in); height 2.67m (8ft 9in)

Weight: 1586kg (3490lb) loaded

Armament: 2 x 7.7mm (0.303in) Vickers MGs; Four x 9kg (20lb) bombs

▼ Gloster Gladiator Mk I

Norwegian Air Force, 1939

The Norwegian air force received 12 Gladiator fighters in the form of six Mk I and six Mk II aircraft, and these were entrusted with the air defence of Oslo.

Specifications

Crew: 1

Powerplant: 619kW (830hp) Bristol Mercury VIIIAS air-cooled 9-cylinder radial

Maximum speed: 407km/h (253mph)

Range: 684km (425 miles)

Service ceiling: 9845m (32,300ft)

Dimensions: span 9.83m (32ft 3in); length 8.36m (27ft 5in); height 3.52m (11ft 7in)

Weight: 2272kg (5020lb) loaded

Armament: 4 x 7.7mm (0.303in) Browning MGs

Yugoslavia and Greece
APRIL 1941

Before turning the German forces against the Soviet Union, Hitler decided to secure his southern flank by seizing Yugoslavia, which had turned against the German-Italian axis, and Greece, from which Allied bombers might be able to cripple the Romanian oilfields on which Germany relied.

ALTHOUGH BESET BY internal divisions and a sadly deficient infrastructure, the Yugoslav forces were large and, on paper at least, comparatively formidable at the time of the German invasion of 6 April 1941. The Yugoslav Air Service reached a peak in 1935, when it had 44 squadrons with 440 aircraft, most

▲ **Breguet Bre 19 A2**

Royal Yugoslav Air Force, Kraljevo, 1936

The Bre 19 A2 was obsolete by the time of the German invasion, and was used mainly for reconnaissance purposes. After the fall of the Kingdom of Yugoslavia, 46 aircraft were seized and used by the Croatian Air Force for anti-partisan missions.

Specifications

Crew: 2

Powerplant: 336kW (450hp) Lorraine 12Ed piston

Maximum speed: 214km/h (133mph)

Range: 800km (497 miles)

Service ceiling: 7200m (23,620ft)

Dimensions: span 14.83m (48ft 7in);

length 9.61m (31ft 6in); height 3.69m (12ft 1in)

Weight: 1387kg (3058lb)

Armament: 1 x fixed forward 7.62mm (0.3in) Vickers MG, and mountings for two rear 7.62mm (0.3in) Lewis MGs

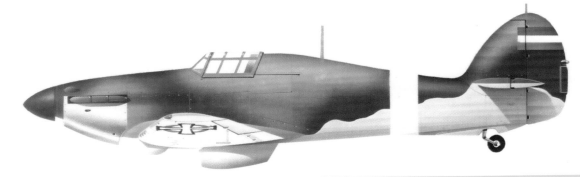

▲ **Hawker Hurricane Mk I**

Royal Yugoslav Air Force, Zemun, April 1941

This is one of 20 Hurricanes built at the factory at Zmaj.

Specifications

Crew: 1

Powerplant: 768kW (1030hp) Rolls-Royce Merlin II liquid-cooled V-12

Maximum speed: 496km/h (308mph)

Range: 845km (525 miles)

Service ceiling: 10,180m (33,400ft)

Dimensions: span 12.19m (40ft 0in); length 9.55m (31ft 4in); height 4.07m (13ft 4.5in)

Weight: 2820kg (6218lb) loaded

Armament: 8 x 7.7mm (0.303in) Browning MGs

of them obsolescent if not obsolete. Hawker Furys and Breguet Bre 19s made up the bulk of the fighter aircraft available.

A major re-equipment programme had been launched, and this included deliveries of the Curtiss P-40B, Hawker Hurricane Mk I and Messerschmitt Bf 109E fighters, as well as the start of licensed production of the Hurricane.

Local effort was responsible for two other fighter types, the Ikarus IK-2 gull-wing monoplane with fixed landing gear, and the more advanced Rogozarski IK-3 monoplane with retractable landing gear. The former entered service in 1939, and eight of the 12 such aircraft were operational in April 1941. The latter entered service in 1940, but only six were operational at the time of the invasion.

Greece

Greece was invaded at the same time as Yugoslavia, and its fighter arm at this time operated the Bloch MB.151 and PZL P.24 fighters from France and Poland. Neither could compete effectively with the German fighters they faced.

⏶ Monoplane wings over Yugoslavia

The Yugoslav Air Force included more than 30 operational Hurricane Mk Is at the time of the German invasion.

⏷ Hawker Fury

35th Fighter Group / 109 Eskadrila / Royal Yugoslav Air Force, April 1941

The 35th and 36th Fighter Groups had 30 operational Furys at the time of the German invasion. Yugoslav Furies did see action against Axis forces. On 6 April 1941, a squadron of Furies engaged with some Messerschmitt Bf 109Es and Messerschmitt Bf 110s. In the resulting conflict, 11 Furies were destroyed – almost the entire squadron – but seven German aircraft also failed to return, though it is possible that some of these were non-combat losses. However, it is certain that at least one of them was lost to ramming by a Fury.

Specifications

Crew: 1	Dimensions: span 9.14 m (30ft);
Powerplant: 477kW (640hp) Rolls-Royce Kestrel	length 8.15m (26ft 9in); height 3.10m
IV V12 engine	(10ft 2in)
Maximum speed: 360km/h (223mph)	Weight: 1637kg (3609lb) loaded
Range: 435km (270 miles)	Armament: 2 x 7.7 mm (0.303in) Vickers
Service ceiling: 8990m (29,500ft)	Mk IV MGs

Co-Belligerent Italy and Brazil
1943–45

When Italy agreed an armistice with the Allies in September 1943, the northern half of the country was still in German hands but the southern portion worked actively with the Allies. Another Allied supporter was Brazil, which sent a small expeditionary force to Italy.

O N 9 SEPTEMBER 1943, as the Allies landed on the Italian mainland just south of Naples, it was revealed that the Italian government had secured an armistice with the Allies, and many Italian squadrons flew south as and when they could to the safety of the Allied-held airfields in the south of Italy. At the same time, the Germans occupied the whole of northern Italy, where a revived fascist state was established under Benito Mussolini, the Italian dictator deposed in July of the same year.

Italian Co-Belligerent Air Force

The forces of this revived state continued to fight alongside the Germans to increasingly little effect, while the Allies permitted the establishment of an Italian Co-Belligerent Air Force (*Aviazione Cobelligerante Italiana*) in southern Italy during October 1943 to fly alongside their own squadrons. That part of the previous Regia Aeronautica now under German control was the National Republican

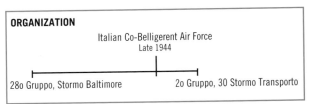

ORGANIZATION

Italian Co-Belligerent Air Force
Late 1944

28o Gruppo, Stormo Baltimore   2o Gruppo, 30 Stormo Transporto

Air Force (*Aeronautica Nazionale Repubblicana*), which was nominally part of the forces of the Italian Social Republic.

By the end of 1943, some 281 Italian warplanes had landed on Allied airfields, but most of these were no longer useful for combat, especially as production was centred in German-held northern Italy and spares were therefore very short. The Italian units were re-equipped with Allied warplanes, and were thereafter employed in tasks such as transport, escort, reconnaissance, sea rescue and limited tactical ground support operations. The Co-Belligerent Air Force flew something in the order of 11,000 missions from

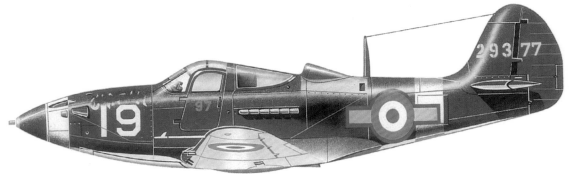

▲ **Bell P-39Q Airacobra**

Italian Co-Belligerent Air Force, 1944

Italy received 149 examples of the Airacobra from US Fifteenth Air Force stocks, and these saw limited operational use in World War II.

Specifications

Crew: 1

Powerplant: 895kW (1200hp) Allison V-1710-85 liquid-cooled V-12

Maximum speed: 605km/h (376mph)

Range: 483km (300 miles)

Service ceiling: 11,665m (38,270ft)

Dimensions: span 10.36m (34ft 0in); length 9.195m (30ft 2in); height 3.785m (12ft 5in)

Weight: 3992kg (8800lb) loaded

Armament: 1 x 37mm (1.46in) M4 cannon, 2 x 12.7mm (0.5in) Browning MGs, 4 x 7.62mm (0.3in) Browning MGs, and 227kg (500lb) of bombs

October 1943 to April 1945. None of its missions was flown over Italy to avoid any possibility of a civil war, the missions instead being flown over the Balkans. It formed the basis for the post-war Italian Air Force, the *Aeronautica Militare Italiana*.

Brazilian flyers

Brazil declared war on Germany in 1942, and in 1943 the 1st Air Fighter Unit was formed from volunteers for service in Italy. The group had four 12-aircraft squadrons, and totalled 350 men, including 43 pilots. After combat training under US supervision in Panama, the group was moved to the United States, transitioned to the Republic P-47D Thunderbolt heavy fighter, and was shipped to Italy, where it arrived in October 1944. The pilots were allocated to the US 350th Fighter Group, in which the Brazilian unit was the 1st Fighter Squadron. This unit flew 2546 sorties in 445 missions.

Carrying the moto 'Senta a Pua' (meaning 'hit 'em hard'), the badge of the Brazilian 1o Gruppo de Caca was designed by the pilots of the unit while in transit to Europe. The green-yellow surrounding represents Brazil, while the red field represents the war skies; the white clouds represent the ground and the blue shield charged with the Southern Cross is the common symbol for the Brazilian armed forces.

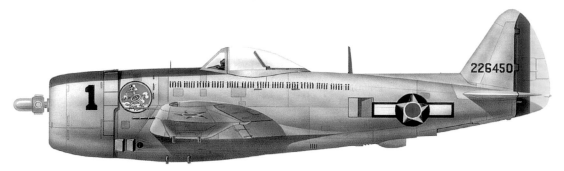

▲ Republic P-47D Thunderbolt

1o Gruppo de Caca / Brazilian Air Force, Tarquinia, Italy, November 1944

The Brazilian Air Force received P-47Ds, all of which fought in Italy.

Specifications

Crew: 1

Powerplant: 1891kW (2535hp) Pratt & Whitney R-2800-59W Double Wasp

Maximum speed: 697km/h (433mph)

Range: 3060km (1900 miles) with drop tanks

Service ceiling: 12,495m (41,000ft)

Dimensions: span 12.42m (40ft 9in); length 11.02m (36ft 2in); height 4.47m (14ft 8in)

Weight: 7938kg (17,500lb) maximum takeoff

Armament: 8 x 12.7mm (0.5in) MGs in wings, plus provision for 1134kg (2500lb) external bombs or rockets

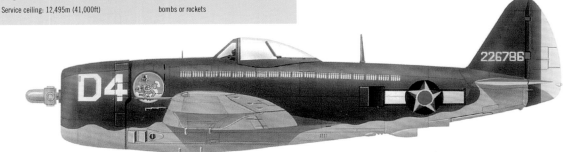

▲ Republic P-47D Thunderbolt

1o Gruppo de Caca / Brazilian Air Force, Tarquinia, Italy, November 1944

The 1ºGAVCA clocked up 5465 combat flight hours from 11 November 1944 to 4 May 1945, mostly in the ground attack role, destroying bridges, ammunition depots and enemy vehicles.

Specifications

Crew: 1

Powerplant: 1891kW (2535hp) Pratt & Whitney R-2800-59W Double Wasp

Maximum speed: 697km/h (433mph)

Range: 3060km (1900 miles) with drop tanks

Service ceiling: 12,495m (41,000ft)

Dimensions: span 12.42m (40ft 9in); length 11.02m (36ft 2in); height 4.47m (14ft 8in)

Weight: 7938kg (17,500lb) maximum takeoff

Armament: 8 x 12.7mm (0.5in) MGs in wings, plus provision for 1134kg (2500lb) external bombs or rockets

Volume Two:
Allied Bombers

Introduction

Most bombers of 1939 were twin-engined
monoplanes with bomb loads in the order of 454 to 2040kg
(1000 to 4500lb) and a range of 4025km (2500 miles) for
the larger types. While Germany concentrated its efforts
on twin-engined aircraft intended primarily for the tactical
role over short ranges, the Allied countries had ambitions
to undertake the strategic as well as tactical roles.
This reached fruition with the development of Bomber
Command in Britain and the introduction of the United States
Eighth Air Force (the 'Mighty Eighth') into the European
theatre from 1942. Although ineffective in the early years of
the war, the combined bomber forces of the United Kingdom
and United States devastated Germany and German
industry, making an important contribution
to the final victory.

◀ **Liberator attack**
A formation of Consolidated B-24 Liberators carry out practice flights against mocked-up targets in the
Libyan desert, July 1943.

THE EARLY-WAR ALLIES were France and the United Kingdom. France had fallen behind the times in the mid-1930s, leaving it with a comparatively large fleet of obsolescent if not obsolete bombers, but was attempting without too much success and at too late a stage to re-equip with new types such as the Lioré-et-Olivier LeO 451, the fastest bomber in 1939.

The fighting in May and June 1940, which led to the defeat of France, also revealed the total inadequacy of the Royal Air Force's (RAF) Fairey Battle single-engined day bomber, which was slow, clumsy in the air, carried only a light bomb load, and was lost in appalling numbers to ground fire. The British also had three supposedly heavy twin-engined bombers: the Armstrong Whitworth Whitley, Handley Page Hampden and Vickers Wellington. Best of these by a considerable margin was the last, whose unusual geodetic structure, covered with fabric, proved to be very sturdy and able to absorb considerable battle damage. The Wellington could carry a substantial bomb load over long distances, and possessed considerable development potential.

Early in 1941 the UK introduced two four-engined heavy bombers, namely the Short Stirling and Handley Page Halifax, and then early in 1942 the Avro Lancaster, which was the best night heavy bomber of the war. Also becoming operational in 1942 was the twin-engined de Havilland Mosquito light bomber, which was of primarily wooden construction and carried no defensive armament as it possessed the speed to evade interception.

▼ Night bomber

The RAF crew of a Wellington Mk III heavy bomber finalize their route to the target before a raid over enemy territory.

Soviet tactical bombers

Soviet bombers, apart from the long-range Ilyushin Il-4, were used mainly for tactical bombing in support of ground forces. The twin-engined tactical bombing capability was initially centred on the obsolescent Tupolev SB-2, succeeded by the high-speed Petlyakov Pe-2 and, from 1943, by the more heavily-armed Tupolev Tu-2. A unique type, built in greater numbers than any other warplane, was the single-engined Ilyushin Il-2 *Shturmovik* attack warplane, in which an armoured 'bath' protected the engine and crew against ground fire.

The 'Flying Fortress'

During 1935 the USA produced the first truly modern all-metal monoplane bomber in the form of the four-engined Boeing B-17. Incorporating five defensive gun positions, this was nicknamed the 'Flying Fortress'. Sturdy and able to cruise at a high speed at high altitude, the B-17 was found in early operations to possess inadequate defensive armament and by mid-1942 had been developed into the far superior B-17G, with greater protection and the armament of 13 12.7mm (0.5in) machine guns, most of them in power-operated positions.

The B-17 was the backbone of the US Army Air Forces' daylight raids against point targets, in which it was supplemented by the four-engined Consolidated B-24 Liberator, but both of these types became truly viable only with the introduction of fighters possessing the range to escort them to and from their targets. First used by the French in May 1940, the Douglas DB-7, known to the British as the Boston and the USAAF as the A-20 Havoc, was a twin-engined attack bomber. The type was then supplemented and finally supplanted by larger twin-engined medium bombers such as the North American B-25 Mitchell and Martin B-26 Marauder, and also the Douglas A-26 Invader attack bomber.

Strategic bombing

Though in itself the epitome of offensive warfare, strategic bombing demanded the creation of defensive tactics. The bombers that carried out the Allies' strategic air offensive against Germany needed a constant stream of revised tactics to counter the German air and ground defences. Because RAF Bomber Command undertook mostly unescorted area bombing night raids, the tactics were different from those of the US Air Forces, whose bombers carried out daylight attacks for precision bombing of point targets. Initially the British bombers were widely dispersed when they flew to their targets and this enabled the German night-fighters of the Kammhuber Line to tackle each succeeding flight as they passed through the line's various radar-controlled 'boxes'. The British countered with the 'bomber stream', which was employed for the first time in the 'thousand-bomber' attack on Köln during May 1942: rather than converging on the target separately, the bombers assembled into one stream to pass through the Kammhuber Line in a column some 70 miles (112km) long and 1220m (4000ft) wide, which made it possible to saturate the defensive capability of the box through which it passed.

Throughout the war several types of electronic warfare equipment were introduced to degrade the German radar and misdirect the German night-fighters. Small spoof raids were also started to draw the night-fighters away from the main raid. The type most successful in the spoof role was the Mosquito, which was too speedy to be intercepted. When bombing real targets, a Mosquito force often attacked in two waves, one at low level co-ordinated with the other making a shallow dive, a tactic that split the defences. The Mosquito was also used for pathfinding, in which high-quality crews arrived just before the main raid to mark the target with special bombs and flares.

USAAF tactics

The USAAF had different tactical solutions to create for the protection of its aircraft. Until long-range fighters became available early in 1944 to escort them, the bombers were dependent on their own defensive armament, and therefore flew in formations designed to maximize their fields of mutual defensive firepower. Thus the numbers of any single formation and the formation's compactness increased as the war progressed. As they were both heavily-armed, the B-17 and B-24 were initially believed to be able to fight their way to and from their targets in formations of six aircraft, four such formations flying together at a distance of 6.4km (4 miles) from each other: this was adequate for bombing as it offered room to manoeuvre, but was defensively poor as German fighters could enter the gaps between the formations.

Thus in September 1942, 18-aircraft groups were introduced, bringing the aircraft closer together

▲ **Douglas bombers**
At the Douglas plant in California, Bostons and Havocs await delivery to the USAAF early in 1942.

and providing a tighter concentration of mutually supporting firepower. However, the formation was difficult to manoeuvre and easily dropped stragglers. The formation was improved in December 1942, but the German fighters were still able to cause a loss rate unsustainable over any length of time. In March 1943, therefore, the basic formation became the 54-aircraft combat wing: three 18-aircraft groups being compacted into a grouping 550m (600 yards) long, 2000m (2200 yards) wide and 810m (2650ft) deep. This aided defence but demanded bombing by formation rather than individual aircraft, and was soon further improved as the 'tucked-in' wing with the aircraft squeezed further together. This yielded a genuinely effective weight of fire and a smaller target for the head-on attacks of the German fighters.

The 'tucked-in' wing lasted to the advent of the long-range escort fighter early in 1944 and the appearance of massed Flak batteries for the defence of German cities early in 1945, each resulting in a change of formation. With fighters covering the bombers from the start to the finish of a raid, self-defence was less important than allowing the bombers to concentrate on more accurate bombing under control of the few aircraft fitted with electronic aids. One such aeroplane led a 12-bomber squadron, with three squadrons constituting an arrow-head group. The final arrangement, introduced in February 1945, comprised a group with four nine-bomber squadrons flying at different altitudes to make it more difficult for the Flak gunner to set their sights and shells.

Chapter 6

France and the Low Countries

Great things were expected of the bomber
during the 1930s, when many believed that bombing
would be the arbiter of any future war. But the bomber was
expensive to build, maintain and operate, so numbers were
comparatively few and, for the most part, the intended bomb
loads were also small. During the 1920s and 1930s,
France had produced several types of extraordinarily ugly,
slab-sided bombers, and only late in the 1930s
began to produce elegant, high-speed bombers such as
those from the Amiot and Lioré-et-Olivier companies.
Belgium and the Netherlands were concerned with defence
rather than offence, and therefore concentrated their limited
resources on light bombers for frontline service.

◀ **Bomb loading**

French ground crew load up a Martin 167 prior to a mission in June 1940. Designed as an attack bomber
in 1938, the US-made Martin XA-22 failed to win any production contracts with the USAAF. In 1939 Martin
looked for buyers overseas, and under the designation Model 167 (named the Maryland) sales were made
to Britain, France, and South Africa.

France
1939–40

The French were strong adherents of the bomber concept in World War I, and retained their faith in the 1920s and 1930s. But their aircraft became increasingly obsolete in concept, and the rearmament of the later 1930s proved too little and too late.

B Y THE MID-1930S, French national security was clearly threatened by the revival of German nationalism under Adolf Hitler, so Pierre Cot, the secretary of the air force, decided that national security was too important for the production of war planes to be left in the hands of private enterprise. In July 1936, the government began to nationalize France's aircraft manufacturing companies to create six large and, it was wrongly estimated, more effective regional groupings. The aircraft engine industry, even though it could not provide the number of powerful engines needed, was not nationalized.

Accelerated production

The announcement of the need to build more than 2500 modern warplanes was the direct government response to a remark by the current commander of the air force. He claimed that less than half of some

1400 frontline aircraft were ready for immediate service, and were in any event mostly obsolescent. Thus France tried to respond militarily to the threat of another European war via an intensive modernization programme in 1938–39.

ORGANIZATION

French Air Force bomber dispositions
May 1940

Zone d'Operations Aeriennes Est (two groupements de bombardement)	Zone d'Operations Aeriennes Sud (none)
Zone d'Operations Aeriennes Nord (two groupements de bombardement and one groupement de Bombardement d'assaut)	Zone d'Operations Aeriennes des Alpes (five groupes de bombardement and one groupement de bombardement d'assaut)

▲ **Potez 540Bn.5**

l'Armée de l'Air

In civil markings and without armament owing to its use in transporting diplomats and negotiators, this was the 228th example of the Potez 540 family. The type first flew in 1933, and production reached 259 aircraft for France. About 70 were still in first-line service in September 1939, but were soon relegated to secondary tasks.

Specifications

Crew: 7

Powerplant: 2 x 515kW (690hp) Hispano-Suiza HS 12 Xirs/Xjrs V-12 liquid-cooled engines

Maximum speed: 310km/h (193mph)

Range: 1250km (777 miles)

Service ceiling: 10,000 m (32,810ft)

Dimensions: span 22.10m (72ft 6in);

length 16.20 m (53ft 2in); height 3.88m (12ft 9in)

Weight: 5950kg (13,115lb) loaded

Armament: 3-5 x 7.5mm (0.29in) MGs in flexible nose, dorsal, and ventral positions; 10 x 55kg (121lb) bombs in bomb bay when loaded for bombing

But it was 'too little, too late' as far as France was concerned. When war did break out in September 1939, the *Armée de l'Air* was still suffering the effects of the total chaos throughout the government, armed forces and industry, which meant that only 826 fighters and 250 bombers were anything like combat-ready. Moreover, many more aircraft were not ready when they ought to have been because of late deliveries and uncalibrated defensive armament and lack of effective bomb sight.

From 10 May 1940, France's lack of modern thinking, aircraft, weapons and communications

▲ Amiot 143M

3e Escadron / Groupe de Bombardement II/35, Pontarlier, September 1939

First flown in the spring of 1935 and built to the extent of 138 aircraft, the Amiot 143 was typical of the French bombers of the mid-1930s with its high-drag lines, fixed landing gear and large ventral gondola.

Specifications

Crew: 5

Powerplant: 2 x 640kW (870hp)

Maximum speed: 310km/h (193mph)

Range: 746km (1200 miles)

Service ceiling: 7900m (25,920ft)

Dimensions: span 24.53m (80ft 5in);

    length 18.26m (59ft 11in);

height 5.68m (18ft 8in)

Weight: 9700kg (21,385lb) loaded

Armament: 4 x 7.5mm (0.295in) MGs in nose

    turret, dorsal turret, forward-fuselage floor

    hatch and rear of ventral gondola; up to

    1600kg (3527lb) bombs

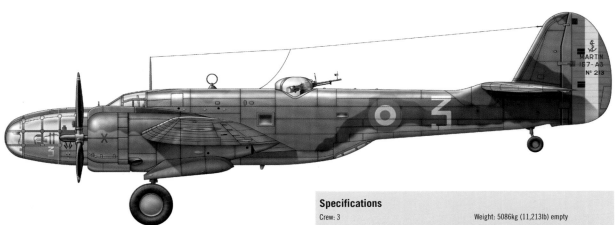

▲ Martin 167A.3

l'Armée de l'Air, 1939–40

Known to the British as the Maryland, the Model 167 was first manufactured for the French in two forms as the Model 167F reconnaissance bomber (115 ordered) and Model 167A.3 attack-bomber (100 ordered, of which 76 were delivered to the UK after the fall of France).

Specifications

Crew: 3

Powerplant: 2 x 894kW (1200hp) Pratt & Whitney

    R-1830-S3C4-G Twin Wasp radial

Maximum speed: 447km/h (278 mph)

Range: 1947km (1210 miles)

Service ceiling: 7925m (26,000ft)

Dimensions: span 18.69m (61ft 4in); length

    14.22m (46ft 8in); height 4.57m (14ft 12in)

Weight: 5086kg (11,213lb) empty

Armament: 1 x 7.62mm (0.3in) Vickers 'K'

    trainable rearward-firing MG in the dorsal

    turretplus 1 x 7.7mm (0.303in) Vickers 'K'

    trainable rearward-firing MG in the ventral

    step position; 4 x 1100kg (500lb) bomb load

BOMBER UNITS OF THE ZONE D'OPERATIONS AERIENNES NORD (ZOAN)		
Unit	Type	Base
GB I/12	LeO 451	Soissons-Saconin
GB II/12	LeO 451	Persan-Beaumont
GB I/34	Amiot 143	Montdidier
GB II/34	Amiot 143	Roye-Amy
GBA I/54	Bre.693	La Ferte-Gaucher
GBA II/54	Bre.693	Nangis

equipment, combined with an almost incredible shortage of many vital hardware elements such as propellers (the result of 'technical problems'), eased the task of the Germans as they advanced through France and destroyed all opposition: on 11 May, for example, nearly 20 French bombers and more than 30 escorting British fighters were shot down in an attempt to stop the Germans from crossing the Meuse river.

This was merely the beginning, for French fighter and bomber strengths became rapidly depleted during May as *Luftwaffe* fighters and ground-based flak units destroyed increasing numbers of the warplanes. Worse was the fact that the squadrons were often out of contact with the army units they were to support, the result in part of the poor coordination of communication between the army and the air force, and in part of the outdated, communications equipment used by the army.

As it became clear that the battle of France was lost, the high command ordered the *Armée de l'Air*'s remnants to withdraw to the French colonies in North Africa – in order, it believed, to continue the fight. In overall terms, during the battle of France, the French lost more than 750 aircraft while the Germans lost more than 850.

Even so, the Germans losses could be made good, and would not prevent the huge defeat inflicted on the French Army.

▲ **Home of the Breguet 693**

An early model Breguet 693 sits in a field at Moteurs Gnome & Rhône, the birthplace of the type.

> This is the emblem of Groupe de Bombardement d'Assaut I/54. The Groupe had a theoretical complement of 13 Breguet 693 aircraft.

▲ **Breguet 693A.2**

Groupe de Bombardement d'Assaut I/54, Montdidier and La Ferte-Gaucher, France, May 1940

GBA I and II/54 were the component halves of the Groupement de Bombardement d'Assaut 18, which was the premier indigenous attack-bomber formation in the northern sector of the French air defence system in May 1940.

Specifications

Crew: 2
Powerplant: 2 x 522kW (700hp)
Maximum speed: 490km/h (304mph)
Range: 1350km (839 miles)
Service ceiling: 4000m (13,125ft)
Dimensions: span 15.37m (50ft 5in);
length 9.67m (31ft 9in);

height 3.19m (10ft 6in)
Weight: 4900kg (10,803lb) loaded
Armament: 1 x 20mm (0.79in) forward-firing
cannon and 4 x 7.5mm (0.295in) MGs in nose
(2), rear cockpit and ventral position; up to
400kg (882lb) of bombs carried internally

French campaign – first phase
MAY 1940

Instead of punching through northern Belgium and along the English Channel coast, as the Allies expected, the Germans drove through the Ardennes in southern Belgium to break through at Sedan before driving to the Channel coast and splitting the Allies in two parts for easy defeat.

THE GERMAN CAMPAIGN FELL into two parts: the battle of the Low Countries and the battle of France, the latter also falling into two phases. As the German forces struck on 10 May into the Low Countries, these called for French and British aid, and the Allies armies moved east, as already planned, to the 'Dyle Line' covering Brussels. Meanwhile, the Germans were driving most of their Panzer

▲ Breguet Bre.693AB.2

4e Escadrille / Groupe de Bombardement d'Assaut II/54, Roy,
May 1940

Making its combat debut on 12 May 1940, the Bre.693 had a disastrous beginning, 10 out of the 11 aircraft being lost or damaged beyond repair.

Specifications

Crew: 2
Powerplant: 2 x 522kW (700hp)
Maximum speed: 490km/h (304mph)
Range: 1350km (839 miles)
Service ceiling: 4000m (13,125ft)
Dimensions: span 15.37m (50ft 5in);
  length 9.67m (31ft 9in);

height 3.19m (10ft 6in)
Weight: 4900kg (10,803lb) loaded
Armament: 1 x 20mm (0.79in) forward-firing
  cannon and 4 x 7.5mm (0.295in) MGs in nose
  (two), rear cockpit and ventral position; up to
  400kg (882lb) of bombs carried internally

Specifications

Crew: 4
Powerplant: 2 x 790kW (1060hp)
Maximum speed: 480km/h (298mph)
Range: 2500km (1554 miles)
Service ceiling: 10,000m (32,810ft)
Dimensions: span 22.83m (74ft 11in);
  length 14.5m (47ft 7in);

height 4.08m (13ft 5in)
Weight: 11,300kg (24,912lb) loaded
Armament: 1 x 20mm (0.79in) trainable
  cannon in dorsal turret; 2 x 7.5mm (0.295in)
  MGs in nose and ventral position; up to
  1200kg (2646lb) of bombs

▲ Amiot 354B.4

4e Escadrille / Groupe de Bombardement II/21, May 1940

First flown in January 1939 and potentially an excellent medium bomber, the Amiot 354 failed to make any real impact: although 900 such aircraft had been ordered, only about 45 had been delivered before the fall of France in June 1940. Several were later adapted as high-speed civil transports.

divisions through the 'impassable' Ardennes. The Germans secured bridgeheads over the Meuse by the 14 May, and moved their armour forward on the night of 15–16 May, heading behind the British Expeditionary Force (BEF) and the French First and Ninth Armies. By 20 May, the Germans had reached the English Channel and established a corridor separating the Allied forces. The Allies fell back around Dunkirk, and after Boulogne and Calais had fallen on 25 and 27 May respectively, the Allies decided to evacuate by sea from Dunkirk.

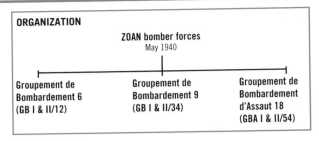

ORGANIZATION

ZOAN bomber forces
May 1940

| Groupement de Bombardement 6 (GB I & II/12) | Groupement de Bombardement 9 (GB I & II/34) | Groupement de Bombardement d'Assaut 18 (GBA I & II/54) |

▲ Bloch MB.174A.3
l'Armée de l'Air, France, 1940

Entering service only in the later part of March 1940, the MB.174 was planned as a reconnaissance attack-bomber, but the 56 aircraft completed were used only in the reconnaissance role, more than half of the 49 operational aircraft being lost by the time of France's capitulation in June 1940.

Specifications

Crew: 3

Powerplant: 2 x 820kW (1100hp)

Maximum speed: 530km/h (329mph)

Range: 1650km (1025 miles)

Service ceiling: 11,000m (36,090ft)

Dimensions: span 17.9m (58ft 9in);

length 12.25m (40ft 3in);

height 3.55m (11ft 8in)

Weight: 7160kg (15,784lb) loaded

Armament: 7 x 7.5mm (0.295in) MGs: two fixed on leading edge of wing, two trainable rearward ones in dorsal position, three trainable rearward ones on ventral wobble mounts; up to 500kg (1102lb) bombs

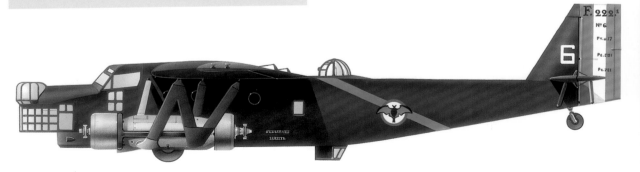

▲ Farman F.222.1Bn.5
l'Armée de l'Air, France, 1940

Some 35 F.222 heavy night-bombers were delivered to the French Air Force: 11 F.222.1s with a short nose and flat outer wing panels and 24 F.222.2s with a longer nose and dihedralled outer wing panels. These were the only four-engined heavy bombers in French service during 1939, equipping three groupes, two in France and the other in West Africa.

Specifications

Crew: 5

Powerplant: 4 x 723kW (970hp)

Maximum speed: 360km/h (224mph)

Range: 2000km (1243 miles)

Service ceiling: 8000m (26,245ft)

Dimensions: span 36m (118ft 1in); length 21.45m (70ft 5in); height 5.19m (17ft 1in)

Weight: 18700kg (41,226lb) loaded

Armament: 3 x 7.5mm (0.295in) MGs: one in nose turret, one in dorsal turret and one in ventral 'dustbin' position; up to 4000kg (8800lb) of either 20 x 200kg (440lb) or 40 x 100kg (220lb) bombs, or a mix of these with 50kg (110lb) bombs

French campaign – second phase
June 1940

With the Low Countries defeated and the northern part of the Allied armies captured or evacuated from Dunkirk, the Germans could concentrate all their efforts on the bulk of the French armies during the course of June 1940.

THE GERMAN PREOCCUPATION with the British evacuation of almost 340,000 men, 120,000 of them French, from Dunkirk in the period up to 4 June offered the French forces south of the Somme river a measure of respite. The French commander-in-chief now attempted to create a defensive system on the line of the Somme and Aisne rivers to protect Paris and the interior of France against the inevitable renewal of the German offensive, but most of the French Army had lost all confidence in its leaders and even in itself. Nor were the remaining Allied forces in any condition to provide help: the

ORGANIZATION

ZOAA bomber forces
May 1940

Groupement de Bombardement 1 (GB I/62 & I/63)

Groupement de Bombardement 6 (GB I & II/31)

Groupement de Bombardement 7 (GB I & II/23)

Groupement de Bombardement 9 (I & II/21)

Groupement de Bombardement 11 (GB I & II/11)

Groupement de Bombardement d'Assaut 19 (GBA II/35 and I & II/51)

BOMBER UNITS OF THE ZONE D'OPÉRATIONS AÉRIENNES DES ALPES (ZOAA)		
Unit	Type	Base
GB I/62 & I/63	Martin 167F	Orange
GB I & II/11	LeO 451, MB.210	Istres-Mas le Rue
GB I & II/21	Amiot 351/354 MB.210	Avignon
GB I & II/23	MB.210	Istres-Le Vallon
GB I & II/31	LeO 451	Lezignan
GBA I & II/51	Potez 633 Bre.691/693	Le Luc
GBA II/35	Potez 633, Bre.691	Briare

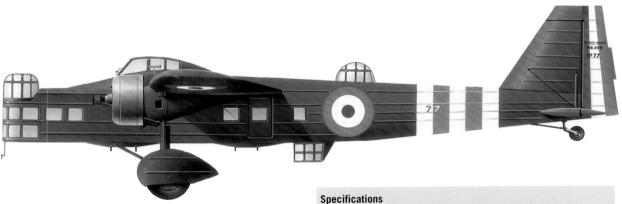

▲ **Bloch MB.200B.4**

Section de Remorquage d'Otange / l'Armée de l'Air, France, June 1940

Entering service late in 1934, the MB.200B.4 was a medium bomber wholly typical of French designers' angular approach to the creation of large aircraft at this time. Deliveries eventually totalled 208 aircraft, all used for training by May 1940.

Specifications

Crew: 4

Powerplant: 2 x 649kW (870hp)

Maximum speed: 285km/h (177mph)

Range: 1000km (621 miles)

Service ceiling: 8000m (26,245ft)

Dimensions: span 22.45m (73ft 8in);

length 16m (52ft 6in);

height 3.9m (12ft 10in)

Weight: 7480kg (16,490lb) loaded

Armament: single 7.5mm (0.295in) trainable MGs in nose, dorsal and ventral positions; up to 1200kg (2646lb) of bombs

British 51st (Highland) Division surrendered at St Valery-en-Caux on 12 June, and the British 52nd (Lowland) Division and the Canadian 1st Division had to be evacuated. The Germans moved south on 4 June, and had crossed the Seine river by 10 June.

Flight from Paris

On 12 June, the French government declared Paris an open city and removed itself to Bordeaux. Winston Churchill's offer of union between the UK and France was rejected, Prime Minister Paul Reynaud

resigned and his successor, Marshal Philippe Petain, accepted German terms on 22 June for an armistice. By this time, German forces had plunged deep into France, reaching western Brittany, the Spanish frontier on the Bay of Biscay, and a line between Limoges and the Swiss frontier near Geneva.

All France north and west of this line was occupied, and a new French government established itself at Vichy in the unoccupied zone. France had been comprehensively defeated, leaving only Charles de Gaulle's Free French to carry on the fight.

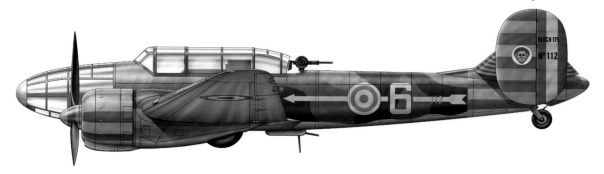

Specifications

Crew: 3

Powerplant: 2 x 850kW (1140hp)

Maximum speed: 540km/h (335mph)

Range: 1600km (994 miles)

Service ceiling: 8000m (26,245ft)

Dimensions: span 17.95m (58ft 11in);

   length 12.43m (40ft 9in);

height 3.55m (11ft 8in)

Weight: 5660kg (12,478lb) loaded

Armament: 7 x 7.5mm (0.295in) MGs: two

   fixed on leading edge of wing, two trainable

   rearward ones in dorsal position, three

   trainable rearward ones on ventral wobble

   mounts; up to 600kg (1323lb) bombs

▲ **Bloch MB.175B.3**

Vichy French Air Force, 1941–42

A development of the MB.174 for the dedicated light attack-bomber role, the MB.175 entered service just before the fall of France. Some 20 aircraft were delivered in June 1940, but none saw combat and 23 of the type saw service with the Vichy French air force. Another 56 were completed for the Luftwaffe as trainers.

The Netherlands and Belgium
MAY 1940

The Dutch and Belgians sought to remain neutral from 1939, relying on small forces and the nature of their countries to deter possible German aggression. It was in vain, and in May 1940 both countries were quickly overrun by larger and more effective German forces.

A**S NOTED ABOVE**, the German campaign in the west fell neatly into two parts, of which the first was the battle of the Low Countries designed to eliminate the Netherlands and Belgium as possible threats to the right flank of the Germans' main thrust and as potential bases for enlarged British forces. But the Netherlands had only eight divisions and some

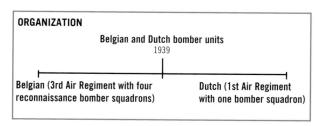

ORGANIZATION

Belgian and Dutch bomber units
1939

Belgian (3rd Air Regiment with four reconnaissance bomber squadrons)

Dutch (1st Air Regiment with one bomber squadron)

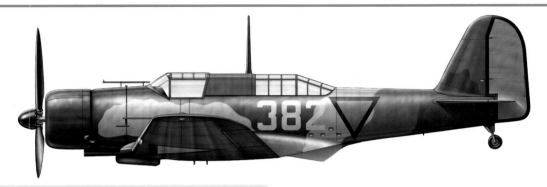

Specifications

Crew: 2

Powerplant: 746kW (1000hp) Wright XR-1820-
32 piston engine

Maximum speed: 410km/h (255mph)

Range: 1240km (773 miles)

Service ceiling: 7780m (25,530ft)

Dimensions: span 12.65m (41ft 6in);
length 10.08m (33ft 1in); height 4.14m
(13ft 7in)

Weight: 2905kg (6404lb)

Armament: 2 x 12.7mm (0.5in) forward-
firing MGs

▲ Douglas (Northrop) Model DB-8A-3N

3rd Fighter Squadron / 2nd Air Regiment, Ypenburg, Netherlands, May 1940

The Dutch Air Force received 18 such aircraft between August and November 1939, and 12 of the aircraft were operational at the time of the German invasion on 10 May 1940. This one was lost on the ground, and of the 11 that took off seven were shot down and the surviving four were later destroyed on the ground.

▲ Fokker T.V

Bomber Squadron / 1st Air Regiment, Schiphol, Netherlands, May 1940

First flown in October 1937 and built to the extent of 16 aircraft intended for the long-range fighter as well as medium bomber roles, the T.V operated only as a bomber. The nine serviceable aircraft flown by the Bomber Squadron on 10 May 1940 were all destroyed during in the following five days.

Specifications

Crew: 5

Powerplant: 2 x 690kW (925hp) Bristol Pegasus
XXVI air-cooled radial engines

Maximum speed: 417km/h (257mph)

Range: 1550km (956 miles)

Service ceiling: 7700m (25,256ft)

Dimensions: span 21m (68ft 11in);

length 16m (60ft 10in);
height 5m (16ft 5in)

Weight: 7250kg (15,950lb) loaded

Armament: 1 x 20mm (0.79in) cannon in nose,
5 x 7.9mm (0.295in) MGs in dorsal, ventral,
both lateral positions and tail cupola; 1000kg
(2205lb) of bombs

125 warplanes, while Belgium had 18 divisions and some 180 aircraft to face altogether more powerful German ground and air forces, the former including three Panzer divisions.

The German campaign against the Low Countries began in the morning of 10 May 1940, when the Germans launched air attacks and parachute landings on Dutch airfields and bridges even as their ground forces moved moved west into the Netherlands and Belgium. This prompted both nations to ask for British and French aid, initially in the form of the pre-planned Allied movement forward to the Dyle Line covering Brussels. Despite their standard recourse in the face of invasion, namely the flooding of key areas and the demolition of bridges over major water courses, the Dutch were soon compelled to back into 'Fortress Holland', bounded by Rotterdam and Amsterdam in the south and north, and the Zuider See and North Sea on the east and west. On 14 May, the German Air Force 'blitzed' the great port city of Rotterdam, and this persuaded the Dutch to surrender after a five-day campaign that had cost the Netherlands some 25 per cent casualties.

Meanwhile, further to the south the Germans had captured Fort Eben Emael, the cornerstone of the Belgian defence, with a gliderborne assault on 11 May, the day on which the bulk of the Belgian Army pulled back toward the Dyle Line. This was no longer of use, however, and the Allies pulled steadily back, Belgium surrendering on the night of 27–28 May.

BELGIAN AND DUTCH BOMBER UNITS			
Unit	Type	Base	Strength
Belgian 1/I/3	Fairey Fox III	Evere	9
Belgian 3/I/3	Fairey Fox III	Evere	9
Belgian 5/III/3	Fairey Battle	Evere	14
Belgian 7/III/3	Fairey Fox VIII	Evere	9
Dutch Bomber Squadron	Fokker T.V	Schiphol	9

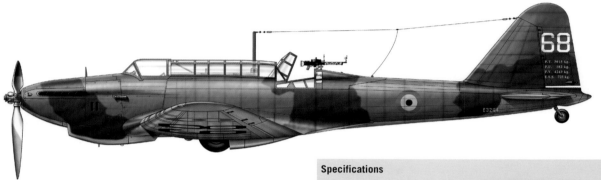

▲ **Fairey Battle Mk I**

5/III / 3rd Air Regiment, Belgium, Evere, May 1940

All 18 Battle Mk I light bombers delivered to Belgium served with this squadron, which had 14 aircraft on strength at the time of the German invasion on 10 May 1940. Six out of nine such aircraft were lost while attacking a bridge over the Albert Canal on 11 May, and the other aircraft were also soon lost.

Specifications

Crew: 3

Powerplant: 2 x 768kW (1030hp) Rolls-Royce
Merlin I Vee piston engines

Maximum speed: 414km/h (257mph)

Range: 1609km (1000 miles)

Service ceiling: 7620m (25,000ft)

Dimensions: span 16.46m (54ft); length 12.9m
(42ft 4in); height 4.72m (15ft 6in)

Weight: 4895kg (10,792lb) loaded

Armament: 2 x 7.7mm (0.303in) Vickers MGs:
one fixed-forward firing in the leading edge of
the starboard wing, one Vickers 'K' trainable
rearward-firing in the rear of the cockpit; up
to 113kg (250lb) bombs carried internally, 2 x
113kg (250lb) carried externally

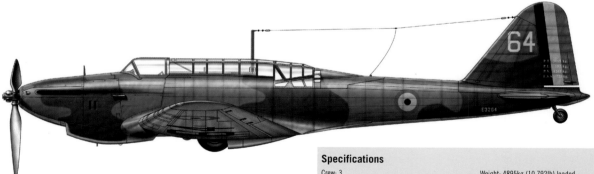

▲ **Fairey Battle Mk I**

5/III / 3rd Air Regiment, Evere, Belgium, May 1940

Like the British, the Belgians found that the Battle was wholly inadequate in speed, agility and armament to survive, let alone operate effectively, against an enemy possessing good fighters and powerful anti-aircraft (AA) defences.

Specifications

Crew: 3

Powerplant: 2 x 768kW (1030hp) Rolls-Royce
Merlin I Vee piston engines

Maximum speed: 414km/h (257mph)

Range: 1609km (1000 miles)

Service ceiling: 7620m (25,000ft)

Dimensions: span 16.46m (54ft); length 12.9m
(42ft 4in); height 4.72m (15ft 6in)

Weight: 4895kg (10,792lb) loaded

Armament: 2 x 7.7mm (0.303in) Vickers MGs:
one fixed-forward firing in the leading edge of
the starboard wing, one Vickers 'K' trainable
rearward-firing in the rear of the cockpit; up
to 113kg (250lb) bombs carried internally, 2 x
113kg (250lb) carried externally

Free French air forces
1940–45

The Free French Forces started with men unwilling to accept the defeat of France in 1940, but grew to include the formations of French colonies retaken by the Allies, and by 1943 were growing strongly in strength and overall capability. Their air force was very useful in 1944–45.

T HE FORCES FRANÇAISES LIBRES (Free French Forces, or FFL) consisted of Frenchmen who had decided to continue fighting against Axis forces after the surrender of France. The FFL were led by the French government-in-exile under Général Charles de Gaulle, and their air arm was the *Forces Aériennes Françaises Libres* (Free French Air Force, or FAFL), distinguished by cross of Lorraine markings. It was on 17 June 1940, five days before the Franco-German armistice was signed, that the first exodus to the UK took place, as 10 men flew from Bordeaux-Mérignac.

Answering the call
Others rallied to de Gaulle from France and French North Africa over the next two years. From a strength of 500 on July 1940, the FAFL had grown to 900 by

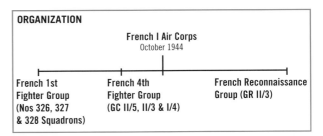

ORGANIZATION

French I Air Corps October 1944		
French 1st Fighter Group (Nos 326, 327 & 328 Squadrons)	French 4th Fighter Group (GC II/5, II/3 & I/4)	French Reconnaissance Group (GR II/3)

1941, including 200 airmen. De Gaulle appointed Colonel Martin Valin as the FAFL's commander in the summer of 1940, but this officer assumed command only on 9 July 1941 from Amiral Emile Muselier.

The FAFL was formed with one mixed unit at Odiham on 29 August 1940. De Gaulle saw one of his first tasks as being the seduction of French

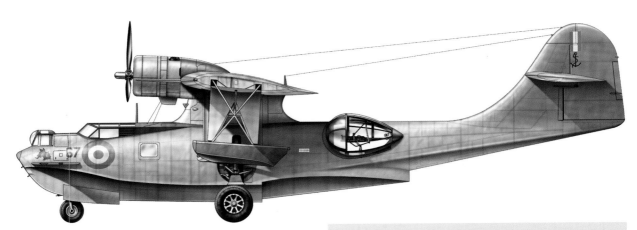

▲ **Consolidated PBY-5A Catalina**

Free French squadron, Morocco, 1943

The French ordered the PBY in 1939 but received no such 'boats' before the fall of France. In 1943, two squadrons (one with Free French and the other with ex-Vichy French personnel) were formed with 28 PBY-5A amphibious flying boats for service off Morocco under operational control of the US Navy.

Specifications

Crew: 7/9

Powerplant: 2 x 895kW (1200hp)

Maximum speed: 288km/h (179mph)

Range: 4096km (2545 miles)

Service ceiling: 4480m (14,700ft)

Dimensions: span 31.7m (104ft);

length 19.47m (63ft 11in);

height 6.15m (20ft 2in)

Weight: 16,066kg (35,420lb) loaded

Armament: 3 x 7.62mm (0.3in) trainable MGs: two in the bow turret, one firing aft of the hull step; 1 x 12.7mm (0.5in) MG in each of the two beam positions; up to 1814kg (4000lb) of bombs or depth charges

The badge of No. 342 Squadron 'Lorraine', RAF, sports the usual Free French cross of Lorraine. The squadron was formed after the French *escadrilles* (squadrons) 'Metz' and 'Nancy' were transferred to the UK from the Mediterranean and combined in April 1943.

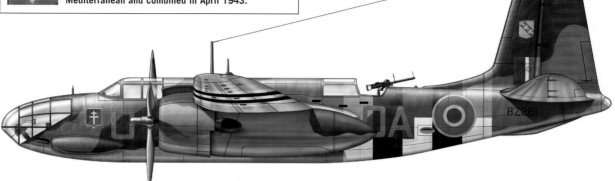

Specifications

Douglas A-20G Havoc

Crew: 3

Powerplant: 2 x 1194kW (1600hp) Wright
 Cyclone R-2600-23 air-cooled radial piston

Maximum speed: 546km/h (339mph)

Range: 1755km (1090 miles)

Service ceiling: 7650m (25,100ft)

Dimensions: span 18.69m (61ft 4in);
 length 14.63m (48ft); height 5.36m (17ft 7in)

Weight: 12,338kg (27,200lb) loaded

Armament: up to 8 x 12.7mm (0.5in) MGs;
 1814kg (4000lb) of bombs

▲ Douglas Boston Mk IIIA

No. 342 Squadron 'Lorraine' / RAF, Hartford Bridge, UK, 1944

No. 342 Squadron was an RAF unit manned by Free French personnel, and was allocated to No. 2 Bomber Group of the 2nd Tactical Air Force (TAF) for service in support of the Allied landings of June 1944 in Normandy, and then the subsequent land campaign.

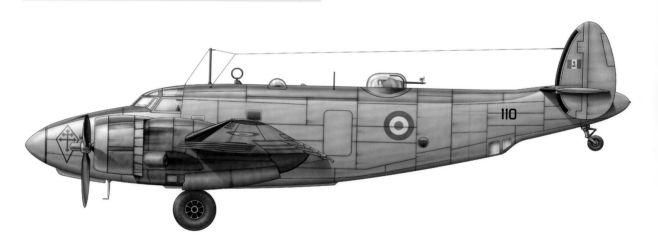

Specifications

Crew: 5

Powerplant: 2 x 1491kW (2000hp)

Maximum speed: 518km/h (322mph)

Range: 2671km (1660 miles)

Service ceiling: 8016m (26,300ft)

Dimensions: span 19.96m (65ft 6in);
 length 15.77m (51ft 9in); height 11m (11ft)

Weight: 15,422kg (34,000lb) loaded

Armament: 5 x 12.7mm (0.5in) MGs: two fixed
 in nose, three fixed in undernose gun pack;
 2 x 12.7 (0.5in) trainable in dorsal turret;
 2 x 7.62mm (0.3in) trainables in rearward
 firing ventral position; bomb load 6 x 227kg
 (500lb) internally, 2 x 454kg (1000lb)
 externally, 1 x MK13-2 torpedo or 6 x 147kg
 (325lb) depth charges

▲ Lockheed PV-1 Ventura

Flottille 6F / Aeronavale, France, 1944–45

The revived French naval air arm operated a small number of PV-1 patrol bombers from 1944, and these were eventually replaced after the end of World War II by Bloch MB.175 aircraft.

colonies from adherence to Vichy France, and an operation was mounted against Dakar in French West Africa. This included the FAFL's *Groupe de Combat Mixte* 1, comprising four squadrons of Bristol Blenheim bombers and Westland Lysander army cooperation aircraft. The operation failed, and the FAFL's envoys were incarcerated at Dakar by the Vichy authorities. However, the forces in Cameroon and Chad rallied to the Gaullist cause.

There were three detachments of French Air Force units based at Fort Lamy, Douala and Pointe Noire with a miscellany of Potez and Bloch aircraft, and they thus became part of the FAFL. However, Gabon remained loyal to Vichy, so, in October 1940, FAFL squadrons set out on photo-reconnaissance and leaflet-dropping missions. The first Vichy-versus-FAFL combats occurred on 6 November 1940, when two Vichy French aircraft tackled two FAFL Lysanders near Libreville, resulting in both aircraft sustaining damage. Two days later, the first FAFL airmen were shot down and taken prisoner. Further north, a mission by the recently formed *Groupe de Bombardement* 1 'Lorraine' on 4 February 1941 ended in disaster when only one of four Blenheims sent to bomb Koufra returned.

Groupe 'Bretagne'

The Groupe 'Bretagne' was formed on 1 January for long-range reconnaissance with the Martin Maryland, army cooperation with the Lysander and transport with Potez aircraft. It was not until

FRENCH SQUADRONS ON THE RAF ESTABLISHMENT, JUNE 1944		
Unit	**Type**	**Base**
No. 329 Sqn	Supermarine Spitfire Mk IX	Merston
No. 340 Sqn	Supermarine Spitfire Mk IX	Merston
No. 341 Sqn	Supermarine Spitfire Mk IX	Merston
No. 342 Sqn	Douglas Boston Mk III	Hartford Bridge
No. 346 Sqn	Handley Page Halifax Mk III	Elvington
No. 347 Sqn	Handley Page Halifax Mk III	Elvington

3 March, however, that the first missions were flown from Uigh-el-Kébir. For most of 1942, the Groupe 'Bretagne' concentrated on liaison and training flights, but from late in 1942 the group's 'Rennes' Squadron engaged Italian forces and operations continued to the fall of Tripoli, Libya, on 23 January 1943.

November 1942 marked the start of the rebirth of the French Air Force as a result of Franklin D. Roosevelt's agreement to deliver 1000 US aircraft. On 1 July 1943 different elements of the French air forces in Africa came under the control of Général Bouscat, who reorganized his command, which included about 20 groupes. The new French Air Force was then active in the Italian campaign, while other elements fought with the RAF in north-west Europe, and a much enlarged and upgraded air force played a major part in the French campaign of 1944–45.

Specifications

Crew: 7

Powerplant: 4 x 1204kW (1615hp) Bristol Hercules XVI

Maximum speed: 454km/h (282mph)

Range: 1658km (1030 miles)

Service ceiling: 7315m (24,000ft)

Dimensions: span 31.75m (104ft 2in); length 21.36m (70ft 1in); height 6.32m (20ft 9in)

Weight: 29,484kg (65,000lb) loaded

Armament: 9 x 7.7mm (0.303in) MGs: one on flexible mount in nose; four each on dorsal and tail turrets; 5897kg (13,000lb) bomb load

▲ Handley Page Halifax Mk III

No. 346 Squadron 'Guyenne' / RAF, Elvington, UK, 1944

No. 346 Squadron was manned by Free French personnel, and in June 1944 was a heavy bomber unit of No. 4 Bomber Group within the Royal Air Force's Bomber Command.

Chapter 7

United Kingdom and Commonwealth

Great things were expected of RAF Bomber Command right from the start of the war, but expectations were initially confounded. Light bombers proved wholly inadequate, medium bombers were very vulnerable by day, bomb weights were too light, and the accuracy of bombing and night navigation was woeful. Gradually the situation improved as night area bombing became the norm, twin-engined medium bombers were replaced by altogether more capable four-engined heavy bombers, and better navigation and bombing equipment were introduced. From later in 1943, Bomber Command became a formidable strategic and, at times, tactical force.

◀ **Flight of Lancasters**

Three Lancaster bombers from No. 207 Squadron fly over British countryside, 1943. The squadron started World War II flying Avro Manchester bombers but switched to Lancasters in June 1942.

RAF Bomber Command
1936–45

The bomber forces with which the UK entered World War II were modest in size and very limited in their capabilities. The light bombers were largely obsolete, and of the medium bombers only the Vickers Wellington offered any genuine capability. There was to be a steep learning curve.

RAF BOMBER COMMAND controlled the RAF's bomber forces, and was formed on 14 July 1936 from the bomber element of the Air Defence of Great Britain. From 12 September 1937 its commander was Air Chief Marshal Sir Edgar Ludlow-Hewitt, replaced on 3 April 1940 by Air Marshal Sir Charles Portal. He, in turn, was replaced on 5 October 1940 by Air Marshal Sir Richard Peirse, and from 22 February 1942, and for the rest of the war, Air Chief Marshal Sir Arthur Harris took over. Bomber Command destroyed a major part of Germany's industries and many of her cities, and it should be noted that many of Bomber Command's personnel and squadrons during the war were not British: a significant proportion came from commonwealth countries or were exiles from occupied Europe.

'Bombers will always get through'

When Bomber Command was created, General Giulio Douhet's aphorism that 'the bomber will always get through' was believed by the public,

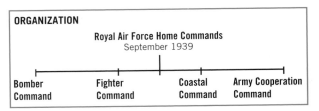

ORGANIZATION

Royal Air Force Home Commands
September 1939

Bomber Command	Fighter Command	Coastal Command	Army Cooperation Command

service personnel and politicians. Until the advent of radar in the late 1930s, this belief was in fact true, for attacking bombers could not be detected early enough for a fighter force to be assembled and intercept the bombers before the latter reached their targets. Some damage might be done by AA guns and by fighters as the bombers turned back after bombing, but this was not an effective defence.

Thus Bomber Command was seen as a force that could threaten an enemy with total destruction, and serve as a deterrent to war. However, even if the bomber could actually get through, its potential for inflicting decisive damage was hugely overrated. The problem was that the British government was basing

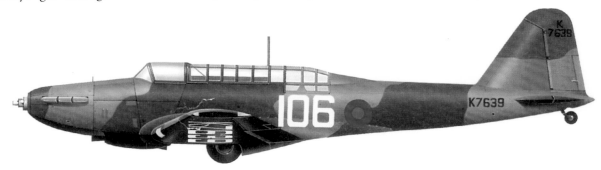

Specifications

Crew: 3

Powerplant: one 768kW (1030hp) Rolls-Royce Merlin II liquid-cooled V-12 piston engine

Maximum speed: 388km/h (241mph)

Range: 1450km (900 miles)

Service ceiling: 7620m (25,000ft)

Dimensions: span 16.46m (54ft 0in); length 12.9m (42ft 4in); height 4.72m (15ft 6in)

Weight: 4895kg (10,792lb) loaded

Armament: 2 x 7.7mm (0.303in) MGs; 113kg (250lb) bomb load

▲ **Fairey Battle Mk I**

No. 106 Squadron, Abingdon, Oxfordshire, August 1938

The Battle was maintained in production well after the time it was appreciated that the type was too slow, too lightly armed (both offensively and defensively) and too lacking in agility for the battlefield bombing role. Such persistence was because there was no successor, and production could not be interrupted.

its data on a casualty rate of 50 per ton of bombs dropped, and thus the government and public saw the bomber as a weapon more terrible than it was in operational reality.

At the start of World War II, Bomber Command was hampered by a lack of size for strategic capability,

The red and blue roundel was most generally associated with night bombers, in which the otherwise standard white intermediate ring was thought too obtrusive and therefore noticeable.

BOMBER COMMAND, NO. 2 GROUP (SEPTEMBER 1939)		
Unit	Type	Base
No. 21 Sqn	Blenheim IV	Watton
No. 82 Sqn	Blenheim IV	Watton
No. 101 Sqn	Blenheim IV	West Raynham
No. 107 Sqn	Blenheim IV	Wattisham
No. 110 Sqn	Blenheim IV	Wattisham
No. 114 Sqn	Blenheim IV	Wyton
No. 139 Sqn	Blenheim IV	Wyton

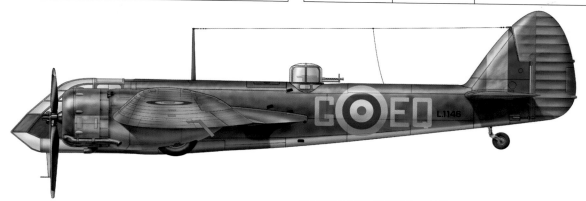

▲ Bristol Blenheim Mk I

No. 57 Squadron / Air Component of the BEF, France, 1939–40

No. 57 Squadron re-equipped from the Hawker Hind single-engined biplane to the Blenheim twin-engined monoplane in 1938, and was transferred to France in September 1939. The unit suffered heavy losses in the first 10 days of the German advance into France as it attacked troop and transport columns, and was then withdrawn to England to recuperate and rebuild.

Specifications

Crew: 3

Powerplant: 627kW (840hp) Bristol Mercury VIII 9-cylinder single-row radial engines

Maximum speed: 459km/h (285mph)

Range: 1810km (1125 miles)

Service ceiling: 8315m (27,280ft)

Dimensions: span 17.17m (56ft 4in); length 12.12m (39ft 9in); height 3m (9ft 10in)

Weight: 4031kg (8839lb) loaded

Armament: 2 x 7.7mm (0.303in) MGs and 454kg (1000lb) bomb load

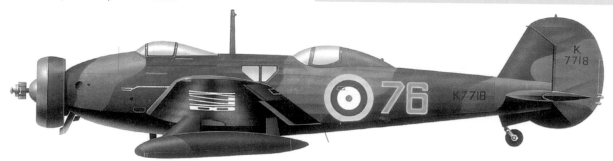

Specifications

Crew: 2

Powerplant: 1 x 708kW (950hp) Bristol Pegasus radial piston engine

Maximum speed: 367km/h (228mph)

Range: 1786km (1110 miles)

Service ceiling: 10,058m (33,000ft)

Dimensions: span 22.73m (74ft 7in); length 11.96m (39ft 3in); height 3.76m (12ft 4in)

Weight: 5035kg (11,100lb) loaded

Armament: 1 x 7.7mm (0.303in) MG and 1 x Vickers MG in rear cockpit; up to 907kg (2000lb) bombs

▲ Vickers Wellesley

No. 76 Squadron, Finningley, Yorkshire, 1939

Designed for the general-purpose role but technically and tactically obsolete by the start of World War II, the Wellesley nonetheless saw limited but useful operational service in North Africa and, more importantly, the Middle East and East Africa during the first part of the war.

the rules of engagement that limited the targets the command was permitted to attack, and a lack of adequate aircraft. The command's standard warplanes at the start of the war were the Battle, Blenheim, Hampden, Wellesley, Wellington and Whitley, and even the best of these, the Wellington,

did not possess the bomb load and range for anything but a limited strategic offensive.

Bomber Command was further reduced in size after the declaration of war. No. 1 Group, with its Battle squadrons, left for France to form the Advanced Air Striking Force (AASF), providing the

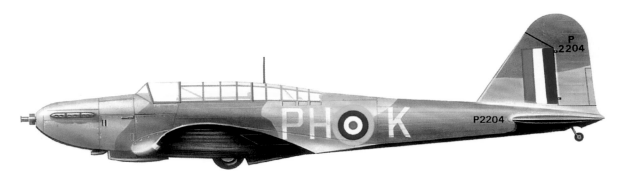

Specifications

Crew: 2

Powerplant: one 768kW (1030hp) Rolls-Royce
  Merlin I inline piston engine

Maximum speed: 414km/h (257mph)

Range: 1609km (1000 miles)

Service ceiling: 7620m (25,000ft)

Dimensions: span 16.46m (54ft 0in);
  length 12.9m (42ft 4in);
  height 4.72m (15ft 6in)

Weight: 4895kg (10,792lb) loaded

Armament: 1 x 7.7mm (0.303in) MG; 1 x
  Vickers K MG; 454kg (1000lb) bomb load

▲ **Fairey Battle Mk I**

No. 12 Squadron / Advanced Air Striking Force / RAF, France, 1939–40

This aeroplane sports the standard day-bomber camouflage and markings of the 'Phoney War' period. The squadron was initially tasked with reconnaissance and leaflet dropping, but from 10 May 1940 was committed, with disastrous losses, against the advancing Germans.

Specifications

Crew: 2

Powerplant: one 768kW (1030hp) Rolls-Royce
  Merlin I inline piston engine

Maximum speed: 414km/h (257mph)

Range: 1609km (1000 miles)

Service ceiling: 7620m (25,000ft)

Dimensions: span 16.46m (54ft 0in);
  length 12.9m (42ft 4in);
  height 4.72m (15ft 6in)

Weight: 4895kg (10,792lb) loaded

Armament: one 7.7mm (0.303in) MG, one
  Vickers K MG; 454kg (1000lb) bomb load

▲ **Fairey Battle Mk I**

No. 218 Squadron / Advanced Air Striking Force / RAF, France, 1939–40

Issued to No. 218 Squadron at Boscombe Down early in 1939, this Battle Mk I went with its squadron to France in September of the same year, flew through the 'Phoney War', and was then lost on 13 May 1940, the fourth day of the German offensive into France.

British Expeditionary Force (BEF) with air striking power, and allowing the Battle to operate against German targets, since it lacked the range to do so from British airfields. The Sitzkrieg (lit. 'sitting down war') between September 1939 and May 1940 affected Bomber Command in France, for its squadrons flew many missions, lost men and aircraft, but did virtually no damage, as most of the missions either failed to find their intended targets, or were limited to the dropping of leaflets rather than bombs. The German attack to the west, launched on 10 May 1940, then changed all this.

▲ Short Stirling Mk I Series 1

No. 7 Squadron / No. 3 Group / RAF Bomber Command, 1940

No. 7 Squadron was the first unit to receive the Stirling, the squadron getting its first aircraft at Leeming in Yorkshire during August 1940. MG-D was the first of the aircraft to be delivered.

Specifications

Crew: 7

Powerplant: 4 x 1030kW (1375hp) Bristol
    Hercules radial engines

Maximum speed: 410km/h (255mph)

Range: 3750km (2330 miles)

Service ceiling: 5030m (16,500ft)

Dimensions: span 30.2m (99ft 1in);

length 26.6m (87ft 3in);

height 8.8m (28ft 10in)

Weight: 31,750kg (70,000lb) loaded

Armament: 8 x 7.7mm (0.303in) Browning
    MGs: two in the nose, four in the tail, two
    dorsal; up to 8164kg (18,000lb) of bombs

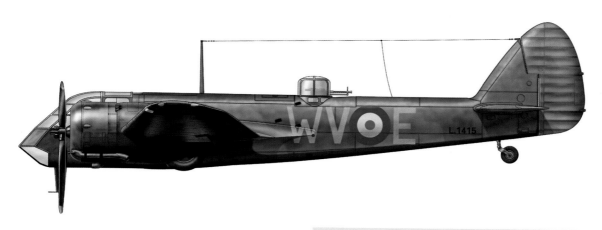

▲ Bristol Blenheim Mk I

No. 18 Squadron / Air Component of the BEF, France, 1939–40

No. 18 Squadron transitioned from the Hawker Hind to the Blenheim in the autumn of 1938, at about the time of the Munich crisis, whose solution delayed the start of World War II for a year. The squadron moved to France in 1939, but by May 1940 had re-equipped with the longer-nose Blenheim Mk IV.

Specifications

Crew: 3

Powerplant: 627kW (840hp) Bristol Mercury VIII
    9-cylinder single-row radial engines

Maximum speed: 459km/h (285mph)

Range: 1810km (1125 miles)

Service ceiling: 8315m (27,280ft)

Dimensions: span 17.17m (56ft 4in);

length 12.12m (39ft 9in);

height 3m (9ft 10in)

Weight: 4031kg (8839lb) loaded

Armament: 2 x 7.7mm (0.3in) MGs; 454kg
    (1000lb) bomb load

'Nickel' leaflet raids
1939–40

Unwilling to attack Germany directly, which would cause the death of civilians and damage to private property, Bomber Command was initially limited to 'attacking' Germany with leaflets designed, futilely, to persuade the German people to reach a peaceful solution with the Allies.

RAF BOMBER COMMAND started with war with night leaflet flights and day reconnaissance of German naval bases. The Whitleys of No. 4 Group carried out the first operation and the other groups shared the second. An important factor of this period of the war was the neutrality of the Netherlands and and Belgium, which prevented any direct approach to Germany from British bases, and thus demanded long approach flights in across the German coast over the North Sea or in the south over France. Dutch and Belgian defences often fired on damaged or lost Whitleys flying over their territory. The leaflet raids continued throughout the 'Phoney War' and were almost free from losses, except those resulting from adverse weather in the long winter nights.

One positive aspect of operations in this period was the high serviceability rate of aircraft maintained by the well-trained ground crew of the prewar era, combined with the fact that the night squadrons were never called upon to dispatch more than a proportion of their available strength. The range of the leaflet flights was increased when some of the Whitleys started to refuel at French airfields in

the early months of 1940, and leaflets were then delivered to cities as distant as Prague, Vienna and Warsaw. It is unlikely that the leaflets had any real effect on German morale, but Bomber Command gained valuable night experience at modest cost.

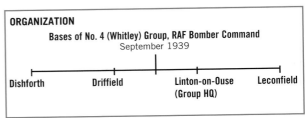

ORGANIZATION

Bases of No. 4 (Whitley) Group, RAF Bomber Command
September 1939

| Dishforth | Driffield | Linton-on-Ouse (Group HQ) | Leconfield |

BOMBER COMMAND, NO. 4 GROUP (SEPTEMBER 1939)

Unit	Type	Base
No. 10 Sqn	Whitley	Dishforth
No. 51 Sqn	Whitley	Linton-on-Ouse
No. 58 Sqn	Whitley	Linton-on-Ouse
No. 77 Sqn	Whitley	Driffield
No. 78 Sqn	Whitley	Dishforth
No. 102 Sqn	Whitley	Driffield

▲ **Armstrong Whitworth Whitley Mk I**

No. 10 Squadron / RAF, Dishforth, Yorkshire, 1939–40

This aeroplane is depicted in the standard camouflage and markings of the period with yellow-ringed fuselage roundels, black under surfaces, and dark-green and dark-earth upper surfaces.

Specifications

Crew: 5

Powerplant: 2 x 593kW (795hp) Tiger IX

Maximum speed: 362km/h (225mph)

Range: 2414km (1315 miles)

Service ceiling: 7925m (26,001ft)

Dimensions: span 25.6m (84ft);

length 21.1m (69ft 3in); height 4.57m (15ft)

Weight: 15,196kg (33,501lb) loaded

Armament: 1 x 7.7mm (0.303in) Lewis gun mounted in front and rear turrets; 1135kg (2500lb) bomb load

From day to night bombing
1940–41

The British bombing effort began in earnest during and after the battle of France, and at first Bomber Command hoped to strike accurately by day against point targets. The losses were so heavy, though, that the command rapidly switched to nocturnal attacks of area targets.

THE FAIREY BATTLE light bomber element of the AASF was badly damaged by German attacks on its airfields at the start of the invasion of France, but not all of this element was caught on the ground, and in the air the Battles proved to be appallingly vulnerable to ground and air fire. On many occasions Battle units were almost wholly destroyed against German chokepoints such as river-crossings.

Defeat in France

The main strength of Bomber Command was itself soon fully committed to battle. France's quick defeat seemed to presage a German invasion of the UK, and as part of its contribution to the Battle of Britain, Bomber Command was tasked with the destruction of the craft being assembled on the southern side of the English Channel for the invasion forces.

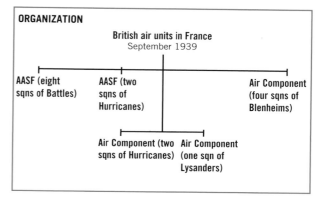

ORGANIZATION

British air units in France
September 1939

AASF (eight sqns of Battles) — AASF (two sqns of Hurricanes) — Air Component (four sqns of Blenheims)

Air Component (two sqns of Hurricanes) — Air Component (one sqn of Lysanders)

This effort was unseen by the British people and never gained any coverage akin to that lavished on Fighter Command, but was nonetheless vital and very dangerous work.

▲ **Vickers Wellington Mk IC**

No. 99 Squadron / No. 3 Group / RAF Bomber Command, Newmarket, Cambridgeshire, 1940

Features of the Wellington Mk IC were two beam guns in place of one ventral gun, and larger main wheels that extended below the engine nacelle when retracted.

Specifications

Crew: 6

Powerplant: 2 x 783kW (1050hp) Bristol Pegasus XVIII 9 cylinder radial engines

Maximum speed: 378km/h (235mph)

Range: 2905km (805 miles)

Service ceiling: 5486m (18,000ft)

Dimensions: span 26.26m (86ft 2in);

length 18.54m (60ft 10in);

height 5.33m (17ft 6in)

Weight: 12,927kg (28,500lb) loaded

Armament: 2 x 7.7mm (0.303in) Browning MGs in both nose and tail; 2 x 7.7mm (0.303in) beam guns; 2041kg (4500lb) bomb load

▲ **Whitley tail gun**

The Armstrong Whitley was notable as the first British bomber to carry a heavy defensive armament, specifically, the manually-operated four-gun tail turret.

From July 1940 to the end of the same year, Bomber Command lost nearly 330 aircraft and more than 1400 men killed, missing or taken prisoner. Bomber Command was also responsible, in part and somewhat indirectly, for the *Luftwaffe's* change of focus away from Fighter Command to the bombing of civilian targets. After a German bomber had become lost and dropped its bombs on London, Prime Minister Winston Churchill

ordered retaliation in the form of a raid on Berlin, the German capital. This very minor effort enraged Hitler, who ordered the *Luftwaffe* to level British cities, so beginning the *Blitz*.

Like the Americans did later in the war, Bomber Command initially tried to fly 'precision' daylight attacks. Several raids late in 1939 were savaged by the well-organized German defences, however, and Bomber Command had perforce to switch to night attacks. This raised a fresh crop of problems, though, with those of the German defences replaced with those of finding the target and attacking it by night. Nocturnal navigation deficiencies in the early years of the war were so great that it was not uncommon for bombers flying by dead reckoning to miss whole urban areas.

Surveys of bombing photographs and other sources during August 1941 indicated that less than 10 per cent of bombs fell within 8km (5 miles) of their intended target. One of Bomber Command's most pressing needs was therefore to develop the technical aids for accurate night navigation.

Bomber Command comprised several groups, starting the war with Nos 1, 2, 3, 4 and 5 Groups. No. 1 Group was detached to France but returned to Bomber Command after the evacuation. No. 2

The yellow outer ring round the tri-colour roundel on the fuselage sides of British day-bombers was standard right into 1941.

▲ **Armstrong Whitworth Whitley Mk V**

No. 77 Squadron / RAF Bomber Command, Linton-on-Ouse, Yorkshire, 1940

This aeroplane carries the standard camouflage of dark-green/dark-earth upper surfaces and black under surfaces, the latter carried unusually high onto the sides of the fuselage.

Specifications

Crew: 5	length 21.1m (69ft 3in);
Powerplant: 2 x 593kW (795hp) Tiger IX	height 4.57m (15ft)
Maximum speed: 362km/h (225mph)	Weight: 15,196kg (33,501lb) loaded
Range: 2414km (1315 miles)	Armament: 1 x 7.7mm (0.303in) Lewis gun
Service ceiling: 7925m (26,001ft)	in front and rear turrets; 1135kg (2500lb)
Dimensions: span 25.6m (84ft);	bomb load

Group consisted of light and medium bombers, and remained part of Bomber Command until 1943, when it was reallocated to the 2nd TAF. Bomber Command also gained two new groups during the war: the Royal Canadian Air Force (RCAF) contributed No. 6 Group, and No. 8 Group was established as the Pathfinder Force to lead the Main Force bombers to their targets.

▼ RAF Bomber Command light bomber squadron, early 1940

The typical British light bomber squadron of September 1939 – May 1940 comprised 12 Bristol Blenheim Mk IV aircraft divided into three flights, each of four aircraft.

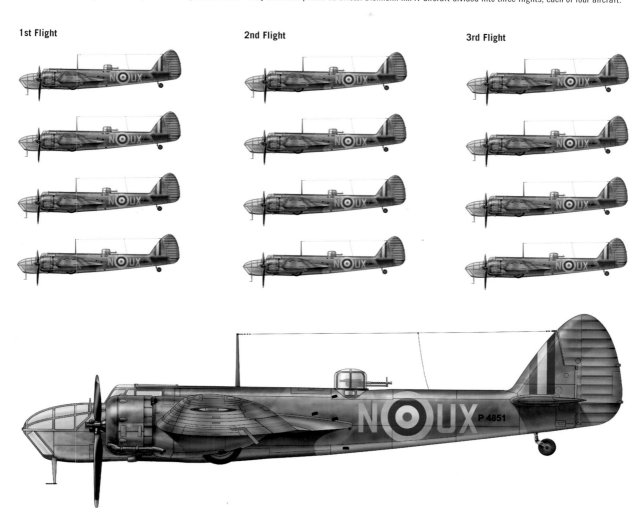

1st Flight

2nd Flight

3rd Flight

▲ Bristol Blenheim Mk IV

RAF Bomber Command, 1939–40

This was an aeroplane of Bristol's third production batch (70 aircraft) of the improved Blenheim Mk IV.

Specifications

Crew: 3

Powerplant: 675kW (905hp) Bristol Mercury XV radial piston engines

Maximum speed: 428km/h (266mph)

Range: 2350km (1460 miles)

Service ceiling: 8310m (27,260ft)

Dimensions: span 17.17m (56ft 4in);

length 12.98m (42ft 7in);

height 3m (9ft 10in)

Weight: 65.32kg (14,400lb) loaded

Armament: 5 x 7.7mm (0.303in) MGs; up to 434kg (1000lb) bombs internally and 145kg (320lb) externally

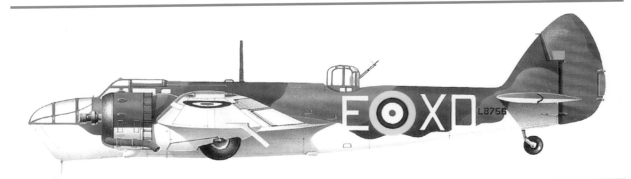

▲ Bristol Blenheim Mk IV

No. 139 Squadron / RAF Bomber Command, Horsham St Faith, Norfolk, 1940
The nose of the Blenheim Mk IV was longer than that of the Mk I to improve the navigator's accommodation, and its upper portion was downward-scalloped on the port side so that the pilot's field of vision would not be degraded. This aeroplane remained in first-line service to 1944, when it was relegated to the training role.

Specifications	
Crew: 3	Dimensions: span 17.17m (56ft 4in);
Powerplant: 675kW (905hp) Bristol Mercury XV	length 12.98m (42ft 7in); height 3m (9ft 10in)
radial piston engines	Weight: 6532kg (14,400lb) loaded
Maximum speed: 428km/h (266mph)	Armament: 5 x 7.7mm (0.303in) MGs; up to
Range: 2350km (1460 miles)	454kg (1000lb) of bombs internally and
Service ceiling: 8310m (27,260ft)	145kg (320lb) externally

Day bombing of German naval bases
1939–40

The British entered the war with the concept that bomber formations could defend themselves against fighter attack by day. Attempts to bomb German naval bases soon suffered unsustainable losses to fighter interception, however, and Bomber Command turned to night bombing.

IN BOMBER COMMAND'S largest operation of the war to date, on 14 December 1939, North Sea shipping searches were flown by 23 Hampdens, 12 Wellingtons and seven Whitleys, while two Blenheims made reconnaissance flights to Sylt. The Wellingtons found a German convoy in the Schillig Roads, north of the port of Wilhelmshaven, but

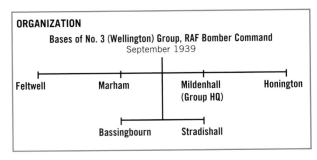

ORGANIZATION
Bases of No. 3 (Wellington) Group, RAF Bomber Command
September 1939

Feltwell — Marham — Mildenhall (Group HQ) — Honington

Bassingbourn — Stradishall

low cloud and poor visibility prevented them from achieving the required bombing position. Even so, the Wellingtons remained in the area for some 30 minutes, flying at low level as they sought to achieve a viable position from which to unload their bombs, and being engaged by flak and also by fighters during this time, losing no fewer than five of their number shot down.

But the RAF was not willing to admit that German fighters had shot down almost half of a formation of

BOMBER COMMAND, NO. 3 GROUP (SEPTEMBER 1939)		
Unit	Type	Base
No. 9 Sqn	Wellington	Honington
No. 37 Sqn	Wellington	Feltwell
No. 38 Sqn	Wellington	Marham
No. 99 Sqn	Wellington	Mildenhall
No. 115 Sqn	Wellington	Marham
No. 149 Sqn	Wellington	Mildenhall
No. 214 Sqn	Wellington	Feltwell
No. 215 Sqn	Wellington	Bassingbourn

Bomber Command's best-armed warplanes, and it was officially claimed that the losses were the result of flak fire. The Germans claimed to the contrary, and admitted that one fighter had been lost. No German vessels were hit, and the other British aircraft saw no action.

Wilhelmshaven raid

On 18 December, 24 Wellingtons were dispatched in another shipping search in the region of Wilhelmshaven, but in this instance the crews were instructed not to attack at any altitude less than 3050m (10,000ft) to escape the worst effects of flak. Some 22 of the 24 aircraft reached the target area and, from an altitude of 3960m (13,000ft), bombed the German ships their crews spotted off Wilhelmshaven. There was no cloud, and the visibility was perfect for bombing.

For the first time in the war, however, German fighters were vectored to this bomber force by a ground controller, who was being given information from a German naval establishment on Heligoland and an experimental 'Freya' radar station of the *Luftwaffe* on the nearby island of Wangerooge. The latter had detected the Wellingtons when they were still 113km (70 miles) distant on their approach. Flak fire caused the bomber formation to spread out

slightly, and the twin-engined fighters of I *Gruppe*, *Zerstörergeschwader* 76 (I/ZG 76) and of II and III/ZG 77, as well as the single-engined fighters of 10. *Staffel, Jagdgeschwader* 26 (10./JG 26), shot down 12 of the Wellingtons, though they also lost two of their own number to the bombers' defensive armament.

The key elements in this action were the superior speed and agility of the fighters, which enabled them to achieve the right firing positions, and their armament, including at least one 20mm (0.79in) cannon, providing greater range than the machine guns with which the British bombers were armed, as well as an explosive shell causing much greater damage in the bombers than the ball ammunition of the British machine guns.

This celebrated action, coming so soon after that of 14 December, had a major impact on the thinking of the commanders of the British bomber arm. Exactly half of the 34 Wellingtons dispatched in the two missions had been shot down in these two actions, and the bombers had not even attempted to penetrate over the mainland of Germany, which was known to be more strongly defended. The conceptual validity of the bomber formation able to protect itself had now been seriously questioned, and thoughts immediately turned to night bombing.

▲ **Vickers Wellington Mk I**

No. 38 Squadron / RAF Bomber Command, Marham, Norfolk, 1940

No. 38 Squadron received its first Wellington twin-engined bombers in 1938, and operated the type in several marks until early in 1942. The Wellington proved very vulnerable to fighter interception in early daylight raids, and was then switched to the night bombing role.

Specifications

Crew: 6

Powerplant: two 1119kW (1500hp) Bristol Hercules XI radial piston engines

Maximum speed: 378km/h (235mph)

Range: 2478km (1540 miles)

Service ceiling: 5791m (19,000ft)

Dimensions: span 26.26m (86ft 2in); length 18.54m (60ft 10in); height 5.31m (17ft 5in);

Weight: 9527kg (21,000lb) loaded

Armament: 6 x 7.7mm (0.303in) Browning MGs in nose and tail and Frazer-Nash ventral positions; either 9 x 227kg (500lb) of bombs, or 2 x 907kg (2000lb) of bombs

Retaliatory raid on Mannheim
DECEMBER 1940

After the *Luftwaffe* had bombed British urban centres, RAF Bomber Command was instructed to retaliate against a German city, and the resulting raid on Mannheim set the pattern for area bombing attacks, which became the staple of Bomber Command for the following four years.

IN ALL PROBABILITY the most interesting British raid of the war to date, the attack made on Mannheim on 16/17 December 1940, resulted from the decision of the War Cabinet that an attack should be carried out on the centre of a German city in retaliation for the recent heavy bombing of English cities such as Coventry and Southampton. Mannheim was selected as the target, and a force of 200 bombers was readied. The threat of deteriorating weather then led to the trimming of the force to 134 twin-engined aircraft in the form of 61 Wellingtons, 35 Whitleys,

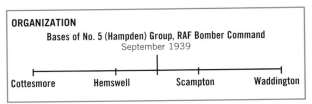

ORGANIZATION
Bases of No. 5 (Hampden) Group, RAF Bomber Command
September 1939

Cottesmore — Hemswell — Scampton — Waddington

29 Hampdens and nine Blenheims. Even so, this was still the British largest force despatched against a single target to date. The attack was started by eight Wellingtons. They used incendiary bombs in

▲ **Night bomber**
This Whitley Mk V of No. 78 Squadron is painted in the overall black used by aircraft engaged in night raids over Germany in the early years of the war.

BOMBER COMMAND, NO. 5 GROUP (SEPTEMBER 1939)		
Unit	Type	Base
No. 44 Sqn	Hampden	Waddington
No. 49 Sqn	Hampden	Scampton
No. 50 Sqn	Hampden	Waddington
No. 61 Sqn	Hampden	Hemswell
No. 83 Sqn	Hampden	Scampton
No. 106 Sqn	Hampden	Cottesmore
No. 144 Sqn	Hampden	Hemswell
No. 185 Sqn	Hampden	Cottesmore

▲ **Blenheims on patrol**

Even in its definitive Mk IV form, the Blenheim was technically obsolete by 1942.

an effort to start fires that would serve as the aiming points for the following crews. For the first time in more than 15 months of war, Bomber Command was attacking a target not primarily of military or industrial nature.

The weather over the target was generally clear, and there was also a full moon. Mannheim's defences were not strong, and Bomber Command's records suggest that anything between 82 and 102 aircraft claimed to have bombed Mannheim. But the attack was unsuccessful, for the 'pathfinder' Wellingtons bombed inaccurately and the largest fires were not in the centre of the city.

Most of the bombs fell in residential areas, 240 buildings being destroyed or damaged by the incendiaries and 236 by HE bombs. The German casualty list totalled 34 dead, 81 injured and 1266

rendered homeless. Of those bombed out, 223 were in the town of Ludwigshafen on the other side of the Rhine. During the raid, Bomber Command lost two Hampdens and one Blenheim, and another four aircraft crashed in England on return.

Specifications

Crew: 4

Powerplant: 746kW (1000hp) Bristol Pegasus
XVII radial piston engines

Maximum speed: 409km/h (254mph)

Range: 3034km (1885 miles)

Service ceiling: 5791m (19,000ft)

Dimensions: span 21.08m (69ft 2in);
length 16.33m (53ft 7in);
height 4.55m (14ft 11in)

Weight: 8508kg (18,756lb) loaded

Armament: 2 x forward-firing and twin 7.7mm
(0.303in) MGs; 1814kg (4000lb) bombs

▲ **Handley Page Hampden Mk I**

No. 106 Squadron / No. 5 Group / RAF Bomber Command, Finningley, Yorkshire, April 1940

The Hampden Mk I was operated by a four-man crew all located in the 'pod' section of the fuselage, which was so narrow that it was impossible for anyone to exchange seats. Thus a badly wounded pilot could not be replaced.

The campaign gathers pace
1941–42

In 1941–42 Bomber Command grew in size and capability, and its night area attacks on German cities began to have a real effect despite the problems associated with accurate navigation and bombing by night. With bomber production increasing steadily, the scene was set fair for 1943.

MANY UNITS and men from Commonwealth and other European countries were evident in the make-up of Bomber Command. Activated on the first day of 1943, No. 6 Group was unique inasmuch as it was not an RAF formation, but rather an element of the RCAF attached to Bomber Command. At maximum, No. 6 Group had 14 bomber squadrons, and in overall terms some 15 different squadrons served with the group. Apart from No. 6 Group, many Canadian personnel served with British and other commonwealth squadrons, and by May 1945 almost 25 per cent of Bomber Command's personnel was provided by the RCAF.

Night navigation
No. 8 Group was activated on 15 August 1942, and its aircraft and crews were instrumental in overcoming Bomber Command's night navigation problems. These problems were dealt with in two fashions: one was the development of an assortment of ever more sophisticated electronic aids to accurate navigation over steadily longer ranges, and the other was the use of the specialized air crews of the Pathfinder Force.

The technical aids were themselves of two types. One was external radio navigation aids such as Gee and the later and extremely accurate Oboe systems, and the other the internal H2S centimetric radar carried in the bombers and providing enough accuracy for bombing as well as navigation. The Pathfinders were a group of elite, specially trained and experienced crews who flew ahead of the main bombing forces, and marked the targets with flares and special marker bombs.

Specifications

Crew: 6	length 18.54m (60ft 10in);
Powerplant: two x 1119kW (1500hp) Bristol	height 5.31m (17ft 5in);
Hercules XI radial piston engines	Weight: 9527kg (21,000lb) loaded
Maximum speed: 378km/h (235mph)	Armament: 8 x 7.7mm (0.303in) Browning
Range: 2478km (1540 miles)	MGs in nose and tail and Frazer-Nash ventral
Service ceiling: 5791m (19,000ft)	positions; either 9 x 227kg (500lb) of bombs,
Dimensions: span 26.26m (86ft 2in);	or 2 x 907kg (2000lb) of bombs

▲ **Vickers Wellington Mk IA**

No. 37 Squadron / RAF Bomber Command, Feltwell, Norfolk, April 1941

The Wellington Mk IA switched from the Mk I's Vickers nose and tail turrets to Nash and Thompson turrets in these two positions. Production mounted to 183 aircraft before Vickers switched to the definitive Wellington Mk IC (2685 built).

Growing command

By the time these developments came about, Bomber Command was also increasing massively in size. In the early days of the war, it was common for raids to consist of a few tens of aircraft, which had a negligible target effect. By late in 1941, however, raids by hundreds of aircraft were being flown on a regular basis.

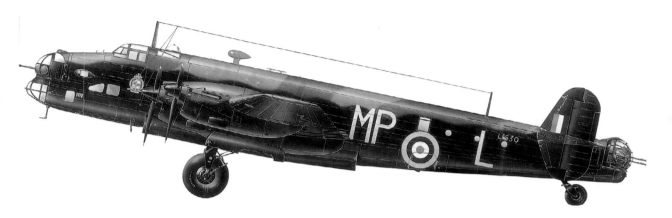

Specifications

Crew: 7

Powerplant: 4 x 954kW (1280hp) Rolls-Royce
  Merlin X inline engines

Maximum speed: 426km/h (265mph)

Range: 2993km (1860 miles)

Service ceiling: 6950m (22,800ft)

Dimensions: span 30.21m (98ft 10in);

length 21.36m (70ft 1in);

height 6.32m (20ft 9in)

Weight: 24,970kg (55,000lb) loaded

Armament: 2 x 7.7mm (0.303in) Browning
MGs; 2 x Vickers 7.7mm (0.303in) K MGs;
6 x 454kg (1000lb), 2 x 907kg (2000lb) and
6 x 227kg (500lb) bombs

▲ Handley Page Halifax Mk I Series 1

No. 76 Squadron / RAF Bomber Command, Middleton St George, August 1941

The major partner of the Avro Lancaster in the UK's heavy night bomber forces of World War II, the Halifax was built to the extent of 6178 aircraft. Though generally associated with the air-cooled powerplant of four Bristol Hercules radial engines, the first marks had four liquid-cooled Rolls-Royce Merlin V-12 engines.

Specifications

Crew: 10

Powerplant: 4 x 895kW (1200hp) Wright
  R-1820-65 engines

Maximum speed: 524km/h (325mph)

Range: 5472km (3400 miles)

Service ceiling: 11,278m (37,000ft)

Dimensions: span 31.62m (103ft. 9in);

length 20.56m (67ft 11in);

height 4.7m (15ft 5in)

Weight: 21,999kg (48,500lb) loaded

Armament: 1 x 7.62mm (0.3in) and
6 x 12.7mm (0.5in) MGs; 2177kg (4800lb)
of bombs

▲ Boeing Fortress Mk I

No. 90 Squadron / RAF Bomber Command, Watton, Cambridgeshire, summer 1941

The Fortress Mk I was based on the USAAF's B-17C, and 20 such aircraft were delivered to the UK. After unsuccessful initial service in the bomber role, the aircraft were transferred to RAF Coastal Command for adaptation as long-range maritime reconnaissance machines.

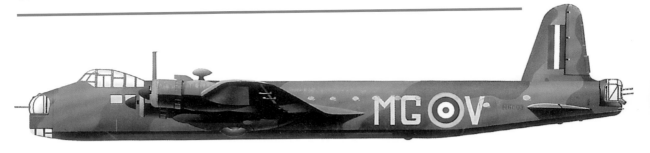

▲ Short Stirling Mk I Series 1

No. 7 Squadron / No, 3 Group / RAF Bomber Command, Oakington, 1941

The Stirling was the UK's first four-engined heavy bomber of World War II, and this aeroplane remained on the strength of No. 7 Squadron until December 1941, when it passed to No. 26 Conversion Flight and later No. 1651 (Heavy) Conversion Unit.

Specifications

Crew: 7

Powerplant: 4 x 1030kW (1375hp) Bristol
  Hercules radial engines

Maximum speed: 410km/h (255mph)

Range: 3750km (2330 miles)

Service ceiling: 5030m (16,500ft)

Dimensions: span 30.2m (99ft 1in);

length 26.6m (87ft 3in);

height 8.8m (28ft 10in)

Weight: 31,750kg (70,000lb) loaded

Armament: 8 x 7.7mm (0.303in) Browning
  MGs: two in the nose, four in the tail, two
  dorsal; up to 8164 kg (18,000lb) of bombs

▲ Armstrong Whitworth Whitley Mk V

No. 78 Squadron / RAF Bomber Command, Croft, late 1941

This aeroplane is depicted in an overall black finish, not standard for Bomber Command, but alleviated by national, squadron, serial and personal markings.

Specifications

Crew: 5

Powerplant: 2 x 854kW (1145hp) Rolls-Royce
  Merlin X inline piston engines

Maximum speed: 370km/h (230mph)

Range: 2414km (1500 miles)

Service ceiling: 7925m (26,000ft)

Dimensions: span 25.6m (84ft);

length 21.49m (70ft 6in); height 4.57m (15ft)

Weight: 15,195kg (33,500lb) loaded

Armament: 4 x 7.7mm (0.303in) MGs in
  powered tail turret and one similar gun in
  nose turret; up to 3175kg (7000lb) of bombs

▲ Handley Page Hampden Mk I

No. 420 'Snowy Owl' Squadron / No. 5 Group / RAF Bomber Command,
Waddington, Lincolnshire, 1941

This Canadian squadron flew the initial version of the Hampden in the night-bomber role until August 1942, and then transferred to the Vickers Wellington.

Specifications

Crew: 4

Powerplant: 2 x 746kW (1000hp) Bristol
  Pegasus XVII radial piston engines

Maximum speed: 409km/h (254mph)

Range: 3034km (1885 miles)

Service ceiling: 5791m (19,000ft)

Dimensions: span 21.08m (69ft 2in);

length 16.330m (53ft 7in);

height 4.55m (14ft 11in)

Weight: 5343kg (11,780lb) loaded

Armament: 2 x 7.7mm (0.303in) MGs, plus up
  to 1814kg (4000lb) bombs

Specifications

Mk IA Crew: 7

Powerplant: 2 x 1312kW (1760hp) Rolls-Royce
 Vulture inline piston engines

Maximum speed: 426km/h (265mph)

Range: 2623km (1630 miles)

Service ceiling: 5850m (19,200ft)

Dimensions: span 27.46m (90ft 1in);
 length 21.13m (69ft 4in);
 height 5.94m (19ft 6in)

Weight: 25,401kg (56,000lb) loaded

Armament: 8 x 7.7mm (0.3i03n) MGs (two each
 in nose and dorsal turrets, four in tail turret);
 up to 4695kg (10,350lb) of bombs

▲ Avro Manchester Mk I

No. 83 Squadron / RAF Bomber Command, Scampton, Lincolnshire,
spring 1942

The mission symbols on the nose of this Manchester indicate it had completed
10 operational sorties by the spring of 1942. The aircraft was to fly a further four
mission before being lost on its fifteenth, a raid against the Blohm und Voss
shipyards in Hamburg.

Specifications

Crew: 2

Powerplant: 2 x 918kW (1230hp) Rolls-Royce
 Merlin XX

Maximum speed: 612km/h (380mph)

Range: 1963km (1220 miles)

Service ceiling: 9449m (31,000ft)

Dimensions: span 16.51m (54ft 2in);
 length 12.43m (40ft 10in);
 height 4.65m (15ft 3in)

Weight: 5942kg (13,100lb) loaded

Armament: none

▲ de Havilland Mosquito PR.Mk I

No. 1 Photographic Unit / RAF, Benson, Oxfordshire, 1941

This was the ninth Mosquito Mk I to be completed, and served with No. 1 PRU until
4 December 1941, when it was lost in the course of an operational mission. The
aeroplane was finished in photo-reconnaissance unit (PRU) blue overall with pale
grey unit code letters.

Dawn of the thousand-bomber raid
1942–43

An inability to bomb accurately with modest numbers of bombers forced the British to switch to the carpet bombing of industrial and urban areas, and the campaign gathered strength in numbers of aircraft and the capabilities of the new generation of heavy bombers.

PROFESSOR FREDERICK Lindemann, the chief scientific adviser to the British government, had the ear of Prime Minister Winston Churchill, who gave Lindemann a seat in the War Cabinet. During 1942, Lindemann presented to the Cabinet a paper that called for the 'aerial bombing of German cities by carpet bombing' as the tactical core of a strategic bombing campaign.

Lindemann advocated carpet, or area, bombing because of Bomber Command's proven inability to strike specific industrial targets or even whole towns and cities with real accuracy. Lindemann had thus decided that the area bombing of major industrial cities was the only way in which Bomber Command could strike effectively at the German war machine.

An inevitable side effect of area bombing would be the destruction of many industrial workers' homes clustered round the factory centres. The housing of the industrial working class was therefore to be targeted because it was more densely packed

and was therefore more prone to major devastation, dislocating the German work force and adversely affecting industrial output.

Controversial policy

This scheme was very controversial within the British political and military leadership even before it was launched. In overall terms, though, it was considered to be implicit within the concept of 'total war' as begun by Germany with its 'terror' attacks on Warsaw, Rotterdam, London and Belgrade. The British Cabinet agreed that bombing was the only course by which the UK could strike directly at Germany in the period before the invasion of north-west Europe, which was still some time away even by the most optimistic assessments.

First thousand bomber raid

Once accepted by the Cabinet, the concept was passed to Harris for action. Harris decided to mount

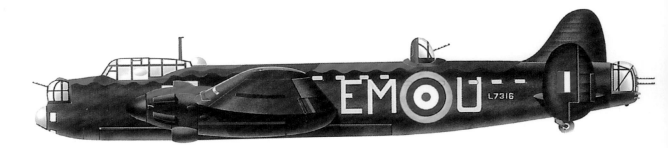

Specifications

Mk IA Crew: 7	length 21.13m (69ft 4in);
Powerplant: 2 x 1312kW (1760hp) Rolls-Royce	height 5.94m (19ft 6in)
Vulture inline piston engines	Weight: 25,401kg (56,000lb) loaded
Maximum speed: 426km/h (265mph)	Armament: 8 x 7.7mm (0.3i03n) MGs (two each
Range: 2623km (1630 miles)	in nose and dorsal turrets, four in tail turret);
Service ceiling: 5850m (19,200ft)	up to 4695kg (10,350lb) of bombs
Dimensions: span 27.46m (90ft 1in);	

▲ **Avro Manchester Mk I**

No. 207 Squadron / RAF Bomber Command, Waddington, Lincolnshire, 1942
The Manchester heavy bomber was not successful in itself, largely as a result of the chronic unreliability of its two under-developed Rolls-Royce Vulture engines, but it paved the way for the Lancaster with four Rolls-Royce Merlin engines.

▲ Avro Lancaster night-bomber
Adequately armed for defence, the Lancaster could carry a heavy bomb load.

▲ Handley Page Halifax B.Mk II

No. 405 Squadron / RAF Bomber Command, Topcliffe, 1942

Nicknamed as the 'Ruhr Valley Express', this was a typical Halifax B.Mk II of the first stages of the Halifax's development life with comparatively small twin fin-and-rudder units characterized by swept leading edges above and below the tailplane.

Specifications

Crew: 7	length 21.36m (70ft 1in);
Powerplant: 4 x 1037kW (1390hp) Rolls-Royce	height 6.32m (20ft 9in)
Merlin X inline engines	Weight: 27,215kg (60,000lb) loaded
Maximum speed: 426km/h (265mph)	Armament: 8 x 7.7mm (0.303in) Browning
Range: 3058km (1900 miles)	MGs in nose, dorsal turret and tail; 6 x 454kg
Service ceiling: 6706m (22,000ft)	(1000lb), 2 x 907kg (2000lb) and 6 x 227kg
Dimensions: span 30.21m (98ft 10in);	(500lb) bombs

a huge raid against Köln on 30 May 1942. For this, the Command had to gather virtually every airworthy aeroplane and crew within its operational and advanced training unit, and so assembled a force of slightly more than 1000 aircraft. Köln was very badly hit, only some 300 houses escaping damage. This first 'thousand-bomber' raid was nonetheless not something which could be repeated

▲ Handley Page Halifax B.Mk II Series 1A

No. 78 Squadron / RAF Bomber Command, Breighton, Yorkshire,
September 1943

Both the Halifax Mks I and II were powered by the Rolls-Royce Merlin liquid-cooled
V-12 engine rather than the Bristol Hercules air-cooled radial engine that became
standard on the considerably more numerous later variants.

Specifications

Crew: 7

Powerplant: 4 x 1036kW (1390hp) Rolls-Royce
  Merlin engines

Maximum speed: 454km/h (282mph)

Range: 3194km (1985 miles)

Service ceiling: 7315m (24,000ft)

Dimensions: span 30.12m (98ft 10in);
  length 21.74m (71ft 4in);
  height 6.12m (20ft 1in)

Weight: 29,484kg (65,000lb) loaded

Armament: 9 x 7.7mm (0.303in) MGs; internal
  bomb load of 6577kg (14,500lb)

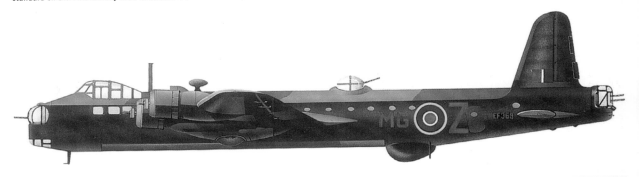

▲ Short Stirling Mk I Series 2

No. 7 Squadron / No. 8 Group (Pathfinder Force) / RAF Bomber Command,
Oakington, summer 1943

Pathfinder Force aircraft marked targets for the Main Force bombers, and had
high-quality crews and aids such as H₂S navigation/bombing radar with its
antenna in a ventral radome.

Specifications

Crew: 7

Powerplant: 4 x 1186kW (1590hp) Bristol
  Hercules XI radial engines

Maximum speed: 410km/h (255mph)

Range: 3750km (2330 miles)

Service ceiling: 5030m (16,500ft)

Dimensions: span 30.2m (99ft 1in)

length 26.6m (87ft 3in);
  height 8.8m (28ft 10in)

Weight: 31,750kg (70,000lb) loaded

Armament: 8 x 7.7mm (0.303in) Browning
  MGs: two in the nose, four in the tail, two
  dorsal; up to 8164kg (18,000lb) of bombs

on a regular basis by the RAF in 1942, and in the
short term had an adverse effect on the strength of
the period's standard raids.

Even so, the raid was of great psychological
importance to the British, and served notice on
the Germans that Bomber Command was on its
way to becoming a formation that could achieve
genuinely strategic bombing results.

This period was notable not only for the major
expansion of Bomber Command in terms of its
strength in aircraft and personnel, but also in the

capability of its first-line aircraft. The year 1942 was
that in which Bomber Command's most important
aircraft of the whole war came into service. Twin-
engined medium bombers were replaced by large
numbers of four-engined heavy bombers such as the
Handley Page Halifax and Avro Lancaster. These
offered longer range, greater speed and heavier
bomb loads. The one major exception to this trend
toward larger aircraft was the superb multi-role de
Havilland Mosquito, a twin-engined fast bomber
that became the major mount of the Pathfinders.

▲ **Lockheed Ventura Mk II**

No. 21 Squadron / RAF Bomber Command, Methwold, mid-1943

A high-speed light bomber of US design and manufacture, the Ventura saw limited British service, primarily for daylight operations over German-occupied Europe. No. 21 Squadron received its first Ventura bombers in mid-1942.

Specifications

Crew: 5

Powerplant: 2 x 1491kW (2000hp) Pratt & Whitney GR-2800-S1A4-G Double Wasp radial piston engines

Maximum speed: 483km/h (300mph)

Range: 1529km (950 miles)

Service ceiling: 7620m (25,000ft)

Dimensions: span 19.96m (65ft 6in); length 15.62m (51ft 3in); height 3.63m (11ft 11in)

Weight: 11,793kg (26,000lb) loaded

Armament: 4 x 12.7mm (0.5in) MGs; 2 x 7.62mm (0.3in) MGs; 1400kg (3000lb) general ordnance or 6 x 147kg (325lb) depth charges or 1 x torpedo

Köln – first 'thousand-bomber' raid
MAY 1942

Though Bomber Command had to 'scrape the bottom of the barrel' to put together the required number, the 'thousand-bomber' attack on Köln marked a significant improvement in Bomber Command's ability to strike hard at major German cities.

ON 30/31 MAY 1942, Bomber Command flew its first 'thousand-bomber raid', its target the city of Köln on the Rhine. Some 1047 bombers were despatched in the form of 602 Wellingtons, 131 Halifaxes, 88 Stirlings, 79 Hampdens, 73 Lancasters, 46 Manchesters and 28 Whitleys. The number of aircraft claiming to have bombed Köln cannot be ascertained with total accuracy, the British official history claiming it was 898 aircraft, but Bomber Command records suggest that 868 aircraft bombed the main target and another 15 other targets. Some 1478 tonnes (1455 tons) of bombs, two-thirds of them incendiaries, were dropped.

German records indicate that 2500 separate fires were started, 1700 of them classified by the local fire brigade as large, but there was no firestorm, as there had been in earlier raids against Lubeck and Rostock, since Köln was essentially a modern city

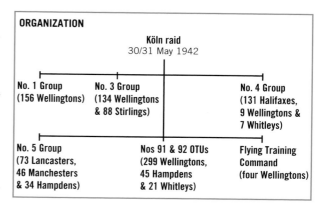

ORGANIZATION

Köln raid
30/31 May 1942

No. 1 Group (156 Wellingtons)	No. 3 Group (134 Wellingtons & 88 Stirlings)	No. 4 Group (131 Halifaxes, 9 Wellingtons & 7 Whitleys)
No. 5 Group (73 Lancasters, 46 Manchesters & 34 Hampdens)	Nos 91 & 92 OTUs (299 Wellingtons, 45 Hampdens & 21 Whitleys)	Flying Training Command (four Wellingtons)

with wide streets and little wooden construction. Local records reveal that the damage included 3330 buildings destroyed, 2090 seriously damaged and 7420 lightly damaged, more than 90 per cent of the damage being the result of fire rather

than blast. Included in these 12,840 buildings were 2560 industrial and commercial buildings. Many of these were small, but 36 large companies suffered a complete loss of production, 70 suffered 50–80 per cent loss and 222 up to 50 per cent loss. Among the buildings classed as totally destroyed were seven official administration buildings, 14 public buildings, seven banks, nine hospitals, 17 churches, 16 schools, four university buildings, 10 postal and railway buildings, 10 buildings of historic interest, two newspaper offices, four hotels,

◀ **Lancaster flight**

A formation of early-production Lancaster Mk Is of No. 44 Squadron form for the photographer some time in 1942.

Specifications

Crew: 7

Powerplant: 4 x 1030kW (1375hp) Bristol Hercules radial engines

Maximum speed: 410km/h (255mph)

Range: 3750km (2330 miles)

Service ceiling: 5030m (16,500ft)

Dimensions: span 30.2m (99ft 1in) length 26.6m (87ft 3in); height 8.8m (28ft 10in)

Weight: 31,750kg (70,000lb) loaded

Armament: 8 x 7.7mm (0.303in) Browning MGs: two in the nose, four in the tail, two dorsal; up to 8164kg (18,000lb) of bombs

▲ **Short Stirling Mk III**

No. 149 Squadron / RAF Bomber Command, Mildenhall, Suffolk, 1942–43

The Stirling Mk III, of which 875 were built, was a simple development of the Stirling Mk I with a different dorsal turret reducing the drag burden faced by the powerplant of four 1189kW (1595hp) Bristol Hercules XI air-cooled radial engines.

▲ **Mosquito B.Mk IV**

No. 139 Squadron / RAF Bomber Command, Marham, Norfolk, 1942

The first bomber variant of the family to enter service, the Mosquito B.Mk IV (273 built) relied on speed rather than guns for defence, and carried a 907kg (2000lb) internal bomb load or, in 54 converted aircraft, one 1814kg (5000lb) bomb. The Mosquito proved itself superbly capable.

Specifications

Crew: 2

Powerplant: 2 x 918kW (1230hp) Rolls-Royce Merlin XX

Maximum speed: 612km/h (380mph)

Range: 1963km (1220 miles)

Service ceiling: 9449m (31,000ft)

Dimensions: span 16.51m (54ft 2in); length 12.43m (40ft 10in); height 4.65m (15ft 3in)

Weight: 5942kg (13,100lb) loaded

Armament: normal internal bomb load 907kg (2000lb)

two cinemas and six department stores. Damage was also caused to 17 water mains, five gas mains, 32 main electricity cables and 12 main telephone routes. So far as the civilian housing stock was concerned, the list of dwelling units (primarily flats and apartments) included 13,010 destroyed, 6360 badly damaged and 22,270 lightly damaged.

The casualty figures for the Köln area are precise, with between 469 and 486 dead, the former

comprising 411 civilian and 58 military casualties, the latter mostly members of flak units. Some 5027 were listed as injured and 45,132 were rendered homeless. The RAF casualties were also high, with 41 aircraft lost: 29 Wellingtons, four Manchesters, three Halifaxes, two Stirlings, one Hampden, one Lancaster and one Whitley. The loss rate of 3.9 per cent was thought acceptable in view of the perfect weather, which aided the German defence.

Specifications

Crew: 6

Powerplant: 2 x 1119kW (1500hp) Bristol
  Hercules XI radial piston engines

Maximum speed: 378km/h (235mph)

Range: 2478km (1540 miles)

Service ceiling: 5791m (19,000ft)

Dimensions: span 26.26m (86ft 2in);
  length 18.54m (60ft 10in);
  height 5.31m (17ft 5in)

Weight: 13381kg (29,500lb) loaded

Armament: 8 x 7.7mm (0.303in) MGs, plus up
  to 2041kg (4500lb) of bombs

▲ Vickers Wellington Mk III

No. 425 'Alouette' Squadron / No. 4 Group / RAF Bomber Command, Dishforth, Yorkshire, September 1942

This Canadian-manned unit flew the first definitive version of the Wellington, the Mk III with Bristol Hercules radial engines rather than Bristol Pegasus radial or Rolls-Royce Merlin V-12 engines (Mks I or II respectively), and introduced a four- rather than two-gun tail turret.

▲ Handley Page Halifax B.Mk II

No. 405 Squadron / RAF Bomber Command, Topcliffe, 1942

Nicknamed as the 'Ruhr Valley Express', this was a typical Halifax B.Mk II of the first stages of the Halifax's development life with comparatively small twin fin-and-rudder units characterized by swept leading edges above the below the tailplane.

Specifications

Crew: 7

Powerplant: 4 x 1037kW (1390hp) Rolls-Royce
  Merlin X inline engines

Maximum speed: 426km/h (265mph)

Range: 3058km (1900 miles)

Service ceiling: 6706m (22,000ft)

Dimensions: span 30.21m (98ft 10in);

length 21.36m (70ft 1in);
  height 6.32m (20ft 9in)

Weight: 27,215kg (60,000lb) loaded

Armament: 8 x 7.7mm (0.303in) Browning
  MGs in nose, dorsal turret and tail; 6 x 454kg
  (1000lb), 2 x 907kg (2000lb) and 6 x 227kg
  (500lb) bombs

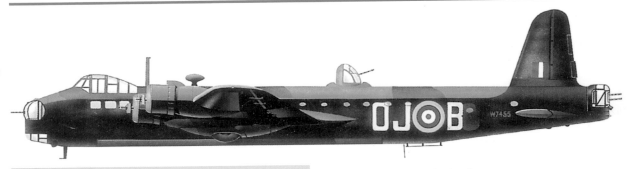

Specifications

Crew: 7

Powerplant: 4 x 1186kW (1590hp) Bristol
Hercules XI radial engines

Maximum speed: 410km/h (255mph)

Range: 3750km (2330 miles)

Service ceiling: 5030m (16,500ft)

Dimensions: span 30.2m (99ft 1in)
length 26.6m (87ft 3in);

height 8.8m (28ft 10in)

Weight: 31,750kg (70,000lb) loaded

Armament: 8 x 7.7mm (0.303in) Browning
MGs: two in the nose, four in the tail, two
dorsal; up to 8164kg (18,000lb) of bombs

▲ **Short Stirling Mk I Series 2**

No. 149 Squadron / RAF Bomber Command, Mildenhall, Suffolk, early 1942
Entering service in August 1940 and built to the extent of 2374 aircraft, the
Stirling was the UK's first four-engined heavy bomber of World War II, and carried
the definitive night-bomber armament of eight machine guns in two-gun nose
and dorsal turrets, and a four-gun tail turret.

The dams raid
MAY 1943

**The attack by modified Lancasters of No. 617 Squadron on a series of dams controlling the flow
of water through the Ruhr was designed to inflict substantial damage and also cut electrical
power generation. The raid was only partially successful, but remains an epic of its type.**

IT WAS ON 21 MARCH 1943 that No. 617 Squadron was
formed, under the command of Wing Commander
Guy Gibson, on the basis of specially selected crews in
No. 5 Group. The squadron then trained intensively
for six weeks for a special operation, namely attacks
using special spinning, cylindrical bombs on a number
of dams controlling the flow of much of the water to
the Ruhr industrial region.

Low level operation

On 16 May, the squadron despatched three waves
of specially modified Lancaster bombers, 19 in total,
each bomber carrying one of the 'bouncing bombs'
developed by Dr Barnes Wallis of Vickers-Armstrong
for attacks on dams. The entire operation was flown
at low level to avoid radar detection and to escape
attack by German night-fighters and so reach the
reservoirs behind the dams, where the bombs were
to be released at a precise air speed, and an exact
and very low altitude above the water. One of the

Lancasters was compelled to turn back at an early
stage of the operation after it struck the sea a glancing
blow that tore off the bomb. Another five aircraft
were shot down or crashed before reaching their
targets, and one was so badly damaged by flak that it
too was compelled to turn back.

This left 12 Lancasters to bomb the dams. The
aircraft of Gibson's crew and four other crews
attacked the Möhne dam and breached it, despite
intense fire from the light flak guns defending the
dam. Three aircraft went on to bomb the Eder dam,
which was also breached. Two aircraft bombed the
Sorpe dam and one the Schwelme dam, but without
causing breaches in their walls. The twelfth aeroplane
could not find its target in misty conditions and
returned to England without dropping its bomb.
Three of the Lancasters were shot down after they
had released their bombs.

The British aircraft losses were thus eight out of the
19 that had been despatched: it is believed that four

were shot down by light flak, one crashed after being damaged by the explosion of its own bomb, two hit electricity cables and crashed, and one went down after hitting a tree as its pilot was dazzled by a searchlight.

Successful operation

Of the 56 crew members in these aircraft, 53 were killed and only three (two of them badly injured) were taken prisoner. For his leadership of this amazing operation and for his courage in attacking the flak positions at the Mohne dam after he had completed his own bombing run, Gibson was awarded the Victoria Cross. Some 34 other men of the Lancaster crews were also decorated.

The breaching of the Mohne and Eder dams was a success. The Mohne reservoir was the major source for the Ruhr some 32km (20 miles) away. The water released caused widespread flooding as well as the disruption of rail, road and canal communications and the interruption of electricity and water supplies.

The Eder reservoir was larger than the Mohne reservoir, but it was 100km (62 miles) from the Ruhr. However, Kassel, which was only 40km (25 miles) distant, and the inland waterway system in the area of Kassel, suffered more than the Ruhr from the breach of the Eder dam. If the aircraft allocated to the Eder dam had instead been allocated to the Sorpe dam,

Specifications

Crew: 7/8	Dimensions: span 31.09m (102ft);
Powerplant: 4 x 1089kW (1460hp) Packard	length 20.98m (68ft 10in);
(Rolls-Royce) Merlin piston engines	height 6.19m (20ft 4in)
Maximum speed: 452km/h (281mph)	Weight: 18,598kg (41,000lb) loaded
Range: 4313km (2680 miles)	Armament: 8 x 7.7mm (0.303in) MGs, up to
Service ceiling: 7460m (24,500ft)	6350kg (14,000lb) bombs

▲ **Avro Lancaster B.Mk III**

No. 617 Squadron / RAF Bomber Command, Coningsby, Lincolnshire, May 1943

Modified to carry the special 'bouncing bomb', this aeroplane was used in No. 617's Squadron's celebrated 'dams raid' of 17 May 1943 against the Mohne, Eder and Sorpe dams. The aeroplane remained in first-line service to December 1943.

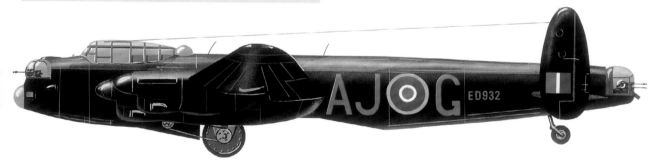

▲ **Avro Lancaster B.Mk III**

No. 617 Squadron / RAF Bomber Command, Coningsby, Lincolnshire, May 1943

Another of the specially adapted 'dams raid' aircraft, this machine was otherwise a standard Lancaster Mk III, of which 3020 were built to a standard differing from that of the Lancaster Mk I only in Packard rather than Roll-Royce Merlin engines.

Specifications

Crew: 7/8	Dimensions: span 31.09m (102ft);
Powerplant: 4 x 1089kW (1460hp) Packard	length 20.98m (68ft 10in);
(Rolls-Royce) Merlin piston engines	height 6.19m (20ft 4in)
Maximum speed: 452km/h (281mph)	Weight: 18,598kg (41,000lb) loaded
Range: 4313km (2680 miles)	Armament: 8 x 7.7mm (0.303in) MGs; up to
Service ceiling: 7460m (24,500ft)	6350kg (14,000lb) bombs

the Germans' believed that there would have been very serious consequences for the Ruhr's industrial production.

But the nature of the Sorpe dam made it a notably difficult target for the 'bouncing bomb', and for this reason it was placed lower down the list of attack priorities. The intact Sorpe reservoir managed to keep the Ruhr supplied with water until the Möhne dam had been repaired. The number of people drowned was some 1294, most of them near the Möhne dam. Neheim-Husten, 8km (5 miles) downstream of the Möhne dam, received the full weight of the flood and at least 859 people died there. It was unfortunate that 493 foreigners (most of them Ukrainian women working on the land), died in their camp at Neheim-Husten. It is believed that 58 or more of the dead were around the Eder dam.

The total number of dead was a new record for a raid on Germany, easily exceeding the 693 people killed at Dortmund in a 596-aircraft raid earlier in May.

▶ **Broken dam**
This aerial photograph shows the floodwater damage sustained by the Möhne dam just days after the attack.

The destruction of Hamburg
JULY–AUGUST 1943

As Germany's second-largest city, Hamburg was deemed worthy of RAF Bomber Command's maximum effort over a 10-day period. Aided by radar navigation and the first operational use of chaff, the four major raids burned the heart out of the ancient port.

HAMBURG WAS GERMANY'S most important port, and by July 1943 it had been attacked 98 times, though never in overwhelming force. This changed in the battle of Hamburg, a series of raids (four British and one US) between 24 July and 3 August 1943. Hamburg lay beyond the range of the 'Oboe' navigation aid, but was a good target for H2S radar.

Harris directed four major raids on Hamburg over 10 nights: 791 aircraft on 24/25 July, 787 aircraft on 27/28 July, 777 aircraft on 29/30 July and 740 aircraft on 2/3 August, with almost 10,160 tonnes (10,000 tons) of bombs being dropped. As a firestorm started during the second raid, it has been claimed that the bombers carried an unusually high proportion of incendiaries with the specific purpose of starting such an event. In fact, slightly under 50 per cent of the tonnage dropped on Hamburg was incendiary, a proportion lower than that used on many of the recent raids against Ruhr targets.

Chaff

The major British tactical advance pioneered over Hamburg was the use of 'Window', or chaff. This was dropped by the bombers to drift towards the ground and saturate the screens of the German interception and flak-laying radars with false echoes. 'Window' had been ready since April 1942, but Bomber Command had not been allowed to use it for fear that the *Luftwaffe* would copy it and use it in raids against England. An understandable fear, but it was the wrong decision, for at this time the *Luftwaffe*'s preoccupation was with the Eastern Front and Bomber Command had lost some 2200 aircraft, many to Germany's radar-assisted defences. In the six major raids (including those on Essen and Remscheid) of the battle of Hamburg, 'Window' probably saved between 100 and 130 Bomber Command aircraft. The German defensive system was rendered obsolete at a stroke.

Specifications

Crew: 7

Powerplant: 4 x 1030kW (1375hp) Bristol
  Hercules radial engines

Maximum speed: 410km/h (255mph)

Range: 3750km (2330 miles)

Service ceiling: 5030m (16,500ft)

Dimensions: span 30.2m (99ft 1in)
  length 26.6m (87ft 3in); height 8.8m (28ft 10in)

Weight: 31,750kg (70,000lb) loaded

Armament: 8 x 7.7mm (0.303in) Browning MGs:
  two in the nose, four in the tail, two dorsal; up
  to 8164 kg (18,000lb) of bombs

▲ Short Stirling B.Mk III

No. 622 Squadron / No. 3 Group / RAF Bomber Command, Mildenhall, Suffolk, 1943

The Stirling was a worthy rather than genuinely capable bomber, and throughout its first-line bomber career suffered from poor payload/range figures and a low service ceiling. By 1943, the type was being relegated to the transport role.

Specifications

Crew: 7

Powerplant: 4 x 1223kW (1640hp) Rolls-Royce
  Merlin XX1V inline piston engines

Maximum speed: 462km/h (287mph)

Range: 4072km (2530 miles)

Service ceiling: 7470m (24,500ft)

Dimensions: span 31.09m (102ft);
  length 21.18m (69ft 6in); height 6.10m (20ft)

Weight: 31,751kg (70,000lb) loaded

Armament: 8 x 7.7mm (0.303in) MGs;
  either one 9979kg (22,000lb) bomb or
  6350kg (14,000lb) of smaller bombs

▲ Avro Lancaster B.Mk I

No. 514 Squadron / RAF Bomber Command, Waterbeach, Cambridgeshire, 1943

Production of the Lancaster Mk I totalled 3444 aircraft by five manufacturers, this aeroplane being one of 919 manufactured by Armstong Whitworth and fitted with H₂S navigation and bombing radar.

Target Peenemünde
AUGUST 1943

Although Bomber Command's everyday 'trade' was area bombing of German cities, every so often there emerged a specific target worthy of rapid destruction. Such a target was Peenemünde, an island off Germany's Baltic coast where much development of 'secret weapons' was undertaken.

ON 17/18 AUGUST 1943, Bomber Command despatched 596 aircraft (324 Lancasters, 218 Halifaxes and 54 Stirlings) against Peenemünde in a raid to destroy the German research establishment off the Baltic coast, at which V-2 rockets were being built and tested.

Master bomber

The raid was carried out in moonlight to improve bombing accuracy in what was the only occasion in the second half of the war when Bomber Command attempted a nocturnal precision raid by large forces against a small target.

For the first time, there was a master bomber to control a major raid. The pathfinder aircraft crews found the target without difficulty, and the master bomber controlled the raid successfully. A diversionary attack by Mosquito light bombers against the city of Berlin drew off most of the German night-fighters for the first two of the raid's three phases.

The initial marking and bombing fell on a camp for forced labourers 2.4km (1.5 miles) south of the first aiming point, but the master bomber and pathfinders quickly brought the bombing back to the main targets, which were bombed successfully. Some 560 aircraft dropped nearly 1829 tonnes (1800 tons) of bombs, of which 85 per cent were HE. This raid probably delayed the V-2 programme by some two months or more, and reduced the scale of the eventual rocket attack. About 180 Germans were killed. Some 500 to 600 foreign workers, mostly

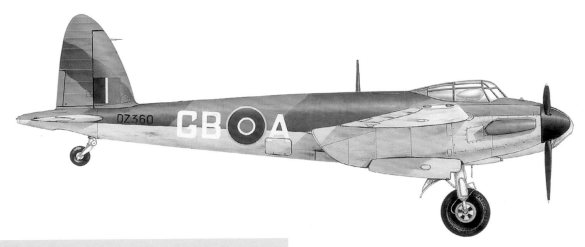

Specifications

Crew: 2	Dimensions: span 16.51m (54ft 2in);
Powerplant: 2 x 918kW (1230hp) Rolls-Royce	length 12.43m (40ft 10in);
Merlin 21 inline piston engines	height 4.65m (15ft 3in)
Maximum speed: 612km/h (380mph)	Weight: 5942kg (13,00lb) loaded
Range: 1963km (1220 miles)	Armament: normal internal bomb load 907kg
Service ceiling: 9449m (31,000ft)	(2000lb)

▲ **de Havilland Mosquito B.Mk IV Series 2**

No. 105 Squadron / RAF Bomber Command, Marham, Norfolk, 1943

With No. 139 Squadron, No. 105 Squadron pioneered the service debut of the Mosquito B.Mk IV Series 2 during 1942, and used the type for high-speed bombing missions over Germany. During World War II, the Mosquito equipped 38 British light bomber squadrons.

▲ **Handley Page Halifax**

Though not as well known as the Avro Lancaster (its primary stablemate in the squadrons of RAF Bomber Command), the Halifax was nonetheless a very capable four-engine heavy bomber.

Polish, were also killed in the labourers' camp. Bomber Command lost 40 aircraft (23 Lancasters, 15 Halifaxes and two Stirlings), representing 6.7 per cent of the force despatched, but this was thought acceptable for so important a target.

Most of the losses were suffered by aircraft of the last wave, when the German night-fighters arrived in strength. This was the occasion on which the Germans employed the novel *schräge Musik* weapon: two forward/upward-firing cannon in the cockpit of Bf 110 night-fighters.

▲ **Handley Page Halifax B.Mk II Series 1 (Special)**

No. 10 Squadron / RAF Bomber Command, Melbourne, Yorkshire, April 1943

The Halifax B.Mk II was a development of the initial Halifax Mk I with more powerful engines and, in some of the 1977 such aircraft, a power-operated dorsal turret carrying four 7.7mm (0.303in) Browning machine guns. A single 7.7mm (0.303in) Vickers K machine gun could be fitted in the nose perspex.

Specifications

Crew: 7
Powerplant: 4 x 1037kW (1390hp) Rolls-Royce
  Merlin X inline engines
Maximum speed: 426km/h (265mph)
Range: 3058km (1900 miles)
Service ceiling: 6706m (22,000ft)
Dimensions: span 30.21m (98ft 10in);
  length 21.36m (70ft 1in);
  height 6.32m (20ft 9in)
Weight: 27,215kg (60,000lb) loaded
Armament: 8 x 7.7mm (0.303in) Browning
  MGs in nose, dorsal turret and tail; 6 x 454kg
  (1000lb), 2 x 907kg (2000lb) and 6 x 227kg
  (500lb) of bombs

Specifications

Crew: 7/8
Powerplant: 4 x 1089kW (1460hp) Packard
  (Rolls-Royce)Merlin piston engines
Maximum speed: 452km/h (281mph)
Range: 4313km (2680 miles)
Service ceiling: 7468m (24,500ft)
Dimensions: span 31.09m (102ft);
  length 20.98m (68ft 10in);
  height 6.19m (20ft 4in)
Weight: 18,598kg (41,000lb) loaded
Armament: 8 x 7.7mm (0.303in) MGs; up to
  6350kg (14,000lb) bombs

▲ **Avro Lancaster B.Mk III**

No. 61 Squadron / No. 5 Group / RAF Bomber Command, Skellingthorpe, mid-1944

The Lancaster was so 'right' from the beginning of its operational career that the two major marks, of which 6464 were built, were the Lancaster Mks I and III that differed from each other only in having British- and US-made Merlin engines.

The flames of victory?
1944–45

In spring 1944 and much against the wishes of its commander, Bomber Command was switched from strategic bombing, undertaken in concert with the USAAF, to tactical work in support of the Normandy campaign. Then it reverted to strategic bombing to the war's end.

BY APRIL 1944, a mightily unwilling Harris had been compelled to bring his strategic offensive to a temporary close as Bomber Command was retasked to tactical targets and the German lines of communications in north-west Europe in the run-up to the Allied invasion of Normandy, launched in June 1944. The campaign against German transport and lines of communication was notably effective, and as the Allies streamed across northern France Bomber

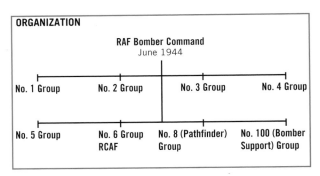

ORGANIZATION

RAF Bomber Command
June 1944

| No. 1 Group | No. 2 Group | No. 3 Group | No. 4 Group |

| No. 5 Group | No. 6 Group RCAF | No. 8 (Pathfinder) Group | No. 100 (Bomber Support) Group |

▼ **British heavy bomber night squadron (June 1944)**

The typical heavy bomber squadron of mid-1944 comprised between 12 and 24 four-engined heavy bombers of the Avro Lancaster or Handley Page Halifax types divided into three four- or eight-aircraft flights.

1st Flight　　　　　　　　　**2nd Flight**　　　　　　　　　**3rd Flight**

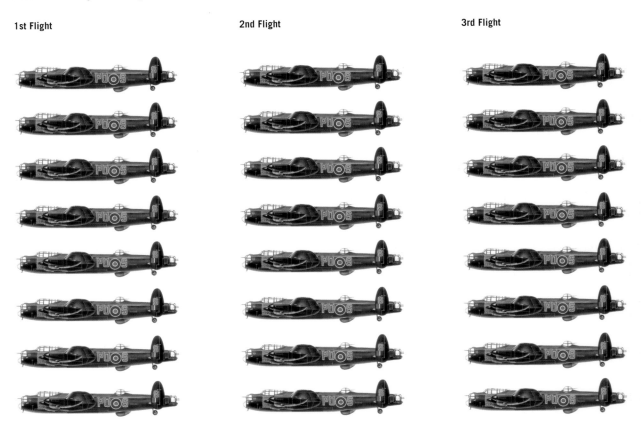

Specifications

Crew: 7

Powerplant: 4 x 1223kW (1640hp) Rolls-Royce
Merlin XXIV inline piston engines

Maximum speed: 462km/h (287mph)

Range: 4072km (2530 miles)

Service ceiling: 7470m (24,500ft)

Dimensions: span 31.09m (102f); length
21.18m (69ft 6in); height 6.10m (20ft)

Weight: 31,751kg (70,000lb) loaded

Armament: 8 x 7.7mm (0.303in) MGs; bomb
load of one 9979kg (22,000lb) bomb or up to
6350kg (14,000lb) of smaller bombs

▲ Avro Lancaster B.Mk I

No. 15 Squadron / RAF Bomber Command, Mildenhall, Suffolk, summer 1944
The Lancaster possessed good payload/range performance, and was the only
British bomber of World War II large enough to carry the 5443kg (12,000lb)
'Tallboy' and 9979kg (22,000lb) 'Grand Slam' earthquake bombs designed to
penetrate deep into the earth or through concrete before detonating.

Command was allowed to revert to its primary task.

From late in 1944, Bomber Command, now with still greater strength and overall capability, was well able to despatch 'thousand-bomber' raids without undue difficulty. Ironically, however, this capability became steadily less needed as the Allied land forces liberated France, Belgium and much of the Netherlands, and plunged into Germany.

Germany's war effort was now crumbling due to exhaustion, lack of adequate manpower, and the decimation of Germany's internal means of land communication (preventing newly made weapons from being delivered to the front), as well as an increasing scarcity of raw materials including, in particular, fuel.

By this time, the German night-fighter arm had ceased to be a significant factor, and the decline of the German day-fighter arm made it possible for Bomber Command to switch a major part of its effort from night bombing to precise, accurate day attacks.

BOMBER COMMAND, NO. 6 GROUP RCAF (JUNE 1944)		
Unit	Type	Base
No. 408 Sqn	Halifax	Linton-on-Ouse
No. 419 Sqn	Halifax	Middleton St George
No. 420 Sqn	Halifax	Tholthorpe
No. 424 Sqn	Halifax	Skipton-on-Swale
No. 425 Sqn	Halifax	Tholthorpe
No. 426 Sqn	Halifax	Linton-on-Ouse
No. 427 Sqn	Halifax	Leeming
No. 428 Sqn	Halifax	Middleton St George
No. 429 Sqn	Halifax	Leeming
No. 431 Sqn	Halifax	Croft
No. 432 Sqn	Halifax	East Moor
No. 433 Sqn	Halifax	Skipton-on-Swale
No. 434 Sqn	Halifax	Croft

BOMBER COMMAND, NO. 100 (BOMBER SUPPORT) GROUP (JUNE 1944)		
Unit	Type	Base
No. 23 Sqn	Mosquito	Little Snoring
No. 85 Sqn	Mosquito	Swannington
No. 141 Sqn	Mosquito	West Raynham
No. 157 Sqn	Mosquito	Swannington
No. 169 Sqn	Mosquito	Great Massingham
No. 192 Sqn	Wellington, Halifax & Mosquito	Foulsham
No. 199 Sqn	Stirling	North Creake
No. 214 Sqn	Fortress	Oulton
No. 239 Sqn	Mosquito	West Raynham
No. 515 Sqn	Mosquito	Little Snoring
No. 1692 Flt	Beaufighter	Great Massingham
No. 1699 Flt	Fortress	Oulton

Specifications

Crew: 7

Powerplant: 4 x 1223kW (1640hp) Rolls-Royce
Merlin XXIV V-12 piston engines

Maximum speed: 462km/h (287mph)

Range: 4070km (2530 miles)

Service ceiling: 7470m (24,500ft)

Dimensions: span 31.09m (102ft);
length 21.18m (69ft 6in); height 6.10m (20ft)

Weight: 16738kg (36,900lb) loaded

Armament: 8 x 7.7mm (0.303in) MGs; bomb
load of either one 9979kg (22,000lb) or up to
6350kg (14,000lb) of smaller bombs

▲ Avro Lancaster B.Mk I

*No. 101 Squadron / No. 1 Group / RAF Bomber Command, Ludford Magna,
Lincolnshire, 1944*

This aeroplane carried the 'Airborne Cigar' radio
equipment, allowing its operators to pass
disinformation to German night-fighters.

Specifications

Crew: 2

Powerplant: 2 x 1253kW (1680hp) Merlin 72
engines

Maximum speed: 668km/h (415mph)

Range: 2888km (1795 miles)

Service ceiling: 10,975m (36,000ft)

Dimensions: span 16.51m (54ft 2in);
length 12.43m (40ft 10in);
height 4.65m (15ft 3in)

Weight: 11,238kg (24,753lb) loaded

Armament: 4 x 227kg (500lb) bombs internally
and one under each wing.

▲ de Havilland Mosquito B.Mk IX

*No. 105 Squadron / No. 8 Group / RAF Bomber Command, Marham, Norfolk,
March 1944*

The Mosquito B.Mk IX was a development of the initial Mosquito B.Mk IV with
more powerful engines, and this machine carries the 'Oboe' navigation system for
accurate long-range navigation in the pathfinder role.

Specifications

Crew: 8

Powerplant: 4 x 895kW (1200hp) Pratt
& Whitney Twin Wasp radial piston engines

Maximum speed: 435km/h (270mph)

Range: 2366km (1470 miles)

Service ceiling: 8534m (28,000ft)

Dimensions: span 17.63m (57ft 10in);

length 12.7m (41ft 8in);

height 4.83m (15ft 10in)

Weight: 11,431kg (25,200lb) loaded

Armament: 4 x 20mm (0.79in) cannon,
7 x 7.7mm (0.303in) MGs; 1 x torpedo and
2 x 113kg (250lb) bombs or 8 x 41kg (90lb)
rocket projectiles

▲ Consolidated Liberator B.Mk VI

*No. 223 Squadron / No. 100 Group / RAF Bomber Command, Oulton,
August 1944*

With its long range, the Liberator was mostly used in the maritime reconnaissance
bomber role by RAF Coastal Command, but its speed and large fuselage also led
to its use by Bomber Command's No. 100 Group in the special duties support role.

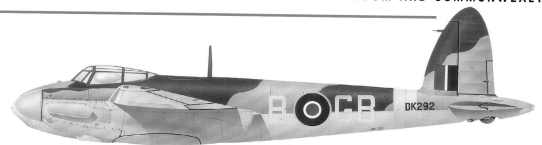

▲ **de Havilland Mosquito B.Mk IV Series 2**

No. 105 Squadron / RAF Bomber Command, Horsham St Faith, 1944

Nos 105 and 139 Squadrons were the units that introduced the Mosquito B.Mk IV series 2 into operational service and, with this type, unescorted high-speed missions over Germany.

Specifications

Mk IV Series II Crew: 2

Powerplant: 2 x 918kW (1230hp) Rolls-Royce
Merlin XX engines
Maximum speed: 612km/h (380mph)
Range: 1963km (1220 miles)
Service ceiling: 9449m (31,000ft)

Dimensions: span 16.51m (54ft 2in);
length 12.43m (40ft 10in);
height 4.65m (15ft 3in)
Weight: 5942kg (13,100lb) loaded
Armament: normal internal bomb load
907kg (2000lb)

BOMBER COMMAND, NO. 1 GROUP (JUNE 1944)

Unit	Type	Base
No. 12 Sqn	Lancaster	Wickenby
No. 100 Sqn	Lancaster	Grimsby
No. 101 Sqn	Lancaster	Ludford Magna
No. 103 Sqn	Lancaster	Kirmington
No. 300 (Pol) Sqn	Lancaster	Faldingworth
No. 460 (Aus) Sqn	Lancaster	Binbrook
No. 550 Sqn	Lancaster	North Killingholme
No. 576 Sqn	Lancaster	Elsham Wolds
No. 625 Sqn	Lancaster	Kelstern
No. 626 Sqn	Lancaster	Wickenby

BOMBER COMMAND, NO. 1 GROUP (MARCH 1945)

Unit	Type	Base	Strength
No. 12 Sqn	Lancaster	Wickenby	20
No. 100 Sqn	Lancaster	Grimsby	19
No. 101 Sqn	Lancaster	Ludford Magna	32
No. 103 Sqn	Lancaster	Elsham Wolds	19
No. 150 Sqn	Lancaster	Hemswell	16
No. 153 Sqn	Lancaster	Scampton	21
No. 166 Sqn	Lancaster	Kirmington	27
No. 170 Sqn	Lancaster	Hemswell	18
No. 300 Sqn (Pol)	Lancaster	Faldingworth	20
No. 460 Sqn, RAAF	Lancaster	Binbrook	27
No. 550 Sqn	Lancaster	North Killingholme	27
No. 576 Sqn	Lancaster	Fiskerton	19
No. 625 Sqn	Lancaster	Kelstern	29
No. 626 Sqn	Lancaster	Wickenby	21

BOMBER COMMAND, NO. 3 GROUP (JUNE 1944)

Unit	Type	Base
No. 15 Sqn	Lancaster	Mildenhall
No. 75 Sqn (NZ)	Lancaster	Mepal
No. 90 Sqn	Stirling & Lancaster	Tuddenham
No. 115 Sqn	Lancaster	Witchford
No. 138 (SD) Sqn	Halifax & Stirling	Tempsford
No. 149 Sqn	Stirling	Methwold
No. 161 (SD) Sqn	Lysander, Hudson & Stirling	Tempsford
No. 218 Sqn	Stirling	Woolfox Lodge
No. 514 Sqn	Lancaster	Waterbeach
No. 622 Sqn	Lancaster	Mildenhall

BOMBER COMMAND, NO. 8 (PATHFINDER) GROUP (1944)

Unit	Type	Base
No. 7 Sqn	Lancaster	Oakington
No. 35 Sqn	Lancaster	Graveley
No. 105 Sqn	Mosquito	Bourn
No. 109 Sqn	Mosquito	Little Staughton
No. 139 Sqn	Mosquito	Upwood
No. 156 Sqn	Lancaster	Upwood
No. 405 Sqn RCAF	Lancaster	Gransden Lodge
No. 571 Sqn	Mosquito	Oakington
No. 582 Sqn	Lancaster	Little Staughton
No. 635 Sqn	Lancaster	Downham Market
No. 692 Sqn	Mosquito	Graveley

Specifications

Crew: 2

Powerplant: 2 x 1253kW (1680hp) Rolls-Royce
 Merlin 72 V-12 piston engines

Maximum speed: 656km/h (408mph)

Range: 2389km (1485 miles)

Service ceiling: 11,280m (37,000ft)

Dimensions: span 16.51m (54ft 2in); length
 12.47m (40ft 11in); height 3.81m (12ft 6in)

Weight: 10,433kg (23,000lb) loaded

Armament: 4 x 227kg (500lb) bombs internally
 and two more under wings or 1 x 1814kg
 (4000lb) bomb

▲ de Havilland Mosquito B.Mk XVI

No. 571 Squadron / No. 8 (Pathfinder) Group / Light Night Striking Force /
RAF Bomber Command, Oakington, 1944

The Mosquito B.Mk XVI, of which 1200 were delivered as the most important
Mosquito light bomber variant, was a development of the limited-production
Mosquito B.Mk IX with a pressurized cockpit for better high-altitude capability.

Specifications

Crew: 7

Powerplant: 4 x 1204kW (1615hp) Bristol
 Hercules XVI radial piston engines

Maximum speed: 454km/h (282mph)

Range: 3194km (1985 miles)

Service ceiling: 7315m (24,000ft)

Dimensions: span 30.12m (98ft 10in); length
 21.74m (71ft 4in); height 6.12m (20ft 1in)

Weight: 29,484kg (65,000lb) loaded

Armament: 9 x 7.7mm (0.303in) machine guns;
 internal bomb load of 6577kg (14,500lb)

▲ Handley Page Halifax B.Mk III

No. 466 Squadron / Royal Australian Air Force / No.4 Group / RAF Bomber
Command, Driffield, Yorkshire, 1944

The yellow-striped fin-and-rudder units were identifying marks of No. 4 Group's
aircraft in 1944.

Taking the war to Berlin
MARCH 1944

**The capital of Germany, Berlin had long possessed a fascination for Bomber Command's
leadership, and the city had been bombed on many occasions. The last major night raid on the
city occurred in March 1944.**

ALTHOUGH MOSQUITOES CONTINUED to attack
the city until 20th April 1945, the last major

British raid on Berlin was delivered on 24/25 March
1944, when 811 aircraft attacked, and in the process

lost 72 aircraft. A strong northerly wind drove the bombers south and scattered them, especially during the homeward flight, when radar-laid flak batteries achieved considerable success – some 50 of the aircraft lost succumbed to the flak. The wind also caused difficulties in marking the target; thus 126 small towns and villages outside Berlin were hit.

Most of the damage occurred in Berlin's south-west area. Much housing was destroyed, about 20,000 people lost their homes, and about 150 people were killed.

No industrial concerns were classed as destroyed, but several important ones were damaged. Although this was the last major raid on Berlin, the city was later bombed by small forces of Mosquitos to keep the Germans off balance.

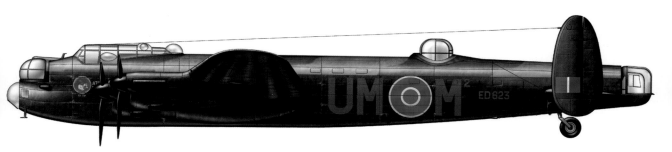

▲ **Avro Lancaster B.Mk III**

No. 626 Squadron / No. 1 Group / RAF Bomber Command, Wickenby, 1944
The Lancaster Mks I and III were fitted defensively with power-operated nose and dorsal turrets, each carrying two 7.7mm (0.303in) machine guns, and a power-operated tail turret carrying four 7.7mm (0.303in) machine guns.

Specifications

Crew: 7/8
Powerplant: 4 x 1089kW (1460hp) Packard
    (Rolls-Royce) Merlin piston engines
Maximum speed: 452km/h (281mph)
Range: 4313km (2680 miles)
Service ceiling: 7460m (24,500ft)

Dimensions: span 31.09m (102ft);
    length 20.98m (68ft 10in);
    height 6.19m (20ft 4in)
Weight: 18,598kg (41,000lb) loaded
Armament: 8 x 7.7mm (0.303in) MGs; up to
    6350kg (14,000lb) of bombs

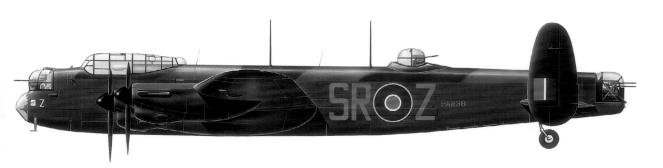

Specifications

Crew: 7
Powerplant: 4 x 1223kW (1640hp) Rolls-Royce
    Merlin XX1V inline piston engines
Maximum speed: 462km/h (287mph)
Range: 4072km (2530 miles)
Service ceiling: 7470m (24,500ft)

Dimensions: span 31.09m (102ft);
    length 21.18m (69ft 6in); height 6.10m (20ft)
Weight: 31,751kg (70,000lb) loaded
Armament: 8 x 7.7mm (0.303in) MGs;
    either one 9979kg (22,000lb) bomb or
    6350kg (14,000lb) of smaller bombs

▲ **Avro Lancaster B. Mk I**

No. 101 Squadron / RAF Bomber Command, Ludford Magna, Lincolnshire, 1944
This aeroplane carries over its fuselage the aerials for the 'Airborne Cigar' electronic warfare system, in which misleading information was radioed to the crews of German night-fighters to divert them from the British bomber streams.

2nd Tactical Air Force
1944–45

Together with the US Ninth Air force, the British 2nd Tactical Air Force (TAF) was vital to the success of the Allied armies during and after the D-Day landings. The 2nd TAF provided the Anglo-Canadian 21st Army Group with decisive tactical air support until the end of the war.

COMMANDED BY Air Marshal Sir Arthur Coningham, who had developed and honed his concept of tactical air support in the North African campaign, the 2nd TAF was a balanced formation with its own three squadrons of reconnaissance aircraft as well as four groups of tactical warplanes, one airborne forces group and one transport group. The most important of these groups were No. 2 Bomber Group with five wings of tactical bombers (13 squadrons), and Nos 83, 84 and 85 Groups with fighters and fighter-bombers. The first two of these groups each had its own three-squadron reconnaissance wing for tactical reconnaissance, and also its own air observation post wing (four and five squadrons respectively) for battlefield reconnaissance and artillery spotting.

In the face of steadily declining German fighter capability, the squadrons of Nos 83 and 84 Groups were used increasingly in the fighter-bomber role with the fixed forward-firing armament of their Spitfire, Typhoon and Tempest warplanes complemented

2ND TACTICAL AIR FORCE, NO. 2 BOMBER GROUP (JUNE 1944)		
Unit	Type	Base
No. 21 Sqn	Mosquito	Gravesend
No. 88 Sqn	Boston	Hartford Bridge
No. 98 Sqn	Mitchell	Dunsfold
No. 107 Sqn	Mosquito	Lasham
No. 180 Sqn	Mitchell	Dunsfold
No. 226 Sqn	Mitchell	Hartford Bridge
No. 305 Sqn (Pol)	Mosquito	Lasham
No. 320 Sqn (Dutch)	Mitchell	Dunsfold
No. 342 Sqn (Fr)	Boston	Hartford Bridge
No. 464 Sqn (Aus)	Mosquito	Gravesend
No. 487 Sqn (NZ)	Mosquito	Gravesend
No. 613 Sqn	Mosquito	Lasham

by loads of bombs and rockets. So while the twin-engined Mitchell and Mosquito medium bombers of No. 2 Group struck close behind the German front

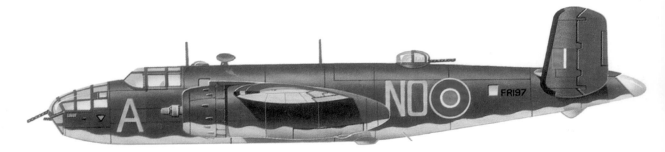

▲ North American Mitchell Mk II

No. 320 (Dutch) Squadron / No. 2 Group / 2nd Tactical Air Force / RAF, Dunsfold, April 1944

The medium bombers of the 2nd TAF's 2nd Bomber Group, including this Mitchell of No. 139 Wing, saw intense employment in the period leading up to the *Overlord* invasion of Normandy in June 1944, and in the following campaign.

Specifications

Crew: 5

Powerplant: 2 x 1268kW (1700hp) Wright Double Row Cyclone radial piston engines

Maximum speed: 470km/h (292mph)

Range: 1979km (1230 miles)

Service ceiling: 8138m (26,700ft)

Dimensions: span 20.57m (67ft 7in); length 16.48m (54ft 1in); height 4.83m (15ft 10in)

Weight: 11,793kg (26,000lb) loaded

Armament: 2 x 12.7mm (0.5in) and 1 x 7.62mm (0.3in) MGs; bomb load of 1814kg (4000lb)

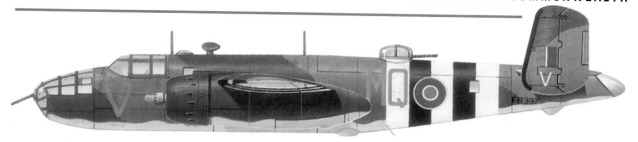

Specifications

Crew: 5

Powerplant: 2 x 1268kW (1700hp) Wright
Double Row Cyclone radial piston engines

Maximum speed: 470km/h (292mph)

Range: 1979km (1230 miles)

Service ceiling: 8138m (26,700ft)

Dimensions: span 20.57m (67ft 7in);
length 16.48m (54ft 1in);
height 4.83m (15ft 10in)

Weight: 11,793kg (26,000lb) loaded

Armament: 2 x 12.7mm (0.5in) and 1 x 7.62mm
(0.3in) MGs; bomb load of 1814kg (4000lb)

▲ **North American Mitchell Mk II**

No. 226 Squadron / 2nd Tactical Air Force, Gilze Rijen, the Netherlands, 1944

The Mitchell medium bomber was of US origins, but used by the RAF in tactical support of the ground forces of the 21st Army Group. By this time the 'invasion stripes' should have been removed, but the pace of operations was too hectic to allow time for this to be done.

lines to isolate the ground forces from reinforcement and resupply, the single-engined fighter-bombers loitered over the battlefield to attack targets of opportunity. Thus the 2nd TAF was able to play a hugely important part in the success of the Canadian First and British Second Armies as they pushed through northwest Europe between June 1944 and May 1945.

Transport conversions
1944–45

As the Lancaster and late-mark Halifax came to predominate in Bomber Command's strength, older aircraft and obsolescent types such as the Stirling were converted for the transport role and, in some cases, further developed specifically for this task late in World War II.

At the time of the Allied invasion of Normandy in June 1944, the British tactical air transport capability was vested in the five squadrons of Transport Command's No. 46 Group with the Douglas Dakota twin-engined transport and Airspeed Horsa assault glider, and with No. 38 Airborne Forces Group of the 2nd Tactical Air Force (TAF) with 10 squadrons of two- and four-engined aircraft towing Horsa assault and Hamilcar logistical transport gliders.

This organization was enlarged and rationalized to meet the requirements of the Arnhem operation of September 1944, and in preparation for the Rhine-crossing operations of 1945 had become Transport Command's Nos 44 to 47 Groups.

By this time, older four-engined bombers, most notably the Handley Page Halifax and Short Stirling, had become available in some numbers

▲ **Vickers Wellington**

The Wellington was a British mainstay throughout the war, first as a bomber and then in the maritime reconnaissance, transport and training roles.

for conversion as transports and heavy glider tugs, and late-production aircraft were completed as the Halifax C.Mk VIII and A.Mk IX, and Stirling A.Mk V, all of which saw useful post-war transport service.

Specifications

Crew: 5

Powerplant: 2 x 854kW (1145hp) Rolls-Royce
Merlin X inline piston engines

Maximum speed: 370km/h (230mph)

Range: 2414km (1500 miles)

Service ceiling: 7925m (26,000ft)

Dimensions: span 25.6m (84ft);
length 21.49m (70ft 6in); height 4.57m (15ft)

Weight: 15,195kg (33,500lb) loaded

Armament: 4 x 7.7mm (0.303in) MGs in
powered tail turret and one similar gun in
nose turret; up to 3175kg (7000lb) of bombs`

▲ Armstrong Whitworth Whitley Mk V

Royal Air Force, 1944

Seen in the standard day-bomber camouflage and markings of the period, this
Whitley Mk V was used for glider-towing, as revealed by the yoke on the rear of the
fuselage and the removal of the guns from the tail turret.

Specifications

Mk VI Crew: 4

Powerplant: 2 x 1186kW (1590hp) Bristol
Hercules XI radial piston engines

Maximum speed: 426km/h (265mph)

Range: 2092km (1300 miles)

Service ceiling: 5485m (18,000ft)

Dimensions: span 23.47m (77ft 0in);
length 18.26m (59ft 11in);
height 4.75m (15ft 7in)

Weight: 10,251kg (22,600lb) loaded

Armament: 2 x 7.7mm (0.303in) Vickers K MGs
in dorsal position

▲ Armstrong Whitworth Albemarle Mk V

*No. 297 Squadron / No. 38 Airborne Forces Group / 2nd Tactical Air Force /
RAF, Brize Norton, Oxfordshire, June 1944*

Some 24 Albemarle aircraft delivered British airborne forces to Normandy in
Airspeed Horsa gliders during the very first stage of the *Overlord* invasion of
France on 6 June 1944.

Specifications

Crew: 7

Powerplant: 4 x 1230kW (1650hp) Bristol
Hercules XV 14-cylinder air-cooled radial
piston engines

Maximum speed: 451km/h (280mph)

Range: 4828km (3000 miles)

Service ceiling: 5182m (17,000t)

Dimensions: span 30.2m (99ft 1in);
length 26.59m (87ft 3in);
height 6.93m (22ft 9in)

Weight: 31,751kg (70,000lb) loaded

Armament: 4 x 7.7mm (0.303in) Browning
MGs in turret

▲ Short Stirling Mk V

*No. 46 Squadron / No. 47 Group / RAF Transport Command, Stoney Cross,
early 1945*

The Stirling Mk V was a purpose-built airborne forces variant, the last to be
manufactured, of the Stirling series. These 160 aircraft had no armament, and
had provision for freight as well as 40 conventional or 20 airborne troops.

Bomber Command: Dresden
JANUARY–MARCH 1945

In the absence of effective enemy flak and fighter opposition, Bomber Command was able to operate by day as well as night in the last months of the war, and to concentrate its power on smaller targets of immediate importance to Germany's continued war effort.

T HE SINGLE MOST controversial attack of Bomber Command's history took place in the early morning of 14 February 1945, and was the bombing of Dresden, essentially a non-military target, in which a huge firestorm erupted. This killed a huge but unquantified number of civilians, most of them refugees fleeing from the Soviets' westward advances.

City targets

The apogee of Bomber Command's effort was March 1945, when it dropped the greatest weight of bombs of any month in the entire war. The major targets, often supplemented by smaller raids on lesser targets, included Mannheim by 478 aircraft on 1 March; Köln by 858 aircraft on 2 March; Kamen and the Dortmund-Ems Canal by 234 and 220 aircraft respectively on 3 March; Chemnitz by 760

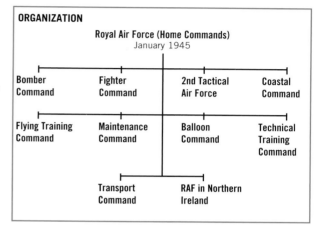

ORGANIZATION

Royal Air Force (Home Commands)
January 1945

Bomber Command	Fighter Command	2nd Tactical Air Force	Coastal Command
Flying Training Command	Maintenance Command	Balloon Command	Technical Training Command
	Transport Command	RAF in Northern Ireland	

aircraft on 5/6 March; Dessau, Hemmingstedt and Harburg by 526, 256 and 234 aircraft on 6/7 March; Hamburg and Kassel by 312 and 262 aircraft on

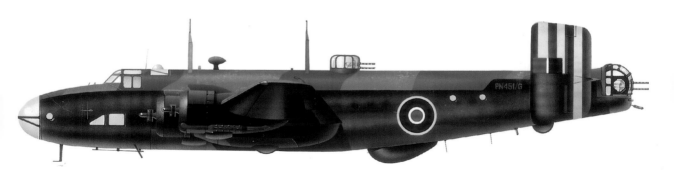

Specifications

Crew: 7

Powerplant: 4 x 1204kW (1615hp) Bristol
  Hercules XVI radial piston engines

Maximum speed: 454km/h (282mph)

Range: 3194km (1985 miles)

Service ceiling: 7315m (24,000ft)

Dimensions: span 30.12m (98ft 10in);
  length 21.74m (71ft 4in);
  height 6.12m (20ft 1in)

Weight: 29,484kg (65,000lb) loaded

Armament: 9 x 7.7mm (0.303in) MGs; internal
  bomb load of 6577kg (14,500lb)

▲ **Handley Page Halifax B.Mk III**

No. 462 (Special Duties) Squadron / Royal Australian Air Force / RAF Bomber Command, Foulsham, Norfolk, early 1945

This aeroplane carries the antennae for the 'Airborne Cigar' radio transmission jamming and disinformation system.

BOMBER COMMAND, NO. 5 GROUP (MARCH 1945)		
Unit	Type	Base
No. 9 Sqn	Lancaster	Bardney
No. 44 Sqn	Lancaster	Dunholme Lodge
No. 49 Sqn	Lancaster	Fiskerton
No. 50 Sqn	Lancaster	Skellingthorpe
No. 57 Sqn	Lancaster	East Kirkby
No. 61 Sqn	Lancaster	Skellingthorpe
No. 83 Sqn	Lancaster	Coningsby
No. 97 Sqn	Lancaster	Coningsby
No. 106 Sqn	Lancaster	Metheringham
No. 207 Sqn	Lancaster	Spilsby
No. 463 Sqn (RAAF)	Lancaster	Waddington
No. 467 Sqn (RCAF)	Lancaster	Waddington
No. 617 Sqn	Lancaster	Woodhall Spa
No. 619 Sqn	Lancaster	Dunholme Lodge
No. 627 Sqn	Lancaster	Woodhall Spa
No. 630 Sqn	Lancaster	East Kirkby

BOMBER COMMAND, NO. 4 GROUP (MARCH 1945)			
Unit	Type	Base	Strength
No. 10 Sqn	Halifax	Melbourne	25
No. 51 Sqn	Halifax	Snaith	31
No. 76 Sqn	Halifax	Holme	40
No. 77 Sqn	Halifax	Full Sutton	47
No. 78 Sqn	Halifax	Breighton	29
No. 102 Sqn	Halifax	Pocklington	20
No. 158 Sqn	Halifax	Lissett	29
No. 346 Sqn (Fr)	Halifax	Elvington	24
No. 347 Sqn (Fr)	Halifax	Elvington	23
No. 466 Sqn (RAAF)	Halifax	Driffield	19
No. 640 Sqn	Halifax	Leconfield	15

▲ **Avro Lancaster B.Mk I**

No. 463 Squadron / Royal Australian Air Force / No. 5 Group / RAF Bomber Command, Waddington, Lincolnshire, spring 1945

This aeroplane carries the yellow-outlined unit code typical of No. 5 Group late in World War II, and was shot down by a German night-fighter in the last Lancaster night raid of the war, on the Tonsberg oil refinery in Norway, on 25/26 April 1945.

Specifications

Crew: 7

Powerplant: 4 x 1223kW (1640hp) Rolls-Royce
Merlin XXIV inline piston engines

Maximum speed: 462km/h (287mph)

Range: 4072km (2530 miles)

Service ceiling: 7470m (24,500ft)

Dimensions: span 31.09m (102f); length
21.18m (69ft 6in); height 6.10m (20ft)

Weight: 31,751kg (70,000lb) loaded

Armament: 8 x 7.7mm (0.303in) MGs; bomb
load of one 9979kg (22,000lb) bomb or up to
6350kg (14,000lb) of smaller bombs

8/9 March; Essen by 1079 aircraft on 11 March; Dortmund by 1079 aircraft on 12 March; Wuppertal and Barmen by 354 aircraft on 13 March; Herne and Gelsenkirchen by 195 and Datteln and Hattingen by 169 aircraft on 14 March; Lützkendorf and Zweibrücken by 244 and 230 aircraft on 14/15 March; Hagen and Misburg by 267 and 257 aircraft on 15/16 March; Nürnberg and Würzburg by 231 and 225 aircraft on 16/17 March; Witten and Hanau by 324 and 277 aircraft on 18/19 March; and Böhlen and Hemmingstedt by 224 and 166 aircraft on 20/21 March. The total of sorties by day on 21 March was 497 aircraft, while the total of sorties by night on 21/22 March amounted to 536 aircraft. Germany's destruction was all but complete.

Bomber Command: final raids
MARCH–MAY 1945

By the last three months of the European campaign, Bomber Command had in effect exhausted its supply of useful targets. Roaming by day as well as night, the command's aircraft completed their destruction of Germany's industries with pinpoint attacks on the last surviving targets.

ON THE NIGHT OF 22/23 MARCH and during the day of 23 March 1945, some 300 Bomber Command aircraft flew small raids. Then, on the night of 23/24 March, 195 Lancaster and 23 Mosquito aircraft of Nos 5 and 8 Groups carried out the last British bombing raid on Wesel, losing no aircraft in the process. It is believed that, for its size, Wesel was by this time the most intensively bombed town in Germany: 97 per cent of the buildings in the town's main area had been destroyed, and the population had fallen to just 1900 persons in May 1945 from a figure of almost 25,000 in September 1939. This attack was part of 537 sorties

BOMBER COMMAND, NO. 3 GROUP (MARCH 1945)			
Unit	Type	Base	Strength
No. 15 Sqn	Lancaster	Mildenhall	22
No. 75 Sqn	Lancaster	Mepal	26
No. 90 Sqn	Lancaster	Tuddenham	21
No. 115 Sqn	Lancaster	Witchford	32
No. 138 Sqn	Lancaster	Tuddenham	20
No. 149 Sqn	Lancaster	Methwold	30
No. 186 Sqn	Lancaster	Stradishall	31
No. 195 Sqn	Lancaster	Wratting Common	30
No. 218 Sqn	Lancaster	Chedburgh	29
No. 514 Sqn	Lancaster	Waterbeach	32
No. 622 Sqn	Lancaster	Mildenhall	22

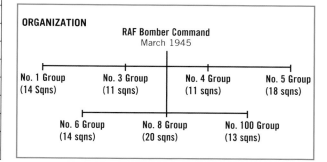

ORGANIZATION

RAF Bomber Command
March 1945

No. 1 Group (14 Sqns)   No. 3 Group (11 sqns)   No. 4 Group (11 sqns)   No. 5 Group (18 sqns)

No. 6 Group (14 sqns)   No. 8 Group (20 sqns)   No. 100 Group (13 sqns)

Specifications

Crew: 7

Powerplant: 4 x 1223kW (1640hp) Rolls-Royce Merlin XXIV inline piston engines

Maximum speed: 462km/h (287mph)

Range: 4072km (2530 miles)

Service ceiling: 7470m (24,500ft)

Dimensions: span 31.09m (102ft); length 21.18m (69ft 6in); height 6.10m (20ft)

Weight: 31,751kg (70,000lb) loaded

Armament: 8 x 7.7mm (0.303in) MGs, bomb load of one 9979kg (22,000lb) bomb or up to 6350kg (14,000lb) of smaller bombs

▲ **Avro Lancaster Mk I**

No. 149 Squadron / No. 3 Group / RAF Bomber Command, Methwold, Norfolk, 1945

The deepened bomb bay and the yellow stripes on the fins indicated that the aeroplane had G-H radar and was the machine of a flight leader.

BOMBER COMMAND, NO. 5 GROUP (MAY 1945)			
Unit	Type	Base	Strength
No. 9 Sqn	Lancaster	Bardney	22
No. 44 Sqn (Rhod)	Lancaster	Spilsby	16
No. 49 Sqn	Lancaster	Fulbeck	19
No. 50 Sqn	Lancaster	Skellingthorpe	17
No. 57 Sqn	Lancaster	East Kirkby	16
No. 61 Sqn	Lancaster	Skellingthorpe	19
No. 106 Sqn	Lancaster	Metheringham	16
No. 189 Sqn	Lancaster	Fulbeck	17
No. 207 Sqn	Lancaster	Spilsby	21
No. 227 Sqn	Lancaster	Balderton	18
No. 463 Sqn (RAAF)	Lancaster	Waddington	21
No. 467 Sqn (RAAF)	Lancaster	Waddington	19
No. 617	Lancaster & Mosquito	Woodhall Spa	42
No. 619	Lancaster	Strubby	17
No. 630 Sqn	Lancaster	East Kirkby	21
No. 83 Sqn (PFF)	Lancaster	Coningsby	22
No. 97 Sqn (PFF)	Lancaster	Coningsby	19
No. 627 Sqn (PFF)	Lancaster & Mosquito	Woodhall Spa	29

BOMBER COMMAND, NO. 6 GROUP (MARCH 1945)			
Unit	Type	Base	Strength
No. 408 Sqn	Halifax	Linton	24
No. 415 Sqn	Halifax	East Moor	24
No. 419 Sqn	Lancaster	Middleton St George	23
No. 420 Sqn	Halifax	Tholthorpe	20
No. 424 Sqn	Lancaster	Skipton-on-Swale	20
No. 425 Sqn	Halifax	Tholthorpe	22
No. 426 Sqn	Halifax	Linton	25
No. 427 Sqn	Lancaster & Halifax	Leeming	28
No. 428 Sqn	Lancaster	Middleton St George	25
No. 429 Sqn	Lancaster & Halifax	Leeming	24
No. 431 Sqn	Lancaster	Croft	20
No. 432 Sqn	Halifax	East Moor	24
No. 433 Sqn	Lancaster & Halifax	Skipton-on-Swale	21
No. 434 Sqn	Lancaster	Croft	24

Specifications

Crew: 7

Powerplant: 1204kW (1615hp) Bristol Hercules
  XVI radial piston engines

Maximum speed: 454km/h (282mph)

Range: 1658km (1030 miles)

Service ceiling: 7315m (24,000ft)

Dimensions: span 31.75m (104ft 2in);
  length 21.36m (70ft 1in);
  height 6.32m (20ft 9in)

Weight: 29,484kg (65,000lb) loaded

Armament: 9 x 7.7mm (0.303in) MGs; up to
  5897kg (13,000lb) bomb load

▲ **Handley Page Halifax B.Mk III**

No. 158 Squadron / RAF Bomber Command, Lissett, 1945

Carrying the nickname Friday the 13th, this was the first Halifax to complete
100 operational sorties, and survived World War II with a total of 128 sorties,
the largest number recorded by any Halifax bomber.

flown in tactical support of the British land forces'
crossing of the Rhine on 24 March.

Razing towns

On the following day, there were attacks on
towns from which the Germans might be able to
reinforce the Rhine front: Hanover was visited by
267 aircraft, Munster by 175, and Osnabruck by
156. On 27 March, attacks were flown against
Paderborn by 268 aircraft, Hamm by 150 and
other smaller areas by 541. On the last day of
March, Hamburg was attacked by 469 aircraft.

The last raid on Berlin was delivered on the night
of 21/22 April, when 76 Mosquitoes flew six separate
raids just before Soviet forces entered the city centre.

Specifications

Crew: 7

Powerplant: 4 x 1223kW (1640hp) Rolls-Royce
 Merlin XXIV V-12 piston engines

Maximum speed: 462km/h (287mph)

Range: 4070km (2530 miles)

Service ceiling: 7470m (24,500ft)

Dimensions: span 31.09m (102ft);
 length 21.18m (69ft 6in); height 6.10m (20ft)

Weight: 16738kg (36,900lb) loaded

Armament: 8 x 7.7mm (0.303in) MGs; bomb
 load of either one 9979kg (22,000lb) or up to
 6350kg (4000lb) of smaller bombs

▲ Avro Lancaster B.Mk I

No. 467 Squadron / Royal Australian Air Force / RAF Bomber Command, 1945

No. 467 Squadron was one of four bomber squadrons of the RAAF to serve with RAF Bomber Command, the others being Nos 460, 463 and 466 Squadrons. However, there were insufficient squadrons to allow the creation of an Australian group like the Canadian No. 6 Group.

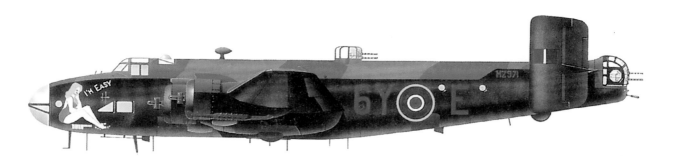

Specifications

Crew: 7

Powerplant: 4 x 1204kW (1615hp) Bristol
 Hercules XVI radial piston engines

Maximum speed: 454km/h (282mph)

Range: 1658km (1030 miles)

Service ceiling: 7315m (24,000ft)

Dimensions: span 31.75m (104ft 2in);
 length 21.36m (70ft 1in);
 height 6.32m (20ft 9in)

Weight: 29,484kg (65,000lb) loaded

Armament: 9 x 7.7mm (0.303in) MGs; up to
 5897kg (13,000lb) of bombs

▲ Handley Page Halifax Mk III

No. 171 (Special Duties) Squadron / No. 100 Group / RAF Bomber Command, North Creake, 1945

This aeroplane was operated in the 'Mandrel', or radio countermeasures, role in the later stages of World War II.

After this, Bomber Command limited itself primarily to raids in tactical support of the army, but the last major strategic raid was the destruction of the oil refinery at Tonsberg in southern Norway by 107 Lancasters during the night of 25/26 April. Another controversial RAF raid occurred on 3 May, when the Cap Arcona, Thielbek and Deutschland were bombed, killing between 7000 and 8000 refugees.

With the surrender of Germany, the Allies could concentrate on Japan. Bomber Command was a significant resource for the proposed invasion of Japan, and plans were prepared to send 30 bomber squadrons to bases on Okinawa, but the nuclear attacks on Hiroshima and Nagasaki occurred before any of the force had been transferred to the Pacific.

Germany's losses
1940–45

The British night bombing campaign against German cities remains one of the most debated aspects of World War II. But Germany had initiated the bombing of civilian centres, and Bomber Command merely responded with the only means the British had to strike directly at Germany.

IN OVERALL TERMS, IT IS ESTIMATED THAT the British and US bombing of Germany killed between 305,000 and 600,000 civilians, some 67 per cent of them succumbing to British attacks, and it was Bomber Command's area bombing campaign that became one of the most controversial aspects of World War II.

Devastated cities

Up to 1942, navigational capability could provide for nothing better than the targeting of an urban area by night bombing. Germany's cities invariably had major industrial districts, and were therefore seen as legitimate targets by the Allies, and especially Bomber Command.

The most destructive single raids in casualty terms were those that caused appalling firestorms in Hamburg (45,000 dead) in 1943 and Dresden (25,000–35,000 dead) in March 1945. Other major raids on German cities that resulted in notably large civilian casualties were those on Darmstadt (12,300 dead), Pforzheim (17,600 dead) and Kassel (10,000 dead).

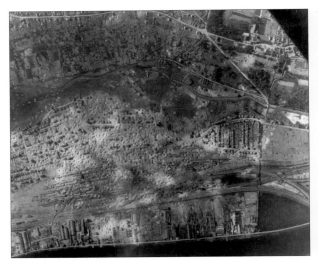

▲ **Rail yard attack**

This aerial photograph shows the devastation caused by Bomber Command's attack on the Juvisy rail yard on the southern outskirts of Paris, 18–19 April 1944. Led by Mosquito pathfinders, 184 Lancasters from No. 5 Group demolished almost the entire track complex.

Specifications

Crew: 7

Powerplant: 4 x 1204kW (1615hp) Bristol Hercules XVI radial piston engines

Maximum speed: 454km/h (282mph)

Range: 3194km (1985 miles)

Service ceiling: 7315m (24,000ft)

Dimensions: span 30.12m (98ft 10in); length 21.74m (71ft 4in); height 6.12m (20ft 1in)

Weight: 29,484kg (65,000lb) loaded

Armament: 9 x 7.7mm (0.303in) MGs; internal bomb load of 6577kg (14,500lb)

▲ **Handley Page Halifax B.Mk III**

No. 640 Squadron / RAF Bomber Command, Leconfield, Yorkshire, 1945

No. 640 Squadron was the highest-numbered of the 36 home-based units to fly the Halifax in the ranks of RAF Bomber Command. This aeroplane has four-gun power-operated dorsal and tail turrets, as well as H_2S navigation/bombing radar.

Bomber Command: casualties
1939–45

Bomber Command carried the war to Germany in a manner that no other element of the British armed forces could attempt. The industrial cost was enormous, but so too was the price that Bomber Command's crews had to pay in men killed, wounded and maimed.

WITH REGARD TO the legality of the campaign, an article in the International Review of the Red Cross stated 'In examining [aerial area bombardment] in the light of international humanitarian law, it should be borne in mind that during the Second World War there was no agreement, treaty, convention or any other instrument governing the protection of the civilian population or civilian property, as the conventions then in force dealt only with the protection of the wounded and the sick on the battlefield and in naval warfare, hospital ships, the laws and customs of war and the protection of prisoners of war.'

The butcher's bill

For its efforts Bomber Command paid a very high price, in the form of 55,573 dead, some 4000 wounded and 9784 taken prisoner. The dead included more than 38,000 RAF aircrew of all nationalities, 9900 men of the RCAF, and more than 1500 men of European countries occupied by the Germans. The manpower strength of the Australian squadrons in Bomber Command represented just 2 per cent of Royal Australian Air Force (RAAF) strength, but the 4050 men killed were 23 per cent

of the total number of RAAF personnel lost in action during World War II: No. 460 Squadron of the RAAF, with an establishment of some 200 men, in fact suffered 1018 deaths in combat during 1942–45 and so was in effect 'destroyed' five times.

On average, of every 100 aircrew serving with Bomber Command, 55 were killed or died of their wounds, three were injured on operations or active service, 12 (some injured) were taken prisoner, two were shot down and were not captured, and 27 survived a complete tour of operations.

In overall terms, Bomber Command flew 364,514 operational sorties and dropped 1.046 million tonnes (1.0305 million tons) of bombs for the loss in action of 8325 aircraft.

The very high casualty figures suffered by the squadrons of Bomber Command, combined with the command's high levels of morale and operational capability, provide very compelling evidence of both the determination and the courage displayed by all

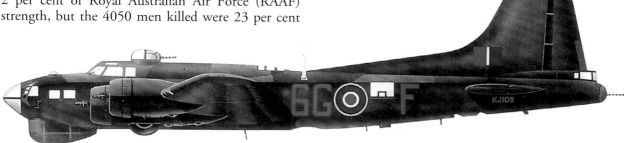

▲ **Boeing Fortress Mk III**

No. 223 (Special Duties) Squadron / No. 100 Group / RAF Bomber Command, Oulton, Norfolk, 1944–45

This aeroplane was operated in the electronic jamming and intelligence-gathering roles in the later stages of World War II.

Specifications

Crew: 8	Dimensions: span 31.62m (103ft 9in);
Powerplant: 4 x 895kW (1200hp) Wright	length 22.25m (73ft); height 4.72m (15ft 6in)
Cyclone GR-1820 radial piston engines	Weight: 29,030kg (64,000lb) loaded
Maximum speed: 451km/h (280mph)	Armament: 13 x 12.7mm (0.5in) MGs in
Range: 4410km (2740 miles)	nose, turrets, waist and tail; up to 5806kg
Service ceiling: 9601m (31,500ft)	(12,800lb) bomb load

aircrew. They took the war to a Germany increasingly better defended by radar-equipped night-fighters and radar-directed anti-aircraft guns.

In statistical terms all aircrew were aware that there was little chance that they would survive through a full tour of 30 operations without being killed, wounded or taken prisoner. This fact was derived from the appreciation that, for much of the war, the loss rate on each mission was in the order of 5 per cent: on average, therefore, one of every 20 aircraft on a mission would be shot down. However, on some missions the loss rate could exceed 10 per cent.

Specifications

Crew: 7

Powerplant: 4 x 1223kW (1640hp) Rolls-Royce
  Merlin XXIV inline piston engines

Maximum speed: 462km/h (287mph)

Range: 4072km (2530 miles)

Service ceiling: 7470m (24,500ft)

Dimensions: span 31.09m (102f);
  length 21.18m (69ft 6in);
  height 6.10m (20ft)

Weight: 31,751kg (70,000lb) loaded

Armament: 8 x 7.7mm (0.303in) MGs;
  1 x 'Grand Slam' 9979kg (22,000lb) bomb

▲ Avro Lancaster B.Mk I (Special)

No. 617 Squadron / RAF Bomber Command, Woodhall Spa, Lincolnshire, early 1945

This aeroplane of the celebrated 'Dambusters squadron' has the cutaway lower fuselage, without bomb bay doors, to carry the 9979kg (22,000lb) 'Grand Slam' earth-penetrating bomb used for the destruction of canals, bridges and viaducts.

▲ Avro Lancaster

The Lancaster was the most important British heavy bomber of World War II, and this No. 635 Squadron aeroplane was used to repatriate POWs at the war's end.

Objectives missed and achieved
1940–45

Bomber Command patently failed in its objective of destroying German civilian morale, and its real strategic successes, while tangible, are very difficult to quantity in any objective fashion. However, the command was certainly of major importance in the last 12 months of the war.

T HE NOTIONAL OBJECT of Bomber Command's effort was to break German civilian morale, and this was not achieved. The bombing was a constant trial to the German people, but the apparently indiscriminate targeting, heavy civilian casualties and widespread damage helped to stiffen German resolve, just as the German Blitz had served to bolster British morale.

In himself, Harris believed that there was a direct relationship between the tonnage of bombs dropped, the areas of city wiped out and military production lost, but in fact the overall effect of Bomber Command's efforts on industrial production is not easy to quantify. The British Bombing Survey at the end of the war was purposefully under-resourced to put matters firmly in the past without due consideration.

The USAAF was concerned with precision attacks, and its analysis highlighted the huge success of US attacks on German synthetic oil production from the spring of 1944 in crippling German transport and military operations. And in attacking targets the

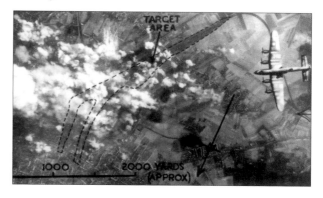

▲ **Bomb bursts**

On 27 December 1944 Bomber Command atacked the Rheydt rail marshalling yard. This photograph shows the target area marked out in a dotted line, with the concentration of bomb bursts over the target.

Germans had to defend, the USAAF knew that its fighters would inflict crippling losses on the Luftwaffe's fighter force. The RAF also contributed to this daylight effort from mid-1944.

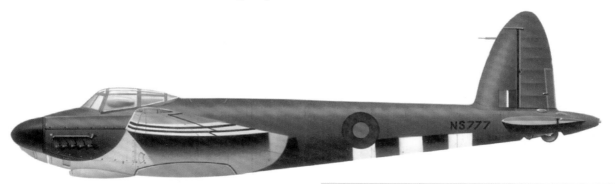

▲ **de Havilland Mosquito PR.Mk XVI**

No. 100 Squadron / RAF, Melsbroek, Belgium, 1944–45

The Mosquito PR.Mk XVI was the photo-reconnaissance counterpart of the Mosquito B.Mk XVI bomber, and as such was the RAF's standard high-altitude reconnaissance aeroplane in the later stages of World War II.

Specifications

Crew: 2

Powerplant: 2 x 1275kW (1710hp) Rolls-Royce Merlin 76 or 77 V-type engines

Maximum speed: 667km/h (415mph)

Range: 3942km (2450 miles)

Service ceiling: 11,742m (38,500ft)

Dimensions: span 16.53m (54ft 2in); length 13.57m (44ft 6in); height 3.8m (12ft 5in)

Weight: 10,419kg (23,000lb) loaded

Armament: none

Specifications

Crew: 8

Powerplant: 4 x 895kW (1200hp) Wright
  Cyclone GR-1820 radial piston engines

Maximum speed: 451km/h (280mph)

Range: 4410km (2740 miles)

Service ceiling: 9601m (31,500ft)

Dimensions: span 31.62m (103ft 9in);
  length 22.25m (73ft); height 4.72m (15ft 6in)

Weight: 29,030kg (64,000lb) loaded

Armament: 13 x 12.7mm (0.5in) MGs in
  nose, turrets, waist and tail; up to 5806kg
  (12,800lb) of bombs

▲ **Boeing Fortress Mk III**

No. 214 Squadron / No. 100 (Bomber Support) Group / RAF Bomber Command, Sculthorpe, Norfolk, 1944–45

The Fortress Mk III was the British version of the USAAF's B-17G, the variant that introduced a chin turret for defence against head-on fighter attacks. The UK took 85 such aircraft for use in the countermeasures, clandestine and decoy roles.

Bomber Command's contribution
1940–45

The increasing scale and capability of Bomber Command's night offensive played a huge part in forcing the Germans to retain substantial numbers of weapons and personnel for the defence of Germany, to the detriment of the frontline and industrial production.

THOUGH IMPOSSIBLE to quantify in any comprehensive fashion, the British night-bomber did achieve real results, but was made difficult by the fact that Germany's industrial base was very strong, and also widely scattered even before a policy of deliberate dispersal was launched. This made complete destruction by area bombing effectively impossible. Moreover, right into 1943 Germany was not even on a full war basis so far as industrial effort was concerned, giving industry considerable leeway in restoring lost production.

A case has been argued for Bomber Command's success in limiting German production of weapons. Whether this is true or not, the German armed forces ultimately did not run out of weapons and ammunition so much as out of useful manpower and transport capability (trucks, locomotives, rolling stock and fuel) with which to move arms and ammunition from the factories to the front.

▲ **Lancaster production**

Undertaken by five British companies and, to a limited extent, the Canadian Victory Aircraft Ltd, manufacture of the Lancaster was aided by the fact that there were comparatively few major variants. Overall production was 7378 aircraft, some of these seeing post-war service with other nations.

Bomber Command's greatest contribution to winning the war derived from the huge diversion of German material and manpower resources into the defence of the *Reich*. By January 1943, for example, some 1000 night-fighters, most of them twin-engined Bf 110 and Ju 88 aircraft, were involved in the defence of Germany.

Perhaps more importantly, by September 1943 the AA defence of Germany involved no fewer than 8875 88mm (3.465in) guns, together with smaller numbers of heavier weapons and about 25,000 20mm (0.79in) and 37mm (1.46in) light flak guns. The '88' was arguably the war's best piece of artillery, and was both an effective AA weapon and a potent battlefield tank destroyer. These weapons would otherwise have been available for service on both the Eastern and Western Fronts.

Manning these guns, the flak regiments in Germany required some 900,000 personnel, and another one million people were committed to clearing wreckage and repairing bomb damage. The military personnel would have been useful at the front, and the civilians were lost to the industrial work force. This diversion of weapons and manpower to the defence of Germany was Bomber Command's greatest contribution to Allied victory. By 1944, defence against the bomber required 30 per cent of German artillery, 20 per cent of heavy shell, 33 per cent of sight and 50 per cent of electro-technical manufacture.

Specifications

Crew: 7/8

Powerplant: 4 x 1089kW (1460hp) Packard (Rolls-Royce) Merlin piston engines

Maximum speed: 452km/h (281mph)

Range: 4313km (2680 miles)

Service ceiling: 7460m (24,500ft)

Dimensions: span 31.09m (102ft); length 20.98m (68ft 10in); height 6.19m (20ft 4in)

Weight: 18,598kg (41,000lb) loaded

Armament: 8 x 7.7mm (0.303in) MGs; up to 6350kg (14,000lb) of bombs

▲ Avro Lancaster B.Mk X

No. 431 'Iroquois' Squadron / Royal Canadian Air Force / No. 6 Group / RAF Bomber Command, Croft, County Durham, early 1945

The Lancaster B.Mk X was the counterpart of the Lancaster B.Mk III manufactured in Canada by Victory Aircraft Ltd. Production totalled 430 aircraft.

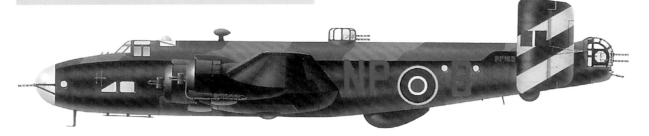

Specifications

Crew: 7

Powerplant: 4 x 1249kW (1675hp) Bristol Hercules 100 engines

Maximum speed: 502km/h (312mph)

Range: 2027km (1260 miles)

Service ceiling: 7315m (24,000ft)

Dimensions: span 31.75m (104ft 2in); length 21.46m (70ft 5in); height 6.32m (20ft 9in)

Weight: 30,872kg (68,000lb) loaded

Armament: 8 x 7.7mm (0.303in) Browning MGs; 5897kg (13,000lb) of bombs

▲ Handley Page Halifax B.Mk VI

No. 158 Squadron / No. 4 Group / RAF Bomber Command, Lissett, April 1945

This was a perfectly standard Halifax night-bomber of the late-war period with H2S navigation and bombing radar, as well as the yellow-striped vertical tail surfaces of No. 4 Group's units (the stripes were used from a time later in 1944).

Mediterranean Theatre
1940–45

British interest in the Mediterranean extended from the Straits of Gibraltar to the coast of Palestine, and from the coast of North Africa to northern Italy. Throughout the war Britain covered this vast region with flying boats and land-based reconnaissance aircraft.

WHEN ITALY ENTERED WORLD WAR II in June 1940, the British had to watch for activities not only in Italy itself and North Africa, but also in the Italian-held Dodecanese islands in the Aegean Sea and the progress of Italy's land campaign against Greece. Other factors that had to be monitored on a constant basis were the dispositions and strengths of the Italian fleet's various components, for these could pose a very real threat to British maritime communications in the Mediterranean, especially the resupply of troops in Egypt.

Battling the Luftwaffe

Despite the success of the British carrierborne air attack on the Italian fleet in Taranto during November 1940, which gave the Royal Navy effective command of the Mediterranean, Italian air power remained a major threat, and one that was supplemented, from a time early in 1941, by

substantial German air strength directed against the British base at Malta as well as British maritime strength and operations.

Gradually, however, the British got the upper hand in the combined sea and air war over the Mediterranean through their combination of astute reconnaissance and well-planned bomber operations. Reconnaissance played a key role on the North African campaign through the discovery of Axis preparations for offensive undertakings, allowing the ground forces to be supported accordingly and the Axis supply dumps and lines of communication to be bombed. The nature of the British air effort changed after the defeat of the Axis in North Africa in May 1943. Major air efforts were required as part of the campaigns in Sicily and Italy, and constant watches still had to be maintained over the western Mediterranean until the autumn of 1944 and then over the Balkans right to the end of the war.

▲ **Bristol Blenheim Mk I**

No. 113 Squadron / RAF, Middle East, Egypt and Greece, 1940–41

No. 113 Squadron switched from the Hawker Hind to the Blenheim in May 1939 at Heliopolis in Egypt, and thereafter flew the type in the first stages of the North African desert campaign after Italy's declaration of war in June 1940. In February 1941, the squadron moved to Greece, where it lost all its aircraft in a devastating German ground attack on 15 April.

Specifications

Crew: 3

Powerplant: 627kW (840hp) Bristol Mercury VIII 9-cylinder single-row radial engines

Maximum speed: 459km/h (285mph)

Range: 1810km (1125 miles)

Service ceiling: 8315m (27,280ft)

Dimensions: span 17.17m (56ft 4in); length 12.12m (39ft 9in); height 3m (9ft 10in)

Weight: 4031kg (8839lb) loaded

Armament: 2 x 7.7mm (0.303in) MGs and 454kg (1000lb) bomb load

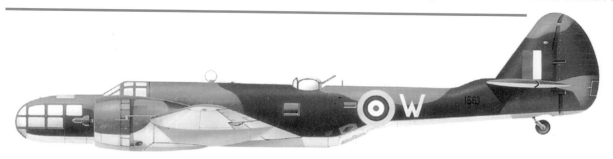

Specifications

Crew: 4

Powerplant: 2 x 895kW (1200hp) Pratt
& Whitney twin Wasp radial piston engines

Maximum speed: 447km/h (278mph)

Range: 2897km (1800 miles)

Service ceiling: 9449m (31,000ft)

Dimensions: span 18.69m (61ft 4in);
length 14.22m (46ft 8in); height 4.57m (15ft)

Weight: 7624kg (16,809lb) loaded

Armament: 4 x 7.7mm (0.303in) Browning
MGs; 2 x single Vickers K MGs; up to 907kg
(2000lb) of bombs

▲ Martin Maryland Mk II

No. 24 Squadron / South African Air Force, Fuka, Egypt, May 1941

The SAAF was a primary operator of the Maryland, and No. 24 Squadron was one
of three detailed for operations over Crete from 23 May. In November 1941, the
squadron transitioned to the more capable Douglas Boston.

Specifications

Crew: 4

Powerplant: 2 x 895kW (1200hp) Pratt
& Whitney twin Wasp radial piston engines

Maximum speed: 447km/h (278mph)

Range: 2897km (1800 miles)

Service ceiling: 9449m (31,000ft)

Dimensions: span 18.69m (61ft 4in);
length 14.22m (46ft 8in); height 4.57m (15ft)

Weight: 7624kg (16,809lb) loaded

Armament: 4 x 7.7mm (0.303in) Browning
MGs; 2 x single Vickers K MGs; up to 907kg
(2000lb) of bombs

▲ Martin Maryland Mk I

No. 431 Flight / RAF, Malta, 1941

Delivered to US standard but fitted with an Armstong Whitworth dorsal turret,
the Maryland Mk I was operated from Malta primarily in the long-range
reconnaissance role deep into the Mediterranean and around Italy's coast.

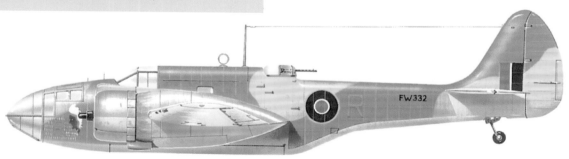

Specifications Mk III

Crew: 4

Powerplant: 2 x 1238kW (1660hp) Wright
Cyclone radial piston engines

Maximum speed: 486km/h (302mph)

Range: 1529km (950 miles)

Service ceiling: 7315m (24,000ft)

Dimensions: span 18.59m (61ft 4in);
length 14.78m (48ft 6in);
height 5.41m (17ft 9in)

Weight: 6895kg (15,200lb) loaded

Armament: 14 x 7.7mm (0.303in) machine
guns; bomb load of 907kg (2000lb)

▲ Martin Baltimore Mk V

No. 232 Wing / RAF, Mediterranean theatre, 1944

A development of the concept embodied in the Maryland, the Baltimore was
designed to European standards. Production totalled 1575 aircraft used mostly in
the Mediterranean theatre with a 907kg (2000lb) bomb load and up to 14 7.7mm
(0.303in) fixed and trainable machine guns.

Coastal Command
1936–45

Given the UK's reliance on the Royal Navy as its first line of defence and on the merchant navy for the trade on which the survival of the UK was dependent, Coastal Command was a vital asset, but nonetheless seldom received the priority it deserved.

COASTAL COMMAND came into existence in July 1936 as part of the major reorganization of the RAF's structure, a reorganization based on the latest official thinking about the probable nature of future war. Coastal Command was created out of the Coastal Area command, which had been established in 1919, and was the organization within the RAF that provided aerial protection for the United Kingdom's maritime interests against submarine, surface warship and aerial threats, and also to visit an aerial threat to any enemy's vessels.

Coastal Command's first commander-in-chief was Air Marshal Sir Arthur Longmore, who was succeeded on 1 September 1936 by Air Marshal Sir Philip Joubert de la Ferte, himself succeeded on 18 August 1937 by Air Marshal Sir Frederick Bowhill. Later commanders were Air Chief Marshal Sir Philip Joubert de la Ferte, once again, from 14 June 1941, Air Marshal Sir John Slessor from 5 February 1943 and, finally in the European context of World War II, Air Chief Marshal Sir William

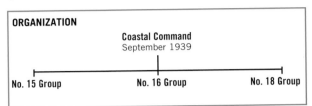

COASTAL COMMAND, NO. 15 GROUP (1939)		
Unit	Type	Base
No. 204 Sqn	Sunderland & London	Mount Batten
No. 210 Sqn	Sunderland & London	Pembroke Dock
No. 217 Sqn	Anson & Tiger Moth	Warmwell
No. 228 Sqn	Sunderland	Pembroke Dock
No. 502 Sqn	Anson	Aldergrove

Sholto Douglas from 20 January 1944. As with the RAF's other major commands, Coastal Command was structured internally into regionally based groups, each comprising a number of squadrons operating

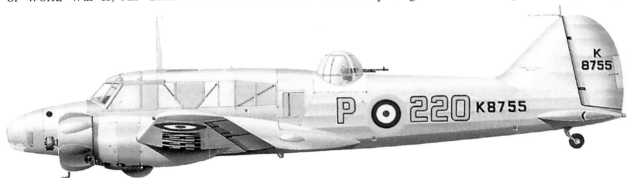

Specifications

Crew: 3

Powerplant: 2 x 261kW (350hp) Armstrong Siddeley Cheetah IX radial piston engines

Maximum speed: 303km/h (188mph)

Range: 1271km (790 miles)

Service ceiling: 5791m (19,000ft)

Dimensions: span 17.22m (56ft 6in); length 12.88m (39ft 7in); height 3.99m (13ft 1in)

Weight: 3629kg (8000lb) loaded

Armament: 2 x 7.7mm (0.303in) MGs; provision to carry up to 163kg (360lb) of bombs

▲ **Avro Anson GR.Mk I**

No. 220 Squadron / RAF Coastal Command, 1938

This Anson is seen in Coastal Command's standard finish and markings of the period immediately before World War II, namely an overall silver dope finish with yellow-outlined roundels, black serials and yellow squadron markings.

from bases close to the UK's long coast. In Coastal Command's youth, other commands had priority for men and equipment, so Coastal Command had to do the best it could with obsolescent aircraft and weapons. The delivery of aircraft was often so limited, indeed, that many units were 'borrowed' from the Fleet Air Arm (FAA) of the Royal Navy, one of the

major beneficiaries of the command's existence, and the command's most important weapon was a small bomb that had to strike a submarine rather than detonate close to it. This bomb also possessed an alarming tendency to 'skip' off the water like a skimmed stone, and in one case even hit and destroyed the aeroplane that had dropped it. Had

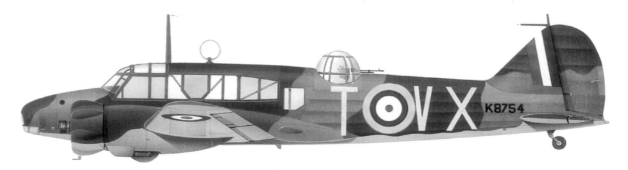

Specifications

Crew: 3/5

Powerplant: 2 x 261kW (350hp) Armstrong
Siddeley Cheetah IX radial piston engines

Maximum speed: 303km/h (188mph)

Range: 1271km (790 miles)

Service ceiling: 5790m (19,000ft)

Dimensions: span 17.2m (56ft 5in);
length 12.88m (42ft 3in);
height 3.99m (13ft 1in)

Weight: 3629kg (8000lb) loaded

Armament: 2 x 7.7mm (0.303in) MGs; up to
163kg (360lb) of bombs

▲ **Avro Anson GR.Mk I**

No. 206 Squadron / RAF Coastal Command, Bircham Newton, 1939–40

No. 206 Squadron received this Anson in 1937, and flew it over the North Sea until 1940 before passing the aeroplane to No. 1 Operational Training Unit. The machine crashed and was lost on 29 August 1940.

Specifications

Crew: 6

Powerplant: 2 x 682kW (915hp) Bristol Pegasus
X radial piston engines

Maximum speed: 249km/h (155mph)

Range: 1770km (1100 miles)

Service ceiling: 6066m (19,900ft)

Dimensions: span 24.38m (80ft);
length 17.32m (56ft 10in);
height 5.72m (18ft 9in)

Weight: 8346kg (18,400lb) loaded

Armament: 3 x 7.7mm (0.303in) Lewis MGs;
up to 907kg (2000lb) of bombs

▲ **Saro London Mk II**

No. 240 Squadron / RAF Coastal Command, Sullom Voe, Shetland, late 1939

This flying boat was built as a London Mk I, but later upgraded to Mk II standard with more powerful engines driving four- rather than two-bladed propellers. The last London biplane flying boats were retired from British service in 1941, some of the machines being passed to the RCAF.

they not been so tragic, many early operations would have been amusing. Nevertheless, on several occasions German submarines were forced to fight off the attentions of Coastal Command aircraft, although the number of times the aircraft found any U-boat was limited.

In 1941 there began experiments of a depth charge that could be dropped from the air, and after successful trials this weapon (soon adapted for shallow detonation after this had been shown to be more useful) rapidly superseded the original bomb. In the same year, the introduction of several types of newer warplane to Bomber Command allowed the command to pass some of its older bomber types, including the Vickers Wellington, to Coastal Command. These acquisitions offered much longer range, making them much more effective. Then the introduction of the Leigh Light in 1942 allowed accurate night attacks, denying U-boats the freedom to recharge their batteries under cover of dark.

▶ **Bristol Blenheim**

The Blenheim Mk IV flew with 11 Coastal Command fighter squadrons, and also with four Coastal Command bomber squadrons in the early part of World War II.

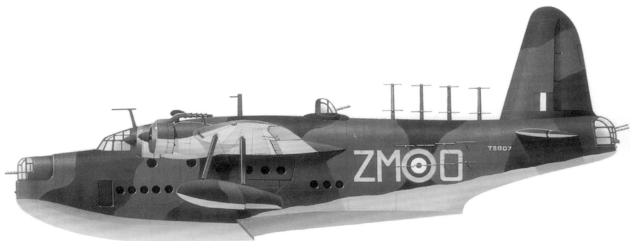

Specifications

Crew: 10

Powerplant: 4x 753kW (1010hp) Bristol Pegasus XXII 9 cylinder single-row radial engines

Maximum speed: 336km/h (209mph)

Range: 4023km (2500 miles)

Service ceiling: 4570m (15,000ft)

Dimensions: span 34.38m (11ft 9.5in); length 26m (85ft 3.5in); height 10.52m (34ft 6in)

Weight: 22,226kg (49,000lb) loaded

Armament: 8 x 7.7mm (0.303in) MGs; internal bomb, depth charge and mine load of 907kg (2000lb)

▲ **Short Sunderland Mk II**

No. 201 Squadron / RAF Coastal Command, Castle Archdale, Co. Fermanagh, Northern Ireland, 1941

Remaining in service to 1944, this flying boat carries the early type of over-fuselage antennae associated with air-to-surface search radar. Operating from Northern Ireland, the squadron's aircraft could range deep into the Atlantic Ocean.

▲ **Short Sunderland Mk I**

No. 230 Squadron / RAF Coastal Command, Mediterranean, 1941

No. 230 Squadron was the first unit to receive the formidable Sunderland general reconnaissance flying boat, taking its first machines during the summer of 1938 before moving to the Mediterranean, where the unit operated for a time from Soudha Bay on the north coast of Crete before the island's fall to the Germans in May 1941.

Specifications

Crew: 10

Powerplant: 4x 753kW (1010hp) Bristol Pegasus XXII 9 cylinder single-row radial engines

Maximum speed: 336km/h (209mph)

Range: 4023km (2500 miles)

Service ceiling: 4570m (15,000ft)

Dimensions: span 34.38m (11ft 9.5in); length 26m (85ft 3.5in); height 10.52m (34ft 6in)

Weight: 22,226kg (49,000lb) loaded

Armament: 8 x 7.7mm (0.303in) MGs; internal bomb, depth charge and mine load of 907kg (2000lb)

Coastal Command – the first shots
1939–40

The advent of World War II found Coastal Command in a very difficult position, for the Command had huge responsibilities but only very meagre resources. Moreover, Bomber Command was very jealous of its own resources, thus denying Coastal Command many aircraft it could have used.

COASTAL COMMAND tried, without much success, to improve its capabilities in the first months of the war, but was aided by the fact that the German naval offensive in the North Atlantic was also slow to gather momentum.

Anti-U-boat operations

From the middle of 1940, however, the Command was faced by a host of often conflicting demands: anti-invasion patrols over the North Sea and English Channel, long-range fighter protection over the South-West Approaches, surveillance of the vast length of coast controlled by the Germans, escort

COASTAL COMMAND, NO. 16 GROUP (1939)		
Unit	Type	Base
No. 22 Sqn	Vildebeest	Thorney Island
No. 42 Sqn	Vildebeest	Bircham Newton
No. 48 Sqn	Anson	Thorney Island
No. 206 Sqn	Anson	Bircham Newton
No. 500 Sqn	Anson, Hind & Tutor	Detling

patrol for convoys, and offensive patrols against U-boats. As the war continued, all of these had to be extended in scope and range, but Coastal

Command had a mere 500 operational aircraft. Most unfortunate of all, given the growing threat of the U-boat, was the fact that of these aircraft a mere 34 were Short Sunderland flying boats able to range more than 800km (500 miles) out into the ocean.

So successful did the U-boat attacks become in the South-West Approaches that convoys were re-routed via the North-West Approaches around the northern tip of Ireland to the ports of Liverpool and Glasgow.

Specifications

Crew: 7

Powerplant: 2 x 686kW (920p) Bristol Pegasus
X 9 cylinder air-cooled radial engines

Maximum speed: 241km/h (150mph)

Range: 1609km (1000 miles)

Service ceiling: 5640m (18,500ft)

Dimensions: span 25.91m (85ft 0in); length
16.71m (54ft 10in); height 6.63m (21ft 9in)

Weight: 8618kg (19,000lb) loaded

Armament: 3 x 7.7mm (0.303in) MGs; up to
454kg (1000lb) of bombs, mines or depth
charges

▲ **Supermarine Stranraer**

No. 240 Squadron / RAF Coastal Command, Pembroke Dock, South Wales, 1940

This squadron operated from Pembroke Dock and Stranraer, with the Stranraer flying boat in the general reconnaissance role until 1941.

Specifications

Crew: 3

Powerplant: 2 x 261kW (350hp) Armstrong
Siddeley Cheetah IX radial piston engines

Maximum speed: 303km/h (188mph)

Range: 1271km (790 miles)

Service ceiling: 5791m (19,000ft)

Dimensions: span 17.22m (56ft 6in);
length 12.88m (56ft 6in);
height 3.99m (13ft 1in)

Weight: 3629kg (8000lb) loaded

Armament: 2 x 7.7mm (0.303in) MGs; provision
to carry up to 163kg (360lb) of bombs

▲ **Avro Anson GR.Mk I**

No. 217 Squadron / RAF Coastal Command, 1939–40

Armed with two 7.7mm (0.303in) machine guns, one in the nose and the other in the manually operated Armstrong Whitworth dorsal turret, the Anson was indifferently armed for defensive purposes, and was replaced in Coastal Command by the Bristol Beaufort from a time late in 1940.

Convoy protection
1940

The Germans soon discovered that the British had switched many convoys further to the north and shifted the focus of their efforts to the new area. Here Coastal Command's task was made all the more difficult by the relative shortage of airfields and flying boat bases.

THE NEW CONVOY lane was soon discovered and the Germans switched their attention to the waters west and north of Ireland. Coastal Command lacked the airfields and flying boat bases to relocate large numbers of aircraft, so this placed a further burden on the already overextended command. Compounding the problem was the fact that in August 1940 the Germans introduced new U-boat tactics, following the target convoy out of the range of its escorts by day, and closing at night for a surface attack undetected by the convoy escorts' sonars.

Radar search

Coastal Command had no immediate answer, as night operations were still tricky, and except in bright moonlight visual detection of a U-boat was difficult. The only real hope lay with air-to-surface search radar, but only about one in six aircraft carried this electronic aid, which was next to useless against all

COASTAL COMMAND, NO. 18 GROUP (1940)		
Unit	Type	Base
No. 201 Sqn	London	Calshot
No. 209 Sqn	Stranraer	Invergordon
No. 220 Sqn	Hudson & Anson	Bircham Newton
No. 224 Sqn	Hudson & Anson	Leuchars
No. 233 Sqn	Hudson & Anson	Leuchars
No. 240 Sqn	London & Lerwick	Invergordon
No. 269 Sqn	Anson	Montrose
No. 608 Sqn	Anson	Thornaby
No. 612 Sqn	Anson, Hector & Hind	Dyce

but a fully surfaced U-boat at a range of less than 4.8km (3 miles).

And even anti-surface vessel (ASV) radar was limited; last-minute visual sighting was still required, as there was no illumination system, and the required

▲ **Bristol Blenheim Mk IVF**

No. 248 Squadron / RAF Coastal Command, North Coates, 1940–41

Used by Fighter Command in small numbers as well as by Coastal Command, the Blenheim Mk IVF was an extemporized fighter created by adapting the standard Mk IV light bomber with a ventral pack carrying four 7.7mm (0.303in) Browning fixed forward-firing machine guns.

Specifications

Crew: 3

Powerplant: 2 x 675kW (905hp) Bristol Mercury XV radial piston engines

Maximum speed: 428km/h (266mph)

Range: 2350km (1460 miles)

Service ceiling: 8310m (27,260ft)

Dimensions: span 17.17m (56ft 4in);

length 12.98m (42ft 7in); height 3m (9ft 10in)

Weight: 6532kg (14,400lb) loaded

Armament: 5 x 7.7mm (0.303in) MGs; 4 x 7.7mm (0.303in) Browning MGs under the hull, up to 434kg (1000lb) of bombs internally and 145kg (320lb) of bombs externally low-altitude release of the depth charge was dangerous under all but perfect conditions for lack of a reliable low-reading altimeter.

Thus convoys had to rely for safety on evasive routing on the basis of intercepted German radio signals, which also made it possible for the British to concentrate air patrols in the areas in which the U-boats were planning to operate. But radio intercepts were not always available or reliable, and shipping losses were often heavy. Between the

beginning of June and the end of 1940, more than 3.04 million tonnes (3 million tons) of British, Allied and neutral merchant shipping were sunk. Some 59 per cent of the total fell victim to U-boats, 12 per cent to Focke-Wulf Fw 200 Condor and other aircraft, and the rest to mines and surface raiders.

During this time, the British losses were more than 2.54 million tonnes (2.5 million tons) greater than replacements. There was an acute need for more and better weapons, aircraft and equipment.

Tipping the balance
1941–42

While 1941 was a year of crisis without much visible hope on the horizon for Coastal Command, there were some notable success and the beginnings of greater capability and a more effective concentration of effort. These changes were to start bearing fruit in the course of 1942.

THE NEEDS OF COASTAL COMMAND also included depth charges designed for air dropping, more radios allowing aircraft/ship communication, longer-range radar and the means (slow-dropping flares or searchlights) to illuminate U-boats at night so that they could be attacked visually. Progress was slow, but progress was nevertheless made.

The start of 1941 was marked by dreadful weather, which was as much a hindrance to German U-boats

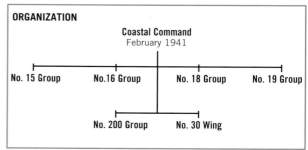

ORGANIZATION

| Coastal Command |
| February 1941 |

| No. 15 Group | No.16 Group | | No. 18 Group | No. 19 Group |

| | No. 200 Group | No. 30 Wing |

▲ **Bristol Beaufort Mk I**

No. 22 Squadron / RAF Coastal Command, 1941–42

Initially based in the UK, No. 22 Squadron and its Beaufort aircraft were shipped to Ceylon during March 1942. The squadron remained in the Far East for the rest of World War II, but transitioned to the Bristol Beaufighter during June 1944.

Specifications

Crew: 4

Powerplant: 2 x 843kW (1130hp) Bristol Taurus VI, XII or XVI radial piston engines

Maximum speed: 418km/h (260mph)

Range: 1666km (1035 miles)

Service ceiling: 5030m (16,500ft)

Dimensions: span 17.63m (57ft 10in); length 13.59m (44ft 7in);

height 13.59m (44ft 7in)

Weight: 9630kg (21,230lb) loaded

Armament: 4 x 7.7mm (0.303in) MGs (two each in nose and dorsal turrets) and, in some aircraft, three additional 7.7mm (0.303in) MGs (one in blister beneath the nose and two in beam positions); up to 1680kg (1500lb) of bombs or mines, or 1 x 728kg (1605lb) torpedo and aircraft as Coastal Command. Convoy losses declined, and Coastal Command was afforded a little more breathing space, but from mid-February the weather improved and British losses increased as Germany committed more U-boats and aircraft, as well as four major surface raiding warships. In April 1941, losses amounted to 654,304 tonnes

(644,000 tons), almost half of them to aircraft. Prime Minister Churchill demanded action, and at last Bomber Command released some obsolete squadrons whose Bristol Blenheims could cover the North Sea and so release Coastal Command squadrons for farther-reaching service. The U-boats moved deeper into the Atlantic to find respite

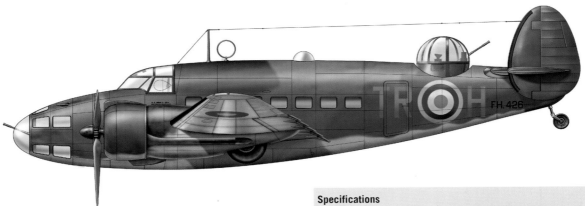

▲ Lockheed Hudson GR.Mk IIIA

No. 59 Squadron / RAF Coastal Command, UK, mid-1942

The Hudson Mk IIIA was the first Hudson model earmarked for RAF service under the terms of the USA's Lend-Lease Act. But of the 800 such aircraft expected only 382 were delivered, the others going to Commonwealth air forces and to the US Army Air Forces (USAAF), in which the type was known as the A-29.

Specifications

Crew: 6

Powerplant: 2 x 890kW (1200hp) Wright Cyclone 9-cylinder radial engines

Maximum speed: 397km/h (246mph)

Range: 3150km (1960 miles)

Service ceiling: 7470m (24,500ft)

Dimensions: span 19.96m (65ft 4in);

length 13.50m (44ft 4in); height 3.62m (11ft 10in)

Weight: 7930kg (17,500lb) loaded

Armament: 7 x 7.7mm (0.303in) Browning MGs (two in nose, two in dorsal turret, two in beam and one ventral); 340kg (750lb) of bombs or depth charges

▲ Lockheed Hudson GR.Mk IIIA

No. 48 Squadron / RAF Coastal Command, UK, 1941–42

With its good speed and comparatively long endurance, the Hudson Mk III had decent defensive as well as offensive armament, and was popular with the men who flew the type.

Specifications

Crew: 6

Powerplant: 2 x 890kW (1200hp) Wright Cyclone 9-cylinder radial engines

Maximum speed: 397km/h (246mph)

Range: 3150km (1960 miles)

Service ceiling: 7470m (24,500ft)

Dimensions: span 19.96m (65ft 4in);

length 13.50m (44ft 4in); height 3.62m (11ft 10in)

Weight: 7930kg (17,500lb) loaded

Armament: 7 x 7.7mm (0.303in) Browning MGs (two in nose, two in dorsal turret, two in beam and one ventral); 340kg (750lb) of bombs or depth charges from aircraft based in the UK and West Africa, and this was reflected in a decline in losses to an average of 127,000 tonnes (125,000 tons) per month in July and August 1941, and a rise in U-boat sinkings as indicated by the loss of five such boats in March.

In June, Joubert returned as leader of Coastal Command, whose situation was improving as better radar was introduced and an aerial searchlight was in its final development. Joubert's first task was to develop the tactics that would make the best use of the new 'weapons'. Over

this same period, Coastal Command's offensive capability, centred on the Bristol Beaufort torpedo-bomber and Bristol Beaufighter heavy fighter, was starting to exercise a significant effect on Germany's coastal shipping. The Beauforts' and Beaufighters' torpedoes supplemented the success of air- and sea-laid mines and the efforts of Bomber Command on German bases and the FAA on German shipping.

▲ Consolidated Liberator GR.Mk I

No. 120 Squadron / RAF Coastal Command, Aldergrove, Northern Ireland, late 1942

The Liberator's long range made it a natural choice for the maritime role, and this machine carries ASV.Mk II air-to-surface search radar as well as a ventral pack with four 20mm (0.79in) cannon for additional anti-submarine punch.

Specifications

Crew: 10
Powerplant: 4 x 895kW (1200hp) Pratt & Whitney Twin wasp radial piston engines
Maximum speed: 488km/h (303mph)
Range: 1730km (1080 miles)
Service ceiling: 8540m (28,000ft)
Dimensions: span 33.53m (110ft);
length 20.22m (66ft 4in);
height 5.49m (18ft)
Weight: 32,296kg (71,200lb) loaded
Armament: 4 x 20mm (0.79in) in ventral position, plus 2 x 12.7mm (0.5in) guns each in dorsal, tail and retractable ball turrets; up to 3629kg (8000lb) bombs

Specifications

Crew: 4
Powerplant: 2 x 746kW (1000hp) Bristol Pegasus XVII radial piston engines
Maximum speed: 409km/h (254mph)
Range: 3034km (1885 miles)
Service ceiling: 5791m (19,000ft)
Dimensions: span 21.08m (69ft 2in);
length 16.33m (53ft 7in);
height 4.55m (14ft 11in)
Weight: 8508kg (18,756lb) loaded
Armament: 2 x 7.7mm (0.303in) forward-firing twin MGs in dorsal and ventral positions; up to 1814kg (4000lb) of bombs

▲ Handley Page Hampden TB.Mk I

No. 489 Squadron / Royal New Zealand Air Force / RAF Coastal Command, Wick, 1942

A machine manufactured in Canada and operated in the torpedo-bomber role, this aeroplane flew anti-ship operations over the northern North Sea and Norwegian Sea in Coastal Command's standard finish of sea-grey upper surfaces and sky-blue under surfaces.

Coastal Command
1942–43

Improvements in aircraft, weapons, electronics and tactics implemented in 1942 made Coastal Command increasingly capable in 1943, and with the advent of the escort carrier to work in the central Atlantic 'black hole' the U-boat was harried day and night right across the Atlantic.

THE ADVENT of the de Havilland Mosquito freed the Bristol Beaufighter for service with Coastal Command, in which the type became a highly useful short-range type using rocket and depth charge armament against German U-boats in the Bay of Biscay. The Beaufighter was also used in attacks on German surface vessels, including the formidable flak vessels used as escorts.

But of greater significance to Coastal Command was the entry to service, to supplement the Short Sunderland flying boat, of the Consolidated Liberator landplane in the very-long-range role. Bomber Command pressure meant that it was 1942 before even a few dozen Liberators were released, and much later still before a single squadron could be allocated to Gander, in Newfoundland, to reach the critical central Atlantic region and allow Coastal Command to cover all the North Atlantic zones. In the middle

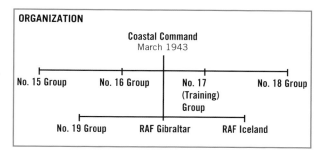

ORGANIZATION

Coastal Command
March 1943

No. 15 Group	No. 16 Group	No. 17 (Training) Group	No. 18 Group

No. 19 Group	RAF Gibraltar	RAF Iceland

of 1942, 45 Boeing B-17Es were transferred to the RAF, by which they were designated Fortress Mk IIs. Probably as a result of the limitations of the Fortress Mk I (B-17C), the RAF decided not to use the Fortress Mk II in its intended high-altitude day bomber role, but to allocate them to Coastal Command for long-range maritime reconnaissance and anti-submarine work.

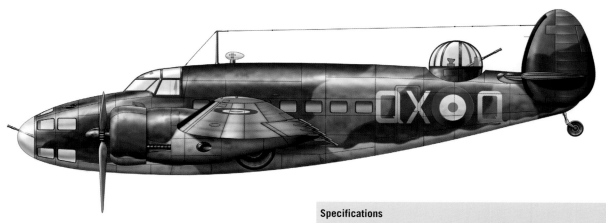

▲ Lockheed Hudson GR.Mk III

No. 233 Squadron / RAF Coastal Command, Aldergrove and St Eval, 1942
Developed from an American civil transport (the Lockheed Model 14) to meet a British requirement for a successor to the Avro Anson, the Hudson proved notably successful in the shorter-range coastal and maritime reconnaissance roles.

Specifications

Crew: 6

Powerplant: 2 x 890kW (1200hp) Wright Cyclone 9-cylinder radial engines

Maximum speed: 397km/h (246mph)

Range: 3150km (1960 miles)

Service ceiling: 7470m (24,500ft)

Dimensions: span 19.96m (65ft 4in);

length 13.50m (44ft 4in);

height 3.62m (11ft 10in)

Weight: 7930kg (17,500lb) loaded

Armament: 7 x 7.7mm (0.303in) Browning MGs (two in nose, two in dorsal turret, two in beam and one ventral); 340kg (750lb) of bombs or depth charges

COASTAL COMMAND, NO. 18 GROUP (JULY 1942)		
Unit	Type	Base
No. 42 Sqn	Beaufort	Leuchars
No. 48 Sqn	Hudson	Wick
No. 86 Sqn	Beaufort	Wick
No. 144 Sqn	Hampden	Leuchars
No. 210 Sqn	Catalina	Sullom Voe
No. 248 Sqn	Beaufighter	Sumburgh
No. 254 Sqn	Hurricane	Dyce
No. 404 Sqn, RCAF	Blenheim	Dyce
No. 455 Sqn, RAAF	Hampden	Leuchars
No. 608 Sqn	Hudson	Wick

By the start of 1943, the improvement in aircraft and tactics, combined with the debut of electronic aids such as centimetric radar and radio direction finding, resulted in a huge improvement in Coastal Command's efficiency: shipping losses fell and U-boat sinkings rose.

However, it was not so much in sinking as steady harassment of the boats that Coastal Command was so effective, for U-boats could no approach their targets by day. This meant that many more convoys remained unmolested.

Specifications

Crew: 7–10

Powerplant: 4 x 895kW (1200hp) Twin Wasp R
14 cylinder radial engines

Maximum speed: 467km/h (290mph)

Range: 3540km (2200 miles)

Service ceiling: 85,340m (28,000ft)

Dimensions: span 33.5m (110ft);

length 20.47m (67ft 2in);

height 5.94m (18ft)

Weight: 29,484kg (65,000lb) loaded

Armament: 10 x 12.7mm (0.5in) Browning MGs
in four turrets and two waist gun positions;
two bomb bays for up to 3629kg (8000lbs)
of bombs

▲ Consolidated Liberator GR.Mk V

No. 224 Squadron / RAF Coastal Command, St Eval, November 1942

Finished in sea-grey and white, with standard national markings and grey serials and squadron codes, this Liberator GR.Mk V has the later type of air-to-surface radar with its antenna in a chin radome.

Specifications

Crew: 8

Powerplant: 4 x 894kW (1200hp) Wright
Cyclone air-cooled radial piston engines

Maximum speed: 480km/h (298mph)

Range: 1835km (1140 miles)

Service ceiling: 10,363m (34,000ft)

Dimensions: span 31.62m (103ft 9in);

length 22.5m (73ft 10in);

height 5.84m (19ft 2in)

Weight: 12,542kg (27,650lb) loaded

Armament: 10 x 12.7mm (0.5in) MGs in nose,
dorsal, ventral, tail and beam; normal bomb
load of up to 2722kg (6000lb) of bombs and/
or depth charges

▲ Boeing Fortress Mk IIA

No. 220 Squadron / RAF Coastal Command, Ballykelly, Northern Ireland, late 1942

A development of the USAAF's B-17F Flying Fortress heavy bomber for British service, the Fortress Mk II was deemed unsuitable for RAF Bomber Command and passed to RAF Coastal Command for the very-long-range maritime role.

▲ Lockheed Hudson GR.Mk VI

RAF Coastal Command, UK, late 1942

During August 1941, RAF Coastal Command introduced a revised colour scheme for its aircraft: the upper surfaces remained dark green and ocean grey, but the undersurfaces were gloss white and the vertical surface matt white.

Specifications

Crew: 5

Powerplant: 2 x 895kW (1200hp) Pratt & Whitney Twin Wasp radial piston engines

Maximum speed: 420km/h (261mph)

Range: 3476km (2160 miles)

Service ceiling: 8230m (27,000ft)

Dimensions: span 19.96m (65ft 6in); length 13.51m (44ft 4in);

height 3.63m (11ft 11in)

Weight: 8391kg (18,500lb) loaded

Armament: 2 x 7.7mm (0.303in) MGs in fixed forward and dorsal turret; 1 x 7.7mm (0.303in) MG in ventral position,; option of 2 x 7.7mm (0.303in) MGs in beam positions; up to 454kg (1000lb) of bombs or underwing rockets

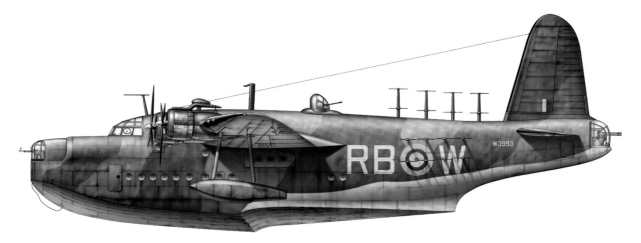

Specifications

Crew: 8-11

Powerplant: 4 x 794kW (1066hp) Bristol Pegasus XVII 9-cylinder radial piston engines

Maximum speed: 341km/h (212mph)

Range: 4828km (3000 miles)

Service ceiling: 4567m (15,000ft)

Dimensions: span 34.39m (112ft 10in); length 26.01m (85ft 4in); height 9.79m (32ft 2in)

Weight: 26,308kg (58,0000lb) loaded

Armament: 1 x 7.7mm (0.303in) Vickers GO MG in nose turret; 2 x 7.7mm (0.303in) Browning MGs in mid upper turret; 4 x Browning MGs in tail turret; optional second nose turret gun; 4 x fixed Browning MGs firing ahead; 2 x 12.7mm (0.5in) Browning MGs firing ahead; 2 x 12.7mm (0.5in) Browning MGs firing from waist hatches; assorted ordnance up to 2250kg (4960lb)

▲ Short Sunderland GR.Mk II

No. 10 Squadron / Royal Australian Air Force / RAF Coastal Command, Mount Batten, April 1942

The primary difference between the Sunderland GR.Mk I and II was the replacement of the former's pair of manually operated 7.7mm (0.303in) Vickers K beam guns by two 7.7mm (0.303in) Browning machine guns in a power-operated dorsal turret. The ammunition supply for the four-gun tail turret was also doubled to 1000 rounds per gun.

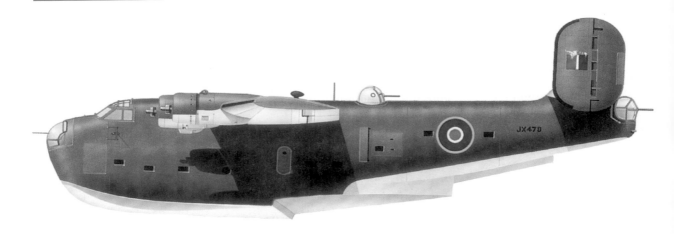

Specifications

Crew: 9

Powerplant: 4 x 895kW (1200hp) Pratt &
  Whitney Twin Wasp radial piston engines

Maximum speed: 359km/h (223mph)

Range: 3814km (2370 miles)

Service ceiling: 6250m (20,500ft)

Dimensions: span 35.05m (115ft); length

24.16m (79ft 3in); height 8.38m (27ft 6in)

Weight: 30,844kg (68,000lb) loaded

Armament: 2 x 12.7mm (0.5in) MGs in bow,
  dorsal and tail turrets, and 1 x 12.7mm
  (0.5in) machine gun in two beam positions;
  up to 5443kg (12,000lb) of bombs, depth
  charges or torpedoes

▲ Consolidated Coronado GR.Mk I

RAF Coastal Command, Beaumaris, 1943

The RAF received 10 examples of the Coronado flying boat but, finding the type unsuitable for the long-range reconnaissance/anti-submarine role, passed the aircraft to No. 231 Squadron of No. 45 Group, based at Boucherville, Toronto, Canada, as transports with accommodation for VIPs and 44 other passengers.

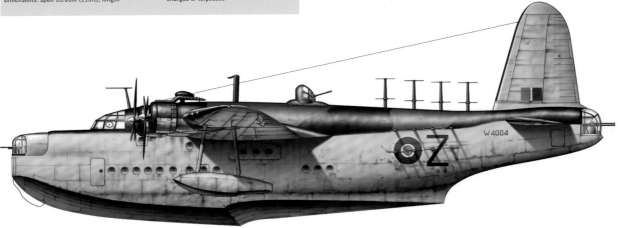

▲ Short Sunderland GR.Mk III

RAF Coastal Command, UK, 1943

Evident on the rear fuselage are the antennae associated with the ASV.Mk II air-to-surface search radar, comprising vertical dipole masts (four above the fuselage) and 16 transmitting loops (eight on each side of the fuselage).

Specifications

Crew: 8–11

Powerplant: 4 x 794kW (1066hp) Bristol
  Pegasus XVII 9-cylinder radial piston engines

Maximum speed: 341km/h (212mph)

Range: 4828km (3000 miles)

Service ceiling: 4567m (15,000ft)

Dimensions: span 34.39m (112ft 10in); length
  26.01m (85ft 4in); height 9.79m (32ft 2in)

Weight: 26,308kg (58,0000lb) loaded

Armament: 1 x 7.7mm (0.303in) Vickers GO MG
  in nose turret; 2 x 7.7mm (0.303in) Browning
  MGs in mid upper turret; 4 x Browning MGs in
  tail turret; optional second nose turret
  gun; 4 x fixed Browning MGs firing ahead,
  2 x 12.7mm (0.5in) Browning MGs firing
  ahead and twin 12.7mm (0.5in) Browning
  MGs firing from waist hatches; assorted
  ordnance up to 2250kg (4960lb)

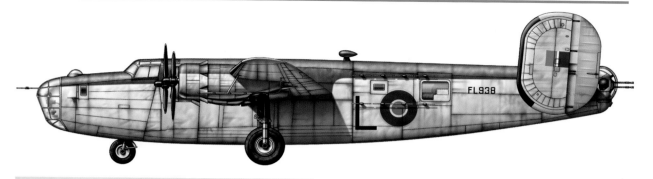

Specifications

Crew: 10

Powerplant: 4 x 895kW (1200hp) Pratt &
  Whitney Twin wasp radial piston engines

Maximum speed: 488km/h (303mph)

Range: 1730km (1080 miles)

Service ceiling: 8540m (28,000ft)

Dimensions: span 33.53m (110ft);

length 20.22m (66ft 4in);
  height 5.49m (18ft)

Weight: 32,296kg (71,200lb) loaded

Armament: 1 x 12.7mm (0.5in) MG in nose,
  2 x 12.7mm (0.5in) MG in beam position,
  4 x 7.6mm (0.303in) MGs in rear turret; also
  5 x 120kg (250lb) depth charges

▲ **Consolidated Liberator GR.Mk V**

RAF Coastal Command, UK, 1943

A maritime reconnaissance version of the USAAF's B-24G heavy bomber, the Liberator GR.Mk V was used on the very-long-range role, and some of the aircraft were later fitted with the Leigh Light installation below the wing for nocturnal location and attack of submarines.

Zones of responsibility
1941–45

The Coastal Command of the period late in World War II was hardly recognizable as the linear descendant of the Coastal Command of 1939. It had expanded enormously in size and overall capabilities, and its advanced aircraft were the dread of every surviving U-boat crew.

DURING THE COURSE of World War II, Coastal Command controlled many subordinate formations. In September 1939, it comprised four groups, of which No. 17 Group was responsible only for the training of Coastal Command aircrews. The other three groups were each allocated the responsibility for coastal operations off a particular part of the British coast: No. 16 Group was responsible for the eastern half of the English Channel and the southern half of the North Sea; No. 18 Group covered the remainder of the North Sea and areas around Scotland, north of a line running north west from the Mull of Kintyre; and No. 15 Group covered the rest of the UK's coast.

New group

In February 1941, the system was changed to allow the introduction of No. 19 Group, the dividing line between Nos 18 and 15 Groups being moved north

COASTAL COMMAND, NO. 16 GROUP (JUNE 1944)		
Unit	Type	Base
No. 143 Sqn	Beaufighter	Manston
No. 236 Sqn	Beaufighter	North Coates
No. 254 Sqn	Beaufighter	North Coates
No. 279 Sqn	Hudson	Strubby
No. 280 Sqn	Warwick	Strubby & Thornaby
No. 415 Sqn, RCAF	Wellington	Bircham Newton
No. 455 Sqn, RAAF	Beaufighter	Langham
No. 489, RNZAF	Beaufighter	Langham
No. 521 Sqn	Ventura & Gladiator	Docking
No. 819 Sqn, FAA	Swordfish	Manston
No. 848 Sqn, FAA	Avenger	Manston
No. 854 Sqn, FAA	Avenger	Hawkinge
No. 855 Sqn, FAA	Avenger	Hawkinge

to a position north-west from Cape Wrath, No. 19 Group then receiving responsibility for the southern part of the area previously allocated to No. 15 Group. In the Irish Sea, No. 19 Group's extended south of a line in about the middle of Cardigan Bay and, in the eastern Atlantic, slightly north of that line.

Coastal Command began to spread its wings further afield with the absorption of elements operating outside the UK. As early as November 1940, the Gibraltar-based No. 200 Group was absorbed into Coastal Command after having been a component of the RAF Mediterranean. The group's squadrons passed temporarily to the operational command of the Allied Forces Headquarters for the November 1942 Allied landing in French northwest, but otherwise remained under Coastal Command control for the rest of the war. No. 200 Group became RAF Gibraltar within Coastal Command during December 1941.

Iceland occupied

RAF units also arrived as British forces occupied Iceland, and given that Iceland's most important air use was as a base for maritime operations, Coastal Command was the lead command organization for what started as No. 30 Wing, but became RAF Iceland in July 1941. Coastal Command reached its maximum extent in mid-1943 after Portugal had granted the UK basing rights in the Azores Islands, which became the home of No. 247 Group, which was entrusted with the task of flying anti-submarine missions over the Atlantic.

In the later stages of World War II, Coastal Command's primary assets in the 'bomber', or long-range anti-submarine, role were the Consolidated Catalina and Short Sunderland flying boats, and the Consolidated Liberator and the Vickers Wellington and Warwick landplanes, all in later variants with more capable electronics and weapons.

The crews of these and other aircraft established close and effective links with the FAA's squadrons operating from escort carriers, especially in the mid-Atlantic area.

COASTAL COMMAND, NO. 19 GROUP (JUNE 1944)		
Unit	Type	Base
No. 10 Sqn, RAAF	Sunderland	Mount Batten
No. 53 Sqn	Liberator	St Eval
No. 58 Sqn	Halifax	St Davids
No. 144 Sqn	Beaufighter	Davidstowe Moor
No. 172 Sqn	Wellington	Davidstowe Moor & Chivenor
No. 179 Sqn	Wellington	Predannack
No. 201 Sqn	Sunderland	Pembroke Dock
No. 206 Sqn	Liberator	St Eval
No. 224 Sqn	Liberator	St Eval
No. 228 Sqn	Sunderland	Pembroke Dock
No. 235 Sqn	Beaufighter	Portreath
No. 248 Sqn	Beaufighter	Portreath
No. 282 Sqn	Warwick	Davidstowe Moor
No. 304 Sqn (Pol)	Wellington	Chivenor
No. 311 Sqn (Cz)	Liberator	Predannack
No. 404 Sqn, RCAF	Beaufighter	Davidstowe Moor
No. 407 Sqn, RCAF	Wellington	Chivenor
No. 415 Sqn, RCAF	Albacore	Winkleigh
No. 461 Sqn, RAAF	Sunderland	Pembroke Dock
No. 502 Sqn	Halifax	St Davids
No. 517 Sqn	Halifax	Brawdy
No. 524 Sqn	Wellington	Davidstowe Moor
No. 541 Sqn	Spitfire	St Eval
No. 547 Sqn	Liberator	St Eval
No. 612 Sqn	Wellington	Chivenor
No. 616 Sqn, FAA	Swordfish	Perranporth
No. 838 Sqn, FAA	Swordfish	Harrowbeer
No. 849 Sqn, FAA	Avenger	Perranporth
No. 850 Sqn, FAA	Avenger	Perranporth

COASTAL COMMAND, NO. 18 GROUP (JUNE 1944)		
Unit	Type	Base
No. 86 Sqn	Liberator	Tain
No. 210 Sqn	Catalina	Sullom Voe
No. 281 Sqn	Warwick	Sumburgh, Wick & Leuchars
No. 330 Sqn (Nor)	Sunderland	Sullom Voe
No. 333 Sqn (Nor)	Catalina & Mosquito	Woodhaven, Sumburgh & Leuchars
No. 519 Sqn	Ventura & Spitfire	Skitten
No. 544 Sqn	Mosquito	Leuchars
No. 618 Sqn	Mosquito	Turnberry

▲ Short Sunderland GR. Mk III

RAF Coastal Command, UK, 1943

This was a Blackburn-built aeroplane. The offensive armament was four 227kg (500lb) or eight 113kg (250lb) bombs carried on racks in the upper part of the fuselage below the wing. In combat the racks were winched out through windowed hatches in the sides of the fuselage to positions inboard of the inner engines.

Specifications

Crew: 8–11

Powerplant: 4 x 794kW (1066hp) Bristol
Pegasus XVII 9-cylinder radial piston engines

Maximum speed: 341km/h (212mph)

Range: 4828km (3000 miles)

Service ceiling: 4567m (15,000ft)

Dimensions: span 34.39m (112ft 10in); length
26.01m (85ft 4in); height 9.79m (32ft 2in)

Weight: 26,308kg (58,0000lb) loaded

Armament: 1 x 7.7mm (0.303in) Vickers GO MG
in nose turret; 2 x 7.7mm (0.303in) Browning
MGs in mid upper turret; 4 x Browning MGs in
tail turret; optional second nose turret
gun; 4 x fixed Browning MGs firing ahead,
2 x 12.7mm (0.5in) Browning MGs firing
ahead and twin 12.7mm (0.5in) Browning
MGs firing from waist hatches; assorted
ordnance up to 2250kg (4960lb)

▲ Vickers Wellington GR.Mk XIV

No. 304 (Polish) Squadron / RAF Coastal Command, Chivenor, late 1944

Operated over the English Channel and eastern part of the Atlantic Ocean, this aeroplane has ASV.Mk III radar (with its antenna in the chin radome), and a Leigh Light installation in an retractable installation that could be lowered from its location in the fuselage just to the rear of the weapons bay.

Specifications

Crew: 5

Powerplant: 2 x 1294kW (1735hp) Hercules
XVII engines

Maximum speed: 402km/h (250mph)

Range: 2816km (1750 miles)

Service ceiling: 4875m (16,0000ft)

Dimensions: span 26.26m (0ft 0in);
length 19.68m (64ft 7in);
height 5.31m (17ft 5in)

Weight: 14,062kg√(31,000lb) loaded

Armament: 2 x 7.7mm (0.303in) Browning
trainable forward-firing MGs in a power-
operated Frazer-Nash F.N.7A nose turret;
2 x 7.7mm (0.303in) Browning trainable
rearward-firing in a power-operated Frazer-
Nash F.N.7A tail turret; 9 x 227kg (500lb)
or 113kg (250lb) bombs, or 2 or 4 x 191kg
(420lb) depth charges, or 2 x torpedoes

In World War II, Coastal Command flew more than 240,000 sorties, sank 212 U-boats and caused the loss of 485,648 tonnes (478,000 tons) of enemy shipping. In exchange, it lost a total of 1777 aircraft and, according to various sources, between 5865 and 10,875 men killed in action, the lower figure possibly not including Commonwealth and Allied aircrew, and men missing and only later declared dead.

Victory in sight
1943–45

Enlarged, equipped with modern aircraft and drawing on the experience of several years of hard operations, Coastal Command's flying boats and landplanes proved the scourge of Germany's U-boat arm and coastal shipping in the later years of the war.

THE STEADILY GROWING capability of Coastal Command started to become evident in August 1942 as the command at last felt itself in a position to divert some of its assets from the UK to points such as northern Russia, which for a time became home to one squadron of Consolidated Catalina twin-engined flying boats and two squadrons of Handley Page Hampden twin-engined torpedo-bombers. These aided the efforts of the Royal Navy in the extremely

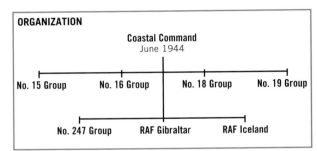

ORGANIZATION

Coastal Command
June 1944

No. 15 Group — No. 16 Group — No. 18 Group — No. 19 Group

No. 247 Group — RAF Gibraltar — RAF Iceland

▲ **Short Sunderland GR. Mk III**

No. 330 (Norwegian) Squadron / RAF Coastal Command, Sullom Voe, Shetland, late 1944

This Norwegian-manned unit was formed in Iceland in April 1941, and transferred to the Norwegian Air Force shortly before it was disbanded in November 1945. The squadron flew several types of aircraft, of which the last was the Sunderland.

Specifications

Crew: 8–11

Powerplant: 4 x 794kW (1066hp) Bristol Pegasus XVII 9-cylinder radial piston engines

Maximum speed: 341km/h (212mph)

Range: 4828km (3000 miles)

Service ceiling: 4567m (15,000ft)

Dimensions: span 34.39m (112ft 10in); length 26.01m (85ft 4in); height 9.79m (32ft 2in)

Weight: 26,308kg (58,0000lb) loaded

Armament: 1 x 7.7mm (0.303in) Vickers GO MG in nose turret; 2 x 7.7mm (0.303in) Browning MGs in mid upper turret; 4 x Browning MGs in tail turret; optional second nose turret gun; 4 x fixed Browning MGs firing ahead, 2 x 12.7mm (0.5in) Browning MGs firing ahead and twin 12.7mm (0.5in) Browning MGs firing from waist hatches; assorted ordnance up to 2250kg (4960lb)

difficult task of getting supply-laden convoys through Arctic waters and past the attentions of German warplanes, warships and U-boats to reach Murmansk and Archangel. It was an almost impossible task, and the convoys were suspended from September, being resumed only in the dark of the period between December 1942 and spring 1943, and the same period in 1943–44. Closer to home, Coastal Command's attack aircraft were taking the war ever more capably and effectively to German coastal shipping and installations, but the decisive theatre remained the convoy routes across the Atlantic.

The advent of longer-range aircraft with more effective equipment, such as a larger number of Sunderland and Catalina flying boats, complemented by land-based aircraft such as the twin-engined Vickers Wellington, had driven the U-boats deeper into the Atlantic for their operations, but the boats were harried to and from their operational areas by shorter-range aircraft to the extent that they had to operate under the water even during their transits, thus increasing their losses and reducing the time they could remain on station. Then the advent of

still longer-ranged aircraft, such as the four-engined Boeing Fortress and Consolidated Liberator, further strengthened Coastal Command and weakened the U-boat arm.

The Germans initially tried to fight it out by installing ever stronger light flak armament on their boats, but Coastal Command responded by the addition of fixed forward-firing batteries of cannon or machine guns to kill the flak gunners. They also added centrimetric radar, which the Germans could not initially detect, to close the range at low level until the U-boat crews, on seeing the oncoming aeroplane, had too little time to submerge their boats before the attack was upon them.

U-boat responses

The Germans then had recourse to expedients, such as the fitting of snorkels to allow extended underwater running, but while this enhanced survivability it further degraded the time the boats could spend on station in the central Atlantic.

Here, too, they were increasingly threatened as the Allies introduced larger numbers of small

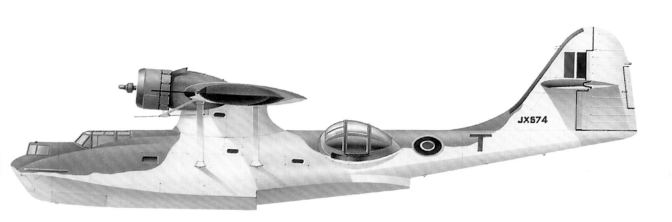

▲ Consolidated Catalina Mk IVA

No. 210 Squadron / RAF Coastal Command, Sullom Voe, Shetland, 1944

No. 210 Squadron operated the Catalina flying boat from April 1941 to the end of World War II, and is credited with the sinking of eight U-boats. This Catalina Mk IVa carries air-to-surface search radar with its antenna under the port wing, and a Leigh Light nocturnal illumination device in a pod under the starboard wing.

Specifications

Crew: 8/9

Powerplant: 895kW (1200hp) Pratt & Whitney radial piston engines

Maximum speed: 306km/h (190mph)

Range: 6437km (4000 miles)

Service ceiling: 7315m (24,000ft)

Dimensions: span 31.7m (104ft); length

19.86m (65ft 2in); height 5.46m (17ft 11in)

Weight: 12,283kg (27,038lb) loaded

Armament: 1 x 7.7mm (0.303in) MG in bow and 2 x 7.7mm (0.303in) MGs in each side blister and in ventral position; up to 907kg (2000lb) of bombs or depth charges.

and comparatively cheap escort carriers carrying specialized anti-submarine aircraft and a few fighters. Despite the dedication of the U-boat crews, the introduction of advanced torpedoes, and the final debut of a new generation of submarines capable of far higher sustained underwater speeds, the tide of battle swayed against the U-boats from mid-1943.

There were still months when the relative fortunes of the two sides moved, but Coastal Command nonetheless had the technical edge over its adversary and, in combination with larger numbers of more effective aircraft, was able finally to crush the real threat which had been posed by the previously dominant U-boats.

▲ Consolidated Liberator GR.Mk VI

No. 547 Squadron / RAF Coastal Command, Leuchars, Fife, 1944–45

Carrying radar and a retractable Leigh Light, and fitted with six 12.7mm (0.5in) machine guns in three power-operated turrets, the Liberator GR.Mk VI had an anti-submarine endurance of 12 hours 30 minutes with a 907kg (2000lb) load of depth charges.

Specifications

Crew: 8

Powerplant: 4 x 895kW (1200hp) Pratt & Whitney Twin Wasp radial piston engines

Maximum speed: 435km/h (270mph)

Range: 2366km (1470 miles)

Service ceiling: 8534m (28,000ft)

Dimensions: span 17.63m (57ft 10in); length 12.7m (41ft 8in);

height 4.83m (15ft 10in)

Weight: 11,431kg (25,200lb) loaded

Armament: 4 x 20mm (0.79in) forward-firing cannon; 6 x 7.7mm (0.303in) forward-firing MGs and 1 x 7.7mm (0.303in) Vickers K MG in dorsal position; 1 x torpedo and 2 x 113kg (250lb) bombs or 8 x 41kg (90lb) rocket projectiles

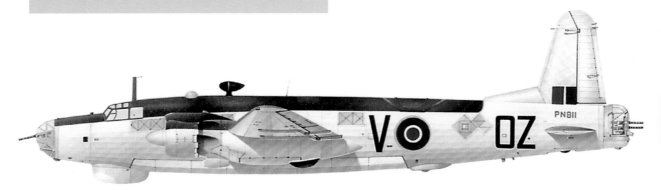

▲ Vickers Warwick GR.Mk V

No. 179 Squadron / RAF Coastal Command, Benbecula and St Eval, 1944–45

No. 179 Squadron, which had flown the Vickers Wellington up to that time, in November 1944 became the first unit to receive the Warwick GR.Mk V. The variant had a modified nose with the antenna for the air-to-surface search in a radome below it, and also carried a retractable Leigh Light installation in the lower fuselage to the rear of the bomb bay.

Specifications

Crew: 7

Powerplant: 2 x 1864kW (2500hp) Bristol Centaurus VI radial piston engines

Maximum speed: 422km/h (262mph)

Range: 4908km (5791 miles)

Service ceiling: 5791m (19,000ft)

Dimensions: span 29.49m (96ft 9in);

length 20.88m (68ft 6in);

height 5.64m (18ft 6in)

Weight: 23,247kg (51,250lb) loaded

Armament: 6 x 7.7mm (0.303in) machine guns (one each in nose, dorsal turrets, four in tail turret); up to 5557kg (12,250lb) of bombs

Specifications

Crew: 7/8

Powerplant: 4 x 1089kW (1460hp) Packard
(Rolls-Royce) Merlin piston engines

Maximum speed: 452km/h (281mph)

Range: 4313km (2680 miles)

Service ceiling: 7460m (24,500ft)

Dimensions: span 31.09m (102ft);
length 20.98m (68ft 10in);
height 6.19m (20ft 4in)

Weight: 18,598kg (41,000lb) loaded

Armament: 8 x 7.7mm (0.303in) MGs; up to
6350kg (14,000lb) bombs

 Avro Lancaster GR.Mk III

School of Maritime Reconnaissance / RAF Coastal Command, St Mawgan,
1945

This aeroplane was not withdrawn from service until October 1956; up to that
time it had been the last operational Lancaster remaining in RAF service.

Fleet Air Arm
1939–45

**From very humble beginnings in 1939, when its carrierborne aircraft operated from just six
ships, the Fleet Air Arm grew enormously in size and capability through World War II, and by
August 1945 flew some 3700 aircraft from shore bases and operated no fewer than 59 carriers.**

THE ROYAL NAVAL AIR SERVICE, which had been
established in 1914 as the Royal Navy's own air
arm, lost its independence in April 1918 when it was
merged with its British Army equivalent, the Royal
Flying Corps, to create the Royal Air Force.

This was the world's first independent air force,
and as such controlled the air units and their
equipment allocated to shore bases and Royal Navy
warships, on which they came under operational
control of the ships' captains. Through the 1920s
and 1930s this became a patently inadequate system,
and in 1937 the Naval Air Branch was returned to
Admiralty control and was soon renamed as the Fleet
Air Arm (FAA).

Carrier force
At the start of World War II, the Royal Navy had six
aircraft carriers with another six being built, and the
FAA comprised just 20 squadrons with a mere 232

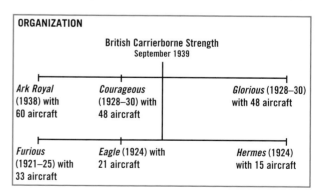

ORGANIZATION

British Carrierborne Strength
September 1939

Ark Royal
(1938) with
60 aircraft

Courageous
(1928–30) with
48 aircraft

Glorious (1928–30)
with 48 aircraft

Furious
(1921–25) with
33 aircraft

Eagle (1924) with
21 aircraft

Hermes (1924)
with 15 aircraft

almost universally obsolete aircraft. By the end of the
war, the strength of the Royal Navy and FAA had
grown to 59 aircraft carriers, 3700 aircraft, 72,000
officers and men, and 56 air stations. The carrier had
replaced the battleship as the navy's capital ship, and
carrierborne aircraft were now decisive offensive and
defensive weapons of naval warfare.

◄ Diving Swordfish

The Fairey Swordfish's primary weapon was a single 730kg (1610lb) torpedo slung beneath the fuselage. Although slow and unmanoeuvrable, the biplane proved very stable during the crucial torpedo run.

The loss of the Courageous in the war's first few weeks highlighted the vulnerability of the carrier when working independently, a factor confirmed by the loss of the Glorious in June 1940. Tactics and weapons were improved, and carriers now operated at the heart of destroyer, cruiser and even battleship escort. The role of the carrier became ever more important as aircraft started to mature as one of the decisive weapons in defeating the U-boat,

surface warships and aircraft. The U-boat threat was a particular concern, as it threatened to sever the maritime supply of materiel across the Atlantic on which the UK so relied.

The same threat faced British transport and supply convoys operating in the Mediterranean and Arctic. The fall of France in June 1940 gave the Germans bases from which their attackers could roam further out into the Atlantic with aircraft as well as warships and U-boats. Only a few ships currently possessed adequate anti-aircraft weapons, and the optimum manner of beating the air threat was the fighter, but

FAA SQUADRONS WITH BLACKBURN SKUA AIRCRAFT (1939)		
Unit	Type	Base
No. 800 Sqn	Skua	Ark Royal
No. 801 Sqn	Skua	Ark Royal & Furious
No. 803 Sqn	Skua	Ark Royal
No. 806 Sqn	Skua	Eastleigh

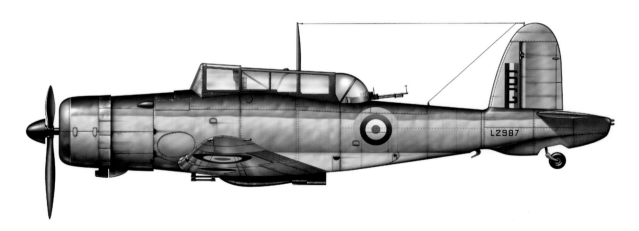

▲ Blackburn Skua Mk II

No. 5 Maintenance Unit, Kemble, 1939

The Skua Mk II was the production variant of the Skua Mk I prototype. Through designed as a carrierborne dive-bomber, the Skua doubled as a naval fighter, but was ineffective in each role and withdrawn from first-line service in 1941.

Specifications

Crew: 2

Powerplant: 664kW (890hp) Bristol Perseus
XII radial engine

Maximum speed: 362km/h (225mph)

Range: 1223km (760 miles)

Service ceiling: 6160m (20,200ft)

Dimensions: span 14.07m (46ft 2in);
length 10.85m (35ft 7in);
height 3.81m (12ft 6in)

Weight: 3732kg (8228lb) loaded

Armament: 4 x 7.7mm (0.303in) MGs in wings;
Lewis rear gun; 1 x 227kg (500lb) bomb
beneath fusilage

there were no carriers available. An interim measure was the Catapult Aircraft Merchant (CAM) ship with a catapult-launched fighter, which had to ditch at the end of its flight. In the event, only 35 CAM ships conversions were completed.

In 1942, there was an urgent demand for a small carrier that could be created swiftly and cheaply as a convoy escort type, and the Admiralty looked to conversions of merchant vessels with their cargo capacities left unaffected.

This became the Merchant Aircraft Carrier (MAC), which by mid-1943 was serving in the Atlantic with aircraft parked on their exposed flightdecks. The MAC ships helped turn the tide against the U-boats, and also paved the way for escort carriers with limited hangar volumes.

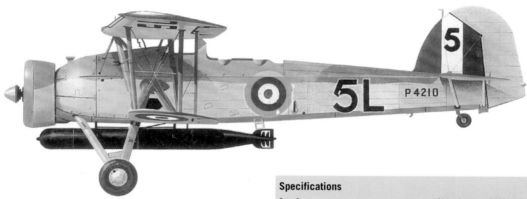

▲ Fairey Swordfish Mk I

No. 820 Squadron / Fleet Air Arm, HMS Ark Royal, 1939

Though slow and not agile when carrying its external torpedo armament, the Swordfish Mk I was very sturdy and had a high level of carrier compatibility.

Specifications

Crew: 3
Powerplant: 1 x 559.3kW (750hp)
  Bristol Pegasus XXX radial piston engine
Maximum speed: 222km/h (138mph)
Range: 879km (546 miles)
Service ceiling: 5867m (19,250ft)

Dimensions: span 12.87m (45ft 6in); length
  10.87m (35ft 8in); height 3.76m (12ft 4in)
Weight: 3406kg (7510lb) loaded
Armament: 2 x 7.7mm (0.303in) MGs; load of
  1 x 457mm (18in) torpedo or 8 x 27.2kg
  (60lb) rocket projectiles

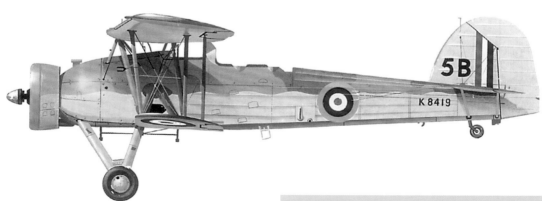

▲ Fairey Swordfish Mk I

No. 824 Squadron / Fleet Air Arm, HMS Eagle, 1939

This aeroplane is depicted in the standard camouflage and markings of the Fleet Air Arm for this period of the war.

Specifications

Crew: 3
Powerplant: 1 x 559.3kW (750hp)
  Bristol Pegasus XXX radial piston engine
Maximum speed: 222km/h (138mph)
Range: 879km (546 miles)
Service ceiling: 5867m (19,250ft)

Dimensions: span 12.87m (45ft 6in); length
  10.87m (35ft 8in); height 3.76m (12ft 4in)
Weight: 3406kg (7510lb) loaded
Armament: 2 x 7.7mm (0.303in) MGs; load of
  1 x 457mm (18in) torpedo or 8 x 27.2kg
  (60lb) rocket projectiles

▲ Fairey Albacore Mk I

No. 826 Squadron / Fleet Air Arm, 1941–43

A more modern iteration of the Swordfish's concept, the Albacore was not as successful. No. 826 Squadron flew convoy escorts from HMS Formidable between November 1940 and April 1941, and was then shore-based in North Africa.

Specifications	
Crew: 3	length 12.13m (39ft 9.5in);
Powerplant: 1 x 794kW (1065hp) Bristol Taurus	height 4.65m (15ft 3in)
II radial piston engine	Weight: 5715kg (12,600lb) loaded
Maximum speed: 259km/h (161mph)	Armament: 1 x 7.7mm (0.303in) Vickers MG
Range: 1320km (820 miles)	and 2 x 7.7mm (0.303in) Vickers K MGs in the
Service ceiling: 6309m (20,700ft)	rear cockpit; 1 x 457mm (18in) torpedo or up
Dimensions: span 15.24m (50ft);	to 907kg (2000lb) of bombs

Fleet Air Arm: operations
1941–45

From 1941, the Fleet Air Arm grew steadily in strength and capability to become a formidable force later in World War II. There were many more carriers, and also large numbers of advanced warplanes, most of them from the United States.

THROUGHOUT THE first part of the war, the FAA's primary strike warplane was the Fairey Swordfish, a technically obsolete biplane that nonetheless proved very successful. It outlasted its Fairey Albacore successor, and was much preferred to the Fairey Barracuda monoplane which, it was hoped, would finally replace the Swordfish.

Attack at Taranto

The Swordfish played a major role in slowing the German battleship Bismarck so that she could be caught and sunk in May 1941, but achieved its greatest single success in November 1940, when 21 Swordfishes launched from HMS Illustrious attacked the Italian fleet in Taranto, sinking one battleship and severely damaging another two as well as one cruiser.

The Swordfish remained in service to the end of the war, even though it was replaced by warplanes

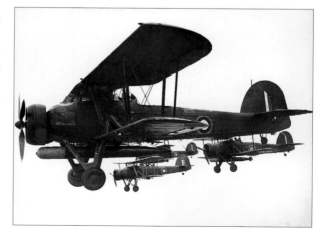

▲ Hunting Swordfish

With its slow speed and steady handling at low altitude, the Swordfish was an ideal platform for the carriage of air-launched torpedoes.

of US origin on larger carriers, for it could operate without difficulty from escort carriers and, armed with eight rockets under its lower wing, remained a potent threat to U-boats.

Torch landings

The FAA participated in all the significant European-theatre joint operations of World War II, including the Allied landings in northwest Africa, Sicily, Italy and Normandy, although in the last operation the FAA's contribution was only small as the invasion area could be covered by aircraft operating from the south of England.

During most of the landings, the FAA flew in tactical support of the troops, spotted for the heavy guns of the battleships, undertook general

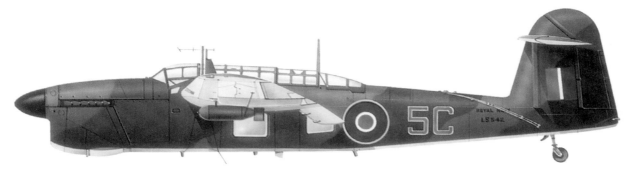

▲ Fairey Barracuda Mk II

No. 785 Squadron / Fleet Air Arm, Crail, 1943

No. 785 Squadron flew the Barracuda in the torpedo-bomber and reconnaissance training roles from April 1943 until after the end of World War II.

Specifications

Crew: 3

Powerplant: 1 x 1222.9kW (1640hp) Rolls-Royce Merlin 32 V-12 piston engine

Maximum speed: 367km/h (228mph)

Range: 1851km (1150 miles)

Service ceiling: 5060m (16,600ft)

Dimensions: span 14.99m (49ft 2in);

length 12.12m (39ft 9in);

height 4.6m (15ft 1in)

Weight: 6396kg (14,100lb) loaded

Armament: 2 x 7.7mm (0.3in) Vickers K MGs in the rear cockpit; 1 x 735kg (1620lb) torpedo, or 4 x 204kg (450lb) depth charges, or 6 x 113kg (250lb) of bombs

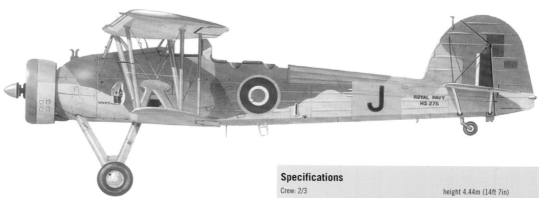

▲ Fairey Swordfish Mk II

No. 1 Naval Air Gunnery School, Yarmouth, Nova Scotia, Canada, 1943

Swordfish aircraft operating in Canada, such as this Swordfish Mk II, generally had the aeroplane's squadron code letter, painted in black on a yellow square, on the side of the rear fuselage.

Specifications

Crew: 2/3

Powerplant: 1 x 559kW (750hp) Bristol Pegasus XXX radial piston engine

Maximum speed: 128km/h (128mph)

Range: 1658km (1030 miles)

Service ceiling: 3260m (10,700ft)

Dimensions: span 13.87m (45ft 6in); length 12.34m (40ft 6in);

height 4.44m (14ft 7in)

Weight: 3679kg (8110lb) loaded

Armament: 1 x 7.7mm (0.303in) MG in forward fuselage; 1 x 7.7mm (0.303in) Lewis MG on Fairey mounting in aft cockpit; 1 x 730kg (1610lb) torpedo or depth charges, mines or bombs up to 680kg (1500lb), or up to 8 x rocket projectiles on underwing racks

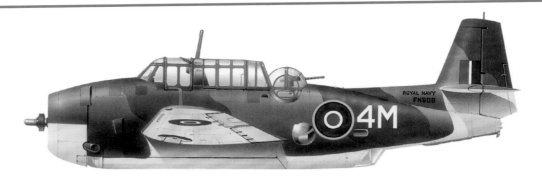

Specifications

Crew: 3

Powerplant: 1 x 1380kW (1850hp) Wright
  Cyclone radial piston engine

Maximum speed: 417km/h (259mph)

Range: 1642km (1020 miles)

Service ceiling: 7010m (23,000ft)

Dimensions: span 16.51m (54ft 2in);
  length 12.19m (40ft);

height 4.78m (15ft 8in)

Weight: 7394kg (16,300lb) loaded

Armament: 2 x 12.7mm (0.5) forward-firing
  MGs in wings, one similar weapon in dorsal
  turret and 1 x 7.62mm (0.3in) MG in ventral
  position; one 871kg (1921lb) torpedo or up to
  907kg (2000lb) of bombs

▲ Grumman Avenger Mk I

NO. 846 Squadron/ Fleet Air Arm, Macrihanish, 1943

The FAA's version of the US Navy's TBF-1B, the Avenger Mk I was flown in the carrierborne and shore-based roles. The British received 408 examples of this excellent torpedo bomber and anti-submarine aeroplane.

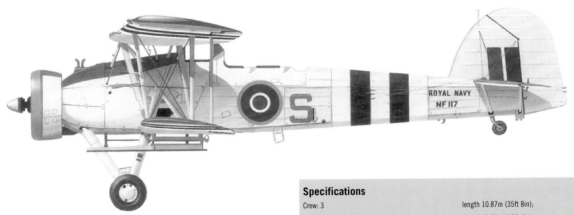

▲ Fairey Swordfish Mk II

No. 811 Squadron / Fleet Air Arm, HMS Biter, mid-1944

Despite its technical obsolescence, the Swordfish outlived the Albacore, created as its successor, and was still effective in a number of roles in 1944.

Specifications

Crew: 3

Powerplant: 559kW (750hp) Bristol Pegasus
  XXX radial piston engine

Maximum speed: 222km/h (138mph)

Range: 879km (546 miles)

Service ceiling: 5867m (19,250ft)

Dimensions: span 12.87m (45ft 6in);

length 10.87m (35ft 8in);
  height 3.76m (12ft 4in)

Weight: 3406kg (7510lb) loaded

Armament: 1 x 7.7mm (0.303in) fixed forward-
  firing MG; 1 x trainable 7.7mm (0.303in) MG
  in rear cockpit; 1 x 457mm (18in) torpedo or
  8 x 27.2kg (60lb) rocket projectiles

reconnaissance and provided fighter cover against potential attacks by Vichy aircraft.

Further afield, the carrierborne assets of the FAA was involved in the British capture of Madagascar from the Vichy French in the Indian Ocean, and the carriers of the British Pacific fleet, serving with the US Navy's Fast Carrier Task Force as Task Force 57, proved very useful in the later amphibious operations of the Pacific theatre, especially the bloody campaign that wrested Okinawa from the Japanese. Here the armoured flightdecks of the British carriers proved invulnerable to the attentions of kamikaze aircraft, unlike those of their US counterparts with unarmoured flightdecks.

▼ British Mediterranean Fleet carrier air wing, mid-1943

This is the air group embarked in the fleet carrier HMS Illustrious in the autumn of 1943, when she served in the Mediterranean Fleet for operations off Italy.

1 x fighter squadron Supermarine Seafire Mk IICs

2 x fighter squadrons Grumman Martlet Mk Vs

1 x fighter squadron Fairey Barracuda torpedo/divebombers

▲ Barracuda's take off

Fairey Barracuda's take-off from an unidentified aircraft carrier in the North Atlantic, probably preparing for the raid against the German battleship Tirpitz in 1944.

Chapter 8

United States

The established doctrine of the US armed forces
has long been to strike at an enemy's main concentrations
of strength as soon as possible and as directly as possible.
For the US Army, this meant the maximum effort to destroy
the enemy's ground forces by direct assault. For the US Army
Air Forces (USAAF), it meant tactical attacks on the enemy's
ground and sea forces, plus the lines of communication
nourishing them, and strategic attacks on the enemy's
sources and stocks of raw materials, war-making industries,
and both internal and external transport systems. The
USAAF became notably adept at both types of bombing
during World War II, in the Pacific as well as European
theatres, and also pioneered the use of nuclear weapons to
bring about the surrender of the Japanese in 1945.

◀ **Boeing B-17 Flying Fortress**
This B-17 has had its port tailplane hit by bombs dropped from other aircraft in its squadron, caught by
the camera over Europe, 1944.

US Eighth Army Air Force
1942–43

The US Eighth Army Air Force (AAF) reached England in the summer of 1942 as the US began to build up its military capability against Germany. Equipped with long-range heavy bombers, the Eighth AAF was to destroy key elements of German industry with precision daylight attacks.

THE HEADQUARTERS OF THE US Eighth AAF came into existence at Savannah, Georgia, on 28 January 1942, and the new air force's bomber formation, the VIII Bomber Command, was then established in England on 22 February 1942, initially at RAF Bomber Command's headquarters at High Wycombe. The Eighth AAF's other commands were the VIII Air Support Command and VIII Fighter Command. During World War II, the headquarters of the Eighth AAF were located at the Wycombe Abbey School for Girls, Buckinghamshire, and this air force was commanded successively by Major-General Carl A. Spaatz, Brigadier-General (soon Major-General) Ira C. Eaker, and Lieutenant-General 'Jimmy' Doolittle. Doolittle was the officer who had led the 'Doolittle raid' of April 1942, when USAAF North American B-25 Mitchell twin-

ORGANIZATION

Eighth Army Air Force
August 1942

| VIII Bomber Command | VIII Fighter Command | VIII Air Support Command |

engined medium bombers had taken off from a US Navy aircraft carrier to make the first air attacks on targets in Japan. The US Eighth AAF finally became the US Air Forces in Europe (USAFE).

First daylight sweep

On 4 July 1942, six crews from the US 15th Bombardment Group (Light), operating with six RAF crews, departed Swanton Morley, Norfolk, on

Specifications
Crew: 8–10
Powerplant: 4 x 895kW (1200hp) Wright turbo-
    supercharged engines
Maximum speed: 510km/h (317mph)
Range: 5150km (3200 miles)
Service ceiling: 10,973m (36,000ft)
Dimensions: span 31.6m (103ft 9in);

length 22.50m (73ft 10in);
height 6.3m (19ft 2in)
Weight: 23,133kg (51,000lb) loaded
Armament: 1 x 7.62mm (0.3in) MG in nose;
    2 x 12.7mm (0.5in) waist MGs; nose, ventral
    and tail turrets each with 2 x 12.7mm (0.5in)
    MGs; 1905kg (4200lb) of bombs

▲ **Boeing B-17E Flying Fortress**
414th Bomb Squadron / 97th Bomb Group / Eighth Army Air Force, Grafton Underwood, September 1942

This has an early pattern of national markings without lateral bars, and early camouflage based on medium-green and earth upper surfaces, and azure blue under surfaces. General Ira C. Eaker, commanding the Eighth AAF, flew in this aeroplane for the first US raid on German-occupied Europe on 17 August 1942.

Boeing B-17E Flying Fortress

The B-17E bore the brunt of the US Eighth AAF's early operations over northwest Europe. The first such aircraft arrived with 97th Bomber Group in July 1942.

VIII BOMBER COMMAND GROUPS (AUGUST 1942)			
Group	Squadrons	Base	Aircraft
92nd Bomb Group	325th, 326th, 327th, 407th BSs	Bovingdon	B-17E/F
301st Bomb Group	32nd, 352nd, 353rd, 419th BSs	Chelveston	B-17F

a daylight sweep against four German airfields in the Netherlands. This was the first occasion on which US airmen had flown in American-built bombers against a German target but, despite being a historical milestone, the raid was not wholly successful, two US-manned aircraft being shot down.

92nd Bomb Group

In August 1942, the 92nd and 301st Bomb Groups arrived to join the swiftly expanding Eighth AAF. The 92nd Bomb Group was the first heavy bombardment group to complete the non-stop deployment flight from Newfoundland to Scotland.

It took some time for the new groups to be made ready for combat, and training in many areas was woefully deficient. As internal argument continued about whether or not to stop the daylight bombing of strongly defended targets in Europe, and also whether or not the bomb loads and defensive armament of the Boeing B-17 Flying Fortress and Consolidated B-24 Liberator were adequate to their tasks, the first B-17 raid of the European war was scheduled for 17 August 1942.

Six B-17E bombers lifted off from Polebrook to undertake a diversionary raid on St Omer, while at Grafton Underwood Colonel Frank A. Armstrong, commanding the 97th Bomb Group, boarded Butcher Shop, piloted by Major Paul Tibbets, and led 11 B-17s to the marshalling yards at Rouen Sotteville in north-western France.

Spaatz had felt confident enough to allow Brigadier-General Eaker to join the crew of Yankee Doodle, lead aeroplane of the second flight of six. Over the Channel, the B-17s were joined by their escort of British Supermarine Spitfire Mk V fighters.

The US aircraft bombed from 7010m (23,000ft): a few bombs fell wide, but the majority landed in the assigned area. Several repair and maintenance workshops were badly damaged. From this very limited start, the Eighth AAF steadily increased the number of its combat groups and its range of targets. The Eighth AAF thus attacked naval targets in France, and worked with RAF Bomber Command for missions into Germany.

Specifications

Crew: 8–10

Powerplant: 4 x 895kW (1200hp) Wright turbo-
supercharged engines

Maximum speed: 510km/h (317mph)

Range: 5150km (3200 miles)

Service ceiling: 10,973m (36,000ft)

Dimensions: span 31.6m (103ft 9in);

length 22.5m (73ft 10in);

height 6.3m (19ft 2in)

Weight: 23,133kg (51,000lb) loaded

Armament: 1 x 7.62mm (0.3in) MG in nose;
2 x 12.7mm (0.5in) waist MGs; ventral and
tail turrets each with 2 x 12.7mm (0.5in)
MGs; 1905kg (4200lb) of bombs

▲ Boeing B-17E Flying Fortress

68th Bomb Goup / US Eighth Army Air Force, UK, autumn 1942

The B-17E introduced the definitive rear fuselage and redesigned vertical tail surfaces of the Flying Fortress family. There were twin 12.7mm (0.5in) machine guns in the dorsal and ventral turrets, and also in the tail position. The other positions carried single guns. Production totalled 512 aircraft.

▲ Consolidated B-24D bombers in flight

The first Liberator variant built in large numbers (2738 aircraft), the B-24D had a framed plexiglas nose without the power-operated turret introduced on the B-24G.

Target Germany
SUMMER 1942 – SPRING 1943

The US Eighth AAF cut its operational teeth with shorter-range missions against targets in occupied France, and encountered strengthening German opposition. From January 1943, the Americans switched their focus to north German targets, and initially met only limited defences.

IT HAD ENJOYED a relatively auspicious start, but by the winter of 1942–43 the US Eighth AAF seemed to be suffering from a measure of official neglect as North Africa and the Pacific took priority for aircraft and reinforcements.

The VIII Bomber Command started with raids against short-range targets in northern France, and from 20 October launched an offensive on the U-boat bases at Lorient, St Nazaire and La Rochelle in western France.

These efforts were escorted up to 65km (40 miles) inland by Supermarine Spitfire Mk VB fighters, but thereafter the bombers had to fight it out alone with the German fighters and radar-directed 88mm

▲ **Loading up**
US ground crew on an English air base prepare a bomb load for a B-17E Flying Fortress before a mission in October 1942.

VIII BOMBER COMMAND GROUPS (DECEMBER 1942)			
Group	Squadrons	Base	Aircraft
44th Bomb Group	66th, 67th, 68th, 506th BSs	Shipdham	B-24D
91st Bomb Group	322nd, 323rd, 324th, 401st BSs	Bassingbourn	B-17F
93rd Bomb Group	328th, 329th, 330th, 409th BSs	Alconbury, Hardwick	B-24D
303rd Bomb Group	358th, 359th, 360th, 427th BSs	Molesworth	B-17F
305th Bomb Group	364th, 365th, 366th, 422nd BSs	Grafton Underwood, Chelveston	B-17F
306th Bomb Group	367th, 368th, 369th, 423d BSs	Thurleigh	B-17F

▲ **Ball turret**

Installed in the ventral position on this B-17E, the ball turret carried two 12.7mm (0.5in) Browning machine guns for lower-hemisphere defence.

(3.465in) and 105mm (4.13in) flak artillery over the often heavily defended targets.

Early operations

At first the US losses were small, but the German fighter pilots were quickly beginning to get to grips with the tactics required for effective attacks on the well-armed US bombers, with special emphasis on high-speed head-on attacks. US losses thus rose from 3.7 per cent in November to 8.8 per cent in December 1942. The VIII Bomber Command was also affected by low aircraft strengths: of the 140 B-17F and B-24D machines on the establishment of the 91st, 93rd, 44th, 305th, 306th and 303rd Bomb Groups (Heavy), only about half were available.

This situation lasted to May 1943, and further degradation of strength resulted from the detachment of many of the 44th Bomb Group's Liberators and the posting of the 93rd Bomb Group to North Africa. At this time, the VIII Fighter Command comprised only the Debden-based 4th Fighter Group (334th, 335th and 336th Fighter Squadrons) with the Spitfire Mk VB. The 56th and 78th Fighter Groups were training in England with the new Republic P-47 Thunderbolt, but would not become available until April 1943.

Shipyard attack

On 27 January 1943, the VIII Bomber Command made its first raid on Germany. The primary target for the 91 B-17s and B-24s of the 91st, 303rd, 305th, 306th and 44th Bomb Groups was the Bremer-

Vulkan Vegesack shipyard, just to the north-west of Bremen, but adverse conditions persuaded the leader to divert to the alternate target, the Germania yard at Wilhelmshaven. Given the intensity of the German fighter reaction to their raids over France, the Americans were surprised by the limited response they encountered on this pioneering attack on Germany.

New armaments, new tactics

However, the increasing capability of German fighter attacks, in particular in head-on attacks, forced the VIII Bomber Command to react: by a time early in spring 1943, more armour was being carried in the B-17F and B-24D, and an additional pair of 12.7mm (0.5in) machine guns was installed around the plexiglas noses.

Since the winter of 1942–43, the tactics had also been changed, and the bombers now flew in tight combat boxes (basic 18/21-aircraft group formation made up of three-aircraft 'vics') with squadrons echeloned vertically to improve the dorsal and ventral turrets' fields of fire.

Already two or more groups were formatting in vertically spaced combat wings (up to 54 bombers), but numbers on operations at present precluded the extensive use of this formation. Thus the German fighters were receiving more concentrated fire as they attacked.

Over the next six weeks, the US VIII Bomber Command flew six missions over Germany: 524 aircraft were despatched, but as a result largely

▲ **Forward fire power**

This nose-on view of the B-17G shows the firepower the Flying Fortress could bring to bear in frontal defence, with two x 12.7mm (0.5in) Browning trainable machine guns in the chin turret and two in the dorsal turret.

of aborted sorties resulting from adverse weather and technical difficulties, only 241 actually attacked and 19 were lost. The VIII Bomber Command's effort to attack Hamm on 2 February 1943 failed because of cloud cover.

Two days later, Emden was attacked by 39 B-17s out of 86 despatched, with five downed. The Wilhelmshaven raid on 26 February saw the loss of seven US aircraft; and on 4 March, 42 out of 85 attacked Hamm, seven of the bombers being lost. The Bremer yard at Vegesack was attacked on 18 March by 76 B-17Fs of the 1st Bomb Wing and 27 Liberators of the 2nd Wing: 97 bombers released 536 454kg (1000lb) bombs from 7315m (24,000ft)

and achieved good concentration, and only two bombers were shot down.

In April 1943, the US 4th, 56th and 78th Fighter Groups became operational with the P-47C and P-47D, but these had a radius of only 280km (175 miles) and were thus limited to escorts over France. Meanwhile, the forces of VIII Bomber Command were increased after the alleviation of pressure in the Mediterranean.

The B-17s of the new 95th, 96th and 351st Bomb Groups became operational on 13 May, and the 94th Bomb Group on the following day, while the 92nd Bomb Group was at last released from its training commitment.

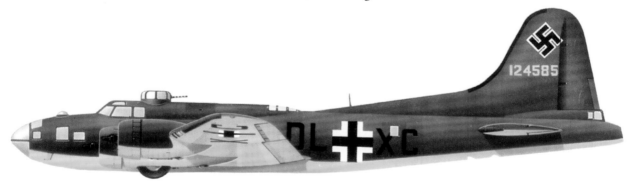

Specifications

Crew: 8–10

Powerplant: 4 x 895kW (1200hp) Wright Cyclone radial piston engines

Maximum speed: 475km/h (295mph)

Range: 2071km (1287 miles)

Service ceiling: 10,975m (36,000ft)

Dimensions: span 31.6m (103ft 9in); length 22.8m (74ft 9in); height 5.85m (19ft 2in)

Weight: 25400kg (56,000lb) loaded

Armament: 12 x 12.7mm (0.5in) guns; 7983kg (17,600) bomb load

▲ **Boeing B-17F Flying Fortress**

360th Bomb Squadron / 303rd Bomb Group / US Eighth Army Air Force, Molesworth, Cambridgeshire, late 1942

This aeroplane force-landed in France on 12 December 1942 after a raid on the Rouen-Satteville marshalling yards, and was repaired by the Germans (as seen here) to be demonstrated to fighter units.

The pace hots up
SPRING–SUMMER 1943

As the pace and weight of the US Eighth AAF's campaign against German war industries increased, so too did its losses, especially as the bombers started to roam deeper inland with longer time spent over Germany. The long-range fighter escort was needed.

T HE FOCKE-WULF factory at Bremen was attacked on 17 April 1943 by 106 out of 115 B-17s and B-24s, 16 being lost. There followed further raids on Bremen, and also on Antwerp, Wevelghem, Kiel, Emden, Flensburg, Wilhelmshaven and Cuxhaven. The attack of 13 June on Kiel marked the beginning of sustained German fighter opposition to the VIII Bomber Command's activities over Germany, and also on their route back to the UK: the VIII Bomber Command lost 26 bombers out of 182 that attacked Kiel and Bremen on this day.

On 22 June, the VIII Bomber Command flew deeper into Germany to attack the synthetic rubber factory at Hüls near Hannover: 235 aircraft were despatched, and 16 of these were brought down by flak and fighters, while 66 other US aircraft were damaged in fighter attacks. The increasing threat of US bombing was reflected on this day by the appearance of another Jagdgruppe, the first unit withdrawn from the Eastern Front to fight the VIII Bomber Command. At last, the acute nature of the Allies' round-the-clock bombing was coming home to the Germans, but more was to come.

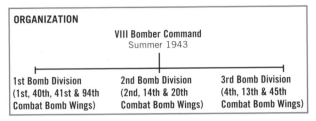

```
ORGANIZATION
                    VIII Bomber Command
                        Summer 1943

1st Bomb Division      2nd Bomb Division      3rd Bomb Division
(1st, 40th, 41st & 94th  (2nd, 14th & 20th      (4th, 13th & 45th
Combat Bomb Wings)     Combat Bomb Wings)     Combat Bomb Wings)
```

First, though, the Eighth AAF had problems to solve: the inadequacy of its Norden bomb sight under European conditions, the limited utility of its 227kg (500lb) and 454kg (1000lb) bombs, and lack of adequate fighter escort. On 12 April, Eaker listed the destruction of U-boat and aircraft manufacture as his command's highest priorities, and the Combined chiefs of staff agreed on 10 June. But first Eaker needed greater bomber strength as well as fighters with the range to escort bombers out and back.

▲ **Boeing B-17F Flying Fortress**
322nd Bomb Squadron / 91st Bomb Group / US Eighth Army Air Force, Bassingbourn, 1943
'The Ragged Irregulars' arrived at Kimbolton in September 1942, but moved to Bassingbourn in the following month and remained there for the rest of the war. The group suffered the heaviest losses of any Eighth AAF unit, with 197 aircraft lost in action, but also claimed the highest number of 'kills' – 420 aircraft.

Specifications
Crew: 8–10
Powerplant: 4 x 895kW (1200hp) Wright Cyclone radial piston engines
Maximum speed: 475km/h (295mph)
Range: 2071km (1287 miles)
Service ceiling: 10,975m (36,000ft)
Dimensions: span 31.6m (103ft 9in); length 22.8m (74ft 9in); height 5.85m (19ft 2in)
Weight: 25400kg (56,000lb) loaded
Armament: 12 x 12.7mm (0.5in) guns; 7983kg (17,600) bomb load

▲ **Box formation**

A group of USAAF B-17s head off for a mission over northern Europe. The US Eighth AAF tried a number of box formations to provide powerful interlocking fields of fire so that the bomber units could defend themselves against fighters.

Specifications

Crew: 8–10

Powerplant: 4 x 895kW (1200hp) Wright
  Cyclone radial piston engines

Maximum speed: 475km/h (295mph)

Range: 2071km (1287 miles)

Service ceiling: 10,975m (36,000ft)

Dimensions: span 31.6m (103ft 9in);
  length 22.8m (74ft 9in);
  height 5.85m (19ft 2in)

Weight: 25400kg (56,000lb) loaded

Armament: 12 x 12.7mm (0.5in) MGs; 7983kg
  (17,600lb) of bombs

▲ **Boeing B-17F Flying Fortress**

359th Bomb Squadron / 303rd Bomb Group / US Eighth Army Air Force, Molesworth, Cambridgeshire, summer 1943

The B-17F was an improved B-17E, with changes including a moulded plexiglas nose, and production totalled 3405 aircraft. This machine has medium-green blotches over the standard olive-drab upper surfaces.

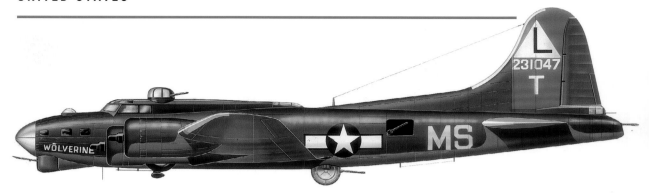

Specifications

Crew: 9–10

Powerplant: 4 x 895kW (1200hp) Wright radial
  engines

Maximum speed: 462km/h (287mph)

Range: 3219km (2000 miles)

Service ceiling: 10,850m (35,800ft)

Dimensions: span 31.62m (103ft 9in);
  length 22.66m (74ft 4in);

height 5.82m (19ft 1in)

Weight: 29710kg (65,000lb) loaded

Armament: 2 x 12.7mm (0.5in) Browning
  trainable MGs in chin, dorsal, ventral and tail
  turrets; 1 x 12.7mm (0.5in) MG in two waist,
  cheek and single dorsal positions; up to
  7983kg (17,600lb) of bombs

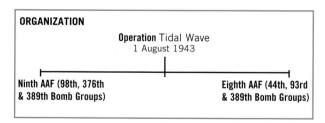

▲ **Boeing B-17G Flying Fortress**

535th Bomb Squadron / 381st Bomb Group / US Eighth AAF, Ridgewell, 1943–44

The 381st Bomb Group's units (532nd, 533rd, 534th and 535th Bomb Squadrons) started to reach the UK in May 1943, and remained at Ridgewell until the group's deactivation in August 1945. The group flew 296 missions.

Objective: Ploiesti

AUGUST 1943

The Romanian oil fields and associated refineries around Ploiesti were one of Germany's primary sources of fuel, and therefore a choice target for destruction. Early efforts achieved nothing, so a major effort was planned and launched at the start of August 1943.

PLOIESTI'S OIL FIELDS and eight associated refineries produced about 10.16 million tonnes (10 million tons) of fuel annually, and were designated a vital strategic target for Allied bombing as early as January 1942 after the first attack had been launched on 23 June 1941 by Soviet bombers. The first US attack was mounted on 11 June 1942 by the 12 Consolidated B-24D Liberator four-engined heavy bombers of the HALPRO detachment in Egypt.

The major USAAF effort was Tidal Wave under the control of Major-General Carl A. 'Toohey' Spaatz's North-West African Air Force. Five groups of B-24 bombers were allocated to the mission, namely the North-West African Air Force's own 98th and 376th Bomb Groups; the Eighth AAF's 44th and 93rd Bomb Groups from the UK; and the 389th Bomb Group, initially allocated to the Eighth AAF but diverted while still in the United States. The

ORGANIZATION		
	Operation Tidal Wave 1 August 1943	
Ninth AAF (98th, 376th & 389th Bomb Groups)		**Eighth AAF (44th, 93rd & 389th Bomb Groups)**

plan called for the mission to be despatched from Benghazi for a low-level attack, in the hope of taking the Germans and Romanians by tactical surprise.

Departure

Some 178 B-24s lifted off on 1 August, and over the Mediterranean separated into five streams for the approach flight, which was already being monitored by the alert Germans. The 376th Bomb Group and the following 93rd Bomb Group made navigational

EIGHTH AAF ELEMENTS IN 'TIDAL WAVE'		
Unit	Squadrons	Aircraft
44th Bomb Group	66th, 67th, 68th, 506th BSs	B-24
93rd Bomb Group	328th, 329th, 330th, 409th BSs	B-24
389th Bomb Group	564th, 565th, 566th, 567th BSs	B-24

▲ **Consolidated B-24 Liberator**

This remains a classic photograph of a formation of B-24 bombers on a mission, in this instance B-24J aircraft against a Romanian oil refinery at Ploiesti some time in 1944.

errors and headed for Bucharest before realizing the fact and turning back, only six aircraft of the 376th Bomb Group then bombing Ploiesti while the other aircraft attacked targets of opportunity.

The 44th and 98th Bomb Groups made accurate approaches, but were faced by fully alerted defences. The 389th Bomb Group also bombed with good accuracy. Over the target area and on their exit the bombers were engaged by fighters, and losses were 41 over the target and another 13 on approach or departure.

Limited damage

Some 40 per cent of the Ploiesti refinery capacity was destroyed, but as the Germans needed only 60 per cent of refinery capacity to process the available oil, the results of the raid were minimal – within a few days, the Germans had restored production to its previous levels.

Ploiesti exercised a fascination for the Americans, and over the following year another 20 raids were launched against the refineries and the complex's transport system before the refineries shut down on 24 August 1944. In the course of 7500 bomber sorties, the Americans dropped about 13,716 tonnes (13,500 tons) of bombs on Ploiesti and lost a total of 350 heavy bombers.

Specifications

Crew: 10

Powerplant: 4 x 895kW (1200hp) Pratt
& Whitney radial piston engines

Maximum speed: 488km/h (303mph)

Range: 1730km (1080 miles)

Service ceiling: 8540m (28,000ft)

Dimensions: span 33.52m (110ft);

length 20.22m (66ft 4in);

height 5.46m (17ft 11in)

Weight: 27216kg (60,000lb) loaded

Armament: 1 (or 3) x 12.7mm (0.5in) nose

MGs; 6 x 12.7mm (0.5in) MGs: two in dorsal

turret, two in retractable ball turret, two in

waist positions; 3629kg (8000lb) of bombs

▲ **Consolidated B-24D Liberator**

93rd Bomb Group / US Eighth Army Air Force, Hardwick, Norfolk, 1943

'The Travelling Circus' reached Hardwick in December 1942 after spending three months at Alconbury, and remained at this base for the rest of the war. The 93rd Bomb Group possessed the distinction of flying more missions – totalling 396, including 49 from North Africa – than any other Eighth AAF bomb group.

Schweinfurt and Regensburg
AUGUST 1943

These two undertakings were planned in concert so that the German defences would be saturated and major damage would be inflicted on vital war industries. It was a bold plan, but also a plan that went badly wrong and led to very substantial Eighth AAF losses.

THIS DOUBLE mission was conceived as an ambitious plan to cripple the German aircraft industry, and was based on two large forces attacking separate targets in order to dilute the *Luftwaffe*'s fighter response. After being postponed several times as a result of adverse weather, the *Juggler* mission was flown on 17 August, the anniversary of the Eighth AAF's first bombing mission. This was the Eighth AAF's 84th mission, and launched 376 bombers of 16 bombardment groups against German heavy industry well beyond the range of escorting fighters. By this time, the B-17 force had been expanded four-fold and was now organized into the 1st and 4th Combat Bomb Wings (CBWs), which were soon to be redesignated as bomb divisions.

The manufacture of the Messerschmitt Bf 109 fighter was centred in Regensburg, and and almost all production of ball bearings was located in Schweinfurt. In its original form, *Juggler* also

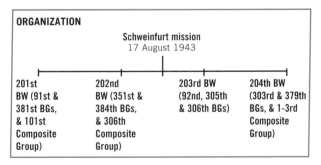

envisaged an attack on the Bf 109 factory at Wiener Neustadt in Austria by B-24 bombers, but this mission was in fact flown separately on 13 August. On 17 August, the 4th CBW would attack the fighter factories in Regensburg and then fly on to bases in North Africa, thereby catching the German defences off balance. Following close behind the 4th CBW, the 1st CBW would turn north-east and bomb the ball-bearing factories of Schweinfurt, and by doing so catch the German fighter force on the ground rearming and refuelling after its endeavours against the 4th CBW. P-47 fighters would be able to escort the bombers only as far as Eupen in Belgium. The take-off of the 1st CBW was delayed by fog, so the 4th CBW was therefore well ahead of it.

Fighter response

The Regensburg force was led by the 4th CBW's commander, Colonel Curtis E. LeMay, and comprised seven B-17 groups totalling 146 aircraft. About 15 minutes after it crossed the coast, the Regensburg force encountered the first German fighter response, which continued with growing intensity nearly all the way to the target area. After 90 minutes of combat, the German fighter force broke off the engagement since its aircraft were low on fuel and ammunition, but it had already shot down or fatally damaged at least 15 bombers.

The flak over Regensburg was light and the weather clear, and of the remaining 131 bombers, 126 dropped 303.53 tonnes (298.75 tons) of bombs on the fighter factories with great accuracy. The surviving aircraft then headed south to cross the Alps, losing another eight aircraft.

In all, 24 bombers were lost and more than 60 of the 122 survivors that arrived in Tunisia had suffered battle damage. The 1st CBW, commanded and led

▲ **Boeing B-17 Flying Fortress**

Almost tailless, this B-17 of the VIII Bomber Command nonetheless made it home safely after a raid on St Omer, France, in 1943.

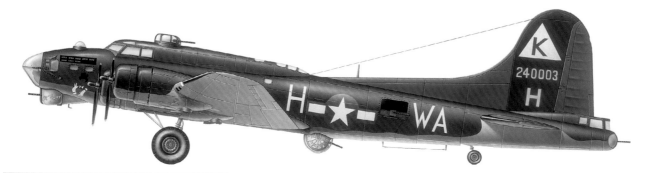

▲ **Boeing B-17G Flying Fortress**

602nd Bomb Squadron / 398th Bomb Group / US Eighth Army Air Force, Nuthampstead, 1943

The 398th Bomb Group comprised the 600th, 601st, 602nd and 603rd Bomb Squadrons, and deployed from the USA to the UK during April 1944. The group remained at Nuthampstead throughout the war, and redeployed to the USA in May and June 1945 after flying 195 missions.

Specifications

Crew: 9/10

Powerplant: 4 x 895kW (1200hp) Wright radial engines

Maximum speed: 462km/h (287mph)

Range: 3219km (2000 miles)

Service ceiling: 10,850m (35,800ft)

Dimensions: span 31.62m (103ft 9in); length 22.66m (74ft 4in);

height 5.82m (19ft 1in)

Weight: 29710kg (65,000lb) loaded

Armament: 2 x 12.7mm (0.5in) Browning trainable MGs in chin, dorsal, ventral and tail turrets; 1 x 12.7mm (0.5in) MGs in two waist, cheek and single dorsal positions; up to 7983kg (17,600lb) bombs by Brigadier-General Robert B. Williams, comprised nine B-17 groups organized into three provisional combat wings, and followed the same route as the Regensburg force. The first German fighters attacked after the bombers crossed the coast, and over Germany twin-engined fighters joined the battle as more than 300 fighters opposed the raid.

Schweinfurt attacked

The attacking force diverged from the morning's route at Mannheim, alerting the German defenders that the target was Schweinfurt. Losses among the 57 B-17 bombers of the leading wing were so severe that many among its airmen considered the possibility that the wing might be annihilated before reaching the target.

However, 24km (15 miles) from Schweinfurt the opposing fighters, after shooting down 22 bombers, disengaged and landed to rearm and refuel in order to attack the force on its way back. Some 8km (5 miles) from Schweinfurt, the flak lofted a barrage into the path of the bomber force.

At 1459, some 40 B-17 bombers remained as the leading wing dropped its bombs on the target area, followed over a 24-minute period by the remainder

REGENSBURG FORCE, EIGHTH AAF			
Wing	Group	Base	Sent/lost
403rd BW	96th Bomb Group	Snetterton Hall	21/0
403rd BW	388th BG	Knettishall	21/1
403rd BW	390th BG	Framlingham	20/6
401st BW	94th BG	Bury St Edmunds	21/1
401st BW	385th BG	Great Ashfield	21/3
402nd BW	9th BG	Horham	21/4
402nd BW	100th BG	Thorpe Abbotts	21/9

of the force. Each wing found increasingly heavy smoke from preceding bomb explosions a hindrance to accuracy. Three bombers had been shot down by flak over Schweinfurt.

Fifteen minutes after leaving the target, each element of the force circled to rebuild its formation, then continued west. At 15:30, the German fighters renewed their attacks. From 16:30, P-47 and Spitfires covered the withdrawal, claiming 20 fighters shot down, but eight more bombers were lost before the force reached the North Sea, where three more crash-landed. The Schweinfurt force lost a total of 36 bombers.

US Eighth Army Air Force
1944–45

From the spring of 1944, the US Eighth AAF was withdrawn from its strategic role and retasked, together with RAF Bomber Command, to the tactical role in support of the forthcoming invasion of Europe. Only after this could the Eighth AAF complete its strategic task over Germany.

On 4 January 1944, the Boeing B-17 and Consolidated B-24 four-engined heavy bombers flew their last missions as part of the US VIII Bomber Command. On this date, the US Eighth AAF and the US Fifteenth AAF, the latter operating from bases in Italy, were combined under central command, namely the new US Strategic Air Forces (USSTAF) with its headquarters at Bushey Hall. In effect, this was a redesignation of the Eighth AAF. The VIII Bomber Command in turn was re-designated as the Eighth AAF on 22 February of the same year and then went out of existence. General Carl Spaatz returned to England

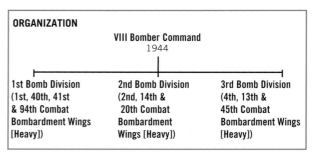

to command the USSTAF. At the same time, Major-General 'Jimmy' Doolittle passed command of the Fifteenth AAF to Major-General Nathan F.

Twining and assumed command of the new Eighth AAF at High Wycombe. Doolittle's thinking was direct and simple: 'Win the air war and isolate the battlefield.' Spaatz and Doolittle planned to employ the USSTAF in a programme of carefully coordinated attacks under the designation Operation *Argument*. This daylight effort would be supported by Bomber Command's nocturnal programme, and

its target was the whittling down of the German aircraft industry as quickly as possible.

By mid-1944, the Eighth AAF had climbed to a strength of more than 200,000 personnel as the human side of an establishment comprising, at its peak, 40 groups of heavy bombers, 15 groups of fighters and four groups of specialized support aircraft. This allowed the Eighth AAF to launch, on a

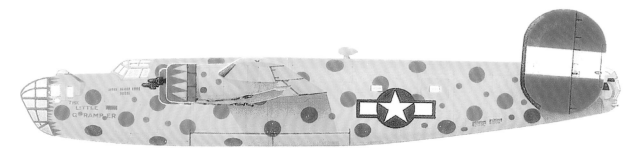

Specifications

Crew: 10

Powerplant: 4 x 895kW (1200hp) Pratt & Whitney Twin wasp radial piston engines

Maximum speed: 488km/h (303mph)

Range: 1730km (1080 miles)

Service ceiling: 8540m (28,000ft)

Dimensions: span 33.53m (110ft);

length 20.22m (66ft 4in); height 5.49m (18ft)

Weight: 32,296kg (71,200lb) loaded

Armament: 1 (usually 3) x 12.7mm (0.5in) nose MG, plus 2 x 12.7mm (0.5in) MGs each in dorsal, tail and retractable ball turrets; 2 x MGs in waist positions; up to 3629kg (8000lb) of bombs

▲ **Consolidated B-24D Liberator**

491st Bomb Group / US Eighth Army Air Force / North Pickenham, Norfolk, 1944

Each Liberator group possessed one garishly coloured aeroplane designed to facilitate the formation of the group over the UK before the aircraft set off across the English Channel or North Sea to their target. Created out of 'war weary' machines, the unarmed assembly aircraft then returned home.

Specifications

Crew: 8–10

Powerplant: 4 x 895kW (1200hp) Wright Cyclone radial piston engines

Maximum speed: 475km/h (295mph)

Range: 2071km (1287 miles)

Service ceiling: 10,975m (36,000ft)

Dimensions: span 31.6m (103ft 9in); length 22.8m (74ft 9in); height 5.85m (19ft 2in)

Weight: 25400kg (56,000lb) loaded

Armament: 12 x 12.7mm (0.5in) MGs; 7983kg (17,600lb) of bombs

▲ **Boeing B-17F Flying Fortress**

388th Bomb Group / US Eighth Army Air Force, 1944

This B-17F landed in Rinkaby in neutral Sweden on 29 February 1944, and was later adapted in that country as a 14-passenger transport aeroplane with the markings seen here. This revised aeroplane operated in the civil transport role from 6 October 1944.

UNITED STATES

1ST AIR DIVISION (MAY 1945)		
Unit	HQ	Groups
1st Bomb Wing	Bassingbourn	91st, 381st, 398th BGs
40th Bomb Wing	Thurleigh	92nd, 305th, 306th BGs
41st Bomb Wing	Molesworth	303rd, 379th, 384th BGs
94th Bomb Wing	Polebrook	351st, 401st, 457th BGs
67th Fighter Wing	Walcot Hall	20th, 352nd, 356th, 359th, 364th FGs

regular basis, more than 2000 four-engined bombers and more than 1000 escorting fighters on a single day's mission to several targets. Within the context of the USSTAF's overall command, the Eighth AAF was primarily responsible for the 'Big Week' air offensive over Germany, the escort fighters tackling the *Luftwaffe*'s fighter arm directly as the German fighters sought to destroy the bombers, which had German aircraft manufacturing facilities as their targets. The heavy bombers of the Eighth AAF also flew missions deep into the heart of Germany, and undertook daylight attacks on Berlin.

Tactical raids
Before the Allied invasion of France in June 1944, the heavy bomb groups of the Eighth AAF conducted tactical raids in preparation for, and in tactical support of, Allied ground forces in and behind the

invasion area. They also helped in the airborne assault on Arnhem in the Netherlands during September 1944, and attacked German ground forces during the 'Battle of the Bulge' at the end of the year.

These missions were completed only at a high cost, however, for 50 per cent of the USAAF's casualties in World War II were suffered by the Eighth AAF: 26,000 dead and more than 21,000 wounded. The cost paid by the Eighth AAF, and also its significance in the Allied effort over Europe, is attested by the fact that the personnel of this air force received 17 Medals of Honor, 220 Distinguished Service Crosses and 442,000 Air Medals. The Eighth AAF included 261 fighter aces, 31 of them with more than 15 'kills' each.

Final raids
The Eighth AAF's last raid was flown on 25 April 1945, when B-17s attacked the Skoda armaments factory at Pilsen in Czechoslovakia, and B-24s attacked four railway facilities in the area round Hitler's retreat at Berchtesgaden, and the Fifteenth AAF attacked the mountain passes to prevent German troops from escaping from Italy.

After the end of the war in Europe, some combat units began to move to the Pacific theatre. The HQ of the Eighth AAF reached Okinawa on 16 July 1945, but the Eighth AAF saw no Pacific service.

Specifications

Crew: 2
Powerplant: 2 x 1253kW (1680hp) Merlin 72 engines
Maximum speed: 668km/h (415mph)
Range: 2400km (1300 miles)
Service ceiling: 11,000m (37,000ft)

Dimensions: span 16.52m (54ft 2in); length 12.43m (44ft 6in); height 5.3m (17ft 5in)
Weight: 6490kg (14,300lb) empty
Armament: none

▲ **de Havilland Mosquito PR.Mk XVI**
653rd Bomb Squadron (Light) / US Eighth Army Air Force, Watton, Norfolk, 1944
The aeroplane was used for weather reconnaissance and visual assessment of bombing attacks. It was completed in PRU blue with black/white 'invasion stripes' on its under surfaces, and its USAAF association was revealed by the national markings, the red tail unit and the 653rd Bomb Squadron's marking on the fin.

Reducing the German fighters

FEBRUARY 1944

To succeed in its strategic bombing campaign, the Eighth AAF needed to be able to reach its targets and bomb accurately. It was therefore a priority that escort fighters were able to accompany the bombers to and from the target, and destroy the German fighter arm.

OPERATION *ARGUMENT* was a six-day major air offensive undertaken between 20 and 25 February 1944 by General Carl Spaatz's US Strategic Air Forces in Europe (Major-General James 'Jimmy' Doolittle's US Eighth AAF in the UK and Major-General Nathan H. Twining's US Fifteenth AAF in Italy), Major-General Hoyt S. Vandenberg's US Ninth AAF in the UK and Air Chief Marshal Sir Arthur Harris' RAF Bomber Command.

It was directed against German fighter strength and production – in this 'Big Week' effort, the Allies used their bombers to attack Germany's major aircraft production centres as the escorting fighters

▶ **Boeing B-17 Flying Fortress**
The two waist gunners of the B-17 operated in exposed positions, and therefore had warm suits and oxygen masks to cope with the conditions at high altitude.

Specifications

Crew: 9–10

Powerplant: 4 x 895kW (1200hp) Wright radial engines

Maximum speed: 462km/h (287mph)

Range: 3219km (2000 miles)

Service ceiling: 10,850m (35,800ft)

Dimensions: span 31.62m (103ft 9in); length 22.66m (74ft 4in);

height 5.82m (19ft 1in)

Weight: 29710kg (65,000lb) loaded

Armament: 2 x 12.7mm (0.5in) Browning trainable MGs in chin, dorsal, ventral and tail turrets; 1 x 12.7mm (0.5in) MG in two waist, cheek and single dorsal positions; up to 7983kg (17,600lb) of bombs

▲ **Boeing B-17G Flying Fortress**
452nd Bomb Group / US Eighth Army Air Force, Deopham Green, 1944
An unusual distinction of the 452nd Bomb Group was that it had more commanding officers, nine in all, than any other bomb group. The group started to reach the UK in December 1943, and remained at Deopham Green until August 1945. The group's 728th, 729th, 730th and 731st Bomb Squadrons flew a total of 250 missions.

on the ground and in the air. The planners designed the operation as the means to lure the *Luftwaffe* into a decisive battle by launching massive attacks on the German aircraft industry. By defeating the *Luftwaffe*, the Allies knew they would have air superiority for the planned *Overlord* amphibious assault on the mainland of Europe.

▲ **Friendly fire?**

These bombs have been dropped from a Boeing B-17 toward a sister aeroplane flying at lower altitude.

used the opportunity to tackle the German fighters that took off to challenge the Allied bomber crews.

The Allied offensive destroyed substantial numbers of German fighters, though the real importance of the battle lay not so much in inflicting severe losses on the *Luftwaffe*, but in forcing the Germans to use irreplaceable fuel supplies and to suffer the loss of yet more experienced pilots at a time when their flying schools were wholly unable to make good such losses with adequately trained replacements.

On 20 February, the US Strategic Air Forces, the US Ninth AAF and RAF Bomber Command started a series of missions against German air-related targets

▲ **Boeing B-17G Flying Fortress**
602nd Bomb Squadron / 379th Bomb Group / US Eighth Army Air Force, Nuthampstead, 1944
The B-17G introduced staggered waist gun positions to provide the gunner with more room, and this aeroplane had radar in place of the ventral 'ball' turret.

Specifications

Crew: 9–10

Powerplant: 4 x 895kW (1200hp) Wright radial engines

Maximum speed: 462km/h (287mph)

Range: 3219km (2000 miles)

Service ceiling: 10,850m (35,800ft)

Dimensions: span 31.62m (103ft 9in); length 22.66m (74ft 4in);

height 5.82m (19ft 1in)

Weight: 29710kg (65,000lb) loaded

Armament: 2 x 12.7mm (0.5in) Browning trainable MGs in chin, dorsal, ventral and tail turrets; 1 x 12.7mm (0.5in) MG in two waist, cheek and single dorsal positions; up to 7983kg (17,600lb) of bombs

▲ **Boeing B-17G Flying Fortress**
91st Bomb Group / US Eighth Army Air Force, Bassingbourn, 1944
The B-17G was essentially an improved B-17F with a remotely controlled chin turret, armed with two 12.7mm (0.5in) Browning machine guns, to cope better with German fighters making head-on attacks.

Specifications

Crew: 10	length 20.47m (67ft 2in);
Powerplant: 4 x 895kW (1200hp) Pratt &	height 5.49m (18ft)
Whitney Twin wasp radial piston engines	Weight: 25,401kg (56,000lb) loaded
Maximum speed: 467km/h (290mph)	Armament: 2 x 12.7mm (0.5in) Browning
Range: 5955km (3700 miles)	trainable MGs each in nose, dorsal, ventral
Service ceiling: 8535m (28000ft)	'ball' and tail turrets, and one each in beam
Dimensions: span 33.53m (110ft);	positions; up to 5806kg (12,800lb) of bombs

▲ **Consolidated B-24H Liberator**

406th Bomb Squadron / 'Carpetbaggers' Special Operations Group /
US Eighth Army Air Force, Cheddington, 1944

This squadron specialized in the nocturnal delivery of leaflet 'bombs', which were laminated paper cylinders, each holding 80,000 leaflets and designed to burst in the air at an altitude between 305m (1000ft) and 610m (2000ft).

'Big Week'
19–25 FEBRUARY 1944

The 'Big Week' campaign was designed to whittle down Germany's fighter strength and cripple Germany's fighter production capability. The campaign was costly for the Americans, but achieved considerable successes, including a strong psychological blow to the Germans.

IN THE 'BIG WEEK' of Operation *Argument*, the USAAF flew heavily escorted missions against airframe manufacturing and assembly plants and other targets in many German cities, including Leipzig, Braunschweig, Gotha, Regensburg, Schweinfurt, Augsburg, Stuttgart and Steyr.

In six days, the bombers of the Eighth and Ninth AAFs flew more than 3250 sorties, the US Fifteenth

▲ **Weary but safe**
The crew of a Boeing B-17G flying Fortress leave their aeroplane to the ground crew after returning from their latest mission.

USAAF RAIDS DURING 'BIG WEEK'			
Date	**Target**	**Sent**	**Lost**
19/20 February	Leipzig & others	921	79 (8.6%)
20/21 February	Stuttgart & others	826	10 (1.2%
21/22 February	various	69	1 (1.4%)
22/23 February	various	134	0
23/24 February	various	22	0
24/25 February	Schweinfurt	1070	36 (3.4%)

AAF more than 500, and Bomber Command some 2350 sorties. The Allied bombers dropped almost 20,320 tonnes (20,000 tons) of bombs and seriously disrupted German fighter production, preventing or delaying the manufacture of hundreds of aircraft at a time when these were badly needed on the Eastern Front and in Italy.

The whole effort cost the US forces 226 heavy bombers and 28 fighters, while Bomber Command lost 157 aircraft. The Allies found the six-day effort costly, the Eighth AAF's losses in February amounting to almost 20 per cent, but this was more than offset by the Germans' loss of two months of fighter production.

Specifications

Crew: 9–10

Powerplant: 4 x 895kW (1200hp) Wright radial engines

Maximum speed: 462km/h (287mph)

Range: 3219km (2000 miles)

Service ceiling: 10,850m (35,800ft)

Dimensions: span 31.62m (103ft 9in);
length 22.66m (74ft 4in);
height 5.82m (19ft 1in)

Weight: 29710kg (65,000lb) loaded

Armament: 2 x 12.7mm (0.5in) Browning trainable MGs in chin, dorsal, ventral and tail turrets; 1 x 12.7mm (0.5in) MG in two waist, cheek and single dorsal positions; up to 7983kg (17,600lb) of bombs

▲ Boeing B-17G Flying Fortress

324th Bomb Squadron / 91st Bomb Group / US Eighth Army Air Force, Bassingbourn, 1944

'The Ragged Irregulars' started to reach the UK from September 1942, settling first at Kimbolton before moving to Bassingbourn in October 1942 for the rest of the war. The group's four squadrons were the 322nd, 323rd, 324th and 401st Bomb Squadrons, and the group flew 340 missions under seven commanders.

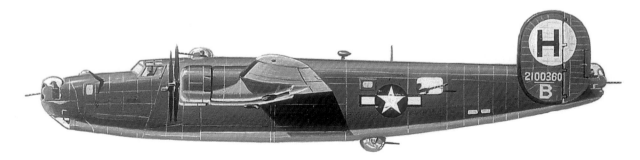

Specifications

Crew: 10

Powerplant: 4 x 895kW (1200hp) Pratt & Whitney Twin wasp radial piston engines

Maximum speed: 467km/h (290mph)

Range: 5955km (3700 miles)

Service ceiling: 8535m (28000ft)

Dimensions: span 33.53m (110ft);
length 20.47m (67ft 2in);
height 5.49m (18ft)

Weight: 25,401kg (56,000lb) loaded

Armament: 2 x 12.7mm (0.5in) Browning trainable MGs in nose, dorsal, ventral 'ball' and tail turrets, and one each in beam positions; up to 5806kg (12,800lb) of bombs

▲ Consolidated B-24J Liberator

446th Bomb Group / US Eighth Army Air Force, Bungay, early 1944

The 'Bungay Buckaroos' group comprised the 704th, 705th, 706th and 707th Bomb Squadrons, and began to reach the UK in November 1943. The group remained at Bungay for the rest of the war, and was redeployed to the USA in June and July 1945 after flying 273 missions.

Another consequence of *Argument* was the Germans' decision to increase still further their dispersion of several industries, particularly aircraft and ball-bearing manufacture, despite the monetary cost and the further dislocation of production. Although this ultimately enabled the Germans to continue and indeed step up fighter production, it also rendered the industry extremely vulnerable to another factor, namely systematic attacks on the transportation network on which dispersed production was reliant.

Morale booster

The week-long offensive also seriously eroded the morale and capability of the *Luftwaffe*. US air crews claimed more than 600 German fighters destroyed and thus achieved almost immediate air superiority, and the *Luftwaffe* never recovered from the loss of so high a proportion of its steadily diminishing pool of skilled fighter pilots. The Germans were therefore forced, in effect, to concede air superiority over occupied Europe and Germany itself to the Allies. The 'Big Week' also bolstered the confidence of US strategic bombing crews.

Until that time, Allied bombers had tended to avoid contact with the *Luftwaffe* whenever possible, but from this time onward the US planners deliberately sought to force the *Luftwaffe* into combat with growing numbers of P-51 escort fighters, which possessed the range to escort the bombers to and from distant targets. This policy allowed the USAAF to consider attacks on Berlin, the German capital. Raiding the German capital, Allied leaders reasoned, would damage important industries and bring the *Luftwaffe* to battle.

Berlin attacks

Thus, on 4 March the USSTAF launched the first of several attacks against Berlin, the fierce air battles which resulted causing heavy losses on each side. But while the Allies could make good their losses without appreciable delay, the Germans could not achieve this and therefore grew steadily weaker. By the spring of 1944, the Allied strategic forces had attacked U-boat construction yards, aircraft factories, transportation and other industrial facilities with limited success. They had fought the *Luftwaffe* in the skies over Europe and, despite suffering severe losses, had never turned back.

When the combined bomber offensive officially ended on 1 April 1944, and the focus of the strategic air effort was switched to support *Overlord,* Allied airmen were well on the way to achieving air superiority over all of Europe.

▲ Consolidated B-24H Liberator

566th Bomb Squadron / 389th Bomb Group / US Eighth Army Air Force,
Hethel, spring 1944

'The Sky Scorpions' group comprised the 564th, 565th, 566th and 567th Bomb Squadrons, which started to arrived in the UK in June 1943. The group flew 321 missions, 14 of them from North Africa, and was inactivated in September 1945.

Specifications

Crew: 10	length 20.47m (67ft 2in);
Powerplant: 4 x 895kW (1200hp) Pratt &	height 5.49m (18ft)
Whitney Twin wasp radial piston engines	Weight: 25,401kg (56,000lb) loaded
Maximum speed: 467km/h (290mph)	Armament: 2 x 12.7mm (0.5in) Browning
Range: 5955km (3700 miles)	trainable MGs in nose, dorsal, ventral 'ball'
Service ceiling: 8535m (28000ft)	and tail turrets, and one each in beam
Dimensions: span 33.53m (110ft);	positions; up to 5806kg (12,800lb) of bombs

Taking the war to Berlin
FEBRUARY–APRIL 1945

A city without the concentrations of war-making industries that the USAAF saw at their primary targets, Berlin did not receive much in the way of American bombing attention until 1945. Then, against the wishes of its commander, the Eighth AAF was ordered to make several raids.

AFTER ITS FAILURE in the battle of Berlin, which involved 16 raids between 18 November 1943 and January 1944 and yielded no major results other than the loss of many bombers and their crews, RAF Bomber Command sensibly decided to avoid Berlin for most of 1944, when its resources were in any case largely diverted to targets in western Germany, France and Belgium in support of the Allied invasion of France in June 1944.

Nevertheless, it was deemed useful to maintain at least a presence over Berlin, thus ensuring that its defences against air attack would not be moved to protect other possible targets, so regular nuisance raids were continued by both the RAF and the USAAF.

Berlin targetted
It was only in early 1945 that Berlin again became a major target for Allied bombing attack. As the

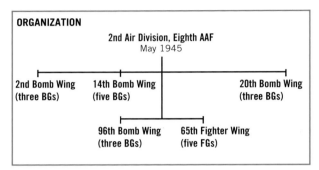

ORGANIZATION

2nd Air Division, Eighth AAF
May 1945

2nd Bomb Wing (three BGs)	14th Bomb Wing (five BGs)	20th Bomb Wing (three BGs)

96th Bomb Wing (three BGs)   65th Fighter Wing (five FGs)

Soviet forces closed on Berlin from the east, the RAF carried out a series of attacks on cities in eastern Germany, swollen with refugees from farther east, to disrupt communications and put more strain on Germany's dwindling manpower and fuel resources. Then a force of almost 1000 B-17 bombers of the Eighth AAF, escorted by large numbers of P-51 single-engined fighters, attacked the German railway system in Berlin during 3 February in an effort to prevent movement of the Sixth *Panzerarmee*, which intelligence sources believed to be travelling through the German capital by rail to fight the Soviet forces on the Eastern Front.

Collateral damage
The raid killed between 2500 and 3000 people, and left another 120,000 persons homeless. This was one of the few occasions on which the USAAF undertook an area attack on a city centre. Lieutenant-General James Doolittle, commanding the Eighth AAF, had objected to the plan but had been overruled by General Carl Spaatz, commanding the US Strategic Air Forces, and General Dwight D. Eisenhower, the supreme commander of the Allied forces in Europe.

The reasoning of Doolittle's two superiors was that the raid might achieve useful military results, but would also help to convince the Soviet Union that the Western Allies were seeking to support them actively. During this raid, Kreuzberg (the

▲ **Top gun**
Forward-firing defensive armament was crucial to the success of the Fortresses' missions. This was finally addressed in the B-17G, which included four machine guns in two turrets as well as two manually operated cheek guns.

newspaper district), Mitte (the central area, as suggested by its name), and other areas such as Friedrichshain were all severely damaged. Among the several government and Nazi party buildings that were also hit were the Reich chancellery, the party chancellery and the headquarters of the Gestapo secret police organization. The Unter den Linden, Wilhelmstrasse and Friedrichstrasse areas were all effectively destroyed.

There was another major US raid on 26 February, and this left another 80,000 persons homeless. The US raids continued until April, when the Soviet forces had reached the outskirts of Berlin, and during the final days of the war the Soviet air forces also bombed Berlin.

Big raid

The largest of the Eighth AAF's raids on Berlin took place on 18 March, when 1327 bombers of three air divisions were committed, together with powerful escort forces. On this occasion the Germans felt that the tactical and weather conditions were favourable for the use of a significant number of Messerschmitt Me 262 jet-powered fighters, each armed with

four 30mm (1.18in) cannon. The 1st and 3rd Air Divisions were each attacked by a group of between 10 and 20 Me 262s, which shot down eight bombers within the US losses of 24 bombers on the day. Two Me 262s fell.

Estimates of the dead in Berlin as a result of air raids range from 20,000 to 50,000, the former being more probable. The comparatively low death count for Berlin resulted in part from the city's distance from airfields in the UK, which made the launching of major raids difficult before the liberation of France in late 1944, and in part to the high strength and quality of the city's air defences and shelters.

2ND AIR DIVISION, EIGHTH AAF (MAY 1945)		
Wing	Headquarters	Groups
2nd BW	Hethel	389th, 445th, 453rd BGs
14th BW	Shipdham	44th, 392nd, 491st, 492nd, 489th BGs
20th BW	Hardwick	93rd, 446th, 448th BGs
96th BW	Horsham St Faith	458th, 466th, 467th BGs
65h FW	Saffron Walden	4th, 56th, 355th, 361st, 479th FGs

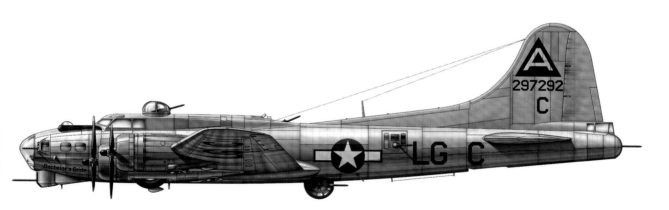

▲ Boeing B-17G Flying Fortress

322nd Bomb Squadron / 91st Group / US Eighth Army Air Force, Bassingbourn, late 1944–early 1945

The decline of the German fighter arm meant that from April 1944 USAAF bombers increasingly flew in a natural metal finish, reducing cost, maintenance, weight and drag, and boosting performance slightly.

Specifications

Crew: 9/10

Powerplant: 4 x 895kW (1200hp) Wright radial engines

Maximum speed: 462km/h (287mph)

Range: 3219km (2000 miles)

Service ceiling: 10,850m (35,800ft)

Dimensions: span 31.62m (103ft 9in); length 22.66m (74ft 4in);

height 5.82m (19ft 1in)

Weight: 29710kg (65,000lb) loaded

Armament: 2 x 12.7mm (0.5in) Browning trainable MGs in chin, dorsal, ventral and tail turrets; 1 x 12.7mm (0.5in) MG in two waist, cheek and single dorsal positions; up to 7983kg (17,600lb) of bombs

Specifications

Crew: 9/10

Powerplant: 4 x 895kW (1200hp) Wright radial
engines

Maximum speed: 462km/h (287mph)

Range: 3219km (2000 miles)

Service ceiling: 10,850m (35,800ft)

Dimensions: span 31.62m (103ft 9in);
length 22.66m (74ft 4in);

height 5.82m (19ft 1in)

Weight: 29710kg (65,000lb) loaded

Armament: 2 x 12.7mm (0.5in) Browning
trainable machine guns in chin, dorsal,
ventral and tail turrets, 1 x 12.7mm (0.5in)
machine guns in two waist, cheek and single
dorsal positions, up to 7983kg (17,600lb)
bombs

▲ **Boeing B-17G Flying Fortress**

364th Bomb Squadron / 305th Bomb Group / 40th Combat Wing /
US Eighth Army Air Force, 1944–45

Based in Grafton Underwood, the 305th Bomb Group was first activated in
November 1942, and flew its final mission on 25 April 1945. The group dropped
10,144kg (22,363lb) of ordnance over occupied Europe, flying more than 9000
sorties. The 364th Bomb Squadron used the markings 'WF'.

Suppressing the V-2
1944–45

**Once the threat of the German 'V-weapons' was appreciated, the Allies made strenuous efforts
to destroy the production facilities and launch sites. As part of this effort, the US Eighth
AAF visited Peenemünde on three occasions during the course of 1944.**

AFTER THE BRITISH attack on Peenemünde in
Operation *Hydra* on the night of 17/18 August
1943, the Germans deliberately fabricated 'evidence'
of bomb damage in the area, in an effort to persuade
the Allies that this target had in fact been destroyed
beyond the point of any continued operational
viability. They created a number of larger craters in
the sand, deliberately blew up a number of lightly
damaged and minor buildings, and went so far as to
paint simulations of charred beams on the roofs of
undamaged buildings.

Even so, the US Eighth AAF was committed to
three attacks on Peenemünde during 1944, largely
in an effort to ensure that there was no production
of hydrogen peroxide for fuel, one of the essential
ingredients used in the rocket engine of the V-2
ballistic missile, at this site.

The first of these three attacks, which was flown
on 18 July 1944, employed 377 B-17 Flying
Fortress four-engined heavy bombers to attack
the experimental establishment at Peenemünde,
the scientific headquarters at Zinnowitz, and the
marshalling yards at Stralsund. The effort of the
bombers was significantly aided by a previous
weather reconnaissance, which had established that
the conditions were just right for the bombers.
Such pre-raid reconnaissance was a new feature in
USAAF planning, and paid handsome dividends.
The US forces lost three B-17s and had another 64
of the aircraft damaged.

The escort for the raid was provided by 297 P-38
Lightning twin-engined and P-51 Mustang single-
engined fighters, and these claimed the destruction
of 21 German fighters for the loss of three P-51s

and another damaged so badly that it had to be scrapped after returning to the UK. General Spaatz commented: 'The finest example of precision bombing I have ever seen.'

Second raid

The second raid, flown on 4 August, also struck at targets in the Peenemünde area. This undertaking involved 221 B-17s against Peenemünde itself, 110 against the airfield at Anklam and 70 against aircraft manufacturing facilities also at Anklam. Three B-17s were lost, one damaged irreparably, and 94 more damaged. The escort force this time comprised 250 P-51 fighters, of which just 223 actually took part on the operation. The Mustangs claimed the destruction of four German fighters and another four damaged on the ground, for the loss of nine of their own number and one more damaged irreparably.

The third raid, on 25 August, committed 376 B-17s against targets in the Peenemünde area: 146 of the bombers attacked the experimental establishment at Peenemünde once again, 108 bombed the airfield at Neubrandenburg and 71 more bombed the airfield at Anklam; 21 other bombers attacked the airfield at Parow, and five

▲ **Boeing B-17G Flying Fortress**

533rd Bomb Squadron / 381st Bomb Group / US Eighth Army Air Force, Ridgewell, Essex, 1944

The 381st Bomb Group comprised the 532nd, 533rd, 534th and 535th Bomb Squadrons, and reached the UK in June 1943. The group flew 296 missions from Ridgewell before returning to the USA in May and June 1945.

struck at targets of opportunity. Of these B-17s, five were lost and another 75 damaged. On this occasion, the bombers were escorted by 171 P-47 Thunderbolt and P-51 single-engined fighters, and these claimed 36 German aircraft destroyed and another 28 damaged on the ground for the loss of just two of their own number.

Specifications

Crew: 9–10

Powerplant: 4 x 895kW (1200hp) Wright radial engines

Maximum speed: 462km/h (287mph)

Range: 3219km (2000 miles)

Service ceiling: 10,850m (35,800ft)

Dimensions: span 31.62m (103ft 9in); length 22.66m (74ft 4in);

height 5.82m (19ft 1in)

Weight: 29710kg (65,000lb) loaded

Armament: 2 x 12.7mm (0.5in) Browning trainable MGs in chin, dorsal, ventral and tail turrets; 1 x 12.7mm (0.5in) MGs in two waist, cheek and single dorsal positions; up to 7983kg (17,600lb) bombs

▲ **Boeing B-17G Flying Fortress**

711th Bomb Squadron / 447th Bomb Group / US Eighth Army Air Force, Rattlesden, 1945

This is a late-production example of the B-17G with a revised tail position. The 447th Bomb Group comprised the 708th, 709th, 710th and 711th Bomb Squadrons, which reached Rattlesden, the group's only English base, in November 1943. The group returned to the USA in August 1945 after flying 257 missions.

The firebombing of Dresden
FEBRUARY 1945

In one of the most controversial campaigns of the strategic air war, the Western Allies bombed Dresden in February 1945. The physical destruction caused by the night and day raids was huge, but the casualties, though still very large, were not as great as has been claimed.

THE ALLIED BOMBING of Dresden, led by Bomber Command of the Royal Air Force and followed by the Eighth AAF of the USAAF, on 13/15 February 1945, remains one of the most controversial Allied campaigns of World War II. Though largely unmilitarized and only little damaged in earlier raids, Dresden was believed early in 1945 to possess the transport network along which the Germans could have passed reinforcements to the Eastern Front. The Western Allies therefore came to the conclusion that the city had to be destroyed despite the fact that it was filled with a possible 200,000 refugees fleeing the Soviet advance from the east.

The railway yards, near the city centre, had already been attacked twice by the Eighth AAF in daylight raids: on 7 October 1944 with 71 tonnes (70 tons) of HE bombs, and once again on 16 January 1945 with 325 tonnes (320 tons) of bombs, including 41.6 tonnes (41 tons) of incendiaries. The new campaign was to have been started by the Eighth AAF during the day of 13 February, but bad weather

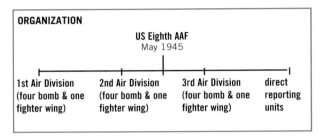

ORGANIZATION

US Eighth AAF
May 1945

| 1st Air Division (four bomb & one fighter wing) | 2nd Air Division (four bomb & one fighter wing) | 3rd Air Division (four bomb & one fighter wing) | direct reporting units |

prevented USAAF operations during this day. Thus RAF Bomber Command carried out the first raid during the night of 13/14 February.

Then, from just after midday on 14 February, 311 B-17s dropped 783 tonnes (771 tons) of bombs on Dresden, with the railway yards as their aiming point. During this US raid, there was a brief but intense dogfight between US and German fighters around Dresden. The Eighth AAF resumed its attack on 15 February. During the British attack and the two US attacks, some 3962 tonnes (3900 tons) of bombs were dropped.

▲ **Silver flyers**
Camouflage began to disappear from the Eighth AAF's Flying Fortresses from early 1944. These B-17Gs are from the 381st Bomb Group, based at Ridgewell in the UK.

The attacks were designed to create a firestorm: first, a considerable weight of high-explosive (HE) bombs was used to blow the roofs off buildings and so expose the timbers within them; second, incendiary bombs were dropped to ignite the exposed timbers; and third, more HE bombs were dropped to deter the firefighting services. In Dresden, the bombings created a self-sustaining firestorm, with temperatures peaking at more than 1500°C (2700°F). After an area had caught fire, the air in the area immediately above it became very heated and rose rapidly, cold air then being drawn in at very high speed at ground level, sucking other flammable materials into the firestorm and sustaining it.

Devastation

After the main firebombing campaign of 13/15 February, there were two other USAAF attacks on the city's railway marshalling yards: on 2 March 406 B-17s dropped 955 tonnes (940 tons) of HE and 143 tonnes (141 tons) of incendiary bombs, and on 17 April 580 B-17s dropped 1578 tonnes (1554 tons) of HE and 167 tonnes (165 tons) of incendiary bombs. A German police report shortly after the attacks stated that the old town and the inner eastern suburbs had been engulfed in a single fire that had destroyed almost 12,000 buildings, including residential barracks. The report also said that the raid

3RD AIR DIVISION, EIGHTH AAF (MAY 1945)		
Wing	Headquarters	Bomb groups
4th BW	Bury St Edmunds	94th, 447th, 448th, 487th BGs
13th BW	Horham	95th, 100th, 390th BGs
45th BW	Snetterton Heath	96th, 388th, 452nd BGs
93rd BW	Mendlesham	34th, 385th, 490th, 493rd BGs
66th FW	Sawston Hall	55th, 78th, 339th, 353rd, 357th FGs

had destroyed 24 banks, 26 insurance buildings, 31 stores and retail houses, 640 shops, 64 warehouses, two market halls, 31 large hotels, 26 public houses, 63 administrative buildings, three theatres, 18 cinemas, 11 churches, six chapels, five building of cultural and historical significance, 19 hospitals and other medical facilities, 39 schools, five consulates, one zoological garden, one water works, one railway facility, 19 postal facilities, four tram facilities and 19 river craft of various sizes.

Almost 200 factories were damaged, 136 of them badly. The number of dead is difficult to fix, and estimates have varied between 25,000 and 60,000 or more, but modern scholarship suggests a figure toward the lower end of the range between 25,000 and 35,000.

Specifications

Crew: 9/10

Powerplant: 4 x 895kW (1200hp) Wright radial engines

Maximum speed: 462km/h (287mph)

Range: 3219km (2000 miles)

Service ceiling: 10,850m (35,800ft)

Dimensions: span 31.62m (103ft 9in); length 22.66m (74ft 4in);

height 5.82m (19ft 1in)

Weight: 29710kg (65,000lb) loaded

Armament: 2 x 12.7mm (0.5in) Browning trainable MGs in chin, dorsal, ventral and tail turrets; 1 x 12.7mm (0.5in) MGs in two waist, cheek and single dorsal positions; up to 7983kg (17,600lb) bombs

▲ **Boeing B-17G Flying Fortress**

386th Bomb Squadron / 487th Bomb Group / US Eighth Army Air Force, Lavenham, 1945

The 487th Bomb Group comprised the 836th, 837th, 338th and 839th Bomb Squadrons, which started to reach Lavenham from the USA in July 1944. The group remained at the same base until July and August 1945, where it redeployed to the USA after completing 185 missions.

US Ninth Army Air Force
1943–45

The Ninth AAF of North African service was replaced in October 1943 by a new Ninth AAF based in the UK for support of the US ground forces during and after the *Overlord* invasion of Normandy. The force grow enormously in the winter of 1943–44.

On 16 October 1943, the headquarters of the original US Ninth AAF was inactivated in Egypt and a new headquarters activated in the UK at Burtonwood under the command of Lieutenant-General Lewis H. Brereton, who was succeeded on 7 August 1944 by Major-General Hoyt S. Vandenberg. Initially controlling assets that had previously been part of the Eighth AAF's establishment, but soon swollen enormously by the arrival in the UK of other tactical air units, the new Ninth AAF was created to provide tactical air support for the Allies' planned *Overlord* invasion of German-occupied north-west Europe, and in the periods before, during and after the invasion. As such, the Ninth AAF became a decisive factor in the tactical air power equation in western Europe. With its formation in England, the Ninth AAF was entrusted with the provision of the full range of tactical air support requirements for the US Army in north-western Europe, leaving the Eighth AAF to concentrate its efforts on the strategic bombing mission.

New tactical air force

The core of the new Ninth AAF was created during November 1943 by the transfer from the Eighth AAF of tactical bomber, fighter and troop carrier groups. This transfer created the following: Brigadier-General Samuel E. Anderson's IX Bomber Command with four bomb groups of Martin B-28 Marauder twin-engined medium bombers; Brigadier-General Elwood R. Quesada's IX Fighter Command with one reconnaissance group flying variants of the Lockheed P-38 Lightning twin-engined fighter and three fighter and fighter-bomber groups flying the North American P-51 Mustang single-engined fighters; and Brigadier-General Paul L. Williams' IX Troop Carrier command with three groups of Douglas C-47 twin-engined transport aircraft.

In February 1944, one of the IX Fighter Command's Mustang groups was replaced by

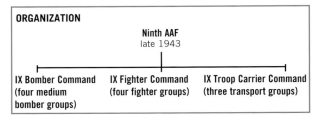

another flying the Republic P-47 Thunderbolt single-engined heavy fighter and fighter-bomber, and the IX Fighter Command was itself later divided into Major-General Quesada's IX Tactical Air Command with an eventual nine groups to support the US First Army, and Brigadier-General Otto P. Weyland's XIX Tactical Air Command, which had an eventual seven groups to support the US Third Army. This division of responsibilities was eventually formalized on 1 August 1944.

IX BOMBER COMMAND (LATE 1943)			
Group	Headquarters	Squadrons	Type
322nd BG	Andrews Field	449th, 450th, 451st,452nd BSs	B-26
323rd BG	Earls Colne	353rd, 454th, 455th, 456th BSs	B-26
386th BG	Great Dunmow	552nd, 553rd, 554th, 555th BSs	B-26
387th BG	Chipping Ongar	556th, 557th, 558th, 559th BSs	B-26

US ATTACK BOMBER ARMAMENT		
Type	Guns	Disposable
Douglas A-20G	9 x 12.7mm (0.5in)	1814kg (4000lb)
Douglas A-26B	18 12.7mm (0.5in)	2722kg (6000lb)
Douglas DB-7B	7 x 7.7mm (0.303in)	907kg (2000lb)
Martin B-26G	11 x 12.7mm (0.5in)	1814kg (4000lb)
North American B-25J	13 x 12.7mm (0.5in)	1814kg (4000lb)

The Ninth AAF grew rapidly during the winter of 1943/44 and the spring of 1944. Thus by the end of May, when its last combat group became operational, the Ninth AAF had grown to no fewer than 45 operational groups with some 5000 aircraft.

Together with its all-important ground support units, without which the air units could not have kept flying, the Ninth AAF thus had a personnel strength of more than 200,000, a total greater than that of the Eighth AAF strategic air force at the same time.

Specifications

Crew: 2–3
Powerplant: 2 x 1193kW (1600hp) Wright
    radial piston engines
Maximum speed: 546km/h (339mph)
Range: 1754km (1090 miles)
Service ceiling: 12,338m (27,200ft)
Dimensions: span 18.69m (61ft 4in);
    length 14.63m (48ft);

height 5.36m (17ft 7in)
Weight: 12,338kg (27,200lb) loaded
Armament: 6 x 12.7mm (0.5in) fixed forward-
    firing MGs in nose; 2 x 12.7mm (0.5in) MGs
    in power-operated dorsal turret; 1 x manually
    operated 12.7mm (0.5in) MG in ventral
    position; up to 1364kg (3000lb) of bombs

▲ **Douglas A-20G Havoc**

646th Bomb Squadron / 410th Bomb Group / US Ninth Army Air Force, Gosfield, 1944

The 410th Bomb Group (Light) comprised the 644th, 645th, 646th and 647th Bomb Squadrons, and with the 409th and 416th Bomb Groups (Light) comprised the IX Bomber Command's 97th Combat Bomb Wing (Medium).

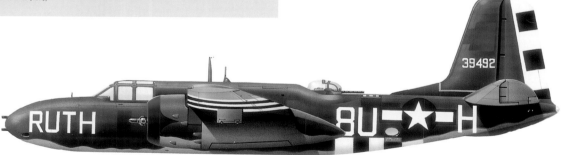

Specifications

Crew: 2–3
Powerplant: 2 x 1193kW (1600hp) Wright
    radial piston engines
Maximum speed: 546km/h (339mph)
Range: 1754km (1090 miles)
Service ceiling: 12,338m (27,200ft)
Dimensions: span 18.69m (61ft 4in);
    length 14.63m (48ft);

height 5.36m (17ft 7in)
Weight: 12,338kg (27,200lb) loaded
Armament: 6 x 12.7mm (0.5in) fixed forward-
    firing MGs in nose; 2 x 12.7mm (0.5in) MGs
    in power-operated dorsal turret; 1 x manually
    operated 12.7mm (0.5in) MG in ventral
    position; up to 1364kg (3000lb) of bombs

▲ **Douglas A-20G Havoc**

646th Bomb Squadron / 410th Bomb Group / US Ninth Army Air Force, Gosfield, 1944

The A-20G was a two/three-seat attack bomber, and in addition to its three defensive machine guns (two in the dorsal turret and one in the ventral position) carried six 12.7mm (0.5in) fixed forward-firing machine guns in the nose, as well as 1361kg (3000lb) of bombs in the lower-fuselage weapons bay.

Specifications

Crew: 2–3

Powerplant: 2 x 1193kW (1600hp) Wright
   radial piston engines

Maximum speed: 546km/h (339mph)

Range: 1754km (1090 miles)

Service ceiling: 12,338m (27,200ft)

Dimensions: span 18.69m (61ft 4in);

length 14.63m (48ft); height 5.36m (17ft 7in)

Weight: 12,338kg (27,200lb) loaded

Armament: 6 x 12.7mm (0.5in) fixed forward-
   firing MGs in nose; 2 x 12.7mm (0.5in) MGs
   in power-operated dorsal turret; 1 x manually
   operated 12.7mm (0.5in) MG in ventral
   position; up to 1364kg (3000lb) of bombs

▲ **Douglas A-20G Havoc**

Unknown bomber group / US Ninth Army Air Force, UK, early 1944

With 2850 aircraft built, the A-20G was the most numerous of the A-20 variants, and was a development of the A-20D with a gun-carrying 'solid' nose for improved low-level attack capability.

Softening northern Europe
SPRING 1944

Before *Overlord* could be launched and hope to achieve success, the Allied air forces had to weaken the German defences and also cripple France's transport system, making the arrival of German reinforcements slow and laborious. Here the Ninth AAF came into its own.

THE FIRST OPERATIONAL task undertaken by the Ninth AAF lay within the context of the 'Pointblank' directive issued in January 1943 by the Allied leaders to fix the tasks to be undertaken by their air forces.

Degrading the Luftwaffe

Working in tandem with the Eighth AAF, the Ninth AAF was to attack German troop concentrations and military installations, as well as the transport system of northwest Europe, with the IX Bomber Command's aircraft, and to destroy the strength of the *Luftwaffe* on the ground and in the air.

The *Luftwaffe*'s degradation was to be undertaken with the aid of the excellent North American P-51 Musatangs of IX Fighter Command, which would decimate the German fighters that rose to tackle the US bombers.

Ground support role

The Ninth AAF also had to prepare for its major role, which would be the direct tactical support of the US ground forces in the coming invasion. As part of this preparation, the 357th Fighter Group and its P-51 Mustang fighters were transferred to the Eighth AAF in exchange for the 358th Fighter Group and its heavier Republic P-47 Thunderbolt fighter-bombers. The Thunderbolt was an excellent ground attack aircraft and ideal for the role.

The Ninth AAF's missions now grew steadily in pace and intensity, and came to involve attacks on railway marshalling yards; the rail lines themselves, together with the bridges and tunnels they traversed; canal and river barges; airfields; industrial facilities; military installations along and behind the entire north and north-west coasts of France; and other targets in France, Belgium and the Netherlands.

▲ Douglas A-20G Havoc
This A-20G served with a unit of the Ninth AAF, which recorded more than 100,000 combat hours in the run-up to D-Day on 6 June 1944.

Specifications

Crew: 7

Powerplant: 2 x 1432kW (1920hp) Pratt
& Whitney radial piston engines

Maximum speed: 45km/h (282mph)

Range: 1851km (1150 miles)

Service ceiling: 6400m (21,000ft)

Dimensions: span 21.64m (71ft);

length 17.75m (58ft 3in);
height 6.55m (21ft 6in)

Weight: 16,783kg (37,000b) loaded

Armament: 7 x 12.7mm (0.5in) MGs: one in
the nose, two in dorsal turret, two in tail
turret and two waist guns; 1818kg (4000lb)
of bombs

▲ Martin B-26C Marauder
557th Bomb Squadron / 387th Bomb Group / US Ninth Army Air Force,
Chipping Ongar, Essex, 1944
One of the four groups constituting the Ninth AAF's 98th Combat Bomb Wing
(Medium), the 387th Bomb Group (Medium) was itself composed of the 556th,
557th, 558th and 559th Bomb Squadrons, all based at Chipping Ongar.

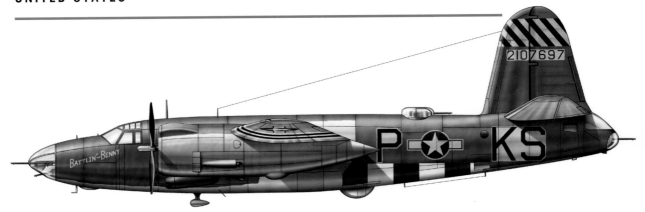

Specifications

Crew: 7

Powerplant: 2 x 1491kW (2000hp) Pratt
 & Whitney radial piston engines

Maximum speed: 455km/h (283mph)

Range: 1770km (1100 miles)

Service ceiling: 6035m (19,800ft)

Dimensions: span 21.64m (71ft);

length 17.09m (56ft 1in);

height 6.20m (20ft 4in)

Weight: 17,327kg (38,200lb) loaded

Armament: 11 x 12.7mm (0.5in) MGs in fixed
 forward-firing, trainable nose and waist
 mounts, power-operated dorsal and tail
 turrets; up to 1813kg (4000lb) of bombs

▲ **Martin B-26C Marauder**

557th Bomb Squadron / 387th Bomb Group / US Ninth Army Air Force,
Chipping Ongar, 1944

Part of the 98th Combat Bomb Wing (Medium), the four squadrons of the 397th
Bomb Group flew the B-26C version of the Marauder medium bomber, itself
identical to the B-26B except for being built in Omaha rather than Baltimore.

Operation *Overlord*
JUNE 1944

The Allied invasion of Normandy was launched on 6 June 1944. Over the ships and men of the invasion forces there roamed the bombers, fighters and fighter-bombers of the Allied tactical air forces. Within them, the Eighth AAF had a major part to play in support of the US landings.

THE ALLIED TACTICAL air forces mustered 2434 fighters and fighter-bombers, together with some 700 light and medium bombers, for the Normandy campaign in the hands of the US Ninth AAF and British 2nd Tactical Air Force. This force first struck against the Germans during the preparatory campaign undertaken before D-Day. Some 60 days before the scheduled start of the invasion, the Allied air forces began their interdiction attacks against rail centres in a campaign that increased steadily in intensity right up to the eve of the invasion and was further enhanced in capability by the collaboration of the Allies' heavy bomber forces.

The campaign against the bridges of northern France began 46 days before D-Day. It was intended to ensure that the forthcoming land battlefield was isolated from the rest of German-occupied Europe by cutting the bridges over the Seine river below Paris and of the Loire river below Orleans, as well as those over a number of other major and minor rivers and canals. In this task, fighter-bombers proved more effective than medium or heavy bombers, largely because their manoeuvrability allowed them to make pinpoint attacks in a fashion impossible for their larger counterparts with bombing runs in straight and level flight. The fighter-bombers also had the speed, firepower and agility to evade or dominate the *Luftwaffe*'s limited resources in France and the Low Countries. Though flak and fighters brought down some of the fighter-bombers, the loss rate was considerably less than it would have been with conventional attack by level bombers.

By 21 days before D-Day, the Allied air forces were attacking German airfields within a radius of

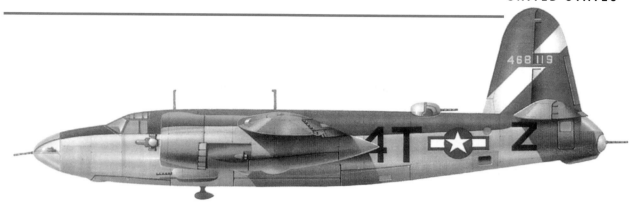

Specifications

Crew: 7

Powerplant: 2 x 1491kW (2000hp) Pratt
  & Whitney radial piston engines

Maximum speed: 455km/h (283mph)

Range: 1770km (1100 miles)

Service ceiling: 603500m (19,800ft)

Dimensions: span 21.64m (71ft);

length 17.09m (56ft 1in);

height 6.20m (20ft 4in)

Weight: 17,327kg (38,200lb) loaded

Armament: 11 x 12.7mm (0.5in) MGs in fixed
forward-firing, trainable nose and waist
mounts, power-operated dorsal and tail
turrets; up to 1813kg (4000lb) of bombs

▲ Martin B-26G Marauder

585th Bomb Squadron / 394th Bomb Group / US Ninth Army Air Force,
Cambrai, France, 1944

Another element of the Ninth AAF's 98th Combat Bomb Wing (Medium), based
at Boreham before D-Day, the 394th Bomb Group (Medium) moved its 584th,
585th, 586th and 587th Bomb Squadrons to France as soon as suitable airfields
were available.

210km (130 miles) of the area of Normandy selected
for the initial lodgement, and this effort was also
sustained up to the eve of *Overlord*.

On D-Day itself, 6 June 1944, the IX Troop
Carrier Command flew more than 2000 sorties to
deliver the paratroopers and infantry-filled gliders
of the US 82nd and 101st Airborne Divisions to
Normandy. Other elements of the Ninth AAF,
namely the IX Bomber Command and IX Tactical
Air Command, carried out massive air attacks with
B-25 Mitchell and B-26 Marauder medium bombers,
and with P-47 Thunderbolt and P-51 Mustang
fighter-bombers.

Air cover during the amphibious assault of the
Allied forces on the beaches of France during the
morning of 6 June was flown mostly by P-38
Lightnings, which encountered almost nothing in
the way of German 'trade'. During the assault, a total
of 171 British and US fighter squadrons undertook
a variety of tasks in support of the invasion: 15 flew
shipping cover, 54 provided cover over the assault
beaches, 33 were committed to bomber escort and
offensive fighter sweeps, 33 hit targets inland of the
assault beaches and 36 provided direct air support to
invading forces. Of greater importance by far, given
that the German air opposition was almost non-
existent, was the direct support provided to the forces
landed in Normandy.

▲ Bombing run

A Martin B-26B of the 556th Bomb Squadron, 387th Bomb Group, releases a stick
of bombs over a target in German-occupied Europe.

The French campaign
JUNE–SEPTEMBER 1944

The Ninth AAF helped the US First Army to consolidate its lodgement in Normandy, expand this by taking the Cotentin peninsula and then break out at St Lô and Avranches, and then supported the US Twelfth Army Group as it raced across France toward western Germany.

A S THE US TROOPS came ashore on 'Omaha' and 'Utah' Beaches, they discovered that the air and naval bombardments of the German coastal defences had failed to destroy a considerable portion of those defences. This was especially evident on 'Omaha' Beach, where the US forces suffered heavy casualties and were badly delayed.

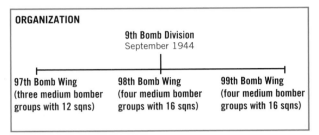

ORGANIZATION

	9th Bomb Division September 1944	
97th Bomb Wing (three medium bomber groups with 12 sqns)	98th Bomb Wing (four medium bomber groups with 16 sqns)	99th Bomb Wing (four medium bomber groups with 16 sqns)

Invasion support

Despite a series of attacks by heavy and medium bombers in the early hours of 6 June, the invading troops were checked on the beach itself. The air commanders had predicted that the air and naval bombardments would not wholly destroy the German defensive positions, but the army commanders had believed otherwise and were now sadly disabused. It was only the success of fighter-bombers in later battlefield operations that then restored the confidence of army commanders in the efficacy of air support.

Throughout the advance from the Normandy lodgement, it was the fighter-bomber that emerged as being more useful in the ground-attack role than the heavy or even the medium bomber. With the lodgement secure, the Ninth AAF's tactical air units

▲ **Martin B-26 Marauders**
The 'PN' codes identify these B-26B medium bombers as aircraft of the 449th Bomb Squadron, 322nd Bomb Group. This latter was the first B-26 group to be assigned to the European theatre.

then provided the air support for the US forces' break-out from the beach-head.

Contact cars

The most significant development in terms of tactical air support during the Normandy campaign was the establishment of a system of close liaison between air and armoured forces. In the Italian campaign, the British had initiated the use of 'contact cars' to operate as mobile air/surface control posts, and continued this successful practice in Normandy. Thus tactical air units always knew the exact position of the relevant British and German forces. The contact cars worked with reconnaissance aircraft, reducing the time required to summon air support. Brigadier-General Quesada developed a comparable system for the US forces in Normandy.

Shortly before the break out from St Lô to Avranches, Quesada felt that General Omar N. Bradley was unwilling to concentrate his armoured strength in the face of the Germans' strong defences. He therefore offered Bradley potent air support for an armoured concentration, from dawn to dusk, if he was provided with an armoured vehicle in which the relevant radio equipment and an air force pilot could be located for real-time communication with the fighter-bombers, which would be loitering overhead. Bradley agreed, and an initial two M4 Sherman medium tanks were modified. The concept worked

excellently, and immediately became a standard feature of the operations of the US First Army, and then of the US Twelfth Army Group.

By early in August 1944, most of the Ninth AAF's fighter and bomber groups had been moved to bases in France and assigned to support of the new US Twelfth Army Group. These groups were then assigned to tactical air commands which were allocated to specific armies: Brigadier-General Richard E. Nugent's XXIX Tactical Air Command supported the US Ninth Army in the north, Major-General Quesada's IX Tactical Air Command supported the US First Army in the centre, and Major-General Weyland's XIX TAC supported the US Third Army in the south.

Air cover over the US-controlled areas on the continent was provided by the new IX Air Defense Command, and bomber support by Major-General Anderson's 9th Bomb Division with three wings of 45 squadrons. As the land campaign moved west, the groups of the Ninth AAF kept pace with it in a succession of moves within France, then the Low Countries and finally western Germany. This ensured that the tactical air groups were always within range and, perhaps more importantly, could respond with minimum reaction time to emergencies.

▲ Martin B-26B Marauder
598th Bomb Squadron / 397th Bomb Group (Medium) / US Ninth Army Air Force, Dreux, France, September 944
Based at Rivenhall before D-Day but moving to France when this became feasible, the 397th Bomb Group was one of the 98th Combat Bomb Wing (Medium)'s four groups, and consisted of the 596th, 597th, 598th and 599th Bomb Squadrons.

Specifications

Crew: 7	length 17.75m (58ft 3in);
Powerplant: 2 x 1432kW (1920hp) Pratt	height 6.55m (21ft 6in)
& Whitney radial piston engines	Weight: 16,783kg (37,000b) loaded
Maximum speed: 453km/h (282mph)	Armament: 7 x 12.7mm (0.5in) MGs: one in
Range: 1851km (1150 miles)	the nose, two in dorsal turret, two in tail
Service ceiling: 6400m (21,000ft)	turret and two waist guns; 1818kg (4000lb)
Dimensions: span 21.64m (71ft);	of bombs

Germany defeated

JANUARY–MAY 1945

The beginning of 1945 found the Germans at the end of their tether after their offensive in the 'Battle of the Bulge' had been defeated. The warplanes of the Ninth AAF kept pounding at German tactical targets, and the US ground forces drove the Germans steadily back to the east.

DURING OPERATION *Dragoon*, the Franco-American invasion of southern France in August 1944, two fighter groups of the Ninth AAF were transferred to Major-General Ralph Royce's US/Free French 1st Tactical Air Force (Provisional), which had been created specifically to provide air support for the invasion force's advance to the north along the line of the Rhone river.

Battle of the Bulge

In the following month, as part of the intertwined but failed Operations Market and Garden to secure a crossing of the lower Rhine in the area of Arnhem in the Netherlands, the Ninth AAF transferred the whole of its IX Troop Carrier Command (14 groups with C-47 transports) to the Allied First Airborne Army in September 1944.

In December 1944 and January 1945, the fighters and bombers of the Ninth AAF played a decisive part in defeating the German offensive in the 'Battle of the Bulge': the Germans had timed the start of the offensive for adverse weather that would keep the Allied air forces on the ground, but fell behind schedule and were then caught and crushed with the aid of Allied air power as soon as the weather cleared sufficiently for the bombers and fighter-bombers to carry out ground attacks.

In overall terms, its support for the US Twelfth Army Group as this drove across France and through Luxembourg and Belgium toward the Netherlands and western Germany, had been the heyday of the Ninth AAF's existence in terms of its capabilities and the support provided. There was much very hard fighting on the ground, but the Ninth AAF was

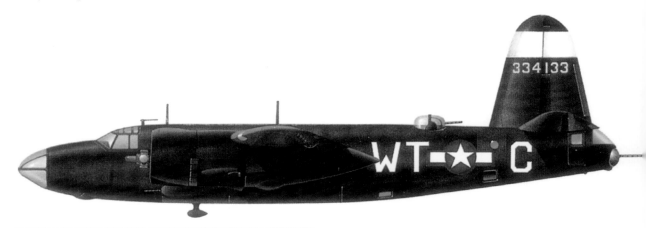

▲ Martin B-26G Marauder

456th Bomb Squadron / 323rd Bomb Group (Medium) / US Ninth Army Air Force, Laon, France, late 1944

Another element of the four-group 98th Combat Bomb Wing (Medium), and based at Horham before D-Day, the 323rd Bomb Group (Medium) comprised the 453rd, 454th, 455th and 456th Bomb Squadrons all flying in the medium bomber role.

Specifications

Crew: 7

Powerplant: 2 x 1491kW (2000hp) Pratt & Whitney radial piston engines

Maximum speed: 455km/h (283mph)

Range: 1770km (1100 miles)

Service ceiling: 6035m (19,800ft)

Dimensions: span 21.64m (71ft);

length 17.09m (56ft 1in);

height 6.20m (20ft 4in)

Weight: 17,327kg (38,200lb) loaded

Armament: 11 x 12.7mm (0.5in) MGs in fixed forward-firing, trainable nose and waist mounts, power-operated dorsal and tail turrets; up to 1813kg (4000lb) of bombs on hand to provide accurate and timely air support wherever the terrain permitted this and the weather made flying possible.

Glider operations

During the spring of 1945, the troop carrier groups of the Ninth AAF were instrumental in the delivery of paratrooper and glider units during the Allies' Operation *Varsity* assault crossing of the Rhine river on 24 March 1945: this was the single largest airborne operation in history, and its worst aspect was the 28 per cent losses suffered by the Curtiss C-49 Commando transports making their debut in Europe.

The Ninth AAF continued to provide its now-traditional level of tactical support to the ground forces of the US Army right to the end of the European war in May 1945, but was then cut back by rapid demobilization. Most personnel were returned to the USA and their units inactivated. Others were assigned to the new US Air Forces in Europe (USAFE) command on ex-*Luftwaffe* bases for occupation duties. Some transport units were relocated to France. Finally, the Ninth AAF was inactivated at the headquarters of the USAFE on 2 December 1945.

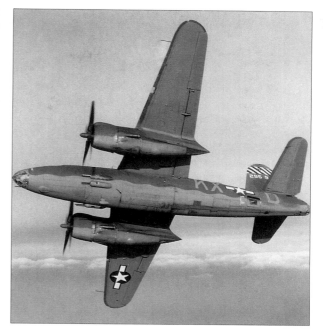

▲ **Bombing run**

This Martin B-26B-50-MA served with the 558th Bomb Squadron, flying 29 missions with the 'Mighty Eighth', before transferring to the Ninth Air Force in August 1944.

▲ **Douglas A-26B Invader**

552nd Bomb Squadron / 386th Bomb Group / US Ninth Army Air Force, Beaumont sur Oise, France, April 1945

Part of the 99th Combat Bomb Wing (Medium), the 386th Bomb Group (552nd, 553rd, 554th and 555th Bomb Squadrons) had been based at Great Dunmow before D-Day, but switched from the B-26 to the A-26 after arriving in Europe.

Specifications

Crew: 3

Powerplant: 2 x 1491kW (2000hp) Pratt & Whitney radial piston engines

Maximum speed: 600km/h (373mph)

Range: 2253km (1400 miles)

Service ceiling: 6735m (22,100ft)

Dimensions: span 21.34m (70ft);

length 15.62m (51ft 3in);

height 5.56m (18ft 3in)

Weight: 15,876kg (35,000lb) loaded

Armament: 6 x 12.7mm (0.5in) MGs: two each in nose, dorsal and ventral positions; up to 1814kg (4000lb) of bombs

US Air Forces in North Africa and the Mediterranean
1942–45

The North African and Italian campaigns of World War II were seen by the Americans largely as a 'sideshow', since they did not commit the main weight of the US forces directly against the primary enemy, Germany. Even so, three numbered air forces operated in this theatre.

THE ALLIED CAMPAIGNS in North Africa and Italy were supported by three numbered air forces: the Ninth, Twelfth and Fifteenth AAFs. The first was essentially a tactical air force, the second was a more evenly balanced formation, and the third was dedicated almost exclusively to the strategic role. This reflected the fact that as World War II continued, the offensive air forces of the USAAF were progressively classified as strategic or tactical.

The former's mission was to attack the enemy's war effort (in essence, weapon manufacture, supplies of essential raw materials and fuel, and transportation) deep behind the front. The mission of the latter was to support the ground forces (in or immediately behind the frontline) with objectives normally chosen through a process of cooperation with the field forces. In Europe, the Eighth AAF was the first

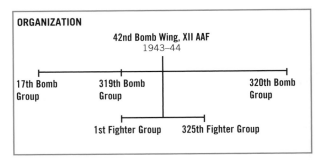

ORGANIZATION

42nd Bomb Wing, XII AAF
1943–44

17th Bomb Group   319th Bomb Group   320th Bomb Group

1st Fighter Group   325th Fighter Group

of the USAAF's strategic air forces, with a mission to pave the way for an invasion of continental Europe from the UK. The Eighth AAF originally included a number of tactical units, but many of these were transferred to the Twelfth AAF, which was formed in the UK during the autumn of 1942 as a tactical air force to provide air support for the Allied invasion

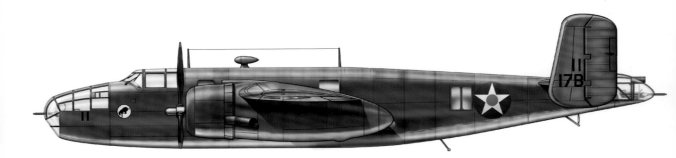

▲ **North American B-25A Mitchell**

17th Bomb Group (Medium) / USAAF, McChord Field, 1942

The 17th Bomb Group was the first USAAF unit to receive the new B-25 medium bomber (24 built). Production of the following B-25A, with self-sealing fuel tanks, totalled only 40 aircraft.

Specifications

Crew: 5

Powerplant: 2 x 1268kW (1700hp)

Maximum speed: 483km/h (300mph)

Range: 3219km (2000 miles)

Service ceiling: 7163m (23,500ft)

Dimensions: span 20.7m (68ft);

length 16.2m (53ft); height 0m (0ft)

Weight: 14,061kg (31,000lb) loaded

Armament: 1 x 7.6mm (0.3in) nose-mounted MG; 4 x 12.7mm (0.5in) MGs (pair in top and pair in bottom turret); 1361kg (3000lb) of bombs

of French north-west Africa in November of the same year.

The USAAF had begun planning for the development of a significant US air power capability in the Middle East as early as January 1942 in response to a request from the British. The first unit to arrive was designated as HALPRO and, under command of Colonel Harry A. Halverson, comprised 23 Consolidated B-24D Liberator four-engined heavy bombers with carefully selected crews.

HALPRO raids

On 12 June 1942, 13 of the the HALPRO B-24s took off from Fayid, Egypt to bomb the oil fields at Ploiesti in Romania. Only 12 aircraft actually completed the the attack at dawn. Four of the 13 landed at the Iraqi base designated for the task, three landed at other Iraqi airfields, two landed in Syria, and four were interned in Turkey. Though damage to the target was negligible, the raid was significant because it was the first USAAF combat mission in the North African and European theatres of operations in World War II.

On 15 June, seven HALPRO aircraft attacked units of the Italian fleet attempting to intercept a convoy from Alexandria to Malta. The Liberators achieved at least one direct hit on the battleship *Littorio*, but the convoy did not reach Malta because of the threat of the Italian warships.

On 17 June, HALPRO became part of the new US Army Forces in the Middle East, commanded by Major-General Russell L. Maxwell. The new command comprised HALPRO and a detachment of Boeing B-17Ds from the 7th Bomb Group at Allahabad in India under the command of Major-General Lewis H. Brereton.

The B-17Ds had been assigned to the China-Burma-India Theatre to attack targets in Japan from airfields in China. But the British loss of Burma allowed the Japanese to cut the Burma Road, and this prevented the logistical support of the bombers, which were therefore diverted to India.

To Egypt

On 2 July 1942, additional B-17Es from the 7th Bomb Group arrived from India at Lydda, Palestine, and on 20 July the B-24s and B-17s were formed into the 1st Provisional Group in Cairo. Soon after this, the USAAF deployed to this theatre the Curtiss P-40F single-engined fighter-bombers of the 57th Fighter Group, the North American B-25C twin-engined medium bombers of the 12th Bombardment Group (Medium), and the B-24D four-engined bombers of the 98th Bombardment Group (Heavy), together with a number of Douglas C-47 Skytrain twin-engined transport aircraft, to bases in Egypt and Palestine. US Air Forces in the Middle East (USAFIME) units took part in the British victory at

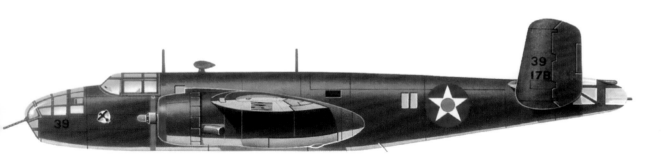

▲ **North American B-25A Mitchell**

34th Bomb Squadron / 17th Bomb Group (Medium), Pendleton, Oregon, 1942
The 17th Bomb Group was operational with the US Twelfth AAF before the end of December 1941, the month in which the United States entered World War II. Within a year, the Twelfth AAF would be in action in North Africa.

Specifications

Crew: 5	length 16.2m (53ft); height 0m (0ft)
Powerplant: 2 x 1268kW (1700hp)	Weight: 14,061kg (31,000lb) loaded
Maximum speed: 483km/h (300mph)	Armament: 1 x 7.6mm (0.3in) nose-mounted
Range: 3219km (2000 miles)	MG; 4 x 12.7mm (0.5in) MGs (pair in top
Service ceiling: 7163m (23,500ft)	and pair in bottom turret); 1361kg (3000lb)
Dimensions: span 20.7m (68ft);	of bombs

the second battle of El Alamein in November 1942, and its operations demonstrated the importance of having in this theatre a heavy bomber capability as well as tactical air assets. On 12 November 1942, the USAFIME was terminated and succeeded by the US Ninth Air Force, under the command of Lieutenant-General Frank M. Andrews, with triple tactical tasks: winning air superiority, denying the Axis forces the ability to resupply or make good their losses, and the provisiong of close air support for the Allied forces in North Africa.

Ninth AAF structure

At this time, the Ninth AAF North Africa comprised the IX Bomber Command, IX Fighter Command and 316th Troop Carrier Group. The IX Bomber Command controlled the 12th Bomb Group (Medium) with B-25C squadrons detached to the RAF, 98th Bomb Group (Heavy) with B-24Ds, 340th Bomb Group (Medium) with B-25Cs, and 376th Bomb Group (Heavy) with B-24Ds (previously the 1st Provisional Group USAAF).

The IX Fighter Command controlled the 57th Fighter Group with squadrons detached to RAF, 79th Fighter Group and 324th Fighter Group: all of these groups had P-40F fighter-bombers. By the end of 1942, some 370 aircraft had reached the Ninth Air Force. While the great majority were the B-24, B-25 and P-40 aircraft already mentioned, there were also more than 50 C-47 twin-engined transports, making it possible to create an effective local air transport service.

▲ **Consolidated B-24 Liberator**
The B-24D Teggie Ann kicks up the dust of a Libyan base while preparing for a mission. These aircraft were finished in a light shade known as desert pink.

First Ploiesti raid
JUNE 1942

The HALPRO raid on the Romanian oil facilities at Ploiesti was the first attack by bombers of the USAAF against a target in continental Europe. The raid was small and ineffective, but showed that Ploiesti was within range of North African bases, and that the USAAF meant business.

COMMANDED BY Colonel Harry A. Halverson, CHALPRO (Halverson Project no. 63) was a provisional unit equipped with 23 examples of the new Consolidated B-24D Liberator four-engined

heavy bomber, a type already making a good name for itself as a long-range bomber as a result of the considerable efficiency of its high-aspect-ratio wing. This range capability suggested the initial deployment of the B-24D for operations against Japan. HALPRO therefore left its base in Florida to reach the Tenth AAF in Burma. From here, it was proposed that the aircraft should be based around Chengtu in the province of Szechwan in China, and from a forward base at Chekiang launch a raid or raids on Tokyo, the capital of Japan.

However, after it had reached Khartoum in Sudan, HALPRO was instructed to wait since the April 1942 'Doolittle raid' on Japanese targets, undertaken by B-25 Mitchell bombers launched from a US Navy aircraft carrier, had persuaded the Japanese that the aircraft must be operating from China, and they therefore launched an offensive toward Chekiang.

Specifications

Crew: 10

Powerplant: 4 x 895kW (1200hp) Pratt & Whitney Twin wasp radial piston engines

Maximum speed: 467km/h (290mph)

Range: 5955km (3700 miles)

Service ceiling: 8535m (28000ft)

Dimensions: span 33.53m (110ft);

length 20.47m (67ft 2in); height 5.49m (18ft)

Weight: 25,401kg (56,000lb) loaded

Armament: 2 x 12.7mm (0.5in) Browning trainable MGs in nose, dorsal, ventral 'ball' and tail turrets, and one each in beam positions; up to 5806kg (12,800lb) of bombs

▲ Consolidated B-24D Liberator

98th Bomb Group / IX Bomber Command / USAAF, Benghazi, Libya, 1943

On 20 February 1943, this aircraft became lost and landed inadvertently on the Italian airfield at Pachino in Sicily, where it was captured after an earlier attack on Naples.

Specifications

Crew: 10

Powerplant: 4 x 895kW (1200hp) Pratt & Whitney Twin wasp radial piston engines

Maximum speed: 467km/h (290mph)

Range: 5955km (3700 miles)

Service ceiling: 8535m (28000ft)

Dimensions: span 33.53m (110ft);

length 20.47m (67ft 2in); height 5.49m (18ft)

Weight: 25,401kg (56,000lb) loaded

Armament: 2 x 12.7mm (0.5in) Browning trainable MGs in nose, dorsal, ventral 'ball' and tail turrets, and one each in beam positions; up to 5806kg (12,800lb) of bombs

▲ Consolidated B-24D Liberator

376th Bomb Group / 47th Bomb Wing / US Fifteenth AAF, Libya, 1943

This aeroplane, wearing a desert-pink finish under its mix of US and British national markings, was on the strength of the 'Liberandos', or 376th Bomb Group, during their attack of 1 August 1943 on the Romanian oil fields at Ploiesti.

HALPRO was then ordered to proceed to Fayid near the Great Bitter Lake in Egypt, and prepare for a raid on Ploiesti before flying south-east to a base in British Iraq, a distance of some 4185km (2600 miles). There were no accurate maps, the raid would be flown at night, and the crews were wholly inexperienced in combat. They were also flying aircraft of a variant that had not been blooded.

Limited success

Thirteen aircraft took off late in the night of 11/ 12 June, and 12 of these reached the vicinity of the target, where they bombed without success but also without loss over the target before departing to a number of safe locations. Eight bombs fell into the Black Sea, two on Constanza, six on Ploiesti, six on Teisani and several on Ciofliceni. In total, three people were killed.

There was no publicity of the type that had followed the 'Doolittle raid', but the USAAF had entered combat over Europe in a raid that confirmed its ability to strike at distant targets.

US Ninth Army Air Force: Mediterranean operations
1942–45

The Ninth AAF cut its operational teeth in North Africa in support of the British Eighth Army, and moved steadily west with the advance to meet forces, including the new Twelfth AAF, moving from the west. The Allied junction in Tunisia spelled the end for the Axis forces in North Africa.

THE FIGHTERS OF THE Ninth Army Air Force supported the westward drive of the British Eighth Army across Egypt and Libya, with bomber escort as well as ground-attack and dive-bombing missions against Axis airfields, lines of communication and troop concentrations. The Ninth AAF also attacked shipping and harbour installations in North Africa, Sicily, Italy, Crete and Greece as part of the Allied effort to cut the supply lines used by the Axis powers to nourish their forces in North Africa.

In February 1943, after the Axis forces had been compressed into Tunisia, the Germans took the offensive and pushed through the Kasserine Pass before being stopped. Units of both the US Ninth and Twelfth AAFs were involved in this part of the campaign, in which the Allies checked the Kasserine Pass and other Axis thrusts before driving the surviving German and Italian forces back into a coastal lodgement around Bizerta and Tunis. Here the last Axis forces surrendered in May.

The victory not only ended the North African campaign, but gave the Allies the use of Tunisia as the springboard from which to launch an

ORGANIZATION

US 9th AAF
Spring 1943

| IX Bomber Command (two heavy & two medium bomb groups) | IX Fighter Command (three fighter groups) | 316th Troop Carrier Group |

IX BOMBER COMMAND UNITS

Unit	Type	Aircraft type
12th Bomb Group	Medium	B-25C
98th Bomb Group	Heavy	B-24D
340th Bomb Group	Medium	B-25C
376h Bomb Group	Heavy	B-24D
57th Fighter Group	Fighter-bomber	P-40F
79th Fighter Group	Fighter-bomber	P-40F
324th Fighter Group	Fighter-bomber	P-40F

amphibious descent on Sicily as the prelude to an assault on Italy proper. Following the Allied victory in Tunisia, Ninth AAF groups attacked airfields and rail facilities in Sicily and Italy.

Transport elements of the Ninth AAF were involved in Operation *Husky,* the Allied amphibious invasion of Sicily, delivering paratroopers and flying reinforcements to the ground forces. The heavy bomber elements also participated in the *Tidal Wave* low-level attack on the oil refineries at Ploiesti on 1 August 1943. In August and September 1943, Ninth AAF units in North Africa were transferred to the Twelfth AAF as preparations were made for the reconstitution of the Ninth AAF in the UK for service in and after the *Overlord* invasion of Normandy. The Ninth AAF was inactivated in Egypt on 16 October 1943.

In mid-1942, a series of Allied planning meetings was held to develop an overall strategy for the prosecution of the war in North Africa against Germany and Italy, whose forces held the central coastal part of North Africa, with the Vichy French colonial forces holding the portion farther to the west and round onto the Atlantic coast of French Morocco south-west of the Strait of Gibraltar.

The first step in this process was to be Operation *Torch,* the landing of the Allied First Army in French north-west Africa during November 1942, to take French North Africa and then advance east to meet the British Eight Army advancing from the east.

Specifications

Crew: 5	length 16.2m (53ft); height 0m (0ft)
Powerplant: 2 x 1268kW (1700hp)	Weight: 18,960kg (41,800lb) loaded
Maximum speed: 457km/h (284mph)	Armament: 2 x 12.7mm (0.5in) nose-mounted
Range: 3219km (2000 miles)	MGs; 4 x 12.7mm (0.5in) MGs (pair in top
Service ceiling: 7163m (23,500ft)	and pair in bottom turret); 2359kg (5200lb)
Dimensions: span 20.7m (68ft);	of bombs

▲ **North American B-25C Mitchell**

487th Bomb Squadron / 340th Bomb Group / USAAF, Catania, Sicily, September 1943

Wearing a mix of USAAF and RAF markings, the latter exemplified by the fin flashes, this aeroplane has desert-sand upper surfaces and sky-blue under surfaces.

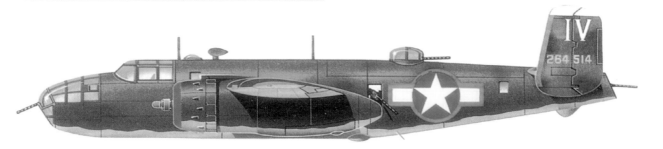

Specifications

Crew: 5	length 16.2m (53ft); height 0m (0ft)
Powerplant: 2 x 1268kW (1700hp)	Weight: 18,960kg (41,800lb) loaded
Maximum speed: 457km/h (284mph)	Armament: 2 x 12.7mm (0.5in) nose-mounted
Range: 3219km (2000 miles)	MGs; 4 x 12.7mm (0.5in) MGs (pair in top
Service ceiling: 7163m (23,500ft)	and pair in bottom turret); 2359kg (5200lb)
Dimensions: span 20.7m (68ft);	of bombs

▲ **North American B-25C Mitchell**

81st Bomb Squadron / 12th Bomb Group / USAAF, Gerbini, Sicily, August 1943

By this time, the Allies had taken Sicily and were quickly developing its facilities, and especially its air bases and airfields, to accommodate the tactical warplanes that would be required for the September 1943 invasion of the Italian mainland at Salerno, and the operations which would follow that.

US Twelfth Army Air Force
1942–45

Because Operation *Torch* required a new air organization to provide enough manpower and equipment, plans for the creation and outfitting of a new Twelfth AAF were developed alongside the preparations for the invasion proper and subsequent campaign.

T HE TWELFTH AAF was activated on 20 August 1942 at Bolling air base in Maryland, and on 23 September 1942 Brigadier-General James 'Jimmy' Doolittle formally assumed command of the Twelfth AAF with Colonel Hoyt S. Vandenberg as his chief of staff. Barely four months after it had been conceived, the Twelfth AAF was able to make its first contributions to World War II, for when the North African invasion was launched on 8 November 1942, the Twelfth AAF was ready to undertake the role intended for it by providing tactical air support for the Allied First Army as it moved to link with the British Eighth Army and encompass the overwhelming defeat of the Axis forces in North Africa by May 1943.

XII Bomber Command reactivated

The XII Bomber Command was activated at MacDill air base in Florida on 13 March, was assigned to the Twelfth AAF in August and transferred, without personnel and equipment, to High Wycombe in England, where it was re-established. It moved to Tafaraoui in Algeria on 22 November 1942 in the immediate aftermath of the Torch landings in

ORGANIZATION

US Twelfth AAF
Summer 1944

| XII Bomber Command (four bomb wings) | XII Tactical Air Command (one heavy bomber, two medium bomber & one fighter wings) | XXII Fighter Command (three fighter wings) |

5TH BOMB WING, TWELFTH AAF (1943–44)

Unit	Type	Aircraft type
2nd Bomb Group	Heavy bomber	B-17
47th Bomb Group	Attack bomber	A-20 & A-26
97th Bomb Group	Heavy bomber	B-17
98th Bomb Group	Heavy bomber	B-24
99th Bomb Group	Heavy bomber	B-17
301st Bomb Group	Heavy bomber	B-17
376th Bomb Group	Heavy bomber	B-24
463rd Bomb Group	Heavy bomber	B-17
483rd Bomb Group	Heavy bomber	B-17
1st Fighter Group	Fighter	P-38
14th Fighter Group	Fighter	P-38
82nd Fighter Group	Fighter	P-38
325th Fighter Group	Fighter	P-38
68th Recce Group	Reconnaissance	varied

North Africa. The Twelfth AAF later saw large-scale action over Sicily, Italy and southern France in support of the US Fifth and Seventh Armies and their allies. The Twelfth AAF acquired an excellent reputation, and by VE-Day in May 1945 had flown some 430,680 sorties, claimed the destruction of 2857 German and Italian aircraft, and lost 2667 of its own aircraft.

With hostilities over, the Twelfth AAF was inactivated at Florence, in northern Italy, on 31 August 1945. The Twelfth AAF had incorporated

▲ **North American B-25 Mitchells**

A section of B-25 Mitchells gets airborne from Sousse in Tunisia, some time late in 1943, for a mission to Italy.

three subordinate formations, namely the XII Bomber Command, XII Tactical Air Command (originally XII Air Support Command) and XXII Tactical Air Command.

The XII Bomber Command was operational in the Mediterranean theatre until 1 November 1943, when most of its manpower was withdrawn, but it then received additional personnel in January 1944 and was operational once more to 1 March 1944

before being inactivated in Corsica on 10 June 1944. The XII Tactical Air Command was initially planned as the XII Ground Air Support Command on 10 September 1942, activated on 17 September, assigned to the Twelfth AAF as the XII Air Support Command, and redesignated as the XII Tactical Air Command in April 1944.

The command moved to French Morocco on 9 November 1942 as part of the Torch campaign,

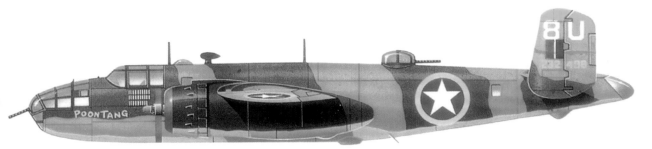

Specifications

Crew: 5	length 16.2m (53ft); height 0m (0ft)
Powerplant: 2 x 1268kW (1700hp)	Weight: 18,960kg (41,800lb) loaded
Maximum speed: 457km/h (284mph)	Armament: 2 x 12.7mm (0.5in) nose-mounted
Range: 3219km (2000 miles)	MGs; 4 x 12.7mm (0.5in) MGs (pair in top
Service ceiling: 7163m (23,500ft)	and pair in bottom turret); 2359kg (5200lb)
Dimensions: span 20.7m (68ft);	of bombs

▲ North American B-25C Mitchell

488th Bomb Squadron / 340th Bomb Group / US Twelfth AAF, Sfax, Tunisia, April 1943

With a disruptive olive-drab pattern over the original desert sand finish, this B-25C has the yellow ring round the national markings (used in North Africa up to June 1943) and British fin flashes. The dorsal turret was adopted on the B-25B.

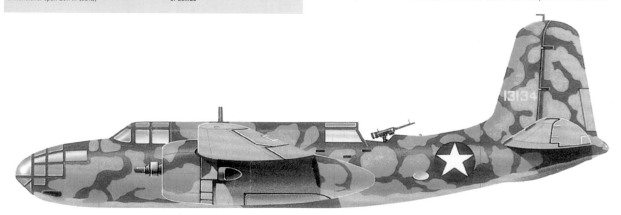

▲ Douglas A-20B Havoc

84th Bomb Squadron / 47th Bomb Group / US Twelfth AAF, Mediouna, Morocco, December 1942

The A-20B light attack bomber was the USAAF's counterpart of the DB-7A delivered by Douglas to the French Air Force. The aeroplane could carry 1179kg (2600lb) of bombs internally, and had two fixed forward-firing machine guns.

Specifications

Crew: 2–3	Weight: 9414kg (20,710lb) loaded
Powerplant: 2 x 1192kW (1600hp) Wright radials	Armament: 2 x 12.7mm (0.5in) forward-firing
Maximum speed: 563km/h (350mph)	MGs in forward fuselage; 1 x 12.7mm (0.5in)
Range: 3701km (2300 miles)	MG in flexible dorsal position; 1 x 7.62mm
Service ceiling: 8687m (28,500ft)	(0.3in) MG in ventral tunnel; 2 x rearward-
Dimensions: span 18.69m (61ft 4in);	firing 7.62mm (0.3in) MGs in engine nacelles;
length 14.63m (48ft); height 5.51m (18ft 1in)	1179kg (2600lb) bombs

and served operationally in the Mediterranean and European theatres until May 1945. It then remained in Europe as part of the US Air Forces in Europe until inactivated at Bad Kissingen in Germany on 10 November 1947.

The XXII Tactical Air Command was activated on 5 March 1942, and redesignated as the XII Fighter Command in May 1942 before becoming the XXII Tactical Air Command in November 1944. The command was assigned to the Twelfth AAF during August 1942 and moved to Wattisham in England during September before reaching Tafaraoui in Algeria on 8 November 1942. The command was operational in the Mediterranean until the end of the war, and was inactivated at Pomigliano in Italy on 4 October 1945.

57TH BOMB WING, TWELFTH AAF (1944)		
Unit	Type	Aircraft type
12th Bomb Group	Medium bomber	B-25
310th Bomb Group	Medium bomber	B-25
319th Bomb Group	Medium bomber	B-25
321st Bomb Group	Medium bomber	B-25
340th Bomb Group	Medium bomber	B-25
47th Bomb Group	Attack bomber	A-20 & A-26
57th Fighter Group	Fighter-bomber	P-40
79th Fighter Group	Fighter-bomber	P-40

Specifications

Crew: 7

Powerplant: 2 x 1400kW (1900hp) Pratt & Whitney R-2800-43 radial engines

Maximum speed: 4600km/h (287mph)

Range: 4590km (2850 miles)

Service ceiling: 6400m (21,000ft)

Dimensions: span 21.65m (71ft); length 17.8m (58ft 3in); height 6.55m (21ft 6in)

Weight: 17,000kg (37,000lb) loaded

Armament: 12 x 12.7mm (0.5in) Colt-Browning MGs; 1800kg (4000lb) bomb load

▲ **Martin B-26B Marauder**

444th Bomb Squadron / 320th Bomb Group / US Twelfth Army Air Force, Decimomannu, Sardinia, 1945

Operating primarily over northern Italy, the aircraft of the 444th Bomb Squadron all gained shark's mouth markings on the forward fuselage during the last months of the war.

▲ **Douglas A-20 Havoc light attack bombers**

These A-20Bs were flown by the 84th Bomb Squadron, 47th Bomb Group, from the base at Mediouna, Morocco, during December 1942. Large patches of brown were applied over the original olive-drab finish to create a makeshift but nonetheless effective North African camouflage.

US Fifteenth Army Air Force
1943–45

The Fifteenth AAF was established on 1 November 1943 in Tunis. It was conceived specifically as a strategic rather than tactical air force.

THE FIFTEENTH AAF began combat operations on 2 November, the day after its establishment, under the command of Major-General Doolittle, whose previous command, the Twelfth AAF, was now led by Major-General Carl Spaatz and, from 21 December of the same year, Major-General John K. Cannon.

The Fifteenth AAF was not an altogether new formation, for it drew its initial forces from the IX Bomber Command when the Ninth AAF was relocating to the UK to become a tactical air force for north-west European operations, and through a diversion of other bomb groups that had originally been destined for service with the Eighth AAF in England.

The Fifteenth AAF moved to Bari in south-eastern Italy on 1 December 1943, and operated from a growing number of bases in this flat region in raids over German-held northern Italy, Germany, Austria, Hungary and the Balkans.

European remit

The Fifteenth AAF grew quickly and strongly in power and, with the Eighth AAF and RAF Bomber Command, became one of the primary weapons in the Allied strategic air offensive against German targets in occupied Europe and Germany. The Fifteenth AAF eventually grew to six Boeing B-17 and 15 Consolidated B-24 groups, and it lost some 2110 of its aircraft, while its seven fighter groups claimed 1836 German aircraft destroyed. The Fifteenth AAF was inactivated in Italy on 15 September 1945.

Specifications

Crew: 10

Powerplant: 4 x 895kW (1200hp) Pratt & Whitney Twin wasp radial piston engines

Maximum speed: 467km/h (290mph)

Range: 3380km (2100 miles)

Service ceiling: 8535m (28,000ft)

Dimensions: span 33.53m (110ft); length 20.47m (67ft 2in); height 5.49m (18ft)

Weight: 32,296kg (71,200lb) loaded

Armament: 2 x 12.7mm (0.5in) Browning trainable MGs in nose, dorsal, ventral 'ball' and tail turrets, and one MG in each beam position; up to 5806kg (12,800lb) of bombs

▲ **Consolidated B-24J Liberator**

449th Bomb Group / US Fifteenth Army Air Force, Mediterranean Theatre, late 1944

With its wing characterized by a high aspect ratio, the B-24 was aerodynamically efficient, and its primary advantage over the B-17 was therefore greater range.

US maritime operations
1941–45

Before World War II, the maritime defence of the United States had been largely a prerogative of the US Army Air Corps, which commissioned aircraft such as the Boeing B-17 for this purpose. In World War II, the primary responsibility switched steadily to US naval aviation.

JUST FOUR DAYS after Germany's invasion of Poland started World War II, President Franklin D. Roosevelt declared the neutrality of the USA, and also that nation's intention of ensuring this neutrality, by force if necessary.

Roosevelt was, in fact, strongly pro-British, and the US military of the period was poorly prepared for real military operations. The US Navy was ordered to establish a Neutrality Patrol to 555km (345 miles) off the US east coast, running south along the boundary of the Caribbean. The entry of any foreign warship entering the zone was to be reported immediately, and a force, more imposing on paper than in reality, was available to enforce the patrol: four battleships, five cruisers, some 40 destroyers and two aircraft carriers.

In fact, most of the required patrol work fell on the shoulders of five flying boat squadrons supported by four tenders. In all, 36 Consolidated PBY and 18 older Consolidated P2Y flying boats were based at Newport, Rhode Island; Norfolk, Virginia; and in Cuba and Puerto Rico. Detachments were also sent to Charleston, South Carolina, and Key West, Florida. In 1940, two patrol squadrons were commissioned at Norfolk.

Convoy protection

A support organization was established in March 1941 as the Support Force Atlantic Fleet destroyers and a patrol wing of five squadrons. Directed to prepare for operations in northern waters, the patrol crews practised convoy escort and anti-submarine warfare. The intent was to prevent German commerce raiders and U-boats from severing the maritime route linking the USA and UK. Elements of Patrol Squadron 52 (VP-52) arrived at Argentia in Newfoundland during mid May 1941. Only six days after their arrival, the news that the German

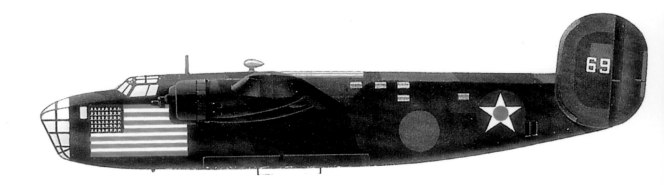

▲ **Consolidated LB-30B**

Unknown squadron / USAAF, Bolling Field, 1941

This was an aeroplane ordered by the British as a night bomber but taken over by the USAAF before delivery to the UK and adapted as a transport. The RAF roundels were overpainted but just evident on the fuselage sides, and large US flags were painted on each side of the nose and above the fuselage to indicate neutrality.

Specifications

Crew: 10

Powerplant: 4 x 895kW (1200hp) Pratt & Whitney Twin wasp radial piston engines

Maximum speed: 467km/h (290mph)

Range: 5955km (3700 miles)

Service ceiling: 8535m (28000ft)

Dimensions: span 33.53m (110ft); length 20.47m (67ft 2in); height 5.49m (18ft)

Weight: 25,401kg (56,000lb) loaded

Armament: N/A

battleship Bismarck had sunk the British battle-cruiser Hood in the Denmark Strait led to the lift-off of 11 of VP-52's PBYs to search for the German warship, but the aircraft became lost and scattered, and it was several days before they all returned to Argentia.

Hunting the Bismarck

Some 17 PBY pilots had been sent to the UK in April to instruct Coastal Command of the RAF in Catalina operations. US Navy pilots then started to fly search missions with Coastal Command squadrons, one of these men being Ensign Leonard B. Smith, who was assigned to No. 209 Squadron at Lough Erne in Northern Ireland. Flying his second operational sortie, Smith spotted the German battleship. The Catalina's crew watched the Bismarck for the next four hours, awaiting relief. Each of the next two Catalinas to arrive on station also had a US Navy pilot on board, and finally a British battleship and cruiser force caught and destroyed the Bismarck. British and US cooperation continued during the summer as six new Martin PBM Mariners of VP-74 and six PBY-5s of VP-73 moved to Skerjafjord in Iceland during August.

US FIRST-LINE AIR STRENGTHS			
Date	USAAF	USN & USMC	Total
January 1942	1622	1915	3573
January 1943	3174	8268	11,442
January 1944	4911	13,065	17,976
January 1945	5827	14576	20,403
July 1945	7260	14648	21,908

Though supported by a US Navy tender, the aircraft also used RAF moorings, and the area of the Atlantic that could be covered was radically increased. In October, four Catalinas also deployed to Greenland for three weeks.

Three aircraft carriers were also involved in the Neutrality Patrol, operating from Norfolk, Virginia, for most of the period. The Ranger, Wasp and Yorktown undertook periodic sorties into the Atlantic and Caribbean, but these were more training exercises than operational cruises. The Wasp was at sea on 7 December 1941 with the Yorktown's VF-5 fighter squadron on board. The Yorktown was rushed to the Pacific, and VF-5 did not catch up with its parent air group for more than six months.

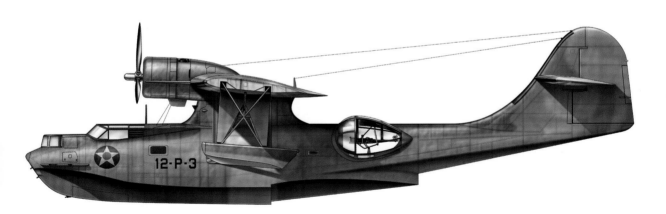

▲ Consolidated PBY-5

VP-12 (Patrol Squadron 12) / US Navy, 1942

Long-ranged and reliable, the flying boats of the PBY series were at the heart of the US Navy's maritime reconnaissance capability in World War II. And with the ability to carry two torpedoes, or four depth charges or four 454kg (1000lb) bombs, the PBY was also a very useful 'bomber'.

Specifications

Crew: 7–9

Powerplant: 2 x 895kW (1200hp)

Maximum speed: 288km/h (179mph)

Range: 4096km (2545 miles)

Service ceiling: 4480m (14,700ft)

Dimensions: span 31.7m (104ft);

length 19.47m (63ft 11in);

height 6.15m (20ft 2in)

Weight: 16,066kg (35,420lb) loaded

Armament: 3 x 7.62mm (0.3in) trainable MGs: two in the bow turret, one firing aft of the hull step; 1 x 12.7mm (0.5in) MG in each of the two beam positions; up to 1814kg (4000lb) of bombs or depth charges

Specifications

Crew: 7

Powerplant: 2 x 1300kW (170hp) Wright
R-2600-12 14-cylinder radial engines

Maximum speed: 330km/h (205mph)

Range: 4800km (3000 miles)

Service ceiling: 6040m (19,800ft)

Dimensions: span 36m (118ft);

length 23.50m (77ft 2in); height 5.33m
(17ft 6in)

Weight: 25,425kg (56,000lb) loaded

Armament: 4 x 12.7mm (0.5in) MGs (one
each in nose and dorsal turrets, blisters
amidships), plus 1800kg (4000lb) of bombs
or depth charges or 2 x Mark 13 torpedoes

▲ Martin PBM-1 Mariner
VP-74 / US Navy, USA, 1942

The PBM-1 was the first production model of the Mariner family, and only 20 of this variant were built. The PBM-1 was equipped with retractable wing landing floats that were hinged inboard. The following PBM-3 had longer nacelles, each possessing a bay for four 227kg (500lb) bombs or depth charges, and fixed rather than retractable underwing stabilizing floats.

Anti-submarine warfare
1942

The squadrons and airmen of the US Navy soon found that the intensity of real combat operations off the USA's eastern seaboard and over the North Atlantic was considerably more taxing than the Neutrality Patrol, but after a slow start started to come to grips with the task.

NOW THE USA was no longer neutral, and US Naval Aviation was faced with altogether more pressing demands on two fronts. The war in the Atlantic was primarily an anti-submarine effort. For the first 18 months of the US entry into World War II, anti-submarine warfare squadrons were exclusively land-based.

U-boat threat

Though based extensively on each side of the Atlantic, the aircraft had only modest ranges, and this left large holes in the trade routes in which the U-boats could operate with little fear of air attack. Once Germany had declared war on the USA on 11 December 1941, Admiral Karl Dönitz ordered his packs of U-boats to start operating in US waters from January 1942. Here the U-boats found perhaps their best hunting of the whole war. Ill-prepared

▲ Consolidated PBY-6A
Production of this amphibious flying boat totalled 235 machines. Some 48 were delivered to the USSR, and 75 to the USAAF, by which the type was known as the OA-10B.

for hostilities, the Atlantic coast continued to glow with city lights and navigational beacons operating normally, and many ships sailed independently and without escort.

The U-boats sank 26 ships off the US and Canadian coasts in January 1942. In February, the U-boats slipped into the Gulf of Mexico, attacking oil tankers and other merchant ships, and achieving 42 sinkings.

A shooting war

The situation improved but little in the rest of 1942, for Allied shipping losses were greater than new construction. However, measures were being implemented to improve the situation, albeit only slowly. Some parts of the Neutrality Patrol were already in position as the shooting war started. Patrol Wing Seven covered the northern routes from Newfoundland and Iceland, Patrol Wing Five operated from Norfolk, Virginia, and Patrol Wing Three flew from the Panama Canal Zone.

With some foresight, Natal in Brazil had been prepared as an anti-submarine warfare (ASW) base during December 1941, and by late in 1942 three patrol squadrons were based there. Eventually they

▲ **Catalina blister gunner**

Possessing good fields of fire and observation, the blister gunner/observer provided a measure of defence against beam attacks and watched the sea.

were joined by Martin PBMs and Lockheed Venturas of Fleet Air Wing 16 during 1943.

Meanwhile, the German U-boats continued to enjoy success in its campaign in US east coast waters.

Specifications

Crew: 7–9

Powerplant: 2 x 895kW (1200hp) engines

Maximum speed: 288km/h (179mph)

Range: 4096km (2545 miles)

Service ceiling: 4480m (14,700ft)

Dimensions: span 31.7m (104ft);

length 19.47m (63ft 11in);

height 6.15m (20ft 2in)

Weight: 16,066kg (35,420lb) loaded

Armament: 3 x 7.62mm (0.3in) trainable MGs: two in the bow turret, one firing aft of the hull step; 1 x 12.7mm (0.5in) MG in each of the two beam positions; up to 1814kg (4000lb) of bombs or depth charges

▲ **Consolidated PBY-5 Catalina**

VP-44 (Patrol Squadron 44) / US Navy, 1942

The large blistered transparencies on the waist of the PBY's hull to the rear of the wing pylon provided excellent vantage points for a pair of observers, each armed with a single 7.62 or 12.7mm (0.3 or 0.5in) Browning trainable machine gun.

May was the worst month to date, with 72 ships sent to the bottom. While few U-boats were lost, the patrol squadrons did score occasional successes. During the summer, for example, a PBY of VP-73 scored a direct hit with a depth charge on the wooden deck planking of a surfaced U-boat. The charge was pushed overboard, sank to its preset detonation depth and exploded, sinking the boat.

Specifications

Crew: 6

Powerplant: 2 x 750kW (1000hp) Wright R-1820-53 radial engines

Maximum speed: 346km/h (215mph)

Range: 1850km (1150 miles)

Service ceiling: 7280m (23,900ft)

Dimensions: span 27.3m (89ft 6in); length 17.6m (57ft 10in); height 4.6m (15ft 2in)

Weight: 10,030kg (22,123lb) loaded

Armament: 3 x 7.62mm (03in) MGs, plus a bom load of up to 2200kg (4500lb)

▲ **Douglas B-18B Bolo**

Unknown squadron / USAAF, USA, 1942

Lacking adequate coastal and maritime reconnaissance aircraft when it entered the war, the USAAF converted 122 B-18A bombers as B-18B anti-submarine aircraft with search radar (antenna in the nose radome) and the Magnetic Anomaly Detector Mk IV with its sensor to the rear of the tail unit.

North Atlantic operations
1943–44

Despite all their efforts to out-think and outfight the Allied air squadrons, the U-boat arm was steadily matched in 1942 and outmatched in 1943. By 1944, the US Navy's patrol bomber and anti-submarine squadrons were in the ascendant, and there was nothing the Germans could do.

S LOWLY AND METHODICALLY, the ASW squadrons assimilated their experience and evolved an effective tactical method. The advent of new equipment, such as improved search radar, more effective weapons and more efficient aircraft, was critical. The submarine war was perhaps the most technological of all, and small improvements in detection or warning equipment gave each side a useful if temporary advantage.

Perhaps best-suited for the long-range ASW role was the Consolidated Liberator four-engined bomber.

Designed for the US Army Air Corps as the B-24, the Liberator became the US Navy's PB4Y-1, later evolved into the PB4Y-2 Privateer with a single than twin vertical tail surfaces. With exceptional range and the ability to carry heavy offensive and defensive armament, the PB4Y was a very capable submarine hunter and killer. But so were aircraft as different as the PBM Mariner flying boat and the slow, and generally under-rated, 'blimp' airship.

Another way in which the U-boat was countered was the 1942 creation of 15 inshore patrol squadrons

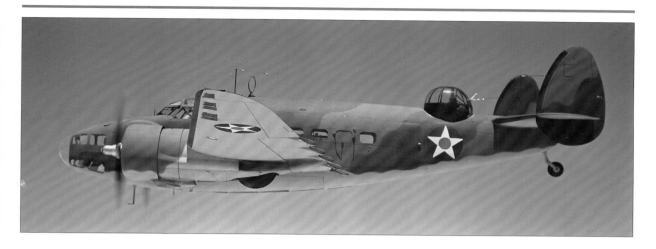

▲ **A-29 submarine hunter**

The first submarines sunk by US aircraft were claimed by US Navy patrol VP-82, equipped with A-29s originally intended for British use under the Lend-Lease scheme.

for service along the USA's eastern seaboard and in the Caribbean. Another 15 such squadrons were also established for service along the USA's western seaboard, at Coco Solo in the Panama Canal Zone, and Pearl Harbor.

On 17 October 1942, these inshore patrol squadrons came under the control of the patrol wings. Originally equipped with the Vought OS2U floatplane, the squadrons were bolstered by the arrival of Douglas SBD Devastators for the ASW role. By the middle of 1944, the U-boat threat had largely disappeared, and the inshore patrol squadrons were steadily inactivated, all having disappeared by the end of World War II.

Central Atlantic operations

In the Atlantic theatre, the establishment of new bases helped to close the 'Atlantic Gap' in which air

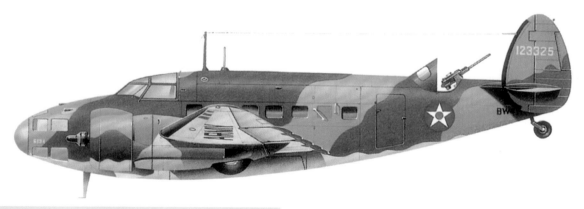

Specifications

Crew: 6

Powerplant: 2 x 820 kW (1100 hp) Wright Cyclone 9-cylinder radial engines

Maximum speed: 397km/h (246mph)

Range: 3150km (1960 miles)

Service ceiling: 7470m (24,000ft)

Dimensions: span 19.96m (65ft 6in); length 13.51m (44ft 4in); height 3.62m (11ft 10in)

Weight: 7930kg (17,500lb) loaded

Armament: 4 x 9.7mm (0.303in) Browning MGs, 2 in nose, 2 in dorsal turret; 340kg (750lb) of bombs or depth charges

▲ **Lockheed A-29**

Unknown group / USAAF, USA, 1943

While early examples of Hudson repossessed by the USAAF for service with the designation A-29 retained the Boulton Paul turret specified by the British, later aircraft such as that seen here had an open gunner's position with a 12.7mm (0.5in) machine gun. The British camouflage and serial were retained.

patrol had previously been impossible. Airfields in the West Indies, along the Brazilian coast and finally on Ascension Island did much to enhance the overall level of protective air cover that could be provided to convoys. New aircraft and improved technology could not in themselves ensure the defeat of the U-boat, however. Before the end of 1942, US Navy patrol squadrons were operating on both sides of the Atlantic. Fleet Air Wing 15's two original squadrons were operational from Casablanca and Port Lyautey in French Morocco within hours of the Vichy French surrender of 11 November.

Squadrons of Lockheed Ventura twin-engined and Liberator four-aircraft patrol aircraft increasingly supplemented the PBY in the first half of 1943, covering the North Atlantic convoys routes from Iceland to Morocco as far as their ranges permitted. But the Germans were themselves slightly on the ascendant once more. As the Allied coastal air patrols increased, *Luftwaffe* maritime aircraft became increasingly aggressive during May 1943. While Focke-Wulf Fw 200 and other long-range aircraft had previously been content to shadow convoys and radio reports of their positions, courses and speeds, they now attacked ships more frequently in the Bay of Biscay, diverting Allied squadrons from ASW work to

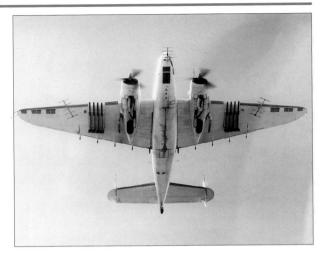

▲ **Lockheed Hudson**

This view of a Hudson Mk IV shows developments to boost capability: the eight under-wing rocket projectiles were potent submarine killers, and ASV.Mk II radar (antennae under the wing and on the nose) was a capable search equipment.

convoy air defence. In the summer, the U-boats were ordered to fight it out with aircraft: fitted with ever heavier batteries of light flak weapons, they remained on the surface and resisted as they made high-speed passage to and from their operational areas.

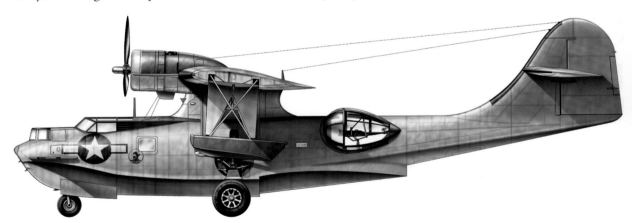

Specifications

Crew: 7–9

Powerplant: 2 x 895kW (1200hp) engines

Maximum speed: 288km/h (179mph)

Range: 4096km (2545 miles)

Service ceiling: 4480m (14,700ft)

Dimensions: span 31.7m (104ft);

length 19.47m (63ft 11in);

height 6.15m (20ft 2in)

Weight: 16,066kg (35,420lb) loaded

Armament: 3 x 7.62mm (0.3in) trainable MGs: two in the bow turret, one firing aft of the hull step; 1 x 12.7mm (0.5in) MG in each of the two beam positions; up to 1814kg (4000lb) of bombs or depth charges

▲ **Consolidated PBY-5A**

Unknown squadron / US Navy, mid war years

The general versatility of the PBY series was enhanced in the PBY-5A variant by the adoption of retractable tricycle landing gear to turn the type from a pure flying boat into an amphibian also able to use conventional runways.

Losses on both sides were heavy: for instance, the Gibraltar-based FAW-15 made 16 attacks on U-boats during the first half of June 1943, claiming five kills, but lost one PBY and three Liberators to the U-boats' flak guns.

Biscay patrols

Flights over the Bay of Biscay and the approaches to the Mediterranean now regularly encountered aggressive patrols of Junkers Ju 88s. Meanwhile, FAW-7 had been located to Dunkeswell in Devon as the US Navy's most important ASW unit in the UK, and here, late in July, the original VP-103 and VP-105 with Liberators were supplemented by the VP-63 squadron flying a variant of the PBY with MAD (magnetic anomaly detection) gear for the detection of submerged submarines. The wing's start was problematic, with a number of losses and only limited success. But things started to improve

from August, in which only two merchant ships sunk in areas patrolled by US Navy aircraft. Even so, the wing's aircraft generally operated alone, and were never a match for the faster and better armed aircraft which the *Luftwaffe* operated over the area. On sighting a German (and sometimes aggressively neutral Spanish) warplanes, therefore, the pilots of PBY and PB4Y aircraft generally turned west in an effort to use their machines' greater range to outstay the opposition. The solution was found in the movement to Agadir in Morocco of a pair of well-armed and considerably faster and agile Venturas to take over the PBYs' patrol route.

Operating under the direction of RAF Coastal Command, Fleet Air Wing 7 played a major role in the D-Day landings in Normandy in June 1944 with dawn-to-dusk patrols, helping to ensure that not one of the thousands of Allied vessels was lost to U-boat attack in the three weeks after D-Day.

End of Atlantic operations
1944–45

By mid 1943 the Germans had lost the technological race on which success in the Battle of the Atlantic hinged. From this point to the German capitulation in May 1945, substantial numbers of U-boats were sunk, usually with all hands, as the Allies maintained their sea and air superiority.

FROM LATE 1943 the rate at which men and equipment reached the UK from North America paved the way for the June 1944 invasion of France. This fact was evident to the Germans, who tried every expedient that they could think of to reassert their offensive in the Atlantic. They therefore made several attempts at reviving the fortunes of their numerically important Type VII class U-boat force, including much heavier anti-aircraft batteries, radar detection equipment, and the addition of the *Schnorchel* (snorkel) device to allow them to run underwater off their diesel engines and so reduce the chances of detection by radar.

None of these expedients was genuinely effective, however, and by the autumn of 1943 Allied air power was so strong that the U-boats were being attacked in the Bay of Biscay as they left or tried to return to port. The development of German torpedoes was also stepped up, paving the way for weapons

U-BOAT LOSSES, ATTRIBUTED TO US NAVY				
Year	1942	1943	1944	1945
Sunk/captured	9	43	16	2

US NAVY AVIATION, ATLANTIC OPERATIONS				
Aircraft types	Action sorties	Tons bombs dropped	Enemy aircraft destroyed	Aircraft lost
Carrierborne	1,103	174	40/40	32/8
Land-based	58	3	2/0	12/1
Overall totals	1,161	177	42/30	44/9

which ran a pre-programmed course criss-crossing the convoy path. Perhaps the most dangerous were the electrically powered G7e/T4 Falke acoustic-homing torpedo and G7es/T5 Zaunkönig (known to

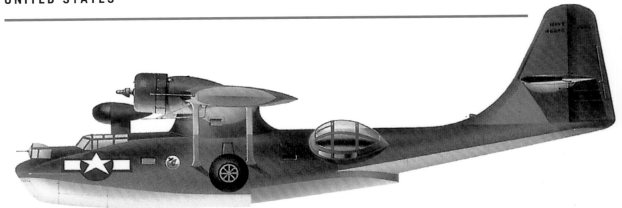

▲ Consolidated PBY-6A Catalina

US Navy, 1944–45

This was an amphibious flying boat (built by Convair in New Orleans) of the type designed by Consolidated on the basis of the PBY-5A with the revised nose and tail unit created for the PBN-1 Nomad, a development of the PBY-5 by the Naval Aircraft Factory. The PBY-6A was generally deemed the best Catalina variant.

Specifications

Crew: 7–9

Powerplant: 2 x 895kW (1200hp) engines

Maximum speed: 288km/h (179mph)

Range: 4096km (2545 miles)

Service ceiling: 4480m (14,700ft)

Dimensions: span 31.7m (104ft);

length 19.47m (63ft 11in); height 6.15m

(20ft 2in)

Weight: 16,066kg (35,420lb) loaded

Armament: 3 x 7.62mm (0.3in) trainable MGs: two in the bow turret, one firing aft of the hull step; one 12.7mm (0.5in) MG in each of the two beam positions; up to 1814kg (4000lb) of bombs or depth charges

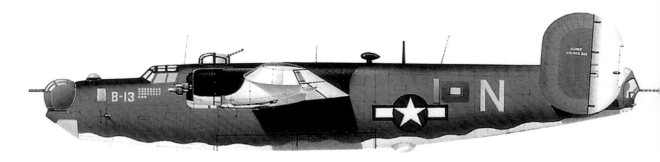

Specifications

Crew: 10

Powerplant: 4 x 895kW (1200hp) Pratt & Whitney Twin wasp radial piston engines

Maximum speed: 467km/h (290mph)

Range: 5955km (3700 miles)

Service ceiling: 8535m (28000ft)

Dimensions: span 33.53m (110ft);

length 20.47m (67ft 2in); height 5.49m (18ft)

Weight: 25,401kg (56,000lb) loaded

Armament: 2 x 12.7mm (0.5in) Browning trainable MGs in nose, dorsal, ventral 'ball' and tail turrets, and one each in beam positions; up to 5806kg (12,800lb) of bombs

▲ Consolidated PB4Y-1

VPB-110 / US Navy, Devon, UK, winter 1944

Operated in the long-range patrol bomber role out over the southwestern Approaches to the UK and farther afield into the Atlantic, this aeroplane has non-specular sea-blue upper surfaces, intermediate blue vertical surfaces and insignia-white under surfaces.

the Allies as the GNAT, or German Navy Acoustic Torpedo), which homed on the propeller noise of a target. Late-war developments were the *Elektroboot* series, comprising the Type XXI and short-range Type XXIII classes. The design was finalised in January 1943 but production started only in 1944–45. The Type XXI ran at 17 knots submerged, but full-scale production began only in 1944 and only

one combat patrol was carried out by a Type XXI boat before the war ended.

Even if the new boats and new weapons had been available in larger numbers, the strength of the Allied air forces, on both sides of the Atlantic, on islands such as Iceland and the Azores, and on large numbers of escort carriers dedicated to the anti-submarine role, would have made their task impossible.

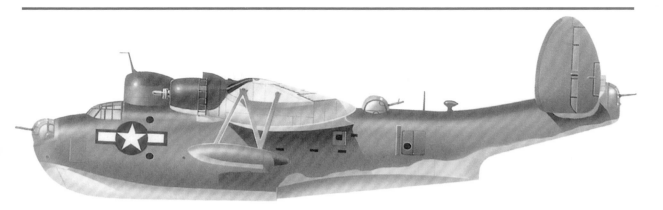

Specifications

Crew: 7

Powerplant: 2 x 1300kW (170hp) Wright
  R-2600-12 14-cylinder radial engines

Maximum speed: 330km/h (205mph)

Range: 4800km (3000 miles)

Service ceiling: 6040m (19,800ft)

Dimensions: span 36m (118ft);

length 24.50m (80ft); height 5.33m
  (17ft 6in)

Weight: 25,425kg (56,000lb) loaded

Armament: 4 x 12.7mm (0.5in) MGs (one
  each in nose and dorsal turrets, blisters
  amidships), plus 3629kg (8000lb) of bombs
  or depth charges or 2 x Mark 13 torpedoes

▲ **Martin PBM-5 Mariner**

US Navy, 1945

With two rather than four engines, and a bomb load of 3629kg (8000lb) rather than 5443kg (12,000lb), the Mariner was smaller and lighter than the heavyweight Coronado, and was designed for operations over shorter ranges. Again, the radar was located above the hull just to the rear of the flight deck.

Carrier operations
1942–44

While it was the war in the Pacific theatre that captured most of the attention for aircraft carrier operations, US Navy carriers were also involved in the North African and European theatres in a tactical role in support of the land forces.

THE FIRST US CARRIER involved in the European war was the USS *Wasp*, which left the US east coast late in March 1942 and reached the British base at Scapa Flow on 4 April. After taking on 47 Supermarine Spitfire land-based fighters for delivery as reinforcements for the British bastion on the Mediterranean island of Malta, the USS *Wasp* undertook the first delivery on 20 April. The carrier returned to its base in Scapa Flow, Scotland, some six days later. Facing overwhelming German and Italian air strength, Malta's air units suffered a heavy rate of losses, and a second reinforcement was launched on 2 May, 47 more Spitfire fighters being delivered on 9 May. The *Wasp* returned to the United States almost immediately after this and prepared to redeploy into the Pacific. The USS *Ranger* also ferried fighters, but in this instance Curtiss P-40 Warhawk fighter-

bombers of the US Army Air Forces: the carrier delivered 68 such aircraft to the Gold Coast in West Africa during April, and a second batch of aircraft in June.

Operation Torch

Soon after this, the USS *Ranger* embarked its air group and began to train for the most ambitious naval operation yet conducted in the African and European theatres: three groups of simultaneous amphibious landings by Anglo-US forces in Morocco and Algeria early in November 1942 as Operation *Torch*. Supporting the US portion of the undertaking were four carriers operating in three task groups, with 62 Douglas SBD-3 and Grumman TBF-1 bombers and 109 Grumman F4F fighters. Floatplanes operating from battleship and cruisers were also committed for the scouting, observation and search-and-rescue roles.

The US landings were centred on and round Casablanca. The USS *Ranger* and the escort carrier USS *Suwanee* operated to the west of Casablanca while two other smaller carriers, the USS *Sangamon* and USS *Santee*, operated to the west of the northern and southern landing areas respectively. The experience of most naval fliers was distinctly limited, but the task force had been assembled and dispatched so rapidly that there had been almost no opportunity to train in any realistic manner, and some pilots had not flown in two weeks.

More important that the experience of the aircrews, however, was the way in which the Vichy French armed forces would react: all agreed that they would fight the British, but opinion was divided as to their reaction to the Americans. The Vichy air force and naval air arm approached some 200 aircraft, including many US-built Martin and Douglas bombers and Curtiss fighters, and many of the Vichy French pilots were veterans of the Battle of France.

Landings begin

The landings began at dawn on 8 November, and to reduce the chances of triggering any reaction, the US aircrew were forbidden to shoot unless first fired upon. Matters got off to a poor start as a flight of seven fighters from the USS *Santee* became lost and ran low on fuel. One ditched in the sea and five crash-landed ashore: six of the pilots eventually reached safety, but one disappeared and was later reported killed. The pilots of the USS *Ranger*'s VF-4 and VF-9 soon discovered that that they could not dogfight the agile French fighters, and also encountered automatic weapons fire from the ground.

The focus of the undertaking in this part of French Morocco was Casablanca harbour, in which lay the French battleship *Jean Bart*, whose 381mm (15in) guns supplemented the efforts of the shore batteries. Eighteen of the USS *Ranger*'s dive-bombers attacked the port's naval facilities, submarine moor¬ings and the *Jean Bart*. The battleship was hit and damaged, and one submarine was sunk. When a French light cruiser, escorted by destroyers, emerged from Casablanca in a sortie against the US naval force, SBD and F4F warplanes attacked with bombs and machine gun fire at low level, and the cruiser and two destroyers had to be beached to prevent their sinking.

The subsidiary objectives, Fedala and Safi in the north and south respectively, were captured on the first day of Operation *Torch*. During this period SBD and TBF bombers flew anti-submarine patrols

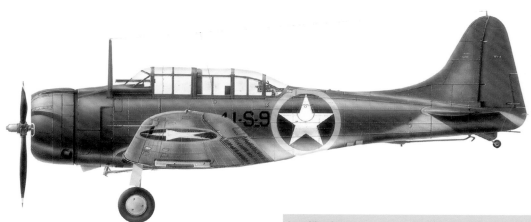

▲ **Douglas SBD-3 Dauntless**

VS-41 / USS Ranger, Northwest Africa, November 1942

The slightly ragged yellow circling of the US National insignia was applied by hand on all US Navy aircraft involved in Operation Torch, the Allied landings in French north-west Africa.

Specifications

Crew: 2

Powerplant: 895kW (1200hp) Wright R-1820-60 radial engine

Maximum speed: 410km/h (255mph)

Range: 1243km (773 miles)

Service ceiling: 7780m (25,5300ft)

Dimensions: span 12.65m (41ft 6in); length 10.08m (33ft 1in); height 4.14m (13ft 7in)

Weight: 4843kg (10,676lb) loaded

Armament: 2 x 12.7mm (0.5in) forward-firing machine guns

and attacked Vichy French airfields and defensive positions. Casablanca's batteries continued to fire on the American forces during 9 November, and nine SBDs from the USS *Ranger* attacked them with 454kg (1,000lb) bombs, scoring two direct hits which finally put the *Jean Bart* out of action. The French surrender came early on the morning of 11 November. As far as the US Navy was concerned, Operation *Torch* had been invaluable in providing its aircrews with a relatively mild introduction to combat. Ground support tactics had been proved in real operations, and anti-submarine techniques tested, not least as the TBFs of the USS *Suwanee* sank at least one Vichy French boat at sea.

In the air, the unblooded F4F pilots achieved a kill/loss rate of about 5/1 after learning very rapidly that mutual support and the maintenance of high speed were vital. But the losses of carrierborne warplanes to ground fire and operational causes were heavy. As its aircraft losses had reached almost 25 pecent over a three-day period, the task force could have sustained operations for only a very short time longer.

Norwegian operation

The next operation undertaken by a US Navy carrier in European waters took place almost a year later, and this again involved the air group of the USS *Ranger*. Collaborating with the British Home Fleet, the USS *Ranger* was involved in an attack on German shipping in and around the harbour of Bodø on the Norwegian coast. The US carrier reached position about dawn on 3 October 1943, closely escorted by a powerful Royal Navy force, and here launched two waves of warplanes: 20 SBDs followed by 10 TBFs, each escorted by six to eight F4Fs.

After a low-level approach to reduce the chances of detection by radar, each wave climbed to attack altitude within visible distance of the coast, and the bombers then attacked coastal targets and shipping anchored in the harbour. There was no aerial opposition over the target area. Between them, the SBDs of VB-4 and the TBFs of VT-4 destroyed six ships and damaged another three. The attackers lost three of their number, and one fighter was badly damaged. This very successful undertaking marked the end of the USS *Ranger*'s combat career, for the carrier was then used as a training carrier off the west coast of the United States for the rest of the war.

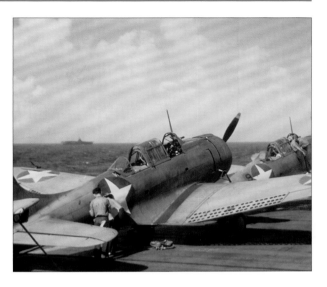

▲ **Douglas SBDs in the Atlantic**
Douglas SBD Dauntless divebombers sit aboard USS Yorktown while on Atlantic patrol in 1943. USS Ranger can be seen in the background.

Final raids

The next, and indeed final, undertaking by US carriers in the European theatre took place in the Mediterranean, where two escort carriers provided air support for Operation *Dragoon*, the invasion of southern France. Here both the carriers and their aircraft were different from those that had been used in Operation *Torch*. By August 1944 the escort carriers USS *Tulagi* and USS *Kasaan Bay* each had a squadron of Grumman F6F-5 Hellcat fighters far superior to the F4F machines they replaced. Each of the carriers had 24 of these large fighter-bombers. On 15 August, the first day of the landings, the two American squadrons flew 100 sorties, directing naval gunfire against German troop concentrations and supply routes. In the succeeding days the wide variety of missions undertaken including low-altitude bombing, machine-gun strafing, attacks on ground targets with rockets, and armed reconnaissance. The two squadrons were operational over the south of France for 13 days, and in this time lost 11 F6Fs, including five on 20 August, but in exchange had destroyed more than 800 road vehicles and 84 locomotives.

So ended US carrier aviation's operations against the western Axis powers, but the escort carriers' war against the U-boats continued.

Chapter 9

Soviet Union

A leading exponent of the concept of long-range bombing during the 1930s, a period in which it developed some of the world's first genuinely heavy bombers, the Soviet Union then stepped back from the notion of the strategic bomber and decided to concentrate its efforts on tactical bombing with light and medium bombers. Validated in the Spanish Civil War (1936–39) by machines such as the Tupolev SB-2, the new Soviet concept was based on fast bombers operating at no greater than medium altitude over and immediately behind the battlefield, providing the ground forces with immediate and short-term support. The concept proved useful but limited, and late in World War II the Soviet Union began once again to consider long-range strategic heavy bombing.

◀ Ilyushin Il-2
Well protected, possessing adequate performance and agility, but notably well armed with cannon, machine guns, light bombs and rocket projectiles, the Il-2 was a war-winning battlefield weapon.

Soviet Frontal Aviation
1941–43

In the first months of the war, the FA (Frontal Aviation) lost the majority of its aircraft on the ground and in the air. Even so, the surviving Soviet light and medium bomber elements fought with courage, if not with great skill, but achieved little and had to be almost wholly rebuilt.

THE LIGHT AND MEDIUM bomber elements of the FA (Frontal Aviation), representing the vast majority of the bombing capability available to the Soviet Union, were tasked from the very start of hostilities with attacks on German tactical targets right on the battlefield, and only slightly later and also to a lesser degree with rear-area targets such as airfields, troop, artillery and vehicle (especially armoured) concentrations, and chokepoints typified by bridges and railway junctions.

Flying as a mix of many obsolescent and few modern aircraft, the Soviet bomber regiments initially operated largely by day and without fighter escort, although fighters started to become available, initially to no great effect, after about the first month of the campaign. The bombers' losses were very great, and their successes minimal. They did, however, have the

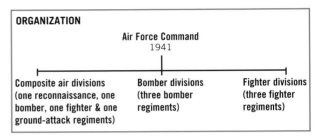

ORGANIZATION

Air Force Command
1941

| Composite air divisions (one reconnaissance, one bomber, one fighter & one ground-attack regiments) | Bomber divisions (three bomber regiments) | Fighter divisions (three fighter regiments) |

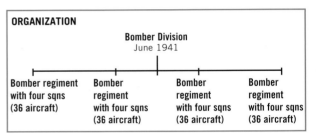

ORGANIZATION

Bomber Division
June 1941

| Bomber regiment with four sqns (36 aircraft) | Bomber regiment with four sqns (36 aircraft) | Bomber regiment with four sqns (36 aircraft) | Bomber regiment with four sqns (36 aircraft) |

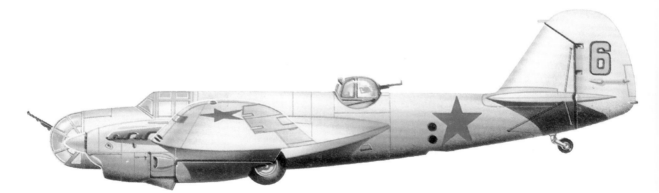

Specifications

Crew: 4

Powerplant: 2 x 619kW (830hp) M-100 V-12 piston engines

Maximum speed: 410km/h (255mph)

Range: 1200km (746 miles)

Service ceiling: 8500m (27,885ft)

Dimensions: span 20.33m (66ft 9in); length 12.27m (40ft 3in);

height 3.25m (10ft 8in)

Weight: 5732kg (12,636lb) loaded

Armament: 2 x 7.62mm (0.3in) MGs in nose turret; 1 x 7.62mm (0.3in) ShKAS MG in dorsal turret and 1 x 7.62mm (0.3in) ShKAS MG in ventral position; maximum bomb load 1000kg (2205lb)

▲ **Tupolev SB-2M**

Unknown bomber regiment / Soviet Air Force, 1941–42

Developed for high-speed bombing, and eventually built to the extent of 6967 aircraft, the SB-2 series is here exemplified by an aeroplane in winter camouflage. The ANT-40 prototype first flew in October 1934, and the type made its combat debut on the Republican side in the Spanish Civil War (1936-39). Always powered by liquid-cooled engines, though initially with frontal rather than chin radiators, the SB-2 was obsolescent by 1941 but remained in first-line service to 1944.

effect of clearing from the Soviet inventory the high proportion of inferior types. Thus they facilitated the entry of more modern bombers as and when these were delivered from the factories uprooted from western Russia in the face of the German advance and relocated to the safety of areas lying to the east of the Ural mountains.

The rate and weight of the Soviet bombing attacks increased steadily from the end of August 1941, although they tended still to be made against short-range tactical targets: to this extent the bombers attacked essentially the same types of targets as the ground-attack aircraft, and in tactical terms the

Specifications

Crew: 4	height 3.25m (10ft 8in)
Powerplant: 2 x 619kW (830hp) M-100 V-12	Weight: 5732kg (12,636lb) loaded
piston engine	Armament: 2 x 7.62mm (0.3in) machine guns
Maximum speed: 410km/h (255mph)	in nose turret, 1 x 7.62mm (0.3in) ShKAS in
Range: 1200km (746 miles)	dorsal turret and 1 x 7.62mm (0.3in) ShKAS
Service ceiling: 8500m (27,885ft)	in ventral position; maximum bomb load
Dimensions: span 20.33m (66ft 9in);	1000kg (2205lb)
length 12.27m (40ft 3in);	

▲ **Tupolev SB-2M**

Unknown bomber regiment / Soviet Air Force, 1941–42

This is a somewhat atypical example of the SB-2M fast bomber with no dorsal turret (its location being fitted with a sliding transparency) and the original type of ventral protection by means of a 7.62mm (0.3in) ShKAS machine gun in a ventral hatch position.

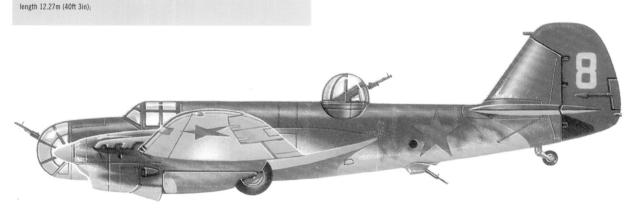

Specifications

Crew: 4	height 3.25m (10ft 8in)
Powerplant: 2 x 619kW (830hp) M-100 V-12	Weight: 5732kg (12,636lb) loaded
piston engines	Armament: 2 x 7.62mm (0.3in) MGs in nose
Maximum speed: 410km/h (255mph)	turret; 1 x 7.62mm (0.3in) ShKAS MG in
Range: 1200km (746 miles)	dorsal turret and 1 x 7.62mm (0.3in) ShKAS
Service ceiling: 8500m (27,885ft)	MG in ventral position; maximum bomb load
Dimensions: span 20.33m (66ft 9in);	1000kg (2205lb)
length 12.27m (40ft 3in);	

▲ **Tupolev SB-2bis-3**

Unknown bomber regiment / Soviet Air Force, 1942–43

This is an example of the final production version of the SB-2 fast bomber with an MV-3 dorsal turret and remotely controlled ventral barbette, each carrying one 7.62mm (0.3in) ShKAS machine gun. The aeroplane is depicted in standard summer camouflage.

efforts of the ground-attack and bomber regiments can be regarded as little more than an extension of the fire plan ordained for the Soviet long-range artillery.

While short-range attack remained a major part of the bombers' efforts, the importance of targets deeper in the Germans' rear gradually registered with the Soviets and the number of attack on such targets increased. Typical of such efforts were the raids delivered on German-held airfields in the region of Kiev on 21–26 July 1941. In these raids the number of attacking bombers was between three and 10, and some of the crews managed to make good tactical use of cloud to conceal their approaches. The bombing was then carried out at various altitudes, without fighter escort and without any attempt at evasive manoeuvres, and in most of the attacks all of the Soviet bombers were destroyed by the German fighters and/or anti-aircraft fire without inflicting anything but very minor damage, which in no way impeded the tempo of German air operations.

Increased production

So remained the basic nature of Soviet bombing operations until well into 1942. Numbers of more modern aircraft were being delivered, and the flying schools were beginning to churn out an ever-increasing flood of pilots and other aircrew, but the newer bombers were often delivered before they were in fact fully ready for service, and the aircrews were both short of flying experience and lacking in operational training before they were committed to operations. The *Luftwaffe*, on the other hand, was flying fully developed fighters in the hands of highly experienced pilots, and the toll they exacted from the Soviet bombers continued to be very high.

The toll was also exacerbated by the Soviet demand that the vast majority of bombing efforts were directed against targets in or immediately behind the battlefield, where the density of the German fighters and flak guns was greatest.

Nevertheless, the Soviet tactical bombing arm did slowly begin to become more effective as the last teething problems of the new-generation bombers were eliminated, and as aircrews gained experience, where they survived, and could thus pass on the fruits of their survival to fresh aircrews. The Soviet tactical bombing effort thus began to improve late in 1942 and early in 1943. It was increasingly well coordinated within the overall operational plan to provide the infantry, armour and artillery with the support they needed to check the Germans advances and start to develop their own strategic offensives, which the Germans lacked the strength to beat back.

Specifications

Crew: 11	height 6.20m (20ft 4in)
Powerplant: 1100kW (1350hp)	Weight: 27,000kg (59,400lb) loaded
Maximum speed: 443km/h (276mph)	Armament: 2 x 20mm (0.79in) ShVAK cannons
Range: 3600km (2245 miles)	(dorsal and tail turret); 2 x 12.7mm (0.5in)
Service ceiling: 9300m (30,504ft)	UBT MGs (engine nacelles); 1 x 7.62mm
Dimensions: span 39.10m (128ft 3in);	(0.3in) ShKAS MG (nose turret); up to 4000kg
length 23.59m (77ft 5in);	(8800lb) of bombs

▲ **Petlyakov Pe-8**

Unknown bomber regiment / Soviet Air Force, 1943

The only genuinely long-range heavy bomber operated by the Soviet Union in World War II, the Pe-8 was built to the extent of only 79 aircraft for service from 1940. The type was well armed both defensively and offensively, but suffered constantly from powerplant problems.

Facing *Barbarossa*

June–December 1941

The German *Barbarossa* invasion of the Soviet Union caught the Soviets completely by surprise, with their forces deployed too far forward in a cordon behind the frontier. The Germans swept forward, killing and capturing vast numbers of Soviet personnel on their way to Moscow.

THE *BARBAROSSA* INVASION started on 22 June 1941, and the Germans swept all before them as their infantry and armoured forces, supported by tactical warplanes, punched through the Soviet line and began a series of pincer envelopments that killed or captured vast number of men and took huge amounts of weapons and equipment.

The pace of the advance slowed later, but the Germans were poised outside Moscow in November, only to be denied the prize by the onset of winter and the determination of the Soviet government and forces, and then falling back.

During this period, the FA's bomber regiments made many attacks, but to no real effect. Each attack was made by a squadron of typically six to eight but never more than 10 aircraft flying at between 600m

ORGANIZATION

Composite Air Division
June 1941

| Reconnaissance regiment (four sqns with 36 aircraft) | Fighter regiment (four sqns with 48 aircraft) | Ground-attack regiment (four sqns with 48 aircraft) | Bomber regiment (four sqns with 36 aircraft) |

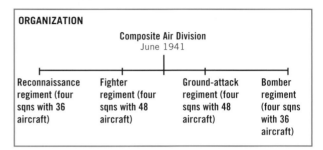

▷ **Shturmovik fighter-bomber**

In combination with its successor (the Ilyushin Il-10), the Ilyushin Il-2 is the single most produced military aircraft design in all of aviation history. A total of 36,163 were built by the Soviets during World War II.

Specifications

Crew: 2

Powerplant: 1 x 1134kW (1520hp)

Maximum speed: 486km/h (302mph)

Range: 1100km (683 miles)

Service ceiling: 8800m (28,870ft)

Dimensions: span 14.30m (46ft 11in);

length 10.46m (34ft 4in);

height 3.80m (12ft 6in)

Weight: 3273kg (7216lb) loaded

Armament: 4 x 7.62mm (0.3in) fixed wing MGs and 1 x 7.62mm (0.3in) MG in dorsal turret; 400kg (880lb) of bombs

▲ **Sukhoi Su-2**

Unknown regiment / Soviet Air Force, 1941–42

Designed as a light reconnaissance bomber role with ground-attack capability, the Su-2 was built to the extent of 500 or slightly more aircraft in 1940–42. Early operational experience against German fighters revealed that the Su-2 lacked the performance, agility, armament and protection for battlefield survival.

(1970ft) and 825m (2700ft) in tight formation, despite the attentions of flak. The attacking squadron sometimes attempted to manoeuvre in formation, and tended to become more widely spaced only after the arrival of German fighters.

The whole attack was delivered in level flight 'by the book', with a rigid adherence to a preconceived plan that made no allowance for the realities of the tactical situation. In combination with the slow speed of the formation, this resulted in very heavy losses, many such formations losing all of their number. Moreover, the inaccuracy of the bombing, even from the low altitude from which it was delivered, meant that the results of most attacks were very poor.

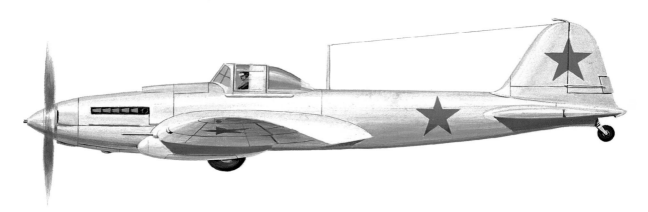

▲ Ilyushin Il-2

Unknown attack regiment / Soviet Air Force, winter 1941–42

The original version of the Il-2, first flown in TsKB-55P prototype form during December 1940, was rushed into service during 1941 as a single-seater with the gun armament of two 20mm (0.79in) ShVAK cannon with 420 rounds and two 7.62mm (0.3in) ShKAS machine guns with 1500 rounds.

Specifications

Crew: 2

Powerplant: 1 x 1320kW (1770hp) Mikulin AM-38F liquid-cooled inline engine

Maximum speed: 404km/h (251mph)

Range: 800km (497 miles)

Service ceiling: 6000m 19,685ft)

Dimensions: span 14.6m (47ft 11in); length 11.60m (39ft); height 3.4m (11ft 2in)

Weight: 6360kg (14,023lb) loaded

Armament: 2 x 20mm (1.79in) ShVAK cannon and 2 x 7.62mm (0.3in) MGs

Night harassment
1941–45

The Soviets were adept at exploiting the equipment they did possess in useful quantities, even if this equipment was technically obsolete. One such type of aeroplane was the old training and liaison biplane, which was used to disturb the Germans' opportunity to rest at night.

THE SOVIETS were quick to appreciate that they could achieve good results at minimal cost by simple harassment of the Germans at night using obsolete biplanes such as the Polikarpov Po-2 (or U-2).

Silent attack

Equipped with a single defensive machine gun and carrying a small load of bombs, often of the anti-

NIGHT HARASSMENT AIRCRAFT			
Type	Engine	Bomb load	Speed
Polikarpov U-2VS	1 x radial	200kg (441lb)	147km/h (91mph)
Polikarpov R-5	1 x V	400kg (882lb)	228km/h (142mph)
Yakovlev UT-2	1 x radial	light bombs	192km/h (20mph)

personnel bomblet type, an irregular stream of these aircraft at intervals of between five and 15 minutes would cruise over the German lines at a height of between 225m (740ft) and 1500m (4920ft) to drop their bombs and fire at anything evident on the ground. The U-2 aircraft often made a gliding approach to arrive without warning, and then gunned their engines as they dropped their bombs before turning back.

The Germans' direct casualties were small, but the effort had a cumulative effect in keeping the Germans psychologically off balance and disturbing their opportunity to rest. As such, an obsolete aircraft performed a militarily useful service.

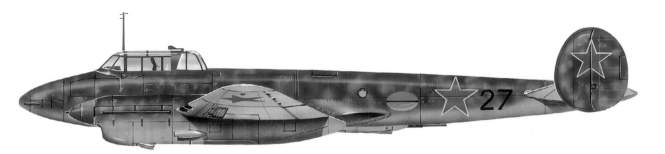

Specifications

Crew: 3	height 4m (13ft 2in)
Powerplant: 2 x 820kW (1100hp)	Weight: 8496kg (12,943lb) loaded
Maximum speed: 540km/h (336mph)	Armament: 2 x 7.62mm (0.3in) ShKAS MGs in
Range: 1500km (932 miles)	nose and 1 x 7.62mm (0.3in) ShKAS MG in
Service ceiling: 8800m (28,870ft)	ventral or dorsal station; maximum bomb
Dimensions: span 17.16m (56ft 4in);	load 1200kg (2646lb)
length 12.66m (41ft 7in);	

▲ Petlyakov Pe-2FT

Unknown dive-bomber regiment / Soviet Air Force, 1943

Fast, agile and well protected, the Pe-2 was one of the finest warplanes to serve with any of the combatants in World War II. The original crew was three, but the bomb-aimer's glazed position in the nose was later removed as redundant, leaving the pilot and gunner as the two members of the crew.

▲ Polikarpov U-2VS

Unknown Polish-manned regiment / Soviet Air Force, 1942

Built to the extent of 33,000 or more aircraft, the Po-2 was a 'maid-of-all-work' aeroplane in a host of variants. The U-2VS was the night harassment variant.

Specifications

Crew: 2	length 8.17m (26ft 10in);
Powerplant: 1 x 75kW (100hp)	height 3.10m (10ft 2in)
Maximum speed: 156km/h (97mph)	Weight: 890kg (1962lb) loaded
Range: 400km (249 miles)	Armament: 1 x 7.62mm (0.3in) rear-facing MG
Service ceiling: 4000m (13,125ft)	and up to 250kg (551lb) of bombs under the
Dimensions: span 11.4m (37ft 5in);	lower wing.

Checking the German offensive
1942–43

In 1942, the Germans switched their focus south, where they hoped to reach the Caspian Sea and secure the oilfields of the Caucasus. Time and distance slowed the advance, and then Hitler decided that the objective was to be Stalingrad, where the Germans suffered a huge defeat.

THE LURE OF THE Caucasian oilfields drew the Germans' primary offensive of 1942 off to the south-east and into a vastness of open country and great heat. Suffering from acute strategic indecision as the Soviet forces melted away and no tangible benefit accrued from his armies' efforts, Hitler then decided that the industrial city of Stalingrad on the Volga river should be taken.

A trap is sprung

As the exhausted Germans approached and entered Stalingrad, the Soviets prepared a major counterstoke, which trapped the German Sixth Army and part of the Fourth Panzer Army in the city, where some of the war's bloodiest fighting took place. *Reichsmarschall* Hermann Göring assured Hitler that his *Luftwaffe* could keep the garrison supplied, but Soviet pressure and deteriorating weather meant that this was not achieved.

The remnants of the starving garrison surrendered in February 1943, and with them disappeared

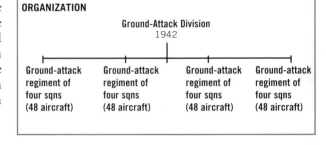

ORGANIZATION

Ground-Attack Division
1942

Ground-attack regiment of four sqns (48 aircraft)	Ground-attack regiment of four sqns (48 aircraft)	Ground-attack regiment of four sqns (48 aircraft)	Ground-attack regiment of four sqns (48 aircraft)

Germany's last real chance of victory on the Eastern Front. Throughout 1942, the quality of the Soviet bombing effort improved, but only slowly and hesitantly.

Each bomber unit generally flew in a V formation of between 12 and 30 aircraft, followed at a varying distance by the next unit probably at a different altitude, while the rare attacks by complete bomber divisions were normally made with the regiments abreast of each other. The attack was generally started at dawn or at midday, and the last attack of the day,

Specifications

Crew: 2

Powerplant: 1 x 1320kW (1770hp) Mikulin Am-38F liquid-cooled inline piston engine

Maximum speed: 404km/h (251mph)

Range: 600km (375 miles)

Service ceiling: 5945m (19,500ft)

Dimensions: span 14.6m (47ft 11in); length 11.6m (38ft 0.5in); height 3.4m (11ft 1in)

Weight: 6360kg (14,021lb) loaded

Armament: 2 x 37mm (1.46in) cannon, 2 x 7.62mm (0.3in) MGs; 1 x 12.7mm (0.5in) MG in rear cockpit; 200 x 2.5kg (5.5lb) PTAB anti-tank bombs, or 8 x RS-82 or RS-132 rockets

▲ **Ilyushin Il-2m3**

Unknown attack regiment / Soviet Air Force, Stalingrad Front, 1943

The aircraft of the Il-2 series were known universally by the soubriquet Shturmovik, meaning 'assaulter' or 'attacker'. The weight of the protective armour incorporated in each aeroplane was typically 990kg (2183lb), and much of this also served a structural purpose.

▲ **Ilyushin Il-2 attack aircraft, 1942**

Reliable, easy to maintain and simple to manufacture in large numbers (it was produced in only a small number of variants), the Il-2 was rugged, as demanded by the indifferent quality of the airfields from which it had to operate, and became the heart of the Soviet ground-attack capability at low level over the armoured battlefield.

often the most intense, was always delivered before the fall of night.

The attack altitude was varied in accordance with circumstances, including the tactical situation and the weather, and were recorded by the Germans between rare lower and upper limits of 300m (985ft) and 8000m (26,245ft). Targets in or close behind the frontline were normally attacked from between

1000m (3810ft) and 2500m (8200ft), while those farther to the rear were tackled by bombing from between 3000m (9845ft) and 4000m (16,405ft).

All of the aircraft bombed simultaneously under command of the lead bomb-aimer, and the bombs were of the light and medium types. Several attacks were made until the whole bomb load had been dropped, and then the bombers turned for home.

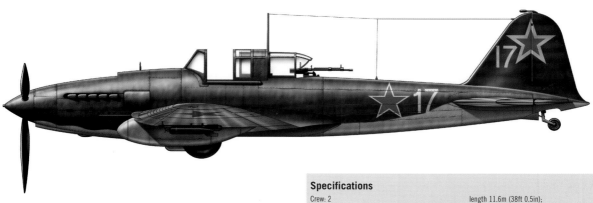

▲ **Ilyushin Il-2m3**

Unknown attack regiment / Soviet Air Force, 1943–44

The original Il-2 single-seater had offered good offensive capability but, despite its sturdy structure and much armour, proved vulnerable to fighter attack from the rear. The Il-2m3 introduced a gunner with one 12.7mm (0.5in) machine gun, and formations of Il-2m3 aircraft could put up a powerful weight of defensive fire.

Specifications

Crew: 2	length 11.6m (38ft 0.5in);
Powerplant: 1 x 1320kW (1770hp) Mikulin	height 3.4m (11ft 2in)
Am-38F liquid-cooled inline piston engine	Weight: 6360kg (14,021lb) loaded
Maximum speed: 404km/h (251mph)	Armament: 2 x 23mm (0.9in) VYa-23 cannon,
Range: 600km (375 miles)	2 x 7.62mm (0.3in) MGs, 1 x 12.7mm (0.5in)
Service ceiling: 5945m (19,500ft)	rear-mounted MG; and 8 x 82mm (3.2in)
Dimensions: span 14.6m (47ft 11in);	RS-82 or 132mm (5.2in) RS-132 rockets

Soviet Frontal Aviation
1943–45

The qualitative improvement of the FA's bombing capability in the last two years of the war mirrored that of the Soviet Union's fighter and ground-attack capabilities, albeit on a smaller scale and reflecting the importance placed by the Soviets on battlefield air power.

B Y THE MIDDLE OF 1943, the improvements in Soviet tactical bombing that had become discernible in the previous 18 months were becoming more pronounced. While tactical bombing still lagged somewhat behind fighter and ground-attack operations in the repertoire of Soviet air power capabilities, the Germans were the first to admit that it nonetheless achieved useful results.

Bomber development

The slower pace of the bomber arm relative to the fighter and ground-attack arms reflected a number of factors: industrial limitations meant that all three air elements could not be developed at the same rate, the development of the bomber arm presented problems not typical of the fighter and ground-attack arms, Soviet military doctrine emphasized the importance

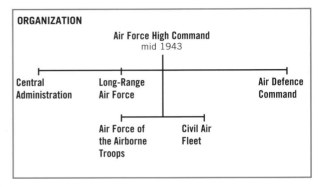

ORGANIZATION

Air Force High Command
mid 1943

Central Administration — Long-Range Air Force — Air Defence Command

Air Force of the Airborne Troops — Civil Air Fleet

of battlefield rather than rear-area air power, and for attacks on Germany's cities and industrial base the Soviets could leave matters to the Western Allies.

Even though the bomber arm lagged behind the fighter and ground-attack arms, it benefited

Specifications

Crew: 2

Powerplant: 1 x 1320kW (1770hp) Mikulin Am-38F liquid-cooled inline piston engine

Maximum speed: 404km/h (251mph)

Range: 600km (375 miles)

Service ceiling: 5945m (19,500ft)

Dimensions: span 14.6m (47ft 11in); length 11.6m (38ft 0.5in);

height 3.4m (11ft 1in)

Weight: 6360kg (14,021lb) loaded

Armament: 2 x 23mm (0.9in) VYa-23 cannon, 2 x 7.62mm (0.3in) MGs, 1 x 12.7mm (0.5in) rear-mounted MG; and 8 x 82mm (3.2in) RS-82 or 132mm (5.2in) RS-132 rocket projectiles

▲ **Ilyushin Il-2m3**

Unknown attack regiment / Soviet Air Force, 1944

A decisive tactical warplane built to the extent of some 36,250 aircraft, the Il-2 was an excellent aeroplane in the ground-attack and anti-armour roles. It reached its definitive form as the Il-2m3 with a gunner added behind the pilot for rearward protection. The gunner's glazing was not infrequently removed to improve the field of fire for the one or occasionally two 12.7mm (0.5in) machine guns. The slogan on the side of the fuselage translates as 'Avenger'.

considerably from the decline of the German fighter and anti-aircraft artillery branches in achieving useful results. It is estimated that by March 1944 the Soviet tactical bomber arm totalled some 4560 aircraft, including about 1810 nocturnal harassment machines and excluding about 860 long-range

bombers (February 1944 figure). The latter almost doubled to about 1600 in January 1945.

During September 1944, the tactical bomber arm comprised six bomber corps with 30 bomber divisions incorporating 110 bomber regiments, these figures rising to seven, 35 and 135 respectively by

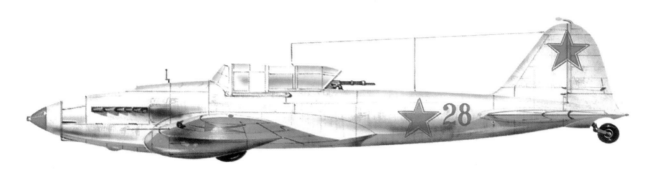

▲ Ilyushin Il-2m3

Unknown attack regiment / Soviet Air Force, winter 1943–44

Seen in winter camouflage, this Il-2m3 retains the gunner's glazing. The wing carried two 23mm (0.9in) VYa-23 cannon and two 7.62mm (0.3in) machine guns and eight 82mm (3.2in) or four 132mm (5.2in) rocket projectiles, while the bomb load was six 100kg (220lb) bombs or a smaller number of lighter bombs, the later including anti-armour bomblets.

Specifications

Crew: 2

Powerplant: 1 x 1320kW (1770hp) Mikulin
   Am-38F liquid-cooled inline piston engine

Maximum speed: 404km/h (251mph)

Range: 600km (375 miles)

Service ceiling: 5945m (19,500ft)

Dimensions: span 14.6m (47ft 11in);

length 11.6m (38ft 0.5in);
   height 3.4m (11ft 2in)

Weight: 6360kg (14,021lb) loaded

Armament: 2 x 23mm (0.9in) VYa-23 cannon,
   2 x 7.62mm (0.3in) MGs, 1 x 12.7mm (0.5in)
   rear-mounted MG; and 8 x 82mm (3.2in)
   RS-82 or 132mm (5.2in) RS-132 rockets

▲ Tupolev Tu-2S

Unknown bomber regiment / Soviet Air Force, 1943–45

The Tu-2 series was optimized for mass production by a demand for the minimum number of parts, the use of very accurate drawings and tooling to ensure accuracy of fit, and pre-prepared wiring looms and pipe runs. The result was a major reduction in the number of man hours required to build each aeroplane.

Specifications

Crew: 4

Powerplant: 2 x 1380kW (1850hp) Shvetsov
   ASh-82FN radial piston engines

Maximum speed: 547km/h (340mph)

Range: 2000km (1243 miles)

Service ceiling: 9500m (31,170ft)

Dimensions: span 18.86m (61ft 11in);

length 13.8m (45ft 4in);
   height 4.56m (14ft 11in)

Weight: 12,800kg (28,219lb) loaded

Armament: 2 x 20mm (0.79in) ShVAK cannon
   in wing roots; 3 x 12.7mm (0.5in) UBT MGs
   (one in both dorsal positions and ventral
   station); max. bomb load 3000kg (6614lb)

the end of the year. At the same time, the long-range bomber arm comprised nine corps with 18 divisions incorporating 48 regiments. At this time, the establishment of the bomber regiment was 33. However, most squadrons in fact had between three and five more aircraft, and also a number of crews in reserve as combat attrition replacements.

Improved capabilities

The growing experience that helped to make the tactical bomber arm more capable was reflected in the fact that, by September 1944, the Soviets reckoned that some 70 per cent of their crews could be deemed experienced. Another way of looking at the same trend is provided by losses, which had been 5100 aircraft in 1943 and 5200 in 1944, the very slight increase in losses being considerably more than offset by the numbers of aircraft in service.

The role in which the Soviets employed their tactical bomber arm reflected not only their overall military philosophy but, of course, the nature of the land war on the Eastern Front. Up to the end of 1942, the Soviets had in general responded to German offensives, and mustered significant bomber strength in the areas in which the Germans were trying to effect a breakthrough.

After the surrender of the German Sixth Army at Stalingrad in February 1943, however, the Soviets generally had the strategic initiative, and therefore grouped their bomber strength to support their own great offensive movements. Up to April 1944, the ADD was concentrated primarily in the north for attacks on Finland, but after that time it was shifted south to the area of Kiev to support the great offensives through Ukraine and Poland and into the northern Balkans.

Ground support

Over the same period, the tactical bomber arm was grouped to support the efforts within the various grand schemes by fronts (army groups), armies and corps. By this stage of the war, there was a high level of coordination between the ground forces and their supporting air strength, and the bombers were able to go about their tasks increasingly unmolested by German fighters because of the latter's declining capability and the conduct of bombing operations with fighter escort or, over the battlefield, in collaboration with fighter patrols.

Night bombers

A notable feature evident from the middle of 1944 was the greater use made of night bombing of all types, and the commitment of the Soviet bombers to attacks deeper in the German rear areas. For the latter, several waves of bombers were employed,

Specifications

Crew: 4	height 4.56m (14ft 11in)
Powerplant: 2 x 1380kW (1850hp) Shvetsov	Weight: 12,800kg (28,219lb) loaded
ASh-82FN radial piston engines	Armament: 2 x 20mm (0.79in) ShVAK cannon
Maximum speed: 547km/h (340mph)	in wing roots and 3 x 12.7mm (0.5in) UBT
Range: 2000km (1243 miles)	MGs (one each in both dorsal positions and
Service ceiling: 9500m (31,170ft)	ventral station); maximum bomb load of
Dimensions: span 18.86m (61ft 11in);	3000kg (6614lb)
length 13.8m (45ft 4in);	

▲ **Tupolev Tu-2S**

Unknown bomber regiment / Soviet Air Force, possibly Kalinin front, 1943–45

The subject of protracted development, as indicated by a first flight in January 1941 but entry into service only at a time early in 1944, the four-seat Tu-2 was a superlative medium attack bomber and ground-attack warplane. More than 1000 aircraft were delivered before the end of World War II, and more than 1500 after the war. The Tu-2S was the first full-production model, and the dorsal and ventral positions each carried 12.7m (0.5in) machine guns.

▼ Soviet bomber regiment / Frontal Aviation, 1943–44

The regiment was the smallest tactical unit of the Soviet Air Force, and in organizational terms was subordinated to the air division or, in some cases, was controlled directly by an air army. The bomber regiment comprised three bomber squadrons, each with an establishment of 11 aircraft, giving the bomber regiment a total establishment of 33 aircraft, a figure often exceeded by up to five aircraft later in the war.

1st Squadron

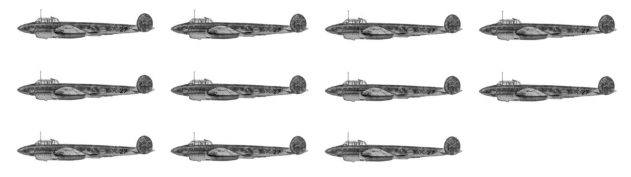

2nd Squadron

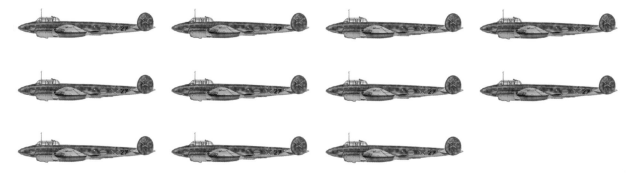

3rd Squadron

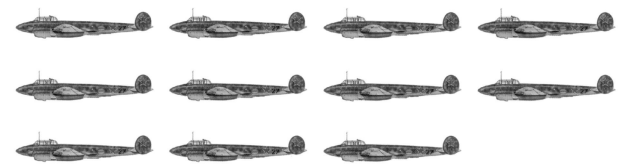

each wave comprising one regiment that attacked in a tight concentration at altitudes between 2000m (6560ft) and 4000m (13,125ft), all of the aircraft releasing their bombs in level flight on receipt of the order from the leading aeroplane. Bombing accuracy was better than it had been in 1943 and the first part of 1944, but was still not as great as that achieved by the Western Allies, and losses to flak were heavy.

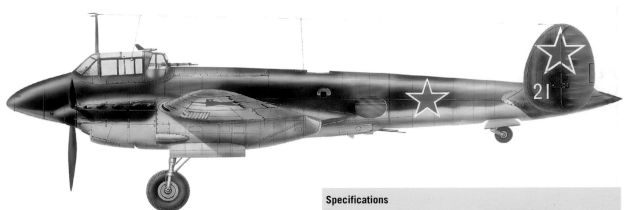

▲ **Petlyakov Pe-2 Series 359**

Unknown dive-bomber regiment / Soviet Air Force, 1944–45

This is an example of a late variant with individual ejector exhaust stubs.

Specifications

Crew: 3	height 4m (13ft 2in)
Powerplant: 2 x 820kW (1100hp)	Weight: 8496kg (12,943lb) loaded
Maximum speed: 540km/h (336mph)	Armament: 2 x 7.62mm (0.3in) ShKAS MGs in
Range: 1500km (932 miles)	nose and 1 x 7.62mm (0.3in) ShKAS MG in
Service ceiling: 8800m (28,870ft)	ventral or dorsal station; maximum bomb
Dimensions: span 17.16m (56ft 4in);	load 1200kg (2646lb)
length 12.66m (41ft 7in);	

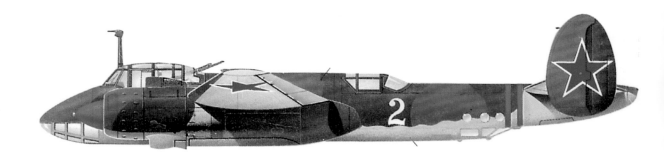

Specifications

Crew: 4	length 13.8m (45ft 4in);
Powerplant: 2 X 1380kW (1850hp) Shvetsov	height 4.56m (14ft 11in)
ASh-82FN radial piston engines	Weight: 12,800kg (28,219lb) loaded
Maximum speed: 547km/h (340mph)	Armament: 2 x 20mm (0.79in) ShVAK cannon
Range: 2000km (1243 miles)	in wing roots,;3 x 12.7mm (0.5in) UBT MGs
Service ceiling: 9500m (31,170ft)	(one in both dorsal positions and ventral
Dimensions: span 18.86m (61ft 11in);	station); max. bomb load of 3000kg (6614lb)

▲ **Tupolev Tu-2S**

Unknown bomber regiment / Soviet Air Force, summer/autumn 1944

With two 20mm ShVAK cannon in the wing roots, and rearward defence provided by three 12.7mm (0.5in) UBT machine guns (single guns in the two dorsal and one ventral positions), the Tu-2S had good gun armament and provision for a standard bomb load of 3000kg (6614lb) carried internally or overload of 4000kg (8814lb), including two 500kg (1102lb) weapons under the wing roots.

Drive to victory
1943–45

Germany's defeat at Stalingrad made the Soviet Union's eventual victory all but certain, though there was still more than two years of bitter fighting still to come. During this period, the Soviet bomber arm matured slowly but steadily as a potent adjunct to the Soviet ground forces.

AFTER ITS VICTORY at Stalingrad, the Soviet Army drove forward to retake the region between the Don and Donets rivers, in the process creating the great Kursk salient, which the Germans tried but failed to retake during July 1943 in their last major attempt to regain the initiative on the Eastern Front. The Soviets then swept across the Dniepr river to re-enter Ukraine in the south, freeing Leningrad from siege in the north, liberating south Ukraine in spring 1944, and Belorussia and north Ukraine in the summer before moving into Poland during late summer 1944.

Without real pause, the Soviets then moved into the northern Balkans and retook the Baltic states in the south and north respectively, and then in January 1945 moved remorselessly into Germany proper, where their capture of Berlin on 2 May 1945 signalled the end of the 'Great Patriotic War'.

Operations in the Crimea

Throughout this series of grand offensives, which placed huge demands on men and machines, and required a vast logistical effort that seldom faltered in any major way for more than a short period, the ground forces were covered by the fighter arm of the V-VS, and supported by the heavier warplanes of the same service's ground-attack and bomber arms.

The nature of the bombing undertaken by the bomber arm of the V-VS in these decisive later stages

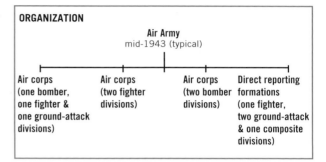

SOVIET LIGHT AND MEDIUM BOMBER AIRCRAFT			
Type	Engines	Bomb load	Speed
Ilyushin Il-2m3	1 x V	600kg (1323lb)	404km/h (251mph)
Nyeman R-10	1x V	300kg (661lb)	370km/h (230mph)
Petlyakov Pe-2FT	2 x V	1200kg (2465lb)	540km/h (336mph)
Sukhoi Su-2	1 x radial	600kg (1323lb)	378km/h (235mph)
Tupolev SB-2	2 x V	1000kg (2205lb)	410km/h (255mph)
Tupolev Tu-2S	2 x radial	3000kg (6614lb)	547km/h (340mph)
Yakovlev Yak-4	2 x V	600kg (1323lb)	540km/h (335mph)

SOVIET GROUND ATTACK AIRCRAFT, 1941–45	
Year	Total
1941	1543
1942	8219
1943	11,177
1944	11,110
1945	c. 5500
Total	37,549

of the war can first be discerned in the campaign of the first part of 1944, which aimed for the expulsion of the Germans from Crimea and the recapture of the great fortress city of Sevastopol.

The campaign fell into four parts, and in the first of these (the German withdrawal into Sevastopol and the unsuccessful Soviet attempt to storm the city) bombers were not used at all. Thereafter the air tactics employed by the bombers focused on using long-ranged and more heavily armed counterparts of those used by the ground-attack arm.

In the second phase of the campaign, the Soviets attempted to take Sevastopol in a major assault. Long-range support was provided by bombers operating from airfields in the area of Kiev to deliver day and night attacks on targets located deep in Germany's fortified area round Sevastopol, but the accuracy of the bombing was poor and the Germans losses, in men and materiel, were therefore small.

In the third phase of the campaign, the Soviet bombers undertook a carefully pre-planned offensive against the fortress of Sevastopol and the German airfields in the fortified area round Sevastopol. This third phase, flown primarily by day, was more successful than the second phase.

The fourth and final phase was flown over the western Crimea as the Germans tried to evacuated

Specifications

Crew: 3

Powerplant: 2 x 820kW (1100hp)

Maximum speed: 540km/h (336mph)

Range: 1500km (932 miles)

Service ceiling: 8800m (28,870ft)

Dimensions: span 17.16m (56ft 4in);

length 12.66m (41ft 7in);

height 4m (13ft 2in)

Weight: 8496kg (12,943lb) loaded

Armament: 2 x 7.62mm (0.3in) ShKAS MGs in nose and 1 x 7.62mm (0.3in) ShKAS MG in ventral or dorsal station; maximum bomb load 1200kg (2646lb)

▲ Petlyakov Pe-2FT
Unknown dive-bomber regiment / Soviet First Air Army, spring 1945

The Pe-2FT was the first standard variant of the Pe-2 series, of which 11,427 examples were delivered between early 1941 and the end of World War II. The Pe-2 was the Soviets' most important tactical bomber of World War II, and the slogan on the side of this aeroplane translates as 'Leningrad-Konigsberg'.

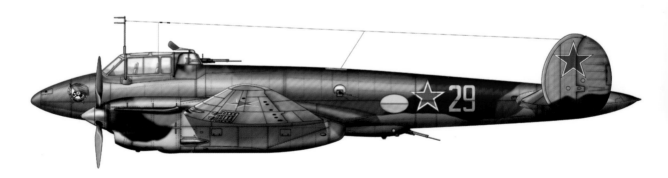

Specifications

Crew: 3

Powerplant: 2 x 820kW (1100hp) Klimov

Maximum speed: 540km/h (336mph)

Range: 1500km (932 miles)

Service ceiling: 8800m (28,870ft)

Dimensions: span 17.16m (56ft 4in);

length 12.66m (41ft 7in);

height 4m (13ft 2in)

Weight: 8496kg (12,943lb) loaded

Armament: 2 x 7.62mm (0.3in) ShKAS MGs in nose and 1 x 7.62mm (0.3in) ShKAS MG in ventral or dorsal station; maximum bomb load 1200kg (2,646lb)

▲ Petlyakov Pe-2FT
Unknown dive-bomber regiment / Soviet Air Force, 1944–45

The vane above the forward edge of the MVT turret immediately to the rear of the cockpit was an aerodynamic balance area to offset the drag of the 12.7mm (0.5in) machine gun as the turret was traversed, and so obviate the need for the turret to be power-operated.

their forces by sea to Ukraine. Here the main targets of the Soviet bombers were the ports the Germans were using for the evacuation, and the troop transports plying to and from these ports.

This phase of the bombing effort was successful, the bombs killing large numbers of troops awaiting evacuation, sinking two 3048-tonne (3000-ton) transport ships as well as larger numbers of 1016- tonne (1000-ton) transport vessels. This tactical pattern was repeated, with changes as demanded by the situation, in other areas wherever the Germans tried to make a stand and then withdraw in the face of overwhelming Soviet ground strength. The basic element of the Soviet bombing attacks was a double concentration on the German-held area and its associated lines of communication.

▲ Ilyushin Il-10
Unknown attack regiment / Soviet Tactical Air Force, Poland 1945
The Il-10 was the second-generation successor to the classic Il-2 Shturmovik, and retained only its predecessor's basic concept. It had an improved engine and enclosed rear-gunner's cockpit, as well as heavier armaments.

Specifications
Crew: 2
Powerplant: 1 x 1492kW (2000hp)
Maximum speed: 530km/h (329mph)
Range: 800km (497 miles)
Service ceiling: 7250m (23,785ft)
Dimensions: span 13.4m (43ft 12in);
   length 11.06m (36ft 4in);

height 4.18m (13ft 9in)
Weight: 6535kg (14,407lb) loaded
Armament: 2 x 7.62mm (0.3in) MGs; 2 x 23mm
   (0.9in) cannon on wings and 1 x 20mm
   (0.8in) cannon or 12.7mm (0.5in) MG in
   dorsal position; up to 500kg (11290lb) bombs
   and 4 x rockets

Specifications
Crew: 2
Powerplant: 1 x 1492kW (2000hp)
Maximum speed: 530km/h (329mph)
Range: 800km (497 miles)
Service ceiling: 7250m (23,785ft)
Dimensions: span 13.4m (43ft 12in);
   length 11.06m (36ft 4in);

height 4.18m (13ft 9in)
Weight: 6535kg (14,407lb) loaded
Armament: 2 x 7.62mm (0.3in) MGs; 2 x 23mm
   (0.9in) cannon on wings and 1 x 20mm
   (0.79in) cannon or 12.7mm (0.5in) MG gun in
   dorsal position; up to 500kg (11290lb) bombs
   and 4 rockets

▲ Ilyushin Il-10
Unknown attack regiment / Soviet Air Force, 1945
Total Soviet production of the Il-10 to 1949 (when the tooling was transferred to Czechoslovakia for the manufacture of 1200 B-33 and BS-33 trainers), and of the Il-10M in 1951–55, was 4966 aircraft.

Soviet Long-Range Aviation
1939–45

During the 1930s, the Soviet Union allowed its air force to become a semi-independent force, and this expanded its belief in the desirability of long-range bombing. The situation did not last long, however, and for most of World War II long-range aviation was a very limited asset.

IN 1935, THE SOVIET authorities allowed the slight disentanglement of the air force from the army and navy, of which it had been a part. By the following year, it had established itself as a semi-independent force in terms of its structure, but was still required to cooperate with the two older services and furnish them with the type of air support they needed.

This emphasis stemmed from a factor at the very heart of Soviet military thinking, namely that it was the forces on the ground that were the arbiters of war, and therefore that air power should be an adjunct of these. Even so, the V-VS (Soviet Air Force) had already started to experiment with a long-range heavy bomber capability designed to secure strategic results. The effort had been spurred by Soviet attempts to create, primarily for political and social reasons, a generation of very large and moderately advanced multi-engined aircraft whose existence

▲ **Petlyakov Pe-8**

A Pe-8 bomber used to transport diplomats to Britain refuels at an RAF base somewhere in Scotland, 1942.

would highlight the scientific and industrial advances being made by the Soviet Union. These technical developments led to the Tupolev TB-1 and TB-3, and the Kalinin K-7 heavy bombers, and it was these

Specifications

Crew: 4	length 14.8m (48ft 6in);
Powerplant: 2 x 821kW (1100hp) 88B radial piston engines	height 4.10m (13ft 6in)
	Weight: 10,000kg (22,046lb) loaded
Maximum speed: 410km/h (255mph)	Armament: 12.7mm (0.5in) MGs in nose,
Range: 2600km (1616 miles)	dorsal turret and ventral positions; maximum
Service ceiling: 10,000m (32,810ft)	bomb load 1000kg (2205lb)
Dimensions: span 21.44m (70ft 4in);	

▲ **Ilyushin Il-4**

Unknown bomber regiment / Soviet Air Force, 1945

Initially known as the DB-3F, the Il-4 was built to the extent of 5256 aircraft in a programme extending from 1941 to 1945. Differentiated from predecessor variants by its more streamlined and glazed nose, the Il-4 provided the backbone of the Soviet Union's longer-range bomber capability throughout World War II.

SOVIET LONG-RANGE BOMBERS			
Type	Engines	Bomb load	Speed
Ilyushin DB-3F (Il-4)	2 x radial	2500kg (5511lb)	507km/h (305mph)
Petlyakov Pe-8	4 x V or radial	4000kg (8818lb)	438km/h (272mph)
Tupolev TB-1	2 x V	3000kg (6614lb)	198km/h (121 mph)
Tupolev ANT-3	4 x V	4000kg (8818lb)	288km/h (179mph)

ungainly machines that constituted the Soviet heavy bomber arm in the late 1930s.

Further operational thinking and technical development had by now started the pendulum swinging back toward the tactical bomber able to intervene directly over the battlefield. The 'modern' aeroplane, of light alloy construction with a cantilever monoplane wing, retractable landing gear and enclosed accommodation, was by now standard, and the new generation of Soviet bombers was developed on the basis of this concept.

Bomber types

The Petlyakov Pe-8 was created as a four-engined heavy bomber, but was then built only in very small numbers, while far more ambitious manufacture was undertaken of twin-engined medium bombers typified by the Ilyushin DB-3 (Il-4), Petlyakov Pe-2 and Yermolayev Yer-2 and Yer-6 as successors to the

pioneering Tupolev SB-2, which saw service in the Spanish Civil War on the Republican government side. The process of rebuilding the V-VS' bomber force with modern aircraft and the tactics to serve the ground forces over the battlefield was still incomplete as German forces invaded the Soviet Union in June 1941. Even though the Soviets had more than four times as many aircraft as the Germans, the aircraft's general obsolescence and the poor training of their crews meant that those which managed to get into the air were shot down in droves. Large numbers were also destroyed on the ground.

The situation of the Soviet Union became ever more critical in the first four months of the war as the Germans drove steadily east, and the Soviets had recourse to all manner of expedients in an effort to stem the German tide. One of these expedients was the committal of bomber units to unescorted attacks in daylight against German forces shielded by potent anti-aircraft artillery under an umbrella of *Luftwaffe* fighters. The Soviet bomber force was largely destroyed in vain efforts to inflict tactical reverses on the Germans. After the immediate crisis had passed, a smaller and leaner long-range bomber arm was created in March 1942 as the ADD (Long-Range Aviation). The ADD's two main types were a few Pe-8 aircraft for limited long-range attacks and altogether larger numbers of Il-4s for more numerous medium-range efforts. In December 1944, the ADD came under the direct control of the V-VS as the Eighteenth Air Force.

▲ Tupolev Tu-2S

Unknown bomber regiment / Soviet Air Force, 1944–45

The Tu-2 was an outstanding design, in which great care had been taken to minimize drag. The result was high performance on modest power.

Specifications

Crew: 4

Powerplant: 2 X 1380kW (1850hp) Shvetsov ASh-82FN radial piston engines

Maximum speed: 547km/h (340mph)

Range: 2000km (1243 miles)

Service ceiling: 9500m (31,170ft)

Dimensions: span 18.86m (61ft 11in);

length 13.8m (45ft 4in);

height 4.56m (14ft 11in)

Weight: 12,800kg (28,219lb) loaded

Armament: 2 x 20mm (0.79in) ShVAK cannon in wing roots; 3 x 12.7mm (0.5in) UBT MGs (one in both dorsal positions and ventral station); max. bomb load of 3000kg (6614lb)

Soviet Naval Air Force
1941–45

The task of the Soviet Naval Air Force was, not surprisingly, the protection of ships and naval facilities from the attentions of Axis warplanes, and attacks on Axis shipping, especially in the Arctic Ocean, the Baltic Sea and the Black Sea as well as on major rivers.

LIKE THE V-VS, the Soviet Naval Air Force was structured and equipped for tactical support, and where necessary the two forces could assume a limited part of each other's roles. In the last two years of the war, for example, the Germans found that V-VS bombers were notably active in the anti-ship role. Up to 1943 it was mainly in the Black Sea that the Soviet Naval Air Force operated, but its attentions were spread more widely after that, and in 1944–45 the service was strongly evident in the Baltic Sea and the Arctic Ocean.

Medium-altitude bombing

The primary Soviet targets were convoys, supply vessels and troop transports, and attacks on German warships and naval installations were altogether less frequent. A type of target much favoured by the Soviets was the seaborne evacuation, in which

ORGANIZATION

Morskaya Aviatsiya
mid 1944

| Northern Fleet Air Force | Baltic Fleet Air Force | Black Sea Air Force | Pacific Fleet Air Force |

the sinking of a laden transport not only cost the Germans the troops being evacuated, but the subsequent use of the ship for further evacuations.

The bombers of the Soviet Naval Air Force operated in regiments, squadrons and flights according to the importance of the target, and the standard tactic was medium-altitude level bombing at between 3000m (9845ft) and 4000m (13,125ft). Only occasionally was dive-bombing used, Petlyakov Pe-2 warplanes then being employed

▲ **Handley Page Hampden TB.Mk I**

Unknown bomber regiment / Northern Fleet Air Force / Soviet Naval Air Force, Vaenga, Murmansk, October 1942

The Soviet Union took over 10 or more of these aircraft when the British pulled out the personnel of the two torpedo-bomber squadrons deployed temporarily to the Soviet Union earlier in 1942 for anti-shipping operations off northern Norway.

Specifications

Crew: 4

Powerplant: 2 X 746kW (1000hp) Bristol Pegasus XVIII radial piston engines

Maximum speed: 409km/h (254mph)

Range: 3034km (1885 miles)

Service ceiling: 5790m (19,000ft)

Dimensions: span 21.08m (69ft 2in); length 16.33m (53ft 7in); height 4.55m (14ft 11in)

Weight: 8508kg (18,756lb) loaded

Armament: 1 x 7.7mm (0.303in) Vickers or Browning fixed forward-firing MGs in port side of upper fuselage; 7.7mm (0.3in) Vickers K trainable forward-firing MGs in nose, dorsal position, ventral positions; 907kg (2000lb) of bombs, or 4 or 6 x 227kg (500lb) bombs or mines, or 1 x 457mm (18in) Mk XII torpedo in dives at between 60 and 70 degrees. The size of bomb carried was generally between 150kg (331lb) and 250kg (551lb), and the aircraft of each flight followed the leader to release their bombs at an altitude of about 1000m (3280ft). Wherever possible, the bombers had strong fighter escort to provide protection, and the aircraft also carried parachute-retarded fragmentation bombs for release over German fighter units as a (questionable) means of self-defence. Torpedo-bombing by Ilyushin Il-4s and Douglas A-20s became standard only late in the war.

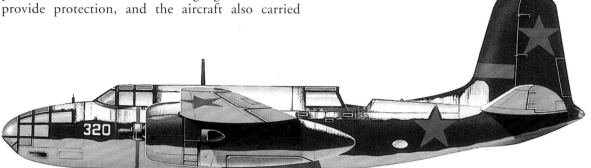

Specifications

Crew: 3

Powerplant: 2 x 1193kW (1600hp) Wright
  radial piston engines

Maximum speed: 510km/h (217mph)

Range: 1521km (945 miles)

Service ceiling: 7225m 23,700ft)

Dimensions: span 18.69m (61ft 4in);

length 14.63m (48ft); height 5.36m (17ft 7in)

Weight: 10,964kg (24,127lb) loaded

Armament: 6 x 12.7mm (0.5in) Browning M2
  fixed forward-firing MGs; 2 x similar weapons
  in power-operated dorsal turret, and one
  rearward-firing through ventral tunnel; up to
  1814kg (4000lb) of bombs

▲ **Douglas A-20C**

Unknown bomber regiment / Northern Fleet Air Force / Soviet Naval Air Force, 1944

The Soviet Union received 665 and 48 examples respectively of the A-20B and A-20C variants of the Havoc, known to the British as the Boston, and made extensive first-line use of these aircraft.

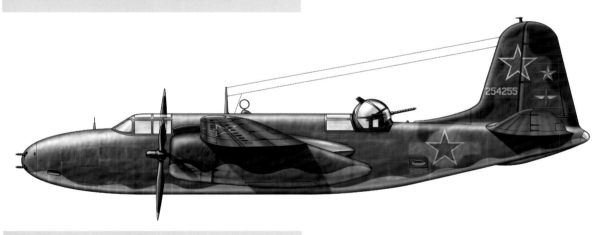

Specifications

Crew: 3

Powerplant: 2 x 1193kW (1600hp) Wright
  radial piston engines

Maximum speed: 510km/h (217mph)

Range: 1521km (945 miles)

Service ceiling: 7225m 23,700ft)

Dimensions: span 18.69m (61ft 4in);

length 14.63m (48ft); height 5.36m (17ft 7in)

Weight: 10,964kg (24,127lb) loaded

Armament: 6 x 12.7mm (0.5in) Browning M2
  fixed forward-firing MGs, and 2 x similar
  weapons in power-operated dorsal turret, and
  one rearward-firing through ventral tunnel;
  up to 1814kg (4000lb) of bombs

▲ **Douglas A-20G**

Unknown bomber regiment / Soviet Naval Air Force, March 1944

The Soviet Union received 3125 aircraft of the DB-7 series as part of US Lend-Lease deliveries, many of them receiving a number of local modifications such as the Soviet dorsal turret evident here. The Soviet Naval Air Force operated its aircraft in the anti-ship role from the Arctic Ocean to the Black Sea.

Appendices

Neither Germany nor Japan expected or planned for long wars of attrition when they launched their attacks on Poland in 1939 and at Pearl Harbor in 1941. The miscalculation was to cost them dearly when Allied industrial capabilities rapidly increased from late 1942.

▼ **Combat strengths, all countries**

World War II saw sophisticated weaponry being created in unprecedented numbers. Nowhere was that more true than in the air, with tens of thousands of combat aircraft being deployed in the later years of the war. (Rounded figures are estimates.)

FRONTLINE COMBAT AIRCRAFT, COMPARATIVE STRENGTHS (1939–45)					
Date	Germany	USA	USSR	UK	Total Allied
September 1939	2,916	–	–	1,660	1,660
August 1940	3,015	–	–	2,913	2,913
December 1940	2,885	–	–	1,064	1,064
June 1941	3,451	–	8,105	3,106	11,211
December 1941	2,561	4,000	2,495	4,287	6,782
June 1942	3,573	1,902	3,160	4,500	9,562
December 1942	3,440	4,695	3,088	5,257	13,040
June 1943	5,003	8,586	8,290	6,026	22,902
December 1943	4,667	11,917	8,500	6,646	27,063
June 1944	4,637	19,342	11,800	8,339	39,481
December 1944	5,041	19,892	14,500	8,395	42,787
April 1945	2,175	21,572	17,000	8,000	46,752

▼ German aircraft losses by type

Few German pilots who took part in the Luftwaffe's early victories in Poland, France, the Balkans and the Soviet Union could have predicted the unsustainable losses they would suffer later in the conflict.

GERMAN AIRCRAFT LOSSES BY TYPE (1939–45)	
Type	Total
Fighter	41,452
Night fighter	10,221
Ground attack	8,548
Bombers	22,037
Transport	6,141
Reconnaissance	6,733
Trainers	15,428

▼ Soviet aircraft losses

Soviet Air Forces suffered dreadfully in the early stage of the war. The consistent quality of the Luftwaffe opposition meant that loss rates remained high until the end of the conflict.

USSR COMBAT AIRCRAFT LOSSES (1941–45)	
Period	Total
21 June – 30 Nov 1941	12,652
1 Dec – 30 April 1942	7,099
1 May – 31 Oct 1942	14,601
1 Nov – 30 June 1943	17,690
1 July – 31 Dec 1943	20,741
1 Jan – 31 May 1944	13,386
1 June – 31 Dec 1944	20,283
1 Jan – 8 May 1945	?
Total	106,652

▷ Aircraft losses, totals for all countries

Combat losses accounted for only part of the totals of aircraft destroyed in World War II. Operational service was hard, and rough fields, bad weather and mechanical failures accounted for almost as many aircraft as the enemy.

◁ Yak-9 fighters

The inscription on the side of these Yak-9s, 'Little Theatre: Front', indicates that they were donated by Moscow's Little Theatre in 1943.

▼ USAAF aircraft losses

The contrast between the Pacific and European theatres was at its height in 1944, where the Germans were destroying nine American aircraft for every one lost to the Japanese.

US AIRCRAFT OPERATIONAL LOSSES (1942–45)			
Year	Europe	Pacific	Total
1942	141	344	485
1943	3,028	819	3,847
1944	11,618	1,671	13,289
1945	3,631	1,699	5,330
Total	18,418	4,533	22,951

▼ Polish aircraft losses

The first Blitzkrieg campaign saw much of the Polish Air Force destroyed on the ground, and although those aircraft that did get into the air fought hard, they were no match for the Luftwaffe. By the end of September the few remaining operational aircraft had fled to Romania.

POLISH AIRCRAFT LOSSES (SEPTEMBER 1939)	
Type	Total
Fighter	116
Dive-bomber	112
Bombers	36
Reconnaissance	81
Transport	9
Seaplane	21
Other	23

ALL OPERATIONAL LOSSES (1939–45)			
Country	Lost in action	Damaged	Total
Finland	251	352	603
France	413	479	892
Germany	69,583	47,001	116,584
Italy	3,269	2003	5,272
Japan	–	–	38,105
Netherlands	–	–	81
Poland	–	–	398
UK	–	–	22,010
USA	–	–	22,951
USSR	–	–	106,652

▼ RAF fighter strengths by theatre

Early in the war the bulk of RAF fighter strength was reserved for the defence of the home islands. As the war expanded worldwide, fighting units saw action in increasing numbers in all of the major theatres.

RAF COMBAT FIGHTER SQUADRONS (1939–45)					
Date	UK	NW Europe	Med	Far East	Total
September 1939	41	4	6	4	55
July 1940	65	–	8	4	77
December 1941	114	–	29	13	156
December 1942	93	–	47	19	159
December 1943	83	–	49	29	161
September 1944	58	48	41	29	176
March 1945	46	51	33	30	160

▼ FAA fighter/fighter-bomber strengths by theatre

The Fleet Air Arm was very much a poor relation of the RAF at the outbreak of war, but it was to grow twenty-fold over the course of the conflict to play an important part in maritime warfare.

FLEET AIR ARM FIGHTER SQUADRONS (1939–45)			
Date	Total	Far East	Aircraft
September 1939	3	–	36
September 1940	7	–	78
September 1941	13	–	129
September 1942	27	–	252
September 1943	32	–	339
September 1944	37	4	645
April 1945	39	26	826
September 1945	40	32	739

▼ Eastern Front, combat aircraft

The onset of Operation Barbarossa in the summer of 1941 saw the Soviet air forces reduced to parity with the Luftwaffe by the time of the battle for Moscow, but Soviet production had outstripped the Germans within a year.

SOVIET AND GERMAN FRONT-LINE COMBAT AIRCRAFT (1941–45)		
Date	German	Soviet
June 1941	2,130	8,100
July 1941	1,050	2,500
December 1941	2,500	2,500
May 1942	3,400	3,160
November 1942	2,450	3,100
July 1943	2,500	8,300
January 1944	1,800	8,500
June 1944	1,710	11,800
January 1945	1,430	14,500
April 1945	1,500	17,000

▼ USAAF fighter combat groups by theatre

In US usage, a combat group was a formation consisting of two or more squadrons, with two or more groups forming a wing. By far the largest proportion of American combat strength during World War II was deployed to Europe and the Mediterranean, though large numbers were due to be transferred to the Pacific when the Japanese surrendered in 1945.

USAAF FIGHTER COMBAT GROUPS STATIONED OVERSEAS BY THEATRE (1941–45)						
Date	Pacific	CBI	UK	NW Europe	Med	Total
December 1941	4	–	–	–	–	4
December 1942	7	2	4	–	10	23
December 1943	10	4	17	–	13	44
September 1944	9	6	16	17	12	60
March 1945	12	6	9	21	10	58

▲ **Spitfire Mk VC**
Serving with the Desert Air Force (DAF) in 1943, this Spitfire of No. 43 Squadron is parked at a captured Italian airfield at Comiso, Sicily.

▼ **Fighter production, all Allied and Axis forces**
In terms of economic output, the Axis powers were no match for the Allies, with the United States alone producing more aircraft than Germany, Italy and Japan combined. Albert Speer's miraculous industrial reorganization in the face of heavy Allied bombing increased German production fivefold between 1942 and 1944, but even this could not match the combined industrial might of the USA, the Soviet Union and the British Empire.

ANNUAL ALLIED MILITARY AIRCRAFT PRODUCTION (1939–45)				
Year	USA	USSR	UK	Total
1939	–	–	1,324	1,324
1940	1,162	4,574	4,283	10,019
1941	4,416	7,086	7,064	18,566
1942	10,769	9,924	9,849	30,542
1943	23,988	14,590	10,727	49,305
1944	38,873	17,913	10,730	67,516
1945	20,742	c 9,000	5,445	35,187
TOTAL	99,950	63,087	49,422	212,459

ANNUAL AXIS MILITARY AIRCRAFT PRODUCTION (1939–45)				
Year	Germany	Italy	Japan	Total
1939	605	?	?	?
1940	2,746	1,155	?	?
1941	3,744	1,339	1,080	6,163
1942	5,515	1,488	2,935	9,938
1943	10,898	528	7,147	18,573
1944	26,326	–	13,811	40,137
1945	5,883	–	5,474	11,357
TOTAL	55,727	4,510	30,447	90,684

▼ Bomber aircraft production, all Allied and Axis forces

Bombers are essentially offensive weapons, but although Germany was the aggressor in the early stages of the war, it did not produce as many aircraft of this type as the British. Albert Speer's rearmament program in the later stages of the war meant that German production increased, even in the face of intense Allied attacks, but the entire Axis production throughout the war was matched by the production of United States industry in 1944 alone. The British also built more bombers than the Germans, though the Soviets concentrated more on fighters and ground-attack aircraft.

ANNUAL ALLIED BOMBER AIRCRAFT PRODUCTION (1939–45)				
Year	USA	USSR	UK	Total
1939	–	–	1837	?
1940	623	3571	3488	7682
1941	4115	3748	4668	12,531
1942	12,627	3537	6253	22,417
1943	29,355	4074	7728	41,157
1944	35,003	4186	7903	47,092
1945	16,087	c 2,000	2812	20,899
TOTAL	97,810	21,116	34,689	153,615

ANNUAL AXIS BOMBER AIRCRAFT PRODUCTION (1939–45)				
Year	Germany	Italy	Japan	Total
1939	737	?	?	?
1940	2852	640	?	?
1941	3373	754	1461	5588
1942	4502	566	2433	7501
1943	4789	103	4189	9081
1944	1982	–	5100	7082
1945	–	–	1934	1934
TOTAL	18,235	2063	15,117	35,415

▲ Rest and relaxation

US aircrews watch as a B-17 Flying Fortress from the 1st Combat Wing (Heavy) lands at an East Anglian air base following an attack on a German munitions factory in the Autumn of 1943.

TONS BOMBS DROPPED AND SORTIES FLOWN BY ALLIED AIR FORCES IN EUROPE (AUGUST 1942 – MAY 1945)									
	Bomber Command			US Eighth Air Force		US Fifteenth Air Force		Balkan Air Force	
Date	Tons	Day Sorties	Night Sorties	Tons	Sorties	Tons	Sorties	Tons	Sorties
Aug 1942	4162	186	2454	151	114	–	–	–	–
Sept	5595	127	3489	189	183	–	–	–	–
Oct	3809	406	2198	278	284	–	–	–	–
Nov	2423	127	2067	604	519	–	–	–	–
Dec	2714	200	1758	340	353	–	–	–	–
TOTAL 1942	**18,703**	**1046**	**11,966**	**1411**	**1453**	–	–	–	–
Jan 1943	4345	406	2556	594	338	–	–	–	–
Feb	10,959	426	5030	568	526	–	–	–	–
Mar	10,591	284	5174	1483	956	–	–	–	–
Apr	11,467	316	5571	858	449	–	–	–	–
May	12,290	360	5130	2555	1672	–	–	–	–
Jun	15,271	–	5816	2330	2107	–	–	–	–
Jul	16,830	–	6170	3475	2829	–	–	–	–
Aug	20,149	–	7807	3999	2265	–	–	–	–
Sept	14,855	–	5513	7369	3259	–	–	–	–
Oct	13,773	–	4638	4548	2831	–	–	–	–
Nov	14,495	–	5208	5751	4157	5392	1785	–	–
Dec	11,802	–	4123	10,655	5973	7752	2039	–	–
TOTAL 1943	**157,367**	**1792**	**62,736**	**44,185**	**27,362**	**13,144**	**3824**	–	–
Jan 1944	18,428	–	6278	10,532	6367	11,051	4720	–	–
Feb	12,054	45	4263	16,480	9884	6747	3981	–	–
Mar	27,698	18	9031	19,892	11,590	10,176	5996	–	–
Apr	33,496	10	9873	22,447	14,464	21,256	10,182	–	–
May	37,252	16	11,353	32,450	19,825	30,355	14,432	–	–
Jun	57,267	2371	13,592	54,204	28,925	27,466	11,761	–	–
Jul	57,615	6298	11,500	40,784	23,917	32,183	12,642	132	2509
Aug	65,855	10,271	10,013	44,120	22,967	27,859	12,194	277	3437
Sept	52,587	9643	6428	36,332	18,268	20,856	10,056	480	3698
Oct	61,204	6713	10,193	38,961	19,082	16,257	9567	430	3416
Nov	53,022	5055	9589	36,091	17,003	17,297	9259	342	4604
Dec	49,040	3656	11,239	36,826	18,252	18,757	10,050	761	4653
TOTAL 1944	**525,518**	**44,096**	**113,352**	**389,119**	**210,544**	**240,260**	**114,840**	**2422**	**22,317**
Jan 1945	32,923	1304	9603	34,891	16,702	6784	4002	395	2460
Feb	45,889	3685	13,715	46,088	22,884	24,508	13,444	1085	4690
Mar	67,637	9606	11,585	65,962	31,169	30,265	14,939	1086	3954
Apr	34,954	5001	8822	41,632	20,514	29,258	15,846	1561	4546
May	337	1068	349	–	2276	84	42	101	373
TOTAL 1945	181,740	20,664	44,074	188,573	93,545	90,899	48,273	4228	16,023
GRAND TOTAL	**883,328**	**67,598**	**232,128**	**623,288**	**332,904**	**344,303**	**166,937**	**6650**	**38,340**

▼ RAF medium/heavy bomber strengths by theatre

Medium and heavy bombers are the primary offensive weapon of any air arm. The Royal Air Force was a firm believer in the efficacy of the heavy bomber as a strategic platform, but it was not until the introduction of large numbers of heavy four-engined bombers in 1942 that Bomber Command was able to hit German industry hard. The 'UK (other)' column refers mainly to Coastal Command squadrons.

RAF MEDIUM AND HEAVY BOMBER SQUADRONS (1939–45)						
Date	Bomber Command	UK (other)	NW Europe	Med	Far East	Total
September 1939	37	3	–	2	2	44
July 1940	38	3	–	2	2	45
December 1941	50	12	–	7	3	72
December 1942	60	17	–	14	7	98
December 1943	72	19	–	21	8	120
September 1944	86	23	1	19	9	138
March 1945	96	30	2	16	15	159

▼ RAF light bomber strengths by theatre

Light bombers formed a high proportion of the RAF's bomber inventory at the beginning of World War II, but experiences in France in 1940 showed that such aircraft had no place in a modern strategic bombing campaign. Later in the war light bombers returned to favour, primarily as tactical weapons operating in support of armies on the ground.

RAF LIGHT BOMBER SQUADRONS (1939–45)					
Date	UK	NW Europe	Med	Far East	Total
September 1939	12	6	8	5	31
July 1940	19	–	9	4	32
December 1941	22	–	10	2	34
December 1942	8	–	17	9	34
December 1943	17	–	13	5	35
September 1944	12	3	7	6	28
March 1945	8	9	6	5	28

▼ USAAF bomber combat groups by theatre

The Group was the basic tactical unit of the American air forces. Usually consisting of three or four squadrons with up to 72 aircraft in heavy units and 96 aircraft in lighter units, Bomb or Bombardment Groups were classified as Very Heavy (operating Boeing B-29s or Consolidated B-32s and only used in the Pacific); Heavy (equipped with Boeing B-17s or Consolidated B-24s); Medium (using North American B-25s or Martin B-26s) and light (flying Douglas A-20s or A-26s). Ground attack aircraft such as the Republic P-47 Thunderbolt and P-38 Lightning were classified as fighters.

USAAF BOMBER COMBAT GROUPS BY THEATRE (1941–45)						
Date	Pacific	CBI	UK	NW Europe	Med	Total
December 1941	3	–	–	–	–	3
December 1942	8	2	11	–	9	30
December 1943	14	3	34	–	17	68
September 1944	19	7	44	9	27	106
March 1945	30	6	43	9	27	115

▼ RAF Bomber Command operational strength

The actual number of aircraft available for operations was much lower than the total number on strength, with many bombers being unserviceable, under repair or being used for operational conversion and training.

AVAILABLE CREWS											
Date	Hampden	Blenheim	Mosquito	Wellington	Whitley	Stirling	Halifax	Manchester	Lancaster	US Type	Total
Sept 1939	71	140	–	77	61	–	–	–	–	–	280
Nov 1941	150	79	–	250	62	18	17	31	–	3	506
May 1942	27	29	–	214	15	45	62	15	29	44	417
Jan 1943	–	–	17	128	–	56	104	–	178	99	515
Mar 1944	–	–	58	–	–	63	328	–	594	–	974
Apr 1945	–	–	203	–	–	–	353	–	1087	–	1609

▼ USAAF bomber strengths by type (1939–45)

The USAAF grew to become the largest bomber force in the history of air warfare during the course of World War II, fielding an extremely high proportion of B-17 and B-24 heavy bombers.

USAAF BOMBER AIRCRAFT BY TYPE (1939–45)			
Date	Heavy	Med & Light	Total bombers
December 1939	39	738	777
December 1940	92	639	731
December 1941	288	1544	1832
December 1942	2079	3757	5836
December 1943	8118	6741	14,859
December 1944	13,790	9169	22,959
August 1945	13,930	8463	22,393

▼ Total bombs dropped by weight (1942–45)

Although the US Eighth Air Force flew more sorties than RAF Bomber Command, the larger payload of the British bombers meant that they actually dropped more bombs.

BOMB TONNAGES DROPPED IN EUROPE		
Year	Bomber Command	US Eighth Air Force
1942	18,703	1411
1943	157,367	44,185
1944	525,518	389,119
1945	181,740	188,573
Totals	883,328	623,288

▼ FAA torpedo-bomber strengths by theatre

The bomber strength of the Fleet Air Arm in 1939 was provided by the Fairy Swordfish torpedo bomber. These were later supplemented by the Albacore, Barracuda and Avenger.

FLEET AIR ARM TORPEDO-BOMBER SQUADRONS (1939–45)			
Date	Total	Far East	Aircraft
September 1939	12	2	140
September 1940	19	–	169
September 1941	29	–	198
September 1942	28	1	209
September 1943	29	1	349
September 1944	37	6	549
April 1945	27	8	500
September 1945	27	14	205

Index

Page numbers in *italics* refer to illustrations, photographs and tables.

INDEX

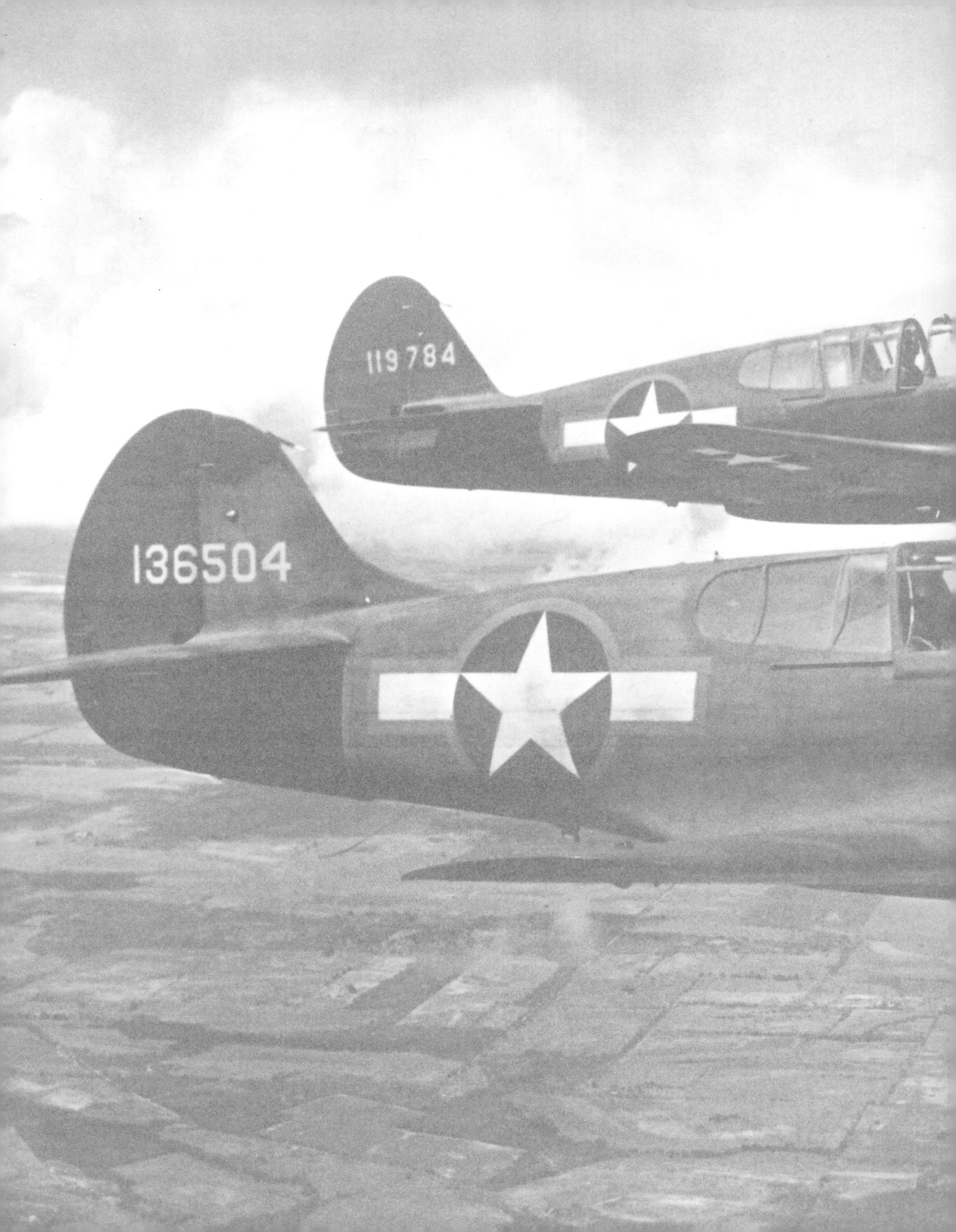
119784
136504